FIX YOUR

CHEVROLET

ALL MODELS

1978 to 1968

By

BILL TOBOLDT

Member, Society of Automotive Engineers
Associate Member, Automotive Engine Rebuilders Association

SOUTH HOLLAND, ILLINOIS
THE GOODHEART-WILLCOX CO., INC.
Publishers

INTRODUCTION

FIX YOUR CHEVROLET is a handbook of time and money-saving information for Chevrolet, Chevelle, Chevette, Corvette, Monte Carlo, Nova, Camaro and Vega owners and mechanics.

It describes simplified tune-up procedures; tells how to locate trouble and make many adjustments and repairs without the use of expensive equipment.

FIX YOUR CHEVROLET covers shortcut methods of removing defective parts and installing new ones; tells you how to make emergency repairs if your car "conks out," and how to get better than normal Speed, Power and Economy. It also covers the use of Special Speed Equipment.

When discussing service procedures, this book identifies the various Chevrolet engines by displacement; 250 cu. in., 350 cu. in., etc., rather than by names such as the Impala, Bel Air, Nova. The names identify the complete chassis, which in most cases is available with a choice of engines. For this reason, it is necessary to determine the displacement of the engine to be repaired before selecting the repair procedure which is applicable.

FIX YOUR CHEVROLET is based on material obtained from many sources, particularly from topflight Chevrolet mechanics throughout the country, from the Chevrolet Motor Division, General Motors Corporation, and from many tool and equipment manufacturers.

Bill Toboldt

New styling and improved performance are features of 1978 Corvette on its 25th anniversary. Wrap-around rear glass area is 3 1/2 times larger than before. Optional high performance 5.7 L (350 cu. in.) engine has an 8.9 to 1 compression ratio and delivers 220 hp @ 5200 rpm.

CONTENTS

TUNE-UP TIPS 7

IGNITION TUNE-UP 15

CARBURETOR AND FUEL SYSTEM
SERVICE. 43

SHORTCUTS ON ENGINE DISASSEMBLY . . . 71

SIMPLIFIED ENGINE REPAIRS 85

VALVE ADJUSTING 119

COOLING SYSTEM KINKS 125

EXHAUST SYSTEM SERVICE 137

QUICK TESTS ON BATTERIES 143

SIMPLIFIED GENERATOR SERVICE 147

STARTER SERVICE 159

LIGHTING SYSTEM SERVICE 165

ACCESSORIES AND INSTRUMENT
SERVICE 175

QUICK CLUTCH SERVICE 197

TRANSMISSION SERVICE 203

PROPELLER SHAFT AND UNIVERSAL
JOINTS. 233

SHORTCUTS ON REAR AXLE SERVICE 237

SHOCK ABSORBERS AND SPRING
SERVICE 247

SHORTCUTS ON WHEEL ALIGNMENT
AND STEERING. 255

QUICK SERVICE ON BRAKES. 269

HINTS ON LUBRICATION AND TIRES 301

EMERGENCY TROUBLE SHOOTING 309

TIPS ON BODY SERVICE. 315

MORE SPEED AND POWER. 329

MECHANICAL AND TUNE-UP
SPECIFICATIONS. 343

SERVICING VEGA, MONZA, CHEVETTE . . .349

INDEX 364

TUNE-UP
TIPS

To get maximum performance and best fuel mileage, special care must be taken when doing a tune-up job. While accuracy and precision are required, doing a good tune-up job on a Chevrolet, Chevelle, Chevette, Chevy II, Camaro, Corvette, Monte Carlo and Nova is not difficult.

WHEN TO DO A TUNE-UP JOB

Generally, a tune-up job is needed after about 10,000 miles of operation. However, starting with the 1975 models equipped with High Energy Ignition, this service interval is greatly extended. Plan to tune-up when there is a noticeable drop in fuel mileage and engine performance.

Since fuel consumption is so dependent on type of driving, it is im-

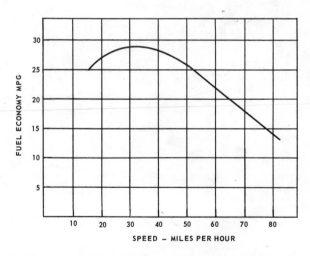

Fig. A-1. Note how fuel economy drops as speed increases.

possible to state what fuel mileage can be expected from various Chevrolet-built cars. Naturally, a driver who maintains a steady, conservative speed will get many more miles per gallon than will the driver who is always driving as fast as possible, regardless of conditions. See Fig. A-1.

Fix Your Chevrolet

It will be found that cars used mostly in city stop-and-go driving will have lower fuel economy and require a tune-up job more frequently than cars used mostly on trips of ten miles or more. The reason is that on trips of short duration, the engine does not reach full operating temperature. Consequently, valves will tend to stick, compression will drop, and operation of the engine will be rough and more fuel will be required.

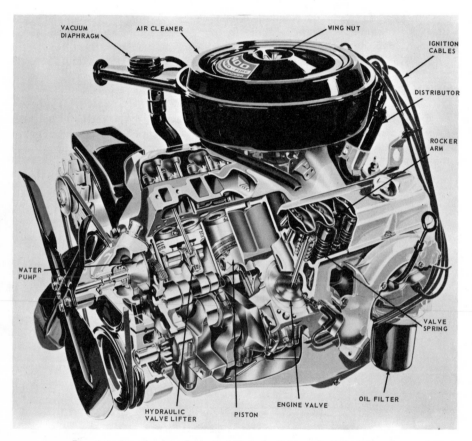

Fig. A-2. Cutaway view of a typical Chevrolet V-8 engine, 1970–1978.

In many cases a tune-up job is advisable every 10,000 miles, or possibly sooner, if maximum performance and economy are desired.

Leaving the tune-up go for a longer period will invariably result in hard starting, poor fuel economy, and possibility of roadside failure.

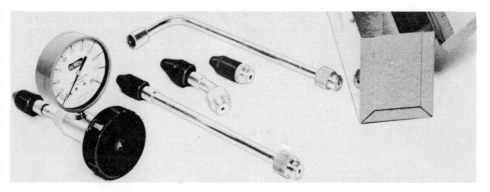

Fig. A-3. Typical compression gauge with special adapters for use with different type engines.

FIRST STEP IN TUNE-UP

The first step in a tune-up job is to make sure the valves are not sticking. Then check compression.

A good way to make sure the valves are free and are not sticking is to take advantage of one of the special oils that are available and designed to free sticking valves.

While instructions with different brands of such lubricants vary somewhat, the usual procedure is to bring the engine up to operating temperature. Then remove the air cleaner from the carburetor and with the engine running at a fast idle, the contents of a can of a tune-up oil is poured slowly and steadily into the air intake of the carburetor. As this is done the engine speed should be increased. Huge clouds of smoke will come from the exhaust, so this operation must be done out-of-doors. It is usually advisable to use the tune-up oil when it will not be necessary to use the car for several hours. In that way the tune-up oil will have ample time to dissolve any gum on the valve stems, and in that way sticking will be eliminated.

When the car is started after using the tune-up oil, it will be found that the engine will idle more smoothly and stepped-up performance will result. A compression test can now be made. It will be safe to assume that there will be no compression loss due to sticking valves.

HOW TO MAKE A COMPRESSION TEST

The first step is to remove the air cleaner, Fig. A-2, and this is held to the carburetor by means of the wing nut. After removing the wing nut, the air cleaner can be lifted from the carburetor. Then block the throttle and choke in the wide-open position. Remove all the spark plugs and then insert the compression gauge, Fig. A-3, into each of the spark plug holes in turn, Fig. A-4. Crank the engine through at least four compression strokes to obtain highest possible reading.

Fix Your Chevrolet

Check and record the compression of each cylinder. The compression should read as indicated in the accompanying table. Variations between the highest and lowest reading cylinders should be less than 20 lbs.

Compression Pressure at Cranking Speed

Car Model	Displacement	Compression Pressure, psi
1976-1978	1.4 L (85 cu. in.)	145
1976-1978	1.6 L (98 cu. in.)	145
1978	151 cu. in. Four	*
1962-1970	153 cu. in. Four	130
1962-1968	194 cu. in. Six	130
1978	196 cu. in. V-6	145
1978	200 cu. in. V-6	*
1963-1970	230 cu. in. Six	130
1978	231 cu. in. V-6	*
1966-1978	250 cu. in. Six	130
1975-1976	262 cu. in. V-8	155
1968-1970	302 cu. in. V-8	190
1976-1978	305 cu. in. V-8	155
1968-1973	307 cu. in. V-8	150
1963-1969	327 cu. in. V-8	160
1966-1968	327 cu. in. V-8 (350 hp)	150
1968-1971	350 cu. in. V-8	160
1969-1970	350 cu. in. V-8	190
1971	350 cu. in. V-8 (all except 330 hp)	160
1971	350 cu. in. V-8 (330 hp)	150
1972	350 cu. in. V-8 (all except 255 hp)	160
1972	350 cu. in. V-8 (255 hp)	150
1973-1975	350 cu. in. V-8 (all except 245 hp)	160
1973-1975	350 cu. in. V-8 (245 hp)	150
1976-1978	350 cu. in. V-8	150
1966-1970	396 cu. in. V-8	160
1970-1976	400 cu. in. V-8	160
1972	402 cu. in. V-8	160
1966-1970	427 cu. in. V-8	160
1969-1970	427 cu. in. V-8 (425, 430, 435 hp)	150
1972-1976	454 cu. in. V-8 (215, 235, 270 hp)	160
1970-1971	454 cu. in. V-8 (345, 360 hp)	160
1970-1971	454 cu. in. V-8 (425, 450 hp)	150

* Lowest cylinder pressure must be at least 70 percent of highest.

If one or more cylinders read low or uneven, pour about a tablespoonful of engine oil on top of each piston in each low reading cylinder. This oil is poured into the spark plug hole. Crank the engine several times and recheck the compression. If the compression comes up but does not reach

Fig. A-4. Checking compression on a V-8 engine.

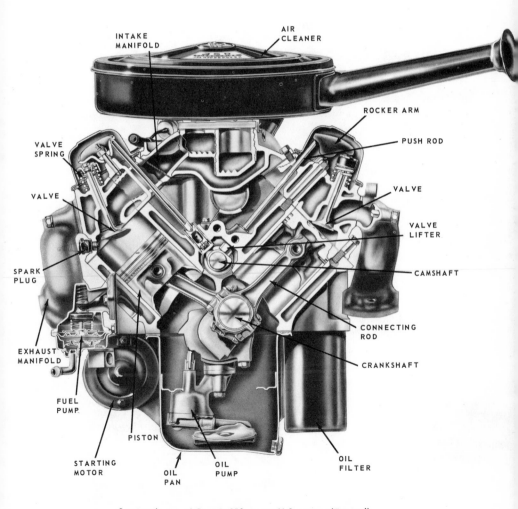

Sectional view of Camaro 350 cu. in. V-8 engine. (Typical)

11

normal, the rings and pistons are probably worn and reconditioning would be needed. If the compression does not improve, the valves are sticking or are seating poorly.

If two adjacent cylinders indicate low compression and injecting oil does not increase the compression, the cause may be a head gasket leak between the cylinders. Engine coolant and/or oil in cylinders could result in case of such a defect.

The compression check is important because an engine with low or uneven compression cannot be tuned successfully to give peak performance. Therefore, it is essential that improper compression be corrected before proceeding with an engine tune-up. If a weak cylinder cannot be located with the compression test, it is desirable to make a cylinder balance test.

CYLINDER BALANCE TEST

To make a cylinder balance test, the engine is operated on a few cylinders at a time while the remaining spark plugs are grounded. The usual method of grounding the spark plugs is by means of a special wiring

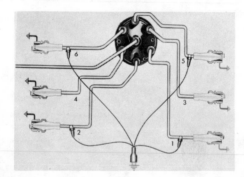

Fig. A-5. Method of shorting out cylinders when making a cylinder balance test. Do not make this test on engines in cars equipped with a catalytic converter.

harness, Fig. A-5. If such a harness is not available, the wires can be disconnected from the spark plugs and held against any convenient point on the engine by means of a spring-type clothespin.

Do not perform a cylinder balance test on late model engines in cars equipped with a catalytic converter. Misfiring created by the test would cause unburned fuel to be exhausted from the cylinder which, in turn, would result in overheating of the catalytic converter.

In addition to the wiring harness, a vacuum gauge, Fig. A-6, or a tachometer can be used to accurately determine the performance of the cylinders in operation. If instruments are not available, simply estimate and compare the changes in engine speeds as the spark plugs are shorted out.

Tune-up Tips

Fig. A-6. Type of vacuum gauge used to check engine performance.

To perform the cylinder balance test procedure, connect a vacuum gauge to the intake manifold of the engine. Start the engine and operate it at a fast idle. Then, by means of the wiring harness, or other means, ground all the cylinders except the two being tested.

Divide the firing order in half and arrange one half over the other. The cylinders to be tested together appear one over the other. For example, V-8 firing order 1-8-4-3-6-5-7-2 should be arranged as follows:

$$\frac{1-8-4-3}{6-5-7-2} = 1\text{-}6,\ 8\text{-}5,\ 4\text{-}7,\ 3\text{-}2.$$

The L-Six firing order would be arranged:

$$1\text{-}5\text{-}3\text{-}6\text{-}2\text{-}4 = \frac{1-5-3}{6-2-4} = 1\text{-}6,\ 5\text{-}2,\ 3\text{-}4.$$

Firing order of Chevy II, Vega and Chevette would be arranged:

$$1\text{-}3\text{-}4\text{-}2 = \frac{1-3}{4-2} = 1\text{-}4,\ 3\text{-}2.$$

The reading on the vacuum gauge should be essentially the same for each pair of cylinders being tested. If one pair of cylinders shows a vacuum reading materially lower than the others, that pair is weak and should be further checked to see which cylinder is at fault. This can be done by first increasing the speed of the engine and then shorting first one cylinder and then the other. The cylinder which gives the lowest vacuum reading is then at fault.

The difficulty may be caused by low compression, faulty ignition to that cylinder, or possibly an air leak at the intake manifold.

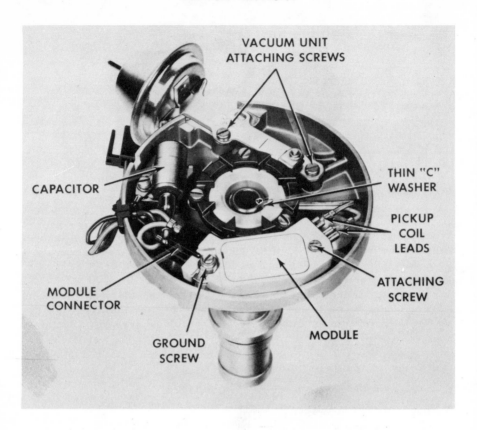

VACUUM UNIT
ATTACHING SCREWS

CAPACITOR

THIN "C"
WASHER

PICKUP
COIL
LEADS

ATTACHING
SCREW

MODULE
CONNECTOR

MODULE

GROUND
SCREW

All of the 1975–1978 models are equipped with GM's High Energy Ignition (HEI) system. This is a pulse-triggered, transistor-controlled, inductive discharge system. A magnetic pickup assembly located inside the distributor contains a permanent magnet, a pole piece with internal teeth and a pickup coil. The system's electronic module is a solid state unit containing five complete circuits. It is serviced as a complete unit only. When replacing the module, a special silicone grease (provided with replacement part) must be applied to the metal mounting surface. HEI system is free from routine servicing and maintenance.

IGNITION
TUNE-UP

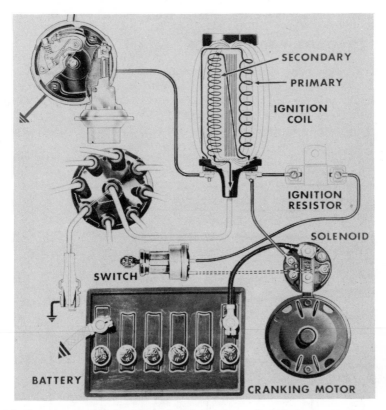

Fig. B-1. Typical wiring diagram of Chevrolet ignition system. Note block type ignition resistor. On recent models this is replaced with a single resistor wire.

The ignition system, Fig. B-1, is designed to supply the spark that ignites the combustible mixture in the combustion chamber. The ignition system is easily serviced.

QUICK TEST OF SPARK

There are many types of expensive equipment available for testing the spark. However, a satisfactory method requiring no equipment, is to disconnect the high tension cable at one of the spark plugs. Then, with the engine operating, hold the end of the spark plug wire about one-quarter inch away from some metal portion of the engine, such as the exhaust manifold, or the cylinder block. A strong spark should jump from the end of the wire to the engine. If the spark will not jump that distance, or is weak or intermittent, the ignition system requires servicing. Before disconnecting the wire at the spark plug, be sure to observe the precaution given in the paragraph "Checks and Care of Ignition Cable." Also make sure that there are no leaks from the fuel system.

WHAT TO DO ABOUT SPARK PLUGS

Spark plugs used with breaker point ignition should perform well for about 10,000 miles. Plugs in 1975 and later models with High Energy Ignition should last up to 22,500 miles. However, continued use of old plugs results in hard starting and increased fuel consumption. Fig. B-2. Also

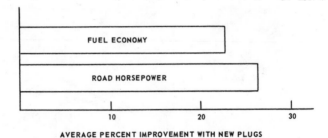

Fig. B-2. Note improvement in fuel economy and road horsepower when new spark plugs are installed.

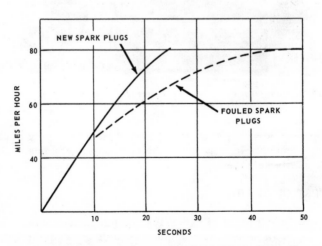

Fig. B-3. When spark plugs are fouled, acceleration drops off.

under wide open throttle conditions, maximum power will not be developed, Fig. B-3. Spark plugs that have a sooty insulator can be easily cleaned and put back into service, but plugs on which the electrodes are worn should be replaced with new ones.

When spark plug insulators are covered with soot, it is an indication that the engine requires servicing of some sort, or the wrong kind of spark plug is being used. The correct type of spark plug for use on Chevrolet engines is given in the accompanying table.

Spark Plug Type
Original Equipment

Car Model	Displacement	Spark Plug Model	Spark Plug Gap	Distributor Gap +
1962-1968	153 cu. in. Four	AC 46N	.035 in.	.016 in.
1962-1968	194 cu. in. Six	AC 46N	.035 in.	.016 in.
1963-1969	230 cu. in. Six	AC 46N	.035 in.	.016 in.
1966-1969	250 cu. in. Six	AC 46N	.035 in.	.016 in.
1968	302 cu. in. V-8	AC 43	.035 in.	.016 in.
1968	307 cu. in. V-8	AC 45S	.035 in.	.016 in.
1968	327 cu. in. V-8 250 hp	AC 44S	.035 in.	.016 in.
1968	327 cu. in. V-8 All others	AC 44	.035 in.	.016 in.
1968	427 cu. in. V-8 430 hp	AC 43XL	.035 in.	.016 in.
1968	427 cu. in. V-8 All others	AC 43N	.035 in.	.016 in.
1969-70	153 cu. in. Four	AC R46N	.035 in.	.016 in.
1970	230 cu. in. V-8	AC R46T	.035 in.	.016 in.
1970	250 cu. in. V-8	AC R46T	.035 in.	.016 in.
1971	250 cu. in.	AC R46TS	.035 in.	.016 in.
1969	302 cu. in. V-8	AC R43	.035 in.	.016 in.
1969	307 cu. in. V-8	RC R45	.035 in.	.016 in.
1970	307 cu. in. V-8	AC R43	.035 in.	.016 in.
1971	307 cu. in.	AC R45TS	.035 in.	.016 in.
1969	327 cu. in. 210 hp	AC R45S	.035 in.	.016 in.
1969	327 cu. in. 235 hp	AC 45S	.035 in.	.016 in.
1969-1970	350 cu. in. 255, 300, 350 hp	AC R44	.035 in.	.016 in.
1969-1970	350 cu. in. 370 hp	AC R43	.035 in.	.016 in.

Car Model	Displacement	Spark Plug Model	Spark Plug Gap	Distributor Gap +
1971	350 cu. in. 245 hp	AC R45TS	.035 in.	.016 in.
1971	350 cu. in. 270, 330 hp	AC R44TS	.035 in.	.016 in.
1969-1970	396 cu. in. V-8	AC R44N	.035 in.	.016 in.
1971	400 cu. in.	AC R44TS	.035 in.	.016 in.
1971	402 cu. in.	AC R44TS	.035 in.	.016 in.
1969	427 cu. in. V-8 335 hp	AC R44N	.035 in.	.016 in.
1969-1970	427 cu. in. V-8 390, 400, 425 hp	AC R43N	.035 in.	.016 in.
1969-1970	427 cu. in. 430 hp	AC R43XL	.035 in.	.016 in.
1969-1970	427 cu. in. 435 hp	AC RC42N	.035 in.	.016 in.
1970	454 cu. in. 345 hp	AC R44T	.035 in.	.016 in.
1970	454 cu. in. V-8 360, 390, 450 hp	AC R43T	.035 in.	.016 in.
1971	454 cu. in.	AC R42TS	.035 in.	.016 in.
1972-1974	250 cu. in.	AC R46T	.035 in.	.016 in.
1972-1973	307 cu. in.	AC R44T	.035 in.	.016 in.
1972-1974	350 cu. in.	AC R44T	.035 in.	.016 in.
1972-1974	400 cu. in.	AC R44T	.035 in.	.016 in.
1972	402 cu. in.	AC R44T	.035 in.	.016 in.
1972-1974	454 cu. in.	AC R44T	.035 in.	.016 in.
1975	250 cu. in.	AC R46TX	.060 in.	HEI
1975	All V-8s	AC R44TX	.060 in.	HEI
1976	All V-8s	AC R45TS	.045 in.	HEI
1976-1977	1.4 L (85 cu. in.)	AC R43TS	.035 in.	HEI
1976-1977	1.6 L (97.6 cu. in.)	AC R43TS	.035 in.	HEI
1976-1977	140 cu. in. Four	AC R43TS	.035 in.	HEI
1976-1978	250 cu. in. Six	AC R46TS	.035 in.	HEI
1977-1978	305 cu. in. V-8	AC R45TS	.045 in.	HEI
1977-1978	350 cu. in. V-8	AC R45TS	.045 in.	HEI
1978	1.6 L (98 cu. in.)	AC R43TS	.035 in.	HEI
1978	151 cu. in. Four	AC R43TSX	.060 in.	HEI
1978	196 cu. in. V-6	AC R46TSX	.060 in.	HEI
1978	200 cu. in. V-6	AC R45TS	.045 in.	HEI
1978	231 cu. in. V-6	AC R46TSX	.060 in.	HEI

+ Specified gap refers to used points; new points, .019 in.
HEI High Energy Ignition

NOTE: When setting distributor gap on older engines, set dwell (cam angle) to 28 to 32 deg. If dwell meter is not available, connect a test lamp to primary lead at distributor. Rotate distributor shaft until one cam lobe is under center of rubbing block on breaker lever. Turn adjusting screw, Fig. B-18, until lamp lights, then back off one-half turn.

Careful examination of the spark plugs will usually disclose whether the plug is the correct type for the kind of service in which the car is being used and also the general condition of the engine will be revealed. Typical conditions are shown in Figs. B-4, B-5, B-6 and B-7.

The terms "hot" and "cold" as applied to spark plugs, indicate that

Fig. B-4. Left. Spark plug fouled by excessive oil. Fig. B-5. Right. When spark plug insulator is covered with dry soot, an excessively rich fuel mixture is indicated.

the temperature of a certain plug is hotter than another plug. The higher the temperature of a spark plug, the less tendency there is for soot to collect on the insulator. The spark plugs listed in the table are for normal driving. If the car is driven at high speeds for prolonged periods, a "colder" type spark plug should be used. Or if the car is used exclusively in slow speed stop-and-go city driving, a warmer type plug may be more satisfactory.

Fig. B-6. Left. When spark plug insulator has burned appearance, the plug is too "hot" for that particular engine and a "cooler" running plug should be installed. Fig. B-7. Right. When the spark plug gap is worn as shown, new plugs should be installed.

The plug shown in Fig. B-7 is definitely worn out, as indicated by the eroded condition of the firing point or gap. The center electrode should be flat with sharp edges, and the side electrodes should not have a groove or show other signs of spark wear. In an emergency, a plug with worn electrodes can be put back into service by filing the end of the center electrode so that it is perfectly flat. If there is a groove worn in the side electrode, it should be removed with a file.

When the spark plug insulator has a rusty, brown or greyish powder deposit, or when the insulator is light brown around the tip, the plug has the correct heat range and is operating satisfactorily.

Fig. B-8. To effectively clean spark plugs, specialized equipment is advisable.

CLEANING AND CHECKING SPARK PLUGS

The best way to clean spark plugs is by means of special equipment, as shown in Fig. B-8. If this is not available, the soot should be scraped from the insulator and from the interior of the metal body of the spark plug as much as possible. After the spark plug is cleaned, it should be carefully examined to make sure that the insulator is not cracked at any point, or has other defects. In addition, it is important to check the condition of the firing point or gap, as an excessively worn gap, Fig. B-7, will reduce the effectiveness of the plug and it is usually advisable to install a new one. A gap is worn when the end of the center electrode is rounded and when the side electrode has a groove worn in it.

ADJUSTING THE SPARK PLUG GAP

When adjusting the spark plug gap, never attempt to bend the center electrode as this invariably results in breaking the insulator. Only the side electrode should be bent when adjusting a spark plug gap. Combination gauges and adjusters are available at nominal cost. Fig. B-9 shows one type of tool which also includes a file for filing the electrodes, as well as a gauge to use in adjusting the gap and a hook with which to bend the side electrode. It should be pointed out that by the time the electrodes

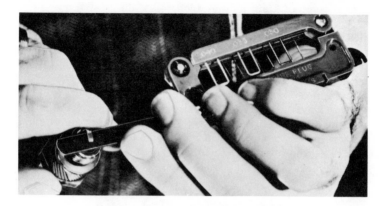

Fig. B-9. One type of spark plug gap gauge which includes a file used to true plug gap and a tool for bending the side electrode.

are worn to a degree that filing is needed, it is better to install new plugs. Higher voltages are needed to jump the gap of worn electrodes and consequently misfiring and hard starting will result.

The gap should be adjusted to specified amount, .035 in., and care should be exercised that this adjustment is made with accuracy. Either a round wire type gauge, Fig. B-9, or a flat sealer type gauge can be used. However the round wire type is preferred when measuring the gap of worn firing points.

REMOVING AND INSTALLING SPARK PLUGS

Before removing a spark plug it is first necessary to disconnect the spark plug wire. Do not pull on the wire itself because the wire connection may be damaged. Instead grasp, twist and pull the molded cap only in order to disconnect the wire. Then carefully blow all the dust and dirt which may be surrounding the spark plug. If this dirt is not removed it will drop into the combustion chamber and eventually damage the engine valves. The spark plug can then be unscrewed from the cylinder head. A 13/16 in., (some plugs 5/8 in.) "deep" socket wrench is used to remove the spark plugs. Special deep sockets with sponge rubber lining in the upper end designed to grip the plug insulator and also reduce the possibility of cracking the insulators are available.

Before installing the spark plugs make sure that the spark plug threads and surface contacting the head are clean. This is particularly important as any dirt may result in compression leakage, but also make the spark plug operate at higher than normal temperatures with attendant misfiring and short life.

When tightening the spark plugs, the factory specifies 20 to 25 ft. lb. torque. That is 20 to 25 lb. exerted at the end of a one foot wrench, or 40 to 50 lb. at the end of a six inch wrench.

REMOVING THE DISTRIBUTOR CAP AND ROTOR

In order to replace ignition breaker points, the condenser or rotor, it is first necessary to remove the distributor cap.

There are three different methods used to hold the distributor cap in place on the Chevrolet cars. The design shown in Fig. B-10 is used primarily on the Chevrolet V-8 engine. To remove this type of cap all that is necessary is to press down on the latch and give it a half turn with a screwdriver, as shown in Fig. B-10.

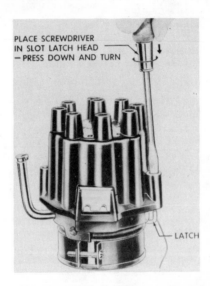

PLACE SCREWDRIVER
IN SLOT LATCH HEAD
— PRESS DOWN AND TURN

LATCH

Fig. B-10. Removing cap from distributor used on V-8 engines.

Fig. B-11 shows the distributor cap clip used on the 1962 and earlier six cylinder models. Two clips are provided, one on each side of the distributor cap. They are released by prying them away from the cap.

The cap used on the 1963-1974 four and six cylinder distributors is held by two conventional screws, Fig. B-12. Removing these screws permits removal of the cap.

After removing the distributor cap on any distributor it should be cleaned carefully and then thoroughly inspected. Check to be sure that it

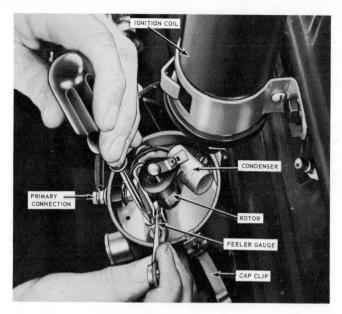

Fig. B-11. Method of adjusting breaker point gap on distributor used on 1962 and earlier Chevrolet Six. Note clips used to hold cap in place.

Fig. B-12. Typical of distributors used on 1963–1974 four and six cylinder engines.

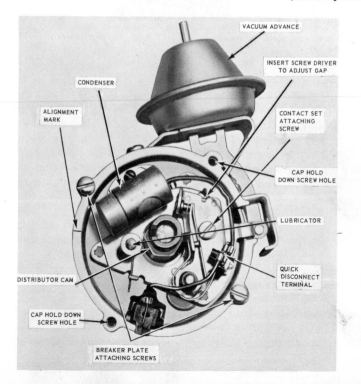

is not cracked at any point. Particular attention should be paid to any evidence of charring between the firing points on the interior of the cap. Such a condition results from arcing of the spark. Also make sure the interior of the towers are clean and are not corroded. Any evidence of corrosion should be removed. The easiest way to do this is to roll some fine grain abrasive paper around a pencil and use this as a hone to remove the corrosion, Fig. B-13.

If the cap is cracked, or if there has been any arcing between the points in the interior of the cap, or if the interior of the towers cannot be cleaned, a new cap should be installed.

Fig. B-13. Using a piece of fine emery cloth on a pencil to clean towers of distributor cap.

With the cap removed, the rotor can then be removed. On the type distributor used on the V-8 engines, Fig. B-14, the rotor is held in place by two screws which enter the centrifugal advance mechanism. Removing these screws permits lifting the rotor from its position. On other distributors, Fig. B-11, the rotor is pulled vertically from the top of the distributor shaft. On this latter type of construction, if the spring contact on top of the rotor is defective, a new rotor should be obtained. Also if the firing end of the rotor is badly erroded, the rotor should be replaced.

REPLACING THE CONDENSER

The condenser, Figs. B-11, B-12 and B-14, is replaced at the same time that the regular points are replaced. To remove a condenser, all that is necessary is to remove the attaching screw and disconnect the short wire which connects the condenser to the breaker points. On late model V-8 distributors, the condenser and breaker points form a single assembly and are removed together.

Specialized equipment is needed to test a condenser, but as the cost of a new condenser is relatively low, they are usually discarded without

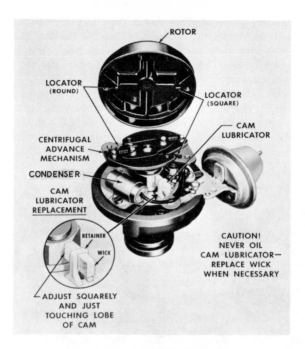

Fig. B-14. Details of V-8 distributor. Cam lubricator on recent models has changed to the round type as used on six cylinder distributors.

testing whenever ignition breaker points are replaced. A defective condenser will cause severe arcing of the breaker points, resulting in a scorched or smoky appearance of the points, accompanied with misfiring.

REPLACING BREAKER POINTS

Ignition breaker points should be replaced when the contacts are badly burned, Fig. B-15, or when there is excessive metal transfer from one point to the other. Metal transfer is considered excessive when it equals or exceeds the gap width or approximately 0.015 in.

Fig. B-15. Note pitted condition of these ignition breaker points.

Burned points are generally the result of a defective condenser or the result of an accumulation of oil and dirt on the points. This is usually caused by oil bleeding from the distributor base bushing onto the points, by excessive or improper cam lubricant being thrown on the points, or neglecting to clean the points periodically.

Excessive metal transfer from one point to the other is generally caused by incorrect point alignment, incorrect voltage regulator setting, wrong type of condenser, or a radio condenser installed to the distributor side of the coil, or extended operation at speeds other than normal.

Chevrolet 307 cu. in. V-8 engine equipped with 2-barrel carburetor and fitted with Controlled Combustion System.

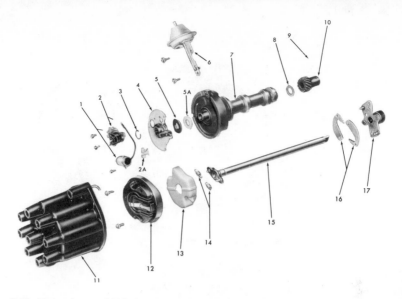

Fig. B-16. View of typical V-8 distributor. 1–Condenser. 2–Contact point assembly. 2A–Cam lubricator. 3–Retaining ring. 4–Breaker plate. 5–Felt washer. 5A–Plastic seal. 6–Vacuum advance unit. 7–Housing. 8–Shim washer. 9–Drive gear pin. 10–Drive gear. 11–Cap. 12–Rotor. 13–Radio shield. 14–Weight springs. 15–Main shaft. 16–Advance weights. 17–Cam weight base assembly.

Breaker points which have a smooth gray surface are still serviceable and will make contact over the entire contacting area.

On the six cylinder and four cylinder models, the distributors are readily accessible and the breaker points may be replaced without removing the distributor from the engine. On the V-8 engines, the distributors are not so accessible. Consequently, most mechanics prefer to remove the distributor from the engine, as this will permit a more careful examination of the condition of the breaker points, and also simplify the adjustment of the breaker point gap.

Naturally, if the distributor is to be overhauled or tested on a distributor test bench, it will be necessary to remove the unit from the engine.

HOW TO REPLACE BREAKER POINTS

Eight Cylinder Engine Distributor: The contact point set is replaced as one complete assembly and only the dwell angle (breaker point gap) requires adjustment after replacement. The breaker lever spring tension and point alignment are set at the factory and require no further adjustment.

Remove the distributor cap by placing a screwdriver in the slot head of the latch, press down and turn 1/4 turn in either direction. Remove the radio shield 13, Fig. B-16. Remove the attaching screws which hold the base of the contact assembly in place. Remove the primary and condenser leads from the nylon connection, in the contact set, Fig. B-17. Contact set can then be lifted from the distributor.

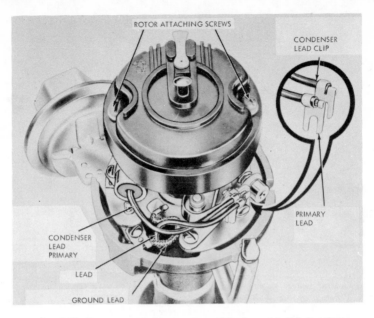

Fig. B-17. Note rotor attaching screws and leads on this V-8 distributor.

To install a new set reverse this procedure. When installing the primary and condenser leads, be sure they are installed as shown in Fig. B-17. Improper installation will cause lead interference between the cap, weight base and breaker advance plate.

On late model cars, the distributor cam lubricator should be rotated 180 deg. every 12,000 miles and replaced every 24,000 miles. On older models with a wick type lubricator for the cam, change the lubricator every 20,000 miles. Use a long nose pliers to squeeze the assembly together at the base and lift it out. Replace it in the same manner, after first wiping all lubricant from the cam. Adjust the cam lubricant wick to just touch the cam lobes. Over-lubricating of the cam can be caused by the wick bearing too hard against the cam surface. Do not apply additional lubricant to the cam.

Crank the engine and observe action of the points to be sure that they open and close as the engine is cranked. Then after installing the distributor cap, operate the engine at idle speed and adjust the points accurately as follows: Using a hex type wrench, turn the adjusting screw, Fig. B-18, in a clockwise direction until the engine begins to misfire, then turn the screw one-half turn in the opposite direction. This will give the approximate dwell angle of 30 deg. which is preferred. If a dwell meter is available, that should be used for adjusting the breaker point gap.

Four and Six Cylinder Distributor 1962-1974: To replace the ignition breaker points on this type of distributor, first release the distributor cap holddown screws, remove cap and rotor. Pull primary and condenser lead wires from contact point quick disconnect terminal, Fig. B-12.

28

Remove contact set attaching screw, lift contact point set from breaker plate. Clean breaker plate of oil sludge and dirt, and place new contact point assembly in position on the breaker plate, and install attaching screw. Be careful to wipe protective film from set prior to installation. Note that the pilot on the contact set must engage matching hole in breaker

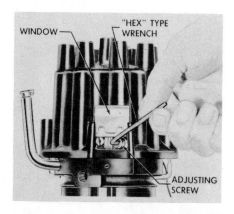

Fig. B-18. Method of adjusting breaker point gap on V-8 distributor.

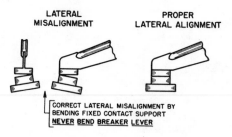

Fig. B-19. Ignition breaker points must be accurately aligned.

plate. Connect primary or condenser lead wires to quick disconnect terminal on contact point set. Check and adjust points for proper alignment and breaker arm spring tension, Fig. B-19. If points require alignment, bend the stationary contact support. The contact spring pressure should be 20 to 23 oz., as measured with a spring balance. Weak spring tension will cause chatter, resulting in arcing and burning of the points and an ignition miss at high speed. Excessive tension will cause undue wear of the contact points. When checking the spring pressure, the scale should be hooked to the breaker lever and the pull exerted at 90 deg. to the breaker lever. The reading should be taken just as the points separate. Pressure can be adjusted by bending the breaker lever spring.

The point opening of new points can be checked with a feeler gauge,

Fix Your Chevrolet

but the use of a feeler gauge on rough or uncleaned breaker points is not recommended as the reading would be inaccurate. Correct point setting for both four and six cylinder distributors is .019 in. for new points and .016 for used points. To adjust the contact point opening, first turn or crank the engine until the breaker arm rubbing block is on the high point of the cam lobe. This will provide maximum point opening. Loosen the contact support block screw, Fig. B-12. Use a screwdriver to move the point support to obtain the correct opening of .019 in. for new points and .016 in. for used points, Fig. B-20. Then tighten the contact support lock screw and recheck the point opening. If available, check the adjustment with a cam angle or swell gauge.

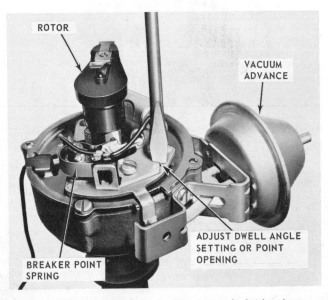

Fig. B-20. Setting breaker point gap on six cylinder distributor.

An exploded view of the distributor used on six cylinder Chevrolet built cars from 1962-1972 is shown in Fig. B-21. The four cylinder distributor is similar in detail.

235 cu. in. 1962-1954 Six Distributor: To replace the ignition breaker points, first remove the distributor cap and rotor, Fig. B-11. Remove the primary wire. Loosen the primary outside spanner nut, and unhook the breaker arm spring from the terminal. Remove contact point lock screw and remove the assembly. Carefully wipe the protective oil film from the contact point of the new set. Place the contact point and support assembly in position over pivot post and adjusting screw, and install lock screw loosely. Place breaker arm over pivot post and hook arm spring over terminal stud. Tighten terminal stud nut securely, and assemble

30

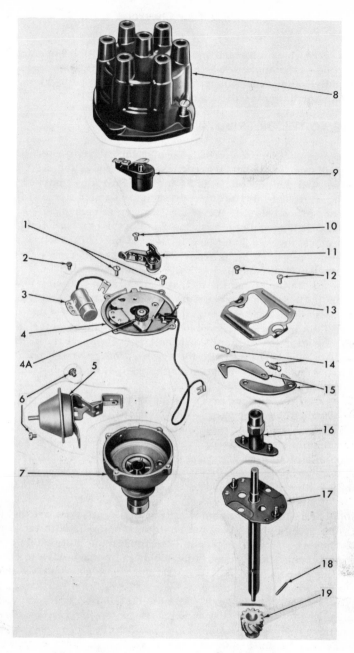

Fig. B-21. Exploded view of typical six cylinder distributor. 1–Breaker plate attaching screws. 2–Condenser attaching screws. 3–Condenser. 4–Breaker plate assembly. 4A–Cam lubricator. 5–Vacuum control assembly. 6–Vacuum assembly attaching screws. 7–Housing. 8–Distributor cap. 9–Rotor. 10–Contact point screws. 11–Contact point assembly. 12–Weight cover screws. 13–Weight cover. 14–Weight springs. 15–Advance weights. 16–Cam assembly. 17–Main shaft assembly. 18–Roll pin. 19–Drive gear.

31

primary wire, lock clip and nut to terminal. Set point opening and align points. Point opening on new points should be .019 in. and used points .016 in. Breaker arm spring tension should be 19 to 23 oz. Replacing rotor and cap completes the operation.

REPLACING THE DISTRIBUTOR

When it is decided to overhaul the distributor, or to check the advance on a distributor test bench, it is necessary to remove the distributor from the engine, and the procedure is as follows: On radio equipped Corvettes, remove ignition shield from over distributor and coil. One bolt is accessible from top of shield, the other two are at rear of shield facing the fire wall. On all models release the distributor cap hold down screws or clips, remove the cap and place it clear of the work area. If necessary, remove the secondary leads from the distributor cap after first marking the cap tower from the lead to No. 1 cylinder. This will aid in the reinstallation of the leads and the cap. Disconnect the primary lead from the coil terminal. Scribe a realignment mark on the distributor bowl and engine in line with the rotor segment. Disconnect the vacuum line to distributor. On the Corvette, also disconnect the tachometer drive cable. Remove the distributor hold down bolt and clamp, Fig. B-22. The distributor can then be lifted from the engine. Note the position of the vacuum advance mechanism relative to the engine, so the distributor can be reinstalled in its original position.

Avoid rotating the engine with distributor removed, as that would necessitate complete retiming of the ignition.

To reinstall the distributor when the engine has not been cranked while the distributor was removed, proceed as follows: Turn the rotor about 1/8 turn in a clockwise direction past the mark previously placed on the distributor housing to locate the rotor. Push the distributor down into position in the cylinder block with the housing in the normal installed position, Fig. B-22.

It may be necessary to remove the rotor slightly to start the gear into mesh with the camshaft gear, but rotor should line up with the mark when the distributor is down in place. Then tighten the distributor clamp bolt snugly and connect the vacuum line. Connect primary wire to coil terminal and install cap. Also install spark plug and high tension wires if they were removed.

If the engine was cranked while the distributor was removed, it will be necessary to position the number one piston in firing position. To do this, remove number one spark plug and with the finger on the plug hole, crank the engine until compression is felt in the number one cylinder. Continue cranking until timing mark on crankshaft pulley lines up with timing tab attached to the engine front cover. An alternate method is to remove the rocker cover (left bank on V-8 engines) and crank engine until number one intake valve closes. Then continue to crank slowly about one-third turn until the timing mark on pulley lines up with timing tab.

Ignition Tune-up

Install distributor in block in normal position, Fig. B-22, noting position of vacuum control unit. Position rotor to point toward front of engine with the distributor housing held in installed position. Then turn rotor counterclockwise approximately one-eighth turn more toward left cylinder bank and push the distributor down to engine camshaft. It may be necessary to rotate rotor slightly until camshaft engagement is felt.

While pressing firmly down on distributor housing, kick starter over a few times to make sure oil pump shaft is engaged. Install hold down clamp and bolt and snug down bolt. Turn distributor body slightly until points just open and tighten distributor clamp bolt. Place distributor cap in position and check to see if rotor lines up with terminal for number one spark plug.

Fig. B-22. Arrow points to distributor clamp screw. Also typical of V-8 construction.

Install distributor cap, check all high tension wire connections and connect spark plug wires, if they have been removed. It is important that wires be installed in their location in the supports. The brackets are numbered to show the correct installation. Wires must be installed as indicated to prevent cross firing. Fig. B-22 shows the location of the wires on the six cylinder model. On V-8 engines follow the numbering on the brackets. Connect vacuum line to distributor and distributor primary wire to coil terminal. The engine can then be started and the timing set.

Fig. B-23. Typical timing marks.

TIMING THE IGNITION

In order to get maximum performance and economy from any of the Chevrolet engines, it is necessary that the ignition timing be set with a high degree of accuracy. If the timing is too far advanced, there is danger of burning holes in the pistons, and if the spark is too far retarded, maximum power will not be attained, and in addition fuel economy will drop.

Ignition timing marks on a 235 cu. in. Six are located on the flywheel and can be seen through an opening in the left side of the flywheel housing. Other engines, four, six and V-8, have the timing marks on the crankshaft pulley or on the vibration damper at the front end of the crankshaft, Fig.. B-23, which is typical of the timing markings at the front end of the engine.

Note the markings on the pads are in 2 deg. increments, with the greatest number of markings on the "A" side of the "O." The "O" marking indicates top dead center of number one cylinder and all before top dead center settings fall on the "A" (advance) side of the "O."

Before attempting to time the engine, the marks should be wiped clean so they are clearly visible. If necessary, chalk the proper mark so it can be clearly seen. The engine is correctly timed when the breaker points

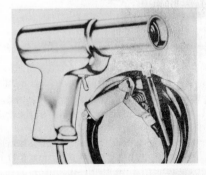

Fig. B-24. One type of timing light.

34

just start to open when the piston is on its compression stroke and the correct degree mark is in alignment with the index mark.

The actual timing is usually done with the aid of a timing light, Fig. B-24. Another method which does not use any special equipment will be described later. Connect the timing light to number one spark plug and to the battery, or follow the instructions accompanying the timing light. Disconnect spark advance hose and plug the vacuum source opening. Start the engine and operate at specified idle speed. Aim timing light at timing marks. Adjust the timing by loosening the distributor clamp and rotating the distributor body as required until correct timing mark is in alignment with pointer. Tighten clamp to hold distributor in position. Stop engine and reconnect vacuum.

If a timing light is not available, a method can be used which requires no special equipment. Crank the engine until number one piston is coming up on the compression stroke. Remove the spark plugs. Compression will be felt by holding your thumb over the spark plug hole when the piston is coming up on the compression stroke. In addition, both intake and exhaust valves will be closed. Continue cranking until the desired timing mark lines up with the index mark. With the ignition cable connected to number one spark plug, place the plug on some metal part of the engine, such as the exhaust manifold. Then loosen the distributor hold down clamp and rotate the distributor body. At the same time, observe the spark plug. Tighten the distributor in position when a spark jumps at the plug gap. The timing will now be set at the correct position.

DISTRIBUTOR SHAFT ROTATION

The distributor shaft on all Chevrolet, Chevy II, Nova, Chevelle, Camaro, Corvette and Monte Carlo engines rotates in a clockwise direction. The location of the distributor cap tower for the No. 1 spark plug cable varies with engine application. Check the location before pulling cables.

FIRING ORDER

Firing order refers to the sequence in which the cylinders fire. In an in-line engine, the cylinders are in numerical order from the front to the rear. In a V-8, the left bank (as viewed from the driver's seat) is given the odd numbers, 1-3-5-7, while the right bank has the even numbers, 2-4-6-8.

The firing order on Chevrolet V-8 engines is 1-8-4-3-6-5-7-2. On in-line six cylinder engines, the firing order is 1-5-3-6-2-4. On the four, it is 1-3-4-2.

Ideally, the objective of cylinder firing order of an in-line engine is to fire consecutive cylinders in the order at alternate ends of the crankshaft. On V-8 engine firing orders, an attempt is also made to alternate cylinder blocks, left and right, for consecutively firing cylinders. This distributes the forces of the power strokes which, in turn, reduces vibration and makes for a smoother running engine.

TRANSISTOR IGNITION

The optional transistor ignition system introduced in 1971 consists of a special distributor, coil and pulse amplifier, Fig. B-25. An iron timer core replaces the conventional breaker cam. It has the same number of equally spaced projections or vanes as the engine has cylinders. The magnetic pickup assembly consists of a ceramic permanent magnet, a pole piece and a pickup coil. The steel pole piece has equally spaced internal teeth, one tooth for each cylinder. The magnetic pickup assembly at the center is rotated (advanced) by the vacuum control unit.

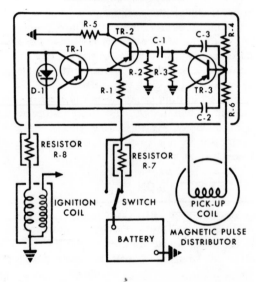

Fig. B-25. Wiring diagram of ignition pulse amplifier.

The timer core is rotated by centrifugal action.

The distributor shaft and bushings are permanently lubricated, so no periodic maintenance is required. To lubricate the upper bushing at the time of overhaul, remove the plastic seal and add SAE 20 engine oil to the packing. The lower bushing is lubricated by the engine through a splash hole in the distributor housing.

To check the ignition coil primary for an open circuit, connect an ohmmeter across the two primary terminals with the battery disconnected. Primary resistance at 75 deg. F. should be between .35 and .55 ohms. Tachometer readings can be made if the manufacturer's instructions so state. Note that when testing the transistor ignition system, a dwell reading cannot be obtained.

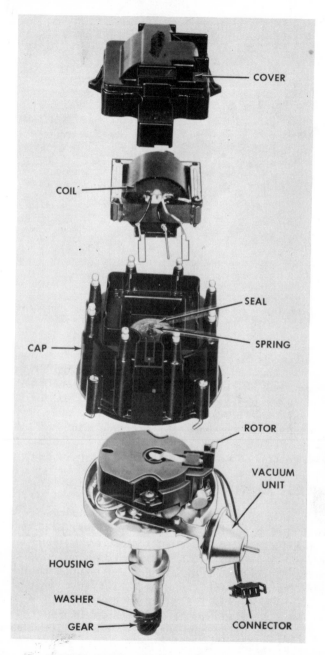

Fig. B-26. High Energy Ignition (HEI) distributor is
used on all engines in all models, starting with 1975.

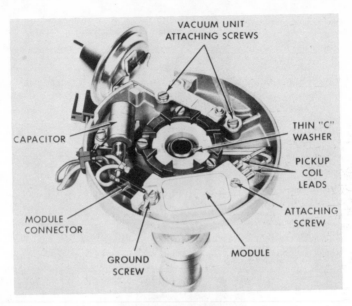

Fig. B-26a. Top view of special ignition distributor with cap removed reveals heart of GM's High Energy Ignition (HEI) system.

The coil secondary winding can be checked for an open circuit by connecting an ohmmeter from the high tension center tower to either primary terminal. To obtain a reliable reading, a scale on the ohmmeter having the 20,000 ohm value within, or nearly within, the middle third of the scale should be used. Secondary resistance at 75 deg. F. should be between 8,000 and 12,500 ohms. If the reading is infinite, the coil secondary winding is open.

A dwell reading cannot be obtained on this type of system.

HIGH ENERGY IGNITION SYSTEM

Starting with 1975 models, all Chevrolet models are equipped with GM's High Energy Ignition (HEI) system, Figs. B-26 and B-26a. Outwardly, the HEI system distributor closely resembles a conventional breaker point distributor. HEI, however, does not have breaker points in its makeup, and the unit installed on V-8 engines has the ignition coil built into the distributor cap. The HEI system used on six cylinder engines has the ignition coil mounted externally.

Chevrolet's High Energy Ignition system is designed to be free of routine maintenance. Not having breaker points eliminates adjustments or parts replacements of that type. The HEI system incorporates an electronic module, which is serviced by complete replacement. Should the need for replacement occur, apply a liberal coating of silicone grease.

A generous quantity is supplied with the replacement unit. Lubrication is necessary to provide adequate cooling of the unit.

The complete HEI distributor is removed in the same manner as the conventional distributor. First, remove the distributor cap and disconnect the vacuum line to the vacuum advance. Then, make a mark on the distributor housing in line with the tip of the rotor. NOTE: This precaution will help insure correct reinstallation. Next, remove the distributor hold-down clamp nut and clamp. Then, lift the distributor from the engine.

Complete distributor testing requires the use of a distributor test stand. If a test stand is not available, check the HEI system to make sure that current is reaching the spark plugs. Disconnect the cable from a spark plug and insert an extension. Using insulated pliers, hold the end of the extension about 1/4 in. from a dry area of the engine block, and crank the engine with the starter. The spark should readily jump the gap. In fact, the HEI system generates nearly twice the voltage of the conventional breaker point system.

The HEI system has points in common with the magnetic pulse distributor shown in Fig. B-26. However, HEI is a complete system with magnetic pulse distributor, integrated circuit electronics and high energy coil all in one factory assembled unit.

To replace the coil: Take off distributor cap. Then remove four screws that secure coil in cap. Remove harness connector and battery wire from side of cap. Push coil leads out of the way. Remove coil. Reverse procedure to install the new coil.

To replace the module: Disconnect wiring harness connector at side of distributor cap. Remove distributor. Remove rotor and disconnect wires from module terminal. Remove two mounting screws and remove module. CAUTION: At installation, coat bottom of new module with dielectric lubricant (furnished with new module) to aid in heat transfer.

CHECKS AND CARE OF IGNITION CABLE

When disconnecting cables from spark plugs or the distributor, pull on the molded cap only. Radio resistor cables have TVRS or the word Radio stamped on the covering. The conductors are made of fabric impregnated with graphite or other material. Pulling on the cable may separate the conductor from the connector at one end or the weather seal may be damaged. Arcing within the cable will occur; misfiring and hard starting result. The resistance of each cable is approximately 24,000 ohms. Never puncture these wires with a probe.

It is very important that the insulation on the cable from the distributor to the spark plugs and from the coil to the distributor be examined carefully, for if this insulation has deteriorated, current will leak and misfiring will result. If the insulation becomes dry so that it is cracked on the surface or is oil soaked, new cables should be installed.

When high tension cables are removed or disconnected, special care must be taken to replace them in their original position. That applies not only to the actual connections from the distributor to the spark plugs, but also to their position in their brackets. If they are placed in the wrong position in the bracket, cross firing from one cable to another will occur and attendant misfiring.

Chevrolet's HEI system can provide up to 35,000V. Because of this higher-than-conventional voltage, the system has large diameter (8mm) spark plug cables. Conventional cables (7mm) should not be used with the HEI system.

The spark plug cables are insulated with a silicone material, which is said to be more heat and moisture resistant than other insulating materials. However, it is softer and more pliable than rubber and more easily damaged by rough handling. HEI cables are gray in color.

Boots on the high tension cables seal tightly to the spark plugs. To remove them, twist the boot about a half turn in either direction to break the seal. Then, pull evenly on the boot and cable to remove them as an assembly. NOTE: Do not try to remove spark plug cables while engine is running. The high voltage could cause a severe shock.

If you want to check for a spark on an engine that fails to start, use an insulated pliers. First, remove the boot and cable as described. Grip the boot with the insulated pliers and hold the cable end about 1/4 in. away from a dry area of the engine block and crank the engine. A spark should jump the gap.

IGNITION RESISTOR

Prior to 1959, a block type resistor was used in the primary circuit of the ignition system, Fig. B-1. This is connected between the ignition and the coil. Since that time a resistance wire is used in place of the block type unit. This primary resistance is cut out of the circuit while the engine is being cranked, but as soon as the engine starts, all the current for the ignition coil passes through the resistor. In that way a full 12V current is supplied to the coils for easy starting.

Should this resistance, either the block type or the wire type, become defective, engine misfiring and eventual complete failure of the engine will result. Be sure to check the resistance when an illusive misfiring occurs. The resistance of the ignition resistor on four and six cylinder cars is 1.8 ohms and on V-8 engines with conventional ignition the resistance is 1.35 ohms, and in the case of transistor ignition systems the resistance of a resistor is .43 and .68 ohms.

CHECKING PRIMARY IGNITION CIRCUIT

Except for defective resistors in the line from the ignition switch to the coil, trouble in the primary ignition circuits is usually confined to loose or dirty connections. Pay particular attention to battery and battery ground connections, making sure they are tight and show no evidence of corrosion.

REPLACING THE IGNITION COIL

When replacing a conventional ignition coil, use care to see that it is correctly connected to the circuit. The center tower is, of course, the high tension connection and is connected to the center tower of the distributor. The other two terminals of the ignition coil are the primary connections. One terminal is marked "+" and the other "-". The negative terminal should be connected to the primary connection of the distributor, and the other or "+" terminal, to the R terminal of the starter solenoid. From the solenoid the connection goes to the starting switch and then to the "+" terminal of the starting battery. The positive terminal of the coil will have two wires connected to it, and the negative terminal will have only one.

While the coil will operate if the primary connections are reversed, full power will not be developed and missing will occur at high engine speeds.

Typical 1973 Chevrolet V-8 engine.

TROUBLE SHOOTING

See also Starting, Engine and Fuel System Troubles.

ENGINE WILL NOT START

Weak battery. Excessive moisture on high tension wiring and spark plugs. Cracked distributor cap. Defective coil or condenser. Worn ignition breaker points. Coil to distributor high tension cable not in place. Loose connections or broken wire in low tension circuit. Incorrect ignition breaker point gap. Defective spark plugs. On cars with seat belt-starter interlock system, be sure seat belts are fastened at each occupied front seat position.

HARD STARTING

Faulty or improperly adjusted spark plugs. Defective or incorrectly adjusted ignition breaker points. Loose connections in primary circuit. Worn or oil soaked high tension wiring. Low capacity condenser. Defective ignition coil. Defective distributor cap. Defective rotor.

ENGINE MISFIRES

Worn or dirty spark plugs. Defective insulation on high tension cables. Defective distributor cap. Poor cylinder compression. Defective or incorrectly adjusted breaker points. Defective coil. Incorrect ignition timing. Defective spark plugs. Defective ignition breaker points.

POPPING, SPITTING, PREIGNITION

Loose wiring. Faulty spark plugs. Over advanced spark timing.

Showing location of temperature switch as installed on 1972–1973 Chevrolet small V-8.

CARBURETOR AND
FUEL SYSTEM SERVICE

The carburetor and fuel system, as a rule, cause every little trouble and require a minimum of attention. A basic fuel system includes:

Fuel Tank	Fuel Pump	Fuel Filter	Intake Manifold
Fuel Line	Carburetor	Air Cleaner	Fuel Gauge

In addition to the foregoing, the fuel system on late model cars includes an emission control system and an evaporative control system. The carburetors on such cars (except those with mechanical cams) are equipped with idle mixture limiter caps. These caps must not be removed and no attempt should be made to adjust the fuel mixture. However, the idle speed must be adjusted to specifications.

Several different types and makes of carburetors are used on the various Chevrolet built cars. Many of these carburetors are illustrated in this chapter, Figs. C-1, C-2 and C-3, for example. In each case the adjustment and other parts are indicated. It will be found that carburetors of Rochester, Holley and Carter are all represented.

Before attempting to do any other work on a carburetor, be sure the ignition system is in good condition and is correctly timed. Engine compression must be up to standard and at full operating temperature before attempting to adjust the carburetor. It is best to drive the engine for fifteen to twenty minutes before adjusting the carburetor to be sure the temperature has stabilized.

In general, poor performance usually results from weak compression, or defective ignition, rather than troubles in the carburetor. Be sure that there are no leaks in the intake manifold or vacuum operated accessories.

PRELIMINARY ADJUSTMENT PROCEDURE

After stabilizing the temperature of the engine by operating for at least fifteen minutes, check torque of carburetor to intake manifold bolts to exclude possibility of air leaks. Similarly, check bolts securing intake manifold to engine block. Also check vacuum lines to any vacuum operated accessories for leaks.

Inspect manifold heat control valve (if used) for freedom of action and correct spring tension.

IDLE SPEED AND MIXTURE ADJUSTMENT

The location of the idle mixture and speed controls is shown in Figs. C-1 and C-2. All carburetor adjustments must be made with the engine at operating temperature and with the distributor vacuum line discon-

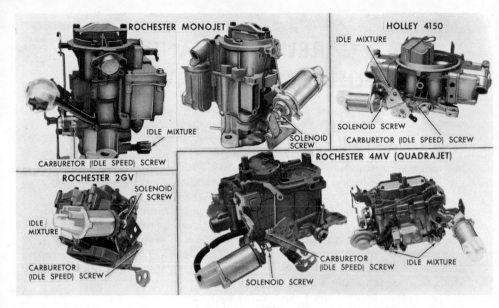

Fig. C-1. Location of idle mixture and speed screws, 1971 carburetors. Typical of 1972-74 carburetors.

nected and plugged.

The procedure for adjusting the idle speed and mixture on single barrel carburetors on cars built prior to 1970 is as follows:

Remove air cleaner, Fig. A-2. If available, connect tachometer and vacuum gauge to engine. Set hand brake and shift transmission into neutral. As a preliminary adjustment, turn idle mixture adjustment lightly to seat, then back out one and one-half turns, Figs. C-1, C-2 and C-3. Be careful not to turn idle mixture screws firmly against seat as damage may result.

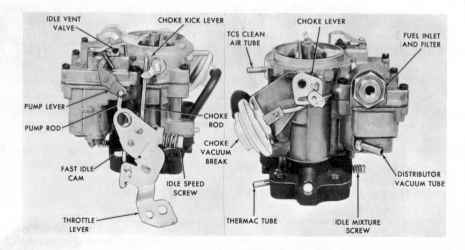

Fig. C-2. Details of Rochester 2GV carburetor.

Carburetor, Fuel System Service

With the engine operating and choke wide open, adjust idle speed screw to specified idle speed. Then adjust idle mixture screw to obtain high vacuum reading. If vacuum gauge is not available, turn idle mixture adjustment in until engine misfires and operates roughly. Then turn idle mixture screw out until the engine lopes due to rich mixture. Then turn in until engine operates smoothly.

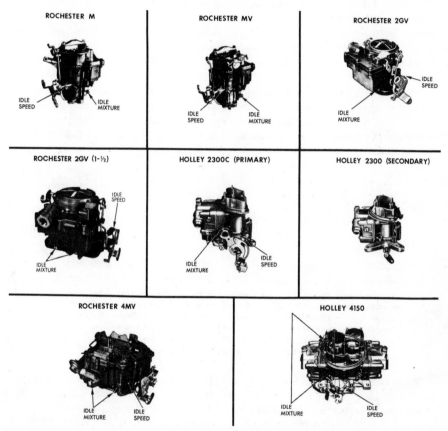

Fig. C-3. Location of idle mixture and idle speed adjustment on additional Rochester and Holley carburetors. See also Fig. C-1.

On air conditioned vehicles, turn air conditioner "off" except on L4 and L6 engines with automatic transmission and 325 and 350 hp 327 cu. in. engines (manual trans.) where idle speed is set with the air conditioner on.

General instructions for idle speed adjustment for engines with idle solenoids is as follows: Adjust idle speed to 500 rpm by adjusting solenoid plunger hex only. Disconnect lead wire at the solenoid and observe idle speed. De-energizing the solenoids allows the throttle lever to seat against the carburetor idle screw. Adjust the carburetor idle screw as necessary to obtain 400 rpm. Then adjust mixture screw in to obtain a 20 rpm drop (lean roll). Then adjust mixture out one-quarter turn.

Dual and four barrel carburetors: On dual and four barrel carburetors there are two idle mixture adjustments. The adjusting procedure is similar to that just described. First turn both needles until they lightly touch the seat. Then back out approximately one and one-half turns. Adjust first one needle and then the other to obtain maximum reading on the vacuum gauge or to obtain maximum idle speed for that particular throttle setting. Then adjust mixture screw in to obtain a 20 rpm drop (lean roll). Adjust mixture screw out one-quarter turn. Repeat for second mixture screw and then readjust the speed screw to obtain the specified idle speed.

1971-1973 carburetor adjustments: Make no attempt to adjust idle mixture on carburetors with idle mixture limiter caps. The only adjustment is for idle speed. On all engines, disconnect distributor spark advance hose and plug vacuum source opening. Disconnect fuel tank line from vacuum canister. Idle speed adjustments are made as follows:

Engine	Manual Trans. in neutral	Auto. Trans. in drive
250 cu. in.	550 rpm	500 rpm
307, 350, 400 cu. in.	600 rpm*	550 rpm#
350 cu. in. Quadrajet	600 rpm*	550 rpm#
350 cu. in. 4 bbl. Holley	700 rpm+	700 rpm+
402 cu. in. Quadrajet	600 rpm	600 rpm
454 cu. in. 4 bbl. Holley	700 rpm%	700 rpm%

* – Air conditioner off. # – Air conditioner on. + – On Corvette: Then turn one mixture screw in to obtain 20 rpm drop. Then back off 1/4 turn, repeat for second screw. % – On all except Corvette adjust mixture screws to obtain maximum rpm, then adjust carburetor speed screw to obtain 700 rpm. Turn one mixture screw in to obtain 20 rpm drop, then back off 1/4 turn. Repeat for other mixture screw. Readjust speed screw to obtain 700 rpm.

Adjusting 1970 carburetors: On all models disconnect and plug distributor line. Turn mixture screw in until lightly contacting seat, then back out four turns. For individual models then proceed as follows:

153 C.I.D.: Set mixture screw to obtain maximum idle rpm. Then adjust idle speed screw to obtain 750 rpm with manual transmisssion on and 650 rpm with automatic transmission. Adjust mixture to obtain 20 rpm drop then back out one-quarter turn. Readjust idle to specified rpm.

230, 250 and 350 (250 hp): Adjust solenoid screw to obtain 830 rpm with manual transmission and 630 rpm with automatic transmission. Adjust mixture screw to obtain 750 rpm with manual transmission and 600 rpm with automatic transmission. Disconnect solenoid. Set carburetor idle screw to obtain 400 rpm. Reconnect solenoid.

307 C.I.D. 400 C.I.D. (265 hp): Adjust idle speed to 800 rpm and solenoid screw to 630 rpm. Adjust mixture screws equally to 700 rpm for manual transmission and 600 rpm for automatic transmission. On auto-

matic transmission cars disconnect solenoid electrically. Set carburetor idle speed screw to 450 rpm and reconnect solenoid.

350 C.I.D. (250 hp): Adjust solenoid screw to obtain 830 rpm with manual transmission and 630 rpm with automatic transmission. Adjust mixture screws equally to obtain 750 rpm with manual transmission and 600 rpm with automatic transmission. Disconnect solenoid electrically set carburetor idle to 450 rpm and reconnect solenoid.

350 C.I.D. (300 hp), 400 C.I.D. (330 hp): Adjust carburetor idle speed screws to 775 rpm with manual transmission and 630 rpm with automatic transmission. Adjust mixture screws equally to obtain 700 rpm with manual and 600 rpm with automatic transmission.

396 C.I.D. 400 C.I.D. (375 hp), 454 C.I.D. (450 hp): Set mixture screws, Fig. C-2, to obtain maximum rpm. Set idle speed screws to obtain 750 rpm with manual transmission and 700 rpm with automatic transmission. Turn one mixture screw in to obtain 20 rpm drop. The back out screw one-quarter turn. Readjust idle speed screw to 750 rpm with manual transmission and 700 rpm with automatic transmission.

396 C.I.D. (350 hp) 454 C.I.D. (345 hp), 454 C.I.D. (360 and 390 hp) with automatic transmission: Adjust idle speed screw to obtain 630 rpm. Adjust mixture screws equally to obtain 600 rpm.

IDLE MIXTURE ADJUSTMENT ON 1974-1978 MODELS

Idle mixture adjustments on recent models with exhaust emission control equipment have been preset at the factory. The carburetors are calibrated to obtain the desired lean air-fuel ratio, then limiter caps are installed. These plastic caps hold the mixture adjustment within a very limited range to avoid over-rich settings and the resulting high levels of air polluting exhaust emissions. Under ordinary conditions, it should not be necessary to remove the idle mixture adjustment limiting caps to obtain a satisfactory idle.

Before suspecting carburetor malfunction, be sure to test the compression pressure of each cylinder and compare the readings with the chart on page 10. Also, check over the ignition system and set ignition timing. Check the operation of the PCV (positive crankcase ventilation) valve. Inspect for vacuum leaks at the intake manifold and at vacuum hose connections. Tighten the carburetor attaching nuts and the intake manifold mounting bolts.

If it is necessary to overhaul the carburetor, follow the instructions provided with the kit of repair parts, which includes limiting caps. After the carburetor has been reassembled and installed on the engine, make the necessary adjustments and install the caps on the idle mixture adjusting screws. Adjustment instructions are provided on a decal located under the hood. The detailed information given includes engine idle speed settings and other important data needed to set up the engine to meet Federal emission standards.

MIXTURE ADJUSTMENT SPECIFICATIONS: 1974 CARBURETORS

	TIMING DEG. BTC @ RPM	SOLENOID ADJ. RPM	LEAN DROP IDLE MIXTURE RPM
250 cu. in. Federal			
Auto. Trans. CCS-EGR	8 deg. @ 600	600 rpm (DR)	650/600 (DR)
Manual Trans. AIR-EGR	8 deg. @ 850	850 rpm (N)	950/850 (N)
250 cu. in. California			
Auto. Trans. AIR-EGR	8 deg. @ 600	600 rpm (DR)	630/600 (DR)
Manual Trans. AIR-EGR	8 deg. @ 850	850 rpm (N)	950/850 (N)
350 and 400 cu. in. Federal 2 bbl.			
Auto. Trans. AIR-EGR	8 deg. @ 600	600 rpm (DR)	650/600 (DR)
Manual Trans. AIR-EGR	4 deg. @ 900	900 rpm (N)	1000/900 (H)
350 and 400 cu. in. Federal 4 bbl.			
Auto. Trans. CCS-EGR	8 deg. @ 600	600 rpm (DR)	650/600 (DR)
Manual Trans. AIR-EGR	8 deg. @ 900	900 rpm (N)	950/900 (N)
350 and 400 cu. in. California 4 bbl.			
Auto. Trans. AIR-EGR	8 deg. @ 600	600 rpm (DR)	630/600 (DR)
Manual Trans. AIR-EGR	4 deg. @ 900	900 rpm (N)	950/900 (N)
454 cu. in. Federal			
Auto. Trans. AIR-EGR	10 deg. @ 600	600 rpm (DR)	630/600 (DR)
Manual Trans. AIR-EGR	10 deg. @ 600	800 rpm (N)	850/800 (N)
454 cu. in. California			
Auto. Trans. AIR-EGR	10 deg. @ 600	600 rpm (DR)	630/600 (DR)
Manual Trans. AIR-EGR	10 deg. @ 800	800 rpm (N)	850/800 (N)
350 cu. in. 4 bbl. Z 28, L 28 Nationwide			
Auto. Trans. AIR-EGR	8 deg. @ 700	700 rpm (DR)	730/700 (DR)
Manual Trans. AIR-EGR	8 deg. @ 700	900 rpm (N)	950/900 (N)
250 cu. in. Federal			
Auto. Trans. EGR-EFE	10 deg. @ 550	550 rpm (DR)	1700 (N)
Manual Trans. EGR-EFE	10 deg. @ 550	850 rpm (N)	1800 (N)
250 cu. in. California			
Auto. Trans. EGR-EFE	10 deg. @ 600	600 rpm (DR)	1700 (N)
250 cu. in. Federal			
Auto. Trans. EGR	8 deg. @ 600	600 rpm (DR)	1800 (N)
Manual Trans. EGR	8 deg. @ 600	850 rpm (N)	1800 (N)
262 cu. in. Federal			
Auto. Trans. AIR-EGR-EFE	8 deg. @ 600	600 rpm (DR)	· · · ·
Manual Trans. AIR-EGR-EFE	8 deg. @ 600	800 rpm (N)	· · · ·
350 cu. in. Federal			
Auto. Trans. EGR-EFE	6 deg. @ 600	600 rpm (DR)	· · · ·
Manual Trans. EGR-EFE	6 deg. @ 800	800 rpm (N)	· · · ·
350, 400 cu. in. Federal			
Auto. Trans. AIR-EGR-EFE	8 deg. @ 600	600 rpm (DR)	1600 (N)
Manual Trans. AIR-EGR-EFE	6 deg. @ 800	800 rpm (N)	1600 (N)
350, 400 cu. in. Corvette			
Auto. Trans. AIR-EGR-EFE	6 deg. @ 600	600 rpm (DR)	1600 (N)
350, 400 cu. in. California			
Auto. Trans. AIR-EGR-EFE	8 deg. @ 600	600 rpm (DR)	1600 (N)
Manual Trans. AIR-EGR-EFE	4 deg. @ 800	600 rpm (DR)	1600 (N)
454 cu. in. Federal			
Auto. Trans. AIR-EGR-EFE	16 deg. @ 600	600 rpm (DR)	1000 (N)

ABBREVIATIONS
AIR — Air injection reactor
BTC — Before top center
CCS — Controlled combustion system

DR — Drive position of auto. trans.
EFE — Early fuel evaporative system
EGR — Exhaust gas recirculation
RPM — Revolutions per minute

FAST IDLE ADJUSTMENT

The fast idle adjustment on Rochester M, 4MV and Holley carburetors is as follows: With the fast idle lever on the high step of cam, and choke valve open with the engine warm, set fast idle to give specified engine rpm. Adjust screw on Rochester 4MV and bend fast idle lever on Rochester M and Holley carburetors. In addition, in the case of the Rochester model 1MV, it is necessary to disconnect the EGR valve signal line and plug it. Also, the air conditioning system must be off.

On Rochester BV carburetor, steps on the fast idle cam are correctly proportioned to give correct speed steps so it is only necessary to have correct relationship between fast idle cam position and the choke valve. If necessary, bend choke valve rod to obtain .050 to .070 in. clearance between lower edge of choke valve and bore of carburetor.

To adjust the fast idle on the Carter AFB carburetor, hold the choke valve closed and index mark of fast idle cam should line up with fast idle adjustment screw. If necessary bend fast idle rod.

CHOKE ADJUSTMENT

If the carburetor is provided with a remote type choke, remove the air cleaner and check to see that the choke valve and rods move freely. Disconnect choke rod at choke lever. Check choke adjustment as follows: On all engines except L6 and 390 hp 427 cu. in. engines, hold choke valve closed and push rod downward to contact stop. The top of rod should be even with bottom of hole in choke lever. On L6 and 390 hp 427 cu. in. engines hold choke valve closed and pull rod upward to end of travel. The

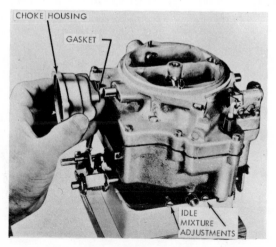

Fig. C-4. Details of Rochester model 4GC carburetor. Note idle mixture adjustment and choke housing.

bottom of rod should be even with top of hole in choke lever. If necessary adjust rod length by bending rod at offset bend. The bend must be such that the rod enters choke lever hole freely and squarely.

Connect rod at choke lever and install air cleaner.

To adjust a vacuum type choke as used on the Rochester 4GC carburetor, Fig. C-4, proceed as follows: Remove air cleaner and make sure that choke valve and mechanism move freely. Loosen choke cover, retaining screws, and adjust choke cover to specifications and tighten retainer screws securely. Replace air cleaner.

In the case of the 2GC carburetor choke: Remove thermostat cover coil. Place idle speed screw on highest step of fast idle cam. Close choke valve by pushing on intermediate choke lever. Edge of coil lever inside housing must align with edge of plug gauge. Bend intermediate choke rod to adjust.

The choke unloader provides a means of unloading raw fuel from the intake manifold if the engine is flooded. To check and adjust the unloader: Remove air cleaner. Depress accelerator pedal and check carburetor to determine whether choke valve is opening. If not, insert prescribed gauge between upper edge of choke valve and air horn casting, Fig. C-5. Hold throttle valve wide open and bend tang on throttle lever until it contacts projection on choke control lever. Remove gauge and again depress accelerator pedal. Choke valve should open prescribed amount.

FLOAT ADJUSTMENT

Most Holley carburetors are provided with a sight plug in the side of the float bowl which permits checking and adjusting the float level without removing the carburetor from the engine. For example, on Holley carburetors used on 1966-69 models, the procedure is as follows: Remove the

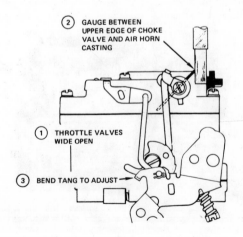

Fig. C-5. Typical choke unloader adjustment.

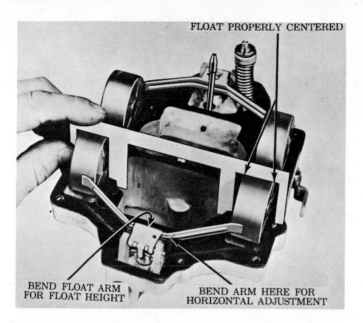

FLOAT PROPERLY CENTERED

BEND FLOAT ARM
FOR FLOAT HEIGHT

BEND ARM HERE FOR
HORIZONTAL ADJUSTMENT

Fig. C-6. Using special gauge to check float level on Rochester 4GC carburetor.
Such gauges usually form part of repair kit of parts.

air cleaner, then remove the fuel level sight plug. With the parking brake on and transmission in neutral, start the engine and allow it to idle. With the car on a level surface, the fuel level should be on a level with the threads at the bottom of the sight plug port, plus or minus 1/32 in. If necessary to adjust, either or both bowls, loosen inlet needle lock screw and turn the adjusting nut clockwise to lower or counterclockwise to raise the fuel level, then tighten the lock screw. One-sixth turn of adjusting nut equals approximately 1/16 in. fuel level change. Allow a minute for fuel level to stabilize and recheck the level at sight plug. Readjust if necessary, until the proper level is obtained, and install sight plug and air cleaner. To insure proper secondary float level setting, it is advisable to accelerate primary throttle slightly and hand operate secondary throttle. This assures a stabilized secondary fuel level.

The float level of Carter and Rochester carburetors is adjusted to a specified height and is measured with the aid of a T-scale or special gauge, Fig. C-6. Such gauges are usually provided with each kit of carburetor repair parts.

CARBURETOR FLOAT LEVEL

Carburetor Make and Model	Primary Float	Secondary Float
1968		
Rochester M, MV	11/32 in.	. . . .
Rochester 2GV	3/4 in.	. . . .
Rochester 4MV (327 cu. in.)	9/32 in.	. . . .

51

Rochester 4MV (396 cu. in.)	3/16 in.	. . . .
Rochester (427 cu. in.)	3/16 in.	. . . .
Holley 2300 (427, 400 cu. in.)	.350 in.	.500 in.
Holley 4150	.350 in.	.500 in.

1969

Rochester M, MV	1/4 in.	. . . .
Rochester 2GV (1 1/4 in.)	27/32 in.	. . . .
Rochester 2GV (1 1/2 in.)	3/4 in.	. . . .
Rochester 4MV (396 cu. in.)	1/4 in.	. . . .
Rochester 4MV (350 cu. in.)	7/32 in.	. . . .
Rochester 2GV (396 cu. in., 1 1/2 in.)	5/8 in.	. . . .

1970

Rochester M, MV	1/4 in.	. . . .
Rochester 2GV (1 1/4 in.)	27/32 in.	. . . .
Rochester 2GV (1 1/2 in.)	23/32 in.	. . . .
Rochester 4MV	1/4 in.	. . . .
Holley 2300	.350 in.	. . . .
Holley 4150	.350 in.	.500 in.

1971

Rochester MV (7041023)	1/16 in.	. . . .
Rochester MV (other than 7041023)	1/4 in.	. . . .
Rochester 2GV (7041024)	1/16 in.	. . . .
Rochester 2GV (7041101 to 7041118)	23/32 in.	. . . .
Rochester 2GV (7041181, 7041182)	25/32 in.	. . . .
Rochester 4MV	1/4 in.	. . . .
Holley	Sight plug	. . . .

1972

Rochester 2 GV (7042111 to 7042118)	23/32 in.	. . . .
Rochester 2 GV (7042831 to 7042838)	25/32 in.	. . . .
Rochester 4 MV	1/4 in.	. . . .

1973

Rochester MV	1/4 in.	. . . .
Rochester 2GV (7043100 to 7043105)	21/32 in.	. . . .
Rochester 2GV (7043111 to 7043118)	19/32 in.	. . . .
Rochester 4MV (7053200, 7043201)	1/4 in.	. . . .
Rochester 4MV (other than 7053200, 7043201)	7/32 in.	. . . .

1974

Rochester MV	.295 in.	. . . .
Rochester 2GV	19/32 in.	. . . .
Rochester 4MV (7044201 to 7044223)	3/8 in.	. . . .
Rochester (other than 7044201, 7044223)	1/4 in.	. . . .

Carburetor, Fuel System Service

1975

Rochester 1MV	11/32 in. . . . .
Rochester 2GC (7045105, 7045106)	19/32 in. . . . .
Rochester (other than 7045105, 7045106)	21/32 in. . . . .
Rochester M4MC (7045200)	17/32 in. . . . .
Rochester M4MC (other than 7045200)	15/32 in. . . . .

1976

Rochester 1MV	11/32 in. . . . .
Rochester 2GC	9/16 in. . . . .
Rochester M4MC, M4ME	13/32 in. . . . .
Rochester M4ME	13/32 in. . . . .

1977

Rochester 1ME (Four)	3/8 in. . . . .
Rochester 1ME (Six - truck)	5/16 in. . . . .
Holley 5210-C	.420 in. . . . .
Rochester 2GC	19/32 in. . . . .
Rochester M4MC	15/32 in. . . . .

1978

Rochester 1ME (Four)	5/32 in. . . . .
Rochester 1ME (Six - truck)	5/16 in. . . . .
Rochester M2ME	1/4 in. . . . .
Rochester 2GC	15/32 in. . . . .
Rochester 2GE	7/16 in. . . . .
Rochester M4MC	15/32 in. . . . .
Holley 5210-C	.520 in. . . . .
Holley 6510-C	.520 in. . . . .

1975-1978 2GC CARBURETOR

All Rochester 2GC carburetors for 1975-1978 provide for exhaust gas recirculation (EGR). Fig. C-7 details the idle system and a vacuum tube beneath the spark tube in the float bowl. A short channel connects the vacuum tube to purge ports located just above the throttle valve in the throttle body bore. When the throttle valve is opened beyond the idle position, the EGR ports are exposed to manifold vacuum. The ports, in turn, are timed to provide the right amount of vacuum to the EGR valve diaphragm to control the amount of exhaust gases introduced into the intake manifold air-fuel mixture.

The fuel vapor canister is purged by ports in the throttle body, Fig. C-7. The timed purge ports are connected from the carburetor bore to a common tube pressed into the throttle body casting. The tube connects directly to the vapor canister through a hose.

Fig. C-8 shows details of idle system on Rochester carburetor.

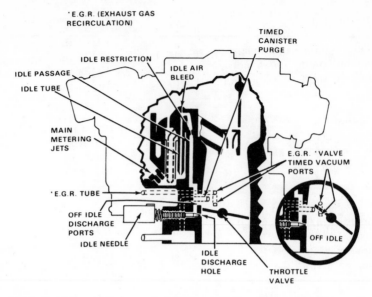

Fig. C-7. Details of idle system of Rochester 2GC carburetor installed on some 1975–1977 Chevrolet engines. Note EGR tube and timed canister purge. Detail of timed vacuum ports is shown in inset.

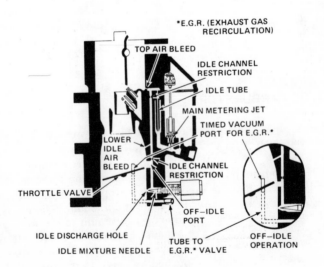

IDLE SYSTEM

Fig. C-8. Idle system of Rochester 1ME Monojet carburetor as installed on 1978 Chevette engine. This single bore, downdraft carburetor uses a triple venturi in conjunction with a plain tube nozzle.

Carburetor, Fuel System Service

The 1975 M4MC/M4MCA carburetor has two idle speeds controlled by an idle stop solenoid. To adjust: Run engine to normal temperature with A/C off. Set parking brake. Block drive wheels. Remove fuel tank hose from vapor canister. Remove and plug vacuum advance hose. Check timing. Reconnect vacuum hose. Remove solenoid wire. With transmission in drive (manual in neutral), turn idle screw to set specified rpm. Reconnect solenoid wire. Crack throttle to extend plunger. Turn plunger to set specified curb idle speed. Reconnect hose to vapor canister.

The 1976-1977 M4MC/M4ME Quadrajet carburetor closely resembles the 1975 model. On 1976-1977 models, a stop solenoid is used on cars with automatic transmission. Also, an adjustable part throttle screw is added to the float bowl.

When adjusting this carburetor, use idle speed screw and adjust engine idle speed according to decal in engine compartment. With the engine at normal operating temperature, the air cleaner in place and air conditioner off, connect a tachometer to the engine. Set parking brake and block drive wheels. Disconnect fuel tank hose from vapor canister. Disconnect and plug vacuum advance hose at distributor. Set ignition timing to specified deg. BTDC at prescribed rpm. Unplug and reconnect vacuum hose at distributor. With automatic transmission in DRIVE or manual transmission in NEUTRAL, turn idle speed screw to obtain specified rpm. Shut off engine and disconnect tachometer. Reconnect fuel tank hose to vapor canister.

To adjust fast idle: Run engine to operating temperature. Place transmission in PARK or NEUTRAL and disconnect and plug vacuum hose at EGR valve. On 454 cu. in. engine, disconnect vacuum hose to front vacuum break unit. Position cam follower lever on highest step of fast idle cam. Turn fast idle screw to obtain specified rpm. Remove plug and reconnect vacuum hose at EGR.

FUEL FILTER SERVICE

Fuel filters on recent model Chevrolets are mounted directly in the fuel inlet of the carburetor. These filters are of two different types. One is a cylindrical element known as the "bronze" type. The other is the paper element type shown in Fig. C-9.

To check these fuel filters, first disconnect the fuel line connection at the inlet fuel filter nut. Remove the inlet fuel filter nut from the carburetor with a 1 in. wrench, preferably of the fitting type. The filter element, Fig. C-9, can then be removed from the carburetor. Check the bronze element for restriction by blowing on the cone end. Element should allow air to pass freely.

Check paper element by blowing on fuel inlet end. If filter does not allow air to pass freely, replace element. Do not attempt to clean filters.

Elements should be replaced if plugged or if flooding of the carburetor occurs. A plugged filter will result in a loss of engine power or rough engine feel, especially at high engine speeds.

Fig. C-9. Paper element type fuel filter as installed on a Rochester carburetor.

Install the spring and the filter element in carburetor. Bronze filters must have small sections of cones facing out. Always install a new gasket or inlet fitting nut and install nut in carburetor and tighten securely.

Filter element should be replaced every twelve months, or 12,000 miles, whichever occurs first.

AIR CLEANER SERVICE

Several different types of air cleaners are used on recent model Chevrolet engines. These include the wire mesh with polyurethane band, oiled paper with polyurethane band, and the oiled paper type. Starting with the 1968 models, most automatic transmission equipped vehicles and emission control systems are provided with a device which thermo-statically controls the temperature of the air entering the air cleaner. The thermostatic valve of the device proportions the air from a heat stove on the exhaust manifold with the cooler air from the engine compartment.

The oiled paper filters, Fig. C-10, used in most air cleaner assemblies have both ends of the paper element bonded with Plastisol sealing material. Oil on the paper causes the element to become discolored by a small amount of dirt. This does not necessarily indicate that the element is plugged or reduced in efficiency. It is advisable to rotate the air cleaner element 180 deg. at 12,000 miles and replace it every 24,000 miles. If the vehicle is operated in very dusty conditions the preceding operation should be performed more frequently.

POLYURETHANE ELEMENT

To remove the filter element for cleaning and inspection, remove the cover wing nut, Fig. A-2, which will then permit the filter element to be lifted from its housing. Visibly check the element for tears and rips, and replace if necessary. Clean all accumulated dirt and grime from air cleaner bottom and cover. Discard air horn to air cleaner gaskets. Remove support screen from element and wash element in kerosene or mineral spirits and squeeze out excess solvent, Fig. C-11.

Never use a hot degreaser or any solvent containing acetone or similar solvent to clean the polyurethane element.

After cleaning with kerosene or mineral spirits, dip the element in light engine oil and squeeze out excess oil.

Never shake, swing or wring the element to remove excess oil or solvent, as this may tear the polyurethane material. Instead squeeze the excess from the element.

Install element on screen support. Using new gasket, replace air-cleaner body over carburetor air horns. Replace the element in the air cleaner. Care must be taken that the lower lip of the element is properly placed in the assembly and that the filter material is not folded or creased in any manner that would cause an imperfect seal.

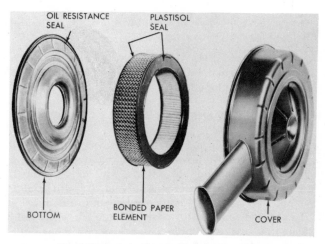

Fig. C-10. Details of paper element type air filter.

OIL WETTED PAPER ELEMENT FILTER

To replace the element of the oil wetted paper type air cleaner, Fig. C-10, first remove the wing nut, washer and cover, Fig. A-2. Remove paper element and discard. Remove bottom section of air cleaner and gasket on air horn of carburetor. Discard air horn gasket. Clean bottom section of air cleaner and cover pieces thoroughly to remove dust and grime. Be sure to check bottom section of air cleaner seal for tears or cracks. Install a new gasket on carburetor air horn and set bottom section of air cleaner on carburetor. Install new paper element on bottom section of air cleaner with either end up. The Plastisol seal is the same material on both ends. Install cover, washer and wing nut to complete the job.

To clean the paper element type filter, tap the element gently against a smooth flat surface to remove any loose dirt. Also if compressed air is available, direct the air gently against the inner side of the element which

Fig. C-11. When cleaning a polyurethane air filter element, it should be squeezed dry, not wrung.

will remove accumulated dirt. Also inspect the element for punctures or splits by looking through the element toward a strong light. If damaged, the element should be replaced.

OIL BATH TYPE AIR CLEANER

Remove the air cleaner assembly. Remove cover and filter element assembly. Empty oil out of cleaner and clean out all oil and accumulated dirt. Wash body with cleaning solvent and wipe dry. Wash filter element by slushing up and down in the cleaning solvent. Dry filter unit with an air hose or let stand until dry. Fill body of cleaner to full mark with SAE 50 engine oil. If expected temperatures are to be consistently below freezing, use SAE 20 engine oil. Assemble filter and cover assembly to body of cleaner. Install cleaner, making sure it fits tight and is set down securely.

THERMOSTATICALLY CONTROLLED AIR CLEANER

This system, Figs. C-12, C-13 and C-14, is designed to improve carburetor operation and engine warm-up characteristics. It achieves this by keeping the air entering the carburetor at a temperature of at least 100 deg. F. or more. The thermostatic air cleaner system includes a temperature sensor, Fig. C-13, a vacuum motor and control damper assembly mounted on the air cleaner, vacuum control hoses, manifold heat stove and connecting pipes. The vacuum motor is controlled by the temperature sensor. The vacuum motor operates the air control damper assembly to regulate the flow of hot air and under-hood air to the carburetor. The hot air is obtained from the heat stove on the exhaust manifold.

Carburetor, Fuel System Service

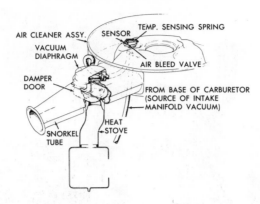

Fig. C-12. Schematic drawing of thermostatically controlled air cleaner.

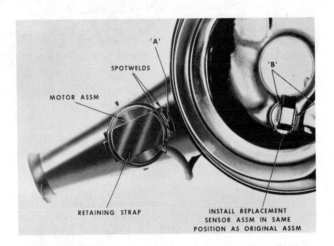

Fig. C-13. Installing replacement sensor assembly.

Visual inspection is made by checking for proper, secure connections at heat pipe and hose connections. Also check for kinked or deteriorated hoses. Repair or replace as required.

Operational inspection is made as follows: Remove air cleaner cover and install thermometer as close as possible to sensor. If engine has been in recent operation allow it to cool to below 85 deg. F. Replace air cleaner cover without the wing nut. Use a mirror if necessary to check the temperature. Start and idle the engine. When control damper assembly begins to open, remove air cleaner cover and observe the temperature reading. Open temperature must be between 85 deg. and 115 deg. F. If damper assembly does not open at the correct temperature, continue with the fol-

Fig. C-14. Chevrolet's 307 cu. in. V-8 features a carburetor hot air system. In operation, heat from exhaust manifold is ducted to air cleaner and snorkel. Thermostat, control valve and damper blend hot and cold air entering carburetor for better air-fuel vaporization.

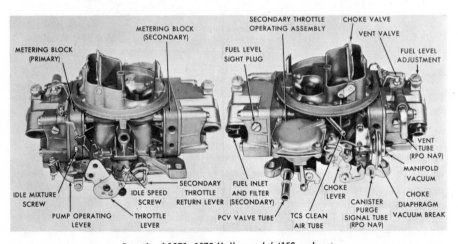

Details of 1970–1972 Holley model 4150 carburetor.

lowing vacuum motor and sensor checks. With the engine off, the position of the control damper assembly should be in the cold air delivery mode. To determine if the vacuum motor is operable, apply at least 9 in. of vacuum (obtained from the intake manifold) to the fitting on the vacuum motor. The control damper should close the cold air passage as long as vacuum is applied (the hot air pipe will be open). If the vacuum motor fails to operate the control damper assembly, with the direct application of vacuum, check to determine if the vacuum motor linkage is properly connected to the door. If the linkage is found satisfactory, then motor replacement is indicated. If the vacuum motor check is found to be satisfactory, then sensor replacement is indicated.

TIPS ON CARBURETOR SERVICE

Most difficulties encountered in the operation of carburetors result from dirt and other foreign material that gets past the fuel filters and forms in the carburetor. It is, therefore, important to make sure that the fuel filters are cleaned at least once each year.

One of the major difficulties arises from moisture that accumulates in the system. This results from condensation. The difficulty is easily overcome by using some of the special preparations that are designed to absorb such moisture. The moisture will then pass through the fine mesh of the filters and the carburetor jets. Such chemicals have various names, but usually imply that freezing of the fuel line will be prevented. Obviously, if this moisture is allowed to accumulate in the fuel system, it will freeze in cold weather with the result that fuel will not reach the carburetor and the engine will not operate. In addition, the fuel pump, filter and carburetor may be damaged by the ice. Moisture that collects in die

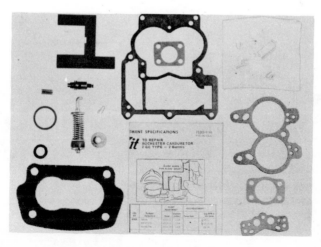

Fig. C-15. Parts contained in a typical kit of parts for overhauling a carburetor. Note illustrated instruction sheet and gauge for setting float level.

cast fuel pumps and carburetors will cause corrosion which will be a cheesy light substance which effectively clogs the system.

CARBURETOR OVERHAUL

Poor fuel economy, rough running engine or rough idle indicate the need for a new or rebuilt carburetor, or you can purchase a kit of repair parts, Fig. C-15, and install them.

Before installing any new parts in a carburetor, it is important that the main body and air horn be carefully cleaned and all the internal passages cleared by blowing out with compressed air. In that connection, a gummy substance frequently forms in the carburetor and it is important that all of it is removed. This is most easily done by special solvents designed for cleaning carburetor parts. Since this gummy substance is formed from the fuel, it is difficult to dissolve it with gasoline or kerosene.

Also before installing new parts in the carburetor, the mating surfaces of the main body and the air horn should be checked to be sure they are true and not warped. This is done with a straightedge, as shown in Fig. C-16. In addition, the two parts should be held together and if one can be rocked on the other, a new unit should be obtained. Unless these two surfaces are true and flat, air leaks will occur and the carburetor will not operate correctly. Be sure to install all new gaskets and other parts contained in the kit.

When disassembling the carburetor, carefully note the position of the various parts, and at the same time study the illustrations contained in the parts kit and the illustrations in this text, so that there will be no confusion when reassembling the unit. Pay particular attention to the location of the ball checks.

Fig. C-16. Checking surface of a carburetor with a straightedge.

QUICK SERVICE ON FUEL PUMPS

Fuel pumps on in-line engines and the V-8 engines are mounted on the right side of the engine. A typical installation on an in-line engine is shown on page 33. Current type fuel pumps are not serviceable and when difficulty occurs, a new fuel pump must be installed. Fig. C-17 shows a typical V-8 fuel pump installation. Plate shown is not used on all cars.

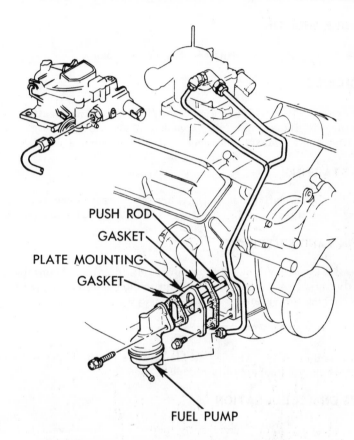

PUSH ROD
GASKET
PLATE MOUNTING
GASKET

FUEL PUMP

Fig. C-17. Current type of fuel pump installation.

Fuel pumps are easily removed. All that is necessary is to first disconnect the fuel lines from the pump and then remove the attaching bolts.

A quick test to see if a fuel pump is operating is to disconnect the fuel line at the carburetor and direct the end into a container. Start the engine and note the length of time required to pump one pint of fuel. On four and six cylinder engines, one pint of fuel should be pumped in thirty seconds, and on the larger engines, one pint in twenty seconds. If little or no fuel is pumped, pump may be defective or line to fuel tank may be obstructed.

If a pressure gauge is available, the fuel pump on the V-8 engine should deliver 5 to 8-1/2 lbs. for the 396 and 427 cu. in. engines, and 5-1/4 to 6-1/2 psi for the smaller V-8s. On the six and four cylinder engines, the fuel pump should develop 3 to 4-1/4 psi.

The fuel pump can also be checked by measuring the volume pumped which should be one pint in 30 to 45 seconds.

TROUBLE SHOOTING

See also Ignition, Starting and Engine sections.

ROUGH IDLE

Incorrect idle mixture. Carburetor float needle not seating. Air leaks in carburetor, intake manifold or gasket. Worn valve stem guides. Leaking cylinder head gasket. Incorrect valve lash. Burned or sticking valves.

HARD STARTING

Choke not operating correctly. Throttle not set correctly. Carburetor dirty and passages restricted. Clogged fuel filter. Clogged air filter.

POPPING AND SPITTING

Manifold heat control valve not properly installed. Manifold heat control valve sticking. Lean mixture. Dirt in carburetor. Clogged fuel filter. Leaky carburetor or intake manifold gaskets.

LACK OF POWER

Air cleaner dirty. Wrong jets for altitude in which car is being operated. Carburetor choke partly closed.

MISSES ON ACCELERATION

Accelerating pump incorrectly adjusted. Vapor vent ball in pump plunger not working. Lean mixture.

EXCESSIVE FUEL CONSUMPTION

Fuel leaks. Worn or incorrect carburetor jets. High fuel level in float bowl. Low engine compression. Worn, burned or sticking engine valves. Incorrect valve lash. Air leaks in carburetor, manifold gasket or intake valve stems. Incorrect spark advance. Fast driving. Dragging brakes. Misaligned wheels. Excessive engine idling. Towing another vehicle or a trailer. Use of air conditioning.

Carburetor, Fuel System Service

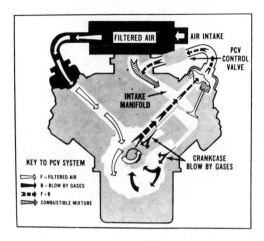

Fig. C-18. Schematic drawing of Positive Crankcase Ventilating (PCV) system.

FUEL PUMP NOISE

Fuel pump loose at mounting. Worn rocker arm. Broken or weak spring.

INSUFFICIENT FUEL DELIVERY

Loose fuel line fittings. Damaged diaphragm. Cracked fuel line.

EXCESSIVE PINGING

Low octane fuel being used. Spark advanced too far. Excessive carbon in combustion chamber.

CRANKCASE AND EXHAUST EMISSION SYSTEMS

Chevrolet uses various systems, or combinations of systems, to reduce emissions resulting from blow-by gases in the crankcase, evaporation of fuel in the tank and carburetor, and noxious gases from the exhaust. The systems include positive crankcase ventilation, evaporative emission control, controlled combustion, air injection reactor, transmission controlled spark, exhaust gas recirculation and early fuel evaporation system. The catalytic converter is covered in the chapter on Exhaust Systems.

These systems have been improved through progressive designing. Their selection for installation is dependent largely on engine size.

The Positive Crankcase Ventilating (PCV) system, Fig. C-18, circulates fresh air from the carburetor air cleaner through the crankcase where it mixes with the blow-by gases. This mixture is carried through the

PCV valve, Fig. C-19, into the intake manifold and to the combustion chambers where it is burned. The entire system must be kept clean and free from sludge. Replace the PCV valve every 12,000 miles or 12 months and the breather filter every 24,000 miles.

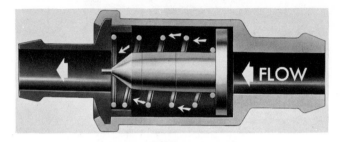

Fig. C-19. Details of Positive Crankcase Ventilating valve (PCV)

To check the condition of the PCV valve, disconnect the ventilating hose at the valve. Block the opening of the valve and note the change in the engine speed. A change of less than 50 rpm indicates a plugged PCV valve and a new valve should be installed.

The Evaporative Emission Control (EEC) system is designed to reduce fuel vapor emissions from the fuel supply tank and carburetor fuel bowl to the atmosphere. All fuel lines must be kept in good condition and free from leakage. The evaporative control system canister, Fig. C-20, is mounted on the left side of the engine compartment. The filter for this system should be replaced every 24,000 miles or 24 months, or more often when vehicle operation is in a dusty area. Check the canister for cracks when replacing the filter.

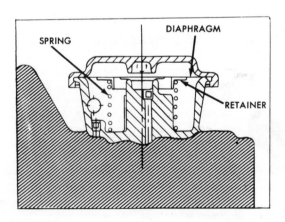

Fig. C-20. Details of canister purge valve in Evaporative Emission Control (EEC) system.

Carburetor, Fuel System Service

The Controlled Combustion System (CCS), Fig. C-21, includes a special air cleaner, Fig. C-14, designed to supply heated air to the carburetor to improve combustion during the engine warm-up period. Both carburetor and distributor are especially calibrated to provide an efficient air-fuel mixture and proper ignition, thereby reducing the generation of excessive hydrocarbons and carbon monoxide.

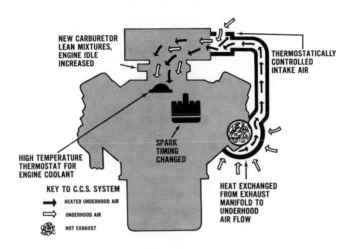

NEW CARBURETOR LEAN MIXTURES, ENGINE IDLE INCREASED

THERMOSTATICALLY CONTROLLED INTAKE AIR

SPARK TIMING CHANGED

HIGH TEMPERATURE THERMOSTAT FOR ENGINE COOLANT

KEY TO C.C.S. SYSTEM

➡ HEATED UNDERHOOD AIR
⇨ UNDERHOOD AIR
🌀 HOT EXHAUST

HEAT EXCHANGED FROM EXHAUST MANIFOLD TO UNDERHOOD AIR FLOW

Fig. C-21. Schematic diagram of Controlled Combustion System (CCS).

The CCS system should be checked every 12,000 miles or 12 months, whichever occurs first. Special care must be observed when doing a tune-up job, particularly in regard to idle mixture adjustment and setting of

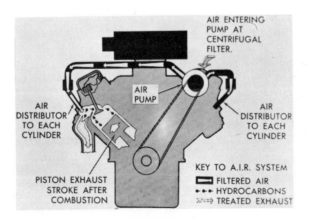

AIR ENTERING PUMP AT CENTRIFUGAL FILTER.

AIR PUMP

AIR DISTRIBUTOR TO EACH CYLINDER

AIR DISTRIBUTOR TO EACH CYLINDER

KEY TO A.I.R. SYSTEM

▭ FILTERED AIR
••• HYDROCARBONS
≈ TREATED EXHAUST

PISTON EXHAUST STROKE AFTER COMBUSTION

Fig. C-22. Schematic drawing of Air Injection Reactor (AIR) system.

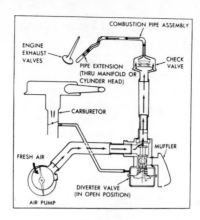

Fig. C-23. Details of diverter valve in Air Injector Reactor (AIR) system.

ignition timing.

The Air Injector Reactor (AIR) system, Fig. C-22, consists of the air injector pump, air injector tubes (one for each cylinder) and an air diverter valve, Fig. C-23. Carburetors and distributors are designed particularly for engines equipped with the AIR system and should not be interchanged.

The AIR system is designed to reduce hydrocarbons (HC) and carbon monoxide (CO) gases in the exhaust. This is accomplished as follows:

Air is compressed by the air pump and fed through the diverter valve and check valve into the air pipe assemblies, Fig. C-23. From here, the compressed air is routed to the exhaust manifold of V-8 engines or the exhaust ports of six cylinder engines. Oxygen in the compressed air mixes with the exhaust gases and most of the hydrocarbons and carbon monoxide

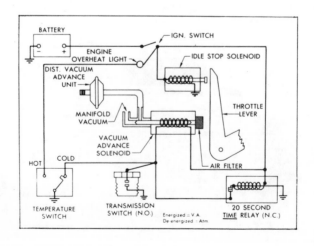

Fig. C-24. Diagram of Transmission Controlled Spark (TCS) system.

gases are burned and pass out through the exhaust system.

During deceleration, the diverter valve is triggered by sharp rises in vacuum to direct air pump output into the atmosphere. This prevents any backfire. The check valves prevent exhaust gases from entering and damaging the injector pump.

When servicing the AIR system, be sure the pump drive belt is correctly adjusted for tension so that no slippage occurs. Inspect all hoses for any sign of deterioration. Replace all defective hoses. Test the check valve by orally blowing through the valve toward the air manifold. Then attempt to suck back through the check valve. Flow should be in one direction only. If not, replace the unit.

Check the condition of all lines, especially the signal line. With the signal line disconnected, a vacuum should be noted with the engine running. With the engine stabilized at idle speed, no air should escape through the muffler. Manually open, then quickly close the throttle. A momentary blast of air should discharge through the muffler. Replace defective valves.

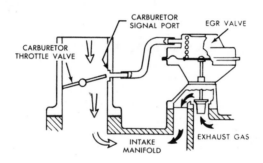

Fig. C-25. Schematic of Exhaut Gas Recirculating (EGR) system.

The Transmission Controlled Spark (TCS) system, Fig. C-24, is used only on cars equipped with a manual transmission. With this system, control of exhaust gas is accomplished by preventing vacuum advance of ignition timing when the vehicle is operating in reverse, neutral or low forward speeds.

With TCS, vacuum advance is controlled by a solenoid operated valve, which is energized by grounding a normally open switch at the transmission. When the solenoid is in the non-energized position, vacuum to the distributor advance unit is shut off and the distributor is vented to the atmosphere. When the solenoid is energized, the vacuum port is uncovered and the plunger is seated at the opposite end, shutting off the clean air vent.

The vacuum advance solenoid is controlled by two switches and a time relay. The solenoid is energized in the high forward gear by a transmission-operated switch. A thermostatic coolant temperature switch is used to provide override below 93 deg. F. The time relay is incorporated in the circuit to energize the vacuum advance solenoid for approximately 20 seconds after the ignition switch is turned on. However, the solenoid will remain energized as long as the temperature is below 93 deg. F.

A malfunction of the idle stop solenoid will cause the engine to stall at idle. Poor high gear performance may result from an inoperative vacuum advance solenoid, inoperative time relay, temperature switch or transmission switch.

The Exhaust Gas Recirculating (EGR) system, Fig. C-25, is used to reduce the emission of oxides of nitrogen (NOx) from the engine exhaust. These emissions occur at high temperature. Therefore, to reduce the formation of NOx, a slight reduction in peak operating temperature is required. This is accomplished by casting exhaust gas passages into the intake manifold. These passages are used to conduct the exhaust gas to the combustion chambers in amounts controlled by a vacuum modulated shutoff and metering valve.

Rough idling may be caused by exhaust deposits holding the EGR valve in the open position. Clean the valve with a wire brush. Do not use a solvent. Also be sure the air passages in the inlet manifold are clean.

EARLY FUEL EVAPORATION SYSTEM

The EFE system consists of a heat control valve at the flange of the exhaust manifold, an actuator and a thermal vacuum switch mounted in the water outlet housing where it directly controls vacuum. With coolant temperature below 180 deg. F., manifold vacuum is applied to the actuator which, in turn, closes the EFE valve. This routes hot exhaust gases to the base of the carburetor to improve fuel vaporization. When the coolant temperature reaches 180 deg. F., vacuum to the actuator is shut off.

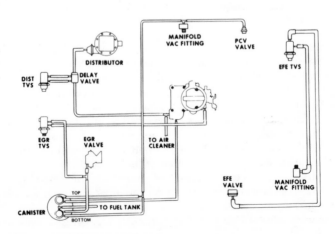

Layout of emission control systems on 250 cu. in. Six.

Shortcuts on
ENGINE DISASSEMBLY

Fig. D-1. Sectional view of 1963–1970 Chevrolet 230 cu. in. engine. Typical.

This chapter deals with short cut methods of removing different engine parts and their reinstallation. Details of servicing procedures for repairing these individual parts, together with further information of disassembling after these parts are removed are given in the chapter on Simplified Engine Repairs.

HOW TO REMOVE THE CYLINDER HEAD

In-line Chevrolet engines with push rods include the 153, 194, 230, 235 and 250 cu. in. power plants, Figs. B-22 and D-1. The procedure for removing the cylinder head is basically the same:

Drain the cooling system and disconnect the radiator upper hose. Remove the air cleaner. Disconnect the accelerator and choke linkage from the carburetor. Disconnect fuel and vacuum lines at the carburetor. Disconnect wire harness from the engine temperature sending unit. Disconnect wires and remove spark plugs. Remove ignition coil on L6 engines only. On the 135, 194, 230 and 250 cu. in. engines, disconnect exhaust pipe at manifold flange, then remove manifold bolts and clamps and remove the manifold and carburetor as an assembly.

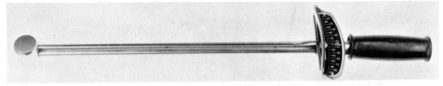

Fig. D-2. Always use a torque wrench to tighten cylinder head bolts to the specified torque.

On the 235 cu. in Six, remove bolts and clamps that attach manifold assembly to cylinder head and pull manifold assembly off the manifold studs. Also remove intake pilot sleeves.

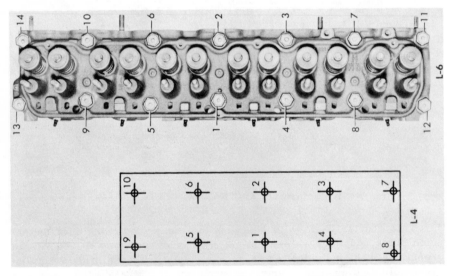

Fig. D-3. Correct sequence for tightening cylinder head bolts on 194, 230, 250 cu. in. six cylinder engines (upper) and 153 cu. in. four cylinder engine (lower). Torque for all these engines is 90 to 95 ft. lb.

On all engines remove battery ground strap. On engines with positive crankcase ventilation, remove air cleaner attachment to rocker arm cover. Remove rocker arm cover.

On the 235 cu. in. Six, remove rocker arm assembly. On other in-line engines, including 153, 194, 230 and 250, back off rocker arm nuts, then pivot rocker arm to clear nuts.

Engine Disassembly

On all engines, remove push rods. Identify each rod for reinstallation in original position. Remove cylinder head bolts. Lift off cylinder head. Clean gasket surfaces.

When replacing the cylinder head, use a torque wrench, Fig. D-2, to tighten the bolts to specified torque and in the sequence shown in Fig. D-3.

V-8 Engine Cylinder Head Removal: Drain cooling system and remove air cleaner. Disconnect radiator upper hose and heater hoses. Disconnect throttle rods from carburetor. Disconnect fuel and vacuum lines at carburetor. On overdrive models, disconnect kick-down switch wire from switch. Disconnect and remove ignition coil and distributor. Disconnect battery. Remove spark plugs. Disconnect power brake hose at carburetor when installed. Disconnect crankcase ventilating hoses and air injector reactor hoses, when installed. Disconnect spark advance hose at distributor. Remove temperature indicator unit at intake manifold. Remove fan belts. On 283 cu. in. V-8, Fig. D-4, remove exhaust manifold-to-exhaust crossover pipe stud nuts and allow pipe to drop. Disconnect wires from generator. Remove Delcotron upper bracket.

Remove exhaust manifold. On 283 cu. in. engines, remove choke heat

Fig. D-4. Details of 283 cu. in. V-8 engine.

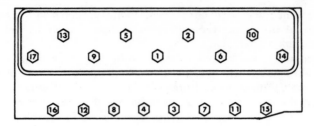

Fig. D-5. Correct cylinder head bolt tightening sequence for 265, 283, 302, 307, 327 and 350 cu. in. engines. Correct torque is 65 ft. lb.

tubes. On all models, remove rocker arm covers, Fig. D-5. Back off rocker arm nuts and pivot rocker arms to clear push rods. Remove push rods. Identify each rod for reinstallation in original position. Be sure push rod seats on solid lifters do not come off of lifters. Snap push rod lower end to one side before lifting to break push rods loose from seats. When reassembling a 348 cu. in. engine, note that exhaust push rods are longer than intake push rods.

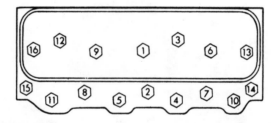

Fig. D-6. Tightening sequence for 396, 402, 427 and 454 cu. in. engines. Torque is 80 ft. lb., except aluminum head short bolts at 65 ft. lb., long bolts at 75 ft. lb.

Remove cylinder head bolts and lift off cylinder heads. On 348 cu. in. models, before removing left cylinder heads, remove generator. On 348 cu. in. and 409 cu. in. engines equipped with air conditioning units remove air compressor before removing right cylinder head. Note: Evacuate air conditioning system before disconnecting the compressor.

When removing cylinder head bolts, note length of each bolt and position from which it was removed so it can be replaced in original position. Cylinder bolt tightening sequences for V-8 engines are shown in Figs. D-6 and D-7. Use no sealers with composition steel gaskets.

When installing the intake manifold on V-8 engines, tighten the bolts in proper sequence, Fig. D-8. Note that bolts are tightened alternately across manifold, starting from center. Torque to 25 to 35 ft. lb.

1976 Chevette cylinder head removal: Remove timing belt. Drain cooling system. Disconnect radiator hoses and heater hoses. Remove air cleaner and accelerator cable support bracket. Disconnect spark plug cables. Remove connections at idle solenoid, choke, temperature sending switch and Delcotron. Raise vehicle. Disconnect exhaust pipe at manifold. Lower vehicle. Remove bolt holding dipstick bracket to manifold. Disconnect fuel line at carburetor. Remove ignition coil. Remove cam covers and camshaft housing attaching studs. Remove rocker arms, guides and valve lash adjusters, placing them in a rack in sequence to maintain original order. Remove cam carrier. Remove manifold and cylinder head assembly.

When reassembling Chevette engine, use sealer on head bolts; use Molycoat on rocker arms.

OIL PAN REMOVAL KINKS

1966-1968 six cylinder models: On Chevelle, it is necessary to remove engine from chassis before oil pan can be removed. On other models: Disconnect battery positive cable. Remove through bolts from front engine mounts. Drain coolant from radiator. Disconnect radiator hoses at radiator. Remove engine cooling fan. Drain engine oil. Remove starter.

On vehicles equipped with automatic transmission, disconnect cooler lines at transmission and remove converter housing underpan. Disconnect steering rod at idler lever, then swing away steering linkage for oil pan clearance. Rotate crankshaft until timing mark on torsional damper is at 6 o'clock position. Using a suitable jack with a block of wood to protect oil pan, raise engine high enough to insert 2 in. x 4 in. wooden blocks under engine mounts, then lower engine on blocks. Remove oil pan and discard gaskets and seals.

1969-1974 six cylinder models: On 1969 Chevelle with manual transmission, it is necessary to remove engine from chassis before removing oil pan. On other models: Disconnect battery positive cable. Remove upper

Fig. D-7. Correct torque for tightening cylinder head bolts on 348 and 409 cu. in. V-8 engines is 60 to 70 ft. lb. Correct sequence is indicated.

radiator mounting panel or side mount bolts. On 1969 models: Remove through bolts from engine front mounts. Place a heavy piece of cardboard between fan blades and radiator core. Disconnect fuel line at fuel pump. Raise vehicle and drain oil.

Disconnect and remove starter. Remove flywheel underpan or converter housing underpan. On most models, disconnect steering rod at idler arm lever and swing away linkage. Rotate crankshaft until timing mark on vibration damper is at 6 o'clock position. On 1971-1975 models: Remove bolts attaching brake line to front crossmember and move brake line away from crossmember.

Using a suitable jack and a block of wood to protect oil pan, raise front of engine and insert a 2 in. x 4 in. block of wood under engine mounts. On following models, remove front engine mounts: 1970-1972 Chevelle, 1971-1973 Chevrolet, 1972-1975 Nova. On 1969 Nova, remove hood hinge front bolts, swing hood up, then use a hoist to raise engine

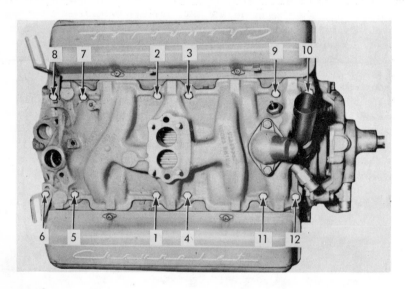

Fig. D-8. Typical tightening sequences of intake manifold bolts on V-8 engines. Correct torque is 25–35 ft. lb. A pilot tool made of wood and inserted in hole for distributor shaft will help guide the manifold in place and reduce the possibility of the manifold and seals slipping out of place.

approximately 2 in.

With engine raised, remove oil pan bolts and lower pan.

1969-1970 Chevelle with 390 cu. in. V-8 engine: Disconnect battery positive cable. Remove air cleaner, oil dipstick and radiator cap. Remove radiator shroud and upper mounting panel. Place a heavy piece of cardboard between radiator core and fan. Disconnect engine ground straps at engine. Remove fuel pump and plug line from tank. Disconnect accelerator control cable from engine. Place hook, Fig. D-9, and suitable 4 ft. chain over cowl. Install bolt through holes in hook and center link of chain.

Raise vehicle on hoist, drain oil and remove oil filter. Disconnect starter brace at starter. Remove starter. Remove propeller shaft and plug rear of transmission. On all floor shift manual transmissions, re- move two bolts securing shift lever to linkage. On all other models, dis- connect transmission linkage at transmission. Disconnect speedometer cable and back-up lamp connector. On manual transmissions, disconnect clutch cordon shaft at frame. On automatic transmission cars, disconnect oil cooler lines, detent cable, rod or switch wire and modulator pipe.

Remove crossmember bolts and place jack under engine. Raise engine and move crossmember toward rear of engine. On engines with single exhaust, remove crossover pipe. On engines with dual exhaust, disconnect exhaust pipes. Remove flywheel housing cover. Remove transmission attaching bolts and remove transmission. On manual transmission models, remove flywheel housing and throw-out bearing. Remove engine mount through bolts. Raise engine at rear approximately 4 in. Attach each end of chain to flywheel bell housing bolts (manual transmission) or transmission mounting bolts (automatic transmission). Lower engine jack and move it to front of engine. Raise front of engine about 3 in. and

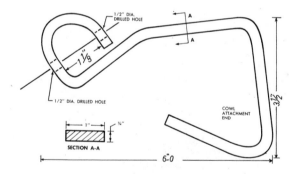

Fig. D-9. Drawing of fabricated hook.

insert 2 in. blocks of wood under front engine mounts, Fig. D-10. Rotate engine until timing marks on torsional damper are at 6 o'clock. Remove oil pan bolts and remove pan.

1969-1978 Chevrolet, Camaro, Monte Carlo, Nova and Chevelle, ex- cept with 396 cu. in. engine: Disconnect battery. Remove distributor cap. Remove fan shroud retaining bolts or upper radiator mounting panel or side mount bolts as needed. Place heavy piece of cardboard between radiator core and fan. Raise vehicle on hoist and drain oil. Disconnect exhaust pipe or crossover pipe. On vehicles equipped with automatic transmission, remove converter housing underpan and splash shield. On

Fig. D-10. Note blocks of wood used to keep engine in raised position while oil pan is being removed.

most models, disconnect steering idle lever at the frame and swing down steering linkage for oil pan clearance. Rotate crankshaft until timing mark on vibration damper is at 6 o'clock position.

Disconnect starter brace at starter. Remove inboard starter bolt and loosen outboard starter bolt. Swing starter outboard to provide clearance. On small V-8 engines, remove fuel pump and plug fuel line. Remove through bolts from engine front mounts.

On all except Nova 307 and 350 cu. in. engines, use block of wood between jack and oil pan and raise engine. On Nova 307 and 350 engines, use special screw type jack, Fig. D-11, to raise front of engine. Engine should be raised until wood blocks of 4 in. on Chevrolet, 2 in. on Nova and 3 in. on Chevelle, can be inserted under engine mounts. Lower engine on blocks, Fig. D-10. Then remove oil pan bolts and lower pan to floor.

1970-1972 Chevelle with 396 cu. in. V-8 engine: Disconnect battery positive cable. Remove air cleaner, dipstick and distributor cap. Disconnect radiator shroud and upper mounting panel. Place a piece of heavy cardboard between radiator and fan blades. Disconnect engine ground strap at engine. Disconnect accelerator control cable. Place a hook fabricated from steel strap iron, Fig. D-9, with a suitable chain over cowl. Install a bolt through holes in hook and center link of chain (to be used later to support rear of engine). Raise vehicle on hoist and drain engine oil. Remove drive shaft and plug rear of transmission. On floor shift models, remove two bolts securing shift lever to linkage. On other models, disconnect linkage at transmission. Disconnect speedometer cable and back-up lamp switch. On manual transmission, disconnect cordon shaft at frame. On automatic transmission, disconnect cooler lines, detent cable, rod or switch wire and modulator pipe.

Remove crossmember bolts and place jack under engine. Raise engine and move crossmember toward rear of vehicle. On engines with single

Fig. D-11. A special screw type jack is used to support front of engine while removing pan on Nova engines.

exhaust, remove crossover pipe. On dual exhaust engines, disconnect exhaust pipes. Remove flywheel housing cover. Remove transmission attaching bolts and remove transmission. On manual transmission models, remove flywheel cover housing and throw-out bearing. Remove engine mount through bolts.

Raise engine at rear approximately 4 in. Attach ends of chain, which pass through end of fabricated hook on cowl, to bell housing bolts (manual transmission) or transmission mounting bolts (automatic transmission). Lower engine and move jack to front of engine. Raise front of engine and insert 2 in. wooden blocks under front engine supports, Fig. D-10. Rotate crankshaft until timing mark on torsional balancer is at 6 o'clock position. Remove pan bolts and lower pan.

1973-1978 Corvette: Disconnect battery positive cable. Remove engine oil dipstick and tube. Raise vehicle on hoist. Drain engine oil. Disconnect steering linkage at frame and lower linkage. Remove oil pan bolts and remove oil pan. Discard used gaskets and seals.

1976 Chevette: To remove oil pan, first remove heater housing assembly from front dash. Remove engine mount nuts, pull back engine mount wire restraints. Remove radiator upper support and fan shroud. Raise vehicle and drain crankcase oil. Remove pan bolts. Raise engine, then remove oil pan.

HOW TO REMOVE CONNECTING RODS

To remove connecting rods it is first necessary to remove the cylinder head and oil pan. Carefully note the identification numbers on each of the connecting rods and caps. If numbers are not visible center punch rods and caps with appropriate number of punch marks for identification.

If a ridge has been worn at the top of the cylinder bore, Fig. D-11a, this must be removed by special cutter before the rods are removed. If this is not done, the pistons will be damaged as the assemblies are removed. Before removing ridge, crank engine until piston is at bottom of its stroke and place an oiled rag on the top of the piston. As the ridge is removed with the cutter, the metal chips will be caught on the rag. At

The 1978 Monza 2 + 2 sport hatchback with dual rectangular headlamps.

completion of ridge removal, crank engine until piston is at top and re-move rag with chips. Remove a connecting rod cap and push rod and piston up and out of cylinder. Replace cap on rod and remove remaining rods in a similar manner. Always place connecting rod caps on original rods and do not mix bearing inserts.

REMOVING THE TIMING CASE COVER

Removal of the timing case cover requires considerable disassembly

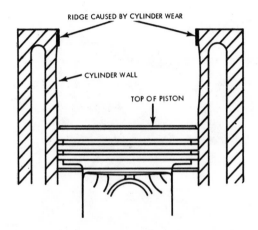

Fig. D-11a. Ridge in cylinder above ring travel area must be cut flush before piston assembly can be removed.

work. The operation is basically the same on all Chevrolet built engines, four, six and eight models.

Remove the radiator and fan belt. On most late model V-8 engines, remove fan shroud and water pump. On all models except the Chevy II four cylinder, remove harmonic balancer. On Chevy II four cylinder, remove fan pulley. On all models, remove oil pan. On most V-8s, remove water pump. On 235 cu. in. Six remove two bolts installed from back through front main bearing. Then remove timing case bolts and cover.

On all models, except the 235 cu. in. Six engine, the front cover seal can be replaced without removing the cover. Remove vibration damper. Pry out old seal. Install new seal so that open end of seal is toward inside of cover. Fig. D-12 shows a new oil seal being driven into position with the cover removed.

1976-1977 Chevette crankcase front cover removal: First, remove timing belt upper front cover, crankshaft drive pulley, lower timing belt cover and crankshaft sprockets. Disconnect battery negative cable at battery. Remove the fan. Remove cover retaining screws and nuts.

Withdraw cover from vehicle. Then, loosen Delcotron and A/C compressor; remove drive belts. Remove crankshaft-to-pulley bolt and washer; pull off crankshaft pulley. Loosen idler pulley bolt to loosen idler pulley. Remove timing belt from sprockets. Remove three screws securing camshaft sprocket cover to cam carrier. Inspect camshaft seal. Remove timing belt sprocket bolt and washer. Remove camshaft sprocket. Then, remove crankshaft timing belt sprocket. Remove three oil pan bolts and remaining attaching bolts. Remove old crankcase cover gasket and front portion of oil pan gasket.

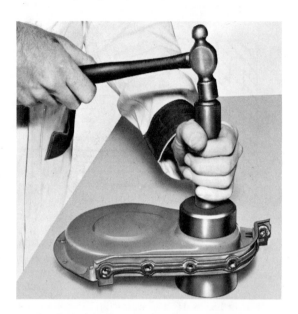

Fig. D-12. Installing an oil seal in timing case cover.

REMOVING THE ENGINE

Removal and installation of an engine becomes necessary when a rebuilt engine is installed. As an engine assembly weighs six to seven hundred pounds, an overhead beam capable of supporting such a weight, together with a chain hoist is necessary.

The basic procedure applicable in general to all engines is as follows: Drain the cooling system, crankcase and transmission. Scribe alignment marks on the hood around the hinges, and remove the hood from the hinges. Remove the radiator hoses and heater hoses on models so equipped. Remove battery and battery cables. Remove fan shroud on cars so equipped. On Power Glide and Turbo-Glide models, remove and plug oil cooler lines. Remove radiator core.

Engine Disassembly

Disconnect starter and generator wires, engine to body ground strap, oil pressure indicator wire at sending unit on block, and ignition coil wires. Disconnect vacuum line to power brake unit.

Remove temperature indicator element wire. Remove oil filter assembly. Remove air cleaner. Remove air conditioning on cars so equipped. Note that special equipment is needed to evacuate the air conditioning system before it can be removed. Disconnect fuel and vacuum lines. On eight cylinder models it is necessary to remove the distributor cap. If the car has power steering, this unit should be removed. Disconnect carburetor control rod from bell crank and throttle valve lever on transmission, if the car has an automatic transmission.

Remove exhaust pipe flange nuts and lower exhaust pipes and muffler. Remove road draft tube, if so equipped.

Remove exhaust crossover pipe and manifold heat valve from right hand exhaust manifold on eight cylinder models. Remove transmission control rods. On overdrive models, disconnect wires and cables. Remove clutch control bell crank and control rods and conventional transmission

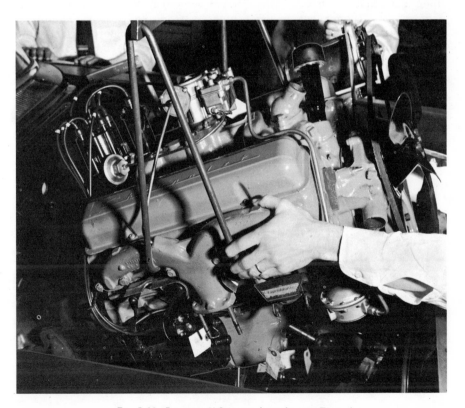

Fig. D-13. Removing V-8 engine from chassis. Typical.

models. On automatic transmission models, remove oil filler tube and plug the opening. Disconnect speedometer cable at the transmission. Remove the propeller shaft. Raise engine to take weight off front mounts and remove front mount through bolts. Remove rear mount to crossmember bolts. Raise engine to take weight off rear mounts, then remove crossmember.

If eye bolts fitting the cylinder head bolts are available, these should be screwed into the cylinder head for attaching the lifting hooks from the hoist. If not, use a chain sling around the engine. The engine and transmission, Fig. D-13, can then be lifted from the vehicle as a unit.

Starting with 1968 models, all V-8 engines are equipped with two, strap-type lifting rings, one at the right rear of the engine and the other at the left front. These straps make it unnecessary to remove the valve rocker arm covers when raising the engine.

1976-1977 Chevette engine removal: After removing hood, remove battery and drain coolant. Disconnect radiator hoses and heater hoses. Disconnect engine wiring harness at bulkhead. Remove radiator upper support, then radiator. Remove air cleaner assembly. Disconnect fuel line, transmission throttle linkage and accelerator cable. Remove A/C compressor. Disconnect exhaust pipe at manifold. Raise vehicle on hoist. Remove flywheel dust cover or converter underpan. On automatic transmission cars, remove converter-to-flywheel bolts. Remove converter housing or flywheel housing-to-engine retaining bolts. Lower vehicle. Install floor jack under transmission. Remove safety straps from front engine mounts and remove engine mount bolts. With suitable hoist, remove engine from vehicle. Pull engine forward to clear transmission while slowly lifting engine.

Simplified
ENGINE REPAIRS

General repair work on the Chevrolet, Chevelle, Chevy II, Nova, Camaro and Corvette engines is not difficult. In this chapter of Fix Your Chevrolet instructions covering the repair of different parts of the engine, applicable to all Chevrolet built engines, will be discussed.

In order to recondition or replace an engine part, it is, of course, necessary to first disassemble the engine, either partly or completely. Removal procedure was discussed in the preceding chapter. This chapter will be devoted to servicing and disassembly of the different parts after they have been removed from the engine.

WHEN SHOULD VALVES BE RECONDITIONED?

Due to incorrect valve tappet clearance, gummy valve stems, defective hydraulic valve lifters, the use of low octane fuel, unequal tightening of the cylinder head bolts, etc., valve life is often materially shortened. As a result, the face and seat of the valve become burned and pitted, as shown

Fig. E-1. Example of badly burned and carboned valve. Carbon under valve head usually indicates worn valve guide or defective seal.

in Fig. E-1. As a further result, compression of the combustible gases will not reach its maximum value. In extreme cases it will be necessary to replace the valve and also the valve seat. In cases not so extreme, the valve and seat can be reconditioned to give many more thousands of miles of useful service.

It is necessary to recondition the valves of Chevrolet built engines when compression tests indicate the valves are leaking. Leaking valves will also be indicated by loss of power and reduced fuel economy.

With regard to valve reconditioning, most mechanics without modern shop equipment prefer to remove the cylinder head and send it to an automotive machine shop where all the work of reconditioning the valves and cylinder head will be performed. This will not only save time, but a precision job will be performed.

HOW TO REMOVE ENGINE VALVES

Before removing the valves, it is necessary to remove the cylinder head from the engine. After removing the cylinder head, as explained in the preceding chapter, procedure for removing the valves from the 153,

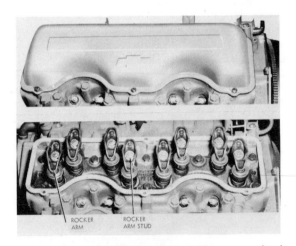

Fig. E-2. Details of types of rocker arms used on V-8 engines and in-line Sixes, except the 235 cu. in. Six.

194, 230 and 250 cu. in. in-line engines, and all the V-8 engines is as follows:

Swing the rocker arm on the rocker arm stud so it does not cover the end of the valve stem, Fig. E-2, or remove the rocker arm nuts, rocker arm bolts and rocker arms.

To remove the valves from the cylinder head, a C-type valve spring compressor is used, Fig. E-4. While it is possible to compress the valve springs by pressing down on the valve spring retainers with two screwdrivers, this is a difficult and tedious method. With the valve springs compressed, the valve locks, cap and seal are removed.

Any valve with a bent stem, or a stem that is worn more than .002 in. should be replaced.

Fig. E-3. Detailed view of typical rocker arm and shaft construction.

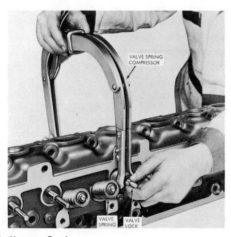

Fig. E-4. Using a C—clamp type compressor to remove engine valves.

Micrometers are used to measure the wear on valve stems. First measure the diameter on the valve stem of a new valve, or the unworn portion of an old valve. This is then compared to the diameter of the worn portion of the old valve.

Wear in excess of .002 in. will result in poor seating of the valve. In addition, air and oil will be drawn past the valve stem. The air will dilute the fuel mixture and the oil will cause increased oil consumption.

If the valve is not bent, or the stem worn, the valve can be refaced.

Fig. E-5. One type of valve refacing machine.

This is done on a valve refacing machine, Fig. E-5. Any automotive machine shop will perform this operation at a low cost. After a valve is refaced, the head should be checked to make sure it is not too thin. If the edge of the valve head is less than 1/32 in. thick, Fig. E-6, the valve should be replaced.

In addition to refacing the valve, the valve seat should also be reconditioned. Special valve seat reconditioning equipment is available for doing such work. By using 30, 45, and 60 deg. seat cutters, the proper seat width of 1/16 in. can be obtained.

The angle of the valve seats and valves of the different Chevrolet built engines is as follows:

	Intake		Exhaust	
	Seat	Face	Seat	Face
Engine	Angle	Angle	Angle	Angle
Corvair (1960-1968)	45	44	45	44
Chevette (1976-1977)	46	45	46	45
Others	46*	45	46*	45

*Aluminum heads 45 deg.

RECONDITIONING VALVES WITHOUT SPECIAL EQUIPMENT

It is possible to recondition valves and valve seats without the use of special equipment, but the final job is not as satisfactory as is the case when special equipment is used. However, it is often resorted to when an auto machine shop is not immediately available, or when the costs are of major importance.

The procedure is to use fine carborundum powder, or special valve grinding compound, and grind or lap the valve to the seat. A very light coating of a valve grinding compound is placed on the face of the valve, and the valve is placed in position in the cylinder head. Then with a valve lapping tool, the valve is rotated back and forth on its seat. The valve lapping tool is basically a vacuum cup attached to the end of a short handle. The valve grinding compound grinds away the metal of both the seat and the valve until both are smooth and free from pits or other defects.

To keep the valve grinding compound evenly distributed, the valve should be raised occasionally from its seat and given a half-turn before the lapping process is renewed. Only light pressure should be placed on the valve during the grinding process.

The lapping is continued until all of the pit marks are ground away from both the valve and its seat. If the valves are badly pitted, it will be found that a groove will be ground in the face of the valve during the lapping process. Such a condition is not desirable, as the valve will then quickly pit again. The groove affords a place for carbon and other combustion products to lodge. That is why refacing the valve head and seat is the preferred method.

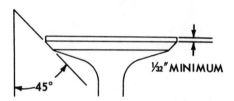

45°   1/32" MINIMUM

Fig. E-6. If edge of valve is less than 1/32 in. thick, valve should be replaced.

When the lapping process is completed, great care must be exercised to remove all traces of the grinding compound. Should any of the compounds remain in the intake valve seat, it will be drawn into the engine and cause rapid wear of all parts. On the exhaust valve it will cause the stem to be worn and in turn the valve will seat poorly, resulting in compression loss followed by burning of the valve and seat.

The width of the intake valve seat should range from .060 in. to .080 in., while the limits of exhaust valve seat width should range from .070 in. to .090 in. This is important because if the seats are too narrow, the valves will operate at too high a temperature and will soon become burned. If the seat width is too wide, there is a tendency for carbon to lodge on the seat and the valve will soon become pitted and not hold compression.

The finished valve seat should contact the approximate center of the valve face. This can be determined by placing a slight amount of Prussian Blue on the valve seat. Set the valve in position and rotate the valve with light pressure. The Blue will be transferred to the face of the valve and show clearly whether it is centered or not.

Another point to check on an engine valve is the condition of the end of the valve stem. If the end of the valve stem is rough, it will be difficult to accurately adjust the valve tappet clearance. When necessary, the end of the valve stem can be ground on the same machine that refaces the valve face.

As pointed out previously, it is possible to recondition valves by hand grinding but a better job can be done by using specialized equipment. Consequently many car owners and operators of small garages, not having their own equipment, take advantage of the facilities of the automotive machine shop. This is particularly true in the case of overhead type en-

Fig. E-7. One method of checking strength of valve spring.

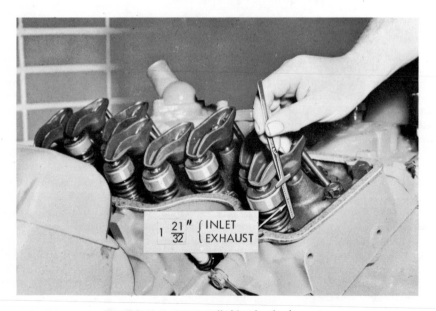

$1 \frac{21}{32}''$ { INLET
EXHAUST

*Fig. E-8. Measuring installed height of valve spring.
Indicated dimension does not apply to all engines.*

gines, such as Chevrolet. In such cases all that is necessary is to remove the cylinder heads from the engine and take them to the machine shop where the head will be completely disassembled, cleaned and reconditioned.

QUICK CHECKS ON SPRINGS

Check the condition of the valve springs. If any are weak, full power will not be developed, particularly at higher engine speeds. Special spring compression strength testers are available, Fig. E-7. However, a fairly accurate check can be made by comparing the lengths of new and used springs. The end of the spring should be flat, and neither flatness nor length should vary more than 1/16 in.

After the valve and seat have been reconditioned, the valve springs will not exert as much pressure. Since a reconditioned valve seats deeper, the spring will not be compressed as much and the assembled height of the spring will be greater.

Therefore, it is necessary to measure the length (assembled height) of the valve spring after it is reassembled in the engine, Fig. E-8. If it exceeds the specified amount, install a spacer between the cylinder head and valve spring to restore the spring's normal compression.

Assembled Valve Spring Height

Engine	Height	Engine	Height
1.4 L (85 cu. in.)	1.25 in. (32 mm)	327 cu. in. 67-68	1-5/32 in.
1.6 L (98 cu. in.)	1.25 in. (32 mm)	350 cu. in. 67-69	1-5/32 in.
140 cu. in. 77	1-9/16 in.	350 cu. in. 70-74	1-23/32 in.
151 cu. in.	1-21/32 in.	350 cu. in. 74	1-5/8 in.
153 cu. in.	1-21/32 in.	160, 185 hp	
194 cu. in.	1-21/32 in.	350 cu. in. 74-76	1-23/32 in.
196 cu. in.	1-21/32 in.	245, 250 hp	
200 cu. in.	1-23/32 in.	350 cu. in. (in)	1-23/32 in.
231 cu. in.	1-23/32 in.	77-78 (ex)	1-19/32 in.
250 cu. in.	1-23/32 in.	396 cu. in.	1-7/8 in.
302 cu. in.	1-5/32 in.	400 cu. in. 70	1-7/8 in.
305 cu. in. (in)	1-23/32 in.	400 cu. in. 71-76	1-23/32 in.
77-78 (ex)	1-19/32 in.	402 cu. in. 71-72	1-23/32 in.
307 cu. in. 68-73	1-5/32 in.	427 cu. in.	1-7/8 in.
307 cu. in. 74	1-5/8 in.	454 cu. in.	1-7/8 in.

REPLACING VALVE STEM SEAL OR VALVE SPRING

Occasionally it is necessary to replace a valve seal, or a valve spring, without doing any work on the valve itself, and this can be done as follows: Remove rocker arm cover, and the spark plug, rocker arm and push rod on the cylinders to be serviced. Apply compressed air to the spark plug hole to hold the valves in place.

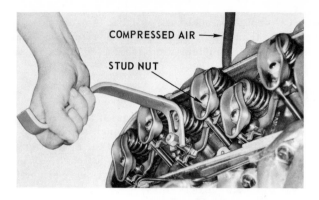

Fig. E-9. Illustrating method of compressing valve spring in order to replace oil seals or springs without removing head from engine. Note compressed air hose which supplies air pressure at spark plug hole.

A tool to apply the compressed air to the cylinder can be made from an old spark plug by removing the porcelain insulator from the plug. Then using a 3/8 in. pipe tap, cut threads in the remaining portion of the spark plug. A compressed air hose adaptor can then be screwed into the spark plug and the spark plug in turn into the cylinder head.

Compress the valve spring as shown in Fig. E-9. Then with the spring compressed, remove the valve locks, valve tap, valve shield, and the valve spring and damper. Also remove the valve stem oil seal. A new seal and spring can then be installed. A light coat of oil on the seal will help prevent twisting.

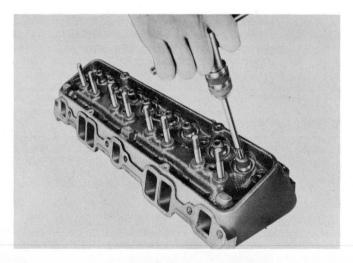

Fig. E-10. Reaming a valve guide.

WHAT TO DO ABOUT VALVE GUIDES

Only the 235 cu. in. Chevrolet Six, built in 1962 and earlier, is provided with the removable type valve guide. On other engines, valve guide holes are accurately reamed directly in the cylinder head. This has the advantage of cooler operating valves. However, when the valve guide holes in the cylinder head become worn more than .0045 in., it is necessary to recondition the holes by reaming, or by knurling, and then installing new valves with oversized valve stems. As this is a precision operation, it is generally necessary to have such work done by an automotive machine shop. Fig. E-10 shows a guide being reamed. Valves with oversized stems are available for intake and exhaust valves in the following oversizes, .003 in., .015 in., .030 in.

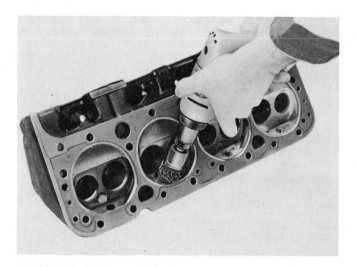

Fig. E-11. Cleaning carbon from cylinder head with a wire brush driven by an electric drill.

CLEANING THE CYLINDER HEAD

Before assembling the valves to the cylinder head, the head should be thoroughly cleaned. Carbon and combustion deposits should be removed from the combustion chambers. This can be done by scraping with a putty knife, or by means of an electric drill equipped with a wire brush, Fig. E-11. Be sure all carbon accumulations are removed, as any particles remaining may result in preignition. Also all grease should be removed from the outer side of the cylinder head and the water jacket thoroughly flushed to remove all traces of rust accumulation. All carbon accumulations must also be removed from the top of the piston.

It is also essential to check the surface of the cylinder head that mates with the cylinder block. This can be done with a straightedge and a feeler or thickness gauge. The straightedge should be held diagonally and then across the center of the cylinder head while checking the clearance between the straightedge and the cylinder head by means of a feeler gauge. Warpage should not exceed .003 in. in any six inches, or .006 in. overall.

In addition, the cylinder head should be carefully examined for any cracks, particularly around the valve seats and around the water jacket. Special spray-on type chemicals are available which will help greatly in revealing any cracks that may be present. While the head is off, it is also an excellent time to check and make sure the core plugs are tight and have not rusted. If there is any indication of rust around any of the core plugs, they should be replaced as explained in the Chapter on Cooling Systems.

It also pays to clean the interior of the water jacket so as to be sure that all rust accumulations are removed and in that way reduce the possibilities of overheating. This can be done by filling the cylinder head with radiator cleaning solution, which is allowed to remain in the head for approximately twenty-four hours.

HOW TO INSTALL PISTON RINGS

After the connecting rod and piston assemblies are removed from the engine, they should be thoroughly cleaned in a solvent designed for cleaning engine parts. If such special solvent is not available, kerosene can be used, but that is not nearly as effective as commercial cleaning solvent. After the assemblies have been cleaned, the rings can be removed as they will not be used again. The usual practice is to grab the end of the ring with a pair of pliers and pull out. In the case of cast iron rings, this will break the ring so that both parts are easily removed from the groove. Steel rings are removed in the same manner, but instead of breaking, the ring can be easily worked out of the groove and once one end is free, the

Fig. E-12. Cleaning piston ring groove with a special tool.

rest will easily spiral out of the groove. Always be sure to remove the steel expander ring from the bottom of each groove where such rings are used. Then with the rings removed from each piston, the groove can be thoroughly cleaned. The preferred method of cleaning is to use a special ring groove cleaning tool, such as is illustrated in Fig. E-12. Such tools quickly cut the carbon from the groove without danger of scratching or otherwise damaging the sides of the ring groove.

If such a tool is not available, a substitute method is to use a broken segment of a cast iron piston ring. This is used as a scraper. This method is long and tedious and there is also a possiblility of marring the surface of the sides of the ring grooves. This could result in loss of compression. It also tends to increase oil consumption.

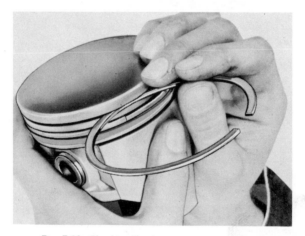

Fig. E-13. Checking fit of piston ring in ring groove.

It should be pointed out that if new piston pins are fitted, that most shops will not bother to clean the piston and rod assemblies. Instead they send them to an automotive machine shop to clean the assemblies, and install the new pins and rings. Or, if desired, the ring installation can be left to the mechanic doing the actual overhaul job. In general, when new rings are found to be necessary, it is always advisable to install new piston pins at the same time. The reason being that the pins generally wear out about the same time as the rings do.

Before installing new rings on the pistons, or fitting new piston pins, the pistons should be carefully checked to make sure they are in good condition and are still serviceable. In addition, the difference in diameter between the piston and the cylinder wall should be checked. This is known as piston clearance and is discussed in later paragraphs.

When examining the piston, make sure the ring grooves are in good condition, that the sides of the grooves are smooth, and without any groove worn by the rings. The sides of the grooves must be at right angles with the center line of the piston. A good method of checking the grooves is to roll a new piston ring around the groove, Fig. E-13. It should roll freely, without binding, but also without any side play. If the clearance between the side of the ring and the piston groove exceeds .005 in., Fig. E-14, the piston should be discarded. However, if desired, the pistons can be placed in a lathe and the grooves trued. A spacing ring is then inserted to compensate for the amount of metal removed from the side of the groove. When checking pistons, make sure there are no burned areas around the ring lands. In addition, make sure there are no cracks. If the piston of the steel strut type, make sure the strut has not become loose.

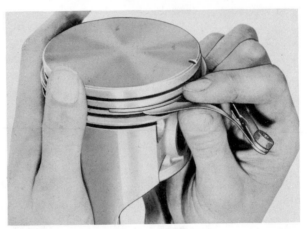

Fig. E-14. Checking clearance of ring in groove with a feeler gauge.

Spongy, eroded areas near the top of the pistons are usually caused by detonation or preignition. A shiny surface on the thrust surface of the piston, offset from the center line between the piston pin holes, can be caused by a bent connecting rod. Replace pistons that show signs of excessive wear, wavy ring lands, fractures and/or damage from detonation or preignition.

FITTING PISTON RINGS

Replacement type piston rings are designed to compensate for a certain amount of wear in the cylinders. The claims made by some manufacturers are extreme, but in general, replacement type rings should not be installed in the cylinders that have more than .010 in. taper, or .005 in. out-of-round. For details on measuring cylinder wear, see paragraph entitled "Should Cylinders be Reconditioned."

When selecting a piston ring set for an engine, it is necessary to select the proper size. To do this, position the ring in the cylinder bore in which it is going to be used. Push the ring down into the bore area where normal ring wear is encountered. Use the head of a piston to position the ring in the bore so the ring is square within the cylinder wall. Be careful to avoid damage to the ring or cylinder bore.

Measure the gap between the ends of the ring with a feeler gauge, as shown in Fig. E-15. The size of this gap is dependent on the make of the piston ring, and also on the diameter of the cylinder bore. In general this gap should be .003 in. for each inch of diameter. In other words, the correct ring gap for a 3 in. bore cylinder should be three times .003 in. or .009 in.

Fig. E-15. Measuring end gap of piston ring with a feeler gauge.

The side clearance of the piston ring in the groove should not be less than .001 in. for both oil and compression rings.

Piston rings are easily installed on the pistons. Some mechanics use special ring spreader tools, which, of course, make the installation quite simple, and without any danger of breaking the ring. Other mechanics will not use a special tool, but will spread the rings by hand. On the cast iron type rings, the procedure is to place a thumb over each end of a ring and spread the end of the ring apart. This will enlarge the diameter sufficiently so that it can be slid down over the piston to its proper groove. Be careful to follow the manufacturer's instructions so each ring is placed in the correct groove. In some designs it is necessary that one side of the ring be toward the top of the piston. If rings are not placed in the proper groove and with the right side up, excessive oil consumption will result.

When placing piston rings on the pistons, make sure the gaps are as indicated in Fig. E-32. In that way, the ring gaps are not in a row. Consequently, blow-by through the gaps is kept to a minimum.

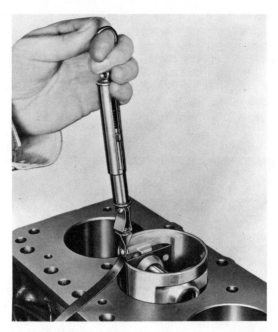

Fig. E-16. Checking piston clearance with a feeler gauge and spring balance to measure the pull.

ARE NEW PISTONS NECESSARY?

When new piston rings are installed without reconditioning the cylinders, it is seldom necessary to install new pistons. Naturally, if the ring lands are badly worn, or if the pistons have been badly damaged as a result of preignition, and excessive blow-by, new pistons will be required. When the original pistons are in good condition, they can be used again if expanded to desired clearance between piston and cylinder.

The normal piston clearance at the skirt is listed below. However, on the high performance models, skirt clearance is increased materially.

Engine (cu. in.)	Skirt. (in.)	Engine (cu. in.)	Skirt (in.)
85 (1.4 L)	.001-.002	327	.0005-.0011
98 (1.6 L)	.001-.002	350 (1968-1970)	.0005-.0011
140	.0018-.0028	350 (1971-1978)	.0007-.0017
151	.0025-.0033	350 (245 hp)	.0036-.0042
153	.0006-.0010	396	.0018-.0026
196	.0008-.0020	400	.0014-.0020
200	.0005-.0015	402	.0018-.0026
231	.0008-.0020	427	.0009-.0015
250	.0005-.0011	454	.0024-.0034
305	.0017-.0042	454 (235 hp)	.0018-.0028
307	.0005-.0011	454 (425 hp)	.0040-.0050

MEASURING PISTON CLEARANCE

One method of measuring piston clearance is to use one-half in. wide feeler gauge stock. Such a feeler gauge of the desired width and thickness can be secured in lengths of approximately 12 in. long. The procedure is to place the feeler gauge along the side of the piston, 90 deg. around the piston from the piston pin. The piston and feeler gauge are then inserted into the cylinder bore, Fig. E-16. If the clearance is correct, the piston should push the cylinder with light pressure, but it should lock if a feeler gauge of .001 in. more than standard clearance is used. Another method is to measure the pull required to pull the feeler gauge from between the piston and the cylinder wall. The feeler gauge should be pulled straight up and out by means of a scale, Fig. E-16, and the reading should be between 7 and 18 lb. If less than that amount, the clearance is excessive and if more than that amount the clearance is insufficient.

Still another method of measuring the piston clearance is to use micrometers, Fig. E-17. In this case the diameter of the cylinder bore is measured with inside micrometers, and the diameter of the piston is measured with outside micrometers. When measuring the cylinder bore, it is measured across the width of the engine, and the diameter of the piston is measured across its thrust faces. The difference between the two diameters will then be the piston clearance.

If the clearance is in excess of the amount specified, the pistons should be expanded sufficiently to obtain the desired clearance. Automotive machine shops have the necessary equipment for expanding the pistons.

Fig. E-17. Measuring piston diameter with outside micrometers.

CHECKING PISTON PINS

It is often difficult to determine whether a piston pin requires replacement. In general, a piston pin knock will sound very much like a loose valve tappet, and in many cases is worse when the engine is cold, than after it has reached operating temperature. However, when a car has traveled a distance sufficient to require replacement of piston rings and bearings, it will be poor economy not to replace the piston pins also. Furthermore, when new piston rings have been installed, and particularly when pistons have been expanded, piston pins with only a slight amount of excess clearance will cause a knock. This knock will in some cases disappear after the piston rings have been run in.

When examining the condition of the piston pins, any appreciable looseness or wear is sufficient cause for rejection. An inexperienced mechanic will sometimes confuse side play of the pins and the piston boss with pin wear.

The method of judging the fit of new pins will depend largely on the method used in fitting the pins. When a hone is used to fit the pins, they will seem to be relatively loose. If a reamer is used for fitting the pins, they will appear to be tighter than if they have been fitted by the hone method.

When the hone method is used, the end of the rod will drop quickly of its own weight when the assembly is held by the piston. If the reamer method is used to fit the pin, the rod will not drop of its own weight when the assembly is held by the piston.

BE SURE TO CHECK ROD ALIGNMENT

Along with the job of fitting the piston pin, is the job of checking the connecting rods for alignment. Obviously, if the rod is bent, or twisted, the piston will not move in a straight line at right angles to the center line of the crankshaft. The equipment for aligning connecting rods forms part of every well equipped shop.

If the equipment is not available, an approximation of the trueness of the connecting rod can be obtained by viewing the movement of the upper end of the connecting rod, as the engine is cranked. To do this, the oil pan is removed and the rod and piston assemblies are in position on the crankshaft. While the engine is cranked by the starter, the mechanic underneath the engine views the movement of the upper end of the connecting rod. This should remain centrally located on the piston pin, with equal clearance on each side of the piston pin bosses, and the end of the connecting rod. If the end of the connecting rod moves back and forth between the piston bosses, or if it remains pressed firmly against one of the bosses, the rod is bent.

TIPS ON REPLACING ENGINE BEARINGS

After the connecting rods have been removed from the engine, it is important to check the connecting rod bearings to determine whether they can be used again. It is often difficult to determine the condition of a bearing, and many bearings are discarded when actually they still retain many miles of useful life. First of all, the color of bearing surface is no gauge of the condition of the bearing.

In many cases the bearing surface will be stained a dark gray, or black. Such bearings are usually still serviceable. If any of the bearing metal has dropped from the backing, the bearing should be discarded. Also if the bearing surface is deeply grooved, scratched or pitted, replacement is indicated. If the back of a bearing which contacts the connecting rod or cap shows areas that are black, it indicates that there was dirt between the shell and the rod and the bearing should be replaced. If there are

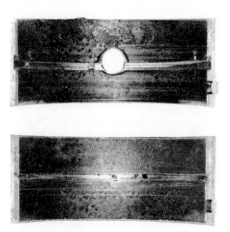

Fig. E-18. Example of worn engine bearings. In case illustrated, the bearings have been worn and gouged as the result of dirt.

groove marks on the back of the bearing shell, the shell has been slipping in the rod, and such bearing should also be replaced. An illustration of a bearing that has failed is shown in Fig. E-18.

Another test for a bearing is to measure the thickness of the shell. Such measurements are made with special micrometers, with a button on

Fig. E-19. Note grooves worn in these engine bearing journals as the result of dirt in the oil.

the rounded end of the anvil. Manufacturers of bearings provide specifications giving the thicknesses of different bearings. One of the best methods of determining the condition of a bearing is to make an oil leak test. This test is described later in this chapter.

CHECKING THE CRANKSHAFT

Before replacing any connecting rod bearings, the connecting rod bearing journal should be carefully measured for wear and roughness. Ordinary three inch outside micrometers are used for measuring connecting rod journals. The throws or journals should be measured at several points along their length to check for taper, and also measured at two points at right angles to each other to see if they are out-of-round.

Generally accepted limits for taper and out-of-round are .001 in. and .0015 in., respectively. If the wear exceeds these values, the crankshaft should be reground. If there is any roughness as shown in Fig. E-19, the journal should be reground. When journals are tapered, out-of-round or scored it will be impossible to fit the bearing correctly with the result that the bearing will knock, lose an excessive amount of oil, and will soon fail completely.

Equipment is available for reconditioning connecting rod journals without removing the crankshaft from the engine.

RODS MUST FIT BEARINGS

When overhauling an old engine, it is often found that a previous mechanic has filed down the bearing caps in an effort to make a worn-out bearing last a little longer. The result of this is that the bearing bore of the connecting rod is no longer round, and it will be impossible to install a new bearing shell. When such a condition is found, it will be necessary to rebore the big end of the connecting rod in order to return true circularity.

It is important that a bearing shall be a snug fit in the connecting rod. To insure such a fit in the conventional connecting rod, bearing manufac-

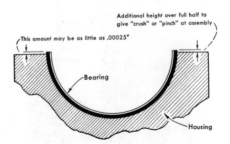

Fig. E-20. Bearing shells should extend approximately .00025 in. above surface of bearing cap, prior to being bolted in position.

turers make the bearing half slightly bigger than an exact half. As a result, the bearing half will extend slightly beyond the edge of the bearing cap. This is known as bearing crush, and is illustrated in Fig. E-20.

Conventional type bearings are keyed to the connecting rods, and are often adjusted by the feel or drag as the rod is swung back and forth on the connecting rod journal.

Some mechanics use "Plastigage" for checking the fit of these bearings. Plastigage consists essentially of slender rods of plastic. A short length of Plastigage is placed between the bearing journal and the bearing, and the connecting rod caps are tightened to approximately 65 ft. lb. tension. The connecting rod is then removed and the width of the crushed Plastigage is compared with a gauge provided by the manufacturer, Fig. E-21. The gauge reading gives the clearance of the bearing directly in thousandths of an inch.

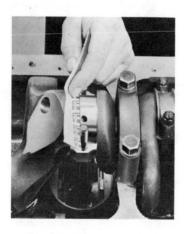

Fig. E-21. Checking engine bearing clearance by means of Plastigage.

HOW TO FIT ROD BEARING

Another method of fitting connecting rod bearings is to place a piece of .002 in. metal feeler stock that is one-half inch wide and 7/8 in. long between the bearing and the crank pin as shown in Fig. E-22. Bolt the connecting rod on the crank pin but with the piston end down, instead of in the conventional manner. Then with the rod bolts tight, the piston end of the rod is swung back and forth, presenting some resistance. If no resistance is felt, the clearance is excessive. If the rod cannot be swung back and forth on the crank pin, the clearance is too little. The correct clearance is obtained when the piston is swung to approximately a horizontal position and then will gradually sink to a vertical position. Be sure to remove the piece of shim stock from between the bearing and bearing journal before the final assembly of the rod to the crankshaft.

USE TORQUE WRENCH ON ROD NUTS

After all of the connecting rod bearings have been adjusted, the bearing cap nuts should be tightened to the correct torque, as specified in the table at the back of this book.

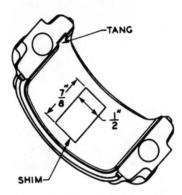

Fig. E-22. Using a piece of .002 in. thick feeler stock to check clearance of engine bearing.

CHECKING AND REPLACING MAIN BEARINGS

The usual procedure when replacing main bearings, is to replace one bearing at a time, leaving the other bearings to support the shaft. After removing the bearing cap, the upper half of the bearing shell must be removed from the cylinder block. There are several ways in which this can be accomplished without removing the crankshaft. A putty knife or some similar tool with a bent blade can be used to rotate the bearing shell around the shaft until it can be removed. Another method is to bend a cotter pin, as shown in Fig. E-23. Insert the eye end of the cotter pin in the oil hole in the bearing journal. Rotate the crankshaft, and the bent end of the cotter pin will force out the bearing shell.

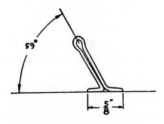

Fig. E-23. Method of bending a cotter pin so it can be used to remove upper half of main bearing shell.

Caprice Classic and Impala models carry over engine and drive train combinations for 1978 with lower axle ratios to improve fuel economy.

Fig. E-24. Using special micrometers to measure diameter of crankshaft without removing shaft from the engine block.

After both halves of the bearing shell have been removed, the crankshaft journal should be checked for wear. Special micrometers are required to check these journals, Fig. E-24. Conventional micrometers cannot be used, as they will not reach up and measure the full diameter. If the journal has more than .001 in. taper, or is more than .0015 in. out-of-round, the crankshaft should be reground. To do this, it will have to be removed from the engine. The correct torque for the main bearing bolts is given in the specification tables at the back of this book.

When the proper size main bearing shells are obtained, the upper one is slid into place in the upper half of the bearing journal. Then the lower half is placed in the cap and the cap installed.

To check main bearing clearance, the Plastigage method can be used or a piece of shim stock, as described in the section devoted to fitting rod bearings.

WHEN SHOULD MAIN BEARINGS BE REPLACED

Main bearings should be replaced when they are worn to such an extent that the engine will knock, or when there is excessive oil leakage, as indicated by an oil leak test. Main bearing knocks will become most evident when the engine is under a heavy load, such as when pulling a steep grade.

HOW TO MAKE AN OIL LEAK TEST

One of the best methods of checking engine bearings for proper fit and wear, and also to determine when they need replacing, is to make an oil pressure, or oil leak test, as shown in Fig. E-25. Such a test will also show whether the entire engine lubricating system is clear and unobstructed so as to permit a full flow of oil to all the engine bearings.

The equipment for making such a test as illustrated, is designed to supply oil under pressure to the engine lubricating system.

106

Engine Repairs

Basically the equipment consists of a small tank of about five gal. capacity. This is partly filled with oil of SAE 30 grade. Compressed air is then applied to the tank until the pressure reaches approximately 25 lb., or the normal operating oil pressure of the engine. By means of suitable tubing, the tank is connected to the engine oil system. The engine is then cranked slowly and at the same time the engine bearings and the entire oiling system are carefully observed. Under these conditions, copper alloy bearings in good condition will leak at a rate of approximately 50 drops per minute. Engine bearings leaking oil at a faster rate, particularly those leaking in a steady stream, have too much clearance. Bearings showing a slower leakage than 30 drops per minute may have insufficient clearance, or the oil line to the bearing may be clogged. Babbitt type bearings should leak at a rate of 20 to 150 drops per minute.

In addition to the main and rod bearings, it is important to observe other bearings which may receive pressure lubrication, such as camshaft bearings and piston pin bearings. It is also important to check the plug at the rear of the camshaft rear bearing. This plug will occasionally get loose and excessive oil leakage will occur. As this oil will drop down past the rear main bearing, it is often mistaken for a leaking rear main bearing.

Fig. E-25. Making an oil pressure test on an engine to determine condition of engine bearings.

Instead of a pressure tank for making this test, some mechanics will use an oil pump. The intake of the pump is immersed in a pan of oil, and the outlet is connected to the engine oiling system. An electric drill is then used to drive the pump.

Regardless of the type of equipment used in making this test, it is important that the oil used is not heavier than SAE 30. In addition it is important that the oil is not cold, but should be at least 75 deg. F.

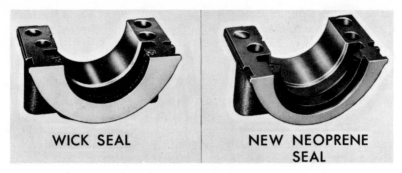

WICK SEAL   NEW NEOPRENE
                              SEAL

Fig. E-26. Illustrating two types of rear main bearing oil seals.

REPLACING REAR MAIN OIL SEALS

To prevent leakage of oil from the rear main bearing, special seals are provided. Typical seals are illustrated in Figs. E-26 and E-27. The wick type seal, Fig. E-26 was used as original equipment on the 235 cu. in. six cylinder engine, and also on the V-8 prior to 1959. A lip type rubber molded seal over a steel core is now available for replacement of the wick type seal used originally. This seal must be installed in sets of two per engine, and is so supplied. To replace the wick type seal, first remove the

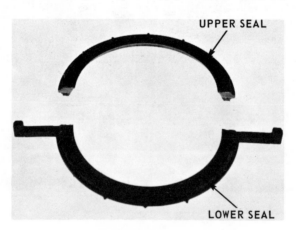

UPPER SEAL

LOWER SEAL

Fig. E-27. Note side extension on this oil seal.

bearing cap and pry the old seal from the bearing cap, using a small screwdriver. Loosen the remaining bearing caps to allow the crankshaft to drop slightly. In some cases it will be necessary to use a lever, placed between the crankshaft and the cylinder block to force the crankshaft down. Using a screwdriver or a blunt punch, push the seal out of the upper bearing sufficiently to pull it out completely with the end of a pair of pliers. Rotating the crankshaft in the same direction will often help pull the seal out.

To replace the wick type seal with a lip type rubber molded seal, after removing the wick type seal, first make sure that the upper and lower grooves are clean. Inspect the crankshaft seal contact area, and remove any imperfections with a fine oilstone. Dip the new seal in engine oil. Handle seals carefully to avoid marring the lip surfaces. Insert the upper seal in groove in engine block with lip of seal toward the front of the engine. Rotate the seal into the groove. Install the lower seal in the bearing cap with the lip toward the front of the engine.

To replace the neoprene type seal used on V-8 engines and illustrated in Fig. E-26, first remove the rear main bearing cap. Remove oil seal from groove, prying from bottom, using a small screwdriver. Always clean crankshaft surface before installing a new seal. New seals should be well lubricated with engine oil on lip only. Be careful not to get oil on

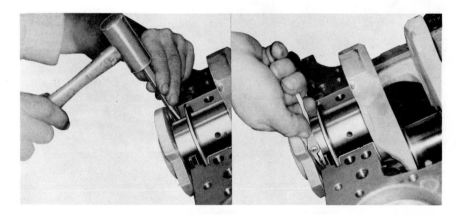

Fig. E-28. Using a pin punch to drive the oil seal (left) and then pliers to pull it through the remainder of the way.

parting line surface as this is treated with adhesive. The lip should face toward the front of the engine. With finger and thumb, roll seal into place being careful not to cut bead on back of seal with seal tangs at parting line.

Always replace upper and lower seal as a unit.

To replace the upper half of the seal, use a small hammer and tap a brass pin punch on one end of the seal until it protrudes far enough to be removed with pliers, Fig. E-28.

Always wipe crankshaft surface clean before installing a new seal.

Lubricate the lip of a new seal with engine oil, taking care to keep oil off the parting line surface. Gradually push with a hammer handle, while turning the crankshaft, until seal is rolled into place. Be careful the seal tangs at parting line do not cut bead on back of seal. Use sealer at parting

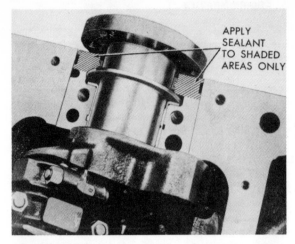

APPLY
SEALANT
TO SHADED
AREAS ONLY

Fig. E-29. Sealer should be applied to the area indicated and also to the bearing cap in order to prevent leakage of oil.

Fig. E-30. Using a dial gauge to check a cylinder for taper and out-of-round.

Fig. E-31. Piston, ring and rod assembly being installed in a cylinder. Note ring compressor used to compress rings into their grooves.

line on cap half of seal. Install the rear main bearing cap with new seal and torque to specifications.

Be sure to use sealer at parting line of cap half of seal and seal area of cylinder block as shown in Fig. E-29.

SHOULD CYLINDERS BE RECONDITIONED?

In most cases cylinders will require reconditioning only after 100,000 miles of operation or when the cylinder is more than .003 in. out-of-round, or when the taper exceeds .006 in.

It should be pointed out that when the car is used mostly in city driving, which consists of short trips of less than five miles, engine wear increases more rapidly than it does on long trips of many miles duration.

The most satisfactory method of determining the wear in a cylinder is to use a dial gauge as shown in Fig. E-30. The measurement is taken across the cylinder and the reading of the gauge is noted as it is moved up and down for the entire length of piston travel. This will measure the taper which should not exceed .010 in. Then measure the fore-and-aft diameter and the difference between that and the taper will give the amount of out-of-round which should not exceed .005 in.

Cylinders can be reconditoned either by means of a boring bar or by means of a cylinder hone. Boring bars are generally used when considerable metal must be removed. Final finish is usually made with a hone.

Automotive machine shops with necessary equipment will do the reconditioning. However, even when cylinder wear is not excessive, the glaze should be removed from the cylinders before installing new piston rings. If the glaze is not removed from the cylinders, the engine will continue to use considerable oil. Removing the glaze is accomplished by means of deglazing hone. The hone is driven by an electric drill, and all that is necessary is to move the rotating hone several times up and down the cylinder until the glaze is removed.

If a deglazing hone is not available, it is advisable to use a relatively fine abrasive paper and rub the surface of the cylinder to remove the glaze. The abrasive paper should be moved spirally around the cylinder bore when deglazing by hand.

Before deglazing the cylinders, cloth should be placed over each of the crankshaft throws so that abrasive particles from the hone will be caught in the cloth.

INSTALLING CONNECTING ROD ASSEMBLIES

After the main bearings have been replaced, new rod bearings selected, pins fitted, pistons expanded, and rings installed on the pistons, the connecting rod and piston assemblies are ready to be installed in their original cylinders. To do this, it is necessary to use a ring compressor as shown in Fig. E-31. This is essentially a sleeve, which compresses the piston rings in their grooves, so the pistons can be replaced in the cylinders. Before compressing the rings, however, the piston and rings should be given a liberal coating of engine oil. Similarly, the cylinders should be covered with oil. With the rings compressed, insert the connecting rod and piston assembly in the top of the cylinder. The assembly will be prevented from dropping through the cylinder by the pressure of the expanded piston against the cylinder walls and by the ring compressor. The assembly is driven the rest of the distance into the cylinder by tapping the top of the piston with the handle of a heavy hammer, Fig. E-31.

On all engines except the 348 cu. in. V-8, be sure the indentation mark or arrow on top of the piston is toward the front of the engine. On the 348 cu. in. V-8 engine, the indentation mark on the top of the piston should be toward the front of the engine on the left bank of cylinders, and to the rear on the right bank of cylinders.

It is important that the gaps of the piston ring should be correctly located around the piston, as indicated in Fig. E-32.

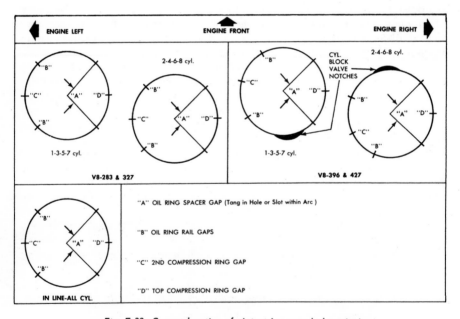

Fig. E-32. Correct location of piston ring gaps is important.

When installing rod and piston assemblies, one mechanic should be underneath the engine to guide the lower end of the connecting rod so it does not strike and mar the connecting rod throw on the crankshaft.

If it proves difficult to force the piston fully into the cylinder, the trouble is probably caused by the piston rings not having been compressed into their respective grooves, with the result that the rings are extending over the edge of the cylinder. In such cases, remove the ring compressor and then making sure that none of the rings have been damaged, again compress the rings carefully and install the piston assembly in the cylinder.

Always check and double check to be sure that the rod and piston assemblies have been correctly assembled and placed in their respective bores from which they were originally removed. On V-8 engines install with connecting rod bearing tang slots on side opposite cam shaft. In-line engines must have pistons with the piston notch facing front of engine. Unless assembly and installation is made correctly, there will be danger of the valves striking the top of the piston and doing considerable damage.

TIGHTENING CONNECTING ROD CAPS

When installing and tightening connecting rod bolts, it is important to place the caps on the rods from which they were originally removed, and also in their original relative position. Be sure to apply a liberal coating of oil to the crankshaft throw before attaching the connecting rod and cap. The socket used to tighten the nuts must be of the thin wall type, as there is very little clearance. Some mechanics will tighten these nuts as much as possible. This is poor practice as it distorts the bearings and connecting rod caps with the result that they are no longer round. Under such conditions, oil leaks from the bearings, bearing life will be materially shortened and oil consumption increased. A torque wrench can always be used to tighten connecting rod nuts.

WHEN TO REPLACE TIMING CHAINS

The life of a timing chain, Fig. E-33, is normally in excess of 100,000 miles. A worn timing chain will first be indicated by a whirring and rattling noise from the front of the engine. In cases of extreme wear, the tim-

Fig. E-33. Typical timing chain installation.

ing chain may be so loose, it will jump from one position to another on the sprockets with the result that the timing of the ignition and camshaft will be altered. When this happens, the engine will fail to operate, or if it does operate, performance will be very poor.

HOW TO REPLACE TIMING CHAINS

The timing chain, as used on V-8 engines, is easily replaced after removing the radiator, hydraulic balancer, and timing case cover. Crank the engine until timing marks on the sprocket are in line, as shown in Fig. E-33. Remove the three camshaft sprocket to camshaft bolts. Then remove the camshaft sprocket and timing chain together. The sprocket is a light press fit on the camshaft. A light blow with a plastic faced hammer on the lower edge of the ridge of the sprocket should free it.

When installing the timing chain and sprocket, be sure the timing marks are in alignment, Fig. E-33. Do not drive the sprocket on the camshaft, as this will push on the sealing plug at the rear end of the shaft, causing an oil leak. Instead draw the camshaft sprocket into position by tightening the three bolts in rotation.

HOW TO REPLACE TIMING GEARS

Timing gears are used on all Chevrolet in-line engines, including the 153, 194, 230, 235 and 250 cu. in. engines, Fig. E-34. These gears seldom require replacement.

The camshaft gear is a press fit on the camshaft, and it is necessary to remove the camshaft from the cylinder block to remove the gear.

Fig. E-34. Typical timing gear installation. A method of checking gear lash with a feeler gauge is illustrated.

Fig. E-35. Installing oil seal in timing case cover.

FRONT COVER OIL SEAL

In case of oil leakage from the front cover, it is necessary to install a new oil seal and gasket. The procedure is to remove the cover, and pry out the old seal. Then install a new seal so the open end of the seal is toward the inside of the cover, and drive it into a position with a round drift of the diameter which fits the seal, Fig. E-35.

The replacement of the front cover oil seal can be made either with the cover removed, or with the cover still installed on the front of the engine. If the cover is still on the front of the engine, the procedure is to remove the crankshaft pulley and hub or torsional damper after which the seal can be pried from the cover with a large screwdriver, taking care not to damage the seal surface on the cover. The new seal is then installed in the same manner as previously described herein.

HYDRAULIC LIFTER CHECKS

Hydraulic valve lifters are available as either standard or optional equipment on all Chevrolet built engines, except the 409 cu. in. V-8. Hydraulic valve lifters seldom require attention, particularly if the engine oil is changed at frequent intervals. Fig. E-36 shows the details of hydraulic valve lifters used on recent model Chevrolet built engines.

It is normal for hydraulic valve lifters to be noisy when the engine is first started. That results from the oil having drained from the lifter, but as soon as the lifters are again filled with oil the noise will disappear. However, if the noise persists, servicing is required. An easy way to locate a noisy valve lifter is to use a piece of garden hose, approximately

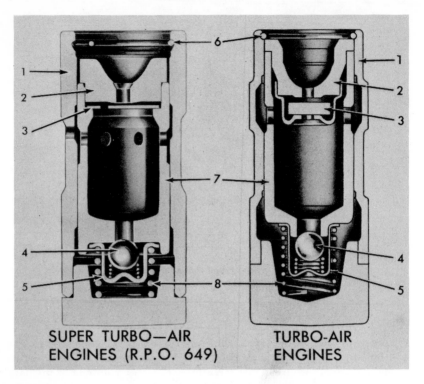

SUPER TURBO—AIR
ENGINES (R.P.O. 649)

TURBO-AIR
ENGINES

Fig. E-36. Types of hydraulic valve lifters. 1—Lifter body. 2—Push rod seat. 3—Valve. 4—Ball check. 5—Ball retainer. 6—Lock ring. 7—Plunger. 8—Check ball spring.

4 ft. long. Place one end of the hose near the end of each valve, with the other end of the hose being held to your ear. By following this procedure, noisy valve lifters can easily be located, as the garden hose acts as a stethoscope. Another method of locating a nosy lifter is to place a finger on the edge of the valve spring retainer on each valve in turn. Lifters not operating correctly will give a distinct shock each time the valve seats.

Each hydraulic lifter is a matched assembly. If the parts of one lifter are intermixed with those of another, improper valve operation will result and the lifter will be noisy. It is, therefore, necessary to keep the parts of each valve lifter separated so that they will not be mixed with the parts of other lifters. Also keep the lifter assemblies in proper sequence so they can be installed in their original position.

To disassemble a hydraulic valve lifter, grasp the lock ring, Fig. E-36, at the upper end of the lifter with a pair of long-nosed pliers to release it from the groove. It may be necessary to depress the plunger slightly in order to release the lock ring. After removing the lock ring, the other parts are easily removed from the lifter body.

In general, when hydraulic valve lifters have seen enough mileage so they are no longer operating quietly, it pays to install a complete new unit rather than to attempt to salvage the old ones. However, in cases where the cost factor is of major importance, by thoroughly cleaning the individual parts of the hydraulic lifters with solvent, they can be reassembled and placed back in service.

Instructions covering the adjustment of hydraulic valve lifters are given in the Chapter on Valve Tappet Adjustment.

DO NOT MIX PARTS

Regardless of what part of the engine is being assembled, it always pays to carefully observe the relative position of each part. Whenever possible the parts should be marked so they can be reassembled in their original position. This applies particularly to such parts as engine valves, hydraulic valve lifters, rocker arms, piston and rod assemblies, and engine bearings.

TROUBLE SHOOTING

See also Chapters on Fuel, Ignition and Electrical Systems.

LACK OF POWER

Incorrect valve lash. Sticking valves. Leaking valves. Valve springs weak or broken. Valve or ignition timing incorrect. Leaking cylinder head gasket. Worn pistons, rings and cylinder walls. Low compression.

Fig. E-37. Parts of a typical hydraulic valve lifter.

EXCESSIVE OIL CONSUMPTION

Oil leaks, check all gaskets and oil lines. Clogged oil return from rocker arm chamber. Clogged crankcase ventilating system. Leaking rear main bearing. Worn rings, pistons and cylinder walls. Worn valve stems and guides. Worn valve stem seals. Defective vacuum diaphragm on dual type fuel pumps.

HARD STARTING

Low engine compression. Excessive friction. Heavy engine oil. Valves holding open. Leaking manifold gasket. Loose carburetor mountings.

POPPING, SPITTING, DETONATION

Excessive carbon in combustion chamber. Valves sticking. Incorrect valve lash. Valves too thin and overheating. Weak valve springs. Incorrect valve timing. Clogged water jackets. Restricted exhaust ports in cylinder head. Cylinder head gasket blown between cylinders. Clogged muffler and exhaust system.

ROUGH ENGINE IDLE

Incorrect valve lash. Valve loose in guides. Valves not seating properly. Sticking valves. Leaking head gasket. Cracks in exhaust port.

MISSING ON ACCELERATION

Incorrect valve lash. Burned valves. Sticking valves. Leaking manifold gaskets. Low compression. Leaking head gasket.

ENGINE NOISE

Worn main bearings will give a heavy thumping noise, which is loudest on slow heavy pull. Worn rod bearings will give a sharp knock which is loudest at speeds of about 40 mph and as the engine goes from a pull to a coast. Worn pistons will give a sharp knock or slap which is worse when the engine is cold and decreases as the engine reaches operating temperature. Worn piston pins will act very much the same as a worn piston. Loose or worn engine mounts will cause a heavy thump particularly on sudden acceleration.

VALVE
ADJUSTING

In order to get maximum power from engines with mechanical lifters, it is essential that the valve lash of these lifters be accurately adjusted. Valve lash is the distance between the end of the rocker arm and the end of the valve stem.

MECHANICAL VALVE LIFTER ADJUSTMENT

Mechanical lifters are used on the 235 cu. in. Six and also as standard or special equipment on the 248, 302, 409 and 427 cu. in. V-8 engines. Correct valve lash on the Six is .006 in. for the intake valves and .015 in. for the exhaust. On the 348 and 409 cu. in. engines, the lash is .012 in. and .018 in. for the intake and exhaust respectively. On the 427 cu. in. engines the lash is .022 and .024 in. On the 302 cu. in. engines both valves are adjusted to .030 in.

On the 330 hp version of the 350 c.i.d. engine and 425 hp version of the 454 c.i.d. engine mechanical lifters are also used. In the case of the 350 c.i.d. engine the intake valve clearance is .024 in., and the exhaust is .030 in. The valve clearance for the 454 c.i.d. engine is .024 in. and .028 in. for the intake and exhaust valves respectively.

Before attempting to adjust valve lash, normalize the temperature of the engine. The best method of doing this is to drive the car for about 5 miles, or until the engine oil temperature remains the same for about 5 minutes.

Adjustment of the clearance between the end of the valve stem and the rocker arm is made by first loosening the lock nut on the rocker arm, Fig. F-1, and turning the adjustment until the proper clearance is obtained between the end of the rocker arm and the end of the valve stem. The clearance is measured by means of a feeler gauge.

MECHANICAL LIFTERS ON V-8 ENGINES

To adjust the mechanical valve lifters as used on V-8 engines, proceed as follows: Crank engine until mark on torsional damper lines up with the center or "O" mark on the timing tab and the engine is in the number one firing position. This may be determined by placing fingers on number one cylinder valve as the mark on the damper comes near the "O" mark on the front cover. If the valves are not moving, the engine is in the number one firing position. If the valves move as the mark comes up to the timing tab, the engine is in number six firing position and the crankshaft should be rotated one more revolution to reach the number one position.

Fig. F-1. Adjusting mechanical valve tappets on Chevrolet 235 cu. in. Six. Note feeler gauge in mechanic's left hand.

With the engine in number one firing position, as determined above, adjust the following valves to specifications with a feeler gauge, Fig. F-2: Exhaust valves 4 and 8, Intake valves 2 and 7. Turn the crankshaft one-half revolution clockwise and adjust the following valves to specifications with a feeler gauge: Exhaust valves 3 and 6, Intake valves 1 and 8.

Turn the crankshaft one-half revolution clockwise until the pointer

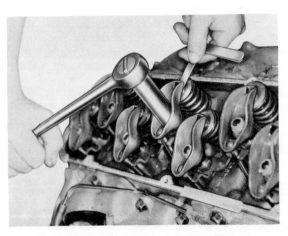

Fig. F-2. Adjusting valve lash on pivot type rocker arms.

Valve Adjusting

"O" mark and the torsional damper mark are again in alignment. This is number 6 line position. With the engine in this position, adjust the following valves to specifications with a feeler gauge: Exhaust valves 5 and 7, Intake valves 3 and 4.

Turn crankshaft one-half revolution clockwise and adjust the following valves to specifications with a feeler gauge: Exhaust valves 1 and 2, Intake valves 5 and 6.

The valve lash should be adjusted with the engine hot and running, and only after the engine has reached full operating temperature.

HYDRAULIC LIFTERS

A typical hydraulic valve lifter is shown in Figs. E-36 and F-3. Hydraulic valve lifters very seldom require attention. The lifters are extremely simple in design, the adjustments are not necessary and servicing of the lifters requires only that care and cleanliness be exercised in the handling of parts.

Locating noisy hydraulic valve lifters was discussed in the previous chapter. The general types of valve lifter noise are as follows:

Hard rapping noise: Usually caused by the plunger becoming tight in the bore of the lifter body to such an extent that the return spring can no longer push the plunger back up to the working position. Probable causes are: Excessive varnish or carbon deposit causing abnormal stickiness. Galling or pickup between plunger and bore of lifter body, usually caused by an abrasive piece of dirt or metal wedging between plunger and lifter body.

Moderate rapping noise: Probable causes are: Excessively high leakdown rate. Leaking check valve seat. Improper adjustment.

General noise throughout the valve train: This will in most cases be a definite indication of insufficient oil supply or improper adjustment.

Clicking noise; Intermittent clicking: Probable causes are: A microscopic piece of dirt momentarily caught between ball seat and check valve ball. In rare cases the ball itself may be out-of-round or have a flat spot. Improper adjustment.

In most cases where noise exists in one or more lifters, all lifter units should be removed, disassembled, cleaned in a solvent, reassembled and reinstalled in the engine. If dirt, corrosion, carbon, etc. are shown to exist in one unit, it probably exists in all units, thus it would on be a matter of time before all lifters cause trouble.

Hydraulic valve lifters can be removed after first removing the intake manifold. Then remove the rocker arms and push rods after which the valve lifters can be lifted from the engine.

TIPS ON HYDRAULIC LIFTER SERVICE

Thoroughly clean all parts in cleaning solvent, and inspect them carefully. If any parts are damaged or worn, the entire lifter assembly should be replaced. If the lifter body wall is scuffed or worn, inspect the cylinder block lifter bore; if the bottom of the lifter is scuffed or worn, inspect the camshaft lobe; if the push rod seat is scuffed or worn, inspect the push rod.

Note that the inertia valve and retainer in the hydraulic lifter installed in the turbo air engines should not be removed from the push rod seat. To check the valve, shake the push rod seat and inertia valve assembly and the valve should move.

Plungers and other parts of hydraulic lifters are not interchangeable; they are a selective fit at the factory. Should a plunger or lifter body become damaged, it is necessary to replace the entire unit. The plunger must be free in the lifter body. A simple test for this is to be sure the plunger will drop of its own weight in the body.

When disassembling a hydraulic valve lifter, be sure the parts are not mixed and are returned to the same unit. A unit is easily disassembled by removing the retainer, shown in Fig. E-36 and F-3, after which the other parts can be pulled from the body of the unit. When replacing a hydraulic valve lifter, be sure to fill the assembly with SAE 10 oil before completing the installation.

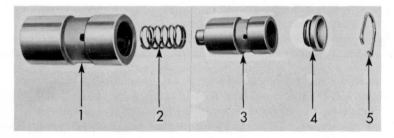

Fig. F-3. Parts of typical valve lifter. 1—Body. 2—Spring.
3—Plunger and ball check. 4—Push rod seat. 5—Retainer.

Hydraulic valve lifters are easily removed. In the case of V-8 engines, remove the rocker arm cover attaching screws and remove the rocker arm cover. Also remove the intake manifold. Back off the rocker arm nuts until the arms can be swung away from the push rods. Remove the push rods. The hydraulic valve lifters can then be lifted from their places in the cylinder block.

A similar procedure is to be followed when removing the hydraulic valve lifters from six cylinder engines.

ASSEMBLING HYDRAULIC LIFTERS

Place the ball check on small hole in bottom of plunger. Insert check ball spring on seat in ball retainer and place retainer over ball so spring rests on the ball. Carefully press the retainer into position in plunger with a blade of a small screwdriver.

Place the plunger spring over the ball retainer and slide the lifter body over the spring and plunger, being careful to line up the oil feed holes in the lifter body and plunger. Fill the assembly with SAE 10 oil, then insert the end of a 1/8 in. drift pin into the plunger and press down solid. At this point, oil hole in lifter body and plunger assembly will be in alignment. Do not attempt to force or pump the plunger.

Insert a 1/16 in. drift pin through both oil holes to hold the plunger down against the lifter spring tension. On the type illustrated as turbo-air in Fig. E-36, the drift pin must not extend inside the plunger. Remove the 1/8 in. drift pin. Refill assembly with SAE 10 oil. Install the metering valve and push rod seat or push rod seat and inertia valve, as the case may be, Fig. E-36. Install the push rod seat retainer, press down on the push rod seat and remove the 1/16 in. drift pin from the oil holes. Lifter is now completely assembled, filled with oil and ready for installation.

Before installing any new lifters, be sure to coat the bottom of the lifter with Molykote or its equivalent to prevent scoring of the lifter.

ADJUSTING HYDRAULIC VALVE LIFTERS

When rocker arm assemblies or valve lifters have been removed and replaced on an engine, it is then necessary to make an initial adjustment of each valve lifter. This adjustment must be made when the lifter is on the base circle of the cam, following this procedure:

Crank engine until mark on torsional damper aligns with center or "O" mark on the timing tab and the engine is in the number one firing position. This may be determined by placing fingers on the number one cylinder valve as the mark on the damper comes near the "O" mark on the front cover. If the valves are not moving, the engine is in the number one firing position. If the valves are moving, as the mark comes up to the timing tab, the engine is in the number six firing position and the crankshaft should be rotated one more revolution to reach the number one position.

Valve adjustment is made by backing off the adjusting nut, (rocker arm stud nut) until there is play in the push rod and then tighten nut to just remove all push rod to rocker arm clearance. This may be determined by rotating push rod with fingers as the nut is tightened, Fig. F-4. When the push rod does not readily move in relation to the rocker arm, the clearance has been eliminated. The adjusting nut should then be tightened an additional one turn on older models and 3/4 turn on 1976-1977 models to place the hydraulic lifter plunger in the center of the travel. No further adjustment is required.

With the V-8 engine in number one firing position, as determined above, the following valves may be adjusted: Exhaust 1, 3, 4, 8. Intake 1, 2, 5, 7. Crank the engine one revolution until the pointer and the "O" mark are again in alignment. This is number six firing position. With the engine in this position, the following valves may be adjusted: Exhaust 2, 5, 6, 7. Intake 3, 4, 6, 8.

On six cylinder engines the procedure for cranking the engine so that the engine is on the base circle of the camshaft's lobe is slightly different, and is as follows:

Mark distributor housing with chalk, at each cylinder position (plug wire) then disconnect plug wires at spark plugs and coil and remove distributor cap and plug wire assembly (if not previously done).

Crank engine until distributor rotor points to number one cylinder position and breaker points are open. Both valves on number one cylinder may now be adjusted.

Fig. F-4. Adjusting hydraulic valve lifter.

Back out adjusting nut until lash is felt at the push rod, then turn in adjusting nuts until all lash is removed. This can be determined by checking push rod side play while turning adjusting nut, Fig. F-4. When play has been removed, turn adjusting nut in one full additional turn in order to center lifter plunger.

Adjust the reamining valves, one cylinder at a time, in the same manner.

Firing order of the six cylinder engines is 1-5-3-6-2-4; V-8 engines 1-8-4-3-6-5-7-2; four cylinder engines 1-3-4-2.

Cylinders are numbered in sequence from front to rear. In the case of V-8 engines, the left bank (as viewed from the driver's seat) has uneven numbers; right bank, even numbers.

COOLING SYSTEM
KINKS

Chevrolet engines are designed to operate with permanent type anti-freeze in the cooling system, regardless of seasonal temperature. Only in this way will efficient operating temperature be maintained.

Many troubles that may occur in engine cooling system can be eliminated by draining and flushing cooling system every two years (or more often), then refilling with permanent type antifreeze affording protection to at least -20 deg. F. Permanent antifreeze provides protection against rusting as well as freezing, and the rust protection is extremely important. In addition to antifreeze, install an inhibitor and sealing compound each autumn as further protection against rusting.

A pressurized cooling system, Fig. G-1, is provided on all models by a pressure type radiator cap, Fig. G-2. With the 15 lb. pressure cap, coolant temperatures of up to a boiling point at 247 deg. F. are provided.

When radiator cap is removed or loosened, system pressure drops to atmospheric. When this occurs, heat which has caused water temperatures to be higher than 212 deg. F. will convert water into steam. Steam that forms will be ejected from radiator filler. The mechanic should be careful to avoid being burnt when removing the cap.

Coolant level should be maintained in conventional down flow radiator at one inch below bottom of filler neck when cooling system is cold, or at bottom of filler neck when system is warm. With cross flow radiators, coolant level should be maintained 3 in. below the bottom of the filler neck when the system is cold.

On vehicles with coolant recovery system, Fig. G-3, coolant level is checked by observing fluid level in reservoir (radiator cap need not be removed). The coolant level should be at "Cold Full" mark when cooling system cools, and coolant is at ambient temperature. When engine reaches operating temperature, level should be at "Hot Full" mark on reservoir which is made of a transparent plastic.

It is very important that the correct level be maintained at all times. If there is repeated coolant loss, check condition of pressure radiator cap. Check cooling system for loose hose connections, defective hoses, gasket leaks. See trouble shooting section at end of chapter.

DRAINING THE COOLING SYSTEM

Every two years the cooling system should be serviced by flushing with clear water, then completely refilled with a fresh solution of water and a high quality permanent type glycol base antifreeze. This will help prevent the formation of rust and sludge in the system.

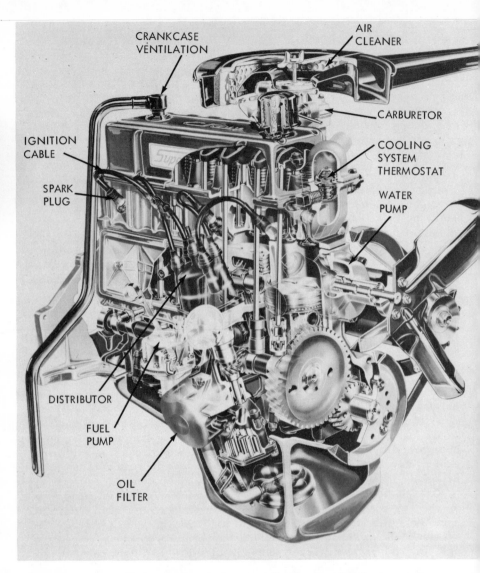

CRANKCASE
VENTILATION

AIR
CLEANER

CARBURETOR

IGNITION
CABLE

COOLING
SYSTEM
THERMOSTAT

SPARK
PLUG

WATER
PUMP

DISTRIBUTOR

FUEL
PUMP

OIL
FILTER

Fig. G-1. Details of 153 cu. in. four cylinder engine. Note location of cooling system thermostat, water pump and fan. Typical of other engines.

To drain the cooling system on all but early 1973 models, there is a drain cock at the bottom of the radiator. On early 1973 models it is necessary to disconnect the radiator lower hose. Drain cocks in the cylinder block should be opened. On in-line engines, there is a single drain cock. On V-8 engines, there is a drain cock on each side of the engine. Late 1973 and subsequent models have a radiator drain cock.

After the system has been drained, it should be thoroughly flushed to remove all traces of rust and old coolant. If a strong stream of water is available, it is advisable to reverse flush the system. That is done by disconnecting the upper hose, removing the thermostat, Figs. G-1 and G-3, then applying the water pressure at the bottom of the radiator so that the water flows from the bottom to the top. Also apply the water pressure at the top of the engine so that the water will flow from the top of the engine and out the bottom.

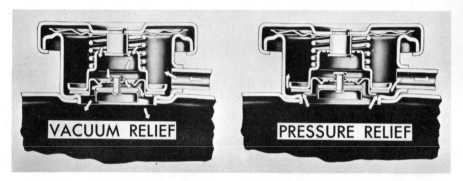

Fig. G-2. Sectional views of pressure type radiator cap. The vacuum relief relieves the vacuum created when the engine cools. The pressure relief allows excessive pressure to be relieved out the radiator overflow.

After flushing with clear water, the system should be filled with water and a permanent type antifreeze as explained later in this chapter. In addition, add a cooling system inhibitor and sealer of high quality. This will retard the formation of rust and scale.

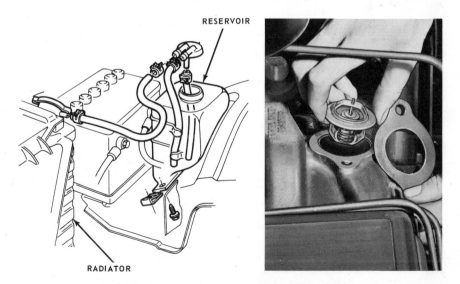

Fig. G-3. Left. Coolant recovery system. Right. Removing thermostat.

It is desirable to remove the cooling system thermostat from the system before flushing to insure a free flow of water. The cooling system thermostat is located at the forward end of the cylinder head, Fig. G-1 and Fig. G-3, where the hose connection for the radiator is located.

WHEN THE SYSTEM GETS CLOGGED

Tests for a clogged radiator can be made by warming the engine, then stop the engine and feel the surface of the radiator. On down flow radiators, the radiator should be hot at the top and warm toward the bottom. Cross flow radiators should be hot on the left side and warm at the right. On both types, there should be an even temperature change from warm to hot. Cold spots indicate a clogged radiator. Water pump operation can be checked by squeezing the upper hose while the engine is running. A pressure surge should be felt.

A defective cylinder head gasket may allow exhaust gases to leak into the cooling system. This is particularly damaging to the system as the gases combine with the water to form acids which are harmful to the radiator and engine. Such a condition will result in severe overheating.

IF ANTIFREEZE GETS IN LUBRICATING SYSTEM

As the result of a defective cylinder head gasket, or a cracked water jacket, the coolant may get into the engine crankcase. If the coolant is of the ethylene glycol type, a heavy gummy substance will be formed in the engine crankcase and it will be necessary to clean the entire lubricating system. First the engine oil should be completely drained, the oil filter removed, and the crankcase filled with a mixture of approximately three quarts of SAE 10W motor oil and two quarts of butyl cellulose. That material can be obtained from a chemical supply company. The engine should be run at idling speed for thirty minutes, paying particular attention to the oil pressure and then immediately drained. A flushing solution of approximately three quarts of SAE 10W oil and two quarts of kerosene should then be circulated through the engine at idling speed for approximately five minutes and then completely drained. If the engine cannot be cranked because of the contaminated oil, run hot water from a steam Jennie through the cooling system which will soften the glycol in the oiling system so that the engine can be cranked.

QUICK CHECK FOR LEAKS

To check for exhaust leaks into the cooling system, drain the system until the water level stands just above the top of the cylinder head. Then disconnect the upper radiator hose and remove the thermostat and fan belt. Start the engine and quickly accelerate several times. At the same time note any appreciable water rise, or appearance of bubbles, which are indicative of exhaust gases leaking into the cooling system.

Cooling Systems

Small water leaks in the cooling system can be fixed by means of special preparations designed to stop such leaks. Instructions covering the use of such chemicals supplied by the manufacturer should be carefully followed.

In the case of leaking core plugs, Fig. H-4, these should be replaced. There are a number of these core plugs located throughout the engine water jacket and in some cases they are rather difficult to reach. To remove a rusted core plug, drive a screwdriver or other pointed tool into the center of the plug and pry it from the engine block. After carefully cleaning the recess, a new plug is installed by driving it into position with a drift approximately the same diameter as the plug. Before driving the plug into position, the recess is carefully coated with a suitable cement.

Fig. G-4. Applying pressure to the cooling system as a check for leaks.

Most water leaks in a cooling system are clearly visible to the eye. However, to locate some leaks it is necessary to apply pressure to the cooling system. Such pressure can be applied by means of special equipment such as is shown in Fig. G-4. If the pressure applied to the system as indicated by the gauge is maintained, there is no leak present and water is probably being lost through the radiator cap and overflow. But if the pressure is not maintained there is leakage somewhere and if it cannot be seen by the eye, it is probably at a defective cylinder head gasket.

Mid-size 1978 Malibu Classic Coupe is set on a 108 in. wheelbase and is powered by a 95 hp, 3.3 litre (200 cu. in.) V-6 engine.

CHECK RADIATOR CAP

It is important that the radiator cap be checked seasonally to be sure that it is operating correctly. Radiator caps used on Chevrolet built engines from 1958 to 1965 are designed to open at 13 lb. pressure and air conditioned cars at 15 lb. pressure. From 1966, the 15 lb. caps were used throughout.

The pressure at which these caps will open can be tested by using a special tester, Fig. G-5. Such a tester applies pressure to the cap and unless these caps open at the specified value, the pressure may become so great that the radiator will burst. This usually occurs at the seam of the radiator tank. If the caps open at a pressure lower than the specified value, coolant will be lost and overheating result.

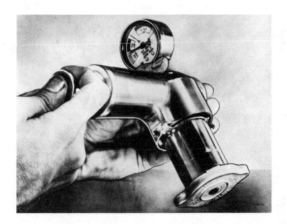

Fig. G-5. Checking a radiator cap with special tester which applies air pressure.

CLEANING THE COOLING SYSTEM

When the coolant in the cooling system appears rusty, the system should be cleaned with one of the chemicals available for that purpose. Directions for using that particular cleaner should be carefully followed.

In the event that no special cleaning preparation is available, oxalic acid in crystal form can be used, but special care must be taken to thoroughly flush all traces of this from the system, and then use a good rust inhibitor. One-half pound of oxalic acid is usually sufficient to clean the cooling system.

In cases of persistent overheating it may be necessary to remove the radiator and have it cleaned by a specialist in such work. In such cases, it is usually advisable to remove the cylinder head also and have it reconditioned, which includes cleaning the water jacket. While the cylinder head is removed, the water jacket and cylinder block should be scraped as

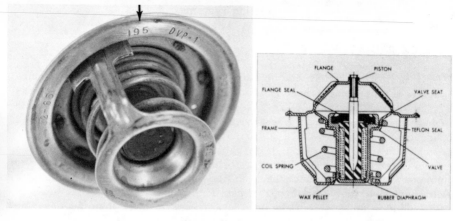

Fig. G-6. Left. Cooling system thermostat marked with temperature at which it is designed to open. Right. Sectional view of pellet type cooling system thermostat used on recent models.

clean as possible and flushed repeatedly to remove as much rust as possible. The interior of the water jacket can be reached through the openings in the top of the cylinder block. If necessary, the core plugs can be removed from the side of the cylinder block, which will also aid in reaching the interior of the water jacket with the scraper.

CHECKING RADIATOR FLOW

If there is any doubt about the condition of the radiator, it can be checked by filling it with water after it is removed and then seeing how fast the water will flow from the lower outlet. A radiator in good condition will have water flowing from the outlet reach a height of approximately 6 in. If the water fails to come out in a strong stream, it is definite that the radiator passages are clogged and that the radiator should be reconditioned or replaced.

FILLING THE RADIATOR

Filling the radiator of a warm engine presents no difficulty, but when the engine is cold, the thermostat is closed and little coolant will reach the water jacket surrounding the engine. It, therefore, becomes necessary to fill the radiator as much as possible, then start the engine. When it has reached operating temperature, the thermostat will open permitting the coolant from the radiator to enter the water jacket. It will then be possible to add more coolant to the radiator so the system is filled completely.

WHAT TO DO ABOUT THERMOSTATS

Starting with the 1968 models, a 195 deg. thermostat was standard equipment on all Chevrolet water cooled engines. Prior to that time a 180 deg. thermostat was used. Alcohol and methanol antifreeze solutions are not recommended for use in the 1968 models. Such coolants would require a thermostat operating at a lower temperature. As shown in Fig. G-6, the thermostat is marked to indicate the temperature at which it is designed to open.

Thermostats are located in the water outlets in the engine, Fig. G-1 and Fig. G-3. To remove a thermostat, first drain the system until the water level is below the thermostat. Then remove the water outlet elbow, or the elbow to which the radiator upper hose is connected. The thermo-

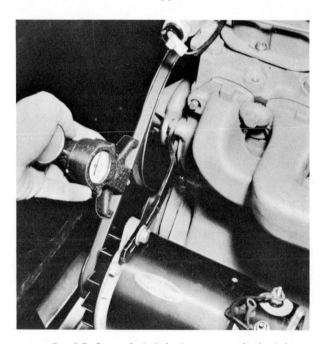

Fig. G-7. One method of checking tension of a fan belt.

stat can then be lifted from the engine, Fig. G-3. At room temperature the valve of the thermostat should be in the closed position. If there is any doubt regarding the condition of the thermostat, place it in a pan of water. The thermostat should be open when the water reaches the specified temperature.

CHECKING THE FAN BELT

Fan and accessory belts when properly adjusted will operate for at least 25,000 miles without giving any trouble. But it is well to anticipate their failure, as the belt not only drives the fan, but also the water pump and the generator. Accessory belts are also important. As a result, should the fan belt break, not only will the engine overheat but the battery will soon become discharged. In addition to checking the tension of the belts, examine the belt to be sure that there are no cracks at any point, or lumps which would indicate deterioration.

To adjust tension of the fan belt, loosen bolts at generator slotted bracket. Pull the generator away from the engine until the desired belt tension is obtained. Special testers are available, Fig. G-7, to check the tension of the belts, but when such equipment is not available, apply a light pressure midway between the water pump pulley and the generator pulley. The belt should deflect 5/16 in. on four cylinder and six cylinder models, and 13/16 in. on the V-8 models, Fig. G-8. Do not use a pry bar against the alternator case as this may distort or crack the case.

Fig. G-8. A simple method of checking tension is to measure the deflection of the belt.

WHICH TYPE ANTIFREEZE?

Regardless of whether freezing temperatures are expected, cooling system protection should be maintained at least to -20 deg. F. in order to provide adequate corrosion protection and proper temperature indicating light operation. Every two years, the system should be serviced by flushing with water, then completely refilling it with a high quality ethylene glycol type antifreeze. Add a high quality rust inhibitor and sealer. Also check and add inhibitor and sealer every year.

Alcohol and methanol types antifreeze or just plain water are not recommended for use in Chevrolet engines at any time, because the pressurized system raises the boiling point.

The use of the ethylene glycol antifreeze permits the use of a 195 deg. thermostat and a 15 lb. radiator cap. This in turn permits safe engine operating temperature of 252 deg. F.

To make sure that there is sufficient antifreeze in the cooling system to provide protection against freezing, the coolant should be checked with a hydrometer, Fig. G-9. Such checks should be made several times during the winter driving season.

Fig. G-9. Checking the antifreeze in the cooling system.

KINKS ON WATER PUMP SERVICE

Water pumps give good service for many thousands of miles of operation and need replacement only after they start to leak, as a result of failure of the seal and scoring of the shaft. While replacement parts are available for rebuilding water pumps, most mechanics prefer to install a new or rebuilt pump rather than take the time to rebuild the worn unit. To disassemble a water pump requires a puller to remove the hub and drive pulley from the shaft and a press, Fig. G-10, to push the shaft from the impeller.

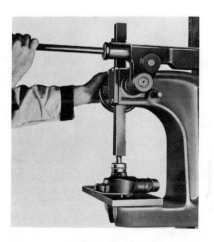

Fig. G-10. Pressing impeller and shaft from a water pump housing.

The procedure for removing the water pump is as follows: First drain the radiator and remove the water inlet hose from the pump. Remove the fan belt. On cars equipped with heaters, remove the hose from the pump housing. Remove the water pump to cylinder block attaching bolts and then remove the pump from the engine.

COOLANT RECOVERY SYSTEM

A coolant recovery system has been developed especially for recreational vehicles operating under severe conditions. This converts the conventional pressure vented system into one that is closed, but which compensates for coolant expansion and returns the coolant to the radiator when system cools. In that way the possibility of overheating is greatly reduced.

TROUBLE SHOOTING

CAUSES OF OVERHEATING

Restricted radiator passages. Restricted water jacket in engine. Restricted hose connections. Defective cooling system thermostat. Defective radiator cap. Lack of coolant. Loose fan belt. Water pump inoperative. Incorrect valve or ignition timing. Brakes dragging. Improper grade and viscosity of engine oil. Restricted exhaust system. Restricted air flow through radiator. Leaking cylinder head gasket. Radiator capacity too small for car equipped with air conditioning.

Towing a trailer or other vehicle, particularly in warm weather will often cause overheating, as will operation of the air conditioning system particularly for prolonged periods when the vehicle is not in motion.

LOSS OF COOLANT

Leaking radiator. Loose or damaged hose connections. Leaking water pump. Loose or damaged heater hose. Leaking heater unit. Leaking cylinder head gasket. Cracked cylinder head. Core plugs in cylinder and cylinder head loose or rusted. Wrong type or defective radiator cap.

CIRCULATION SYSTEM NOISY

Defective fan belt. Defective water pump shaft bearings. Fan blades loose or bent. Improper fan to shroud clearance.

OVERCOOLING

Defective thermostat.

EXHAUST SYSTEM
SERVICE

The exhaust system includes the exhaust manifold, muffler, connecting pipes and, in some cases, a resonator. In addition, the 1975 and later models are fitted with a catalytic converter, Fig. H-1.

Single exhaust setups use an exhaust manifold, Fig. H-2, an exhaust pipe and muffler assembly, and a tail pipe that extends back to a point below the left side of the rear bumper. An exhaust crossover pipe is used on V-8 models to connect the two exhaust manifolds.

On dual exhaust systems, two exhaust pipe and muffler assemblies are used together with two resonators and two tail pipes. Each assembly is connected to its own exhaust manifold, and carries the exhaust gases to the rear of the vehicle.

The life of mufflers and pipes is dependent largely on the type of service in which the vehicle is used. If it is used mostly in city type stop-and-go driving, with few trips exceeding five miles, the muffler will soon be rusted out. In most cases on dual muffler installations on V-8 engines, the maximum mileage under such conditions is seldom in excess of 10,000 miles. On single muffler jobs, 20,000 to 25,000 miles may be expected.

The reason for such short muffler life is that on short trips, condensed moisture from the engine exhaust gases collects in the mufflers and pipes. This moisture is highly acidic and corrosive. As a result the pipes and mufflers are soon corroded and have to be replaced.

If the car is driven mostly on longer trips, the mufflers and pipes will get hot enough to evaporate this moisture. Consequently, corrosive action is retarded and exhaust system parts will last longer.

Mufflers and pipes used on single exhaust systems will last much longer than a dual muffler installation, because all the exhaust gases pass through the single muffler, and as a result its temperature reaches a higher value more quickly, and the corrosive moisture will be evaporated sooner.

Mufflers and pipes should be replaced before they are rusted completely through, for if there are any leaks in the system, the exhaust gases, which are poisonous, will escape into the interior of the car where they may cause the death of the occupants, or a serious accident if the driver becomes affected by the gas.

The different sections of the pipes and mufflers are telescoped together and supported by brackets, Fig. H-1. The removal of worn exhaust pipes and mufflers is not complicated, but it is sometimes difficult be-

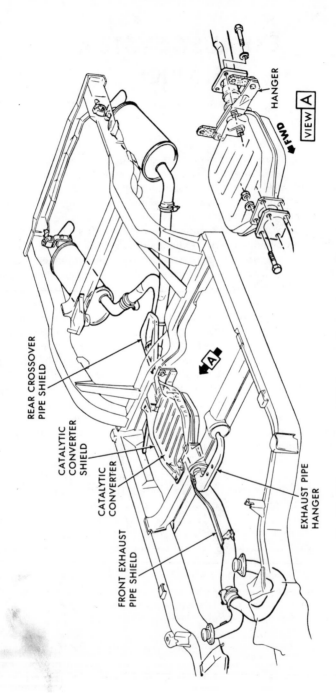

REAR CROSSOVER
PIPE SHIELD

CATALYTIC
CONVERTER
SHIELD

CATALYTIC
CONVERTER

FRONT EXHAUST
PIPE SHIELD

EXHAUST PIPE
HANGER

HANGER

FWD

VIEW A

Fig. H-1. Exhaust system on 1975 Corvette, showing location of catalytic converter.

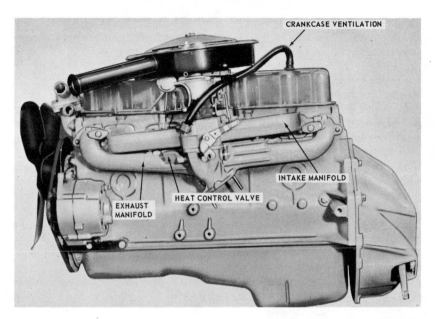

Fig. H-2. Exhaust manifold and heat control valve as installed on in-line six cylinder engine.

cause various sections are rusted together. To disassemble the system so that replacement can be made, it is usually necessary to cut them apart with a hacksaw or a chisel, as shown in Fig. H-3.

Before cutting at the rear exhaust pipe, measure service muffler exhaust pipe end, and make certain to allow 1-1/2 in. for engagement of the rear exhaust pipe into service muffler pipe.

The procedure for removing mufflers and pipes is as follows: First apply penetrating oil to all the bolts and nuts of the support brackets and

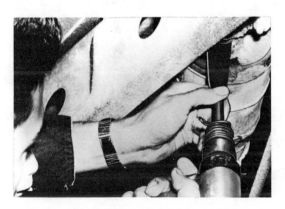

Fig. H-3. Cutting a tail pipe from a muffler.

clamps. Separate the pipes from the muffler either by cutting with a hacksaw or chisel after having jacked up the rear of the car with a bumper jack so as to provide as much clearance between the rear axle and the body as possible. Then remove the clamps from the exhaust pipes, mufflers and tailpipes, permitting removal of the various parts. The car should be jacked up as high as possible, to allow ample room between the rear axle and the lower side of the body, so that the long tail pipe can be maneuvered into position. When making the installation of new pipes and mufflers, the usual procedure is to first install the exhaust pipe, then the muffler, and finally the tail pipe.

All exhaust systems used on the Chevrolet from 1968 are of a split system in which all components (exhaust pipes, mufflers, resonators and tail pipes) can be separated by removing clamps. All other models have at least two components that cannot be separated by merely removing a clamp.

All V-8 single exhaust systems incorporate a cross-under exhaust pipe in which either the left or right exhaust pipe crosses under the engine oil pan to join the rest of the system.

Dual exhaust systems are available as regular production or optional equipment on all models. Chevrolet and Camaro offer an optional "deep-tone" system which eliminates the resonators.

MANIFOLD HEAT CONTROL VALVE

The manifold heat control valve, Figs. H-2 and H-4, is designed to provide a certain amount of heat to the intake manifold in order to improve the air-fuel mixture reaching the combustion chamber. It is controlled by

Fig. H-4. Manifold heat control valve.

a thermostatic coil and counterweight and velocity of exhaust gas through the exhaust manifold. The thermostatic coil is installed in a manner which will maintain sufficient tension on the valve shaft to keep the valve in a closed position when the engine is cold.

In the cold position, hot gases from the exhaust circulate up and around the hot spot chamber in the intake manifold. This in turn helps vaporize fuel passing down through the intake manifold, resulting in smooth engine performance. Should the heat control valve become stuck in either the open or closed position, the car performance will be affected.

The operation of the heat control valve should be inspected at every lubrication and oil change, by moving the counterweights through the complete arc of its travel.

Note that in Fig. H-2 the manifold heat control valve for six cylinder in-line engines is placed immediately below the carburetor, and is on the left side of the engine. The manifold heat control valve for eight cylinder engines is located on the right side of the engine.

If the shaft of the heat control valve is sticking, it can be freed by applying special solvents, or penetrating oil, and also by tapping the shaft back and forth in the manifold.

Note that on eight cylinder engines it may be necessary to remove the heat control valve flange to free the inboard end of the valve shaft.

CATALYTIC CONVERTER

All current cars are equipped with a catalytic converter as part of the exhaust system. This emission control device is designed to reduce hydrocarbon and carbon monoxide pollutants from the exhaust gas stream. On 1976 Chevette, the converter is attached with a hanger mounted to the transmission mounting adapter assembly. Periodic maintenance of the catalytic converter is not required. In the case of 1975 models, special equipment is required when removing and installing a catalytic converter.

PULSE AIR VALVE SYSTEM

Some 1977 engines are equipped with a Pulse Air Valve System, Fig. H-5, that utilizes a pulse air valve and a check valve for each port. In operation, the engine creates a pulsating flow of exhaust gases. These pulsations are positive or negative, depending on whether the exhaust valve is seated or not. If there is a vacuum in the exhaust system, the check valve will remain open and fresh air will be drawn in and mixed with the exhaust gases. During high engine rpm, the check valve will be closed.

A hissing noise while the engine is running will indicated a defective pulse valve or an exhaust manifold leak. If one or more check valves has failed, exhaust gas will enter the carburetor through the air cleaner and cause poor driveability.

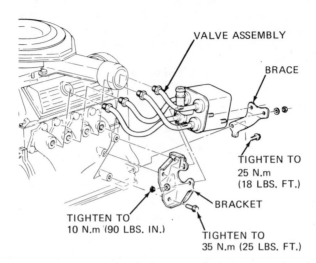

VALVE ASSEMBLY

BRACE

TIGHTEN TO
25 N.m
(18 LBS. FT.)

BRACKET

TIGHTEN TO
10 N.m (90 LBS. IN.)

TIGHTEN TO
35 N.m (25 LBS. FT.)

Fig. H-5. Details of pulse air valve system that permits fresh air to enter the exhaust gases under certain conditions.

If exhaust gases pass through the pulse air valve, the excess is transmitted to the valve body (indicated by burned paint on the body). Rubber hose will also deteriorate, and pieces of rubber may enter the carburetor, making cleaning imperative.

The 1978 Nova Custom four door sedan replaces the 1977 Concours. The 4.1 litre (250 cu. in.) Six rated at 110 hp is standard equipment.

Quick Tests on
BATTERIES

If headlamps do not light to normal brilliance when engine is not running or when the engine is not cranked at normal speed, the first point to check is the starting battery.

First of all, the battery connections must be clean and tight. Corroded terminals or loose connections provide a high resistance in the circuit, so that full voltage is not available for lighting, starting and ignition.

The battery terminals and cable connections should be cleaned by scraping with a knife, or brushed with a wire bristle brush.

The top surface of the battery must also be kept clean and dry as any moisture and/or dirt will permit current leakage, and is a major cause of discharged batteries.

The level of the electrolyte should also be checked every 1000 miles and should never be permitted to get below the top of the battery plates.

All 1977 and 1978 models are equipped with a long life, sealed battery that does not require the addition of water throughout its life.

COMMON CAUSES OF FAILURE

If the battery tests good but fails to perform satisfactorily in service (for no apparent reason), consider the following important factors that may point to the cause of the trouble: Vehicle accessories inadvertently left on overnight. Slow speed driving of short duration. Vehicle electrical load that exceeds alternator capacity. Defect in charging system, such as high resistance, slipping fan belt, faulty alternator or voltage regulator.

ELECTROLYTE INDICATOR

The Delco battery used as standard equipment on older models, and often as a replacement unit, features an electrolyte level indicator. Each vent plug has a transparent rod extending through the center. When the electrolyte level is correct, the lower tip of the rod is immersed, and the top of the rod will appear very dark. If the level falls below the lower tip of the rod, the top will glow.

The indicator reveals at a glance if water is needed without the necessity of removing the vent plugs. The level indicator is used only in one cell, the second cell cap from the positive battery post, because when the electrolyte level is low in one cell, it is normally low in all cells.

Fumes from a starting battery are highly explosive; therefore never use an open flame to see the level of the electrolyte in the battery. Use only a flashlight to check the level.

HOW TO TEST THE BATTERY

In the past one of the most popular methods of testing the condition of the battery was by means of a voltmeter. However, since all modern starting batteries have a hard cover over the entire surface of the top of the battery, a hydrometer is now the preferred method, as it permits testing the condition of each cell of the battery. This is a reliable test and the hydrometer is low in price.

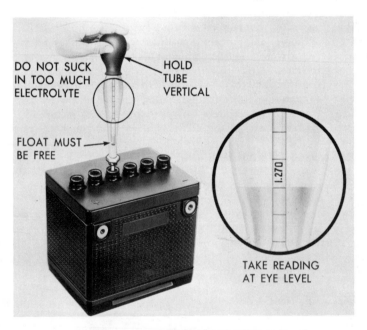

Fig. J-1. Using hydrometer to check the condition of the battery.

A hydrometer, Fig. J-1, should be used only when there is sufficient electrolyte above the battery plate to fill the hydrometer tube. Do not take hydrometer readings immediately after filling a battery with distilled water. Instead place the battery on charge or drive the car for about an hour or two. Normal battery activity will then disburse the water to the electrolyte.

Batteries

To check the condition of a battery with a hydrometer, the tube of the instrument is placed in the opening of the filler plug and electrolyte is drawn into the instrument by means of the suction bulb, as shown in Fig. J-1.

Draw the electrolyte into the tube and force it out several times to bring the temperature of the hydrometer float to that of the electrolyte. Then draw in just enough electrolyte to lift the float. Read the specific gravity of the electrolyte on the float, Fig. J-1. A specific gravity of 1.275 to 1.285 indicates a full charged battery. A reading of 1.230 to 1.240 incicates approximately 60 percent charge. If the specific gravity varies more than .025 between cells of the battery, the battery should be replaced.

Some batteries supplied to warm climates have a specific gravity reading of 1.260 when fully charged. In such cases, the battery is plainly marked.

Batteries that are not fully charged will freeze at low temperatures, while a fully charged battery will not freeze until the temperature reaches -90 deg. F.

Specific Gravity	Freezing Temperature
1.280	-90 deg.
1.250	-62 deg.
1.200	-16 deg.
1.150	+ 5 deg.
1.100	+19 deg.

CHARGING BATTERIES

If the car owner lives in an isolated area, where service stations are at some distance, it pays to have a battery charger of some type available for charging batteries in an emergency. Battery chargers are available for charging a single battery. Instructions for charging the battery, which accompany the charger, should be carefully followed.

EVIDENCE OF OVERCHARGING

If it is necessary to add water to the battery at frequent intervals, it is an indication that the battery is being overcharged. In such cases, a careful check of the voltage regulator should be made and it should be either readjusted or a new unit installed.

INSTALLING THE BATTERY

When installing a battery, it is particularly important that only the negative terminal of the battery be grounded. A battery that is installed backwards (with positive terminal grounded) will burn out the rectifiers on alternating current systems. Also, the battery will be quickly ruined because of the reversal of the charge.

The positive terminal is indicated with a plus sign, and the negative terminal with a minus sign, Fig. J-1. These markings are either placed directly on the top of the battery posts or on the battery case adjacent to the terminal.

When it is difficult to start an engine, it is sometimes desirable to use an additional battery for a quick start. In such cases, the positive terminal of the additional battery should be connected to the positive terminal of the car battery, and the negative terminal of the additional battery to the negative terminal of the car battery. The starting switch is then used in the usual manner.

1976 FREEDOM BATTERY

The starting battery used on 1976 cars has more electrolyte than conventional batteries, and water does not have to be added. There are no vent plugs in the cover. The battery is completely sealed, except for two small vents on the side to permit small amounts of gases to escape when necessary. A charge indicator in the cover shows the state of charge.

DELCOTRON INTEGRATED CIRCUIT REGULATOR

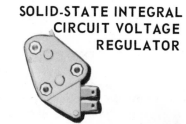

SOLID-STATE INTEGRAL CIRCUIT VOLTAGE REGULATOR

SEPARATE VOLTAGE REGULATOR

INTEGRAL REGULATOR DELCOTRON

Details of 1974 Delcotron integrated circuit regulator are shown. The 1975 system is similar except that a 40 ohm resistor has been added to the warning indicator system. Purpose of resistor is to provide a definite warning indicator light in case of an open field circuit.

Simplified
GENERATOR SERVICE

The following instructions are limited primarily to determining whether trouble exists in the generator (alternator), regulator or battery.

Knowing the location of the trouble, a new unit, as needed, can then be obtained and installed and properly adjusted. This same policy is followed by many service shops.

Fig. K-1. Showing location of alternator on V-8 engine.

Before making any tests on a generator (alternator), or regulator, the battery should be carefully checked as outlined in the Chapter on Quick Tests on Batteries. If the battery and its connections prove to be in good condition, and the generator (alternator) drive belt is also correctly adjusted, then tests on the generator (alternator) and regulator should be made.

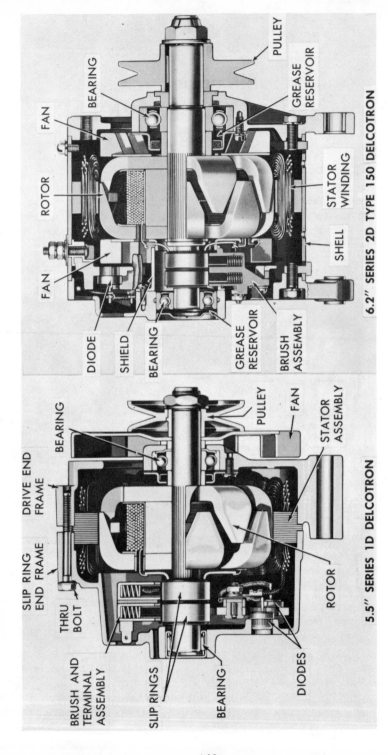

BEARING

PULLEY

GREASE
RESERVOIR

FAN

ROTOR

STATOR
WINDING

FAN

SHELL

6.2" SERIES 2D TYPE 150 DELCOTRON

DIODE

SHIELD

BEARING

GREASE
RESERVOIR

BRUSH
ASSEMBLY

SLIP RING
END FRAME

DRIVE END
FRAME

BEARING

PULLEY

FAN

STATOR
ASSEMBLY

THRU
BOLT

BRUSH AND
TERMINAL
ASSEMBLY

SLIP RINGS

BEARING

DIODES

ROTOR

5.5" SERIES 1D DELCOTRON

Fig. K-2. 1968–1970 types of Delcotron alternating current generators. Previous models were similar.

Generator Service

THE ALTERNATOR

The Delcotron alternator was first provided as optional equipment on the 1962 models. In 1963, it was adopted for all models. The alternator is mounted on the side of the engine. Fig. K-1 shows a typical installation.

Two types of alternators are shown in Fig. K-2, and diagrams of connections are shown in Fig. K-3 and Fig. K-4. Another alternator has a built-in solid state regulator which requires no adjustment, Fig. K-2a. It was introduced as standard equipment on the 1969 Corvette and, since 1973, is standard equipment on all models.

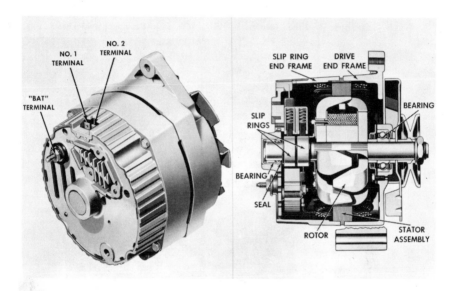

Fig. K-2a. Series 10-S1 Delcotron has solid state regulator built into end frame. First used in 1969, it is now standard equipment on all models.

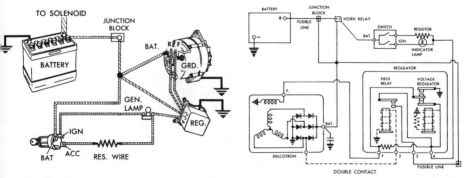

Fig. K-3. Left. Typical alternator wiring diagram.   Fig. K-3a. Right. Voltage circuitry of double contact voltage regulator (1970).

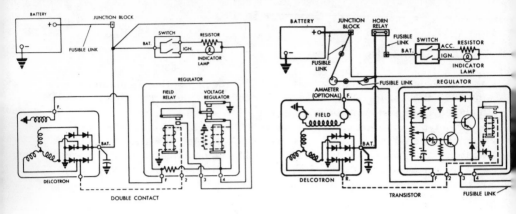

Fig. K-4. Circuitry of voltage regulators, 1968–1969. Left—Double contact system.
Right—Transistor system.

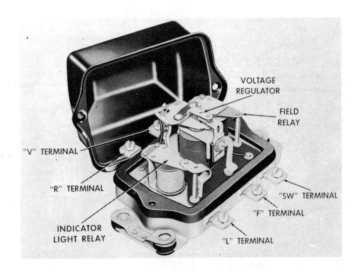

Fig. K-5. Regulator with light indicator relay as used with Delcotron on 1962 models.

The alternator, Fig. K-1 and Fig. K-2, generates alternating current and is provided with six rectifier diodes, located in the slip ring end frame. The diodes change the alternating voltage to direct voltage, which appears at the outlet terminal of the alternator. Conventional direct current instruments can be used for testing the output of the alternator.

The system used in 1962 was provided with a regulator, Fig. K-5, which included an indicator light relay. Starting with the 1963 models, a two unit, double contact regulator was used, Fig. K-6, and some installations were provided with a transistor type voltage regulator, Fig. K-7. The double contact regulator is used on all models of the Delcotron up to and including the 52 amp. model, while a transistorized regulator is used on the 62 amp. system.

150

Generator Service

SPECIAL PRECAUTIONS NECESSARY

There are several precautions which must be emphasized when working on the alternator system. First of all, in installing a battery, always make sure the ground polarity of the battery, alternator and regulator are the same. On the Chevrolet models, the negative terminal of the battery must be grounded.

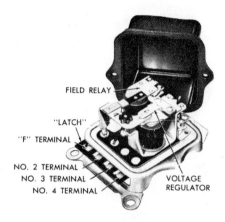

Fig. K-6. Double contact, two unit regulator.

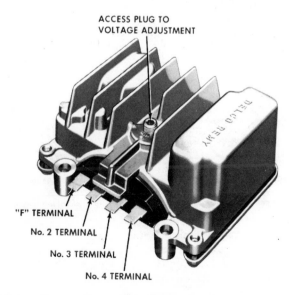

Fig. K-7. Note location of voltage adjustment on this transistor type regulator.

When connecting a booster battery, make certain to connect the correct battery terminals together. That is, the positive terminal of the booster battery must be connected to the positive terminal of the battery in the car, and the two negative terminals will be connected together. Also when connecting a charger to the battery, connect positive terminal of the charger to the positive terminal of the battery and the negative terminal of the charger to the negative terminal of the battery.

Never operate the alternator on open circuit. Make certain that all connections in the system are tight and clean. Never short across or ground any of the terminals on the alternator or the regulator. Do not attempt to polarize the alternating current Delcotron.

PINPOINTING TROUBLE IN THE ALTERNATOR

It is a simple matter to determine whether failure to generate voltage lies in the alternator or the regulator. Unplug the connector from the alternator which will expose the relay (R) terminal and the field (F) terminal. Connect a jumper from the generator (F) terminal to the BAT terminal, and in this way full field current will be applied to the alternator. Turn on all possible accessory loads, such as headlights, etc. Then with the en-

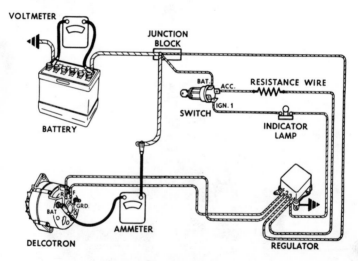

Fig. K-8. Note connections of voltmeter and ammeter when checking output of Delcotron.

gine at a fast idle, if the indicator lamp or ammeter on instrument panel shows a charge, the regulator is defective. If no charge is shown, then the alternator is probably defective. Knowing which of these two units is defective, a new part is then easily substituted.

A more accurate test is shown under the paragraph headed Output Check.

Another test, which may be used to isolate the Delcotron, its companion regulator, and the wiring harness for testing, is known as the "Dynamic Test." After checking for a loose drive belt and a defective battery, proceed as follows:

Start the engine and operate at a fast idle of approximately 1500 to 2000 rpm. Make sure that all accessories, lights, etc. are disconnected from the circuit. With the engine still operating, disconnect the battery ground cable. If the engine stops, the alternator is probably defective. If the engine continues to operate, either the regulator or wire harness is defective.

To determine if harness or regulator is defective, remove wiring push-on connector from the regulator and install a known good regulator. Be sure to ground the regulator to the vehicle.

Repeat the previous check of disconnecting the battery ground cable. If indicator lamp remains on with the engine idling, check for open resistor. If indicator lamp operates normally, regulator is shown to be defective.

OUTPUT CHECK

To make a complete current output test of an alternator, first make sure the drive belt is adjusted to the proper tension. Then disconnect the battery ground cable from the battery. Connect an ammeter between alternator BAT terminal and disconnect lead as shown in Fig. K-8. Connect a tachometer from distributor terminal of coil to ground. Reconnect battery ground cable. Connect a voltmeter across battery.

Turn on all possible accessory loads. Apply parking brake firmly. Start engine. Adjust engine idle to approximately 500 rpm with the transmission in drive position. At this engine speed, generator output should be approximately 10 amp. or over. Shift transmission to park and increase engine speed to approximately 1500 rpm and output should be 30 amp. or over.

If output is low in either of the preceding tests, try supplying field current directly to cause full generator output. This is done by unplugging the connector from the generator and connecting a jumper from the generator (F) terminal to BAT terminal. Retest at 500 rpm and 1500 rpm as described previously. If output is still low, generator is faulty and should be replaced. If output is now O.K. when using the field jumper, trouble is in the regulator or wiring harness.

DELCOTRON DIODE AND FIELD TEST

A diode is a device which rectifies the alternating current to direct. Diodes can be easily tested without special equipment, other than a 12V battery and a small lamp bulb. These are used as a test set to see if current will flow through the diodes. First separate the three stator leads at the (Y) connection. Test the rectifiers with the 12V battery and a test

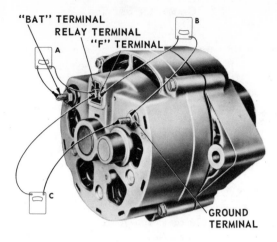

"BAT" TERMINAL
RELAY TERMINAL
"F" TERMINAL
A
B
C
GROUND
TERMINAL

Fig. K-9. Meter connections for checking diodes and field.

lamp by connecting one side of the test lamp to the positive battery post. Connect the other side of the lamp to a test probe with the other test probe connected to the negative battery post.

Contact the outer case of the diode with one probe, and the other probe to the wire at the center of the rectifier. Reverse the probes, moving the probes from rectifier outer case to the rectifier wire, and the probe from the rectifier wire to the rectifier outer case. If the test lamp lights in one direction, but does not light in the other direction, the rectifier is satisfactory. If the lamp lights in both directions, the rectifier is shorted and should be replaced. If the test lamp does not light in either direction, the rectifier is open and will also have to be replaced.

Another method of testing the diodes is to use an ohmmeter. This naturally is a much more accurate test. The procedure is as follows: First disconnect the battery ground cable at battery. To test the positive diodes, connect the ohmmeter as shown at A in Fig. K-9, that is between the (R) terminal and the BAT terminal, and note the reading. Then reverse the leads at the same terminal and note this reading. The meter should read high resistance in one direction and low in the other.

To test the negative diodes connect the ohmmeter as shown at C in Fig. K-9, that is between the (R) terminal and the GRD terminal, and note the reading, then reverse the leads and note this reading. Meter should read high in one direction and low in the other.

A high or low reading in both directions indicates a defective diode.

DELCOTRON OPEN FIELD CHECK

To check for an open field in a Delcotron alternator, connect the ohmmeter as shown at B in Fig. K-9. That is from the (F) terminal to the GRD terminal stud and note the reading on the lowest scale of the ohmmeter. The meter should read 7 to 20 ohms. If the meter reads zero or excessively high resistance, the Delcotron is faulty.

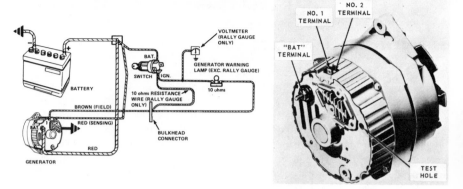

Fig. K-10. Left. Diagram of 10-SI series generator and 1978 charging system. Fig. K-11. Right. Location of terminals and test hole in 10-SI generator.

ADJUSTING ALTERNATOR REGULATOR VOLTAGE

Regulators used on recent model cars with Delcotrons are shown in Figs. K-6 and K-7. To adjust these types of regulators proceed as follows: Connect a 1/4 ohm 25 watt fixed resistor into the charging circuit at the junction block as shown in Fig. K-12.

Operate the engine at about 1500 rpm, or above for at least 15 minutes of warmup. Then cycle the regulator voltage control (by disconnecting and reconnecting regulator connector) and read the voltage.

If the voltage is 13.5 to 15.2 volts, the regulator is in good condition. If the voltage is not within those limits, leave engine running at 1500 rpm and disconnect four terminal connector, Fig. K-6, and adjust the voltage to 14.2 to 14.6. This is done with the high beam headlights and heater blower on for five to ten minutes. Then disconnect four terminal connector and reinstall regulator cover and reinstall connector. Cycle regulator voltage by disconnecting and reconnecting regulator connector. Read voltage. A reading between 13.5 and 15.2 volts indicates a good regulator.

Caution: Be sure four terminal regulator connector is disconnected when removing or installing cover. This is to prevent regulator damage by short circuit.

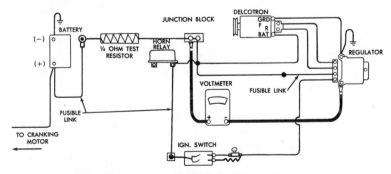

Fig. K-12. Diagram of connections for voltage setting on alternators.

SERVICE TIPS ON 10-SI DELCOTRON

The 10-SI series Delcotron alternator shown in Fig. K-2a features a solid state regulator that is mounted in the alternator end frame. This Delcotron was first used as standard equipment on the 1969 Corvette. Its use was gradually expanded until all Chevrolets were so equipped. All regulator components are enclosed in a solid mold and this unit, along with the brush holder, is attached to the slip ring end frame. The regulator voltage setting never requires adjustment, and no provision for adjustment is provided. Rotor bearings contain a sufficient supply of lubricant, eliminating the need for periodic lubrication.

A basic wiring diagram of the series 10-SI Delcotron is shown in Fig. K-10. If engine cranks slowly and specific gravity readings of battery are low, the trouble may be determined by making the following checks after making sure all wiring is in good condition, and fan belt is tight. Then connect a voltmeter in the circuit at the "BAT" terminal of the alternator. Operate engine at approximately 1500 to 2000 rpm and then turn on all electrical accessories. If voltmeter reading is more than 12.8 volts, alternator is not defective. If reading is less than 12.8 volts, ground the field winding by inserting a screwdriver into test hole (not more than 1 in.) in end frame to depress tab, Fig. K-11. If voltage increases to more than 13.0 volts, the regulator is defective.

TROUBLE SHOOTING THE 10-SI DELCOTRON

Most charging troubles show up as a faulty indicator lamp or an undercharged or overcharged battery. So before testing the alternator, first check to be sure that the indicator lamp is not burned out and that the battery is not undercharged because of a faulty ground, or because some accessory has been left on.

Precautions: Do not polarize the alternator. Do not short across or ground any of the terminals in the charging circuit, except as previously noted. Never operate the alternator with the output terminal open circuited. Make sure the alternator and battery are of the same ground polarity. When connecting a charger or booster battery to the vehicle battery, connect negative terminal to negative terminal and positive terminal to positive terminal.

Static Check: Visually inspect alternator drive belt to be sure it is adjusted to proper tension. Visually inspect all connections, including slip-on connections, to be sure they are all clean and tight. Inspect wiring for defective insulation. Be sure mounting bolts of alternator are tight and that it is properly grounded. Check fuses.

Undercharged Battery: Check alternator drive belt for proper tension. Check state of charge of battery with a hydrometer. With all lights and accessories turned off, check to be sure there is no current flowing from the battery.

With ignition switch on, connect a voltmeter from "BAT" terminal to ground, alternator No. 1 terminal to ground, and from No. 2 terminal to ground. A zero reading indicates an open between voltmeter and the battery.

Indicator Lamp Circuit Check: If lamp is on with ignition switch off, disconnect the two leads from the alternator No. 1 and No. 2 terminals. If lamp stays on, there is a short between these two leads. If lamp goes out, replace the rectifier bridge as this condition will cause an undercharged battery. With the switch on, lamp off and engine stopped, this condition will be caused by: a defective rectifier bridge; by reversal of leads on No. 1 and No. 2 terminals; or by an open circuit.

If lamp is on and switch is on with the engine running, the problem could be caused by the same troubles listed under undercharged battery.

Other conditions such as overcharged battery, excessive charging rate, or low charging rate are covered in detail in previous pages.

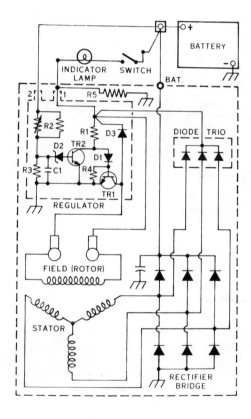

The 10-SI series generator used on 1975 and later models is similar to the 1974 unit, except for a 40 ohm resistor added to the warning indicator circuit. This provides a definite signal in case of an open field circuit.

1977 line of Chevrolet models: Top. Monza Spyder Hatchback. Center. Impala Coupe.
Bottom. Caprice Estate Station Wagon.

STARTER
SERVICE

Two types of starting motors are used on Chevrolet built cars. One type has four field coils, all of which are connected in a series from the motor terminal of the solenoid to the insulated brush. The other type has three field coils connected in series, plus one shunt coil connected from the solenoid motor terminal to the ground. A view of the starting motor is shown in Fig. L-1 and a detailed view is shown in Fig. L-2.

No periodic lubrication of the starting motor or solenoid is required. Since the starting motor and brushes cannot be inspected without disassembly of the unit, no service is required on these units between overhauls.

CHECKS AND ADJUSTMENTS

Although the starting motor cannot be completely checked against specifications while on the car, a check can be made for excessive resistance in the starting circuit.

Place a voltmeter across points in the cranking circuit, Fig. L-3, as outlined below and observe the reading with the starting switch closed and the motor cranking (distributor primary lead grounded to prevent engine firing):

1. From battery positive post to solenoid battery terminal.
2. From battery negative post to starting motor housing.
3. From solenoid battery terminal to solenoid motor terminal.

If the voltage drop in any of the above checks exceeds 0.2 volts, excessive resistance is indicated in that portion of the starting circuit, and the cause of the excessive resistance should be located and corrected in order to obtain maximum efficiency in the circuit.

Caution: Do not operate the starting motor continuously for more than 30 seconds in order to prevent overheating.

When the solenoid, Fig. L-1, fails to pull in, the trouble may be due to excessive voltage drop in the solenoid control circuit. To check for this condition, close the starting switch and measure the voltage drop between the battery terminal of the solenoid and the switch (S) terminal of the solenoid.

1. If this voltage drop exceeds 3.5 volts, excessive resistance in the solenoid control circuit is indicated and should be corrected.

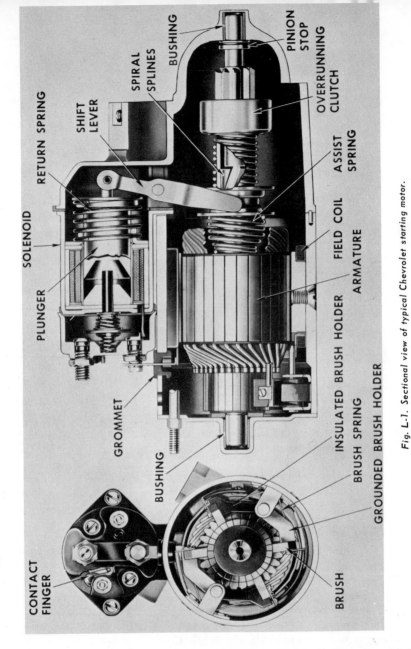

Fig. L-1. Sectional view of typical Chevrolet starting motor.

Labels (clockwise): RETURN SPRING, SHIFT LEVER, SPIRAL SPLINES, BUSHING, PINION STOP, OVERRUNNING CLUTCH, ASSIST SPRING, FIELD COIL, ARMATURE, INSULATED BRUSH HOLDER, BRUSH SPRING, GROUNDED BRUSH HOLDER, BRUSH, BUSHING, GROMMET, PLUNGER, SOLENOID, CONTACT FINGER

2. If the voltage drop does not exceed 3.5 volts, and the solenoid does not pull in, measure the voltage available at the switch terminal of the solenoid.

3. If the solenoid does not feel warm, it should pull in whenever the voltage available at the switch terminal is 7.7 volts or more. When the solenoid feels warm, it will require a somewhat higher voltage to pull in.

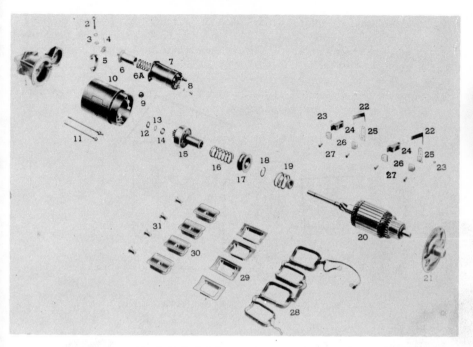

Fig. L-2. Exploded view of starting motor.

1—Drive housing.	12—Thrust collar.	24—Insulated brush holders.
2—Shift lever bolt.	13—Snap ring.	25—Grounded brush holders.
3—Shift lever nut and lock washer.	14—Retainer.	26—Brushes.
4—Pin.	15—Overrunning clutch assembly.	27—Screws.
5—Shift lever.	16—Spring.	28—Field coils.
6—Solenoid plunger.	17—Collar.	29—Insulators.
6A—Solenoid return spring.	18—Snap ring.	30—Pole shoes.
7—Solenoid case.	19—Assist spring.	31—Screws.
8—Screw and lock washer.	20—Armature.	
9—Grommet.	21—Commutator end frame.	
10—Field frame.	22—Brush springs.	
11—Through bolts.	23—Washer.	

STARTING MOTOR AND SOLENOID CHECK

The following checks may be made if the specific gravity of the battery is 1.215 or higher:

1. If the solenoid does not pull in, measure the voltage between the switch (S) terminal of the solenoid and ground with the starting switch closed.

Caution: If the solenoid feels warm, allow to cool before checking.

If the voltage is less than 7.7 volts, check for excessive resistance in the solenoid control circuit. If the voltage exceeds 7.7 volts, remove the starting motor and check:

1. Solenoid current draw; starting motor pinion clearance; and freedom of shift lever linkage.

2. If the solenoid chatters but does not hold in, check the solenoid for an open "hold-in" winding. Whenever it is necessary to replace the starting motor solenoid, always check starting motor pinion clearance.
3. If the motor engages but does not crank or cranks slowly, check for excessive resistance in the external starting circuit, trouble within the starting motor, or excessive engine resistance to cranking.

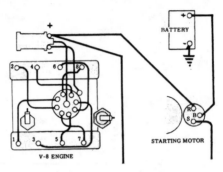

Fig. L-3. Starting circuit diagram for V-8 engines.

STARTING MOTOR REMOVAL

The following procedure is a general guide for all vehicles, and will vary slightly depending on series and model.

Disconnect battery ground cable at battery. Raise vehicle to a good working height. Disconnect all wires at solenoid terminals. Reinstall the nuts as each wire is disconnected, as thread size is different but may be mixed and stripped.

Loosen starter front bracket (nut on V-8 and bolt on L-6), then remove two mount bolts.

Remove the front bracket bolt or nut and rotate bracket clear of work area, then lower starter from vehicle by lowering front end first (hold starter against bell housing and sort of roll end over end).

Reverse the removal procedure to install. Torque the mount bolts to 25-35 ft. lb. first, then torque brace bolt.

TROUBLE SHOOTING

SLOW ENGINE CRANKING SPEED

Partly discharged battery, defective battery, loose or corroded battery terminals. Under capacity cables. Burned starter solenoid switch contacts. Defective starting motor. Heavy oil or other engine trouble causing undue load.

Starter Service

STARTER ENGAGES, BUT WILL NOT CRANK

Partly discharged battery. Bent armature shaft or damaged drive mechanism. Faulty armature or field.

STARTER WILL NOT RUN

Battery discharged. Shorted or open starter circuit. Defective starting motor. Defective solenoid switch.

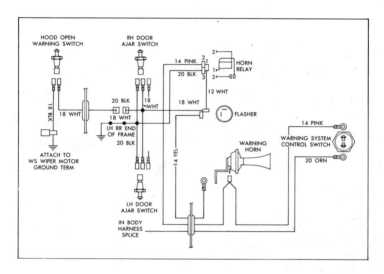

Anti-theft alarm circuit.

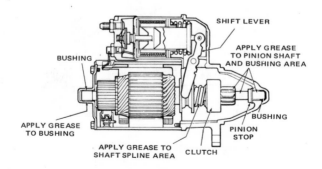

New type starting motor in some 1978 models is similar to previous design, but has field coils and pole shoes permanently bonded to frame.

HEADLAMP AIM

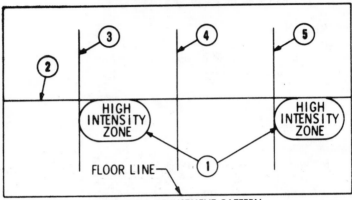

LOW BEAM ADJUSTMENT PATTERN
(VISUAL AIM AT 25 FEET)
5-3/4" TYPE 2 LAMPS (OUTBOARD ONLY) AND 7" TYPE 2 LAMPS

LINE 1	HIGH INTENSITY ZONES.
LINE 2	HORIZONTAL AND VERTICAL AT CENTER OF HEADLAMPS.
LINES 3 & 5	VERTICAL AT CENTER OF HEADLAMPS.
LINE 4	VERTICAL AT CENTER OF CAR.

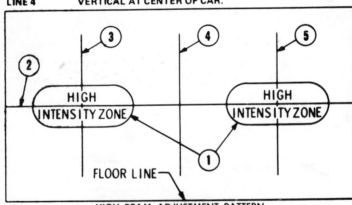

HIGH BEAM ADJUSTMENT PATTERN
(VISUAL AIM AT 25 FEET)
5-3/4" TYPE 1 LAMPS (INBOARD ONLY)

Fig. M-1. Headlamp aiming screen diagram.

LIGHTING SYSTEM
SERVICE

In order to get maximum light from headlights, or any other light on the vehicle, it is important that there be no resistance in the circuit. This can be easily checked by means of a voltmeter. To make a check, remove the head lamp rim, and with the sealed beam unit partly removed from its mounting seat, attach the leads of a low reading voltmeter to the prongs of the sealed beam unit, while it is still inserted in the connector socket.

With the sealed beam connected to the circuit, and after the engine has been stopped and the lights have burned for approximately five minutes, the voltage at the head lamp should not be less than 5.25 volts on 6 volt systems, and 11.25 volts on 12 volt systems. With the lamps burning and the engine warmed up, running at an approximate speed of 20 mph, the voltage at the head lamp should not be less than 6.3 volts, or more than 6.9 volts on 6 volt systems, and 12.3 and 12.5 volts for 12 volt systems. If the voltage is less than indicated, check the condition of the battery, and also clean and tighten all the battery terminals and ground cable. Also check the wires and connections to all lamps, and also at the main headlight switch for high resistance. All connections must be clean and tight.

If the voltage is more than the specified amount, check the adjustment of the voltage regulator.

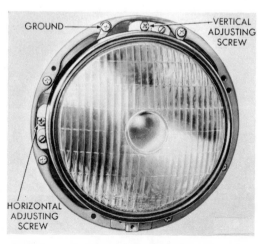

Fig. M-2. Location of vertical and horizontal adjustments on sealed beam head lamp.

CHANGING SEALED BEAM HEADLIGHTS

Because of the construction of the sealed beam headlight, it is hardly possible to install the lamp incorrectly. These lights do not require focusing, and the only adjustment required is to aim them correctly so the light is directed along the road and will not blind oncoming drivers.

While specialized equipment is available for accurately aiming headlights, a satisfactory job can be done by using a screen or wall. The details for laying out such a screen, and aiming the lights are shown in Fig. M-1. Make sure the car is on a level floor and 25 ft. from the screen.

With the car in front of the aiming screen, remove the head lamp rim.

Fig. M-3. Removing retaining ring spring.

Fig. M-4. Removing retaining ring attaching screws.

Fig. M-5. Removing retaining ring, sealed beam unit and mounting ring.

Adjust the top adjusting screw, Fig. M-2, for vertical position of the beam and the side adjusting screw for horizontal position as required. Adjust one head lamp at a time. While adjusting one lamp, cover the other lamp with an opaque cloth so that there will be no confusion.

SEALED BEAM UNIT REPLACEMENT

Remove the screws holding the head lamp bezel in place. With long nosed pliers, remove the retaining spring, Fig. M-3, from the retaining ring. Then remove the retaining ring attaching screws, Fig. M-4. Do not disturb the adjusting screws unless it is necessary to reaim the light after the installation of a new lamp. The retaining ring may now be removed and the sealed beam unit and mounting ring pulled forward, Fig. M-5. Disconnect the connector plug from the sealed beam unit, and remove the unit, Fig. M-6. Install the mounting ring on the new head lamp and attach connector to new sealed beam unit. Make sure that the number or word "top" molded into the lens face is at the top after installation is completed.

In the dual head lamp installations, the inboard unit (No. 1) takes a double connector plug, the outboard unit (No. 2) takes a triple connector plug.

LIGHTING SWITCH

To remove a lighting switch, first disconnect the battery ground cable. Note: On the factory air conditioned Chevy II models, it is necessary to remove the parking brake and the air conditioning control head before proceeding further. On some 1970 models remove left radio speaker.

1977 line of Chevrolet cars: Top. Monte Carlo. Center. Concours four-door sedan. Bottom. Chevelle Malibu Classic.

Fig. M-6. Disconnecting sealed beam unit.

Pull control knob of head lamps to "On" position. Note: On the Corvette only, remove screws at top and left sides of instrument panel, and pull panel forward for access to light switch.

Reach up under instrument panel and depress the switch shaft retainer, Fig. M-8, then remove knob and shaft assembly. Remove ferrule nut and switch assembly from instrument panel.

Remove vacuum hoses from Corvette, also Camaro and Chevrolet, optional head lamp switches. Tag location of hoses for reassembly.

Disconnect the multi-contact connector from the lighting switch. A screwdriver may be inserted in the side of the switch to pry the connector from the switch.

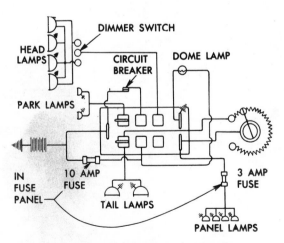

Fig. M-7. Typical lighting switch wiring diagram.

Fix Your Chevrolet

Connect the multicontact connector to the replacement switch. Connect vacuum hoses to head lamp switches and complete switch replacement in the reverse order of removal.

Fig. M-7 shows a typical lighting switch wiring diagram; Fig. M-9, an instrument panel cluster.

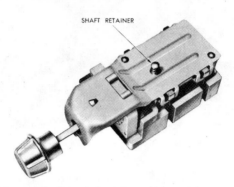

Fig. M-8. Typical lighting switch. Note shaft retainer which must be pressed in to remove switch.

Fig. M-9. Rear of instrument panel cluster — warning devices. Typical.

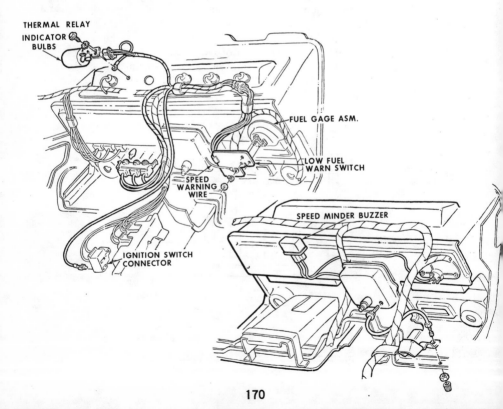

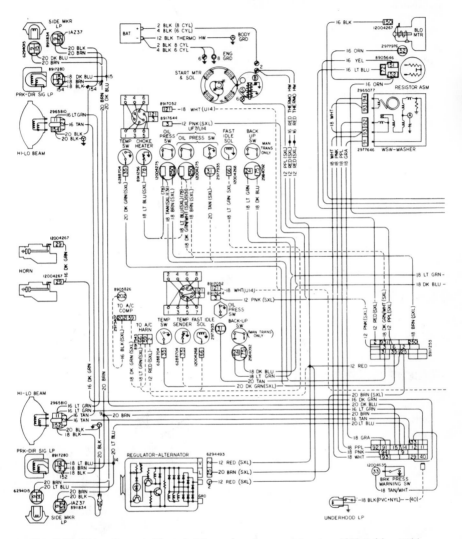

Fig. M-10. Wiring diagram of front lighting and engine compartment on 1978 Malibu, Malibu Classic, El Camino and Monte Carlo.

WIRING DIAGRAMS

A wiring diagram shows circuit layout and electrical connections. Typical front lighting and engine compartment circuits are shown in Fig. M-10. Note that the color of each wire is indicated to simplify tracing the circuits when trouble shooting.

DIMMER SWITCH REPLACEMENT

To replace the headlight dimmer switch, first hold back the upper left corner of the front floor mat. Then disengage the connector lock fingers and disconnect multiplug connector from the dimmer switch, Fig. M-11.

Remove the two screws retaining dimmer switch to toe pan. Connect multiplug connector to new switch and check operation. Then install new switch to toe pan with two screws and replace the floor mat.

Fig. M-11. Typical dimmer switch installation.

BACKUP LAMP SWITCH REPLACEMENT

There are two types of backup lamp switches used on Chevrolet built cars. One is mounted on the mast jacket, and the other on the transmission.

To remove the switch located on the mast jacket (steering column), first disconnect wiring connector at switch terminal. Remove switch at-

Fig. M-12. Backup lamp switch. Left. On mast jacket. Right. On transmission (1978).

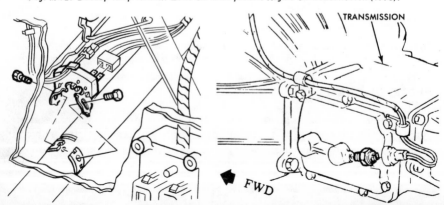

Lighting Systems

taching screws and switch from the mast jacket. Position the new switch on the mast jacket, install retaining screws and reconnect wire connector to switch.

Position gear shift in neutral before assembling switch to mast jacket.

When the backup lamp switch is located on the transmission, first raise the vehicle and then disconnect the switch wiring from the harness wiring at the in-line connector. Remove bolt retaining wiring attaching clip to transmission. Remove wire clip retaining reverse lever rod to switch. Remove screws retaining switch and shield assembly to transmission and remove the switch.

Do not remove transmission to bracket retaining bolts. To install the backup switch, reverse the procedure and check for operation.

To remove the instrument cluster (speedometer and fuel gauge and park assembly), the console must be removed from the vehicle. It is not necessary to remove the speedometer cluster from the console to remove individual units.

TROUBLE SHOOTING

HEADLIGHTS DIM

If the headlights are dim with the engine idling or shut off, the trouble may be: Partly discharged battery. Defective battery. Loose connection in the light circuit. Loose or dirty connections at battery and battery ground. Faulty sealed beam units. High resistance in circuit.

If the headlights are dim with the engine running well above idling speed, check the following: High resistance in lighting circuit. Faulty voltage control unit. Faulty sealed beam units.

LIGHTS FLICKER

Loose connections. Damaged wires in lighting circuit. Light wiring insulation damage, producing momentary short.

LIGHTS BURN OUT FREQUENTLY

Voltage regulator set too high. Loose connections in lighting circuit.

LIGHTS WILL NOT LIGHT

Discharged battery. Loose connections in lighting circuit. Burned out bulbs. Open or corroded contacts in lighting switch. Open or corroded contacts in dimmer switch. Burned out fuse.

CIRCUIT BREAKER CAUSING CURRENT INTERRUPTION

Short in headlight wiring. Short within some light or instrument in use.

HEADLAMP PANEL ADJUSTMENT

The headlamp panel adjustment (not to be confused with the headlamp adjustment) is made as follows:

1. "in-out" loosen screws fastening slotted bracket to underside of headlamp housing assembly, Fig. M-13.

2. "Down" lamp cover top to opening; by turning hex head screw fastened to top of pivot link.

3. "Open" fully extended actuator with rod. (a) remove spring from actuator rod pin. (b) remove cotter pin from rod pin. (c) turn actuator

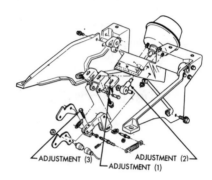

Fig. M-13. Headlamp panel adjustment (Corvette).

rod until bushing hole aligns to forward end of slot in connecting link extended position, with engine idling for vacuum. (d) shut off engine, retract actuator rod and unscrew rod one-half turn to preload actuator rod in link.

4. "Up" (bezel to opening alignment). Loosen jamb nut and turn bumper covered screw up or down to touch, then up one and one-half turns more. Micro switch on linkage must shut off warning lamp when lights are fully extended. Note: The headlamp housing must be properly aligned before headlamps are aimed.

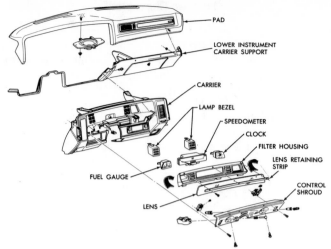

Fig. N-1. Chevrolet instrument panel. (Typical)

ACCESSORY AND
INSTRUMENT SERVICE

All instruments and gauges on recent model Chevrolet vehicles are installed on the instrument panel or console, Fig. M-9, and the entire panel is removable so the individual instrument can be serviced. In general, all indicator or cluster illuminating lamp bulb sockets are clip retained and may be quickly snapped in or out of position.

On some models, when removing the console on which the instruments are mounted, it is also necessary to loosen the upper mast jacket retaining clamp and slide it upward, thus releasing the steering mast jacket. Then loosen the lower mast jacket retaining clamp. Loosen the mast jacket and steering wheel. Unscrew the speedometer cable from the speedometer and unsnap all wiring connectors. Remove the screws attaching the console to the instrument panel and the console can then be removed.

INSTRUMENT PANEL

The instrument panel, Fig. N-1, on recent model Chevrolets incorporates an instrument cluster carrier with controls for the various accessories. Tell-tale lights are in the cluster carrier. Access to those bulbs is from the front of the carrier. After four screws are removed, the shroud comes free of the carrier. Then three screws free the lens, giving access to the bulbs. The bulb has a wedge base and pushes straight in.

Access to cluster illumination bulbs, wiper washer switch, headlamp switch bezel nut, cigar lighter housing, rear window defogger switch, convertible top or rear window switch and left vent control lever assembly is as follows:

1. Disconnect battery ground cable.

2. Remove cigar lighter knob and remove hidden screw in shroud where knob was.

3. Pull on headlight switch, then remove hidden screw above middle of shaft.

4. Remove 2 screws at bottom corners of shroud and lift off shroud. Bulbs can then be pulled out. The far left illumination bulb will require wiper switch loosening for bulb access.

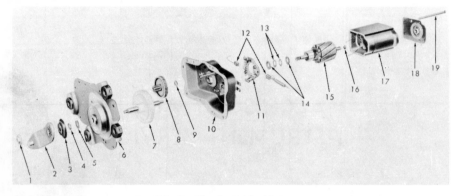

Fig. N-2. Details of windshield wiper motor.

1. Nut.	8. Intermediate gear.	14. Flat washers.
2. Crank arm.	9. Wave washer.	15. Armature.
3. Seal cap.	10. Gear box housing.	16. Thrust plug.
4. Retaining ring.	11. Brush plate assembly and	17. Frame and field.
5. Washer.	mounting brackets.	18. End plate.
6. Gear box cover.	12. Brushes.	19. Tie bolts, two required.
7. Output gear and shaft assembly.	13. Wave washers.	

WINDSHIELD WIPER SERVICE

Regular production Chevrolet cars are equipped with a two-speed electric windshield wiper.

Details of wiper motor and gear box used on recent models are shown in Fig. N-2. While instructions covering the removal of the windshield wiper motor varies with different models, in most cases they can be removed as follows:

Make sure wiper motor is in the Park position. Disconnect washer hoses and electrical connectors from the wiper motor assembly. Remove plenum chamber grille on Chevy II, Nova, Camaro and Corvette models. On Chevrolet models remove the plastic recess cover. Loosen the nuts which retain the drive link to the crank arm ball stud on Chevrolet models. On all other models remove the nut which retains the crank arm to the motor assembly. On Corvette models, it is necessary to remove the ignition shield and distributor cap to gain access to the motor retaining screw assemblies or nuts. Remove the three motor retaining screw assemblies or nuts and remove the motor.

To remove the transmission wiper assembly, Fig. N-3:

Make sure wiper motor is in Park position. Open hood. On Corvettes only, remove rubber plug from front of wiper door actuator, then insert a screwdriver, pushing internal piston rearward to actuate wiper door open. On all models, remove wiper arm and blade assemblies from the transmission. On articulated left-hand arm assemblies, remove carburetor type clip retaining pinned arm to arm blade. Remove plenum chamber air intake grille or screen, if so equipped. Loosen nuts retaining drive rod ball stud to crank arm and detach drive rod from crank arm. Remove transmission retaining screws, or nuts, then lower and drive rod assemblies into plenum chamber. Remove transmission and linkage from plenum chamber through cowl opening.

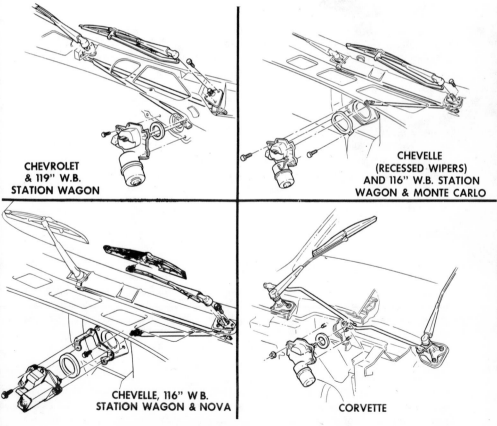

CHEVROLET
& 119" W.B.
STATION WAGON

CHEVELLE
(RECESSED WIPERS)
AND 116" W.B. STATION
WAGON & MONTE CARLO

CHEVELLE, 116" W.B.
STATION WAGON & NOVA

CORVETTE

Fig. N-3. Windshield wiper and linkage details. Typical.

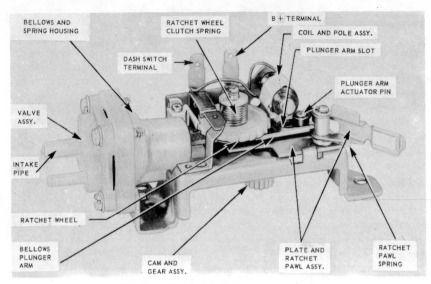

Fig. N-4. Windshield washer pump mechanism.

When trouble is experienced, it is usually advisable to first disconnect the linkage from the motor, and see if the motor will operate without the linkage. If motor does not operate, the trouble is either in the motor, the wiring or switch. Disconnect wiring and run a separate line directly from battery to motor. If motor now operates, the trouble is in the wiring. If the wiper will not shut off, disconnect wiring from dash switch. If motor now shuts off, a defective switch is now indicated. However, if wiper continues to operate, disconnect wiring from the wiper and connect a 12V battery direct to wiper terminal No. 2. Do not connect a jumper wire to terminal No. 1. If wiper now shuts off, check for grounded lead that extends between wiper terminal No. 1 and dash switch.

In case of intermittent operations, check for loose connections and sticking motor brushes.

WINDSHIELD WASHER SERVICE

Details of a current positive type displacement windshield washer pump are shown in Fig. N-4. Area pumps differ in appearance, but the basic pumping action and valve arrangement remain the same. The pump mechanism consists of a small bellows, bellows spring and valve arrangement, driven by a three lobe nylon cam and gear assembly. The wiper motor, Fig. N-2, drives the cam and gear, Fig. N-4.

. The most frequent difficulty encountered in the operation of a windshield washer is clogged nozzles, which in most cases can be cleaned by means of a fine wire inserted into the opening of the nozzle. In addition, make sure the jar has an adequate supply of water solution, that hoses are not damaged, and connections are tight, that the screen at end of jar cover hose is not plugged, and that all electrical connections to washer pump and dash switch are tight.

HIDDEN HEAD LAMPS

The hide-away head lamps on the 1968 models are vacuum operated. The system is controlled by the light switch which controls not only the head lamp electrical circuit, but also the vacuum circuit which operates the head lamp doors. The vacuum source is the intake manifold with a reserve tank so the lamp doors can be operated through one cycle without the engine operating. A relay valve routes vacuum to the actuators. In case of malfunction of the system, there is an over center spring in the linkage to keep the door open or closed. The door can be manually operated from the front of the car by pushing on the housing until the housing locks in the open position. It may not be closed without pushing on the linkage inside the engine compartment.

When aiming these head lamps, operate the engine for one to two minutes after the light has been turned on to insure there is at least 20 in. of vacuum in the system.

A manual valve is incorporated in the system to operate the doors independently of the head lamp (through the head lamp switch) for purposes of bulb replacement, cleaning, etc. The manual valve must be pushed in before the doors will close or operate to the normal light switch circuit.

In case the doors fail to open or close, carefully check the entire vacuum circuit, including the reserve tank for leakage.

To replace the actuator assembly, Fig. N-5, the following procedure on Chevrolet cars is followed:

Actuate doors open by lifting upper cover lid up and back, then lifting lower cover up and back. Remove battery for right side actuator, or remove washer jar and bracket for left side actuator removal. Remove

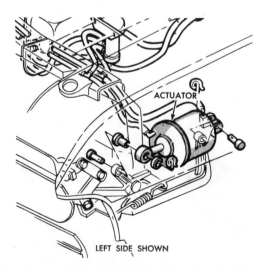

LEFT SIDE SHOWN

Fig. N-5. Actuator assembly for head lamp door, Chevrolet.

front and rear hoses on actuator. Remove front pivot pin retaining washers and pivot pin. Remove actuator rear pivot pin retainer with pin and lift actuator out of vehicle. To replace the actuator, reverse the procedure.

QUICK CHECK ON TURN SIGNAL

The turn signalling lever and cancelling mechanism, Fig. N-6, are located in the turn signal housing adjacent to the steering wheel. The switch requires no adjustment, but in case of malfunction, the steering wheel may be removed and the mechanism checked for defective parts.

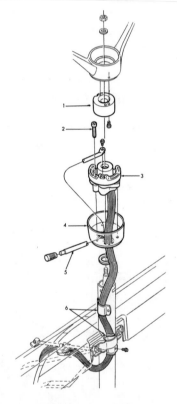

Fig. N-6. Direction signal assembly (Chevrolet). 1—Cancelling cam. 2—Control attaching screw. 3—Control unit. 4—Control housing. 5—Lever. 6—Harness clamps.

A two-bulb flasher is used on the Biscayne and Bel Air passenger cars, and in the Brookwood and Parkwood station wagons. This type flasher operates only two bulbs, the front parking lamp and the tail lamp. A three-bulb flasher is used on Impala cars and Nomad station wagons. The three-bulb flasher operates the front parking lamp and two tail lamps. When installing new flashers, it is important that the correct type be installed. If, when signaling a turn, the indicator light comes on but does not flash, the difficulty may be caused by a burned out parking lamp on that side. The flasher should also be checked.

If, when signalling a turn, the indicator light operation is very rapid, make sure that the correct flasher is installed and that it is in good condition. If, when signaling a turn, both turn indicators come on and stay on, or neither turn indicator turns on, and in either case no clicking is heard, then replace the flasher. Be sure to install the proper type flasher.

If, when signaling a turn, a clicking noise is heard, but the indicator light does not flash, the trouble is probably caused by a defective indicator bulb.

If the horn blows while direction signals are operating, this could most likely be a result of interference between the current signal cancelling pawl and the horn connector assembly which would ground the horn circuit.

If the flashing and cancelling of light is erratic, the trouble is probably caused from the turn signal switch heater being damaged or out of adjustment, and can be eliminated by correct adjustment.

In 1968-1969 models, directional signal assemblies provide as standard production equipment, a lane changing feature and hazard warning system on all model applications. Two different design switches are used. Major difference between the two units is that one type has cancelling and detent springs which are serviceable, otherwise both units are not repairable and must be replaced as an assembly in service.

Due to the integral design relationship of the signal switch and the energy absorbing steering column, which is illustrated in the Chapter on Steering, the switch is involved whenever any service operations are performed on the steering column. The hazard warning unit, even though an integral component of the directional switch assembly, requires the installation of an additional flasher unit in the fuse panel capable of operating six lamps simultaneously, depending upon the vehicle series and model.

TAIL-STOPLIGHT AND BACKUP LIGHT

To remove bulb: Unsnap the socket from the rear of the lamp unit. Replace bulb and snap socket back into place. On station wagon installations, replace bulb by removing lens retaining screws, remove lens and replace bulb.

The stoplight switch is located under the instrument panel and adjacent to the brake panel, Fig. N-7. If the stoplight does not operate when the brakes are applied, the switch can be checked by shorting across the switch terminals. If the bulb is not turned out, the light should light. To replace the switch, disconnect wiring. Remove the lock nut from the plunger end of switch and remove switch. The new switch should be installed in approximately the same position. Adjust switch for proper operation. Electrical contacts should be made when the brake pedal is depressed 5/8 in. from the fully released position.

THEFT DETERRENT SYSTEM

The horn relay-buzzer operates when the driver's door is opened to remind the vehicle driver that the ignition key has been left in the switch. A schematic wiring diagram of this theft deterrent system is shown in Fig. N-8.

With the key fully inserted into the ignition switch, the number four terminal on the horn relay buzzer is connected to the ground through the door switch when the driver's door is opened. Current then flows from the battery through the coil winding, the buzzer contacts, the ignition switch, and the door switch to the ground. Closing the door or removing the key will stop the buzzer action.

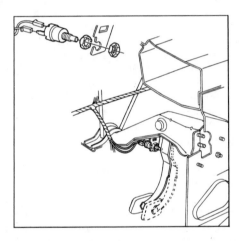

Fig. N-7. Location of stop light switch on Chevrolet. Typical.

When the horn switch is closed, the coil winding is connected to the ground and the armature moves toward the core to close the horn relay contacts. The horns are then connected to the battery and operate accordingly. With the horn switch closed, the buzzer contacts remain separated.

The system can be checked as follows: First be sure that the key is fully inserted into the ignition switch. Then open the driver's door, and observe the dome lamp. If both the dome lamp and buzzer fail to operate, check the door switch for defects. If the dome lamp is on, but the buzzer fails to operate, remove the horn relay buzzer from its mounting and identify the number one and number four terminals. Connect a jumper lead from number four terminal to ground. Slide a probe into the wiring harness connector to make contact if the terminals are of the slip-on type. If the buzzer now operates, check ignition switch wiring and ignition switch for defects. If buzzer does not operate, connect a volt-

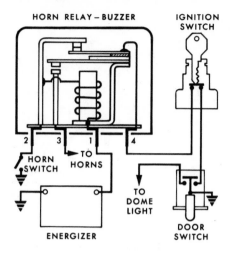

Fig. N-8. Wiring diagram of theft deterrent system.

meter from the No. 1 terminal to the ground. If the reading is zero, the circuit is open between this point and the battery. If a voltage reading is obtained, replace the horn relay-buzzer.

CARE OF SPEEDOMETERS

Speedometers ordinarily require very little attention. Some instruments, however, are provided with a lubrication belt or wick in the speedometer head. In such cases the wick should be saturated with special speedometer oil every 10,000 miles.

Cables used to drive speedometers on recent models do not require lubrication. On older cars, cables should be lubricated every 10,000 miles. To lubricate, disconnect cable at speedometer head. Draw cable from casing and coat with special lubricant. Reinstall cable in casing.

Most difficulty encountered in the operation of speedometers usually originates in the drive cable. The cable may be broken, kinked or in need of lubrication.

To determine what may be the cause of speedometer failure, the easiest method is to remove the cable. If the cable is in good condition, the difficulty is then in the speedometer head. In that case, the usual procedure is to remove the speedometer head and have it repaired by a specialist.

To remove a speedometer cable, disconnect the cable from the back of the speedometer head. This is done by turning back the coupling nut on the speedometer cable casing. The cable can then be withdrawn from the casing.

If the cable has broken, it will be necessary to disconnect the casing at the transmission in order to withdraw the lower portion of the cable.

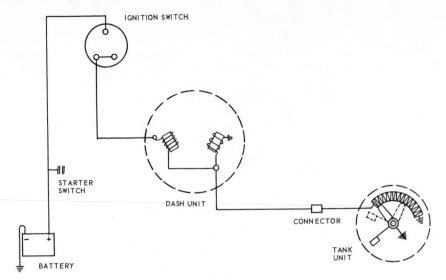

Fig. N-9. Wiring diagram of fuel gauge system.

Cables in good condition should be free from kinks and should not have any frayed or broken wires.

One method of testing a cable for kinks is to hold an end in each of your hands with the cable looped down in front. Then slowly rotate the end of the cable between your fingers. If it is kinked, the cable will "flop" and will not turn smoothly.

Some replacement speedometer cables are cut to the exact lengths and have the necessary fittings secured firmly at each end. In such cases, all that is necessary is to spread a thin coat of speedometer cable lubricant evenly over the lower two-thirds of the cable and insert it into the upper end of the casing, lower end first. Then, connect the upper end of the casing to the speedometer case, making sure the cable tip engages correctly in the speedometer drive member. Tighten the ferrule nut on the casing. Twist the lower end of the cable with your fingers to make sure it turns freely. A sharp twist of the cable should cause the speedometer and needle to register. Finally, connect the lower end of the casing to the transmission making sure that the cable engages in the speedometer driven gear.

When a speedometer cable kit is being used as a replacement, it will be necessary to cut the cable to the desired length and attach the tips. Complete instructions for measuring the cable and attaching the tips are included with the kit.

AIR CONDITIONING SERVICE

Inspect condenser and radiator cores at 2000 mile intervals to be sure they are not plugged with leaves or other foreign material. Check evaporator drain tubes at 2000 mile intervals for dirt or restrictions. At least once a year check the system for proper refrigerant charge and the flexible hoses for brittleness, wear or leaks. Every 2000 miles check sight glass for low freon level. Check tension of the drive belts regularly.

When replacing any of the air conditioning components, the system must be completely purged or drained of refrigerant. The purpose is to lower the pressure inside the system so that the component part can be removed safely. To do this, special equipment is required and the necessary instructions for using the equipment are included with the apparatus.

This same equipment is used when refilling the system with refrigerant.

GENERATOR CHARGE INDICATOR

Instead of an ammeter, some recent model Chevrolet cars are equipped with a charge indicator. If the telltale lamp does not light when the ignition switch is turned on, and the engine not running, the indicator lamp is burned out or the wiring is defective. If the telltale lamp stays on after the engine is started, check generator output. If the lamp stays on at idle speed only, check for low speed idle.

OIL PRESSURE INDICATOR

If the oil pressure indicator light does not come on when the ignition switch is turned on, or if the light stays on after engine is started, either the oil pressure is low, the oil level is low, the wiring or a unit in this circuit is defective.

If telltale light remains on with the engine running, the oil pressure is low. First check oil level, then if pressure is still low remove pressure switch and check oil pressure with a reliable pressure gauge. Another cause might be the electric circuit grounded between telltale light and pressure switch, or oil pressure switch is not operating correctly.

If the telltale lamp is off with the ignition switch on, and the engine not running, then the telltale lamp may be burned out, or there may be an open circuit between light and ignition switch, between light and pressure switch, pressure switch stuck, or the pressure switch not grounded.

FUEL GAUGE

The most common cause of fuel gauge trouble is high resistance in the circuit. Make sure all connections are tight and free from dirt, paint or corrosion.

Since the fuel gauge consists of two remotely located units, and the connecting wires, it is sometimes difficult to determine which unit is at fault.

The easiest way to determine where difficulty is located is to replace the units with new units until the trouble is located. A diagram of connections is shown in Fig. N-9.

TEMPERATURE INDICATOR

The temperature indicator requires very little attention other than making sure all connections are tight and free from dirt. Since the temperature gauge consists of two remotely located units, and the connecting wires, it is sometimes difficult to determine which unit is at fault. Make sure the unit is properly grounded by connecting one lead from a 12 V test lamp to the battery terminal on the starter and the other to the body of the engine unit. If the bulb lights, the unit is properly grounded. Remove test lead from body of the unit and connect lead to terminal of unit. If the bulb lights, the engine unit is internally short circuited and should be replaced.

POWER OPERATED FRONT SEATS (TYPICAL)

Seat adjusters are operated by a 12 volt reversible shunt wound motor. To remove seat for servicing the operating mechanism, first operate seat to full forward position. On four-way or six-way power seats, operate seats to full "up" position. Where front seat safety belts go through seat assembly, remove seat belt floor pan inner anchor plate attaching bolts. Where necessary, remove sill plates, and turn back floor mat and remove seat adjuster to floor pan rear attaching bolts, Fig. N-10. Operate seat

Fig. N-10. Four-way power operated seat. 1—Motor and transmission support. 2—Motor control relay. 3—Adjuster to floor pan front attaching bolt. 4—Ground strap. 5—Adjuster to floor pan rear attaching bolt. 6—Adjuster rear carpet retainer. 7—Adjuster to seat frame attaching bolt. 8—Adjuster track rear lower cover. 9—Adjuster track upper cover. 10—Four-way switch assembly. 11—Motor support attaching screws. 12—Adjuster track cover retainers. 13—Horizontal drive cable (black). 14—Vertical drive cable (blue). 15—Transmission assembly. 16—Motor to transmission coupling. 17—Motor assembly.

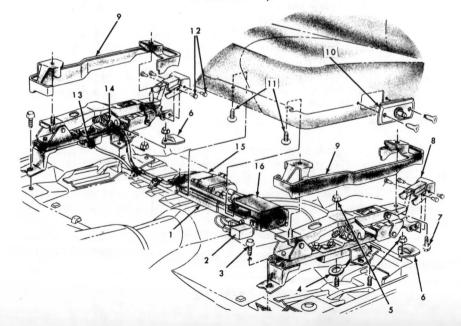

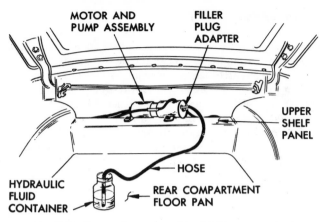

Fig. N-11. Motor and pump assembly of folding top mechanism.

to full rearward position. Remove adjuster-to-floor pan front adjusting bolts. Tilt seat assembly rearward sufficiently to disconnect seat harness feed connector and detach harness from floor pan. Disconnect any wiring. Then lift seat assembly from car.

FOLDING TOP

The hydraulic-electric system used to operate the Chevrolet folding top consists of a 12V reversible type motor, a rotor type pump, two hydraulic lift cylinders and an upper and lower hydraulic hose assembly. The unit is installed in the body directly behind the rear seat back, Fig. N-11.

When filling and bleeding this system, a filler plug adapter is needed. This can be made from a spare reservoir filler plug by drilling a quarter inch hole through the center of the plug. Then install two inch lengths of metal tubing, 3/16 in. i.d. into the center of the filler plug and solder tubing on both sides of the filler plug to form airtight connections.

To fill and bleed the reservoir, place the top in the raised position. Remove pump and motor shield. Place absorbent rags below reservoir at the filler plug. Using a straight-bladed screwdriver, slowly remove filler plug from reservoir, Fig. N-11. Install filler plug adapter to reservoir and attach four or five lengths of 3/16 in. rubber tubing or hose to filler plug tubing. Install opposite end of hose into a container of heavy-duty brake fluid. The container should be placed in the rear compartment body below the level of the fluid in the reservoir.

Operate top to down or stacked position. After top is fully loaded, continue to operate motor and pump assembly approximately 15 to 20 seconds, or until noise level of pump is noticeably reduced. Reduction in pump noise level indicates the hydraulic system is filling with fluid.

Operate top several times, or until operation of top is consistently smooth in both up-and-down cycles.

CRUISE MASTER SPEED CONTROL

The Cruise Master is a speed control system, Fig. N-12, which employs engine manifold vacuum to power the throttle servo unit, Fig. N-13. The servo moves the throttle when speed adjustment is necessary, by receiving a varying amount of bleed air from the regulator unit, Fig. N-14. The regulator varies the amount of bleed air to a valve system, which is linked to a speedometer-like mechanism. The speedometer cable from the transmission drives the regulators, and a cable from the regulator drives the instrument panel speedometer. The engagement of the regulator unit is controlled by an engagement switch located at the end of the turn signal lever. Two brake release switches are provided. An electric

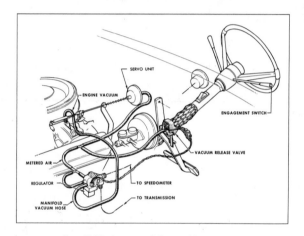

Fig. N-12. Layout of Cruise Master system.

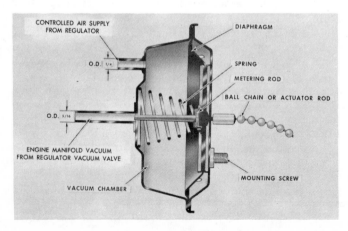

Fig. N-13. Sectional view of servo unit.

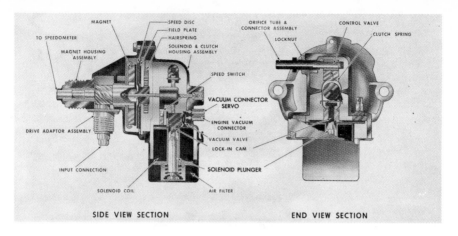

SIDE VIEW SECTION   END VIEW SECTION

Fig. N-14. Details of Cruise Master regulator.

switch disengages the regulator unit, and a vacuum switch decreases the vacuum in the servo unit to quickly return the throttle to idle position. Fig. N-12 shows the location of the system components within the vehicle.

The components of the Cruise Master system are designed to be replaced should they become inoperative. The air filter mounted on the regulator must be replaced at 12,000 mile intervals.

CRUISE MASTER SYSTEM CHECKS

When system will not engage or is otherwise inoperative, check for the following: Brake switch circuit open. Clutch switch circuit open. Blown fuse. Defective engage switch. Vacuum leaks. Vacuum release switch misadjusted. Crossed vacuum and air hose at regulator. Open end wiring. Defective regulator.

Does not cruise at engagement speed, check for orifice tube misadjustment.

System shunts pulses or surges, check for the following: Bead chain loose. Hoses reversed at servo. Kinked or deteriorated hoses. Dirty air filter. Defective and/or improperly positioned drive cables and/or casing assemblies. Defective regulator.

System does not disengage with brake pedal: Brake and/or vacuum switch misadjusted or defective. Defective wiring.

System steadily accelerates or applies full throttle when engaged: Hose interchanged at servo. Manifold vacuum connected directly to outboard tube or servo. Defective regulator. Pinched or plugged air hose that is connected to the outboard tube of servo.

Cannot adjust speed downward with engage button: Defective engagement switch or wiring.

Does not engage or engages at lower than desired speeds: Defective regulator.

Slow throttle return to idle after brake is depressed: Pinched air hose at vacuum release switch.

High engine speed independent of carburetor adjustments, constant air bleed through system: May be caused by: Tight servo chain. Manifold vacuum connected directly to center tube of servo.

System can be engaged at idle by depressing switch but will drop out when switch is released: May be caused by wires reversed at regulator.

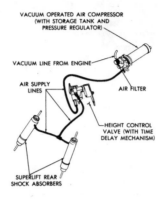

Fig. N-14A. Automatic level control system.

AUTOMATIC LEVEL CONTROL

The automatic level control system is optional equipment and is designed to automatically maintain correct rear trim height of a car under varying load conditions. It is used only in conjunction with the super lift shock absorber which consists of two shock absorbers with pressure lines to a "T" where a fill valve is located. The shocks are inflated with or deflated of compressed air to obtain the vehicle level desired with any given load change.

The automatic leveling system is added to the super lift shock absorbers and supplies its own compressed air. Fig. N-14A consists of a vacuum operated air compressor with pressure regulator and integral storage tank, vacuum line to engine, air intake cylinder, air lines and height control valves.

After completion of work on this system or when servicing other parts of the car and the system is deflated, inflate the reservoir to 140 psi or maximum pressure available through the compression valve.

To make a quick check on the system of the automatic level control, fill the fuel tank. Turn off the engine and add a two passenger load to the rear bumper or tail gate. Maintain the load until the car lifts or at least 20 seconds. After the car lifts remove the load and observe until the car lowers, which it should do in about twenty seconds.

SEAT BELT, STARTER INTERLOCK SYSTEM

The purpose of the seat belt interlock and warning system is to prevent initial engine start until the driver and the front seat passenger have occupied the seat cushion and then engaged the related seat belt buckles before turning the ignition switch on. That is: the seat belt sensor must be actuated prior to engaging the related seat belt buckle switch. Prior to initial start, if the outboard seat sensors and related buckle switch are engaged out of sequence, the interlock relay will prevent the starter operation. Also, the reminder light and buzzer on the instrument panel will be energized if the driver or passenger do not have the seat belt buckle switches engaged with the gear selector in a forward drive position, or while the engine is being cranked after engine stall.

The major components of the interlock and warning system include: logic module; front seat sensor switches; front seat belt buckle switches; seat harness to logic module; front end and floor pan wiring harness; reminder light and buzzer; ignition switch; interlock relay; neutral starter switch; harness connecting components; override control.

In addition to the normal procedure of starting the engine from the driver's seat, buckling the seat belts and turning on the ignition, the engine can also be started by what is called the mechanic's start. This is accomplished with no one in the driver's seat. All that is necessary is to reach into the vehicle and turn the ignition switch to "START" position.

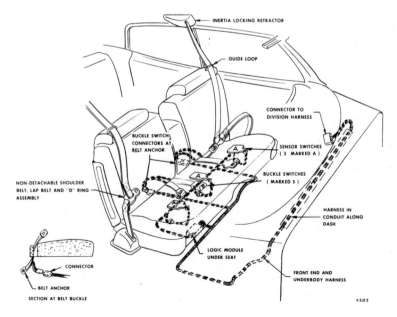

Fig. N-14B. Routing of interlock harness (typical).

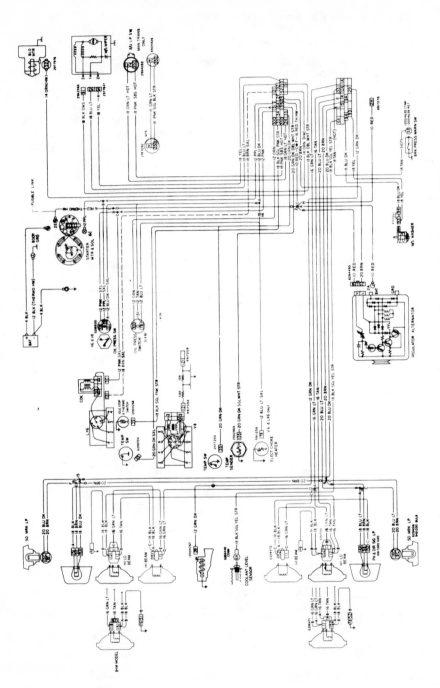

Fig. N-15. Front lighting and engine compartment electrical wiring diagram of 1978 Monza.

The routing of the interlock harness is shown in Fig. N-14B, and the front wiring and engine compartment wiring diagram for late model Chevrolet Monza cars is illustrated in Fig. N-15.

When replacing any of the fasteners of the lap and shoulder belt restraint system, it is emphasized that the attaching parts affect the performance of the vital components and must be replaced with parts having the same part numbers.

Also, the system incorporates an override feature which permits starting the engine in the event of an interlock system malfunction. The control is mounted in the engine compartment. The override control bypasses the interlock system and permits cranking when activated. To activate the override system the following steps must be taken:

1. Turn ignition switch to "ON" position.
2. Depress button on override control.
3. Turn ignition switch to energize starter.

Note that the override button must be released. If retained on the depressed position, the override control will not be activated. After activation, the override control circuit remains closed until the ignition switch is turned to the "OFF" position.

There are two types of interlock logic modules, a relay (electromechanical) type and an electronic type. The belt switches for the electronic type are normally open, while the belt switches for the relay type are normally closed. The units are therefore not interchangeable.

There is a slight drain on the battery when the ignition is in the "OFF" position. To avoid this, the seat belts should remain in the unbuckled position unless the seat(s) are occupied and that no objects be placed on the seats while the vehicle is parked for any length of time.

ENERGY ABSORBING BUMPERS

The energy absorbing bumper as installed on all 1974 models except Camaro and Corvette uses an hydraulic principle to dissipate the energy of impact by converting it to heat energy and pneumatic principles to restore the bumper to its original extended position. It is placed between the front bumper and the frame.

The energy absorbing bumper consists of two main assemblies, the piston tube assembly, Fig. N-16, and the cylinder tube assembly. The piston tube assembly is filled with an inert gas under pressure and consists of a bumper bracket, piston tube, orifice, seal, piston seal, piston and stop ring. The cylinder tube assembly is filled with hydraulic fluid and consists of a frame bracket, cylinder tube, mounting stud and metering pin.

Normally, gas pressure in the piston tube assembly maintains the unit in an extended position. Upon impact, as the energy absorber is collapsed, the hydraulic fluid in the cylinder tube is forced through the orifice. The metering pin controls the rate at which the fluid passes from the cylinder tube through the orifice and into the piston tube. This controlled passage

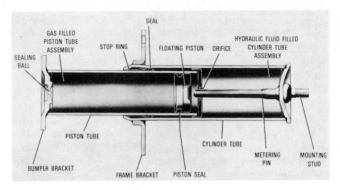

Fig. N-16. Details of energy absorbing bumper.

of the fluid provides the energy absorbing action.

The hydraulic fluid that is forced from the cylinder tube into the piston tube displaces the floating piston. After the impact, the pressure of the compressed gas behind the floating piston forces the hydraulic fluid back into the cylinder tube assembly extending the unit to its normal position.

It must be remembered that when servicing these energy absorbing bumpers that they are under pressure. DO NOT ATTEMPT TO REPAIR. DO NOT WELD. DO NOT APPLY HEAT. Also wear approved safety glasses when performing the following step:

Relieve gas pressure, if unit is to be scrapped, by drilling a small hole in the piston tube near the bumper bracket. The caution label may be used as a locater for drilling. Drill either in front of or through the label.

When a unit is bound-up as a result of a collision in such a way that the Energy Absorbing Device cannot extend, use the following procedure:

1. Stand clear of bumper.
2. Provide positive restrain, such as a chain or a cable.
3. Relieve gas pressure by drilling a small hole in piston tube near bumper bracket.
4. Remove unit from vehicle only after gas pressure has been relieved.

Recommendations to avoid damaging Energy Absorbing Devices:

1. Do not test units by driving vehicle into posts or barriers.
2. Do not rotate a unit unless it is necessary for alignment of unit with bumper bracket.
3. Never immerse unit in solvents.

Diagnosis:

The right and left Energy Absorbing Units are to be diagnosed separatly. The following checks and separate judgements are to be made on each unit.

Leakage: Some oil wetting may be visible due to grease packed in crimp recess between cylinder tube and piston tube. Therefore, a stain or trace of oil in that area is normal. However, if oil is dripping continuously, a leak is indicated and the unit should be replaced.

Damage: Observe the bumper bracket, piston tube, frame bracket and cylinder tube for evidence of collision damage. Scuffing of the piston tube will occur when the unit is stroked and is to be considered normal. If there is obvious damage, the unit should be replaced.

On-Car Test: This test involves compressing each Energy Absorbing Device separately 3/8 in. or more and observing whether the bumper returns to its original position, Fig. N-17. Ignition should be off, the transmission in PARK position, the parking brake set and a brake apply tool holding the service brake. Any suitable barrier can be utilized, such as a pillar, wall, post or anchorable device such as that used for body or frame straightening. The pressure device can be an hydraulic or mechanical jack. The pressure device should be aligned with the unit being tested, Fig. N-16. The jacking slot may be used as a reference point. The pressure device should be positioned squarely with the bumper to avoid slipping.

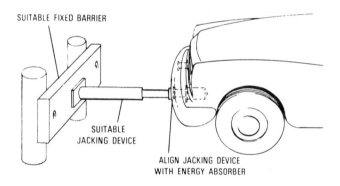

SUITABLE FIXED BARRIER

SUITABLE
JACKING DEVICE

ALIGN JACKING DEVICE
WITH ENERGY ABSORBER

Fig. N-17. Method of testing energy absorbing shock absorber.

Apply pressure to compress the unit at least 3/8 in., using some indicator such as a 6 in. scale to measure the travel. Relieve the pressure and allow the bumper to return to its normal position. This check is to be performed on each unit. If a unit fails to return to its original position it should be replaced.

Driving into posts, walls or pillars to perform this test is not recommended.

CAMARO BUMPER SYSTEM

The Camaro car is not equipped with the hydraulic-pneumatic type of energy absorbing device. Instead, the front and rear face bars are constructed of extruded, polished and buffed aluminum which are supported by steel brackets and employ flat-leaf column springs as the energy managing elements, Fig. N-18.

At the front, additional rigidity is built into the system by use of a tie-bar type reinforcement, located forward of the radiator support. The reinforcing member, attached to the brackets on the ends of the frame rails, spans the distance between the rails. A guide and travel limiting device between the bumper face bars and the center of the leaf spring units directs the impact forces in a horizontal plane. This component restricts upward movement of the face bar, mimimizing front or rear impact damage from the upper edge of the face bars. These brackets also provide additional rigidity during jacking operations.

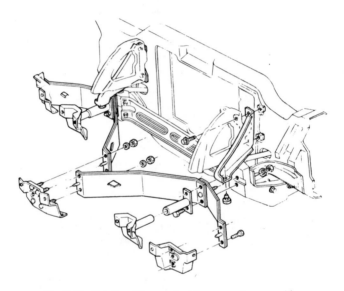

Fig. N-18. Details of Camaro front bumper spring assembly.

Quick
CLUTCH SERVICE

Two designs of the diaphragm spring clutch are used with the different engine-transmission combinations. A third design is a dual plate, heavy-duty clutch option, which is available for all models with higher performance optional V-8 engines.

The clutch assembly is enclosed in a 360 deg. bell housing, which must be removed to gain access to the clutch.

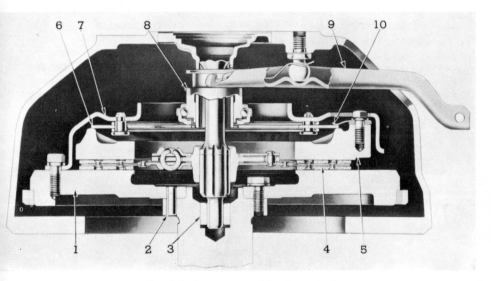

Fig. O-1. Cross section of flat finger clutch.

For engines of lower output, the clutch illustrated in Fig. O-1 is used as standard equipment. V-8 engines equipped with a 4-speed transmission use a bent-finger, centrifugal diaphragm type clutch, Fig. O-2. While the new dual plate heavy-duty clutch option which is available for all models of high performance V-8 engine is shown in Fig. O-3. This new heavy-duty clutch option combines the semicentrifugal bent-finger design and diaphragm type spring, used in regular Chevrolet high capacity clutches, with two conventional dry driven discs separated by a ring type intermediate pressure plate, Fig. O-3. The total disc facing area is 201 sq. in. compared to 123.7 sq. in. for the conventional regular production

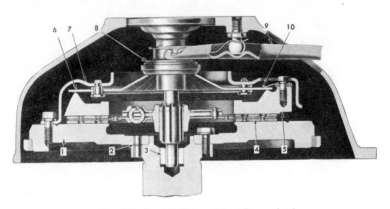

Fig. O-2. Sectional view of bent finger clutch.

unit. The greater total working area of the dual unit permits a reduction of plate load with no loss in efficiency. As a result, pedal effort to disengage the dual unit is approximately one-half of the comparable single disc unit, and clutch life is more than double. In addition, abuse capacity is always measurably greater. A new engine flywheel with a recessed contact area provides the space required to accommodate the second clutch disc and intermediate plate.

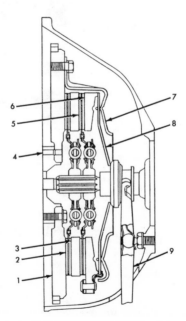

Fig. O-3. Dual plate clutch assembly. 1—Flywheel. 2—Front driven disc. 3—Front pressure plate. 4—Dowel hole. 5—Rear driven disc. 6—Pressure plate. 7—Cover. 8—Retracting spring. 9—Clutch fork.

Clutch Service

Clutch linkage on each of these clutches should be adjusted, unless otherwise specified, so there is one inch free travel, as measured at the clutch pedal pad, before clutch throwout bearing contacts the clutch fingers. In other words, the clutch pedal pad should move one inch before major resistance to movement is felt. This movement of the clutch pedal should be made by hand rather than the foot, as this feel is very sensitive.

CHECKING CLUTCH OPERATION

A clutch that has been slipping prior to free play adjustment may continue to slip right after the new adjustment, due to previous heat damage. Any slippage should then be evaluated as follows: Drive in high gear at 20-25 mph. Depress the clutch pedal to the floor and increase engine speed to 2500-3500 rpm. Engage the clutch quickly by removing foot from pedal, and press accelerator to full throttle. Engine speed should drop noticeably and accelerate with vehicle. If clutch is defective, the engine speed will increase. Be sure not to repeat more than once, or clutch will overheat.

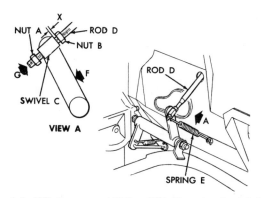

Fig. O-4. 1971 Corvette and 1962 to 1970 Chevrolet clutch linkage.

ADJUSTING 1962-1970 CHEVROLET CLUTCH

Disconnect spring E, Fig. O-4, between clutch push rod and cross-shaft lever. With the clutch pedal against stop, loosen jam nuts sufficiently to allow the adjusting rod to move against the clutch fork until the release bearing contacts the pressure plate fingers lightly. Rotate upper nut B, Fig. O-4, against swivel and back off 4-1/2 turns. Tighten lower nut A to lock swivel against nut B. Install return spring E and check clutch pedal free travel. Pedal free travel should be: Chevrolet 1 in. to 1-1/2 in.; Corvett Standard 1-1/4 in. to 2 in.; Corvett Heavy Duty 2 in. to 2-1/2 in.

1968-1970 CHEVELLE, CAMARO, NOVA AND CHEVY II ADJUSTMENT

Disconnect return spring at clutch fork, Fig. O-5. With clutch pedal against stop: Loosen lock nut C sufficiently to allow the adjusting rod to return out of swivel and against clutch fork, until the release bearing contacts pressure plate fingers lightly. Rotate push rod into swivel three turns and tighten lock nut.

Note: Chevy II and Camaro V-8 engine models use a two-piece push rod. Turn adjusting rod portion of push rod three turns into rod end, then tighten lock nut.

Reinstall return spring and check pedal free travel. Pedal travel should be: Chevelle 1-1/8 in. to 1-3/4 in.; Chevy II and Camaro 1 in. to 1-1/8 in.

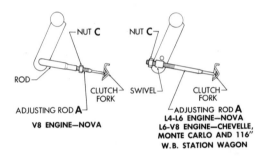

Fig. O-5. 1968–1970 Chevy II, Camaro, Monte Carlo and Chevelle clutch pedal free travel adjustment.

ADJUSTING 1971-1978 CHEVROLET, CHEVELLE, CAMARO CLUTCH

Disconnect return spring at clutch fork, Fig. O-6. Rotate clutch lever and shaft assembly until clutch pedal is firmly against rubber bumper on dash brace. Push outer end of clutch fork rearward until throw-out bearing lightly contacts pressure plate fingers. Loosen lock nut and adjust rod length so that swivel or rod slips freely in gauge hole and increases length until all lash is removed from the system. Remove swivel or rod from gauge hole and insert into lower hole in lever. Install retainer and tighten lock nut. Reinstall return spring. Pedal travel should be 1-1/8 to 1-3/4 in.

With the lower linkage adjusted so outlined, the pedal free travel will range from 1-1/4 in. to 1-5/8 in.

Do not use pedal free travel feel as a method of adjusting the linkage. This is important, because the over center spring feature which, due to its pedal assisting action, tends to give more free travel feel than actually exists. Free travel is from the fully released position of the clutch pedal to the point in depressing the pedal where the release bearing contacts the pressure plate fingers.

Clutch Service

REMOVING THE CLUTCH

1965-1977 models: Support engine and remove transmission. Then, disconnect clutch fork push rod and spring. Remove flywheel housing. Slide clutch fork from ball stud and remove fork from dust boot. Install pilot to support clutch assembly. Prick punch flywheel and clutch cover to permit reassembly in original position. Loosen clutch to flywheel attaching bolts evenly, turning one turn at a time until spring pressure is released. Then, remove bolts and clutch assembly. The 1978 linkage has been altered, Fig. O-7, but basic adjustment remains unchanged.

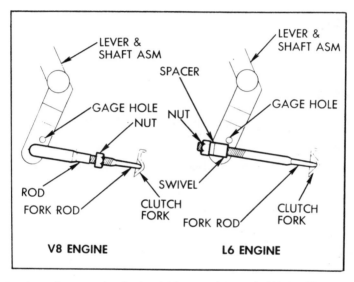

Fig. O-6. Adjustments for clutch pedal free travel. Typical of 1971 to 1977 cars.

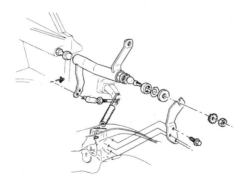

Fig. O-7. Clutch pedal lower linkage as installed on Malibu, Nova and Camaro models.

TROUBLE SHOOTING

CLUTCH FAILS TO RELEASE

Improper adjustment, loose linkage. Weak retracting springs. Faulty pilot bearing. Faulty driven disc.

CLUTCH WORN AND SLIPPING

Insufficient pedal play. Oil soaked facings. Worn splines on clutch gear. Warped pressure plate or flywheel. Weak diaphragm spring.

CLUTCH GRABBING

Oil on clutch facing. Burned or glazed facings. Worn splines on clutch gear. Loose engine mounts. Warped pressure plate or flywheel.

RATTLES AND NOISE

Weak retracting springs. Throw-out fork loose on ball stud or in bearing groove. Worn throw-out bearing.

THROW-OUT BEARING SPINNING WITH CLUTCH ENGAGED

Improper adjustment. Throw-out bearing binding on transmission. Insufficient tension between clutch fork spring and ball stud. NOTE: Clutch throw-out bearing is permanently packed with lubricant. Do not soak in cleaning solvent since this may dissolve lubricant.

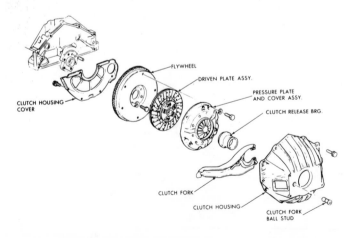

Exploded view of clutch system shows typical components used on late model Chevrolet passenger cars.

TRANSMISSION
SERVICE

Both three-speed and four-speed manual transmissions are available in recent model Chevrolet cars. Typical Muncie and Saginaw transmission models are described and illustrated in this chapter, Figs. P-1 and P-4. While the service procedures given apply particularly to current and recent models, they are also applicable, in general, to older models.

REMOVING THE MANUAL TRANSMISSION

The procedure for removing a manual transmission from the vehicle varies in detail with different models. Generally, proceed as follows:

First, raise car on a hoist or lift, or place car on jack stands. Disconnect speedometer, transmission control linkage and any other "obstructing" accessory equipment and/or electric wiring. Remove propeller

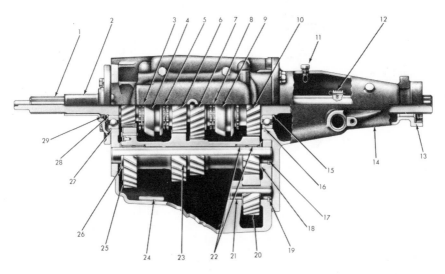

1. Clutch Gear	11. Vent	21. Reverse Idler Shaft
2. Clutch Gear Bearing Retainer	12. Speedometer Gear and Clip	22. Countergear Bearings
3. 3rd Speed Synchronizer Ring	13. Rear Extension Seal	23. Countergear
4. 2nd-3rd Speed Clutch Assy.	14. Rear Extension	24. Case Magnet
5. 2nd Speed Synchronizer Ring	15. Rear Bearing-to-Shaft Snap Ring	25. Anti-Lash Plate Assy.
6. 2nd Speed Gear	16. Rear Bearing-to-extension Snap Ring	26. Thrust Washer
7. 1st Speed Gear	17. Countergear Woodruff Key	27. Clutch Gear Bearing
8. 1st Speed Synchronizer Ring	18. Thrust Washer	28. Snap Ring
9. 1st—Reverse Clutch Assy.	19. Reverse Idler Shaft Woodruff Key	29. Clutch Gear Retainer Lip Seal
10. Reverse Gear	20. Reverse Idler Gear	

Fig. P-1. Cutaway view of three-speed Muncie manual transmission.

shaft assembly. NOTE: On some Camaro models, disconnect exhaust pipe at manifold. Remove crossmember-to-frame attaching bolts. On some models, detach brake control levers.

Remove bolts that retain transmission mount to crossmember. Support engine and raise it slightly while sliding crossmember rearward until it can be removed. Remove shift levers from transmission side cover, Fig. P-3. On floor shift models: Remove stabilizer control lever assembly retaining nut. Push bolt toward transmission until stabilizer rod can be disconnected.

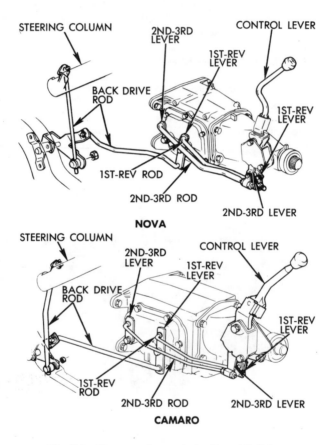

NOVA

CAMARO

Fig. P-1a. Three-speed transmission floor shift linkage.

Remove transmission-to-clutch housing upper retaining bolts. Install guide pins in bolt holes. Then remove lower bolts. Slide transmission rearward and remove it from vehicle.

Transmission can be reinstalled by reversing the removal procedure.

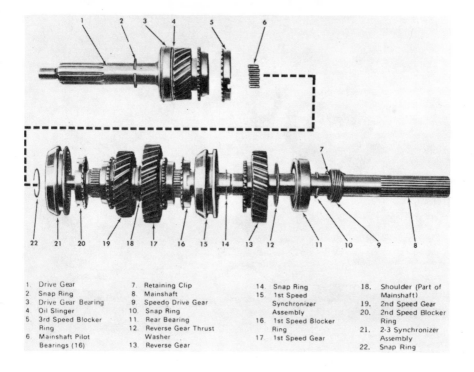

1.	Drive Gear	7.	Retaining Clip	14.	Snap Ring	18.	Shoulder (Part of
2.	Snap Ring	8.	Mainshaft	15.	1st Speed		Mainshaft)
3.	Drive Gear Bearing	9.	Speedo Drive Gear		Synchronizer	19.	2nd Speed Gear
4.	Oil Slinger	10.	Snap Ring		Assembly	20.	2nd Speed Blocker
5.	3rd Speed Blocker	11.	Rear Bearing	16.	1st Speed Blocker		Ring
	Ring	12.	Reverse Gear Thrust		Ring	21.	2-3 Synchronizer
6.	Mainshaft Pilot		Washer	17.	1st Speed Gear		Assembly
	Bearings (16)	13.	Reverse Gear			22.	Snap Ring

Fig. P-2. Main drive gear and mainshaft assembly of Muncie three-speed transmission.

TRANSMISSION DISASSEMBLY

The following procedure pertains particularly to the 1969 to 1975 three-speed Muncie transmission, but it is also helpful in disassembling the case components of other three-speed transmissions.

When disassembling a transmission, arrange each part on the workbench in the order it was removed and in direct relationship to other parts. This will help greatly when reassembling the transmission.

First remove side cover assembly and shift forks. Next, remove main drive gear bearing retainer. Remove drive gear bearing-to-gear snap ring. Figs. P-1, P-3 and P-4. Then remove main drive gear bearing by pulling outward on main drive gear. Drive gear bearing is a slip fit on main drive gear and into case bore. This provides clearance for removal of main drive gear and mainshaft assembly.

Remove transmission case-to-extension housing attaching bolts. Rotate extension housing to left until groove in housing flange lines up with reverse idler shaft. Using a drift, drive reverse idler shaft out of gear and case. Remove drive gear, mainshaft and extension housing by withdrawing assembly from rear opening of transmission case. Take reverse

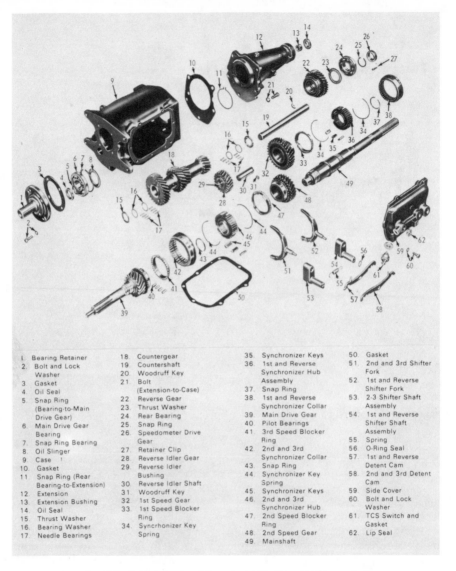

1. Bearing Retainer	18. Countergear	35. Synchronizer Keys	50. Gasket
2. Bolt and Lock Washer	19. Countershaft	36. 1st and Reverse Synchronizer Hub Assembly	51. 2nd and 3rd Shifter Fork
3. Gasket	20. Woodruff Key		52. 1st and Reverse Shifter Fork
4. Oil Seal	21. Bolt (Extension-to-Case)	37. Snap Ring	53. 2-3 Shifter Shaft Assembly
5. Snap Ring (Bearing-to-Main Drive Gear)	22. Reverse Gear	38. 1st and Reverse Synchronizer Collar	54. 1st and Reverse Shifter Shaft Assembly
6. Main Drive Gear Bearing	23. Thrust Washer	39. Main Drive Gear	
	24. Rear Bearing	40. Pilot Bearings	
7. Snap Ring Bearing	25. Snap Ring	41. 3rd Speed Blocker Ring	55. Spring
8. Oil Slinger	26. Speedometer Drive Gear	42. 2nd and 3rd Synchronizer Collar	56. O-Ring Seal
9. Case	27. Retainer Clip	43. Snap Ring	57. 1st and Reverse Detent Cam
10. Gasket	28. Reverse Idler Gear	44. Synchronizer Key Spring	58. 2nd and 3rd Detent Cam
11. Snap Ring (Rear Bearing-to-Extension)	29. Reverse Idler Bushing	45. Synchronizer Keys	59. Side Cover
12. Extension	30. Reverse Idler Shaft	46. 2nd and 3rd Synchronizer Hub	60. Bolt and Lock Washer
13. Extension Bushing	31. Woodruff Key	47. 2nd Speed Blocker Ring	61. TCS Switch and Gasket
14. Oil Seal	32. 1st Speed Gear		62. Lip Seal
15. Thrust Washer	33. 1st Speed Blocker Ring	48. 2nd Speed Gear	
16. Bearing Washer	34. Syncrhonizer Key Spring	49. Mainshaft	
17. Needle Bearings			

Fig. P-3. Exploded view of three-speed Muncie manual transmission.

idler gear from case. Remove drive gear from mainshaft.

Expand snap ring which retains mainshaft rear bearing in extension housing, Fig. P-1. Tap gently on end of mainshaft to remove extension housing from mainshaft.

To disassemble mainshaft: Depress speedometer gear retaining clip and slide gear from mainshaft. Remove rear bearing snap ring from mainshaft groove. Support reverse gear with press plates, and press on rear of mainshaft to remove reverse gear, thrust washer and rear bearing from shaft. When pressing rear bearing, be careful to center gear, washers and bearing on shaft.

Remove first and reverse sliding clutch hub snap ring from mainshaft. Support first gear with press plates, and push on rear of mainshaft to remove clutch assembly, blocker ring and first speed gear. When removing snap rings see that they are not distorted.

Remove second and third-speed sliding clutch hub snap ring from mainshaft. Support second-speed gear with press plates, and press on front of mainshaft to remove clutch assembly, second-speed blocker ring and second-speed gear from shaft.

Use solvent to clean transmission case, extension housing and all parts. Make sure bearings are clean, then lubricate them with light engine oil. Check bearings for roughness of operation by turning them slowly by hand. Inspect all parts. Replace those that show signs of wear.

TO ASSEMBLE MAINSHAFT

Turn mainshaft upward and install parts in correct original relationship, as shown in Figs. P-1 and P-2. NOTE: Both synchronizers are identical, but assembled differently. Install all parts up to and including first and reverse hub and sleeve and synchronizer hub-to-mainshaft snap ring. Turn mainshaft so that rear of shaft is upward. Then install first-speed gear with clutch teeth upward. Follow with remaining parts.

TO ASSEMBLE TRANSMISSION

Load a double row of roller bearings and bearing thrust washers in countergear assembly, using heavy grease to hold rollers in place. Place countergear assembly through rear opening of transmission case, along with thrust washer (tang away from gear) at each end. Then install countershaft and Woodruff key from rear of case. End of shaft must be flush with case. Position reverse idler in case. Expand snap ring in extension case and assemble extension over rear of mainshaft and onto rear bearing. Seat snap ring in rear bearing groove.

Load mainshaft pilot bearings into drive gear cavity and assemble third-speed blocker ring into drive gear clutching surface with its teeth toward gear. Pilot drive gear, pilot bearings and third-speed blocker ring assembly over front of mainshaft assembly. DO NOT assemble bearing to gear. Be sure notches in blocker ring align with keys in second and third synchronizer assembly.

Place extension-to-case gasket on extension, holding it in place with grease and from rear of case, assemble main drive gear, mainshaft and extension to case as an assembly. Rotate extension and install reverse idler shaft and Woodruff key. Install extension to case retaining bolts. Apply sealer to all through bolts.

Install front bearing outer snap ring to bearing and install bearing on stem of main drive gear and into front case bore. Install snap ring to main drive gear and main drive gear bearing retainer and gasket to case. NOTE: Retainer oil return hole should be at bottom. Shift synchronizer sleeves to neutral positions and install cover, gasket and fork assembly to case. Tighten all bolts to 15 ft. lb. torque.

Rotate main drive gear and shift transmission through gears to check for free rotation.

Fig. P-4. Exploded view of three-speed, fully synchronized Saginaw transmission.

DISASSEMBLING THREE-SPEED SAGINAW

To disassemble the fully synchronized three-speed transmission shown in Fig. P-4, first · remove cover attaching screws and remove side cover and shift forks. Remove clutch gear bearing retainer. Remove clutch gear to gear stem snap ring. Then remove clutch gear bearing by pulling outward on clutch gear until a screwdriver can be inserted between bearing snap ring and case to complete the removal. The clutch gear bear-

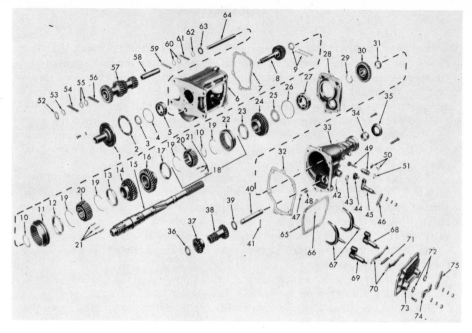

Fig. P-5. Typical four-speed Muncie transmission.

1. Bearing retainer.
2. Gasket.
3. Bearing retainer nut.
4. Bearing snap ring.
5. Main drive gear bearing.
6. Transmission case.
7. Rear bearing retainer gasket.
8. Main drive gear.
9. Bearing rollers and cage.
10. Snap ring.
11. Third and fourth speed clutch sliding sleeve.
12. Fourth speed gear synchronizing ring.
13. Third speed synchronizing ring.
14. Third speed gear.
15. Mainshaft.
16. Second speed gear.
17. Second speed gear synchronizing ring.
18. First and second speed clutch assembly.
19. Clutch key spring.
20. Clutch hub.
21. Clutch keys.
22. First and second speed clutch sliding sleeve.
23. First speed gear synchronizing ring.
24. First speed gear.
25. First speed gear thrust washer.
26. Rear bearing snap ring.
27. Rear bearing.
28. Rear bearing retainer.
29. Selective fit snap ring.
30. Reverse gear.
31. Speedometer drive gear.
32. Rear bearing retainer to case extension gasket.
33. Case extension.
34. Extension bushing.
35. Rear oil seal.
36. Reverse idler front thrust washer (tanged)
37. Reverse idler gear, front.
38. Reverse idler gear, rear.
39. Flat thrust washer.
40. Reverse idler shaft.
41. Reverse idler shaft roll pin.
42. Reverse shifter shaft lock pin.
43. Reverse shifter shaft lip seal.
44. Reverse shift fork.
45. Reverse shifter shaft and detent plate.
46. Reverse shifter lever.
47. Reverse shifter shaft detent ball.
48. Reverse shifter shaft ball detent spring.
49. Speedometer driven gear and fitting.
50. Retainer and bolt.
51. "O" ring seal.
52. Tanged washer.
53. Spacer .050 in.
54. Bearing rollers (20).
55. Spacers (2-.050 in.).
56. Bearing rollers (20)
57. Countergear.
58. Countergear roller spacer.
59. Bearing rollers (20).
60. Spacers (2-.050 in.).
61. Bearing rollers (20).
62. Spacer (.050 in.).
63. Tanged washer.
64. Countershaft.
65. Gasket.
66. Detent cams retainer ring.
67. Forward speed shift forks.
68. First and second speed gear shifter shaft and detent plate.
69. Third and fourth speed gear shifter shaft and detent plate.
70. Detent cams.
71. Detent cam spring.
72. Lip seals.
73. Transmission side cover.
74. Third and fourth speed shifter lever.
75. First and second speed shifter lever.

ing is a slip fit on the gear and into the case bore. This provides clearance for removal of clutch gear and mainshaft assembly. Remove extension to case attaching bolts. Remove reverse idler shaft snap ring. Remove clutch gear, mainshaft and extension assembly together through the rear case opening. Using snap ring pliers, expand snap ring in the extension which retains the mainshaft rear bearing and remove the extension. Use a drift at the front of the countershaft and drive the shaft and its Woodruff key out the rear of the case. There are special tools which will hold the roller bearings in position within the countergear bore. Remove the gear and bearings. Use a long drift through the front bearing case bore and drive the reverse idler shaft and Woodruff key through the rear of the case.

To disassemble the mainshaft, remove the 2nd and 3rd speed sliding clutch hub snap ring from the mainshaft and remove clutch assembly, second speed blocker ring and second speed gear from front of the mainshaft. Remove rear bearing snap ring from mainshaft groove. Support reverse gear with press plates and press on rear of mainshaft to remove reverse gear, thrust washer, spring washer, rear bearing and snap ring from rear of mainshaft.

When pressing rear bearing, be careful to center the gear, washers, bearings and snap ring on mainshaft.

Remove the first and reverse sliding clutch hub snap ring from the mainshaft and remove clutch assembly, first speed block ring and first speed gear from the rear of the mainshaft which completes the disassembly of the mainshaft.

FOUR-SPEED TRANSMISSION DISASSEMBLY

The disassembly procedure for the four-speed Muncie transmission shown in Fig. P-5 is as follows: Remove the transmission side cover and the four bolts, the two bolt lock strips from front bearing retainer, and remove retainer and gasket. Remove the maindrive gear retaining nut after locking up transmission by shifting into two gears. With the transmission gears in neutral, drive lock pin from reverse shifter lever boss and pull shifter shaft out about 1/8 in. This disengages the reverse shift fork from reverse gear.

Remove six bolts attaching the case extension to the case. Tap extension with soft hammer in a rearward direction to start. When the reverse idler shaft is out as far as it will go, move extension to left so reverse fork clears reverse gear and remove extension and gasket.

The reverse idler gear, flat thrust washer, shaft and roller spring pin may now be removed. Remove speedometer gear and reverse gear.

Slide three-four synchronizer clutch sleeve to fourth speed position (forward) before trying to remove mainshaft assembly from case. Carefully remove the rear bearing retainer and entire mainshaft assembly from the case by tapping the bearing retainer with a soft hammer. Unload 17 bearing rollers from main drive gear and remove fourth speed synchronizer blocker ring.

Lift the front half of reverse idler gear and its tanged thrust washer from case. Press main drive gear down from front bearing. From inside

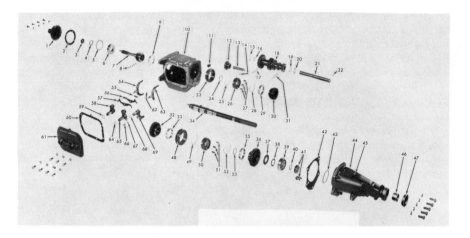

Fig. P-6. Four-speed Saginaw transmission.

1. Bearing retainer.
2. Gasket retainer to case.
3. Oil seal.
4. Snap ring.
5. Snap ring.
6. Clutch gear bearing.
7. Clutch gear.
8. Mainshaft pilot bearing.
9. Fourth speed blocker ring.
10. Case.
11. Filler plug.
12. Reverse idler gear.
13. Reverse idler shaft.
14. Woodruff key.
15. Thrust washer.
16. Needle retainer washer.
17. Needle bearings.
18. Countergear.
19. Needle retainer washer.
20. Thrust washer rear gear.
21. Countershaft.
22. Woodruff key.
23. Synchronizer sleeve.
24. Snap ring hub to shaft.
25. Key retainer.
26. 3-4 synchronizer hub.
27. Clutch keys.
28. Key retainer.
29. Third speed blocker ring.
30. Third speed gear.
31. Needle bearings.
32. Second speed gear.
33. Second speed blocker ring.
34. Mainshaft.
35. First speed blocker ring.

36. First speed gear.
37. Thrust washer.
38. Wave washer.
39. Rear bearing.
40. Snap ring bearing to shaft.
41. Speed drive gear and clip.
42. Gasket extension to case.
43. Snap ring extension.
44. Extension.
45. Vent.
46. Bushing.
47. Oil seal.
48. 1-2 syn. sleeve and rev. gear.
49. Key retainer.
50. 1-2 synchronizer hub.
51. Clutch keys.
52. Key retainer.
53. Snap ring hub to shaft.
54. 3-4 shift fork.
55. Detent spring.
56. 3-4 detent cam.
57. 1-2 detent cam.
58. 3-4 shifter fork.
59. "O" ring.
60. Gasket.
61. Cover.
62. Detent cam retainer.
63. 1-2 shift fork.
64. "O" ring.
65. 1-2 shifter fork.
66. Spring.
67. Ball.
68. "O" ring.
69. Rev. shifter shaft and fork.

case, tap out front bearing and snap ring. From the front of the case press out the countershaft, then remove the countergear and both tanged washers. Remove the 112 rollers, 6.070 in. spacers and roller spacers from countergear. Remove mainshaft front snap ring and slide third and fourth speed clutch assembly, third speed gear, and synchronizing spring from front of mainshaft. Spread rear bearing retainer snap ring and press mainshaft out of the retainer. Remove the mainshaft rear snap ring. Support second speed gear and press on rear of mainshaft to remove rear bearing, first speed gear and sleeve, first speed synchronizer ring, 1-2 synchronizer clutch assembly, second speed synchronizer ring and second speed gear.

FOUR-SPEED SAGINAW TRANSMISSION

To disassemble the four-speed Saginaw fully synchronized transmission, shown in Fig. P-6, first remove side cover attaching screws and remove side cover assembly and shift forks. Remove clutch gear bearing retainer. Remove clutch gear bearing to gear stem snap ring, then re-

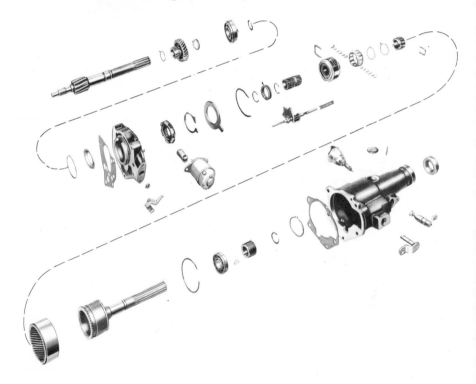

Fig. P-7. Exploded view of overdrive unit.

move clutch gear bearing by pulling outward on clutch gear until a screwdriver or other suitable tool can be inserted between bearing large snap ring and case to complete removal. The clutch gear bearing is a slip fit on the gear and into the case bore. This provides clearance for the removal of clutch gear and mainshaft assembly. Remove extension to case attaching bolts. Remove clutch gear, mainshaft and extension assembly together through the rear case opening. Using snap ring pliers, expand the snap ring in the extension which retains the mainshaft rear bearing and remove the extension. Drive the countershaft and its Woodruff key out the rear of the case. Remove the gear and the bearings.

Remove reverse idler gear stop ring. Using a long drift or punch to the front bearing case bore and drive the reverse idler shaft and Woodruff key to the rear of the case.

QUICK CHECKS ON OVERDRIVE TROUBLES

Details of a typical overdrive unit are shown in Fig. P-7, and the wiring diagram in Fig. P-8.

Troubles with the overdrive may be either mechanical or electrical. Mechanical difficulties will be discussed first.

If the unit does not drive unless locked up manually, the trouble may be caused by broken rollers in the roller clutch, sticking of the roller retainer upon the cam due to worn cam faces.

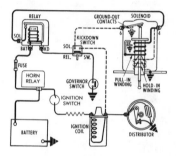

Fig. P-8. Overdrive electrical wiring diagram.

If it does not engage or lock up does not release, the dash control may be improperly connected or the transmission or overdrive improperly aligned. To test for misalignment, be sure that the transmission is not in reverse. Then disconnect the dash control wire from the lock up lever and feel the lever for free forward movement. If the lever can be moved forward more than 1/4 in. it indicates that misalignment probably exists.

If the kickdown switch is improperly adjusted, or the solenoid is improperly installed, or the blocker ring is improperly positioned, it will also result in the overdrive failing to engage or the lockup to release.

If the overdrive engages with a severe jolt or noise, the trouble may be caused by insufficient blocker ring friction.

If the unit free wheels at speeds above 30 mph, the cam roller retainer spring tension may be weak.

Failure of any of the electrical units, or defects in the electrical circuit may cause the system to fail to engage, fail to release or fail to kick down from overdrive.

If the system does not engage, first check the fuse and then the relay, Fig. P-8. Also make sure that the solenoid is operating. Check the kickdown switch and also the wiring between the relay and the kickdown switch. Also check the governor switch and the wiring between the kickdown and the governor switches.

If the system does not release, look for a grounded control circuit between the relay and the governor switch. Also check the relay.

If the system does not kick down from overdrive, check solenoid and make sure the wiring between the switch and coil are in good electrical condition. In addition check the kickdown switch and look for an open circuit in the wiring between the kickdown switch and the number six terminal of the solenoid, Fig. P-8.

Subcompact standard Monza series for 1978 features an 85 hp, 2.5 L (151 cu. in.) Four as standard equipment; a 90 hp, 3.2 L (196 cu. in.) V-6 is optional.

AUTOMATIC TRANSMISSIONS

Automatic transmissions covered by this book include:

1962-73 Aluminum Powerglide	1969-73 Turbo Hydra-Matic 400
1966-69 Turbo Hydra-Matic	1974-76 Turbo Hydra-Matic 375/400
1969-78 Turbo Hydra-Matic 350	1974-76 Turbo Hydra-Matic 250
1973 Turbo Hydra-Matic 375	1976-78 Turbo Hydra-Matic 200

Because of the intricate design of the automatic transmission, major work should be left to the shop having the needed specialized equipment. However, such adjustments that are easily performed are included in this book and when necessary, the transmission can be removed from the vehicle and a factory rebuilt unit installed.

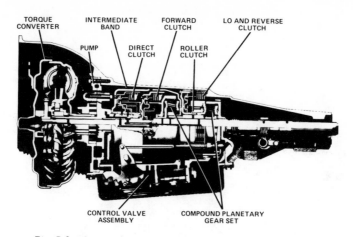

TORQUE CONVERTER — INTERMEDIATE BAND — FORWARD CLUTCH — LO AND REVERSE CLUTCH — PUMP — DIRECT CLUTCH — ROLLER CLUTCH — CONTROL VALVE ASSEMBLY — COMPOUND PLANETARY GEAR SET

Fig. P-8a. Sectional view of Turbo Hydra-Matic 200 transmission.

DRAIN AND REFILL INSTRUCTIONS

Complete drain and refill instructions for automatic transmissions are given on page 303.

1976-1978 TURBO HYDRA-MATIC 200

Model 200 Turbo Hydra-Matic transmission used on the 1976-1977 Chevette is fully automatic, Fig. P-8a. It features a three-element hydraulic torque converter. Its compound planetary gear set has three multiple disc clutches, a roller clutch and a band to provide the required friction elements. Should fluid leakage occur at the rear housing, a new seal can be installed: Remove propeller shaft. Pry out lip oil seal with a screwdriver. Coat outer casing of new lip oil seal with a non-hardening sealer and drive it in place with a circular drift of correct size.

To remove and replace the "200" transmission: First, disconnect negative battery cable and detent cable at the bracket and carburetor. Remove air cleaner and dipstick. On air conditioned cars, remove five heater core cover screws from heater assembly. Disconnect wire connector and, with hoses attached, position heater core cover out of the way. Raise car on hoist. Disconnect propeller shaft, electrical lead to case connector and oil cooler pipes. Disconnect shift control linkage. Support transmission with suitable jack and remove four transmission support bolts. Remove nuts holding converter bracket to support. Disconnect exhaust pipe at rear of catalytic converter. Disconnect exhaust pipe at manifold, then remove exhaust pipe, converter and bracket as an assembly. Remove torque converter underpan. Remove converter-to-flywheel bolts. Lower transmission until jack is barely supporting it and remove transmission-to-engine supporting bolts. Raise engine to its normal position and support it with a jack. Then, slide transmission rearward from engine and lower it away from vehicle.

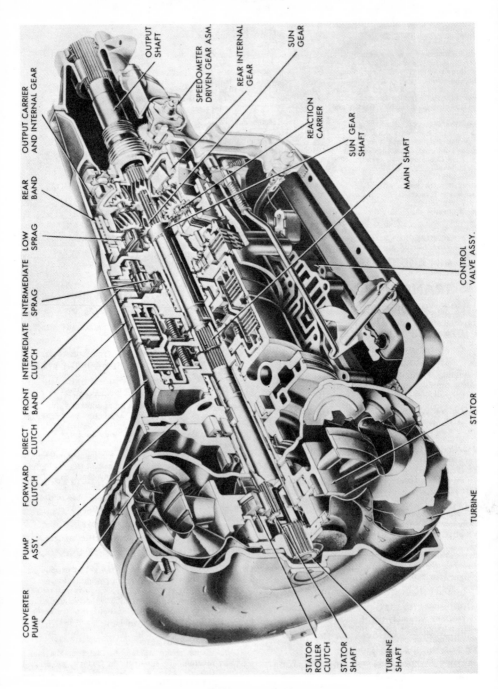

OUTPUT SHAFT

SPEEDOMETER DRIVEN GEAR ASM.

REAR INTERNAL GEAR

SUN GEAR

OUTPUT CARRIER AND INTERNAL GEAR

REACTION CARRIER

SUN GEAR SHAFT

MAIN SHAFT

REAR BAND

LOW SPRAG

INTERMEDIATE SPRAG

INTERMEDIATE CLUTCH

FRONT BAND

DIRECT CLUTCH

FORWARD CLUTCH

PUMP ASSY.

CONVERTER PUMP

CONTROL VALVE ASSY.

STATOR

TURBINE

STATOR ROLLER CLUTCH

STATOR SHAFT

TURBINE SHAFT

Fig. P-9. Turbo Hydra-Matic 400 transmission.

QUICK SERVICE ON 400 AND 400/475 TURBO HYDRA-MATIC

The Turbo Hydra-Matic 400 and 400/475 transmissions are fully automatic units consisting primarily of a three element hydraulic torque converter and a compound planetary gear set. Three multiple-disc clutches, one sprag unit, one roller clutch and two bands provide the friction elements to obtain the desired function of the planetary gear set. Figs. P-9 and P-11 illustrate this transmission.

Check fluid level as indicated in other part of this chapter. Fluid level should be at the full mark with transmission at normal operating temperature. With cold fluid, the level should be approximately 1/4 in. below the "ADD" mark. Only Dexron fluid should be used.

Possible points for oil leakage are the same as those listed for the model 350 Turbo Hydra-Matic transmission.

To check vacuum diaphragm for leakage, insert a pipe cleaner into the vacuum connector pipe as far as possible and check for presence of transmission fluid. If fluid is found, the vacuum modulator should be replaced. If gasoline or water vapor is found in the modulator, the unit should not be changed. To check for atmospheric leakage, apply liquid soap to the crimped seams and the threaded screw seal. Using a short piece of rubber tubing apply air pressure to the vacuum pipe by blowing into the tube. If bubbles appear the modulator should be replaced.

External control connections to the transmission, Fig. P-9, are the manual linkage which selects the desired operating range; the engine vacuum which operates a vacuum modulator unit; and the 12V electrical signal to operate an electrical detent solenoid.

Before disconnecting any linkage, be sure that it is marked so that it can be reassembled in its original position. Also make sure that the engine vacuum line to the transmission is clear and without any leaks. Also be sure that all electrical connections are tight.

The neutral safety switch should be adjusted so that the engine will start in the park or neutral position of the transmission, but will not start in the other positions.

To replace the 1966-1970 Turbo Hydra-Matic transmission, remove the propeller shaft. Disconnect speedometer cable, electrical lead to case connector, vacuum line modulator, and oil cooler pipes.

Also, on Camaro models only, disconnect parking brake cables and remove underbody reinforcement plate on the convertible. Disconnect left exhaust pipe from manifold for clearance. On Corvette models remove both exhaust pipes.

On all models, disconnect shift control linkage. Support transmission with suitable transmission jack. Disconnect rear mount from frame cross member. Remove two bolts at each end of frame cross member (plus through bolt at inside of frame and parking brake pulley on Corvette models). Remove cross member. Remove oil cooler lines, vacuum modulator line, speedometer cable and detent solenoid connector wire at transmission.

Remove convertor underpan. Remove convertor to flywheel bolts. Loosen exhaust pipe to manifold bolts approximately one-quarter turn (Chevrolet and Chevelle). Lower transmission until jack is barely supporting it. Remove transmission to engine mounting bolts and remove oil filler tube at transmission. Raise transmission to its normal position, support engine with jack and slide transmission rearward from engine and lower it away from the vehicle.

The installation of the transmission is the reverse of the procedure.

Fluid leaks at the transmission oil pan may result from the attaching bolts not being correctly torqued. The pan gasket may be improperly installed or damaged, or the oil pan gasket mounting face may be uneven. Leaks at the rear extension may result from attaching bolts not being correctly torqued, the rear seal assembly may be damaged or improperly installed, the gasket seal (extension to case) may be damaged or improperly installed, or the casting may be porous.

Fluid leaks may result from a damaged "O" ring seal at the filler pipe, the modulator assembly "O" ring seal may be damaged, the governor cover gasket and bolts damaged or loose. The speedometer gear "O" ring may be damaged. The line pressure tap plug may be stripped or sealer compound missing. Parking pawl shaft cup plug may be damaged or improperly installed.

Fluid leaks at the front of the transmission may result from a damaged front seal, or the garter spring may be missing. Also pump attaching bolts and seals may be damaged, missing or loose.

If oil comes out the vent pipe, make sure the transmission has not been overfilled or there may be water in the fluid. In addition the pump to case gasket may be mispositioned or otherwise defective.

Transmission leaks caused by aluminum case porosity have been successfully repaired with the transmission in the vehicle by using the following procedure: First road test and bring the transmission to operating temperature. Raise the car, and with the engine running, locate the source of the oil leak. Check for leaks in all operating positions. The use of a mirror will be helpful in finding leaks. Shut off the engine and thoroughly clean area with a solvent and air dry. Following the instructions of the manufacturer, mix a sufficient amount of epoxy cement, which can be obtained from the Chevrolet dealer, to make the repair. While the transmission is still hot, apply the epoxy to the area, making certain that the area is fully covered. Allow the epoxy cement to dry for three hours and retest for leaks.

QUICK SERVICE ON TURBO HYDRA-MATIC 350

The Chevrolet three-speed automatic Turbo Hydra-Matic 350, Fig. P-10, is manufactured for use with engines up to 396 cu. in. displacement.

Four clutch packs and two roller clutches provide the driving force necessary for smooth operation. The direct and forward clutches have in-

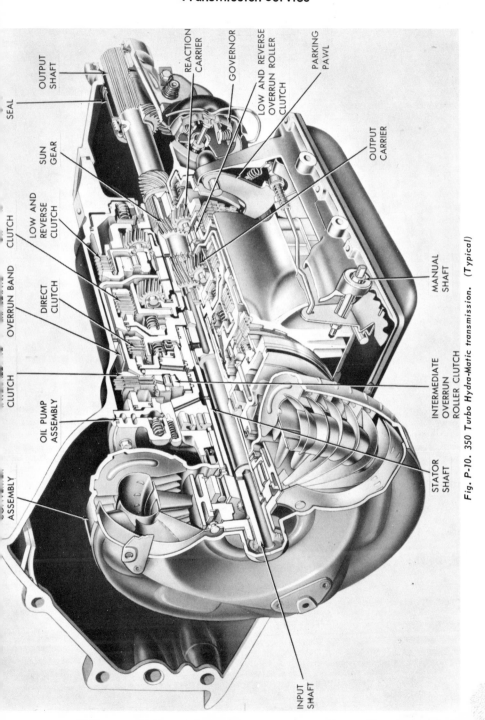

OUTPUT SHAFT SEAL

OUTPUT SHAFT

REACTION CARRIER

GOVERNOR

LOW AND REVERSE OVERRUN ROLLER CLUTCH

PARKING PAWL

SUN GEAR

OUTPUT CARRIER

LOW AND REVERSE CLUTCH

CLUTCH

OVERRUN BAND

DIRECT CLUTCH

MANUAL SHAFT

CLUTCH

OIL PUMP ASSEMBLY

INTERMEDIATE OVERRUN ROLLER CLUTCH

ASSEMBLY

STATOR SHAFT

INPUT SHAFT

Fig. P-10. 350 Turbo Hydra-Matic transmission. (Typical)

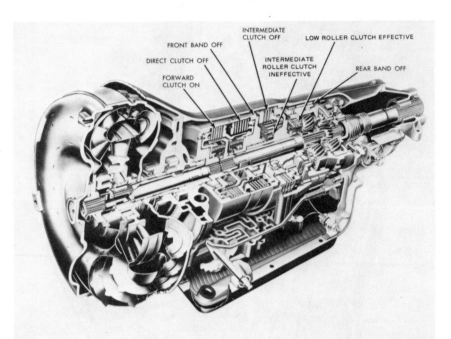

INTERMEDIATE
CLUTCH OFF   LOW ROLLER CLUTCH EFFECTIVE

FRONT BAND OFF

DIRECT CLUTCH OFF   INTERMEDIATE
ROLLER CLUTCH   REAR BAND OFF
INEFFECTIVE

FORWARD
CLUTCH ON

With the selector lever in Drive Range, the forward clutch is applied. This delivers turbine torque to the mainshaft and turns the rear internal gear in a clockwise direction. (Converter torque ratio = approximately 2.:1. at stall).

Clockwise motion of the rear internal gear causes the rear pinions to turn clockwise to drive the sun gear counterclockwise. In turn, the sun gear drives the front pinions clockwise, thus turning the front internal gear, output carrier, and output shaft clockwise in a reduction ratio of approximately 2.5:1. The reaction of the front pinions against the front internal gear is taken by the reaction carrier and one-way roller clutch assembly to the transmission case. (Approximate stall ratio = 5.:1.)

Fig. P-11. Details of 375/400 Hydra-Matic transmission showing operation of components in Drive Range — First Gear. Also study Fig. P-9 for names of parts.

terchangeable parts, thereby keeping service parts to a minimum. Only one band, the intermediate overrun, is utilized with the band being internally adjusted at time of manufacture.

The output shaft contains a yoke seal to permit grease packing of the shaft lines, thereby reducing friction between the output shaft and yoke.

Details of the model 350 Turbo Hydra-Matic are shown in Fig. P-10.

Possible points of oil leaks may occur at the following points: Transmission oil pan leaks resulting from attaching bolts not correctly torqued, damaged pan gasket, pan gasket mounting face not flat. Rear extension leak resulting from attaching bolts not properly torqued, rear seal assembly damaged, "O" ring in extension case damaged, porous casting. Case leak resulting from filler pipe "O" ring damaged, modulator "O" ring seal damaged, governor cover "O" ring seal damaged, speedometer gear "O" ring damaged, manual shift seal damaged. Line pressure tap plug leakage resulting from worn threads or lacking sealing compound. Detent cable "O" ring seal damaged. Front end leak resulting from damaged front seal, pump attaching bolts and seals damaged or loose, converter weld defective, pump "O" ring seal damaged. If oil comes out vent pipe, the trouble may be caused by too much fluid in transmission, water in the fluid, pump to case gasket mispositioned.

1962-1973 ALUMINUM POWERGLIDE

The aluminum Powerglide transmission, Fig. P-12, is a single case aluminum unit. When the manual control is placed in the drive position, the transmission automatically shifts to low gear for initial vehicle movement. As the car gains speed an automatic shift is made to high gear. A forced downshift feature provides a passing gear by returning the transmission to low gear.

The transmission neutral switch should be adjusted so the engine will start when the transmission is in park or neutral position, and will not start when the shift lever is in any other position.

The low band should be adjusted at 12,000 mile intervals, or sooner, if operating performance indicates low band slippage. To adjust the low band, raise the vehicle and place selector lever in neutral. Remove protective cap from transmission adjusting screw. Loosen adjusting locknut one-quarter turn, and hold in this position with a wrench. With a torque wrench, adjust band to 70 in. lb., Fig. P-13, and then back off four complete turns for a band that has been in operation for 6000 miles or more, or three turns for one in use less than 6000 miles. Be sure to hold adjusting screw lock nut at one-quarter turn loose with wrench during adjusting procedure.

Tighten the adjusting screw lock nut to 15 ft. lb. Method of making the adjustment is shown in Fig. P-13.

To remove the Powerglide transmission from the chassis, first place the car on hoist and move oil pan drain plug in order to drain oil. Discon-

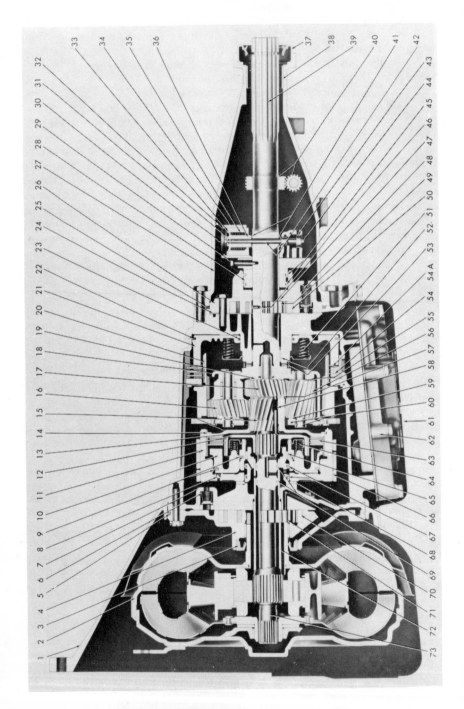

Transmission Service

Fig. P-12. 1962–1972 aluminum Powerglide transmission.

1-Transmission case.
2-Welded converter.
3-Front oil pump seal assembly.
4-Front oil pump body.
5-Seal.
6-Lube relief valve.
7-Oil pump cover.
8-Clutch relief valve ball.
9-Seal.
10-Clutch piston.
11-Clutch drum.
12-Clutch hub.
13-Thrust washer.
14-Clutch flange retaining ring.
15-Low sun gear and clutch flange assembly.
16-Planet short pinion.
17-Planet input sun gear.
18-Planet carrier.
19-Thrust washer.
20-Ring gear.
21-Reverse piston.
22-Outer seal.
23-Inner seal.
24-Extension seal ring.
25-Rear pump wear plate.

26-Rear pump.
27-Extension.
28-Governor hub.
29-Governor hub drive screw.
30-Governor body.
31-Retainer clip.
32-Retainer ring.
33-Retainer ring.
34-Governor springweight.
35-Governor spring.
36-Governor weight.
37-Oil seal.
38-Extension rear bushing.
39-Output shaft.
40-Speedometer drive and driven gears.
41-Governor shaft Belleville springs.
42-Governor shaft.
43-Governor valve.
44-Retaining clip.
45-Seal rings.
46-Drive pin.
47-Rear pump bushing.
48-Rear pump priming valve.
49-Rear pump drive gear.
50-Rear pump driven gear.

51-Reverse piston return springs.
52-Transmission rear case bushing.
53-Thrust bearing.
54-Reverse clutch pack.
54a-Belleville spring.
55-Thrust washer.
56-Planet long pinion.
57-Thrust washer.
58-Splined bushing.
59-Thrust washer.
60-Parking lock gear.
61-Oil pan.
62-Valve body.
63-High clutch pack.
64-Clutch piston return spring.
65-Clutch drum bushing.
66-Low brake band.
67-Seal rings.
68-Thrust washer.
69-Seal rings.
70-Front pump driven gear.
71-Front pump drive gear.
72-Stator shaft.
73-Input shaft.

nect the oil cooler lines (external cooled models), vacuum modulator line and the speedometer drive fitting at the transmission. Tie the lines out of the way. Disconnect manual and throttle valve control lever rods from the transmission. Disconnect propeller shaft from transmission.

Install suitable transmission lift equipment or other lifting device and attach on transmission. Disconnect engine rear mount on transmission extension. Then disconnect the transmission support cross member and slide rearward. Remove cross member on Camaro models.

Remove convertor underpan, scribe flywheel convertor relationship for assembly, then remove the flywheel convertor attaching bolts.

Note the light side of the convertor is denoted by a blue stripe painted across the end of the convertor cover and housing. This marking should be aligned as closely as possible with a like stripe painted on the engine side of the flywheel outer rim (heavy side of engine) to maintain balance.

Support engine at the oil pan rail with a jack or other suitable brace capable of supporting the engine weight when the transmission is removed.

Fig. P-13. Adjusting low band on aluminum Powerglide transmission.

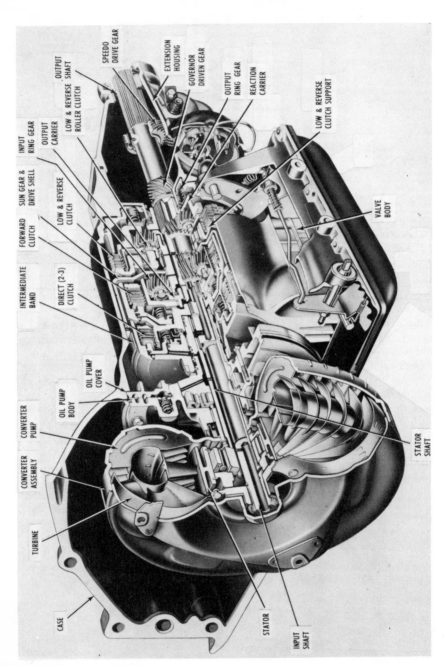

SPEEDO DRIVE GEAR

EXTENSION HOUSING

GOVERNOR DRIVEN GEAR

OUTPUT RING GEAR

REACTION CARRIER

LOW & REVERSE CLUTCH SUPPORT

OUTPUT SHAFT

LOW & REVERSE ROLLER CLUTCH

INPUT RING GEAR

OUTPUT CARRIER

SUN GEAR & DRIVE SHELL

LOW & REVERSE CLUTCH

FORWARD CLUTCH

INTERMEDIATE BAND

DIRECT (2-3) CLUTCH

VALVE BODY

OIL PUMP COVER

OIL PUMP BODY

CONVERTER PUMP

CONVERTER ASSEMBLY

STATOR SHAFT

TURBINE

CASE

STATOR

INPUT SHAFT

Fig. P-14. Details of Turbo Hydra-Matic 250 transmission.

Transmission Service

Lower the rear of the transmission slightly so that the upper transmission housing to engine attaching bolts can be reached using a universal socket with long extension. Remove upper bolts.

On V-8 engines care must be taken not to lower rear of transmission too far as the distributor housing may be forced against the dash causing damage to the distributor. It is best you have an assistant observe clearance of upper engine components while the transmission rear end is being lowered.

Remove remainder of transmission housing to engine attaching bolts. Remove the transmission by moving it slightly to the rear and downward, then remove from underneath the car and transfer to workbench.

Note: Observe convertor when moving the transmission rearward. If it does not move with the transmission, pry it free of flywheel before proceeding.

1968-1969 TORQUE DRIVE TRANSMISSION

The Torque Drive transmission has been released for the Chevrolet II L4 and L6 engine, and the Camaro L6 engine. The Torque Drive transmission is a modified version of the Powerglide transmission with the automatic shifting provisions removed. Lubrication, maintenance and service information is the same as that listed for the aluminum Powerglide.

1974-1976 250 TURBO HYDRA-MATIC

The Turbo Hydra-Matic 250 transmission, Fig. P-14, is a fully automatic unit consisting primarily of a 3-element hydraulic torque converter and two planetary gear sets. Three multiple-disc clutches, one roller clutch and an adjustable intermediate band provide the friction elements required to obtain the desired function of the two planetary gear sets.

Intermediate Band Adjustment: Adjust the intermediate band on the 250 Turbo Hydra-Matic transmission every 24,000 miles (with transmission fluid change). Earlier adjustment may be necessary if operating performance indicates that the intermediate band is slipping.

To make the adjustment: Position selector lever in neutral and raise vehicle. A special tool usually is used to make this adjustment. However, loosen locknut 1/4 turn and hold it in that position. With a torque wrench tighten adjusting screw to 30 inch-pounds. Then, while holding locknut from turning, back off adjusting screw three complete turns. (Use mark on special tool as indicator.) With torque wrench held in position, tighten locknut to 15 foot pounds.

Checking Fluid Level: To determine proper fluid level at normal operating temperature, place vehicle on level floor with selector lever in PARK. Apply parking brake and run engine at normal idle. Remove fluid level dipstick and wipe it clean. Replace dipstick, making sure it is fully seated. Then remove. Fluid level should be at "F" mark.

If the temperature is at or about 70 deg., the checking procedure for measuring the fluid level is the same. However, the dipstick reading should be 1/4 in. below the full mark. It requires one pint of fluid to raise the level from the ADD mark to FULL.

Draining and Refilling Transmission: The oil pan should be drained and the strainer cleaned every 24,000 miles and fresh fluid added to obtain the proper level on the dipstick. Exceptions are if the vehicle is used in heavy city traffic during hot weather; or in commercial use where the engine is idled for prolonged periods; or when the vehicle is used for towing. Then the oil pan should be drained and the strainer cleaned every 12,000 miles.

Drain the fluid immediately after the vehicle has been in operation a sufficient time to bring the transmission to operating temperature.

Proceed as follows:

Raise the vehicle and support the transmission with a suitable jack at the transmission. (Remove transmission cross member on Nova only.) With fluid receptacle placed under the transmission oil pan, remove attaching bolts from front and side of pan. Loosen rear pan attaching bolts approximately four turns.

Carefully pry oil pan loose with screwdriver, allowing fluid to drain. Remove remaining screws and remove oil pan. Discard gasket. Drain fluid from oil pan.

Clean pan with solvent and dry thoroughly with clean compressed air. Remove the two strainer-to-valve body screws, strainer and gasket. Discard gasket. Thoroughly clean strainer assembly in solvent and dry with compressed air. Install new strainer-to-valve body gasket, strainer and two screws. Position new gasket and install oil pan. Tighten thirteen screws and washers, torquing them to 12 ft. lb.

Lower vehicle and add approximately 5 pints of Dexron fluid or equivalent to transmission. With selector lever in PARK position, apply hand brake, start engine and let idle. Do not race engine. Move selector lever through each range, then place selector lever in PARK position and check the fluid level. Add sufficient fluid to bring level to 1/4 in. from full mark on dipstick. Caution: Do not overfill transmission or foaming will result.

Sequence For Diagnosis: 1. Check fluid level. 2. Check detent downshift cable adjustment. 3. Check and correct vacuum line and fittings. 4. Check and correct manual linkage. 5. Road test vehicle.

If engine performance indicates that an engine tune-up is required, this should be performed first because poor engine performance will result in rough shifting or other malfunction.

If there is any indication of a fluid leak, wipe the area carefully. Compare the fluid from the leak to that used in the engine. Fluid leaks from the engine are frequently carried back to the transmission. After cleaning, road test and again check the area.

Possible areas of fluid leakage include: transmission oil pan; extension housing; transmission case leak; leak at front of transmission; front pump housing "O" ring damaged; fluid comes out vent pipe.

A defective modulator may cause: hard upshifts or hard downshifts, delayed shifts; soft upshifts and downshifts; slippage in low, drive and

Transmission Service

reverse; transmission overheating.

Vacuum Diaphragm Leak Test: Insert a pipe cleaner into vacuum connector pipe as far as possible and check for presence of transmission fluid. If fluid is found, replace the modulator. Gasoline or water vapor may find its way in the vacuum side of the modulator. If this is found without the presence of transmission fluid, the modulator is still serviceable.

Atmospheric Leak Test: Apply a liberal coating of soap bubble solution to the vacuum connector pipe seam and to the crimped upper-to-lower housing seam. Using a short piece of rubber tubing, apply air pressure to the vacuum pipe by blowing into the tube. Observe for leak bubbles. If bubbles appear, replace the modulator. DO NOT use compressed air, only lung pressure.

Transmission Clutch Plates: Lined drive plates must be free of pitting, flaking, wear, glazing, cracking, charring or metal particles embedded in surface. Steel driven plates must be free of heat discoloration or scuffing.

Burned Clutch Plates: Burned plates in the forward clutch may result from: a damaged, stuck or missing check ball in clutch housing; clutch piston cracked or missing; low line pressure; pump cover seal rings missing, broken or undersize; case valve face not flat or having porosity between channels.

Intermediate Band: Check for intermediate servo piston seals damaged or missing, low line pressure, case valve body face not flat or porosity between channels.

Direct Clutch: Look for restricted orifice in vacuum line to modulator; damaged, stuck or missing check ball in direct clutch piston; defective modulator spring; clutch piston seals damaged or missing; case valve body face not flat or porosity between channels; clutch installed backwards.

Transmission Slips In All Ranges: Check for low fluid level, water in fluid, bad modulator and/or valve; defective strainer, valve body, pressure regulator, booster valve, manual valve or linkage; porosity or cross leak; worn pump gears or clutch seal rings. Inspect for a porous case or faulty 1-2 accumulator.

Drive Slips, No First Gear: Check for low fluid level; defective modulator, strainer valve body or pressure regulator. Check manual valve and linkage. Other problem areas are: pump gears; clutch seal rings; gasket screen; porous case; 1-2 accumulator; intermediate servo; forward clutch assembly; left and right roller clutch assembly.

Slips 1-2 Upshift: Look for low fluid or faulty modulator, valve, valve body, pressure regulator, booster valve, 1-2 shift valve or 2-3 accumulator. Inspect case for porosity or a cross leak. Other trouble spots include: pump gears, gasket screen, 1-2 accumulator, intermediate servo, intermediate band assembly.

Slips In Reverse: Check for low fluid level, defective modulator or valve, clogged strainer or bad gasket, faulty valve body, gasket, pressure regulator, booster valve, 1-2 shift valve, or manual valve linkage. Look for a porosity cross leak; clutch seal rings; direct clutch assembly; low and reverse clutch assembly.

SYNCHROMESH TRANSMISSION TROUBLE SHOOTING

CAUSE	CORRECTION

SLIPS OUT OF HIGH GEAR

a. Transmission loose on clutch housing.	a. Tighten mounting bolts.
b. Dirt between transmission case and clutch housing.	b. Clean mating surfaces.
c. Misalignment of transmission.	c. Shim between transmission case and clutch housing.
d. Clutch gear bearing retainer broken or loose.	d. Tighten or replace clutch gear bearing retainer.
e. Damaged mainshaft pilot bearing.	e. Replace pilot bearing.
f. Shifter lock spring weak.	f. Replace spring.
g. Clutch gear or second and third speed clutch improperly mated.	g. Replace clutch gear and second and third speed clutch.

SLIPS OUT OF LOW AND/OR REVERSE

a. Worn first and reverse sliding gear.	a. Replace worn gear.
b. Worn countergear bushings.	b. Replace countergear.
c. Worn reverse idler gear.	c. Replace idler gear.
d. Shifter lock spring weak or broken.	d. Replace spring.
e. Improperly adjusted linkage.	e. Adjust linkage.

NOISY IN ALL GEARS

a. Insufficient lubricant.	a. Fill to correct level.
b. Worn countergear bushings.	b. Replace countergear.
c. Worn or damaged clutch gear and countershaft drive gear.	c. Replace worn or damaged gears.
d. Damaged clutch gear or mainshaft ball bearings.	d. Replace damaged bearings.
e. Damaged speedometer gears.	e. Replace damaged gears.

NOISY IN HIGH GEAR

a. Damaged clutch gear bearing.	a. Replace damaged bearing.
b. Damaged mainshaft bearing.	b. Replace damaged bearing.
c. Damaged speedometer gears.	c. Replace speedometer gears.

Transmission Service

NOISY IN NEUTRAL WITH ENGINE RUNNING

a. Damaged clutch gear bearing.   a. Replace damaged bearing.
b. Damaged mainshaft pilot bearing.   b. Replace damaged bearing.

NOISY IN ALL REDUCTION GEARS

a. Insufficient lubricant.   a. Fill to correct level.
b. Worn or damaged clutch gear or counter drive gear.   b. Replace faulty or damaged gears.

TRANSMISSION SERVICING

TROUBLE   CORRECTION

NOISY IN SECOND ONLY

a. Damaged or worn second speed constant mesh gears.   a. Replace damaged gears.
b. Worn or shifted countergear rear bushing.   b. Replace countergear assembly.

NOISY IN LOW AND REVERSE ONLY

a. Worn or damaged first and reverse sliding gear.   a. Replace worn gear.
b. Damaged or worn low and reverse countergear.   b. Replace countergear assembly.

NOISY IN REVERSE ONLY

a. Worn or damaged reverse idler.   a. Replace reverse idler.
b. Worn reverse idler bushings.   b. Replace reverse idler.
c. Damaged or worn reverse countergear.   c. Replace countergear assembly.

EXCESSIVE BACKLASH IN SECOND ONLY

a. Second speed gear thrustwasher worn.   a. Replace thrustwasher.
b. Mainshaft rear bearing not properly installed in case.   b. Replace bearing, lock or case as necessary.
c. Universal joint retaining bolt loose.   c. Tighten bolt.
d. Worn countergear rear bushing.   d. Replace countergear assembly.

EXCESSIVE BACKLASH IN ALL REDUCTION GEARS

a. Worn countergear bushings.

b. Excessive end play in countergear.

a. Replace countergear.

b. Replace countergear thrustwashers.

LEAKS LUBRICANT

a. Excessive amount of lubricant in transmission.

b. Loose or broken clutch gear bearing retainer.

c. Clutch gear bearing retainer gasket damaged.

d. Cover loose or gasket damaged.

e. Operating shaft seal leaks.

f. Idler shaft expansion plugs loose.

g. Countershaft loose in case.

a. Drain to correct level.

b. Tighten or replace retainer.

c. Replace gasket.

d. Tighten cover or replace gasket.

e. Replace operating shaft seal.

f. Replace expansion plugs.

g. Replace case.

POWERGLIDE TROUBLE SHOOTING

OIL BEING FORCED OUT OF FILLER TUBE

a. Oil level too high, aeration and foaming caused by planet carrier running in oil.

b. Split in suction pipe permitting aeration of oil.

c. Damaged suction pipe seal permitting aeration of oil.

d. Ears on suction pipe retainer bent, thereby preventing proper compression of the suction pipe seal, permitting aeration of oil.

e. Bore for suction pipe in housing too deep, thereby preventing proper compression of suction pipe seal, permitting aeration of oil.

f. Sand hole in suction bore in transmission housing or case, permitting aeration of oil.

g. Sand hole in suction cavity in valve body permitting aeration of oil.

POWERGLIDE TROUBLE SHOOTING

Difficulty in shifting from drive to low, and from low to high can be caused by an improperly drilled high clutch feed orifice in the valve body.

Transmission Service

This causes slow application of the clutch. Condition can be diagnosed by connecting pressure gauges to low servo apply, and the release side of low servo.

Slipping and chatter in the low range can be caused by a poor ring fit on the low servo piston. Condition can be checked by connecting pressure gauges to the low servo apply, and the release side of low servo test points. With the selector lever in low range and the brakes set, accelerate the engine to stall speed and if everything is normal, low servo apply gauge should register 160 to 200 lb. and the high clutch gauge should register zero.

In case of high clutch failures, the transmission should be checked carefully, both before and after disassembly. With pressure gauges connected to low servo apply, high clutch and reverse servo test points check the following: 1. With selector in drive, check for slow build up of pressure on high clutch gauge. Slow pressure build up would indicate restriction in high clutch apply orifice. 2. With selector lever in low, check pressure on high clutch gauge. If any pressure is indicated, leakage past the low servo piston ring is indicated. 3. With selector lever in reverse, check pressure on high clutch gauge. If any pressure is indicated, there is probably leakage between the converter out and low servo release channels in the valve body, or a damaged housing-to-valve body gasket. The valve body should be carefully checked for porosity, or sand holes, or a damaged gasket between the transmission housing and the valve body.

If the transmission cannot be shifted into reverse with the engine running, but can be shifted into reverse with the engine stopped, the probable cause is that the accumulator snap ring is out of place.

1977 line of Chevrolet cars: Top. Vega GT. Center. Chevette hatchback Coupe. Bottom. Camaro.

PROPELLER SHAFT, UNIVERSAL JOINTS

Propeller shaft and universal joint design on Chevrolet cars has been changed several times during the past few years. From 1955 to 1957 a single propeller shaft with two universal joints was used. From 1958 to 1964 a two-piece propeller shaft with three universal joints was standard, and from 1965 to date, a single shaft with two universal joints was used on all models. The two joints used currently are lubricated for life.

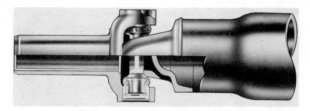

Fig. Q-1. Typical Chevrolet propeller shaft and universal joint.

1965-1978 UNIVERSAL JOINTS AND SHAFT

Fig. Q-1 is typical of the universal joints used in this period. To remove the propeller shaft (Dana) first raise the vehicle and mark relationship of shaft to companion flange and disconnect the rear universal joint by removing the trunnion bearing U-bolts, Fig. Q-2. Tape bearing cups to trunnion to prevent dropping or loss or roller bearings. On Corvette models, remove trunnion U-bolts at transmission yoke also.

Withdraw propeller shaft front yoke from transmission by moving shaft rearward, passing it under the axle housing. Watch for oil leakage from transmission output shaft housing. When reassembling these joints, repack the bearings and lubricate reservoir at end of trunnions with high melting point wheel bearing lubricant and replace the dust seals.

Remove bearing lock rings from the trunnion yoke. Support trunnion yoke on a piece of 1-1/4 in. pipe on an arbor bed. Due to the length of the propeller shaft, it may be more convenient to use a bench vise, for removal and installation, instead of an arbor press. In this case, proceed with disassembly and assembly procedure as with an arbor press.

Using a suitable socket or rod, press trunnion down far enough to drive bearing cup from yoke, Fig. Q-3. Remove dust seals from trunnion, clean and inspect bearing rollers and trunnion. Relubricate bearings with a lithium base chassis lubricant. Make sure reservoir at end of each trunnion is completely filled with lubricant.

Place new dust seals on trunnions and press seal into position. Installation of seal is critical to proper sealing. Special tools are available for installation which prevents seal distortion and assures proper seating of seal.

Partly install one bearing cup into yoke. Place trunnion in yoke and into bearing cup. Install other bearing cup and press both bearing cups into yoke, being careful to keep trunnion aligned in bearing cups. Press bearing cups far enough to install lock rings and install lock rings.

When installing the propeller shaft, make sure it is aligned with companion flange, using reference marks established before the shaft was removed.

To remove the Saginaw propeller shaft, first raise the vehicle sufficiently to permit access to propeller shaft and mark relationship of rear yoke to companion flange. Remove trunnion bearing retaining strap attaching screws from both bearings, Fig. Q-2. Lower rear of propeller shaft, being careful not to dislodge bearing caps from trunnion, and tape bearing caps to trunnion. Withdraw propeller shaft front yoke from transmission by moving shaft rearward, passing it under the axle housing. Watch for oil leakage from transmission output shaft housing.

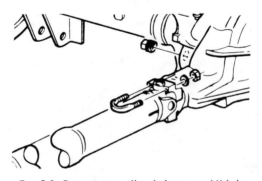

Fig. Q-2. Removing propeller shaft strap and U-bolt.

Because of the elastic properties of the nylon retainers, trunnions must be pressed from the yokes. Pressing the trunnions from the yokes will shear retainers which render the bearing caps unsuitable for reuse. A service kit which employs a snap ring to retain the trunnion must be used when reassembling the propeller shaft.

Remove trunnion at differential end of propeller shaft, using the following procedure: Support trunnion on a press bed so that the propeller shaft yoke can be moved downward. Support front of propeller shaft so that the shaft is in a horizontal position.

Propeller Shaft, Universal Joints

Using a piece of pipe, with an inside diameter slightly larger than 1-1/8 in., press bearing from yoke. Apply force on yoke around bearing until nylon retainer breaks. Continue to apply force until the downward movement of the yoke forces the bearing as far as possible from the yoke.

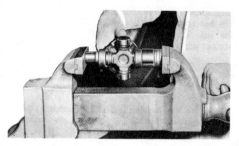

Fig. Q-3. Using bench vise and socket to disassemble a universal joint.

Complete removal of bearing by tapping around the circumference of exposed portion with a small hammer. Rotate propeller shaft so that the opposite bearing may be removed in the same manner. Then remove trunnion from yoke.

1958 TO 1964 UNIVERSAL JOINTS AND SHAFT

To remove the 1958 to 1964 Chevrolet propeller shaft and universal joints, first remove the two bolts attaching center bearing support to frame X-member. Then split the rear universal joint by removing trunnion bearing U-clamps. Tape bearings to keep them from becoming damaged. Remove the propeller shaft and bearing assembly by moving it rearward and to the left passing under the axle housing.

On these models with three universal joints, the angles of the respective shafts are critical and must be checked when any part, such as rear

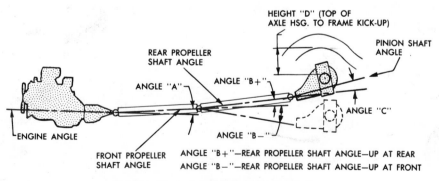

Fig. Q-4. Illustrating propeller shaft angularity.

axle, engine, springs or control arms are removed. Removal of such parts could alter the angle of the propeller shaft and cause severe vibration. These drive line angles are illustrated in Fig. Q-4, and are measured in relation to horizontal or level plane by means of a protractor with a bubble-type spirit level. A positive or negative angle is determined when the imaginary center line of the propeller shaft is above or below the center line of the following section. Angle A is normally positive, that is the engine-transmission center line is down at the rear with relation to the front propeller shaft center line. Angle B is normally negative and angle C is normally positive. The specifications for these angles are as follows:

	Angle A	Angle B	Angle C	Height D
1965 - 1959	2 3/4 deg.	-1 1/4 deg.	3 deg.	6 1/4 in.
1958	2 3/4 deg.	-1 1/4 deg.	2 3/4.deg.	6 3/4 in.

To avoid a lot of work, check the effective angles before removing parts of the engine, rear axle, control arms, rear springs, universal joints, drive shaft center bearing and engine mounts. Then, on reassembly, be sure to reinstall the part in exactly the same as its original position.

The 1976 Chevette propeller shaft is illustrated on page 246. Note that the extension assembly is bolted to the axle housing and is attached to the underbody through a center bearing support.

TROUBLE SHOOTING

EXCESSIVE VIBRATION

Incorrect drive line angles. Worn universal joints. Bent propeller shaft. Universal joint yoke bearings worn. Run-out of pinion flange. Out-of-balance propeller shaft.

EXCESSIVE BACKLASH

Worn universal joints. Worn drive shaft or joint spline. Also check adjustment of rear axle pinion and ring gear.

Shortcuts on
REAR AXLE SERVICE

Details of the rear axle assemblies used in the Chevrolet, Chevelle, Chevy II, Camaro and Corvette cars are shown in Figs. R-1 and R-2. Without specialized equipment it is not advisable to overhaul a rear axle as a high degree of precision is required. However, details of replacing a rear axle shaft and removal of the complete rear axle assembly are provided in this chapter.

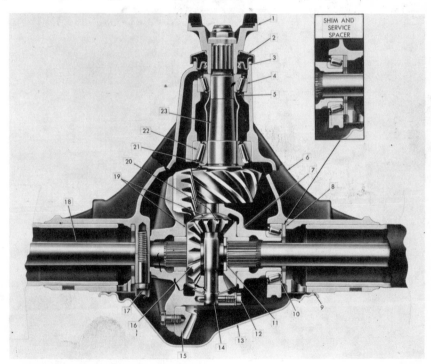

Fig. R-1. Details of rear axle used on 1965 to 1978 Chevrolet, Chevy II, Camaro, Monte Carlo, Nova and Vega. On late model Chevrolet and Camaro axles, a longer pinion bearing spacer is used.

1-Companion flange.	7-Differential case.	13-Cover.	19-Thrust washer.
2-Deflector.	8-Shim.	14-Pinion shaft	20-Differential pinion.
3-Pinion oil seal.	9-Gasket.	15-Ring gear.	21-Shim.
4-Pinion front bearing.	10-Differential bearing.	16-Side gear.	22-Pinion rear bearing.
5-Pinion bearing spacer.	11-"C" lock.	17-Bearing cap.	23-Drive pinion.
6-Differential carrier.	12-Pinion shaft lock bolt.	18-Axle shaft.	

REMOVING THE AXLE SHAFT

The following procedure is recommended for removing the rear axle shaft from 1965 to 1977 Chevrolet, Chevelle, Chevy II, Nova and Camaro models. It also applies to 1976 and 1977 Chevette models.

Raise the vehicle to desired working height and remove the wheel and tire assembly and brake drum. Clean all dirt from area of carrier cover.

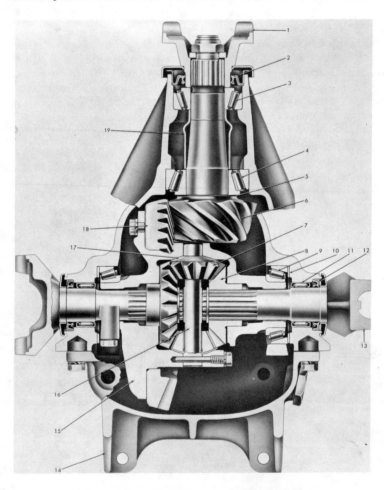

Fig. R-2. Details of Corvette rear axle 1966–1974.

1-Companion flange.	8-Differential side gear.	15-Differential case.
2-Pinion seal.	9-Differential bearing.	16-Differential pinion shaft.
3-Front pinion bearing.	10-Differential bearing shim.	17-Thrust washer.
4-Rear pinion bearing.	11-Yoke bearing.	18-Ring gear.
5-Pinion shim.	12-Yoke bearing seal.	19-Pinion bearing spacer.
6-Pinion.	13-Side gear yoke.	
7-Differential pinion.	14-Carrier cover.	

Drain lubricant from carrier by removing cover. Remove the differential pinion shaft lock screw, Fig. R-1, and the differential pinion shaft. Push flanged end of axle shaft toward center of vehicle and remove the "C" lock, Fig. R-1, from button end of shaft. Pull shaft. Do not damage seal.

To remove B or O type axle shafts, remove bolts attaching retaining plate to backing plate. Attach slide type axle shaft puller and pull axle.

Corvette 1966-1974, Fig. R-2: Disconnect inboard drive shaft trunnion from side of yoke. Bend bolt lock tabs down and remove the four bolts fastening shaft flange to spindle drive flange. Pry drive shaft out of outboard drive flange pinion and remove by withdrawing outboard end first.

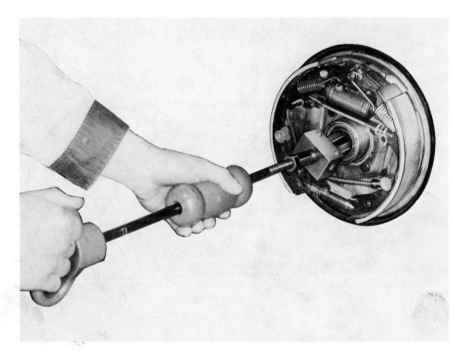

Fig. R-3. One recommended method of removing a rear axle bearing is by use of a slide hammer.

REMOVING REAR WHEEL SEALS AND BEARINGS

Rear wheel oil seals can be removed from the rear axle assembly by using the axle shaft as a removing tool. Insert the button end of the shaft behind the steel case of the oil seal. Then, work the seal out of the axle housing by prying against the back of the seal only, while being careful not to damage the axle housing.

To remove the rear wheel bearing, use a bearing puller or a slide hammer, Fig. R-3. Insert the arms of the tool behind the bearing so that the tangs of the arms engage the bearing outer race. Lock the arms in place and remove the bearing by operating the slide hammer as shown in Fig. R-3.

INSTALLING NEW BEARINGS AND SEALS

Before installing a new bearing, lubricate the rollers and cage with wheel bearing lubricant. Use a driving tool that "fits" the bearing race, Fig. R-4, and drive the bearing in evenly until it bottoms against the shoulder of the axle housing bore. Make sure that it seats around its

Fig. R-4. A driving tool designed for the application should be used to install rear axle bearing and seal.

complete circumference. Pack the cavity between the lips of the oil seal with high melting point wheel bearing lubricant. Position the seal on the driving tool with the lips facing the installed bearing, then start the seal into the axle housing bore. Tap the seal in place until it bottoms against the wheel bearing.

Slide the axle shaft into place, taking care that the splines of the shaft do not damage the lips of the oil seal. Engage the splines on the inner end of the axle shaft with the splines of the differential. Push in on the axle shaft to seat it in the differential assembly. Install the axle shaft "C" lock in the button end of the shaft, then push the shaft outward so that the "C" lock seats in the counterbore of the differential side gear. Insert the differential pinion shaft through the case and pinions, aligning the hole in the shaft. Install the lock screw and torque it to 20 ft. lb. Install a new carrier cover gasket, and bolt the cover in place.

REMOVING 1966-1968 REAR AXLE ASSEMBLIES

On all 1966-1968 models, raise the vehicle to a height that will permit the axle assembly to hang freely. Then, position jack stands under the frame side rails. Disconnect the hydraulic brake lines at the backing plates. Remove the brake hose and line from the carrier cover. Loosen the parking brake equalizer and remove the brake cable. Disconnect the rear universal joint and wire the propeller shaft to the side rail. Support the axle assembly with a jack.

On Chevrolet and Chevelle models, loosen the upper and lower control arm attaching bolts at the axle housing. On Chevrolet models, disconnect the tie rod at the axle. Disconnect the shock absorbers. Lower the axle assembly until the suspension reaches the end of its travel. Then, on Chevrolet models only, disconnect the spring retainer. Withdraw the springs from the vehicle.

On Chevy II and Camaro models, remove the four nuts that secure the lower spring seat to the axle housing, then remove the spring eye attaching bracket and swing the spring to the rear. On Chevrolet and Chevelle models, disconnect the control arm at the axle housing. Lower the axle assembly.

REMOVING 1969-1978 REAR AXLE ASSEMBLY

Use the following procedure to remove the rear axle assembly from a Chevrolet, Chevelle, Monte Carlo, Nova or Camaro: Raise the vehicle and place jack stands under the frame side rails. Remove the rear wheels and support the rear axle housing with a jack to remove the tension from the springs and tie rod. Disconnect the tie rod at the rear axle housing. Also disconnect the propeller shaft at the rear end.

Next, remove the axle U-bolts and spring plate nuts. Disconnect the brake hose. Remove the brake drums and disconnect the parking brake cable. Remove the brake support plate. Then, on vehicles equipped with coil springs, lower the axle housing slowly to relieve tension on the springs. Then, remove the axle assembly from the vehicle. On models equipped with leaf springs, shift the axle assembly to clear the springs when removing the assembly from the vehicle.

The Chevette rear axle assembly is similar in design to other Chevrolet axles. Typically, its axle shafts are retained by C-locks. The major

1976 line of Chevrolet cars: Top. Chevrolet Vega GT Hatchback Coupe. Center. Chevrolet Chevelle Malibu Classic Landau Coupe. Bottom. Chevrolet Monte Carlo Landau Coupe.

difference is that the Chevette has a rear axle extension housing. See illustration on page 246. This housing must be taken down before removing the rear axle housing. Raise vehicle on a hoist. Disconnect propeller shaft from companion flange, then remove shaft from transmission. Place a jack stand under front of rear axle carrier housing. Disconnect center support bracket from underbody. Disconnect extension housing flange from axle housing and carefully remove extension housing. Then, remove the rear axle housing in the usual manner.

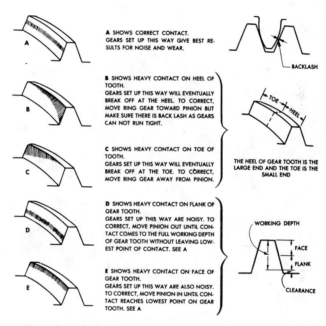

Fig. R-5. Method of obtaining correct mesh of pinion and ring gear.

OVERHAULING REAR AXLE ASSEMBLY

Special gauges and tools should be used to overhaul the differential assembly and rear axle assembly properly. Unless such equipment is available, a noisy rear axle will likely result. Without such equipment it becomes necessary to adjust the mesh of pinion and ring gear by noting the tooth contact, Fig. R-5.

Without specialized equipment an approximation of the correct pinion and ring gear mesh is obtained as follows:

First raise the rear of the car on jacks. Drain and thoroughly clean the lubricant from the gears. After the pinion and ring gears have been wiped clean, paint the ring gear teeth lightly and evenly with red lead or Prussian blue. With the parking brake applied, run the engine slowly with the transmission in first gear and then in reverse. Stop the engine and observe the marks on the gear teeth and compare them, as shown in Fig. R-5. Readjust as indicated and repeat the check with red lead until the desired tooth contact is obtained.

In case of oil leakage at the companion flange nut, pack cavity between high point pinion shaft, pinion flange and pinion washer with sealant. Rear axle oil level should be checked periodically and maintained at the level of the filler plug.

Fig. R-6. Details of Positraction rear axle (Eaton).

1-Ring gear-to-case bolt.	6-Shims.	11-Spring retainer.
2-Differential case.	7-Clutch pack guide.	12-Pinion thrust washer.
3-Side bearing.	8-Clutch disc.	13-Pinion gear.
4-Pinion lock screw.	9-Clutch plates.	14-Pinion shaft.
5-Ring gear.	10-Side gear.	15-Preload spring.

LIMITED SLIP DIFFERENTIALS

Chevrolet cars use two basic types of limited slip differentials: cone type and plate type. The Eaton Positraction unit, Fig. R-6, is plate type. The Borg Warner unit, Fig. R-7, is cone type, as is a third unit made by Dana. Limited slip differentials divide torque equally between both driving wheels under all road surface conditions, which eliminates a major amount of one-wheel slip and affords better traction.

The optionally available Positraction assembly is installed in the conventional carrier to replace the standard differential.

Rear Axle Service

Overhaul procedures for the Positraction equipped axle are for the most part the same as on a conventional axle.

Differential chatter on this device usually results from the use of incorrect lubricant. In some cases the slightest bit of incorrect lubricant is enough to cause considerable chatter. Chevrolet emphasizes the importance of using only lubricants which are specified for the Positraction unit.

Under some operating conditions, where one wheel is on excessively slippery surface, it may be necessary to apply the parking brake slightly to produce enough resistance to the spinning wheel to cause axle lockup.

As a safety precaution, always have both rear wheels jacked up if the engine is to be operated. If only one wheel is jacked up the car will move when the engine is operating and the transmission is engaged.

TROUBLE SHOOTING

EXCESSIVE BACKLASH

Loose wheel bolts. Worn universal joint. Loose propeller shaft to pinion splines. Incorrect ring gear and pinion adjustment. Worn differential gears or case. Worn axle shaft with differential gear splines.

CLUNKING NOISE ON TURNS

Excessive end play in axle shafts.

AXLE NOISE ON DRIVE

Ring gear and pinion adjustment too tight. Pinion bearings rough.

AXLE NOISE ON COAST

Ring gear and pinion adjustment too loose. Pinion bearings rough.

AXLE NOISE ON BOTH DRIVE AND COAST

Pinion bearings rough. Loose or defective differential side bearings. Damaged axle shaft bearing. Worn universal joint. Badly worn pinion and ring gear teeth. Pinion too deep in ring gear. Loose or worn wheel bearings.

AXLE LUBRICANT LEAKS

Axle shaft bearing seals leaking. Pinion shaft oil seal leaking. Differential carrier to housing gasket leaking.

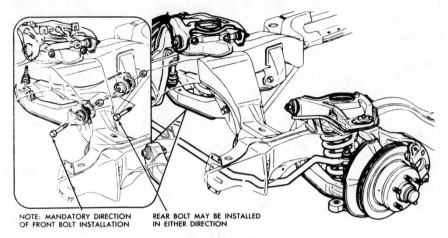

NOTE: MANDATORY DIRECTION
OF FRONT BOLT INSTALLATION

REAR BOLT MAY BE INSTALLED
IN EITHER DIRECTION

1974–1978 front suspension. Typical of Chevrolet, Chevelle, Monte Carlo and Camaro. Previous models are similar.

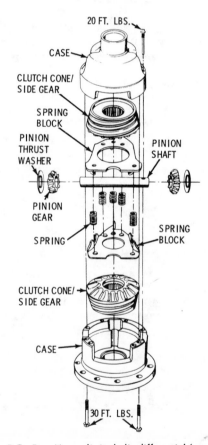

20 FT. LBS.

CASE

CLUTCH CONE/
SIDE GEAR

SPRING
BLOCK

PINION
THRUST
WASHER

PINION
SHAFT

PINION
GEAR

SPRING

SPRING
BLOCK

CLUTCH CONE/
SIDE GEAR

CASE

30 FT. LBS.

Fig. R-7. Borg-Warner limited slip differential (cone type).

SHOCK ABSORBERS AND SPRING SERVICE

In order to maintain a comfortable ride, shock absorbers must be replaced as soon as they no longer control spring rebound. In addition, worn shock absorbers will result in more rapid tire wear, as the wheels will spin when the rebound is not controlled. Of even greater importance is the fact that worn shock absorbers are dangerous, as it is extremely difficult to control a car that is bouncing up and down. Shock absorbers are not re-

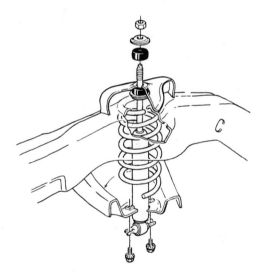

Fig. S-1. Typical front shock absorber installation, all cars except 1962–1967 Chevy II.

paired when they no longer control rebound of the car, instead the complete unit is replaced. So that rebound control is the same on both sides of the car, shock absorbers should always be replaced in pairs.

To determine whether shock absorber replacement is necessary, grasp the bumper of the vehicle and jounce it up and down. If the car continues to jounce up and down after releasing the bumper, the shock absorbers should be replaced.

CHEVROLET, CHEVELLE, CAMARO, NOVA, CORVETTE AND 1968 TO 1976 CHEVY II AND NOVA

To remove the front shock absorbers, Fig. S-1, hold the upper stem from turning with a 1/4 in. wrench. Remove upper stem retaining nut and lock washer. Next remove two bolts holding shock absorber lower pivot to lower control arm and pull shock absorber assembly and mounting out from the bottom. To install the shock absorbers on the Chevrolet, Chevelle, Camaro, Nova, Corvette and Chevy II, place the retainer and rubber grommet in place over the upper stem. Install the shock absorber fully extended up through the lower control arm and spring so that the upper stem passes through the mounting hole in the upper support arm. Install the rubber grommet, retainer and attaching nut over the shock absorber upper stem. With an open-end wrench, hold the upper stem from turning and tighten the retaining nut. Install the two bolts attaching the shock absorber lower pivot to the lower control arm and tighten.

To remove the rear shock absorber on the Chevrolet and Chevelle, raise the rear of the vehicle and support the rear axle assembly. If equipped with superlift shock absorber, disconnect air line from shock absorber. Disconnect shock absorber at upper mounting bracket by removing the two retaining bolts, Fig. S-2. Disconnect shock absorber at lower attaching bracket and remove the shock absorber.

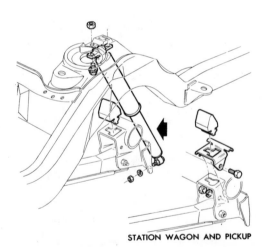

STATION WAGON AND PICKUP

Fig. S-2. Rear shock absorber mounting. (Typical)

To remove the rear shock absorbers from Camaro and Nova cars, raise the vehicle and support axle housing with adjustable jack. Then disconnect the shock absorber at the lower end and then disconnect it at the upper end and withdraw the shock absorber.

CHEVY II 1962-1967

To remove the front shock absorbers on the 1962-1967 Chevy II, Fig. S-3, first place a block between upper control arm and frame side rail. Then raise the vehicle and remove tire and wheel assembly. Disconnect lower shock absorber mounting from lower spring seat. Remove shock absorber and upper mounting bracket bolts, Fig. S-3. Lift shock absorber assembly from the vehicle.

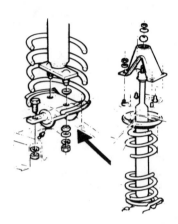

Fig. S-3. Front shock absorber mounting on 1962–1967 Chevy II.

To install the front shock absorber, assemble upper washer and rubber bushing to shock absorber rod, Fig. S-3. Assemble upper mounting bushing washer and nut to rod. Install rubber washers to shock absorber lower seat studs and insert shock absorber and upper bracket assembly to shock

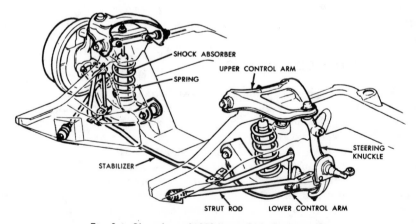

Fig. S-4. Chevrolet and 1970 Monte Carlo front suspension.

249

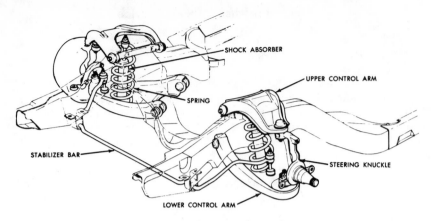

Fig. S-5. Front suspension on 1968–1972 Chevy II, 1964–1972 Chevelle, 1962–1964 Chevrolet. The 1973 suspension is similar.

absorber access hole and position to the lower spring seat. Install washers and nuts.

To remove the rear shock absorbers from a Chevy II 1962-1967, raise the vehicle and support the axle housing with adjustable jack stand. Loosen and remove shock absorber lower mounting bolt from shock absorber eye. Remove shock absorber upper mounting bracket bolts and withdraw shock absorber and brackets. Replacement is accomplished by reversing the procedure.

SPRING SERVICE

Several different types of front suspension systems are used on Chevrolet built cars. These are illustrated in Figs. S-4, S-5, S-6, and S-7.

The rear suspension system of the Chevrolet 1958-1969 is shown in Fig. S-8. The Chevelle also uses coil springs at the rear, but has a different type of control arm, Fig. S-11. Fig. S-9 shows a typical installation of leaf type springs as used on the Nova, Camaro and Chevy II.

Details of the Corvette independent suspension are illustrated in Fig. S-10.

REMOVING FRONT COIL SPRINGS

To remove a front coil spring, place vehicle on hoist and remove wheel and tire assembly. Take off shock absorber. Remove stablizer bar to lower control arm link. Remove strut rod to lower control arm attaching bolts and nuts. Remove tie rod end.

Manufacture steel tool to dimensions shown in Fig. S-5A. Install this tool through shock absorber mounting hole so notch seats over bottom spring coil and bar extends inboard and under inner bushing. Place a 5 in. wooden block between bar and bushing. With a suitable jack, lift up slightly on end of steel tool to remove tension from inner cam bolt, which can then be removed. Lower inner end of lower control arm. Tension must be released before spring can be removed from the car.

The same procedure can be used in reverse to install a spring. In the case of the 1967 Chevy II, it is necessary to use a special spring compressor to remove the spring.

REMOVING REAR COIL SPRINGS

The following procedure applies particularly to Chevrolet rear coil springs, Fig. S-8. In general, it is typical of other installations.

The procedure is as follows: Raise the rear of the vehicle and place jack stands under the frame. Use a jack to support vehicle weight at the

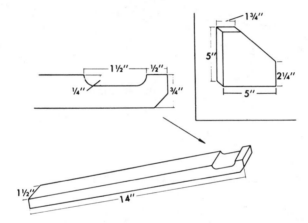

Fig. S-5A. Details of steel bar used when removing front spring.

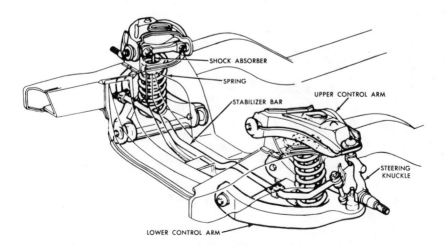

Fig. S-6. Front suspension system on 1967–1971 Camaro and 1970–1978 Nova.

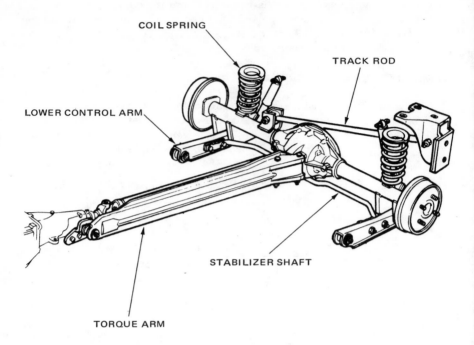

COIL SPRING

TRACK ROD

LOWER CONTROL ARM

STABILIZER SHAFT

TORQUE ARM

Fig. S-7. Details of Vega and Monza rear axle and rear suspension.

rear. Remove both rear wheels. With the car supported so the rear springs are compressed by the weight of the vehicle, proceed as follows: Disconnect both rear shock absorbers from the anchor pin lower attachment. Loosen the upper control arms rear pivot bolt but do not remove the nut.

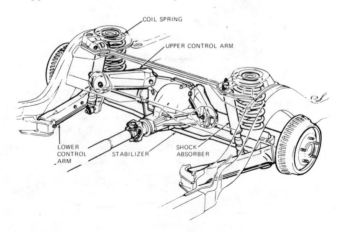

COIL SPRING

UPPER CONTROL ARM

LOWER CONTROL ARM

STABILIZER

SHOCK ABSORBER

Fig. S-8. Rear suspension on 1978 Chevrolet. (Typical)

Shock Absorbers, Spring Service

Loosen both the left and right lower control arm rear attachments, but do not disconnect from axle brackets. Remove the rear suspension tie rod from the studs on the axle tube. Lift the lower seat of both rear coil springs, slightly loosen the nut on the bolt that retains the spring and seat to the control arm. When the nut has been backed off the maximum amount permissible, all threads on the nut should still be engaged on the bolt.

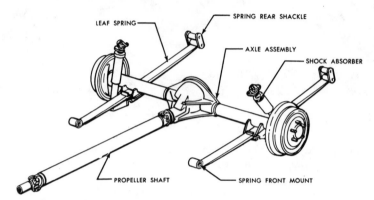

Fig. S-9. *Camaro and Nova rear suspension system. Chevy II is similar.*

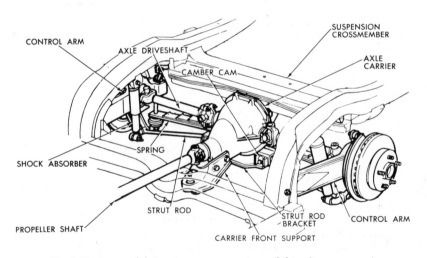

Fig. S-10. *Late model Corvette rear suspension and drive line components.*

CAUTION: Under no condition should the nut at this time be removed from the bolt in the seat of either spring.

Slowly lower the support jack that has been in place under the rear axle, thereby allowing the axle to swing down, carrying the springs out of their upper seat and providing access for spring removal. Remove the

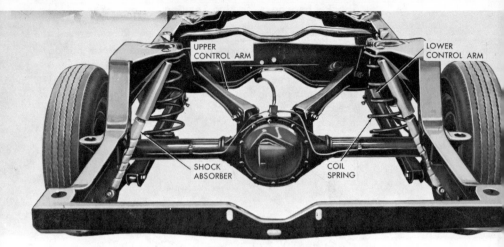

Fig. S-11. Rear suspension system of Chevelle, Monte Carlo and 1971–1972 Chevrolet. The 1973–1976 suspensions are similar.

lower spring attaching rods from each spring, then remove the springs and insulators from the vehicle.

1971-1976 Rear Coil Spring Removal: Raise vehicle on hoist, Fig. S-11. Support vehicle weight so axle can be raised or lowered. Support axle assembly with an adjustable lifting device and disconnect shock absorber at axle bracket. Shock absorber on side opposite need not be disconnected if only one spring is to be replaced. On Chevelle and Monte Carlo models, disconnect brake hydraulic line at the junction block located on the axle housing. Disconnect upper control arm at the axle. Lower axle assembly until suspension reaches end of travel. Then pry lower pigtail over vertical retainer on axle bracket and remove spring and insulator from vehicle.

LEAF SPRING REMOVAL

To remove the leaf springs on Camaro, Nova and 1962-1967 Chevy II vehicles, Fig. S-9, raise rear of vehicle sufficiently to allow axle assembly to hang freely, then support weight of the vehicle at both side rails and near front eye of spring. Raise axle assembly so that all tension is removed from the spring. Loosen and remove shock absorber lower attaching bolt. Loosen the spring eye-to-bracket retaining bolt. Remove the screw securing the spring retainer bracket to the under body. Lower axle sufficiently to permit access to spring retainer bracket and remove bracket from spring.

The spring eye bushing can be replaced without completely removing the spring from the vehicle if necessary.

Shortcuts on
WHEEL ALIGNMENT, STEERING

To do an accurate job of aligning the front wheels requires specialized equipment, and accuracy is a must if tire wear is to be kept to a minimum. In an emergency, however, approximate adjustment can be made without such equipment.

Before altering the alignment of the front wheels, make sure that you know what is causing the tire wear or other steering difficulties. In many cases the difficulty results from some easily remedied cause. Therefore, it is recommended that the following factors be checked, and corrected if necessary, prior to adjusting front wheel alignment.

1. Loose or improperly adjusted steering gear. 2. Steering gear housing loose at frame. 3. Play or excessive wear in spherical joints or steering shaft coupling. 4. Loose tie rod or steering connections. 5. Improper front spring heights. 6. Underinflated tires. 7. Unbalanced wheel and tire assembly. 8. Wheel bearings improperly adjusted. 9. Shock absorbers not operating correctly.

Many authorities recommend that tire pressure be maintained 2 lb. higher than the specified value. This increases tire life and makes the car steer easier, but at a slight sacrifice to riding comfort. Further in regard to tires, make sure the valve cap is in place as it is the cap which seals the valve and prevents leakage of air.

CHECKING THE BALL JOINTS

To check upper ball joint on 1962-1973 models, Fig. T-1, and on Chevette models, Fig. T-5a, the stud must be removed from the steering knuckle. Install a nut on the stud and measure the torque required to turn the stud in the assembly. The specified torque for a new ball stud is 3 to 10 ft. lb. If the readings are too high or too low, replace the ball stud.

Excessive wear of the lower ball joint is indicated if difficulty is experienced when lubricating the joint. If the liner has worn to a degree where the lubrication grooves have worn away, then greater than normal pressure is required to force lubricant through the joint. When this occurs, both lower joints should be replaced.

1974-1976 ball joint: If upper stud has perceptible lateral shake, or if it can be twisted in its socket with the fingers, the upper ball joint should be replaced. The lower ball joint is inspected visually with the weight of the car on the wheels. If the round nipple into which the lubrication fitting is threaded is flush or within the cover surface, the ball joint should be replaced.

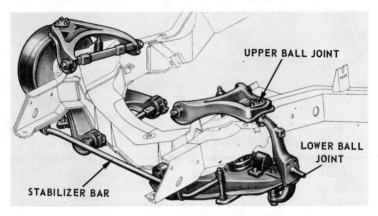

Fig. T-1. Typical front suspension system, (Corvette).

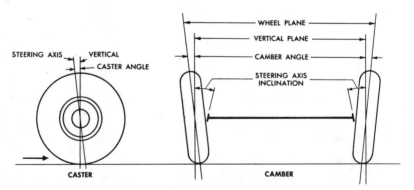

Fig. T-2. Illustrating caster and camber angles.

CASTER, CAMBER AND TOE-IN

The conditions that are included in wheel alignment are caster, camber and toe-in, together with ball joint inclination.

Camber is the amount in degrees the front wheels are tilted outward at the top from the vertical, Fig. T-2.

Toe-in is the amount in fractions of an inch that the wheels are closer together at the extreme front of the car than at the rear.

Caster is the angle of inclination, between the steering axis and the vertical, Fig. T-2. It is considered positive when the steering axis is inclined to the rear.

Toe-in is probably the most important factor affecting tire wear and can be measured to a fair degree of accuracy without specialized equipment.

Before attempting to align the front wheels, the car should always be rolled forward several feet to place the wheels in normal straight ahead running position.

An approximation of the camber angle can be made by placing the car on a level floor and then placing a large carpenter's square against the hub and tire rim. Measure the distance from the square to the rim at the top and also at the bottom. The difference in the distance between these measurements is the camber in inches. There are no factory specifications available for camber measurements of this type. However, the difference in the measurements should be no less than 1/32 in. nor more than 1/16 in. It must be emphasized that checking camber by this method is an emergency method only.

A quite accurate method of measuring toe-in without the use of special equipment is as follows: With the car on a level floor, jack up the front wheels, and with the wheels spinning hold a piece of chalk against the center of the tire tread. Then with the wheels still spinning, hold a pointed tool such as an ice pick, against the chalk mark to scribe a fine line. Do this to both front wheels. Lower the car from the jacks, and roll the car forward several feet. Then suspend a plumb bob from the scribed line at the rear of the tire and make a mark on the floor where it is contacted by the point of the plumb bob. Repeat this operation at the front of the wheel and also on both wheels. Then measure the distance between the two marks at the front of the tires and also at the back of the tires. The difference between these two measurements will be the toe-in, and obviously these

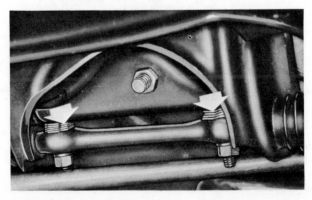

Fig. T-3. Method of adjusting caster and camber on 1970–1977 Chevrolet, 1964–1977 Chevelle, 1963–1977 Corvette, 1970–1977 Monte Carlo, 1968 Chevy II, 1969–1977 Nova and 1967–1977 Camaro.

257

measurements should be made with a high degree of accuracy. Toe-ins for the various models are given in the Specification Pages. Caster can only be measured with specialized equipment.

1970-1978 CHEVROLET, 1964-1978 CHEVELLE, 1963-1978 CORVETTE, 1970-1978 MONTE CARLO, 1968 CHEVY II, 1969-1978 NOVA, 1967-1978 CAMARO WHEEL ALIGNMENT ADJUSTMENTS

The caster and camber adjustments on these cars are made by means of shims between the upper control arm inner support shaft and the support bracket attached to the frame side rail, Fig. T-3.

The addition of shims at the front bolt, or removal of shims at the rear bolt, will decrease positive caster. One shim (1/32 in.) transferred from the rear attaching bolt to the front attaching bolt will change caster approximately one-half degree.

Adding an equal number of shims at both front and rear of the support shaft will decrease positive camber. One shim (1/32 in.) at each location will move camber approximately 1/5th degree on the Chevelle, Camaro and Nova cars; and 1/6th degree on the Corvette.

To adjust for caster and camber, loosen the upper support shaft to cross member nuts, add or subtract shims as required and retighten nuts. Caster and camber can be adjusted in one operation.

Fig. T-4. Caster adjustment on 1965–1969 Chevrolet and 1962–1967 Chevy II.

CHEVROLET 1965-1969, CHEVY II 1962-1967

The caster angle on these cars is adjusted by turning the two nuts at the front of the lower control arm strut rod, Fig. T-4. Shortening this rod will increase caster. Lengthening the rod will decrease caster.

Camber angle is adjusted by loosening the lower control arm pivot bolt and rotating the cam located on this pivot, Fig. T-5. This eccentric cam action will move lower control arm in or out, thereby varying camber.

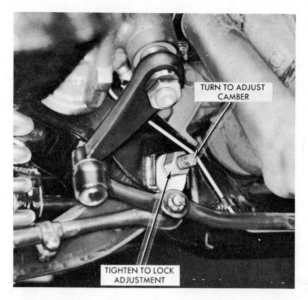

Fig. T-5. Camber adjustment on 1965–1969 Chevrolet. The 1962–1967 Chevy II is similar.

1976-1978 Chevette alignment: Desired camber is + 1/4 deg. $\pm$ 1/2 deg. To increase camber approximately 1 deg., remove upper ball joint, rotate one-half turn, then reinstall it with flat of upper flange on inboard side of control arm, Fig. T-5a. Desired caster angle is 4 1/2 deg. $\pm$ 1/2 deg. To change caster, realign washer between legs of upper control arm. Kits with 3 mm and 9 mm washers are available, Fig. T-5b.

1974-1977 VEGA, 1975-1978 MONZA: Adjust camber and caster by turning cam bolts. Adjust camber first by turning front cam. Adjust caster by turning rear cam. See Vega, Monza section, page 361.

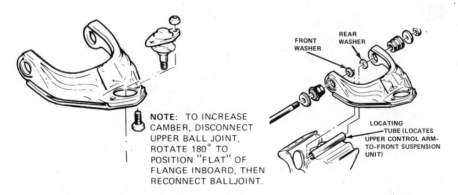

NOTE: TO INCREASE CAMBER, DISCONNECT UPPER BALL JOINT, ROTATE 180° TO POSITION "FLAT" OF FLANGE INBOARD, THEN RECONNECT BALLJOINT.

Fig. T-5a. Left. Chevette camber adjustment. Fig. T-5b. Right. Chevette caster adjustment.

STEERING AXIS INCLINATION ADJUSTMENT

Camber is the outward tilt of the wheel and steering axis inclination is the inward tilt of the steering knuckle. Camber cannot be changed without changing steering axis inclination. Correct specifications are given at the back of this book. If, with the camber correctly adjusted, steering axis inclination does not fall within the specified limits, the knuckle is bent and should be replaced.

If a new knuckle is installed, caster, camber and toe-in should be readjusted.

TOE-IN ADJUSTMENT

Toe-in is checked with the wheels in a straight ahead position. It is a difference of the distance measured between the extreme front and the distance measured between the extreme rear of both front wheels. Toe-in must be adjusted after caster and camber adjustment.

To adjust the toe-in, set the front wheels in a straight ahead position. Loosen the clamp bolts on one tie rod and adjust for the proper toe-in, as given in the specifications. Then loosen the clamp bolts on the other tie rod and turn both tie rods the same amount, and in the same direction, to place the steering gear on its high point, and position the steering wheel in its straight ahead position.

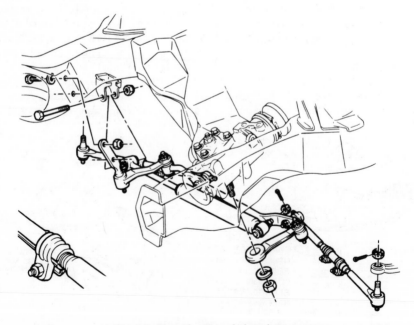

Fig. T-6. Typical steering linkage layout.

After adjusting toe-in, care must be exercised to avoid stabilizer link bolt interference.

On the Chevrolet, position the inboard tie rod clamp slot straight down to 90 deg. rearward to avoid stabilizer link bolt interference. Position outboard tie rod clamp slots as near to tie rod sleeve slots as possible.

On the Chevelle, position all the tie rod clamps with slots straight down to 45 deg. rearward to avoid interference. Bolt heads must be positioned to rear side of clamp.

On the Nova and Camaro, position the inboard tie rod clamps with open end of clamp and slot in line. Clamp open end must be within 15 deg. either side of tie rod sleeve slot. Position relative to ground is unimportant. Position outer clamps open end upward, with bolt top facing the rear and the bolt position 30 deg. either side of horizontal. Position relative to slot is unimportant.

Fig. T-7. Method of freeing ball stud.

SERVICING STEERING LINKAGE

A typical steering linkage is shown in Fig. T-6. It will be noted that each tie rod is of three-piece construction, consisting of the tie rod and two tie rod end assemblies. The ends are threaded into the rod and locked with clamps. Right and left-hand threads are provided to facilitate toe-in adjustment and steering gear centering. Replacement of the tie rod ends should be made when excessive up-and-down motion is evident, or if any lost motion or end play at ball end of stud exists.

To remove tie rod ends, first remove cotter pins from ball studs and remove castellated nuts. To remove outer ball stud, tap on steering arm on tie rod end with a hammer while using a heavy hammer or similar tool as a backing, Fig. T-7. If necessary pull downward on tie rod to remove from steering arm.

Remove inner ball stud from relay rod using same procedure.

To remove tie rod ends from tie rods loosen clamp bolts and unscrew end assemblies.

Installation of the tie rod ends is accomplished by first lubricating the tie rod threads with EP chassis lubricant, and install ends on the tie rod making sure both ends are threaded at equal distance from the tie rod. Make sure that threads on ball stud and in ball stud nuts are perfectly clean and smooth. Install neoprene seals on ball studs.

If threads are not clean and smooth, ball studs may turn in tie rod ends when attempting to tighten nut.

Install ball studs in steering arms and relay rod. Install ball stud nut, and install cotter pins. Lubricate tie rod ends. Adjust toe-in as described previously.

Before locking clamp bolts on the rods, make sure that the tie rod ends are in alignment with their ball studs (each ball joint is in the center of its travel). If the tie rod is not in alignment with the studs, binding will result.

REPLACING THE STABILIZER BAR

Place the vehicle on a hoist and support both front wheels. Disconnect the stabilizer bar, Fig. T-1, from the lower control arm. Remove the stabilizer bar brackets from the frame and remove the stabilizer. Remove the stabilizer link bolts, spacers and rubber bushings from the lower control arms. Inspect the rubber stabilizer link bushings and stabilizer insulator bushings for aging and wear. Replace these bushings if necessary.

If new insulators are necessary, coat stabilizer with recommended rubber lubricant and slide frame bushings into position. Insert stabilizer brackets over bushings and connect to frame. Connect stabilizer rings to link bolts on lower control arms. Then torque bracket bolts and link nuts to 15 ft. lb.

HOW TO BALANCE WHEELS

If specialized wheel balancing equipment is not available, an emergency job which is fairly satisfactory can be done by mounting the wheel to be balanced on the front wheel spindle. The procedure is to first back off on the brake adjustment until the wheel rotates freely. If the wheel bearing adjustment is tight it may be necessary to loosen that adjustment also. With the wheel in position on the spindle, allow it to rotate until it comes to a stop. The heavy area of the wheel will be at the bottom. Temporarily attach a wheel balance weight to the rim at the top. Again allow the wheel to rotate. If the weighted area of the wheel now stops at the bottom, the

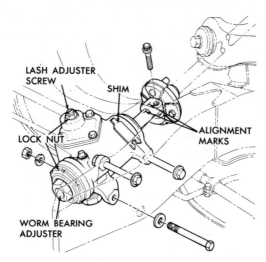

Fig. T-8. Location of steering gear adjustments.

weight is too heavy. Change the weight until the wheel always stops in a different position.

If, for example, it takes three ounces to balance the wheel, take a 1-1/2 oz. weight and place it on the inside of the rim, and another 1-1/2 oz. weight and place it on the outside of the rim.

ADJUSTING THE STEERING GEAR

Before any adjustments are made on the steering gear, make a careful check of the front end alignment, wear of the steering linkage, shock absorbers, wheel balance, and tire pressure. After these have been corrected, adjust the steering gear as follows:

Remove the pitman arm nut and mark the relation of the pitman arm position to the sector shaft. Remove the pitman arm.

Loosen the pitman shaft lash adjuster screw lock nut and turn the adjuster screw a few turns in the counterclockwise direction, Fig. T-8. This removes the load imposed on the worm bearings by the close meshing of rack and sector teeth. Turn steering wheel gently in one direction until stopped by gear, then back away about one turn.

Do not turn steering wheel hard against stops when steering relay rod is disconnected as damage to the ball guides may result.

Disconnect wiring harness at column connector. On vehicles with regular steering, check preload by removing horn button or shroud and applying a torque wrench with a 3/4 in. socket on the steering wheel nut. Total steering gear preload should be 14 in. lbs.

On vehicles with tilt steering columns, it will be necessary to disconnect the steering coupling to obtain a torque reading of the steering column. This reading should then be subtracted from any reading taken on the gear. On vehicles with telescopic steering columns, check preload by removing the horn button and applying torque wrench with a Phillips head adaptor socket on the star-headed screw in the center of the steering wheel.

To adjust worm bearings, loosen worm bearing adjuster lock nut and turn worm bearing adjuster, Fig. T-8, until there is no perceptible end play in the worm. Check pull at steering wheel, readjusting if necessary to obtain proper pull. Tighten lock nut and recheck pull. If the gear feels "lumpy" after adjustment of worm bearings, the bearings are probably damaged.

After proper adjustment of the worm is obtained, and ball mounting bolts securely tightened, adjust lash adjuster screw, Fig. T-8. First, turn the steering wheel gently from one stop all the way to the other, carefully counting the total number of turns. Then turn wheel back exactly half way to center position. Turn lash adjuster screw clockwise to take out all lash in gear teeth and tighten lock nut.

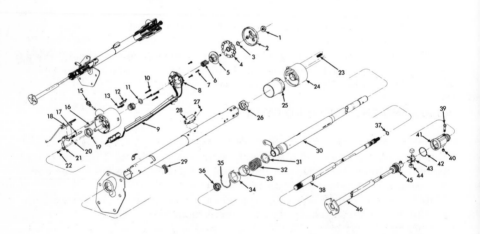

Fig. T-9. Standard steering column for 1971-1978 models. *(Typical)*

1—Shaft nut.	17—Shaft lock bolt.	33—Lower bearing adapter.
2—Cover.	18—Switch rod and rack assembly.	34—Lower bearing reinforcement.
3—Lock plate retaining ring.	19—Thrust cap.	35—Retainer.
4—Lock plate.	20—Shaft lock bolt washer.	36—Lower bearing.
5—Cancelling cam.	21—Shaft lever detent plate.	37—Shaft stop ring.
6—Bearing preload spring.	22—Detent plate screws.	38—Steering shaft.
7—Turn signal screws.	23—Shift lever spring.	39—Pot joint bolt.
8—Turn signal switch.	24—Gearshift lever housing.	40—Nut.
9—Protector cover.	25—Shift shroud.	41—Pot joint cover.
10—Turn signal housing screws.	26—Gearshift housing bearing.	42—Seal retaining ring.
11—Bearing thrust washer.	27—Ignition switch screws.	43—Bearing spring.
12—Key warning switch.	28—Ignition switch.	44—Bearing blocks.
13—Switch clip.	29—Neutral safety or back-up switch retainers.	45—Pot joint seal.
14—Turn signal housing.	30—Shift tube.	46—Intermediate shaft.
15—Ignition switch selector.	31—Thrust spring washer.	
16—Switch rack preload spring.	32—Shift tube thrust washer.	

STEERING WHEEL REMOVAL

To remove the regular production steering wheel, first disconnect battery ground cable. Pull out horn button cap or center ornament and retainer. Remove three screws from receiving cup. Remove the receiving cup, Belleville spring, bushing and pivot ring. Remove the steering wheel nut and washer. Using a special tool which will engage the threaded holes provided in the steering wheel, the wheel can then be pulled.

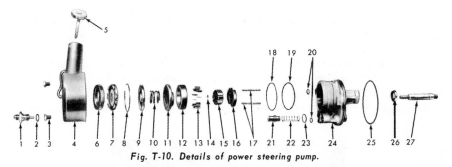

Fig. T-10. Details of power steering pump.

On deluxe type steering wheels, first disconnect the battery ground cable and remove the four attaching screws on underside of steering wheel. Lift steering wheel shroud from wheel and then pull horn wires from cancelling cam tower. Remove steering wheel nut and washer and the wheel can then be pulled with a special tool with anchor screws which can be threaded into the holes provided in the steering wheel.

ENERGY ABSORBING STEERING COLUMN

The energy absorbing steering column in Fig. T-9 is designed to absorb forces resulting from collision. The mast jacket shift tube and steering shaft are designed to collapse under various front impact conditions.

Several different types are used, depending on the type of transmission used. The 1968 model was of the collapsible steel mesh design, while in the 1969 design, Fig. T-9, the jacket features a ball bearing energy absorbing device. Ball bearings imbedded in plastic are pressed between the upper and lower jackets. The steering shaft and shift tube collapse under predetermined loads by sheering injected plastic pins. The 1969 columns also include the ignition lock, ignition switch and antitheft system. The ignition key cannot be removed unless the transmission is in "park" on automatic, or "reverse" on manual shift transmission.

When servicing the energy absorbing steering column, several precautions are necessary.

The outer mast jacket shift tube, steering shaft and instrument panel mounting bracket are designed as energy absorbing units. Because of the design of these components, it is necessary to handle the column with care when performing any serious operation. Avoid hammering, jarring, dropping or leaning on any portion of the column.

When reassembling the column components, use only the specified screws, nuts and bolts and tighten to specified torque. Care should be exercised in using over-length screws or bolts, as they may prevent a portion of the column from compressing under impact.

POWER STEERING SERVICE

Details of the power steering pump are shown in Fig. T-10. While replacement parts are available, most mechanics prefer to replace the entire unit.

It is most important that the correct belt tension be maintained. The belt is correctly adjusted when a 15 lb. force applied to the center of the belt will produce a deflection of 1/2 to 3/4 in., Fig. T-11. To bleed the hydraulic steering system, proceed as follows: Fill oil reservoir to proper

Fig. T-11. Method of adjusting tension of steering pump belt.

level and let oil remain undisturbed for at least two minutes. Start the engine and run only for about two seconds. Add oil if necessary. Repeat above procedure until oil level remains constant during running of engine.

Next raise front end of vehicle so that the wheels are off the ground. Increase the engine speed to approximately 1500 rpm. Turn the wheels right and left, slightly contacting the wheel stops. Add oil to the hydraulic system, if necessary. Lower the car and turn wheels right and left on the ground. Again check the oil level and refill as required. If oil is extremely foamy, allow the vehicle to stand a few minutes with engine off, and repeat the above procedure.

TROUBLE SHOOTING

HARD STEERING

Low air pressure in tires. Lack of lubrication. Improper wheel alignment. Sagging chassis springs. Bent wheel or spindle. Broken wheel bearings. Tight spherical joints. Incorrect steering gear adjustment. Tie rod ends out of alignment.

FRONT WHEEL SHIMMY

Under-inflated tires. Broken or loose wheel bearings. Worn spherical joints. Unbalanced wheels. Steering gear loose. Tie rod ball loose. Loose wheel lugs. Bent wheel. Incorrect wheel alignment.

EXCESSIVE TIRE WEAR

Wheels out of balance. High speed cornering. Incorrect air pressure in tires. Defective shock absorbers. Failure to rotate tires. Grabbing brakes. Excessive acceleration. Incorrect wheel alignment. Violent brake applications.

HARD RIDING

Excessive tire pressure. Seized shock absorber.

ROAD WANDER

Under-inflated tires. Lack of lubrication. Tight steering gear. Incorrect toe-in. Incorrect caster or camber. Worn tire rod ends. Loose relay rod. Worn or incorrectly adjusted steering gear. Loose steering gear housing.

NOISE IN FRONT WHEELS

Loose wheel lugs. Loose or broken brake shoe return spring. Defective front wheel bearings. Scored brake shoes. Lack of lubrication. Blister or bump on tire.

WHEEL TRAMP

Wheel assembly out of balance. Blister or bumps on tire. Defective shock absorbers.

POWER STEERING

HARD STEERING

Power drive belt loose. Low oil level in reservoir.

LOW OIL PRESSURE

Generator drive belt loose. Low oil level in reservoir. Pump defective. Pressure loss in steering control valve. Pressure loss in power cylinder. External or internal oil leaks.

POOR CENTERING OR RECOVERY ON TURNS

Valve spool sticking in valve housing. Incorrect worm thrust bearing adjustment. Sticky cylinder assembly.

OIL PUMP NOISY

Incorrect oil level. Air in system. Reservoir air vent plugged. Dirt in pump. Worn pump parts.

OIL LEAKS

Loose line connections. Faulty "O" ring seals. Hose leaks. Leaking housing. Cylinder seal leaking.

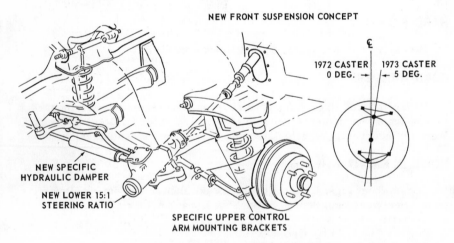

NEW FRONT SUSPENSION CONCEPT

1972 CASTER 0 DEG. → | ← 1973 CASTER 5 DEG.

NEW SPECIFIC HYDRAULIC DAMPER

NEW LOWER 15:1 STEERING RATIO

SPECIFIC UPPER CONTROL ARM MOUNTING BRACKETS

Modifications made in front suspension of 1973 cars.

Quick Service on
BRAKES

In 1963 the Bendix self-adjusting brake, Fig. U-1, was adopted as standard equipment on Chevrolet-built cars. In 1966 four wheel disc brakes of the dual piston type, Fig. U-2, were made standard equipment on the Corvette and optional equipment on the front wheels of other

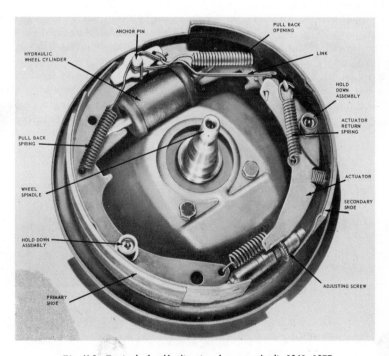

Fig. U-1. Typical of self-adjusting drum type brake 1963–1977.

Chevrolet-built cars. Starting in 1969, the single piston sliding caliper brake, Fig. U-3, was made available for front wheel installation on Chevrolet, Chevelle, Camaro, Monte Carlo and Nova models.

Fig. U-2. Details of four piston, fixed caliper disc brake: 1–Caliper bolts. 2–Bleeder valve. 3–Caliper half. 4–Piston spring. 5–Seal. 6–Assembly. 7–Piston boot. 8–Brake shoes. 9–"O" rings. 10–Caliper half. 11–Retaining pin. 12–Cotter pin.

SERVICING SELF-ADJUSTING DRUM BRAKES

Self-adjusting drum brakes, Fig. U-1, are so designed that the adjusters operate only when the brakes are applied when the vehicle is moving backwards. Although the brakes are self-adjusting, an initial adjustment usually is necessary after the brakes have been relined or whenever the length of the adjusting screw has been changed. The final adjustment is made by using the self-adjusting feature.

To make an initial adjustment, it may be necessary to first retract the adjusting screw. To gain access to the adjusting screw star wheel, knock out the lanced area in the web of the brake drum, using a chisel or similar tool. (This may have been done on a previous relining job.)

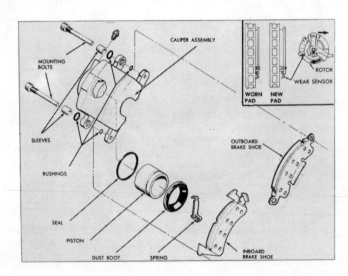

Fig. U-3. Single piston sliding caliper disc brake is available as optional equipment as front brakes. Earlier models did not have wear sensor.

Brake Service

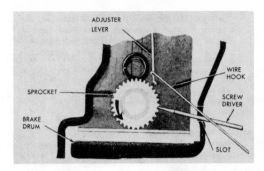

Fig. U-4. Making a manual adjustment on a self-adjusting brake.

Release the actuator from the star wheel by lifting with a small screwdriver or with a wire hook, Fig. U-4. Back off the star wheel with a brake adjusting tool or a screwdriver. Press down on the screwdriver handle to retract the screw and raise up on the handle to expand the screw. Turn the star wheel until there is a slight drag as the wheel of the car is being turned. Then turn the star wheel 1-1/4 turns to retract the brake shoes.

If the lanced area is knocked out, be sure that metal pieces are removed from the drum, then install a new hole cover to prevent contamination of the brakes. Also make sure that the drums are installed in their original position with the drum locating tang in line with the locating hole in the wheel hub.

Make a final adjustment by making numerous forward and reverse stops until a satisfactory brake pedal height results.

REMOVING THE FRONT DRUMS

To remove the front brake drums on Chevrolet, Chevelle, Chevy II, Monte Carlo, Camaro and Nova cars, first jack up the front wheels and remove the wheel cover. Then remove the grease cup from the hub, Fig. U-5. Remove the cotter pin and nut from the end of the wheel spindle. In some cases, it will be necessary to back off on the adjustment of the brakes to provide clearance so the drums can be removed. The procedure for backing off on the adjustment is given in the preceeding paragraphs.

REMOVING THE REAR BRAKE DRUMS

To remove the rear brake drums on Chevrolet, Chevelle, Chevy II, Monte Carlo, Camaro and Nova cars, first remove the wheel covers and the wheels. Loosen check nuts at parking brake equalizer sufficiently to remove all tension from the parking brake cable, Fig. U-6. Remove the spring clips from the wheel studs or, in some cases, the small bolt holding the brake drum to the axle shaft flange. Pull the drum from the studs. In some cases, it may be necessary to back off on the adjustment of the brake

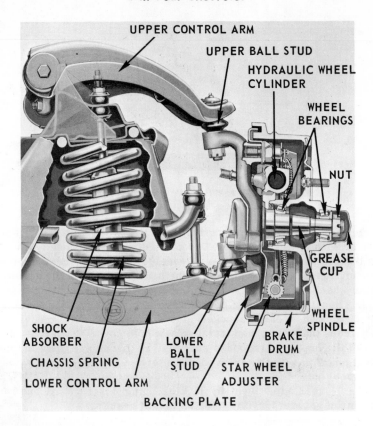

Fig. U-5. *Details of brake and front suspension system. (Camaro)*

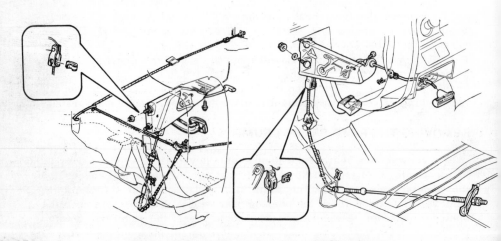

Fig. U-6. *Parking brake system on late model Chevrolet cars.*

to provide additional shoe to drum clearance.

When replacing the drums on late models, make sure the drums are installed in the same position as when removed, with the drum locating tang in line with the locating hole in the drum hub. Do not depress brake pedal while drums are removed.

REMOVING BRAKE SHOES

To remove the brake shoes, first pull the drums as previously described. Then unhook brake shoe, pull back springs from anchor pin and link end, Fig. U-7. A special tool is shown in the illustration. However, a heavy screwdriver can be used as a lever. Remove actuator return spring and link. Remove hold-down pins and springs, Fig. U-8. Remove actuator assembly, Fig. U-1.

Fig. U-7. Unhooking the pull back springs using a special tool.
A heavy screwdriver can also be used.

The actuator, pivot and override spring are an assembly. It is not recommended that they be disassembled for service purposes unless they are broken or otherwise damaged. Separate the brake shoes by removing the adjusting screw and spring. Mark shoe and lining positions if they are to be reinstalled. On rear brakes, remove parking brake lever from secondary brake shoe.

INSPECTION OF BRAKE SHOES

Clean all dirt from the brake drum and backing plate. Use care to prevent dirt from getting into front wheel bearings. Inspect brake drums for

Fig. U-8. Removing the hold down springs.

roughness or scoring, Fig. U-9, and out-of-round, Fig. U-10. Light scratches will not affect brake operation.

Some authorities recommend drum reconditioning if out-of-round exceeds .006 in., others set the limit at 0.010 in. Automotive machine shops have the necessary equipment for reconditioning brake drums.

Inspect Brake Lining: Brakes should be relined when the lining is worn

Fig. U-9. Badly scored brake drums should be reconditioned or replaced.

Fig. U-10. If diameter of brake drum is more than .060 in. oversize, it should be replaced.

Fig. U-11. When brake lining becomes deeply scored, it should be replaced.

to 1/32 in. of the rivet heads which attach the lining to the brake shoes. In the case of bonded (cemented) lining, new shoes should be installed when the lining is worn to 1/16 in. of the shoe platform. Another reason for relining brake shoes is when they become deeply scored, Fig. U-11.

Wheel Cylinder Inspection: Carefully pull lower edge of external wheel cylinder boots from the cylinders to note whether interior is wet with brake fluid. Excessive fluid indicates the wheel cylinder should be reconditioned or replaced. In the case of internal boots, pull a small part of the boot out of the cylinder. If excessive fluid is noted, the cylinder should be reconditioned or replaced.

Brake Flange Plates: Check attaching bolts of brake flange plates (backing plate) to be sure they are tight. Clean all rust and dirt from shoe contact surfaces on flange plate, using fine emery cloth. Apply a light coating of silicone type lubricant to all contact surfaces.

INSTALLATION OF NEW BRAKE SHOES

Before installing new brake shoes and lining, carefully examine lining to make sure there are no nicks or burrs on bonding material. Also check the shoe edge where contact is made with brake flange plate and on any of the contact surfaces. Keep hands clean while handling shoes. Do not permit oil or grease to come in contact with the brake lining or on the brake surface of the brake drum. When working on rear brakes, lubricate parking brake cable.

On rear brakes only, lubricate fulcrum end of brake lever with brake lubricant, then attach lever to secondary shoe. Make sure that lever moves freely. Put a light coating of brake lubricant on pads on flange plate (backing plate) and the threads of the adjusting screw.

Make sure adjusting screw is clean and correctly lubricated. Connect brake shoes together with adjusting screw spring, then place adjusting screw socket and nut in position. Make sure that the proper adjusting screw is used ("L" for left side of vehicle and "R" for right side of vehicle).

The star wheel must be installed with the star wheel nearest to the secondary shoe and the adjusting screw spring inserted to prevent interference with the star wheel. Make sure right hand thread adjusting screw is on left side of car and left hand thread adjusting screw is on right side of car. Make certain star wheel lines up with adjusting hole in brake backing plate. On rear wheels, connect parking brake cable to lever.

Secure the primary brake shoe (short lining-faces forward) first, with the hold-down pin and spring, using special tool or a pair of pliers, Fig. U-8. At the same time, engage the shoes with the wheel cylinder connecting links.

Install and secure the actuator assembly. Attach the secondary shoe by means of the hold-down pin and spring, using a pair of needle nose pliers. On the rear wheels, position the parking brake strut and strut spring. Install the guide plate over the anchor pin. Install the wire link. Take care not to hook the wire link over the anchor pin stud with the regular spring hook tool.

Fasten the wire link to the actuator assembly first, then place it over the anchor pin stud by hand while holding the adjuster assembly in the full down position. Install the actuator return spring. Caution: do not pry actuator lever to install return spring. Ease it into place, using the end of a screwdriver or other suitable flat tool.

If the old pull back (return) springs are nicked, distorted or weak, install new springs. Hook the pull back springs in the shoes, Fig. U-7. Then install the spring from the primary shoe over the anchor pin, and install the spring from the secondary shoe over the wire link end.

After completing installation, make certain the actuator lever functions easily by operating the self-adjusting feature.

Follow the procedure for all wheels. Adjust brakes as previously described.

RECONDITIONING BRAKE DRUMS

Chevrolet cautions that a brake drum more than .006 in. out of round will result in rough brake applications and should be refinished. This condition also makes accurate brake clearance adjustment impossible. Chevrolet service brake drums have a maximum diameter dimension cast into them. This diameter is the maximum wear limit and not a refinish diameter. Do not refinish a brake drum that will not meet the following specifications.

Original Diameter	Maximum Refinish Diameter	Replacement Discard Diameter
9.500 in.	9.560 in.	9.590 in.
11.000 in.	11.060 in.	11.090 in.
12.000 in.	12.060 in.	12.090 in.

SERVICING DISC BRAKES

Chevrolet uses two different types of disc brakes. The dual piston type disc brake, Fig. U-2, is used as standard equipment on all four wheels of the Corvette and some Camaro models. It is also used as optional equipment on the front wheels of 1966-1968 Chevrolet, Chevelle, Chevy II and Nova cars. In 1969-1971, a single piston, sliding caliper brake, Figs. U-3 and U-14, was available for front brakes on these same cars. In 1972 the

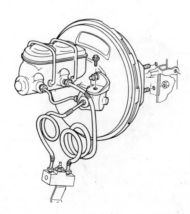

Fig. U-12. Pressure regulating valve on disc brake system.

single piston disc brake was standard equipment on the complete line, except the Vega which has a disc brake of a slightly different type.

DUAL PISTON DISC BRAKE

The dual piston disc brake, Fig. U-2, consists of a fixed caliper, splash shield, mounting bracket, and rotating disc. The caliper assembly contains four pistons and two shoe and lining assemblies. A seal and dust boot are installed in each piston, with a piston spring in the caliper cylinder bore beneath each piston, Fig. U-2. A retaining pin extends through each caliper half and both shoes to hold the shoes and lining in position in the caliper. The disc, which has a series of air vent louvers to provide cooling, is mounted on the front wheel hub.

The Corvette heavy duty option includes a pressure regulator valve, Fig. U-12, mounted in the rear brake line just below the main cylinder. The valve regulates the hydraulic pressure to the rear brakes resulting in simultaneous braking balance between the front and rear brake systems. This valve guards against premature lock-up of rear wheels when brakes are applied.

Shoes with bonded linings should be replaced when the lining is worn to approximately 1/16 in. of thickness. Shoes with linings retained by rivets should be replaced when the lining is worn to approximately 1/32 in. thickness over the rivet heads. To replace the brake shoes on this fixed type caliper disc brake, first siphon two-thirds of the brake fluid from the main cylinder reservoir. If fluid is not removed, insertion of the new full thickness lining will force the pistons back into the housings, displacing fluid into the master cylinder. This will cause the main cylinder to overflow. Do not drain the reservoirs completely or air will be pumped into the system.

Raise the car and remove the wheels. Remove and discard the cotter pin from the inboard end of the shoe retaining pin and slide out the re-

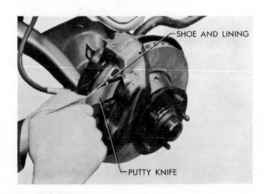

Fig. U-13. Installing brake shoes on fixed caliper disc brake.

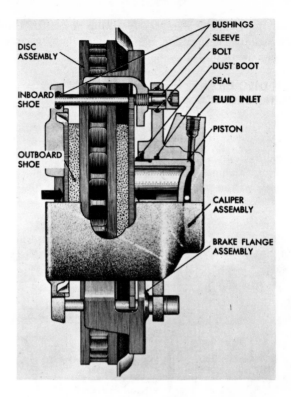

Fig. U-14. Details of sliding caliper disc brake.

taining pin. On Corvette heavy-duty disc brakes, two retaining pins must be removed, one on each end of the caliper assembly. Remove the inboard shoe by pulling up.

Insert the new shoe with lining in position. Use a putty knife to push each piston back as the shoe is inserted, as shown in Fig. U-13. Replace the outboard shoe as described above. When both caliper shoes have been replaced, install the shoe retaining pin throughout outboard caliper half, outboard shoe, inboard shoe and inboard caliper half. Insert a new 3/32 x 5/8 plated cotter pin through the retaining pin and bend back ends of cotter pin.

Repeat above procedure on each wheel where shoes are to be replaced. Refill master cylinder to fluid level and if necessary bleed brake system.

To remove the brake caliper, place car on hoist and remove wheels and disconnect hydraulic brake lining, taping the open tube to prevent entrance of foreign material.

Remove pin and shoe assembly from caliper. Identify inboard and outboard shoe if they are to be reused. Remove the end of the brake hose at bracket by removing U-shape retainer from the hose fitting and withdraw the hose from bracket. The caliper assembly can then be removed by removing the two hex-head bolts.

SINGLE PISTON DISC BRAKE SHOE AND LINING SERVICE

Brake linings should be inspected any time the wheels are removed. Check both ends of the outboard shoe by looking in at each end of the caliper. Maximum wear occurs at the ends of the caliper. At the same time, check lining thickness of the inboard shoe by looking down through the inspection hole at the top of the caliper, Fig. U-14 and U-15.

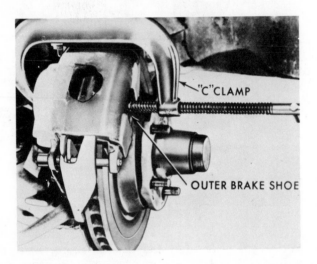

Fig. U-15. Using a C-clamp to aid in pushing back the piston.

If wheels have not been removed, brake pads should be inspected every 12 months or 12,000 miles, whichever occurs first. More frequent checks should be made if driving conditions are severe. Brake pads should be replaced whenever the thickness of any lining is worn within 1/32 in. of the shoe, or rivet head, whichever is applicable.

The outboard shoes have ears near the outer edge which are bent at right angles to the shoe. The top ends of the shoe have looped ears with holes in them which the caliper retaining bolts fit through. The large tab at the bottom of the shoe is bent over at a right angle and fits the cut-out in the inboard section of the caliper. The inboard shoe and lining assembly has ears on the top ends which fit over the caliper retaining bolts. A special spring inside the hollow piston supports the bottom edge of the inboard shoe.

Brake Service

A spring steel scraper, known as the wear sensor, is riveted to the rear edge of each inner brake shoe, Fig. U-3. When the shoe lining has worn to within .030 in. of the rivet heads, the face of the sensor contacts the brake rotor and produces a high frequency squeal. This warning occurs whenever the wheel is rotated. However, if lining wear continues beyond the point at which the linings should be replaced, the warning sound may also cease.

REMOVAL OF DISC BRAKE PADS

When servicing the master brake cylinder, first remove the cover and note level of fluid. If reservoir is more than 1/3 full, it is necessary to syphon enough fluid to bring the level to 1/3 full. This step is needed to prevent overflow of the reservoir when the caliper piston is pushed back into its bore. Discard the fluid that is removed.

Raise the vehicle and remove the front wheels. Push the piston back into its bore by using a C-clamp, as shown in Fig. U-15. Remove the two mounting bolts which attach the caliper to the support, Fig. U-16. Lift the caliper from the disc.

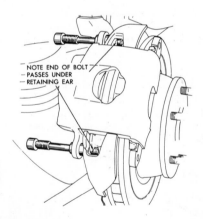

NOTE END OF BOLT PASSES UNDER RETAINING EAR

Fig. U-16. Removing sliding caliper from disc brake.

Remove the inboard shoe. Dislodge the outboard shoe, and position the caliper on the front suspension arm so that the brake hose will not support the weight of the caliper. Mark the position of the disc pads if the same pads are to be reinstalled.

Remove the shoe support spring from the piston. Remove the two sleeves from the inboard ears of the caliper. Withdraw the four rubber bushings from the grooves in each of the caliper ears. Thoroughly clean the holes and bushing grooves in the caliper ears, and wipe any dirt from the mounting bolts.

CAUTION: Do not use any abrasives on bolts as that may damage plating. If the bolts are damaged or corroded, they should be replaced.

Examine the inside of the caliper for evidence of fluid leakage. If any leakage is present, overhaul the caliper. Wipe the inside of the caliper clean, and also the exterior of the dust boot. Check the boot for cuts and other damage.

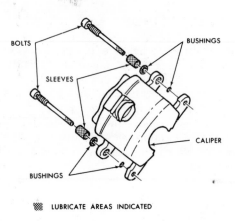

Fig. U-17. Lubricating points on single-piston caliper brake.

CAUTION: Do not use compressed air to clean inside of caliper since it could cause the boot to become unseated.

If original seat pads are being reinstalled, they must be installed in their original positions. Lubricate new sleeves, new rubber bushings,

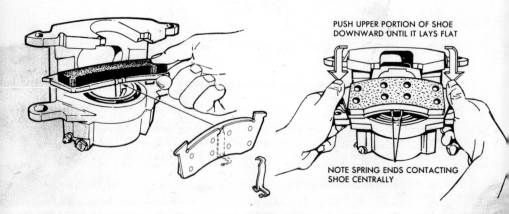

Fig. U-18. Left. Installing support spring. Fig. U-19. Right. Installing shoe to caliper.

bushing grooves and ends of the mounting bolts, using a silicone type lubricant, Fig. U-17. It is essential that new sleeves and rubber bushing be used, and be sure to follow the lubricating instructions to insure proper functioning of the sliding caliper design.

Install the new rubber bushings in the caliper ears. Install the new sleeves in the inboard ears of the caliper. Position the sleeve so that the end toward the shoe and lining assembly is flush with the machined surface of the ear.

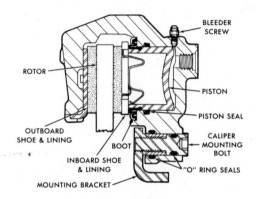

Fig. U-19a. Details of 1976 Chevette front disc brakes.

Install shoe support spring and inboard shoe in center of piston cavity, ig. U-18. Push down until shoe lays flat against caliper, Fig. U-19. osition outboard shoe in caliper with ears at top of shoe, over caliper ars, and engage tab at bottom of shoe in caliper cutout.

With shoes installed, lift up caliper and rest bottom edge of outboard ning on outer edge of brake disc to make sure no clearance exists be- ween tab at bottom of outboard shoe and caliper abutment. Position aliper over brake disc, aligning hole in caliper ears with holes in nounting bracket. Make sure brake hose is not twisted or kinked.

Start caliper mounting bracket bolts through sleeves in inboard aliper ears and through mounting bracket. Make sure ends of bolts pass nder retaining ears on inboard shoe. Push mounting bolts through to ngage holes in outboard shoes and outboard caliper ears, threading olts into mounting bracket. Torque mounting bolts to 35 ft. lb.

Pump brake pedal to seat linings against rotors. Using arc jointed liers, Fig. U-20, bend both upper ears of outboard shoe until no radial learance exists between shoe and caliper housing.

Reinstall front wheels. Lower vehicle. Add brake fluid to within 1/4 in. of top of master cylinder reservoir. Pump brake pedal. Do not move vehicle until a firm brake pedal is obtained. Then, recheck level of luid in master cylinder.

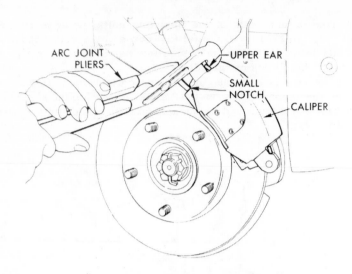

Fig. U-20. Bending outboard shoe upper ears.

1976 Chevette brakes: Front disc brakes are single-piston type. The caliper is retained on its mounting bracket by a single bolt, a sleeve and bushings. No adjustment is required. Details of the Chevette disc brake are shown in Fig. U-19a. Drum brakes are used at the rear. Adjustment is automatic.

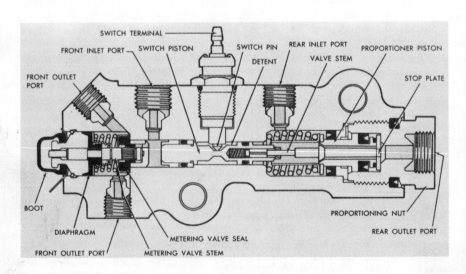

Fig. U-21. Details of combination valve.

COMBINATION VALVE

The combination valve combines the metering valve, the failure warning switch and the proportioner into a single assembly, Fig. U-21. It is installed on all disc brake applications except the Corvette. The metering valve holds off front disc brake applications until the rear brake shoes contact the drums. The failure warning switch is activated if either front or rear brake systems fail. The proportioner improves front-to-rear brake balance at high deceleration. *The proportioner does not operate during brake stops. In case of failure of any of these functions, replace the combination valve. Whenever the valve is removed or replaced, bleed the brake system. The combination valve is mounted either on the frame side rail or under the master cylinder. This valve must be held open whenever the brakes are bled. See instructions on bleeding.

BRAKE DISTRIBUTION SWITCH

The brake distribution switch, Fig. U-22, is used on all front drum brake systems and on the Corvette four wheel disc brake system. The switch is a pressure differential type, designed to light a brake warning light on the instrument panel if either the front or rear hydraulic system fails. The hydraulic brake tubes from the master cylinder outlet ports are connected to the warning light switch.

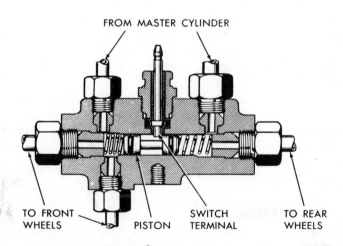

FROM MASTER CYLINDER

TO FRONT WHEELS   SWITCH TERMINAL   TO REAR WHEELS
                PISTON

Fig. U-22. Brake distribution switch in "failed" position.

When hydraulic pressure in both front and rear systems is equal, the switch piston remains centered and does not contact the terminal in the switch cylinder bore. If pressure fails in one of the systems, hydraulic pressure moves the piston toward the inoperative side, Fig. U-22. The shoulder of the piston then contacts the switch terminal to provide a ground for the warning light circuit and light the warning light. The switch is nonadjustable. If defective, it must be replaced.

Fig. U-23. Adjusting parking brake shoe on fixed caliper disc brake.

RECONDITIONING BRAKE DISCS

Servicing of the brake disc is extremely critical due to tolerances required in machining of the disc to insure proper brake operation.

Manufacturing tolerance for flatness and parallelism of the brake disc is held to .0005 in. while lateral run-out of the brake disc surfaces cannot exceed .002 in. total indicator reading.

Excessive lateral run-out of the brake disc will cause a knocking back of the pistons, which will create increased pedal travel and vibration when the brakes are applied. The finish of the frictional surfaces must be maintained at 30-50 micro inches.

It has been found that once a wear pattern has been established, disc brakes are less susceptible to scoring problems than are drum brakes. Disc surface scoring imperfections less than .015 in. in depth have negligible effect on disc brake operation.

The minimum thickness allowable after refinishing is .965 in. for the 1 in. thick disc and 1.215 in. for the 1 1/4 in. thick disc. Refinishing the disc surfaces can be performed if precision equipment is available and the minimum specifications can be maintained.

ADJUSTING PARKING BRAKES

To adjust the parking brake on the fixed caliper type brake, Fig. U-2, proceed as follows:

Place car on hoist and remove the rear wheels. Loosen brake cables at the equalizer until the parking brake levers move freely to the off position with slack in the cables. Turn the disc until the adjusting screw can be seen through the hole in the disc. Insert an adjusting tool or screwdriver through the hole in the disc and tighten the adjusting screw by moving the handle of the tool away from the floor on both right and left sides, Fig. U-23. Tighten until the disc will not move, then back off six to eight notches.

Apply the parking brake two notches from inside the car. Tighten the brake cables at the equalizer to produce a light drag with the wheels mounted. Fully release the parking brake and rotate rear wheels. No drag should be evident with the parking brake released.

Fig. U-24. Method of bleeding hydraulic brakes. Note location of bleeder valve.

BLEEDING THE HYDRAULIC BRAKE SYSTEM

"Bleeding the brakes" is a process whereby any air in the hydraulic system is removed. It is very important that there be no air in the hydraulic system as such air would be compressed instead of transmitting the motion of the fluid. When there is air in the system, the brake pedal will have a spongy feel, instead of the normal solid feel when the brakes are applied. The spongy feel results from the air being compressed.

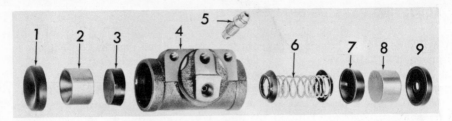

Fig. U-25. Details of typical hydraulic wheel cylinder.

1-Push rod boot.	4-Housing.	7-Piston cup.
2-Piston.	5-Fluid inlet.	8-Piston.
3-Piston cup.	6-Spring.	9-Push rod boot.

To bleed the hydraulic brake system, a small valve is provided at each of the wheel cylinders, Fig. U-25 and Fig. U-26. The valve is operated from the back side of the backing plate.

Brakes should be bled whenever any part of the hydraulic system has been disconnected, or when, on brake application, the pedal has a spongy feel. When bleeding brakes, the master cylinder must always be kept full of new, clean fluid during the entire bleeding process. The left rear wheel cylinder should be bled first, then the right rear, right front and finally the left front, in that order.

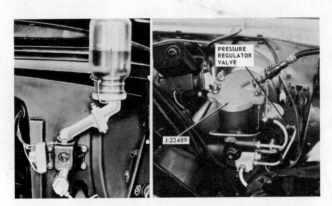

Fig. U-26. Left: Method of filling master cylinder while bleeding brakes. A simpler method is to pour the brake fluid direct from container as needed. Right: A special bleeder is installed on the dual type master cylinder as an aid when bleeding.

The procedure on conventional drum type brakes is to attach a rubber hose to the end of the bleeder screw at the wheel cylinder, Fig. U-24. The tube should fit snugly around the screw so that no air can enter. The free end of the tube is immersed in a jar or container partly filled with clean brake fluid. Then loosen the bleeder screw with a 3/8 in. open-end wrench. Have a helper slowly depress the brake pedal. Just as the brake pedal reaches the end of its travel, close the bleeder valve and allow brake pedal to return slowly to the fully released position. Repeat this procedure until the expelled brake fluid flows in a solid stream in the bleeder hose and no bubbles or contamination are present. Then close the bleeder valve tightly. During the bleeding operation, the level of the fluid in the master cylinder must not be permitted to reach the bottom of the reservoir as that would permit air to enter the system. Note that in systems with dual type master cylinders, the front reservoir is connected to the front brakes and the rear reservoir to the rear brakes.

After bleeding one wheel cylinder, proceed to the next one in order, always making sure that the master cylinder, which is mounted on the dash panel is filled to within one-quarter inch of the top of the reservoir.

Pressure type bleeders which permit one man to bleed the brakes are available, but are relatively expensive. Equipment for maintaining fluid level in the master cylinder during the bleeding operation is shown in Fig. U-26.

When bleeding brakes equipped with power brake units, do not use the vacuum assist. The engine should not be running and the vacuum reserve should be reduced to zero by applying the brakes several times with the engine off before starting the bleeding operation.

The operation of bleeding the four piston type disc brake is the same as described for the conventional Duo Servo system, which was just discussed. The front calipers contain one bleeder valve. The rear calipers on Corvettes contain two bleeder valves, one inboard and one outboard, which necessitates the removal of the rear wheels for bleeding.

Tapping the caliper with a rawhide mallet as the fluid is flowing out may assist in obtaining a good bleeder job.

In regard to the sliding caliper single piston type disc brake, this system includes a pressure metering valve, Fig. U-12, in the front brake system. This valve meters the hydraulic pressure to the front brakes to obtain simultaneous application of the front and rear brakes. The operation of bleeding the front disc brake hydraulic system is the same as the four piston type, except that the spring-loaded end of the pressure metering valve, Fig. U-12, must be depressed while bleeding. This can be done by depressing and holding in the plunger in the end of the valve either by hand or by clamping.

FLUSHING THE BRAKE SYSTEM

The hydraulic system should be flushed annually, or every 10,000 miles, and the procedure is the same as bleeding. However, sufficient fluid should be bled from each line until the fluid is clear and the same as new fluid. When flushing a brake system, it is generally advisable to draw approximately one pint of fluid from the first cylinder bled. This will insure that all fluid from the master cylinder has been drained. On subsequent cylinders, it is then necessary to drain the line until clear fluid is obtained.

QUICK SERVICE ON WHEEL CYLINDERS

The life of wheel cylinders, Fig. U-25, can be prolonged by more frequent flushing of the hydraulic system, and by use of high quality brake fluid. It is necessary to service wheel cylinders when they start to leak fluid. This becomes apparent when the brake pedal gradually goes to the floor when the brakes are applied and pumping the pedal becomes necessary in order to stop the car.

The condition of the wheel cylinders can be checked by removing the brake drums and pulling back the boots from the ends of the wheel cylinder. If the inside of the boot is wet with fluid, it will be necessary to recondition or replace the wheel cylinder.

Kits of the necessary replacement parts are readily available, and the installation of the parts is not difficult.

The procedure, after removing the brake drum and brake shoes, is to pull off the boots from each end of the cylinder. After that, the pistons, cups and springs, Fig. U-25, can be pushed out either end.

If inspection shows that the cylinder bores are pitted or scored, they can be reconditioned. However, many mechanics prefer to install new units, including pistons, cups and boots.

NEW 1978 FEATURES

Some 1978 models are provided with a reservoir for the master cylinder, Fig. U-27. The master cylinder functions in the same manner as before. However, the reservoir attached to the main body of the master cylinder provides greater fluid capacity for the system.

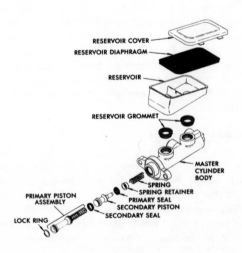

Fig. U-27. New reservoir and method of attachment to master cylinder.

MASTER CYLINDER TIPS

The master or main cylinder, as it is also called, is mounted under the hood on the dash panel. On power brake systems it forms part of the power brake unit. Prior to 1967 a single type master cylinder, Fig. U-28, was used, but starting with the 1967 models, a Duo (split) type master

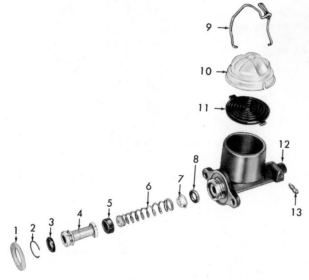

Fig. U-28. Details of single reservoir master cylinder. (Typical)

1-Seal.	6-Spring.	11-Seal.
2-Lock ring.	7-Valve assembly.	12-Body.
3-Secondary cup.	8-Valve seat.	13-Bleeder valve.
4-Piston.	9-Bail wire.	
5-Primary cup.	10-Reservoir cover.	

cylinder, Fig. U-29, was standard equipment. In this design, separate hydraulic systems are provided for the front and rear brakes. If a wheel or brake line should fail at either front or rear of the system, the other part of the system would continue to function. In the split system, there are two entirely separate reservoirs and outlets in a common body, Fig. U-30. The front outlet is connected to the front wheel brakes, and the rear outlet to the rear brakes.

Two types of split master cylinders are used on Chevrolet built cars, Delco-Moraine and Bendix. The capacity of these units varies with different vehicles so it is essential that the make and model of the master cylinder be correctly identified before ordering replacements. Note that the Bendix unit can be identified by a secondary stop piston on the bottom of the casting, Fig. U-30, whereas the stop bolt on the Delco-Moraine is on the inside.

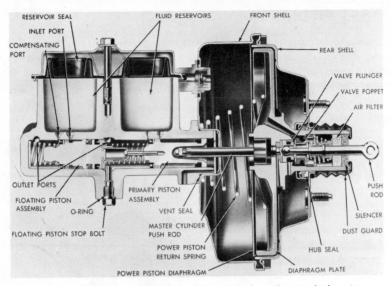

Fig. U-29. Details of Bendix dual master cylinder with power brake unit.

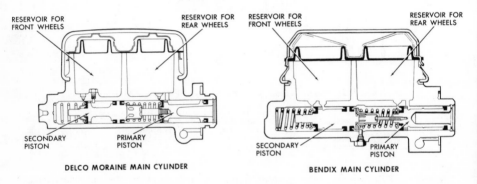

Fig. U-30. Two types of master or main cylinders. The Delco-Moraine is on the left and the Bendix on the right.

In general, master cylinders require servicing when one of the following conditions occurs:

1. All brakes drag.
2. Pedal goes to the floor on brake application.
3. Brakes do not apply.
4. Fluid is found in the boot on the cylinder.

While it is not difficult to overhaul a master cylinder, most mechanics prefer to install a new or rebuilt unit rather than take the time to do the work themselves. However, if it is decided to overhaul the unit, complete instructions are provided with the kit of replacement parts.

Brake Service

When overhauling a master cylinder, care must be taken to keep all parts clean and away from grease and oil. The master cylinder housing must be carefully cleaned using clean brake fluid. Also, all new parts must be dipped in clean fluid before installation.

POWER BRAKE SERVICE

Several different types of power brake units have been used on recent models of Chevrolet built cars, including both single diaphragm type and double diaphragm type.

The single diaphragm Bendix master cylinder is shown in Fig. U-29, and the Delco-Moraine power brake cylinder is shown in Fig. U-31. The Bendix dual diaphragm power brake cylinder is shown in Fig. U-32.

In general these units give very little trouble. When major servicing is required, most mechanics prefer to have the rebuilding done by a specialist or to install a rebuilt unit.

Power brake units are equipped with an air cleaner. See Fig. U-32. Some 1978 models have a filter installed between the vacuum source in the engine manifold and the power brake unit check valve, Fig. U-33.

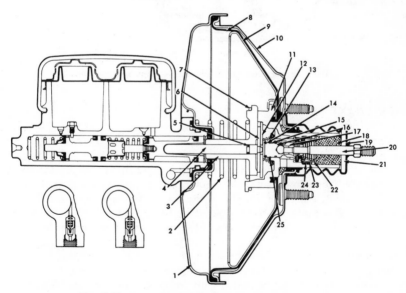

Fig. U-31. Typical Delco-Moraine vacuum power cylinder.

1-Front shell.	10-Rear shell.	19-Boot.
2-Piston return spring.	11-Power piston.	20-Push rod.
3-Reaction retainer.	12-Reaction levers.	21-Silencer.
4-Master cylinder piston rod.	13-Air valve spring.	22-Limiter washer.
5-"O" ring.	14-Reaction bumper.	23-Floating control valve assembly.
6-Reaction plate.	15-Snap ring.	24-Floating control valve retainer.
7-Lock ring.	16-"O" ring.	25-Air valve spring retainer.
8-Diaphragm.	17-Air valve.	
9-Support plate.	18-Air filters.	

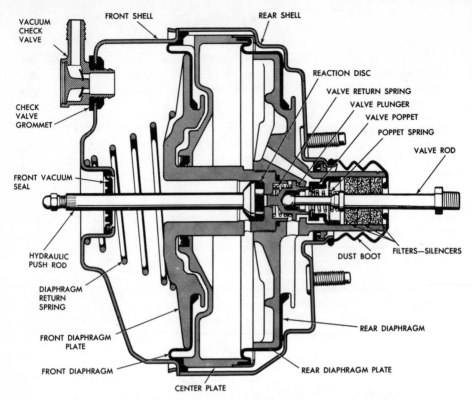

VACUUM
CHECK
VALVE

FRONT SHELL

REAR SHELL

REACTION DISC

VALVE RETURN SPRING

VALVE PLUNGER

CHECK
VALVE
GROMMET

VALVE POPPET

POPPET SPRING

VALVE ROD

FRONT VACUUM
SEAL

HYDRAULIC
PUSH ROD

DUST BOOT

FILTERS—SILENCERS

DIAPHRAGM
RETURN
SPRING

FRONT DIAPHRAGM
PLATE

REAR DIAPHRAGM

FRONT DIAPHRAGM

REAR DIAPHRAGM PLATE

CENTER PLATE

Fig. U-32. Sectional view of Bendix double diaphragm power brake.

POWER BRAKE SERVICE

As previously pointed out, power brake units give very little difficulty. However, a quick check to determine whether the power brake is operating can be made as follows: With the engine not running, apply the brakes ten or twenty times to exhaust the vacuum. Then, while keeping the brake pedal depressed, start the engine. If the power brakes are operating, the brake pedal will move a slight amount so as to further apply the brakes. If the power brake is not operating, no movement of the brake pedal will be noticed when the engine starts. The following checks and inspections can be made:

Check vacuum line and vacuum line connections as well as vacuum check valve in front shell of power unit for possible vacuum loss.

Inspect all hydraulic lines and connections at the wheel cylinders and main cylinder for possible hydraulic leaks.

Check brake assemblies for scored drums, grease or brake fluid on linings, worn or blazed linings, and make necessary adjustments.

Check brake fluid level in hydraulic reservoirs. The reservoirs should be filled to within 1/4 in. of the top. Check for loose mounting bolts at main cylinder and power section.

Check air cleaner filter in power piston extension and replace filter if necessary.

Check brake pedal for binding and misalignment between pedal and push rod.

Note that the push rod, whereby the power brake unit operates the master cylinder, is adjustable. Gauges such as shown in Fig. U-34 can be used for adjusting the push rod. On recent model Delco-Moraine brakes, the dimensions are as indicated. In the case of the Bendix brake, the depth should be 1.220 to 1.225 in.

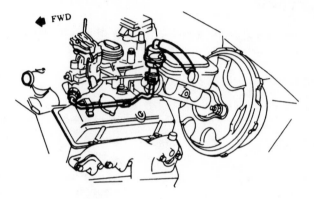

Fig. U-33. Location of special power brake filter on some 1978 models.

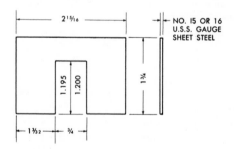

Fig. U-34. Typical gauge for measuring extension of push rod.

CHECKING THE VACUUM

To make sure that full vacuum is reaching the power brake unit, disconnect the vacuum line at the power brake unit and attach a vacuum gauge to the line. Then, with the engine operating at idle speed, note the reading of the gauge. This should be the same as when the vacuum is checked at the intake manifold. Normally this is about 18 in.

TROUBLE-SHOOTING
STANDARD DRUM BRAKE SYSTEM

SYMPTOM AND PROBABLE CAUSE	PROBABLE REMEDY

PEDAL SPONGY

a. Air in brake lines.

a. Bleed brakes.

ALL BRAKES DRAG

a. Improper pedal to push rod clearance blocking compensator port.

a. Adjust clearance.

b. Compensating port in main cylinder restricted.

b. Overhaul main cylinder.

c. Mineral oil in system. .

c. Flush entire brake system and replace all rubber parts.

ONE BRAKE DRAGS

a. Loose or damaged wheel bearings.

a. Adjust or replace wheel bearings.

b. Weak, broken or unhooked brake retractor spring.

b. Replace retractor spring.

c. Brake shoes adjusted too close to brake drum.

c. Correctly adjust brakes.

d. Parking brake adjustment too tight.

d. Readjust parking brake.

EXCESSIVE PEDAL TRAVEL

a. Normal lining wear or improper shoe adjustment.

a. Adjust brakes.

b. Fluid low in main cylinder.

b. Fill main cylinder and bleed brakes.

BRAKE PEDAL APPLIES BRAKES BUT PEDAL GRADUALLY GOES TO FLOOR BOARD

a. External leaks.

a. Check main cylinder, lines and wheel cylinder for leaks and make necessary repairs.

b. Main cylinder leaks past primary cup.

b. Overhaul main cylinder.

BRAKES UNEVEN

a. Grease on linings.

b. Tires improperly inflated.

a. Clean brake mechanism; replace lining and correct cause of grease getting on lining.

b. Inflate tires to correct pressure.

EXCESSIVE PEDAL PRESSURE REQUIRED, POOR BRAKES

a. Grease, mud or water on linings.

b. Full area of linings not contacting drums.

c. Scored brake drums.

a. Remove drums-clean and dry linings or replace.

b. Free up shoe linkage, sand linings or replace shoes.

c. Turn drums and install new linings.

The same types of brake troubles are encountered with power brakes as with conventional or standard brakes. Before checking the power system for source of trouble, be sure to check the braking system as described for a standard brake system.

TROUBLE SHOOTING
POWER BRAKES

SYSTEM TESTS

1. Road test brakes by making a brake application at about 20 mph to determine if vehicle stops evenly and quickly. If pedal has a spongy feel when applying the brakes, air may be present in the hydraulic system. Bleed system as described in this section.
2. With engine stopped and transmission in Neutral, apply brakes several times to deplete all vacuum reserve in the system. Depress brake pedal, hold light foot pressure on pedal and start engine. If the vacuum system is operating pedal will tend to fall away under foot pressure, and less pressure will be required to hold pedal in applied position. If no action is felt, vacuum system is not functioning.
3. Stop engine and again deplete all vacuum reserve in system. Depress brake pedal and hold foot pressure on pedal. If pedal gradually falls away under foot pressure, the hydraulic system is leaking.
4. If the brake pedal travels to within 1 in. of the toeboard, brakes require adjustment or brake shoes require relining.
5. Start engine. With brakes off, run to medium speed and turn off ignition, immediately closing throttle. This builds up vacuum. Wait no less than 90 seconds, then try brake action. If not vacuum assisted for three or more applications, vacuum check valve is faulty.

HARD PEDAL-
VACUUM FAILURE DUE TO:

1. Faulty vacuum check valve.
2. Collapsed vacuum hose.
3. Plugged or loose vacuum fittings, hose or pipes.
4. Leak between vacuum power cylinder and hydraulic master cylinder.
5. Leak in vacuum reservoir tank.

BOUND UP PEDAL MECHANISM
POWER BRAKE UNIT TROUBLE

1. Internal vacuum hose loose or restricted.
2. Jammed sliding air valve.
3. Vacuum leaks in unit caused by loose piston plate screws, loose piston packing, leaks between hydraulic master cylinder and vacuum power cylinder, or by faulty master cylinder piston, or vacuum seal.
4. Defective diaphragm.
5. Restricted air.cleaner.

GRABBY BRAKES (APPARENT OFF-AND-ON CONDITION)

Power Brake unit valve trouble.
    a. Sticking air valve.
    b. Master cylinder piston binding in power piston guide.
    c. Improper number of shims on air valve.
    d. Dented or distorted power cylinder housing.

PEDAL GOES TO FLOOR (OR ALMOST TO FLOOR)

1. Brake adjustment.
2. Fluid reservoir needs replenishing.
3. Power brake hydraulic leakage.
    a. Defective primary or secondary cup.
    b. Defective head nut or head nut gasket.
    c. Cracked master cylinder casting.
    d. Leaks at wheel cylinder in pipes, or in connections.
    e. Defective annular ring on cylinder plug.
4. Faulty master cylinder check valve that has permitted air to enter system causing spongy pedal.

BRAKES FAIL TO RELEASE

1. Faulty check valve at head nut.
2. Excessive friction at seal of master cylinder piston.
3. Excessive friction at power piston cup.

4. Blocked air passage in power piston.
5. Air cleaner blocked or choked.
6. Air valve sticking shut.
7. Broken piston return spring.
8. Broken air valve spring.

TROUBLE SHOOTING
DISC BRAKE

ROUGHNESS OR CHATTER

1. Rotor faces not parallel.
2. Excessive runout of disc.

SQUEAL ON APPLICATION

1. Disc too thin.
2. Wrong type of shoe (lining).

EXCESSIVE PEDAL TRAVEL

1. Piston, shoe and lining assembly not correctly seated.
2. Loose wheel bearing adjustment.
3. Air leak or insufficient fluid in system.
4. Damaged caliper piston seal.
5. Incorrect push rod adjustment.
6. Shoe out of flat more than .005 in.

UNEVEN OR GRABBING BRAKES

1. Seized pistons.
2. Grease or fluid on lining surface.
3. Caliper out of alignment.
4. Incorrect front wheel alignment.
5. Loose caliper.
6. Lining extending beyond end of shoe.

BRAKE RATTLE

1. Excessive clearance between shoe and caliper.
2. Shoe hold-down clips missing.

BRAKE DRAG

1. Seized pistons.
2. Linkage interference causing incomplete pedal return.
3. Defective booster check valve holding pressure in system.
4. Residual pressure in front system.

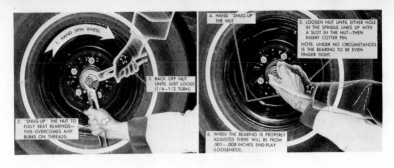

Wheel bearing adjustment procedure.

CALIPER FLUID LEAK

1. Worn piston seal.
2. Scored cylinder bore.
3. Metal clip in seal groove.

NO BRAKES

1. Piston and shoe assembly not correctly seated.
2. Air in system.
3. Insufficient fluid in system.
4. Defective caliper piston seal.
5. Bleeder screw open.

HOW TO ADJUST FRONT WHEEL BEARINGS

In order to get proper steering, good braking and maximum tire life it is essential that the front wheel bearings be correctly adjusted.

To adjust ball type bearings used on older models proceed as follows:

With the wheel raised, remove hub cap and dust cap and then remove the cotter pin from the end of the spindle. While rotating the wheel, tighten spindle nut to 15 ft. lb. of torque. Back off adjusting nut one flat and insert cotter pin. If slot and pin hole do not line up, back off the adjusting nut an additional 1/2 flat or less as required to insert cotter pin. Spin the wheel to check that it rolls freely, then spread end of cotter pin. Bearings should have zero preload and .000 in. to .007 in. end movement when correctly adjusted. Replace dust and hub caps and install wheel.

To adjust the taper roller bearings used on the front wheels of recent model Chevrolet vehicles proceed as follows: These bearings have a slightly loose feel when properly adjusted. They must never be preloaded. Raise the front of the car and spin the wheel to check for unusual noise. If noisy, bearings should be cleaned and inspected prior to adjustment. To check for loose bearing, grasp the wheel at top and bottom and move the assembly in and out. Movement should be less than .008 in.

Remove hub cap or wheel disc from spindle. Remove dust cap from hub. Remove cotter pin from spindle and spindle nut. Adjust bearings as shown in illustration. Insert cotter pin and bend ends against the nut. Cut off extra length to insure ends will not interfere with dust cap. Reassemble dust cap or wheel disc. Lower car to ground.

Hints on
LUBRICATION AND TIRES

The selection of the proper lubricant and its correct application at regular intervals will increase the life of all moving parts and greatly reduce the cost of operation.

ENGINE OIL TO USE

To help assure good cold and hot starting, as well as obtain maximum engine life, fuel economy and oil economy, use the chart that follows to select the proper engine oil for the given conditions.

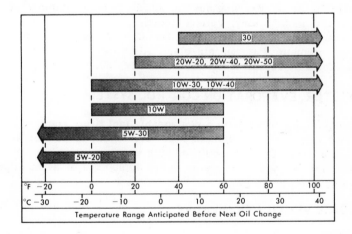

CRANKCASE CAPACITIES

1.4 L Four	4 qt.	200 cu. in. V-6	4 qt.	396 cu. in. V-8	4 qt.
1.6 L Four	4 qt.	231 cu. in. V-6	4 qt.	400 cu. in. V-8	4 qt.
140 cu. in. Four	3 qt.	250 cu. in. Six	4 qt.	402 cu. in. V-8	4 qt.
151 cu. in. Four	3 qt.	305 cu. in. V-8	4 qt.	427 cu. in. Chev.	4 qt.
153 cu. in. Four	4 qt.	307 cu. in. V-8	4 qt.	427 cu. in. Corv.	5 qt.
194 cu. in. Six	4 qt.	327 cu. in. V-8	4 qt.	454 cu. in. V-8	4 qt.
196 cu. in. V-6	4 qt.	350 cu. in. V-8	4 qt.	454 (275 hp) V-8	5 qt.

WHEN TO CHANGE OIL

To insure continued best performance, low maintenance cost and long engine life, change crankcase oil whenever it becomes contaminated with harmful foreign materials. Under normal driving conditions, refill crankcase with fresh oil every six months or every 7500 miles, whichever occurs first. In certain types of service, including trailer hauling, extensive idling, short trip operation in freezing weather (engine not thoroughly warmed up), or in commercial use such as taxicab or limosine service, the oil change interval should not exceed three months or 3000 mi. It is always advisable to drain the crankcase only after the engine has become thoroughly warmed up or reaches normal operating temperature. For vehicles in heavy-duty operation involving continuous starts, stops or prolonged idling, engine oil should be changed every 2500-3000 mi. of operation. The oil filter should be changed at the time of the first oil change, then every second oil change after that.

SERVICING THE AIR CLEANER

Recommended service intervals for engine air filters are as follows: Replace oil wetted paper elements (L-Six engines) every 15,000 mi. Inspect air filters on V-8 engines for leaks, holes or damage after first 15,000 mi. If satisfactory, rotate element 180 deg. from original position. Replace air filter at 30,000 mi. Do not wash, oil, tap or try to clean air filter element with an air blast. Air filter used on 1976 Chevette engines should be removed and replaced every 50,000 miles.

FUEL FILTER, EVAPORATION CONTROL SYSTEM

On engines equipped with a replaceable fuel filter element located in carburetor inlet, replace element every 15,000 mi. or 12 months, whichever occurs first. On cars equipped with an evaporation control system, replace filter in base of canister every 30,000 mi. or 24 months (more often under dusty conditions).

CRANKCASE VENTILATION VALVE

Every 30,000 mi. or 24 months, the crankcase ventilation valve, Fig. V-1, should be replaced. Connecting hoses, fittings and flame arrestor should be cleaned. At every oil change, the system should be tested for proper function and serviced, if necessary.

AIR INJECTOR REACTOR SYSTEM

The air injection reactor system should have A.I.R. pump filter serviced and the drive belt inspected for wear and tension every 30,000 mi. or 24 months, whichever occurs first. In addition, complete effectiveness

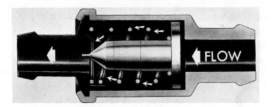

Fig. V-1. Crankcase ventilating valve.

of the system, as well as full power and performance, depends on idle speed, ignition timing, and idle fuel mixture being set according to specifications. A quality tune-up which includes these adjustments should be performed periodically to assure normal engine efficiency, operation and performance.

DISTRIBUTOR LUBRICATION

On four and six cylinder engines, remove distributor cap and rotate lubricator one-half turn at 12,000 mi. intervals. Replace lubricator at 24,000 mi. intervals. On V-8 engines, change cam lubricator end-for-end at 12,000 mi. intervals. Replace lubricator at 24,000 mi.

The High Energy Ignition system on 1975 engines is provided with an oil reservoir that should be maintained in full condition. Inspect reservoir when distributor requires servicing.

AUTOMATIC TRANSMISSION LUBRICATION

Chevrolet states that the only transmission fluid recommended for use in Chevrolet automatic transmissions is fluid identified by the mark Dexron II.

The automatic transmission fluid level should be checked at each engine oil change period. Make the fluid level check with the transmission at normal operating temperature of approximately 180 to 190 deg. F. Have the vehicle on a level surface with the engine idling, selector lever in NEUTRAL position and the parking brake set. If the fluid level is at or below the ADD mark on the dipstick, add sufficient Dexron II to raise the level to the FULL mark. Do not overfill.

Change the transmission fluid and filter every 15,000 mi. (24 000 km) if the car is driven: under heavy city traffic where outside temperature regularly reaches 90 deg. F. (32 C); in very hilly country; in frequent trailer pulling operations; in commercial use. If the vehicle is not used under such severe conditions, change the fluid and filter every 60,000 mi. (96 000 km). Use Dexron II automatic transmission fluid.

To make the change: Remove fluid from the transmission sump and add 2 1/2 qt. (2.36 L) of transmission fluid. Then, operate the transmission through all ranges and recheck the fluid level.

If the automatic transmission is equipped with a sump filter, the filter should be replaced every fluid change.

On heavy-duty service operations using Turbo Hydra-Matic transmissions, drain the converter and sump every 24,000 miles and add approximately 9 qt. of fresh fluid to Chevrolet and Chevelle transmissions, or 7.5 qt. to Nova transmissions.

REAR AXLE LUBRICATION

In standard rear axles (hypoid) use SAE 80 or SAE 90 GL-5 gear lubricant. Straight mineral oil gear lubricants must not be used in these axles.

On Positraction rear axles, use special Positraction lubricant.

STEERING GEAR LUBRICATION

Check the lubricant level in the manual type steering gear every 36,000 miles. If required, add EP chassis lubricant which meets General Motors specifications GM 6031M.

On models equipped with power steering gear, check fluid at operating temperature in pump reservoir. Add GM power steering fluid, or if this is not available use Dextron Automatic Transmission fluid to bring level to full mark on dipstick.

UNIVERSAL JOINT LUBRICATION

Starting with the 1964 models, the Cardan-type universal joints were used which require no periodic maintenance. Prior to that time, it is recommended that the universal joint be disassembled every 25,000 miles, cleaned and lubricated with a high-melting point wheel bearing type lubricant.

GENERATOR AND STARTER LUBRICATION

Alternators which were adopted with the 1963 models require no lubrication.

Direct current generators used prior to that time are provided with an oil cup at each end of the unit which should be filled with engine oil every 1000 miles.

No lubrication of the starter is required as it is equipped with oilless type bearings.

FRONT WHEEL BEARING LUBRICATION

To lubricate the front wheel bearings it is necessary to remove the front wheels, hub and brake drums, as described in the Chapter on Brakes.

Front wheel bearings of the tapered roller type which have been used on Chevrolet built cars since 1961 should be packed, according to latest recommendations, every 30,000 miles with a high-melting point water resistant front wheel bearing lubricant whenever wheel and hub are removed.

Long fibre or viscose type lubricant should not be used.

Also, do not use different kinds of lubricants. Not all lubricants are compatible. Therefore, use clean solvent to remove old lubricant from bearings before repacking the bearings with new lubricant. On cars equipped with disc brakes, use a high melting point lubricant specially formulated for disc brake applications.

TIRE SERVICE

Tire life can be greatly increased by careful and conservative driving habits, by maintaining the specified inflation, and not overloading the vehicle.

High speeds, fast turns, sudden stops and fast acceleration greatly shorten tire life.

With only 25 percent overloading, tire life will be only 64 percent of normal. Fig. V-2 shows the effect of tire pressure on tire life. Note that if the tire is inflated to only 80 percent of normal, (corresponding to about 20 lb. pressure on Chevrolet size tires), tire life is only about 85 percent of what it should be.

Similarly over-inflation will also reduce tire life.

Some authorities advise inflating tires approximately 2 lb. over the recommended pressure to insure better than normal tire life. However, under such conditions there will be some sacrifice of riding comfort.

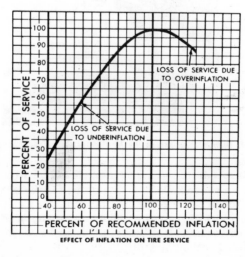

EFFECT OF INFLATION ON TIRE SERVICE

Fig. V-2. Tire pressure must be maintained in order to get maximum mileage from tires.

305

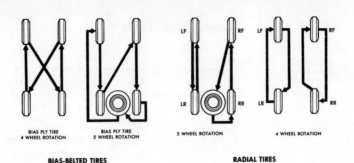

BIAS-BELTED TIRES   RADIAL TIRES

Fig. V-3. Method of rotating tires to obtain increased tire mileage.

Crowned roads, distribution of weight and other factors cause tires to wear at different rates. Therefore, periodic tire rotation is advised, Fig. V-3. Note that different rotation patterns are used for bias belted and radial tires. Rotate bias belted tires every 7500 miles. Rotate radials at the first 7500 miles, then at least every 15,000 miles. Radials tend to wear at a faster rate in the shoulder area, particularly on the front wheels.

CHANGING AND REPAIRING TIRES

To break tire bead from wheel rim, lay tire and wheel assembly on ground under front bumper of car. Place bumper jack between tire and bumper and raise jack to force tire from wheel, Fig. V-4.

Fig. V-4. Method of loosening tire from wheel rim by using bumper jack.

It is difficult to inflate the modern tubeless tire with a hand pump. An air compressor is needed. Before attempting to inflate the tire, it is usually necessary to spread the tire into the rim. This can be done by using a length of rope and a tire iron, or other tool as shown in Fig. V-5. Turning the tool in the tourniquet will spread the tire into the rim and the tire can then be inflated without any difficulty.

There are many different methods of repairing tubeless tires and the manufacturer's instructions should be followed in each case. The Rubber Manufacturers Association has issued a warning against repairing tires with rubber plugs inserted from outside the tire, or using other temporary methods, except in an emergency. A combination vulcanized plug and patch repair applied from inside the tire is the recommended method for permanent repair of punctures, nail holes and cuts up to 1/4 in. confined to the tread only. Section repairs must be made for larger holes in the tread area.

The only way to detect internal damage to a tire is through off-the-wheel inspection. Two out of three tires run even a short distance at turn-pike speed are damaged beyond repair.

Fig. V-5. How to spread tubeless tire into wheel rim, prior to inflation.

The Rubber Manufacturers Association says that tires should never be repaired if they are worn below 1/16 in. tread depth in major grooves, or where inspection shows ply separation; chafer fabric injuries in tubeless tires; broken or damaged bead wires; loose cords on band ply or evidence of having been run flat; tread separation; cracks which extend into the tire fabric; any open liner splice which shows exposed fabric; any tire with a liner showing evidence of having been run under-inflated or excessive overload.

Strict limits have been set by the industry on the use of all temporary repairs, including blow-out patches and areosol sealants as well as plugs. Should such methods be used, the motorist is cautioned not to exceed 50 mph nor drive more than 100 miles before having a permanent vulcanized repair made.

1975 Camaro comes in two models, regular sport coupe and Type **LT** (shown). Featured are wrap-around rear window and more luxurious interior. Type **LT** carries a leather-trimmed seat option.

1975½ Chevelle Laguna S-3 is a sporty intermediate powered by a 350 cu. in. V-8 engine. S-3 has radial ply tires, 15 in. rally wheels and specially tuned suspension. A "soft" urethane panel covers bumper system.

EMERGENCY
TROUBLE SHOOTING

When the car engine suddenly stops, the brakes fail, the horn continues to sound, or some similar trouble occurs, the situation may range from extreme danger to one of annoyance. What to do in such emergencies is described in the following pages. It is hardly possible to describe all possible emergencies that may occur, but the usual ones are listed here, together with suggestions on ways and means of overcoming them. For more details on diagnosing troubles and making permanent repairs, the car owner is referred to other chapters in this volume. In presenting the material in this chapter, it is assumed that the owner has become familiar with automotive terms by studying the other chapters in this book.

ENGINE STOPS SUDDENLY

This condition, often described as the engine "conking out," usually is caused by running out of fuel, and the first check to be made is to note the fuel indicator gauge or light. Another reason is failure of the fuel pump, and still another reason is known as vapor lock. This latter is caused by the fuel vaporizing in the fuel lines, fuel pump, or float chamber of the carburetor. The remedy is to wait until the engine has cooled and then it will start easily.

To check for the failure of a fuel pump takes a bit longer. It is necessary to disconnect the fuel line from the carburetor, and with the end of the fuel line directed into a container, crank the engine for several revolutions. If the fuel pump is working, fuel will spurt from the end of the fuel line in a strong stream.

A loose connection in the primary circuit of the ignition system will also cause the engine to conk out suddenly. A defective switch or a burned resistor are possible causes of this trouble. Wiring around the switch will permit the engine to start in case the switch is defective. If the resistor, or resistor wiring, is burned out, running a wire from the switch connection to the "+" terminal on the coil will permit the engine to start. This should never be done except in the case of extreme emergency, as this will place full battery voltage on the coil, and operation for more than a short time will ruin the coil and ignition breaker points.

ENGINE WON'T CRANK

Among the most common causes of engine cranking difficulties are a defective starting battery, loose or corroded battery connections, poor ground connections or a defective starter solenoid.

In the case of 1974 and 1975 vehicles, be sure to follow instructions regarding sequence of fastening seat belts and starting the engine.

ENGINE CRANKS BUT WON'T START

No fuel in the fuel tank. Defective fuel pump. Check by disconnecting fuel line at carburetor, directing line into a container and cranking the engine. A pump in good condition will deliver a strong stream of fuel.

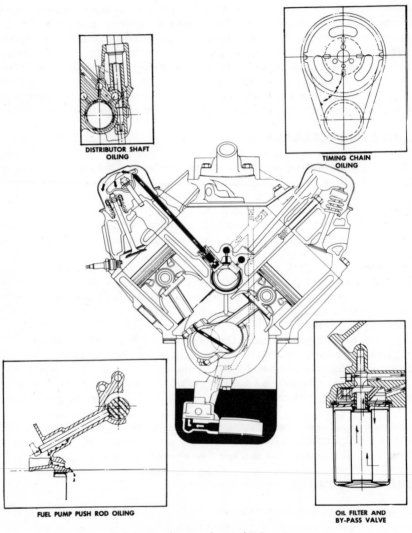

DISTRIBUTOR SHAFT OILING

TIMING CHAIN OILING

FUEL PUMP PUSH ROD OILING

OIL FILTER AND BY-PASS VALVE

Lubrication diagram of typical V-8 engine.

Remove air cleaner and looking into the throat of the carburetor, note if choke plate is closed or open. If the engine is cold the choke plate should be closed. If the engine is hot, the choke plate should be open. Also work the throttle by hand and note if fuel spurts from the accelerating pump nozzle. If no fuel is seen, it indicates that no fuel is reaching the carburetor. Check supply tank and fuel pump. If fuel is seen spurting from the accelerating pump nozzles, the fuel system is apparently in good condition and the trouble is probably in the ignition or starting system.

Excessive moisture on the ignition wiring and/or in distributor. Mop up excess moisture with cloth and then spray with carbon tetrachloride to hasten drying.

Loose or defective connections in primary ignition system. The remedy is to tighten connections.

Burned out primary resistor or resistor wire. Cut unit or wire out of circuit as an emergency measure only. Prolonged operation will ruin coil and breaker points.

Worn or badly adjusted breaker points. Points should be smoothed and cleaned. The correct gap for both V-8 and six is .016 in. If the points are severly pitted, the condition can be improved by filing. A nail file can be used in an emergency.

Dirty or incorrectly adjusted spark plugs will also prevent engine from starting. Correct gap is .035 in.

A flooded carburetor will prevent engines from starting. In most cases a strong odor of fuel will be noted. The best procedure is to wait for about 10 minutes and try again. Or, depress accelerator to floor and hold it there while engine is started in usual manner. In some cases it may be necessary to remove air cleaner and note position of choke plate in the carburetor. If it is in closed position, work carburetor linkage to make sure choke valve will open.

If engine is cranked at lower than normal speed, most likely cause is partly discharged battery, loose, or corroded battery connections.

Failure to have seat belts buckled in correct sequence with starting procedure will also prevent engine starting.

SUDDEN BRAKE FAILURE

If brakes fail suddenly while car is in motion, shut off ignition, apply hand brake, and leave transmission in gear or in drive position, as the case may be. Sudden and complete failure of brakes is caused by a break in the hydraulic line or leakage of fluid at some other point. The only remedy is replacement of defective parts.

SPONGY BRAKE PEDAL

If the brake pedal feels spongy, there is air in the hydraulic line and it is necessary to bleed the system. See the chapter on Brakes for complete instructions for bleeding the system.

BRAKE PEDAL SINKS TO THE FLOOR

If the brake pedal sinks to the floor when the brakes are applied, the trouble is caused by a defective master cylinder or a leak in the system. The remedy is replacement of parts.

BRAKES WILL NOT HOLD

If this condition occurs suddenly and the brakes have been operating satisfactorily before that time, the condition may result from having driven through puddles of water. Condition can be minimized by driving with the brakes lightly applied for a short distance.

BRAKES GRAB

When brakes tend to grab for several applications after the car has been parked for several hours, the trouble is probably caused by moisture absorbed by the brake lining and is a characteristic of many different makes of lining. There are many other causes of grabbing brakes, which are discussed in the Chapter on Brakes.

ALTERNATOR AND GENERATOR FAILURE

When the generator fails as indicated by the warning light on the instrument panel, the first point to check is the belt which drives the fan and generator or alternator. If this belt is loose or broken, the generator or alternator will not be driven at sufficient speed to generate current. As a result, the battery will quickly become discharged, and if the same belt is driving the water pump the engine will overheat with probable damage to the engine bearings, pistons and cylinder walls. The remedy is to tighten the belt by means of the adjuster, or install a new belt as needed.

RADIATOR BOILS OVER

This condition is usually caused by insufficient water in cooling system. Trouble is indicated by the temperature gauge or temperature warning light on instrument panel. It can be caused by leaking radiator, water pump or hose connections, defective core plugs in engine water jacket or by a loose or broken belt driving the water pump and fan.

Shut off engine, let it cool and look for leaks in system. Tighten hose connections if necessary, then place cloth over radiator cap and remove the cap. Remove cap slowly to avoid burst of steam. Start and idle engine. Add water slowly, until system is full. If slight leaks have been noted in radiator core or core plugs, special radiator sealing compounds can be used to stop the leak. Overheating also results from towing another vehicle and use of air conditioner when vehicle is not moving.

HIGH PITCHED SQUEAL

A high pitched squeal when engine is first started and apparently coming from front of engine is often caused by a worn or glazed fan belt, or a water pump seal that needs lubrication. The fan belt can be silenced by applying belt dressing or in an emergency soap can be used. For a complete cure the belt should be replaced. In the case of the water pump seal, it can be lubricated by adding a water pump lubricant and rust inhibitor to the coolant in the radiator.

HARSH RATTLE

A harsh rattling noise at the front of the engine can be caused by a dry or defective fan belt. To check, stop the engine and press together belt on both sides of pulley. A harsh rasp or creaking noise will be made if the belt is dry. Laundry soap can be used as a lubricant on the belt in an emergency.

THROBBING ROAR

A throbbing roar coming from under the car is caused by muffler and pipes that have rusted through, permitting the escape of poisonous gases. Defective parts should be replaced immediately, as the escaping exhaust gases are highly toxic and lethal. Noise is usually accompanied by odor of exhaust gases in the car.

NO LIGHTS

When lights in one circuit, such as headlights, will not light, the trouble is usually caused by a burned fuse or defective circuit breaker. On late models the fuses are located on left-hand air duct, and circuit breaker is built into headlight switch. On older models, headlight switch assembly includes fuses and circuit breaker.

TURN SIGNAL TROUBLE

When there is no blinking action of the turn signal indicator, the trouble is usually caused by a burned out bulb. Check by operating the turn signal first for a left turn, then for a right turn. Walk around the car for each condition and observe each signal. One will probably not be working at all. Replace the bulb to restore operation.

OTHER TROUBLES

For other troubles, together with their solution, the reader is referred to the major trouble shooting sections of this book and also the specific chapters dealing with the different units.

WHAT TO DO WHEN THE ENGINE OVERHEATS

If the engine overheats when you are stuck in bumper-to-bumper traffic or pulling a trailer, turn off the air conditioner. Also, turn on the heater which, in effect, provides an additional radiator. Do not shut off the engine unless you can pull out of the traffic lane. Run the engine at higher rpm to improve air circulation through the radiator.

MAKE YOUR OWN SAFETY CHECK

Check the many conditions contributing to the safety of your car, then make corrections, or have the defects corrected. Before moving the car, check all mirrors for comfortable viewing. The car should be equipped with two side view mirrors and a rear view mirror.

If your inside mirror vibrates when the car is driven on a smooth road, it indicates that some rotating part is unbalanced. Check for a bent wheel or out-of-round condition. Maximum runout for wheels is 1/16 in. radially (out-of-round) and 1/16 in. laterally (wobble). Also, check the tires for runout, and make sure they are in balance. For slow speed driving, static balance usually is satisfactory. For higher speeds, dynamic balancing is advised. Check tire pressures.

Test the steering wheel for excessive play. Check the brakes. With self-adjusting brakes, the height of the brake pedal is not a good gauge of condition. Remove a drum and check the thickness of the lining and condition of the drum. If the pedal is "spongy" when applying the brakes, there is air in the system and service is necessary.

Make sure the engine has ample power for emergency passing. An untuned engine has reduced passing capacity, and economy is seriously affected. It pays to have the engine tuned every 10,000 mi. If you are pulling a trailer, remember that added weight reduces your available power for acceleration and increases stopping distances. Also, the added weight of the trailer will tend to tilt the headlights upward to "blind" approaching drivers. Adjust headlight aim.

For safety's sake, the level of your eyes should be several inches above the steering wheel. Adjust your seat accordingly, or use a cushion.

MORE MILES PER GALLON

A precise engine tune-up is, of course, basic to getting the most miles per gallon. In addition, don't idle the engine unnecessarily. Also, keep the tires inflated to specified pressure, and don't carry excess weight in the car. Up to 1/5 mpg (miles per gallon) is lost for each 100 lb. of excess weight. If you increase driving speed by 5 mph in the 50 to 70 mph range, fuel economy will be reduced by 7 to 9 percent.

Body Service

To remove chewing gum from the upholstery, first harden the gum with an ice cube and then scrape off the particles with a dull knife. If the gum cannot be removed completely by this method, moisten it with benzine or carbon tetrachloride and work it from the fabric with a dull knife while the gum is still moist.

Fruit stains and stains from liquor can usually be removed with very hot water. Wet the stain well by applying hot water to the spot with a clean cloth. If the spot and stain is an old one, it may be necessary to pour very hot water directly on the spot and then follow by scraping and rubbing. However, care must be exercised, as hot water in many cases will discolor the fabric.

To remove blood stains, wash the stain with a clean cloth saturated with cold water until no more of the stain can be removed. Then, if necessary, apply a small amount of household ammonia, using a brush or cloth. Rub the stain again with a clean cloth saturated with water. Do not use hot water or soap on blood stains as they will tend to set the stain, thereby making it practically impossible to remove.

Candy stains, other than stains made from chocolate candy, can be removed by rubbing the surface with a cloth saturated with very hot water. This, if necessary, can be followed with a volatile type of cleaner. In the case of stains made from chocolate candy, use a cloth soaked in lukewarm soap suds and scrape while wet with a dull knife.

If grease or oil has been spilled on the material, as much as possible should be removed by scraping with a dull knife before further treatment is attempted. Grease and oil stains may be removed by rubbing lightly with a clean cloth saturated with volatile cleaner. Be sure all motions are toward the center of the stained area, to decrease the possiblility of spreading the stain. Use a clean white blotter, blot area to remove excess cleaner and loosen grease or oil.

To remove the stains made by paste or wax type shoe polishes, a volatile cleaner is usually needed. Rub the stain gently with a cloth wet with a volatile cleaner until the polish is removed. Use a clean portion of the cloth for each scrubbing operation, and rub the stained area from the outside to the center.

If tar gets on the upholstery, first remove as much as possible with a dull knife. Moisten the spot lightly with a volatile cleaner and again remove as much of the tar as possible with a dull knife. Follow this operation by rubbing the spot lightly with a cloth wet with a cleaner until the stain is removed.

The compositions of different brands of lipsticks vary, making the stains very difficult to remove. In some instances, a volatile cleaner may remove the stain. If some stain remains after repeated applications of the volatile cleaner, it is best to let it dry and try other measures.

Sponge urine stains with clean cloth saturated with lukewarm soap suds (mild neutral soap) and then rinse well by rubbing the stain with a clean cloth dipped in cold water. Then saturate a clean cloth with a solution of one part of household ammonia and five parts water. Apply the cloth to the stain and allow solution to remain on the affected area for one minute, then rinse by rubbing with a clean wet cloth.

Sponge nausea spots with a clean cloth dipped in clear cold water. After most of the stain has been removed by that method, wash lightly with soap (mild neutral) using a clean cloth and lukewarm water. Then rub with another clean cloth dipped in cold water. Household ammonia can also be used in many cases.

WHAT TO DO ABOUT RATTLES

Most squeaks and rattles can be eliminated by carefully going over the car once or twice a year and tightening all the bolts, screws and nuts. This applies particularly to the bolts, nuts and sheet metal screws joining the various panels and shrouds under the hood. Pay particular attention to the bolts attaching the bumper to the frame. Also make sure the door latches and striker plates are tight and correctly adjusted. Rattles and squeaks are sometimes caused by weather stripping and antisqueak material that has slipped out of position. When such a condition exists, apply additional cement or other adhesives and install the material in the proper location to eliminate this difficulty. If necessary, obtain new weather stripping and antisqueak material and install it with a proper type of cement.

HOW TO KEEP THE BODY FROM RUSTING

Whenever possible, the car should be stored in a closed garage so it is protected from the sun, rain and snow. When cars are driven in areas where salt is used on icy roads, care should be taken to wash the car as frequently as possible. Be sure to wash all accumulations from the underside of the fenders.

One of the major causes of car bodies rusting is failure to keep open the drain holes located on the underside of each rocker panel, quarter panel and door, Fig. W-1. These drain holes are provided so that the water will not accumulate within the panels. When the drain holes are not open water will accumulate which will soon rust the panels from the inside. The drain holes become clogged with road dirt and will not drain the water from the interior of the panels.

The door bottom and drain hole sealing strip is attached to the door inner panel over the drain holes by a snap-on fastener at each end of the strip, Fig. W-1. To prevent the strip from adhering from the door inner panel and blocking the drain hole, apply a sparing amount of silicone rubber lubricant on the center section of the sealing strip.

FIXING DUST AND WATER LEAKS

Any unsealed crevice or small opening in the body will permit dust and water to enter the interior. The actual location of the point of entry is often difficult to locate, but by removing the interior trim panel, the source of the leak can usually be found. In many cases dust and rain will leave a trail on the body panel. Water testing a car should be done in sections by spraying water on small areas at a time. In that way, it is possible to locate the points which require sealing. The correct method of water testing is to start at the bottom and work up.

All panel seams, screws, hose and grommets should be carefully closed with body sealer. Check the various openings around the cowl and windshield openings, and apply body sealer where needed. In addition, raise the hood and make sure that there are no openings in the dash panel, which will permit leakage into the driver compartment. Also check the sealer on the door hinges. The body sealer should be filled flush with the pillar post.

Door openings contribute to water leaks in two ways: First, there may be leaks at metal joint seams; and, secondly, the roughness of the door opening metal may not provide a good sealing contact surface for the weatherstrip. Leaks around the weather stripping can be located by the water test, or by using carpenter's blue chalk blown from a testing bulb.

Faulty weather stripping should always be removed and replaced with new. When installing weather stripping, follow the instructions applying to that particular cement. If necessary, build up low areas of the weather stripping by means of rubber shim stock.

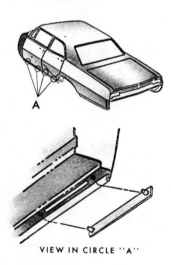

VIEW IN CIRCLE "A"

Fig. W-1. Details of sealing strips on bottom of doors. Drain holes must be kept free to prevent accumulation of water within the panels.

In the case of water leaks around the windshield weather strip, seal the weather strip against the body opening by carefully working a thin coating of windshield rubber sealer between the body edge and the rubber molding. Or, lift the lip of the rubber strip where it contacts the body and use a nozzle type of applicator.

If faulty sealing of the glass to the windshield has caused the leak, apply sealer as far down as possible between the inner weather strip and the glass, for a considerable distance at each side of the leaking point.

To determine the exact location of a dust leak, remove the following trim from inside the vehicle: Floor mats, dash and toe panel pad, and kick pads. Dust leaks should be evident when these pads and mats are removed. Leaks can be sometimes located by putting a bright light under the vehicle body, or checking the interior of the body at joints and weld lines. Light will show through where leaks exist.

Seal all leaks and road test the vehicle on a dusty road to make sure all leaks are sealed. Check for indication of dust leaks around the doors.

Openings that allow dust leaks will also provide water leaks. When checking for water leaks, a helper should be used on the inside of the car to locate the entrance of water while it is applied on the outside.

Water leaks do not always enter the body in the location where they show up. Therefore, back tracking the path of water may be required to show the true entrance of the leak.

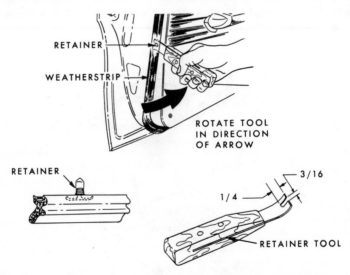

Fig. W-2. Type of tool used and method of removing weatherstrip from doors.

FRONT AND REAR DOOR WEATHER STRIPS

On recent models, both front and rear doors use nylon fasteners to retain the door weather strips. The fasteners are a component part of the weather strip and secure the weather strip to the door by engaging piercings in the door panels. Serrations of the fastener retain the fastener in the piercing and also seal the openings from water entry, Fig. W-2. On certain body styles, the nylon fasteners are used all around the entire perimeter of the door. On other style bodies, the nylon fasteners are used below the belt line only. Weather strip adhesive retains the weather strip around the door upper frame from above the belt line on such bodies, Fig. W-3.

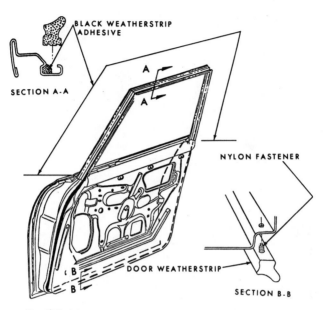

Fig. W-3. Location and type of weatherstrip used on doors.

To disengage nylon fasteners from door panel piercings, use a tool as indicated in Fig. W-2, which permits removal of the weather strip without damaging the serrations on the fasteners so that the weather strip can be reinstalled if desired.

Although a replacement door weather strip will include the nylon fasteners, individual fasteners are available as a service part.

The flat blade tool such as a putty knife can be used to break the cement bond between the door and weather strip.

When installing weather strip, make sure that the nylon fasteners are not damaged and replace those which have been damaged. Also clean off all weather strip and adhesive from the door.

On body styles without door upper frames, position weather strip to door and install plastic fasteners at front and rear end of weather strip.

On sedan styles with door upper frames, position color coded section of weather strip to the door as follows: On front doors, color code should be located at rear upper corner of door upper frame. On rear doors, color coded sections should begin at belt line of door lock pillar and extend upward.

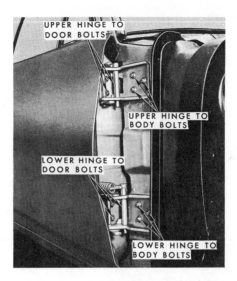

Fig. W-4. Front door hinge attachment. (Typical)

Tap nylon fasteners into door piercings using a hammer and blunt caulking tool.

On Chevelle and Nova sedan styles, apply a bead of black weather strip adhesive to gutter of door frame, Fig. W-3. Allow adhesive to become tacky and then install weather strip.

After all fasteners have been installed on sedan styles, apply weather strip adhesive between door and weather strip outboard surface as needed.

On 1962 and 1963 models, the need for sealing the weather strip clips along the bottom facing is eliminated. On previous models the weather strip clips are also cemented along the bottom and up a short distance on each pillar.

ADJUSTING DOORS

Door hinges are adjustable so as to correctly position the door in the body. There should be approximately 1/8 in. between the edge of the door and the body or body pillar.

On recent models, the front hinges are adjusted through the use of floating anchor plates in the door and front body hinge pillars, Fig. W-4.

Up-and-down and fore-and-aft adjustments are provided at the body hinge pillars. And in-and-out adjustments are provided at the door hinge pillars.

On rear doors, in-or-out and up-or-down adjustment is provided at the door side hinge attaching screws. Fore-or-aft and a slight up-or-down adjustment is available at body side (center pillar) hinge attaching screws, Fig. W-5.

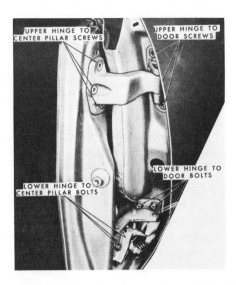

Fig. W-5. Rear door hinge attachment. (Typical)

Before removing any door, use a pencil and mark location of hinges on door or center pillar. On styles equipped with window regulators, or vacuum operated locks, proceed as follows: Remove door trim assembly and inner panel water deflector. Disconnect wire harness connector from regulator motor and/or vacuum hoses from the lock actuator. Remove electric conduit from door, and remove wire harness and/or vacuum hoses from door to conduit access hole.

With door properly supported, loosen upper and lower hinge attaching screws or bolts from the door or center pillar and remove door from the body.

REMOVING DOOR INSIDE HANDLES

Door inside handles are retained by either screws or spring clips. On styles with screw retained handles, the screws are either exposed or covered only with an applied type arm rest that can be removed by the removal of several screws.

On styles with clip retained handles, the clip is either exposed when the arm rest is removed, or else is hidden by the handle, Fig. W-6. Exposed clips can be disengaged from the remote control spindle with a screwdriver. Clips hidden by the handle can be disengaged as follows:

Depress door trim assembly sufficiently to permit inserting tool, Fig. W-6, between handle and plastic bearing plate. With tool in same plane as handle, push tool as indicated to disengage clip. Pull handle inboard to remove from spindle.

To install, engage retaining clip on handle. On ventilator and window

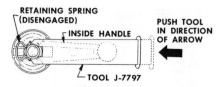

Fig. W-6. Type of tool designed to remove window control handles.

regulator spindles, position handle at same angle as opposite side handle and press handle outboard until clip engages spindle. On remote control spindles, put handle in horizontal position.

HOOD AND REAR DECK LID ADJUSTMENT

The hood is adjusted forward or rearward, or from side to side in the body opening, as follows: Loosen the hinge strap to hood attaching bolts at each hinge, adjust the hood as required, then tighten the bolts.

To adjust rear compartment lid in the body opening, loosen both hinge strap attaching bolts, Fig. W-7. Adjust lid as required, then tighten bolts. To adjust compartment lid at hinge area, install shims between lid inner panel and hinge straps. To raise front edge of lid at hinge area, place shim between lid inner panel and forward portion of one or both hinge straps at C, Fig. W-7. To lower front edge of lid at hinge area, place shim between inner panel and rearward portion of one or both hinge straps at B.

Points 1, 2 and 3 are adjustment points for torque rod E, Fig. W-7.

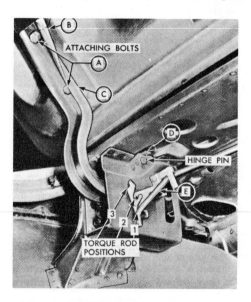

Fig. W-7. Rear compartment hinge and torque rod.

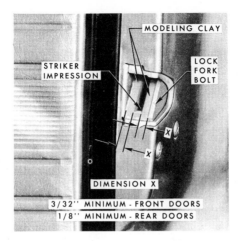

Fig. W-8. Lock to striker engagement.

To adjust the hood up or down, loosen the hinge to body attaching bolts, then shift hood to required position and tighten bolts.

ADJUSTING STRIKER PLATE

To adjust striker up or down, or in or out, loosen striker bolt, and shift striker as required, then tighten striker.

To determine if striker fore-or-aft adjustment is required, proceed as follows: First make sure door is properly aligned. Then apply modeling clay caulking compound to lock bolt opening, as shown in Fig. W-8. Close door only as far as necessary for striker bolt to form an impression in the clay. Do not close door completely as that will make the clay difficult to remove.

Measure striker impression as follows: Striker edge should be centered fore-and-aft as shown, however some tolerances are allowed. In any alignment, it is important that minimum dimensions as outlined in Fig. W-8 are strictly maintained. Spacers are available as service parts and can be used individually or in combination to achieve the desired alignment.

REMOVING TRIM ASSEMBLY

The front and rear door trim assemblies are attached by means of retaining nails attached to the back side of the door trim assembly. To remove the trim, apply masking tape to the door inner panel at trim assembly locations to avoid paint damage when pad is removed. With a clean rubber mallet, tap around entire edge of trim assembly to free trim nails from plastic retainers. Insert a flat blade tool between inner panel and door trim assembly, and carefully loosen trim assembly nails from retainers until trim can be removed from the door.

POWER WINDOW SERVICE

Generally most common failure of power windows to open are "Open" and "Short" circuits. An open circuit is one in which the circuit cannot be completed, due to a broken wire, poor terminal contact or improper ground. A short circuit is one in which the current is grounding before it reaches the operating unit. This creates an overload and actuates the circuit breaker or blows the fuse.

When a short circuit exists in a given circuit, the circuit breaker will be actuated or fuse will blow. However, if the short is located between a switch and an operating unit, the circuit breaker will actuate or the fuse will blow only when the switch is actuated. If the short occurs between the circuit breaker (or fuse) and the switch, the circuit will be inoperative all the time. This will continue until the short is repaired or the battery runs down.

In every case, first check to make sure that the fuse is not blown, and then make sure that the current is reaching the motor. If no current is reaching the motor when the switch is closed, examine the entire circuit for loose or dirty connections, or a broken wire. If none of the windows will operate with the ignition switch on, the probable cause is a short or open circuit in the power feed circuit.

If the right rear door window does not operate from master control switch on left door, or from control switches on right rear door, but the left door window operates, check for an open or short circuit between the right rear door harness and the power window front harness. Also check for a short or open circuit in affected window control switch, or window motor circuit. Also check for possible mechanical failure or bind in window channels. There is also a possibility that the window motor may be defective.

If right door windows will operate from left door master control switch, but will not operate from right door control switches, but left door windows operate, check for open or short circuit in front harness feed wire circuit.

GLASS POLISHING

Minor glass scratches can be effectively removed or substantially reduced by special polishing methods. A low speed (600 to 1300 rpm) rotary polisher is needed together with a wool felt rotary type polishing pad and powered cerium oxide (Glass-Nu or its equivalent) and a wide mouth jar to hold the polish.

The polish is mixed with sufficient water to obtain a creamy consistency. The mixture must be agitated frequently to keep the cerium oxide from settling out. Draw a circle around the scratches on the opposite side of the glass with marking crayon. Also use masking paper where needed to catch drippings or spattered splash.

Saturate the pad with the polish and use a moderate but steady pressure against the surface. Excessive pressure will cause the glass to heat. Should it become heated, allow it to air dry. Do not apply cold water. With a feathering out motion polish the affected area. Never hold the tool in one spot any longer than 30 to 45 seconds. When polishing the windshield glass, care must be taken to avoid excessive polishing, as the optical qualities may be distorted and affect the vision.

WOOD GRAIN TRANSFER

Two types of vinyl grain transfer are used on station wagons. The two types of transfer are not to be used on the same vehicle.

Transfers should not be replaced at temperatures below 65 deg. F. or over 90 deg. F.

Instructions covering the removal and application of such transfer material are included with the material.

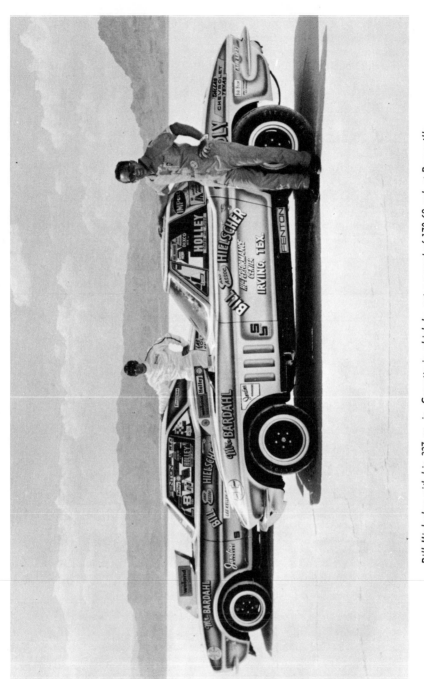

Bill Hielscher with his 327 cu. in. Corvette in which he set a record of 170.69 mph at Bonneville Flats for the B/GT class cars. Co-driver Lee Kelley is on the left. (Holley Carburetor Co.)

MORE SPEED
AND POWER

Stock Chevrolet engines are now available which provide terrific performance. For example, the 427 cu. in. V-8 engine with special carburetion, cams and other refinements develops 435 hp @ 5800 rpm. That is exactly 100 hp more than with standard cams and carburetion. The 396 cu. in. V-8 engine will develop 325 hp @ 4800 rpm, 350 hp @ 5200 rpm and 375 hp @ 5600 rpm depending on the equipment selected. As a result, many men who formerly developed their own engines are using such stock engines instead.

For those who wish to improve the performance of their own engines, there is a large variety of special equipment available which is readily obtainable from specialists in the field. Such special equipment includes:

Special camshafts	Stroked crankshaft
Special intake manifolds	Special exhaust manifold
High lift rocker arms	Magnetoes
Superchargers	Race type spark plugs
Injectors	Carburetors
Lightweight flywheels	Lightweight connecting rods
Roller type valve lifters	High pressure valve springs

FIRST STEPS IN BETTER PERFORMANCE

The basis of improved performance, better acceleration and higher top speed is precision workmanship. Every effort must be made to reduce friction and step up power. It must be remembered that extreme accuracy in setting ignition and carburetion, together with a good valve job, will give better than usual performance.

Contributing largely to stepped-up performance is precision balancing of crankshaft, together with piston and ring assemblies. Special equipment is used for balancing the piston and rod assemblies so that they are all the same weight, Fig. X-1. When they are balanced, their equivalent in weight is attached to the crankshaft, which is then balanced on a crankshaft balancer, Fig. X-2. Such equipment will detect any unbalance of .002 ounce. This far exceeds the 1/2 ounce that is used as a standard on many conventional passenger car engines. Balancing of the crankshaft is so critical and precise that allowance is even made for the weight of the oil in the crank throws.

Such precision balancing permits greatly increased speed and what is equally important it reduces the load on the bearings. As a result, the engine will have many more miles of useful life. When used in normal service, a precision balanced engine will easily deliver in excess of 300,000 miles of trouble-free service. This has been demonstrated many times in the commercial vehicle field.

Fig. X-1. Note special weighing scales in background for weighing pistons and connecting rods, also the set of special rods and pistons in foreground left.

The clearance of bearings and pistons must receive special attention. For street use, main and rod bearing clearance should range from .0025 to .003 in. for most engines. For drag strip operation, a slightly greater clearance should be given. Usually .003 in. has been found to be satisfactory. Side clearance of the rods should be increased to about .003 in.

Intake valves with hollow stems are preferred because of their lighter weight. Sodium filled exhaust valves are considered a must because they can better withstand the higher operating temperatures.

The cylinder block should be "boiled out" to remove all traces of rust and scale from the water jacket and should also be checked with a Magnaflux tester for cracks. Particular attention should be paid to the webbing, main bearing caps, cap bolts and the cylinder head area around the head bolts for stress and cracks. Nicks and scratches should be smoothed away from all surfaces. Grind away any casting flashes.

If a new cylinder block is used, it should also be "boiled out" to be sure there is no casting sand in the waterjacket. New or old, all parts should be checked with a Magnaflux type tester.

More Speed and Power

HINTS ON RAISING COMPRESSION

The answer to the question, how high should compression be raised, depends largely on the compression ratio of the original engine, on the fuel that is to be used, and the type of racing or driving in which the car is to be used. In general, it is seldom advisable to use a compression ratio of over 11 to 1. It must be remembered that recent Federal regulations on exhaust emissions have caused compression ratios of new cars to be lowered.

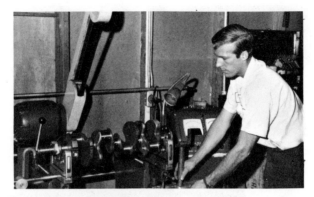

Fig. X-2. One type of special equipment used to balance crankshafts.

When raising compression be sure to check the clearance between the valves in their open position and the top of the piston. If this is not done, the piston may strike the valve with severe damage to the engine.

In the case of the pistons in the 409 cu. in. Chevrolet V-8 engine, these have recessed marks on top to provide the necessary clearance for the valve.

In order to calculate how much the volume of the combustion chamber should be reduced, in order to obtain the desired compression ratio, use is made of the following formula:

$$A = \frac{B}{C-1}$$

Where A is the volume of the combustion chamber, B is the displacement of the cylinder, and C is the desired compression ratio. For example, if it is an eight cylinder engine, with a total displacement of 320 cu. in. (40 cu. in. per cylinder) and the desired compression ratio is 11 to 1, then

$$A = \frac{40}{11-1} = \frac{40}{10} = 4 \text{ cu. in.}$$

the volume of the combustion chamber should then be 4 cu. in. In the case of a flat top piston, which at the top of its stroke is flush with the top of the cylinder block, all the combustion chamber will be in the cylinder head. To measure the volume of the combustion chamber, place the cylinder head on a work bench with the combustion chamber up. Using a spirit level, make sure the gasket surface is perfectly level. Using a chemist's graduate calibrated in tenths of an inch, see how much fluid is required to fill the combustion chamber. The job will be simplified if a piece of clear plastic is clamped firmly to the top of the combustion chamber. Fluid such as brake fluid or kerosene is then poured through a hole in the sheet of plastic.

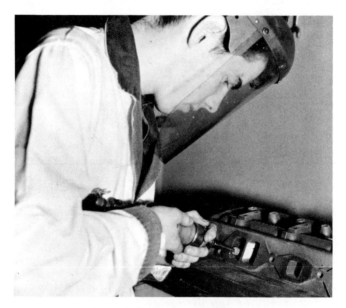

Fig. X-3. Porting a cylinder head.

Boring the cylinders will also increase the compression ratio. In the case of cylinders of about 3-1/2 in. in diameter, when the diameter is increased .060 in. the compression ratio will be increased approximately .2. In general, .060 in. is about the maximum the cylinder can be rebored without danger of breaking through into the water jacket, or at least seriously weakening it.

While working on the combustion chambers, it is important to check the volume of each to be sure they are identical. Any variation in volume will result in a rough running engine, and accompanying vibration and loss of power. Usually, all that is necessary can be accomplished by carefully polishing the surface of the combustion chamber, including the top of the piston. Before deciding on raising the compression of an engine, it is important to decide on what fuel is to be used. Commercial high test gasoline can be used in engines up to approximately 11 to 1. For higher compression ratios it is usually necessary to use special racing fuels.

POINTER ON PORTING

On older engines considerable improvement in performance can be obtained by "porting" the cylinder head, Fig. X-3. That process increases the diameter of the exhaust and intake valve ports in the cylinder head, together with larger diameter valve heads. On more recent models, the factory has used that method of improving the performance of their engine. While the valve ports on stock engines of recent model engines are about as large as possible, some work can still be done on the ports. This is in the form of polishing and making sure that the ports are as much alike as possible.

Special care must be taken so all ports are the same size. A fine emery wheel is used in an electric drill. The wheel must be a fine grit, as the object is to polish rather than to remove metal. Most mechanics use a pair of inside calipers to check the size of the ports to make sure all intake ports are of equal size and that all exhaust ports are of the same size. In some instances, a mechanic will fashion a plug type gauge for checking the size of the ports.

Closely associated with porting is work done on the manifolds, both intake and exhaust. Because of its complex shape, there is not much that can be done to polish the interior of a manifold. The important point is to check to see how the openings in the manifold line up with the openings in the cylinder head. To do this, coat the gasket surface of the manifold with a light coating of Prussian blue and then bolt it in position. When the manifold is removed, some of the blue will have been transferred to the cylinder block, clearly indicating any offset. If the ports do not match up, it will be necessary to enlarge the bolt holes in the manifold so it can be shifted to the desired position. In some cases it may be more desirable to grind the edges of the ports on the manifold so that there will be no overlapping with the ports in the cylinder head. Further in connection with manifolds, many mechanics take advantage of the special speed manifold that has been designed by speed specialists, especially for Chevrolet engines.

Fig. X-4 shows a 1974 Vega set up for Pro Stock racing. A dual quad intake manifold is pictured in Fig. X-5. Fig. X-6 shows a Chevrolet entered in the NHRA Nationals at Indianapolis.

TIPS ON CARBURETION

Some experimentation with carburetor jets is necessary to obtain the best air-fuel ratio. When running without an air cleaner, it usually takes an increase of three to four sizes over standard to get a good mixture. However, the exact mixture will vary with air temperature, altitude, humidity, etc.

When using a 348 cu. in. or a 409 cu. in. Chevrolet engine for the road and dragster work, many mechanics will raise the compression ratio from 1 to 1-1/2 points over stock, and a three carburetor intake manifold with 1-3/16 in. venturi, two-barrel carburetor. A broad recommendation is

Fig. X-4. Vega Pro Stocker driven by S. Schafiroff is tough competition on any track.

1 sq. in. of venturi area for every 40 cu. in. displacement. However, detailed carburetor specifications have to be worked out on a trial testing of each engine.

Some experimentation with carburetion is necessary to obtain the best air-fuel ratio. When running without an air cleaner, an increase of three to four sizes over standard jet size is often required. However, this will vary with different engines and carburetors. It must be remembered that the mixture ratio will also vary with air temperature, altitude and humidity. So it pays to make frequent checks, noting carefully which jet size gives the best performance for each particular weather condition.

Fig. X-5. Special Offenhauser dual quad intake manifold.

With multiple carburetor installations, great care must be taken in the adjustment of the throttle rods so that the opening and closing of the carburetor throttles are correctly synchronized. If this is not done, some cylinders will tend to lag and full power will not be produced.

Fig. X-6. Chevrolet entered at the NHRA Nationals at Indianapolis.

WHAT TO DO ABOUT RODS AND PISTONS

Lightweight aluminum connecting rods, accurately balanced, are available from race parts specialists. However, those not wishing to go to the expense of aluminum connecting rods, should carefully polish and balance connecting rods that are standard equipment with the engine. Pistons must also be accurately balanced, as any variation in the weights of the pistons and rod assemblies will result in vibration and stepped-up bearing loads, Fig. X-1.

Special lightweight pistons are also available. For higher engine speeds, it is necessary to increase the clearance of the pistons in the engines.

Remember that on V-type engines, when replacing pistons and rods, they must weigh the same as the original parts in order to maintain the balance. If the replacement piston and rod assemblies are different weights than the originals, the crankshaft and the reciprocating assemblies will then have to be rebalanced.

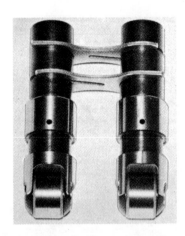

Fig. X-7. Special roller type valve lifters.

VALVES, SPRINGS, CAMS

Valves, springs and cams play an important part in speed and performance.

Valve head diameter should be as large as possible, and in older engines particularly, great improvement in performance can be obtained by cutting larger diameter seats in the cylinder heads and installing larger diameter valves. On more recent model engines, the design has been changed so that larger valves are already incorporated in the design and not much more can be gained in that respect. However, heavier valve springs which will reduce the tendency of valves to bounce at high speeds, are used extensively. Care must be taken that the valve spring height is the same throughout the engine.

It is always important to make sure that the valve head will not strike the piston when the piston is at the top of the stroke. The absolute minimum piston to valve head clearance is .125 in. To check this clearance without dismantling the engine, have the valve lash to the .125 in. clearance. For example, if the valve lash is .025 in. and the piston to valve clearance is .125 in., the total is .150 in. Use a feeler gauge of that thickness and insert it between the valve stem and the rocker arm. Manually turn the engine over twice and if the piston does not hit the valve, you have the proper minimum clearance. Check all eight cylinders. In some cases the pistons may have to be fly cut to provide adequate clearance.

Solid, adjustable valve lifters are used in place of hydraulic lifters and many mechanics prefer lifters of the roller type, Fig. X-7. The rollers are especially heat treated to withstand the higher load of stiffer valve springs and higher speeds. Along with stiffer springs, special heavy-duty valve spring retainers are also used.

In order to get greater valve opening, rocker arms with increased ratios such as 1.5 to 1, or 1.75 to 1, are available.

Installation of a special camshaft is important if increased performance is to be obtained. Racing cams lift the valves higher and hold them open longer than stock camshafts. In that way more air-fuel mixture is drawn into the cylinder. In addition, a larger portion of the burned gases will be expelled from the engine. However, the installation of such a camshaft results in extreme rough idling. There are several different types of cams, each designed for a specific type of operation. No one particular cam provides all the desirable characteristics. Types of cams include road or semi-race, three-quarter grind, full race and super. Road or semi-race cams provide good acceleration with fair idling. Such cams are virtually stock design on current passenger cars.

The full-race cam gives more top speed and acceleration, while the super cam is still more of the same, but both idle very poorly. Naturally, as valves are kept open longer, improved carburetion is a must in order to take full advantage of the faster cam. Also different rear axle ratios are needed to take advantage of the higher engine speeds. If the car is to be used for conventional transportation, as well as speed, the road or semi-cam should be used.

WHAT TO DO ABOUT IGNITION

For sustained high speed driving, many mechanics prefer the use of a magneto. Such magnetos are available in a type that can be substituted directly for the original equipment, Fig. X-8. If the decision is made to stick with battery ignition, a double breaker arm distributor with two ignition coils is preferred.

High Energy Ignition (HEI) became standard in 1975 models. It has no breaker points and has a lot to recommend for high speed operation.

The correct type of spark plugs for sustained high speed driving is critical. The standard equipment spark plugs are usually too hot for such work. As compression is increased and higher speeds maintained, the use of a colder running plug is essential. The best way to determine which is the correct type of spark plug to use is to operate the engine under race conditions, and try spark plugs of different heat range until the correct one is discovered.

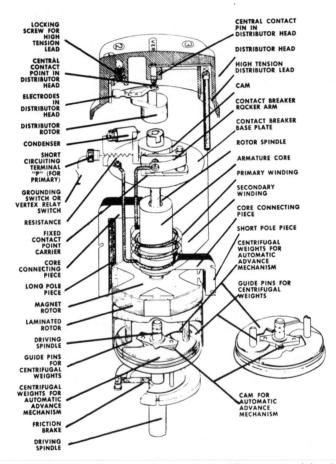

LOCKING SCREW FOR HIGH TENSION LEAD
CENTRAL CONTACT POINT IN DISTRIBUTOR HEAD
ELECTRODES IN DISTRIBUTOR HEAD
DISTRIBUTOR ROTOR
CONDENSER
SHORT CIRCUITING TERMINAL "P" (FOR PRIMARY)
GROUNDING SWITCH OR VERTEX RELAY SWITCH
RESISTANCE
FIXED CONTACT POINT CARRIER
CORE CONNECTING PIECE
LONG POLE PIECE
MAGNET ROTOR
LAMINATED ROTOR
DRIVING SPINDLE
GUIDE PINS FOR CENTRIFUGAL WEIGHTS
CENTRIFUGAL WEIGHTS FOR AUTOMATIC ADVANCE MECHANISM
FRICTION BRAKE
DRIVING SPINDLE

CENTRAL CONTACT PIN IN DISTRIBUTOR HEAD
DISTRIBUTOR HEAD
HIGH TENSION DISTRIBUTOR LEAD
CAM
CONTACT BREAKER ROCKER ARM
CONTACT BREAKER BASE PLATE
ROTOR SPINDLE
ARMATURE CORE
PRIMARY WINDING
SECONDARY WINDING
CORE CONNECTING PIECE
SHORT POLE PIECE
CENTRIFUGAL WEIGHTS FOR AUTOMATIC ADVANCE MECHANISM
GUIDE PINS FOR CENTRIFUGAL WEIGHTS
CAM FOR AUTOMATIC ADVANCE MECHANISM

Fig. X-8. Special magneto designed to be substituted for conventional distributor.

Examination of the spark plug insulator after the plug has been in operation will disclose whether it is of the correct heat range. If the insulator is white to a light amber in color, it is correct for that engine and that particular type of work. However, if the insulator has blistered or is pock-marked, a colder running plug should be substituted.

More Speed and Power

TURNING DOWN FLYWHEELS

The flywheels used on conventional passenger cars are designed to provide smooth low speed idling. As a result they are made relatively heavy. However, the greater inertia reduces acceleration. To overcome this condition, race car mechanics usually reface the flywheel in order to reduce its weight. The amount of metal to be removed depends largely on how much of the smooth idling the owner wishes to sacrifice. In general, the

Fig. X-9. Lightweight flywheel.

maximum that is removed is about one-third of the total weight. However, many mechanics will remove approximately one-quarter of the weight. When refacing a flywheel the metal should be removed from the forward face, in order not to change the surface contacted by the clutch plate. Metal should not be removed from the area of the flywheel contacting the crankshaft flange, as this would affect clutch operation. The starter ring gear should also be left intact. Fig. X-9 shows a special lightweight flywheel designed by race specialists for use on Chevrolet cars.

MORE HIGH SPEED TIPS

The cooling fan consumes a lot of power. At high speeds, up to 5 hp is requred to drive a fan. At road speeds above 35 miles per hour, the fan is not needed to cool the radiator. Consequently, fan blades can be removed unless the car is to be driven in traffic.

Additional savings in power can be made by reducing the battery charging rate to a minimum if the car is fitted with a magneto. If the car is to be used for racing only the battery and generator can be removed. Anything that can be done to reduce the weight of the car will aid materially in improving acceleration, top speed and fuel economy. In this connection, some mechanics will drill 1 in. holes in the frame. Spare tires and wheels are eliminated. Magnesium wheels are also available.

Shock absorbers are of extreme importance, both from the standpoint

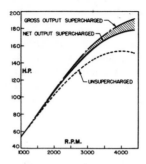

Fig. X-10. Comparison of power developed by supercharged and nonsupercharged engine.

of speed and control of the car. Leaks or defective shock absorbers will permit the driving wheels to spin and increase steering difficulties. For high speed work, different shock absorbers are therefore used. On race cars it is customary to install additional shock absorbers to get the amount of control desired.

SUPERCHARGERS AND TURBOCHARGERS

Superchargers and turbochargers are designed to force more of the air fuel mixture into the combustion chamber than would be drawn in by the normal suction of the pistons. In that way the performance of the engine is

Fig. X-11. Note timing belt for driving the supercharger on this 327 cu. in. Chevrolet engine on exhibition at parts show.

increased, Fig. X-10. Both devices are essentially blowers. The super-charger is driven mechanically by gears or chains, while the turbocharger is driven by the force of exhaust gases. Superchargers have been used for many years, while the turbocharger is a more recent development. The supercharger frequently used on stock engines is the unit developed by General Motors Diesel and is of the Rootes type, Fig. X-11. When used on the Chevrolet V-8 engines it is usually mounted between the banks of cylinders and driven by a chain belt from a sprocket at the front end of the crankshaft.

One of the disadvantages of the supercharger is the power required to drive the unit, Fig. X-10. This naturally cuts down the power available to drive the car. The turbocharger does not have this difficulty as it uses the pressure of the exhaust gases to rotate the veins of the blower.

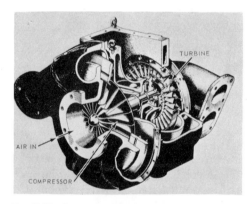

Fig. X-12. Cutaway turbocharger shows typical construction.

One type of turbocharger is shown in Fig. X-12. This cutaway view clearly shows the construction of the turbine, which is driven by exhaust gases and the compressor. Rotational speeds up to 90,000 rpm are attained by some designs. With increased compression resulting from supercharging, there is a tendency toward detonation. As a result, compression ratios are reduced or fuels of higher octane are needed. Improved fuel distribution is an important advantage of supercharging.

FUEL INJECTION

The Chevrolet type fuel injection system, Fig. X-13, comprises three basic assemblies: The intake manifold, the air meter, and the fuel meter-injector nozzle assembly.

In operation, the accelerator pedal controls the volume of air, and the volume of air in turn determines the amount of gas delivered to the fuel injection nozzles. A high pressure pump, submerged in a fuel reservoir,

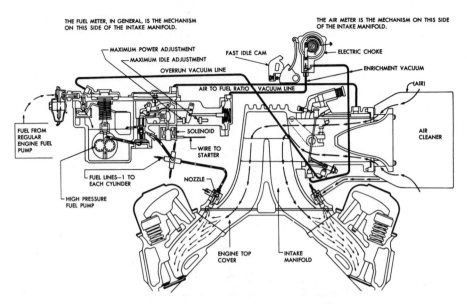

THE FUEL METER, IN GENERAL, IS THE MECHANISM ON THIS SIDE OF THE INTAKE MANIFOLD.

THE AIR METER IS THE MECHANISM ON THIS SIDE OF THE INTAKE MANIFOLD.

MAXIMUM POWER ADJUSTMENT

MAXIMUM IDLE ADJUSTMENT

OVERRUN VACUUM LINE

FAST IDLE CAM

ELECTRIC CHOKE

ENRICHMENT VACUUM

AIR TO FUEL RATIO   VACUUM LINE

(AIR)

FUEL FROM REGULAR ENGINE FUEL PUMP

SOLENOID

WIRE TO STARTER

AIR CLEANER

FUEL LINES—1 TO EACH CYLINDER

NOZZLE

HIGH PRESSURE FUEL PUMP

ENGINE TOP COVER

INTAKE MANIFOLD

Fig. X-13. Operational diagram of Chevrolet fuel injector system.

and driven by the distributor, delivers the fuel to a metering chamber from which there are two outlets. The lower outlet leads to the nozzle, and the upper to an overflow line.

A plunger sensitive to the flow of air in the system meters the amount of fuel directed toward the cylinders. Pressure at the .011 in. orifices of the nozzle measures up to 20 lb. per sq. in. The spray from these nozzles is so fine it cannot be seen by the naked eye, and is directed into the intake ports, immediately before the intake valves. The fuel-air mixture is ignited in the usual way by the spark plug.

LIGHT WEIGHT WHEELS

Special wheels made of aluminum or other light weight alloys are finished to a high degree of accuracy and therefore greatly reduce vibration and materially improve tire life. Equally important, the lighter weight and inertia improve acceleration.

Fig. X-14. Typical light weight wheel.

YEAR AND MODEL	Displacement	Number of Cylinders, Bore and Stroke	Brake Horsepower	Compression Ratio	Compression Pressure	AC Spark Plug Model	Spark Plug Gap	Location of Timing Mark	Breaker Point Open Deg. BTDC	Breaker Point Gap Used Points	Valve Lash Intake	Valve Lash Exhaust
1968	153	4-3.875x3.250	90	8.50	130	46N	.035	V	Od	.016	1 t	1 t
1968	230	6-3.875x3.250	140	8.50	130	46N	.035	V	Od	.016	1 t	1 t
1968	250	6-3.875x3.530	155	8.50	130	46N	.035	V	Od	.016	1 t	1 t
1968	302	V8-4.000x3.000	290	11.00	190	43	.035	V	4	.016	.030	.030
1968	307	V8-3.85x3.250	200	9.00	150	43S	.035	V	2	.016	1 t	1 t
1968	327	V8-4.00x3.250	210	8.75	160	44	.035	V	2g	.016	1 t	1 t
1968	327	V8-4.000x3.250	250	8.75	160	44S	.035	V	4	.016	1 t	1 t
1968	327	V8-4.000x3.250	275	10.00	160	44	.035	V	Od	.016	1 t	1 t
1968	327	V8-4.000x3.250	300	10.00	160	44	.035	V	4	.016	1 t	1 t
1968	327	V8-4.000x3.250	325	11.00	150	44	.035	V	4	.016	1 t	1 t
1968	327	V8-4.000x3.250	350	11.00	150	44	.035	V	4	.016	1 t	1 t
1968	350	V8-4.000x3.480	295	10.25	160	44	.038	V	0	.016	1 t	1 t
1968	396	V8-4.094x3.760	325	10.25	160	43N	.035	V	4	.016	1 t	1 t
1968	396	V8-4.094x3.760	350	10.25	160	43N	.035	V	TC	.016	1 t	1 t
1968	396	V8-4.094x4.760	375	11.00	160	43N	.035	V	4	.016	1 t	1 t
1968	427	V8-4.250x3.760	385	10.25	160	43N	.035	V	4	.016	1 t	1 t
1968	427	V8-4.250x3.760	390	10.25	160	43N	.035	V	4	.016	1 t	1 t
1968	427	V8-4.250x3.760	400	10.25	160	43N	.035	V	4	.016	1 t	1 t
1968	427	V8-4.250x3.760	425	11.00	150	43N	.035	V	4	.016	.024	.028
1968	427	V8-4.250x3.760	430	12.00	150	43XL	.035	V	12	.016	.022	.022
1968	427	V8-4.250x3.760	435	11.00	150	43N	.035	V	4	.016	.024	.028
1969-1970	153	4-3.87x3.25	90	8.50	130	R46N	.035	V	TCd	.016	1 t	1 t
1969-1970	230	6-3.87x3.25	140	8.50	130	R46N	.035	V	TCd	.016	1 t	1 t
1969-1970	250	6-3.87x3.53	155	8.50	130	R46N	.035	V	TCd	.016	1 t	1 t
1969-1970	302	V8-4.00x3.00	290	11.00	190	R43	.035	V	4B	.016	.030	.030
1969-1970	307	V8-3.87x3.25	200	9.00	150	R45S	.035	V	2B	.016	1 t	1 t
1969	327	V8-4.00x3.25	210	9.00	160	R45S	.035	V	2Ae	.016	1 t	1 t
1969	327	V8-4.00x3.25	235	9.00	160	45S	.035	V	2Ae	.016	1 t	1 t
1969-1970	350	V8-4.00x3.48	255	9.00	160	R44	.035	V	TCd	.016	1 t	1 t
1969-1970	350	V8-4.00x3.48	300	10.25	160	R44	.035	V	TCd	.016	1 t	1 t
1969-1970	350	V8-4.00x3.48	350	11.00	160	R44	.035	V	4B	.016	1 t	1 t
1969-1970	350	V8-4.00x3.48	370	11.00	190	R43	.035	V	4B	.016	1 t	1 t
1969	396	V8-4.09x3.76	265	9.00	160	R44N	.035	V	TCd	.016	1 t	1 t
1969	396	V8-4.09x3.76	325	10.25	160	R44N	.035	V	4B	.016	1 t	1 t
1969-1970	396	V8-4.09x3.76	350	10.25	160	R43N	.035	V	TCd	.016	1 t	1 t
1969-1970	396	V8-4.09x3.76	375	11.00	160	R43N	.035	V	4B	.016	.024	.028
1970	400	V8-4.12x3.75	265	9.00	160	R44T	.035	V	4Bj	.016	1 t	1 t
1970	400	V8-4.12x3.75	330	10.25	160	R44T	.035	V	4B	.016	1 t	1 t
1969	427	V8-4.25x3.76	335	10.25	160	R44N	.035	V	4B	.016	1 t	1 t
1969-1970	427	V8-4.25x3.76	390	10.25	160	R43N	.035	V	4B	.016	1 t	1 t
1969-1970	427	V8-4.25x3.76	400	10.25	160	R43N	.035	V	4B	.016	1 t	1 t
1969	427	V8-4.25x3.76	425	11.00	150	R43N	.035	V	4B	.016	.024	.028
1969-1970	427	V8-4.25x3.76	430	12.00	150	R43XL	.035	V	12B	.016	.022	.024
1969-1970	427	V8-4.25x3.76	435	11.00	150	R43N	.035	V	4B	.016	.024	.028
1971	250	6-3.87x3.53	145	8.50	130	R46TS	.035	V	4B	.016	1 t	1 t
1971	307	V8-3.87x3.25	200	8.50	150	R45TS	.035	V	4Bj	.016	1 t	1 t
1971	350	V8-4.00x3.48	245	8.50	160	R45TS	.035	V	2Bk	.016	1 t	1 t
1971	350	V8-4.00x3.48	270	8.50	160	R45TS	.035	V	4Bj	.016	1 t	1 t
1971	350	V8-4.00x3.48	330	9.00	150	R44TS	.035	V	8Bm	.016	.024	.030
1971	400	V8-4.12x3.75	255	8.50	160	R44TS	.035	V	4Bj	.016	1 t	1 t
1971	402	V8-4.12x3.76	300	8.50	160	R44TS	.035	V	8B	.016	1 t	1 t
1971	454	V8-4.25x4.00	365	8.50	160	R42TS	.035	V	8B	.016	1 t	1 t
1971	454	V8-4.25x4.00	425	9.00	150	R42TS	.035	V	8Bm	.016	.024	.028
1972	140	4-3.50x3.625	80 #	8.00	140	R42TS	.035	V	6N	.016	.015	.030
1972	140	4-3.50x3.625	90 #	8.00	140	R42TS	.035	V	6N	.016	.015	.030
1972	250	6-3.87x3.53	110 #	8.50	130	R46T	.035	V	4B	.016	1 t	1 t
1972	307	V8-3.87x3.25	130 #	8.50	150	R44T	.035	V	4BJ	.016	1 t	1 t
1972	307	V8-3.87x3.25	135 #	8.50	150	R44T	.035	V	4BJ	.016	1 t	1 t
1972	350	V8-4.00x3.48	155 #	8.50	160	R44T	.035	V	6B	.016	1 t	1 t
1972	350	V8-4.00x3.48	165 #	8.50	160	R44T	.035	V	6B	.016	1 t	1 t
1972	350	V8-4.00x3.48	175 #	8.50	160	R44T	.035	V	4BJ	.016	1 t	1 t

For explanation of abbreviations see next page.

343

YEAR AND MODEL	Displacement	Number of Cylinders, Bore and Stroke	Net Brake Horsepower @ rpm	Compression Ratio	Compression Pressure	AC Spark Plug Model	Spark Plug Gap	Location of Timing Mark	Breaker Point Open Deg. BTDC	Breaker Point Gap Used Points	Valve Lash Intake	Valve Lash Exhaust
1972	350	V8-4.00x3.48	255@5600	9.00	150	R44T	.035	V	4J	.016	.024	.030
1972	400	V8-4.13x3.75	170@3400	8.50	160	R44T	.035	V	2k	.016	1 t	1 t
1972	402	V8-4.12x3.76	170@3400	8.50	160	R44T	.035	V	k	.016	1 t	1 t
1972	402	V8-4.12x3.76	210@4400	8.50	160	R44T	.035	V	8	.016	1 t	1 t
1972	402	V8-4.12x3.76	240@4400	8.50	160	R44T	.035	V	8	.016	1 t	1 t
1972	454	V8-4.25x4.00	270@4000	8.50	160	R44T	.035	V	8	.016	1 t	1 t
1973 L6	250	6-3.87x3.53	100@3600	8.25	130	R46T	.035	V	6	.016	1 t	1 t
1973 L14	307	V8-3.87x3.25	115@3600	8.50	150	R44T	.035	V	4k	.016	1 t	1 t
1973 L65	350	V8-4.00x3.48	145@4000	8.50	160	R44T	.035	V	8	.016	1 t	1 t
1973 L48	350	V8-4.00x3.48	175@4000	8.50	160	R44T	.035	V	8m	.016	1 t	1 t
1973 Z28	350	V8-4.00x3.48	245@5200	8.50	150	R44T	.035	V	8	.016	1 t	1 t
1973 LF6	400	V8-4.13x3.75	150@3200	8.50	160	R44T	.035	V	8	.016	1 t	1 t
1973 LS4	454	V8-4.25x4.00	245@4000	8.25	160	R44T	.035	V	10	.016	1 t	1 t
1974 L22	250	6-3.87x3.53	100@3600	8.25	130	R46T	.035	V	8	.016	1 t	1 t
1974 L65	350	V8-4.00x3.48	145@3800	8.50	150	R44T	.035	V	0j	.016	1 t	1 t
1974 LM1	350	V8-4.00x3.48	160@3800	8.50	160	R44T	.035	V	4j	.016	1 t	1 t
1974 L48	350	V8-4.00x3.48	185@4000	8.50	160	R44T	.035	V	8j	.016	1 t	1 t
1974 L82	350	V8-4.00x3.48	245@5200	9.00	160	R44T	.035	V	8j	.016	1 t	1 t
1974 LF6	400	V8-4.12x3.75	150@3200	8.50	160	R44T	.035	V	8	.016	1 t	1 t
1974 LT4	400	V8-4.12x3.75	180@4000	8.50	160	R44T	.035	V	8	.016	1 t	1 t
1974 LS4	454	V8-4.24x4.00	235@4000	8.50	160	R44T	.035	V	10	.016	1 t	1 t
1975-1977	140	4-3.50x3.63	78@4200	8.00	140	R43TSX	.060	V	10m	...	1 t	1 t
1975	250	6-3.87x3.53	105@3800	8.25	130	R46TX	.060	V	10	...	1 t	1 t
1975	262	V8-3.67x3.10	110@3600	8.50	150	R44TX	.060	V	8	...	1 t	1 t
1975 2 BBL	350	V8-4.00x3.48	145@3800	8.50	150	R44TX	.060	V	6	...	1 t	1 t
1975 4 BBL	350	V8-4.00x3.48	205@4800	9.00	160	R44TX	.060	V	6j	...	1 t	1 t
1975	400	V8-4.13x3.75	175@3600	8.50	160	R44TX	.060	V	6j	...	1 t	1 t
1975	454	V8-4.25x4.00	215@4000	8.50	160	R44TX	.060	V	16	...	1 t	1 t
1976-1977	85	4-3.23x2.60	52@5200	8.50	145	R43TS	.035	V	10	...	3/4 t	3/4 t
1976	97.6	4-3.23x2.98	60@4800	8.5	145	R43TS	.035	V	10	...	3/4 t	3/4 t
1976	250	6-3.87x3.53	105@3800	8.25	130	R46TS	.045	V	8	...	3/4 t	3/4 t
1976	262	V8-3.67x3.10	110@3600	8.5	155	R45TS	.045	V	6	...	3/4 t	3/4 t
1976	305	V8-3.73x3.48	130@3800	8.5	155	R45TS	.045	V	6	...	3/4 t	3/4 t
1976	350	V8-4.00x3.48	135@3800	8.5	160	R45TS	.045	V	6j	...	3/4 t	3/4 t
1976	350	V8-4.00x3.48	165@3800	8.5	160	R45TS	.045	V	6	...	3/4 t	3/4 t
1976	350	V8-4.00x3.48	180@4000	8.5	160	R45TS	.045	V	8	...	3/4 t	3/4t
1976	350	V8-4.00x3.48	210@5200	8.5	160	R45TS	.045	V	12	...	3/4 t	3/4 t
1976	400	V8-4.12x3.37	175@3600	8.5	160	R45TS	.045	V	8	...	3/4 t	3/4 t
1976	454	V8-4.25x4.00	225@3800	8.5	160	R45TSX	.060	V	12	...	3/4 t	3/4 t
1977	85	4-3.23x2.60	57@5200	8.5	145	R43TS	.035	V	12	...	3/4 t	3/4 t
1977	97.6	4-3.23x2.98	63@4800	8.5	145	R43TS	.035	V	8	...	3/4 t	3/4 t
1977	250	6-3.87x3.53	110@3800	8.25	130	R46TS	.035	V	8	...	3/4 t	3/4 t
1977	305	V8-3.73x3.48	145@3800	8.5	155	R45TS	.045	V	6	...	3/4 t	3/4 t
1977	350	V8-4.00x3.48	170@3800	8.5	150	R45TS	.045	V	8	...	3/4 t	3/4 t
1977	350	V8-4.00x3.48	180@4000	8.5	150	R45TS	.045	V	8	...	3/4 t	3/4 t
1977	350	V8-4.00x3.48	210@5200	8.5	150	R45TS	.045	V	12	...	3/4 t	3/4 t
1978	98	4-3.23x2.98	63@4800	8.6	145	R43TS	.035	V	8	...	na	na
1978	98	4-3.23x2.98	68@5000	8.6	145	R43TS	.035	V	8	...	na	na
1978	151	4-4.0 x3.0	85@4400	8.3	*	R43TSX	.060	V	14	...	**	**
1978	196	V6-3.50x3.40	90@3600	8.0	*	R46TSX	.060	V	15	...	na	na
1978	200	V6-3.50x3.48	95@3800	8.2	*	R45TS	.045	V	8	...	1 t	1 t
1978	231	V6-3.80x3.40	105@3400	8.0	*	R46TSX	.060	V	15	...	na	na
1978	250	6-3.87x3.53	110@3800	8.1	130	R46TS	.035	V	10	...	1 t	1 t
1978	250	6-3.87x3.53	110@3800	8.1	130	R46TS	.035	V	6J	...	1 t	1 t
1978	305	V8-3.74x3.48	145@3800	8.4	155	R45TS	.045	V	4	...	1 t	1 t
1978	305	V8-3.74x3.48	145@3800	8.4	155	R45TS	.045	V	6J	...	1 t	1 t
1978	350	V8-4.00x3.48	170@3800	8.2	150	R45TS	.045	V	6	...	1 t	1 t
1978	350	V8-4.00x3.48	170@3800	8.2	150	R45TS	.045	V	8J	...	1 t	1 t

ABBREVIATIONS APPLICABLE TO TUNE-UP SPECIFICATIONS
Pages 343 and 344

A - After top dead center.
AFB - Carter carburetor model designation.
B - Before top dead center.
d - Applies to cars with manual transmission. With automatic, set timing at 4 deg.
e - Applies to cars with manual transmission. Set timing 2 deg. BTDC on cars with automatic transmission.
F - Flywheel.
f - Applies to cars without A.I.R. Cars with A.I.R. set timing 6 deg. BTDC.
g - Applies to cars with automatic transmission. Set timing at 2 deg. after top dead center on cars with manual transmission.
GC - Rochester carburetor model designation.
H - Adjust valve lash with engine hot.
hy - Hydraulic lifters.
j - Applies to cars with manual transmission. With automatic, set timing at 8B.
J - Set ignition timing at 6 deg. after top dead center on cars with California registration.

k - Applies to cars with manual transmission. On cars with automatic transmission set timing at 6 deg. B.
m - Applies to cars with manual transmission. On cars with automatic transmission set timing at 12 deg. B.
na - Not adjustable.
N - 4 deg. BTDC for California vehicles.
P - Set with engine stopped.
R - 0 deg. K20 Suburban models for California only.
S - For sustained high speeds, adjust intake valve lash .018 in., exhaust valve lash .030 in.
t - Number of turns from zero lash with hydraulic lifters.
TC - Top dead center.
V - Timing mark on vibration damper or on crankshaft pulley.
\# - Net or as-installed horsepower ratings.
* - Lowest cylinder compression pressure must be at least 70 percent of highest cylinder pressure.
** - Tighten rocker arm nut to 20 ft. lb.

WHEEL ALIGNMENT SPECIFICATIONS

YEAR	Caster Degrees	Camber Degrees	Toe-in Inches	Steering Axis Inclination Degrees
Chevrolet				
1965-1966	+1/4	+1/4	1/8 to 1/4	7-1/2
1967-1970	+3/4	+1/4	1/8 to 1/4	7-1/2
1971	-1	+1/2	1/8 to 1/4	...
1972	+1	+1/2	3/16	...
1973-1974	+1	+1L +1/2R	1/16	...
1975	+1-1/2	+1L +1/2R	1/16	...
1976 Belted	+1	+1L +1/2R	1/16	...
1976 Radial	+1-1/2	+1L +1/2R	1/16	...
1977-1978	+3	+3/4	3/16	...
Chevelle				
1965-1970	-1 m	+1/2	1/8 to 1/4	8-1/4
1971-1972	-1	+3/4	1/8 to 1/4	...
1973-1974 Power	0	+1L +1/2R	1/16	...
1973-1974 Manual	-1	+1L +1/2R	1/16	...
1975-1976 Power	+2	+1L +1/2R	1/16	...
1975-1976 Manual	+1	+1L +1/2R	1/16	...
Chevy II				
1962-1967	-1	+1/2	1/4 to 3/8	7
1968	+1/2	+1/4	1/8 to 1/4	8-3/4
Corvette				
1966-1969	+1	+3/4	3/16 to 5/16	7
1971-1972	#	+3/4	#	...
1973 Power	+2-3/4	+3/4	1/16	...
1973 Manual	+1-1/2	+3/4	1/16	...
1974 Power	+2-1/4	+3/4	1/4	...
1974 Manual	#	+3/4	1/4	...
1975-1976 Power	+2-1/4	+3/4	1/8	...
1975-1976 Manual	+1	+3/4	1/8	...
1977-1978	+2-1/4	+3/4	1/4	...
Malibu				
1978 Power	+3	+1/2	1/8	...
1978 Manual	+1	+1/2	1/8	...

YEAR	Caster Degrees	Camber Degrees	Toe-in Inches	Steering Axis Inclination Degrees
Camaro				
1967-1969	+1/2	+1/4	1/8 to 1/4	8-3/4
1971-1972	0	+1	1/8 to 1/4	...
1973-1974 Std.	0	+1L +3/4R	1/16	...
1973-1974 Z28	0	+1L +3/4R	1/16	...
1975-1976	+1	+1	1/16	...
1977-1978				
Nova				
1969-1972	+1/2	+1/4	1/8 to 1/4	8-3/4
1973	+1/2	+1/2	1/16	...
1974	+1/2	+1/4	3/16	...
1975-1976 Power	+1	+3/4	1/16	...
1975-1976 Manual	-1	+3/4	1/16	...
1977-1978 Power	+1	+3/4	1/16	...
1977-1978 Manual	-1	+3/4	1/8	...
Monte Carlo				
1972	+5	+3/4	3/16	...
1973-1974	+5	+1L +1/2R	1/16	...
1977	+1	+1L +1/2R	1/16	...
1978	-3	-1/2	1/8	...
Vega and Monza				
1971-1974	-3/4	+1/4	1/4	...
1975-1976	-3/4	+1/4	-1/16	...
1977	-3/4	+3/16	1/4	...
1978	-3/4	-1/2	1/4	...
Chevette				
1976-1978	+4-1/2	+1/4	1/16	...

m - Applies to all except El Camino, SS and Monte Carlo which are +1/2.
- Caster manual steering +1, Caster power steering 2-1/4. Camber 3/4. Toe-in 3/16 to 5/16. L - Left. R - Right.

ENGINE TIGHTENING SPECIFICATIONS

ENGINE MODEL	Cylinder Head Bolt Torque ft. lb.	Main Bearing Bolt Torque ft. lb.	Connecting Rod Bolt Torque ft. lb.
1966-1970, 153	95	65	35
1966-1970, 230	95	65	35
1966-1977, 250	95	65	35
1966-1968, 327	80	80	35
1966-1968, 396	80	80	50
1966-1968, 427	80	80	50
1967-1968, 350	65	80	35
1968, 302	65	80	50
1968, 307	65	80	50
1969-1970, 302	65	75	50
1969-1974, 307	65	75a	45
1969, 327	65	75a	45
1969-1974, 350	65	75a	45
1969-1970, 396	80	105	45
1969-1970, 427	80	105	50
1970-1974, 400	80	75a	45
1971-1972, 402	80	75	45
1971-1976, 454	80	75	50
1975-1976, 262	65	70a	45
1975-1977, 350	65	70a	45
1975-1976, 400	80	70a	45
1975, 454	80	110	45
1976-1977, 85	60	40-52	34-40
1976-1977, 97.6	60	40-52	34-40
1976, 454	80	110	50
1977, 140	65	70	45
1977, 305	60	65	35
1978, 98 (1.6 L)	60	50	40
1978, 151 (2.5 L)	95	65	30
1978, 196 (3.2 L)	80	100	40
1978, 200 (3.3 L)	65	70	45
1978, 231 (3.8 L)	80	100	40
1978, 250 (4.1 L)	95b	65	35
1978, 305 (5.0 L)	65	80	45
1978, 350 (5.7 L) (L.MI)	65	70	45
1978, 350 (5.7 L) (L.48, L.82)	65	80c	45

a - Outer bolts on 4 bolt caps, 65 ft. lb.
b - LH front head bolt, 85 ft. lb.
c - Outer bolts on 4 bolt caps, 70 ft. lb. (L.82)

Torque specifications are for clean, undamaged and lightly lubricated threads only. Dry, dirty and damaged threads produce friction which prevents accurate measurement of tightening torque.

COOLING SYSTEM AND CRANKCASE SPECIFICATIONS

CAR AND MODEL	Cooling System With Heater Capacity Quarts	Radiator Cap Relief Pressure Lb.	Engine Crankcase Refill Capacity Qt.
Chevrolet			
1966-1968, 153	9	15	4
1966-1968, 230	12	15	4
1966-1968, 250	13	15	4
1966-1968, 396	23	15	4
1966-1968, 427	22	15	4
1968-1970, 302	17	15	4
1968, 307	17	15	4
1968, 427 Corvette	22	15	5
1968-1972, 250	12	15	4
1968, 350 Camaro	18	15	4
1968, 396 Camaro	23	15	4
1968, 327 Camaro	18	15	4
1969-1970, 153	9	15	4
1969-1970, 230	13	15	4
1969-1974, 307	17	15	4
1969, 327	17	15	4
1969-1970, 396	23	15	4
1969-1972, 350	16	15	4
1970-1972, 400	17	15	4
1969-1970, 427 Chevrolet	22	15	4
1969-1970, 427 Corvette	22	15	5
1971-1972, 402	23	15	4
1971-1972, 454	22	15	4
1973-1975, 250	14	15	4
1973-1976, 350	18	15	4
1973-1975, 350 Corvette	19	15	4
1973-1976, 400	18	15	4
1973-1976, 454	25	15	5
1976-1977, 85 Chevette	8-1/2	15	4
1976-1977, 97.6 Chevette	9	15	4
1976-1977, 140 Monza	8	15	3-1/2
1976-1977, 250	14-1/2	15	4
1976, 305	17	15	4
1976-1977, 350 Corvette	20-3/4	15	4
1977-1978, 305 Chevrolet	16	15	4
1977, 305 Monza	18	15	4
1977, 350 Chevrolet	17-1/2	15	4
1978, 98 Chevette	9	15	4
1978, 151	11	15	4
1978, 196	11-1/2	15	4
1978, 200	11-1/2	15	4
1978, 231	14-3/4	15	4
1978, 250	14	15	4
1978, 305 Monza	16	15	4
1978, 350 Chevrolet	16-1/2	15	4
1978, 350 Corvette	21-1/2	15	4

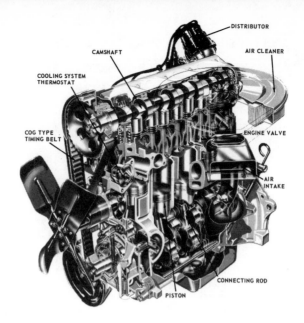

Fig. 1. Details of Vega 140 cu. in. engine.

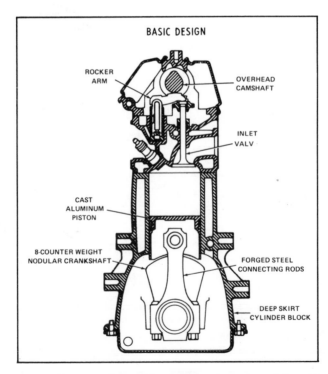

Fig. 1a. Basic design of four cylinder, overhead camshaft, 1.4 L and 1.6 L engines used in Chevette models.

SERVICING VEGA, MONZA, CHEVETTE

Vega, Monza and Chevette models are equipped with four cylinder, overhead camshaft engines. OHC engines are radically different in design and service from other Chevrolet-built engines with the camshaft located in the crankcase. Engines used in Vega, Monza and Chevette cars are: 140 cu. in. (2.3 L) Four, Fig. 1; 85 cu. in. (1.4 L) Four; 98 cu. in. (1.6 L) Four. See Fig. 1a. When servicing other-than-engine parts, follow procedures given earlier for servicing larger Chevrolet models.

IGNITION TUNE-UP

Recent models are equipped with the High Energy Ignition system. Service information on HEI is given in the chapter on Ignition Tune-Up. Details for servicing the breaker point system are as follows:

When ignition breaker points become worn and pitted they must be replaced. See Fig. 2. The procedure is as follows: Release the distributor cap hold-down screws and remove the cap. Remove rotor. Pull the primary and condenser lead wires from the contact point quick disconnect terminal. Remove the contact point set attaching screw. Lift contact point set from the breaker plate. Clean breaker plate of oil smudge and dirt. Install a new set of breaker points by reversing the procedure. Note pilot on contact set must engage matching hole in breaker plate. Check breaker points for proper alignment. See Fig. B-19, page 29. If necessary, bend fixed contact support to obtain alignment of points.

Breaker point gap of new points is 0.019 in. and for used points in good condition is 0.016 in. To set point gap, turn distributor shaft until breaker arm rubbing block is on high point of cam. This provides maximum point gap. Use a screwdriver to move point support to obtain desired gap, Fig. B-20, page 30. Then tighten lock screw. If dwell meter is available, set dwell to 31 - 34 deg.

Later models are equipped with the High Energy Ignition (HEI) system and do not have ignition breaker points. To prepare to service this system, study the ignition section of this text.

CONDENSER REPLACEMENT

Normally a new condenser is installed when the ignition breaker points are replaced. The procedure is to first remove the distributor cap and rotor. Disconnect the condenser lead from the contact point quick disconnect terminal, Fig. 2. Remove the condenser attaching screw and lift the condenser from the breaker plate. The new condenser is installed by reversing the procedure.

REMOVING AND CHECKING THE DISTRIBUTOR

First remove the distributor cap. If necessary, remove the secondary lead wires from the cap after first marking the cap tower for No. 1 cylinder. Disconnect the distributor lead from the coil terminal. Scratch a realignment mark on the distributor bowl and engine in line with rotor segment. Remove the distributor hold-down bolt and clamp, and remove the distributor from the engine. Note position of vacuum advance mechanism relative to the engine. Avoid rotating crankshaft while the distributor is removed from the engine.

Check the distributor centrifugal advance mechanism by turning the distributor rotor in a clockwise direction as far as possible. Then release the rotor to see if it returns quickly to the retard position. Any stiffness in the operation of the spark control will affect ignition timing.

To lubricate the distributor, remove the distributor cap and rotate the lubricator, Fig. 2, one-half turn at 12,000 mile intervals. Replace lubricator after 24,000 miles.

TIMING THE IGNITION

Make all adjustments with engine at operating temperature (choke valve and air cleaner damper door fully open), air conditioner on, vehicle drive wheels blocked and parking brake on. Note: Carburetor idle mixture is preset and "locked in" by the limiter caps. No attempt should be made to adjust the mixture. Do not remove mixture screw caps.

Disconnect fuel tank line from the vapor canister. Disconnect distributor spark advance hose and plug vacuum source opening. Disconnect electrical connection at anti-dieseling solenoid located on carburetor. Operate engine at idling speed of 850 rpm for cars with three speed transmission, 1200 rpm for cars with four speed transmission and 650 rpm on cars with automatic transmission. The markings on the timing tab by the crankshaft pulley are in two degree increments with the greatest number of markings on the BEFORE side of the 0. The 0 marking indicates top dead center and all before top dead center settings fall on the BEFORE (advance) side of the 0.

Adjust the ignition timing by loosening the distributor clamp and rotating the distributor body until the spark occurs at 6 deg. BTDC. If a

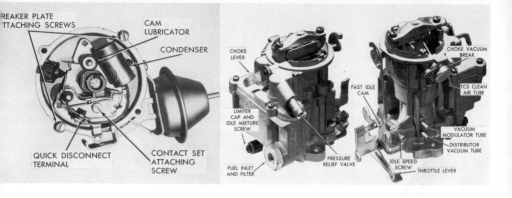

Fig. 2. Left. Note quick disconnect terminal and contact set attaching screw on Vega distributor.
Fig. 3. Right. Adjusting Rochester MV carburetor.

timing light is not available, remove the distributor cap and turn the crankshaft until No. 1 piston is on the compression stroke. Ignition breaker points should start to open at specified degrees before top center as indicated by timing tab. The firing order is 1-3-4-2.

When using a jumper cable to crank engine remotely at starter, disconnect the distributor primary lead from the negative terminal of the coil. Also, turn on the ignition switch. Failure to do this will result in a damaged grounding circuit in the switch.

SPARK PLUGS

To remove spark plug cables, pull only on the boot. Pulling on the cable may cause separation of its conducting core. Use a 5/8 in. deep socket to remove spark plugs. Inspect insulators for cracks and electrodes for wear and erosion. For maximum economy, replace used plugs every 10,000 miles. Check the decal under the hood for plug type and gap.

CARBURETOR TUNE-UP

Rochester carburetors used on Vega and Monza engines include: Mono-Jet, Fig. 3, MV, 1MV, 2GV, Fig. 4, 2GC, 2GE and triple venturi 1ME shown in Fig. C-8. Also used are Holley 5210-C and 6510-C. Carburetors differ between cars with manual and automatic transmissions. Since 1975, carburetors are adapted for use with exhaust gas recirculation (EGR).

First, thoroughly warm up engine for at least 15 minutes if cold. Torque carburetor-to-intake manifold bolts and intake manifold-to-cylinder head bolts to avoid air leaks. Check manifold heat control valve for freedom of action and correct spring tension. Adjust choke as required. Do not tamper with idle mixture screw with black limiter cap. This manufacturer's seal must not be removed unless carburetor is rebuilt.

Check fast idle adjustment with transmission in Neutral and Transmission Controlled Spark (TCS) solenoid disconnected. With full spark to distributor and cam follower tang on highest step of fast idle cam,

351

set fast idle speed at 2400 rpm. To adjust, insert screwdriver in slot on cam follower tang and bend tang until rpm is correct.

Make slow idle speed and mixture settings with engine at normal operating temperature and transmission in Drive. If carburetor has been rebuilt, install red plastic cap on mixture adjusting screw.

Float level on the MV carburetor is 1/16 in.; on the 2GV, 21/32 in.; on the 1MV, 1/8 in.; on the 2GC Federal, 19/32 in.; on the 2GC California, 21/32 in. Dry float setting on the Holley 5210-C is .420 in.

FUEL PUMP

Vega and Monza have an electric fuel pump mounted in the fuel tank. When inoperative or weak, check for: Mechanical defect (pump runs, but does not pump adequately). Open circuit (fuses OK, but pump will not run). Short circuit (fuse or fuses blown).

First check for blown fuses and possibly defective ground. Fuel pump

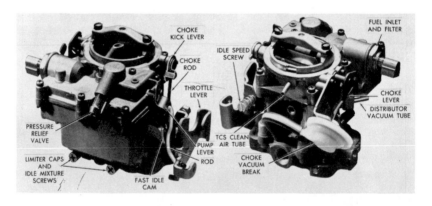

Fig. 4. Details of the model 2GV carburetor used on the 110 hp engine.

ground is located on right side of rear deck lid lock striker. Make sure ground lead is securely attached and making good electrical contact. The electric fuel pump is fused by the pump 20 amp. fuse and the 10 amp. gauge fuse, both located in the fuse panel.

The Chevette has a mechanical fuel pump mounted on the left side of the crankcase. To remove, unscrew the attaching bolts.

FUEL FILTER MAINTENANCE

To service fuel filter, disconnect fuel line connection at inlet fuel filter nut. Remove filter element and spring. Replace with new filter every 12,000 miles or 12 months, whichever comes first. Also replace bronze or paper element if plugged or if flooding occurs.

TIMING BELT REPLACEMENT - 140 CU. IN. ENGINE

To remove timing belt: Remove engine front cover and accessory drive pulley. Drain engine coolant. Loosen water pump bolts to relieve tension on belt. Remove timing belt lower cover. Then, remove belt from camshaft and crankshaft sprockets. Remove water pump.

To install belt: Apply anti-seize compound to water pump attaching bolts. Install water pump, but do not tighten bolts. Align timing mark on camshaft sprocket with notch on timing belt upper cover, Fig. 5. Align crankshaft sprocket timing mark with cast rib on oil pump cover, Fig. 6. Install timing belt on crankshaft sprocket, positioning back of belt in water pump track. Install belt on camshaft sprocket, making sure that both sprockets maintain their indexed positions.

Install timing belt lower cover and adjust belt tension: Place torque wrench with special extension in gauge hole adjacent to left side of water pump, Fig. 7. Apply 15 ft. lb. torque to water pump bolts while maintaining torque on side of pump. Replace remaining parts and refill cooling system.

TIMING BELT REPLACEMENT - 1.4 L AND 1.6 L ENGINES

To remove timing belt on 1.4 litre and 1.6 litre engines: Remove engine front upper and lower covers. Remove crankshaft pulley. Then, loosen idler pulley bolt and remove timing belt from both sprockets.

To install timing belt: Position new belt over crankshaft sprocket. Install crankshaft pulley. Next, position crankshaft at TDC for No. 1 cylinder. Align timing mark on camshaft sprocket with hole in upper

Fig. 5. Left. Timing marks on camshaft and crankshaft sprockets.
Fig. 6. Right. Crankshaft sprocket alignment marks.

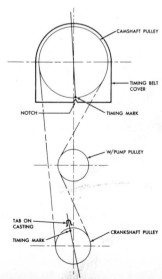

ALLEN WRENCH

Fig. 7. Left. Method of adjusting belt tension. Fig. 8. Right. Valve lash is adjusted by means of an Allen setscrew in the side of the valve lifter.

rear cover. Then, install belt on sprockets and reinstall covers.

To adjust belt tension: Disconnect starting battery and remove radiator support brackets. Remove air conditioner compressor drive belt and upper part of fan shroud. Remove fan belt, fan and fan pulley. Rotate crankshaft clockwise at least one full turn and position it at TDC for No. 1 cylinder. Loosen idler attaching bolt. Then, rotate idler pulley counterclockwise on its attaching bolt until slack is removed from belt. Apply sealer to idler attaching bolt and torque to 15 ft. lb. Using gauge, belt tension should read 55 lb.

ADJUSTING VALVE LASH

Valve lash on 1971-1975 140 cu. in. engines should be adjusted with the engine cold. Intake clearance is 0.014 to 0.016 in. Exhaust clearance is 0.029 to 0.031 in. Adjustment is provided by means of an Allen head screw in the side of the tappet, Fig. 8. This screw has a ground, tapered ramp on one surface and is threaded through the tappet at a 5 deg. angle. The flat, tapered ramp on the screw is square to the tappet axis and parallel to the valve stem tip which contacts the screw. Valve lash is adjusted with tappet on base circle of camshaft lobe and adjusted in one-turn increments. It is mandatory that screw should be turned a complete revolution each time so the flat surface of ramp is always in contact with tip of valve stem. Each revolution will change valve lash 0.003 in.

The 1.4 L and 1.6 L engines and 1976 and later 140 cu. in. engines are fitted with hydraulic lifters. The only specification calls for zero clearance with the valves closed.

OIL PAN REMOVAL

To remove the oil pan from the 140 cu. in. engine: Raise vehicle and drain oil. Support front of engine. Remove front cross member and both frame cross member braces. Disconnect steering idler arm at frame side rail. On air conditioned cars, disconnect idler arm at relay rod.

Mark relationship of steering linkage pitman arm to steering gear pitman shaft and remove pitman arm. Do not rotate pitman shaft while steering arm is disconnected as this will change steering wheel alignment. Remove flywheel cover or converter underpan as applicable. Remove pan-to-cylinder block retaining screws. Tap pan lightly to break sealing bond. Remove oil pan from engine.

To remove the oil pan from 1.4 L and 1.6 L engines: First, remove the heater housing assembly from the front of the dash. Rest the housing on top of the engine. Remove engine mount nuts. Pull back engine mount wire restraints. Remove radiator upper support. On vehicles equipped with air conditioners, remove fan upper shroud. Raise vehicle on hoist and drain crankcase. Remove oil pan attaching bolts. Using a special tool, raise the engine. Remove the oil pan from the engine.

CYLINDER HEAD REMOVAL

To remove cylinder head from 140 cu. in. engine: Remove engine front cover, camshaft cover, timing belt and camshaft timing sprocket. Remove intake and exhaust manifolds. Disconnect coolant hose at thermostat housing. Remove cylinder head bolts and lift off head.

Fig. 9. Sequence to be followed when tightening cylinder head bolts.

To install the cylinder head: Place cylinder head gasket over dowel pins with smooth side of gasket up. With the aid of an assistant, carefully guide cylinder head in place over dowel pins and gasket. Use anti-seize compound on cylinder head bolts. Note that head bolts on spark plug side are approximately 5 5/8 in. long. Those on manifold side are

6 3/8 in. long. Install bolts finger tight, then torque them in sequence, Fig. 9, to 60 ft. lb.

To remove cylinder head from 1.4 L and 1.6 L engines: First remove timing belt as previously described. Drain cooling system. Disconnect radiator upper hose and heater hose at intake manifold. Remove air cleaner and accelerator cable support bracket. Disconnect spark plug cables. Disconnect electrical connections at idle solenoid, choke, temperature sending unit and alternator. Raise vehicle and disconnect exhaust pipe to manifold.

Lower vehicle. Disconnect dipstick tube bracket. Remove cam covers and cam cover-to-camshaft housing attaching stud. Remove rocker arms, guides and valve lash adjusters. NOTE: Be sure to place these assemblies in a rack so they can be reinstalled in same relative positions. Remove cam carrier from cylinder head. Then, remove manifold with cylinder head assembly.

EMISSION CONTROL SYSTEMS

Emission control systems on the Vega include: 1. Positive Crankcase Ventilation (PCV). 2. Controlled Combustion System (CCS). 3. Evaporative Emission Control (EEC). 4. Transmission Controlled Spark (TCS). 5. Air Injector Reactor (AIR). 6. Early Fuel Evaporation (EFE). 7. Exhaust Gas Recirculation (EGR). 8. Catalytic Converter.

Check the PCV system at every oil change to make sure vacuum is drawing vapors from the crankcase. Replace the PCV valve every 24,000 mi. or 24 months; also clean hoses and fittings.

The Controlled Combustion System is designed to increase combustion efficiency through leaner carburetor adjustments and revised distributor calibration. In addition, on the majority of installations, special thermostatically controlled air cleaners are used. Basic servicing of these units is covered in the carburetor and ignition sections.

The Evaporative Emission Control System is designed to reduce fuel vapor emissions that normally vent to the atmosphere from the fuel tank and carburetor fuel bowl. The filter mounted at the bottom of the canister requires replacement every 12,000 miles. Care must be taken that the fuel tank cap is not damaged.

In the Transmission Controlled Spark system, the distributor vacuum advance has been eliminated in the low forward speeds. The control of the vacuum advance is accomplished by means of a solenoid vacuum switch which is energized in the low gears by a grounding switch at the transmission. The TCS system also incorporates a temperature override system which provides full vacuum in all gears when the engine is cold. A thermostatic water temperature switch provides the signal which energizes a normally closed relay, opening the circuit to the solenoid switch, thus providing full vacuum. The system may be checked for proper function by connecting a vacuum gauge between the solenoid and the distributor. Full vacuum should be obtained when the automatic transmission is in "second"; when a four speed transmission is in "third" or "fourth"; when a three speed transmission is in "third."

Emission control systems on 1.4 L and 1.6 L engines include positive crankcase ventilation, exhaust gas recirculation, controlled combustion system, manifold air injection reactor, evaporation control system, carburetor hot air and underfloor catalytic converter. The 1977 models have the pulse air system, Fig. H-5. Other systems are described in the chapter on Carburetor, Fuel System Service.

COOLING SYSTEM

The Vega cooling system is pressurized. The radiator cap is 15 psi type that operates at coolant temperatures up to 247 deg. F.

Maintain the coolant level in cross-flow radiators 3 in. below the bottom of the filler neck when the system is cold. Whether or not freezing temperatures are expected, cooling system protection should be maintained at least to zero deg. F to provide adequate corrosion protection and proper temperature indicating light operation. Flush system every two years with plain water, then refill with permanent glycol base antifreeze and water. Do not use alcohol or methanol base antifreeze.

Late model cooling systems include the coolant recovery system. With this setup, additional coolant is available from a translucent plastic reservoir.

To maintain the coolant recovery system: Check level of coolant in recovery reservoir every 1000 mi. Check level of coolant in radiator every 7500 mi. A faulty system is indicated: 1. If level of coolant in reservoir does not change from cold engine level to hot engine level. 2. If coolant level in reservoir continuously drops below prescribed level. 3. If coolant level in radiator is low, but level in recovery reservoir remains full.

The thermostat is of the 195 deg. type. Cooling system capacity with heater and air conditioning is 6.5 quarts; 1973-1975, 8.6 quarts.

ELECTRICAL SYSTEM

GENERATOR

The 10-SI series Delcotron generator is similar to that shown in Fig. K-2a, page 149. This unit has a solid state regulator that is mounted inside the generator slip ring end frame. The regulator voltage setting never needs adjusting and no provision for adjustment is provided.

STARTING MOTOR

The starting motor used on the Vega is shown in Fig. L-1, page 160. No periodic lubrication of the starting motor solenoid is required. Since the starting motor and brushes cannot be inspected without disassembling the unit, no service is required between overhaul periods.

BRAKES

Disc brakes are standard equipment on Vega, Monza and Chevette. Rear brakes are drum type with leading-trailing shoe design. Rear brake adjustment takes place when parking brake is applied.

When removing disc brake calipers, do not remove the hydraulic line. Lay the caliper on suspension members for support, or hang it from a wire. Do not let the caliper hang by its line.

To remove caliper and replace shoes: Raise vehicle and remove front wheels. Remove and discard mounting pin stamped nuts, Fig. 10. Remove mounting pins and lift caliper from rotor. Slide shoes to mounting sleeve opening and remove shoes, Fig. 11. Remove mounting sleeves and bushing assemblies. Clean caliper and dust boot.

When reassembling: Install new sleeves with bushings on caliper grooves with shouldered end of sleeve toward outside. Install new inner shoe on caliper and slide shoe ears over sleeve. Install outer shoe same

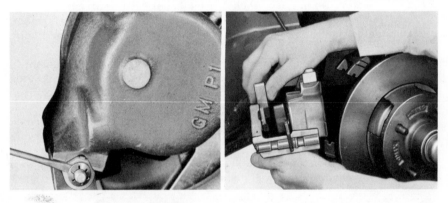

Fig. 10. Left. Removing caliper retainers. Fig. 11. Right. Removing or installing brake shoes on disc type brakes.

way. Mount caliper on vehicle. Remove 1/2 in. of brake fluid from main cylinder, then install mounting pins from inside to outside. Press stamped nuts on pins as far as possible, using a socket that seats on outer edge of nuts. Reinstall front wheels.

REAR BRAKE SERVICING

If rear brake drums cannot be removed, it will be necessary to remove brake adjustment assembly. To gain access to adjuster, knock out lanced area in web of drum. See Fig. 12. Release rod assembly

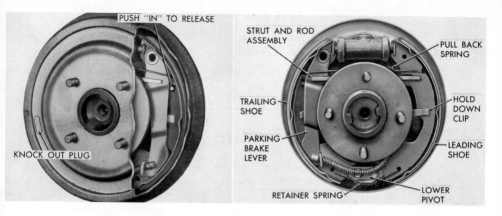

Fig. 12. Left. Location of knock-out-plug (lanced area) and release button on rear brakes of the Vega. Fig. 13. Right. Details of rear brakes.

from trailing shoe by pushing in on rod until it is clear of shoe. Pull back spring will pull shoes toward each other, allowing drum removal. Then, find and discard lanced piece of metal.

Next, release tension from parking brake equalizer. Unhook parking brake cable from lever. Do not allow lever to swing forward as this would "adjust" brakes. Using pliers, remove pull back spring, Fig. 13. Pull shoes from under hold-down clips and remove shoes, strut and adjuster as an assembly. Separate shoes and remove strut and adjuster from trailing shoe. Remove parking brake lever.

To install new brake shoes, reverse the removal procedure. Note that trailing shoe has a hole to accept parking brake lever and an oblong hole to accept adjuster rod. Also, be sure to install pull back spring so that it is over parking brake lever and engaging trailing shoe.

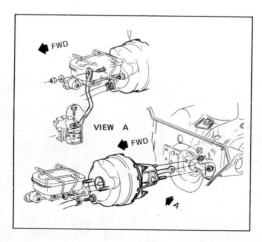

Fig. 13a. Power brake unit used on 1977–1978 Chevette. Vega and Monza unit is similar.

POWER BRAKES

Power brake unit installation on 1977 models is shown in Fig. 13a. Before removal for service, scribe across outer edges of both master cylinder and power unit to insure correct reinstallation.

CLUTCH

The single plate diaphragm spring clutch, Fig. 14, in the Vega is cable operated. To adjust for normal clutch wear: Remove cap from clutch fork ball stud located to right of transmission on clutch housing. Loosen lock nut on ball stud. Turn ball stud counterclockwise to give 0.90 $\pm$ 0.25 in. lash at clutch pedal. Tighten lock nut to 25 ft. lb. torque, being careful not to change adjustment. Install ball stud cap. Check operation.

MANUAL TRANSMISSION

The Vega is equipped with either of two manual transmissions. One is a three speed unit and the other a four speed unit. Both are fully synchronized in all forward speeds and have floor mounted shift controls.

To replace extension oil seal: Raise vehicle on a hoist. Remove propeller shaft and disconnect any items to obtain necessary clearance. Pry seal out of extension. Wash counterbore with cleaning solvent and inspect for damage. Prelubricate sealing lips and coat new seal outside diameter

Fig. 14. Details of the cable operated disc clutch. 1—Clutch cover. 2—Fork ball stud. 3—Lock nut. 4—Ball stud cap. 5—Throwout bearing support. 6—Support gasket. 7—Throwout bearing. 8—Diaphragm spring. 9—Clutch fork. 10—Clutch cable lock pin. 11—Clutch cable. 12—Pressure plate. 13—Driven disc. 14—Pilot bearing. 15—Flywheel.

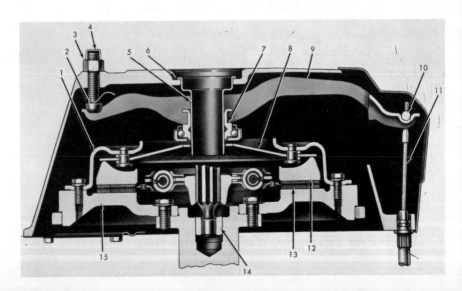

with Permatex or equivalent. Start straight in bore in case extension. Use round drift of appropriate diameter and tap seal into counterbore until flange bottoms against extension.

To remove manual shift transmission: Place shift lever in Neutral position and remove shift lever. Raise vehicle on hoist and drain lubricant. Remove propeller shaft assembly. Disconnect speedometer cable, TCS switch and back-up lamp switch. Remove cross member-to-transmission mount bolts. Support engine with jack stand and remove cross member-to-frame bolts. Remove cross member. Remove transmission-to-clutch housing upper retaining bolts and install guide pins in holes. Remove lower bolts and slide transmission rearward and remove from vehicle.

AUTOMATIC TRANSMISSION

The aluminum Powerglide transmission used through 1973 is similar to the one used on larger Chevrolet models. It is illustrated in Fig. P-12. The manual shifting Torque Drive transmission was also made available with the automatic shifting provisions removed. Lubrication, maintenance and service information are the same. The 1974-1976 models are equipped with the Turbo Hydra-Matic 250 transmission. The 1977 models are set up with the THM 200 automatic transmission illustrated in Fig. P-8a. All of these transmissions are discussed in the transmission section of this text.

REAR AXLE

Rear axle on Vega and Monza is similar to assembly shown in Figs. R-1 and S-8. Axle shaft removal is also similar. To remove rear axle oil seal: Insert button end of axle shaft behind steel case of seal. Pry seal out of bore, being careful not to damage housing. The 1976-1977 Vega and Monza use torque arm rear suspension.

PROPELLER SHAFT

The propeller shaft and universal joints used on the Vega are similar to those shown in Fig. Q-1, page 233. To remove the propeller shaft, raise the vehicle on a hoist and mark the relationship of shaft to companion flange. Disconnect the rear universal joint by removing the trunnion bearing U bolts. Tape the bearing cups to trunnion to prevent dropping and loss of roller bearings. Withdraw propeller shaft front yoke from transmission by moving shaft rearward, passing it under the rear axle housing. Plug rear of transmission to prevent leakage of lubricant.

FRONT WHEEL ALIGNMENT

Camber and caster adjustments on the Vega and Monza are made by the

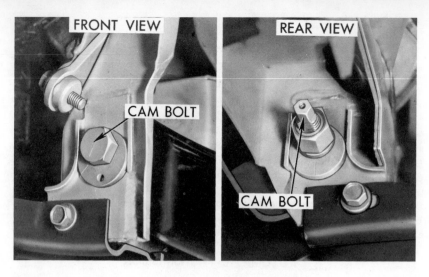

Fig. 15. Camber and caster adjustments.

cam bolts which are the attachment for the lower control arm. To adjust camber: Loosen front lower control arm pivot nut. Rotate cam to obtain correct setting. Caster is adjusted next: Loosen rear lower control arm pivot nut. Rotate cam until correct setting is reached. See Fig. 15. Toe-in is checked last: Loosen clamp bolt nut at each end of each tie rod. Rotate sleeve until correct toe-in is obtained. The sleeve clamps must be positioned between locating dimples at either end of sleeve. Opening in sleeve must not be covered by the clamp. Correct camber is + 1/4 deg., caster is - 3/4 deg. Toe-in is 3/16 in. to 5/16 in.

The procedure for adjusting wheel alignment on Chevette models is detailed on page 259 in the chapter on Wheel Alignment, Steering.

SHOCK ABSORBER SERVICE

To remove the front shock absorbers: Hold shock absorber stem and remove nut, upper retainer and grommet. Raise vehicle on a hoist and remove bolts from lower end of shock absorber. Lower shock absorber from vehicle.

When installing new front shock absorbers: Place lower retainer and rubber grommet in position. Extend shock absorber and install stem through spring tower. Install lower bolts and torque to 20 ft. lbs. Install upper rubber grommet, retainer and nut on shock absorber stem. Hold stem and tighten nut to 12 ft. lbs.

To remove the rear shock absorbers: Raise vehicle on hoist and support rear axle assembly. Remove upper attaching bolts and lower attaching nut, retainer and cushion. Remove shock absorber.

To install a new rear shock absorber, reverse the procedure.

ENGINE SPECIFICATIONS

	140 cu. in. 2.3 L	85 cu. in. 1.4 L	98 cu. in. 1.6 L
Engine bore and stroke	3.501x3.60	3.228x2.606	3.228x2.98
Displacement	140 cu. in.	85 cu. in.	98 cu. in.
Compression ratio 1971-1973	8.5 to 1	----	----
Compression ratio 1974-1977	8.0 to 1	8.5 to 1	8.5 to 1
Compression ratio, 1978	----	----	8.6 to 1
Firing order	1-3-4-2	1-3-4-2	1-3-4-2
Spark plug model	SD	SD	SD
Spark plug gap, 1971-1974	.035 in.	----	----
Spark plug gap, 1975	.060 in.		
Spark plug gap, 1976-1977	.035 in.	.035 in.	.035 in.
Spark plug gap, 1978	----	----	.035 in.
Ignition timing, 1971-72	6 BTDC	----	----
Ign. timing basic eng., 1973	8 BTDC	----	----
Ign. timing Cal., 1974	8 BTDC	----	----
Ign. timing Fed., 1974-77M	12 BTDC	10 BTDC	10 BTDC
Ign. timing Fed., 1974-77A	10 BTDC	10 BTDC	10 BTDC
Ign. timing, 1978	----	----	8 BTDC
Valve lash, intake	.015 in.	Hydr.	Hydr.
Valve lash, exhaust	.030 in.	Hydr.	Hydr.
Idle speed	SD	SD	SD
Cooling system capacity 1971-1974	6.5 qt.	----	----
Cooling system capacity 1975-1977	8.6 qt.	8.5 qt.	9.0 qt.
Cooling system capacity 1978	----	----	9.0 qt.
Crankcase refill capacity	4 qt.	4 qt.	4 qt.
Caster	-3/4	+4 1/2	+4 1/2
Camber	+1/4	+1/4	+1/4
Toe-in	1/8 in.	1/16 in.	1/16 in.

SD See decal under hood.
HEI High energy ignition.
M Manual shift transmission.
A Automatic transmission.

INDEX

A

Accessory service, 175
Air cleaner service, 56, 302
Air conditioning service, 184
Air Injection Reactor system, 68, 302
Alternator
  output check, 153
  pinpointing trouble, 152
  precautions, 151
  regulator voltage adjustment, 155
  service, 147, 149
  trouble shooting, 156
  wiring diagram, 149
Aluminum Powerglide, 221, 223
Antifreeze, 134, 357
Antifreeze in lubricating system, 128
Automatic level control, 190
Automatic transmissions, 215, 361
  drain and refill instructions, 215
  lubrication, 303
Axle oil seal and/or bearing
    replacement, 239, 240
Axle shaft replacement, 238

B

Backup lamp switch replacement, 172
Ball joints, checking, 255
Battery,
  charging, 145
  failure, causes, 143
  installation, 145
  long life, 143
  testing, 143, 144
Body service, 315
Brake disc, reconditioning, 286
Brake drums,
  reconditioning, 277
  removal, 271
Brake master cylinder, 291
Brake service, 269, 358
Brake system, flushing, 289
Brakes, trouble shooting, 296
Breaker point gap,
  adjusting, 23
  setting, 30

Breaker points, replacement, 25, 27
Bumpers, energy absorbing, 193

C

Camber, 256
Carburetion, tips, 333
Carburetor
  air cleaners, 56, 57, 58, 302
  emission controls, 65, 70
  float level table, 51, 52, 53
  hot air system, 58
  overhaul, 61, 62
  overhaul kit, 61, 62
  Rochester GC, 53, 54
  Rochester 1ME, 54
  Rochester M4MC/M4MCA, 55
  service, 43, 49, 53, 55, 351
  service tips, 61
  trouble shooting, 64
Caster, 256
Catalytic converter, 137, 138, 141
C-clamp compressor, 87
Charging battery, 145
Chevrolet cars,
  1978 Corvette, 4
  1978 Monza, 80
  1978 Caprice Classic, 105
  1978 Impala, 105
  1978 Malibu, 130
  1978 Nova, 142
  1977 Monza Spyder, 158
  1977 Impala, 158
  1977 Caprice Station Wagon, 158
  1977 Monte Carlo, 168
  1977 Concours, 168
  1977 Chevelle Malibu, 168
  1977 Monza, 214
  1977 Vega GT, 232
  1977 Chevette, 232
  1977 Camaro, 232
  1977 Vega GT, 242
  1976 Chevelle Malibu, 242
  1976 Monte Carlo, 242
  1975 Camaro LT, 308
  1975 Chevelle Laguna, 308

Index

Choke adjustment, 48
Cleaning the interior, 315, 316, 317
Clutch
  adjustment, 199, 200, 361
  operation, checking, 199
  release bearing, 201
  removal, 201
  service, 197
  throw-out bearing, 201
  trouble shooting, 201
Compression
  gauge, 9
  pressure table, 10
  raising, 331
  test, 9
Condenser, replacement, 24
Connecting rod
  alignment, 100
  assemblies, installation, 111
  caps, tightening, 113
  removal, 81
Controlled Combustion System, 67
Convertible top, 187
Cooling system
  cleaning, 131
  clogging, 128
  draining, 125
  kinks, 125, 357
  leaks, quick check, 128
  recovery system, 125, 357
  thermostat, 126, 127, 357
  trouble shooting, 136, 357
Crankcase
  capacities, 301
  ventilation valve, 65, 302
Crankshaft, checking, 102
Cruise Master
  speed control, 188
  system checks, 189
Cylinder balance test, 12
Cylinder head
  bolt tightening sequence, 72, 74
  cleaning, 93
  removal, 71, 355
Cylinders, reconditioning, 111

D

Delcotron
  alternating current generator, 148
  diode and field test, 153
  open field check, 154

Differential, 243
  limited slip, 244
  Positraction, 244
Dimmer switch replacement, 172
Directional signal assembly, 180
Disc brakes, servicing, 277, 358
Distributor
  cap, removing, 22
  exploded view, 27, 31
  lubrication, 303
  replacement, 32
  rotor, removing, 22
  shaft rotation, 37
Door adjustment, 322
Door inside handle removal, 323
Dual exhaust system, 138
Dual piston disc brake, 278
Dust leaks, 318

E

Early Fuel Evaporation, 70
Electrolyte indicator, 143
Emergency trouble shooting, 309
Emission Control, 65, 356
Energy absorbing bumpers, 193
Energy absorbing steering column, 265
Engine
  bearing replacement, 100
  disassembly shortcuts, 71
  oil, 301
  removal, 82
  repairs, trouble shooting, 85, 117
  valve removal, 86
Evaporative Emission Control, 66
Exhaust emission systems, 65
Exhaust Gas Recirculation, 70
Exhaust manifold and heat control
  valve, 70, 139
Exhaust system service, 137

F

Fan belt check, 133
Firing order, 12, 13, 37
Float adjustment, 49
Four-speed transmission, 210, 212
Fuel economy graph, 7, 16
Fuel filter, 55, 302, 352
Fuel gauge, 184, 185
Fuel injection, 341
Fuel pump, 63, 352
Fuel system service, 43
Fuel system trouble shooting, 63

G

Generator
charge indicator, 185
lubrication, 304
precautions, 151
service, 147, 156
trouble shooting, 156
Glass polishing, 326

H

Head lamp
adjustments, 165
aiming chart, 164
door, actuator assembly, 179
hidden, 179
Headlight
changing, 166
replacement, 167
sealed beam, 166
Hidden head lamps, 179
High Energy Ignition, 14, 38, 40
Hood adjustment, 324
Hydraulic brake system,
bleeding, 287
Hydraulic lifters, 121
assembly, 122
checks, 115
service, 121
Hydraulic valve lifter adjustment, 123
Hydrometer, 144

I

Idle speed and mixture
adjustment, 45, 47
Ignition
breaker points, 29
cable, 39
coil replacement, 41
performance, 337
pulse amplifier unit, 37
pulse amplifier wiring diagram, 38
resistor, 40
system wiring diagram, 15
timing, 34, 350
transistor, 37
trouble shooting, 41
tune-up, 15
Instrument cluster, 175
wiring diagram, 171
Instrument service, 175
Interior, cleaning, 315, 316, 317
Interlock system, seat belt, 191

L

Leaf spring removal, 254
Level control, 190
Lighting switch, 167
wiring diagram, 169
Lighting system
service, 165
trouble shooting, 173
Lighting wiring diagram, 171, 192
Lubrication, 301

M

Magneto, 338
Main bearing
checking and replacing, 104
replacement, 106
Manifold heat control valve, 70, 139
Manual transmission service, 203, 360
Mechanical lifers on V-8 engine, 119
Mechanical valve lifter
adjustment, 119

O

Octane selector, 35
Oil
bath air cleaner, 58
changes, 301, 302
pressure indicator, 185
pan removal, 75, 76, 77, 354
selection, 301
tests, 106, 107
wetted paper air cleaner, 57
Overcharging battery, 145
Overdrive
electrical wiring diagram, 213
quick check, 213

P

Parking brakes, adjusting, 287
Parking brake system, 287
PCV valve, 66
Performance, 329
Piston
pins, check, 99
ring clearance, 97, 98, 99
ring fitting, 96
ring and gap, 97
ring groove cleaning, 94
ring installation, 94
Polyurethane air cleaner, 56
Porting, points, 333
Positive crankcase ventilating
system, 65

Index

Positraction differential, 244
Power brake
  service, 293, 294, 360
  trouble shooting, 297
  vacuum check, 295
Powerglide, 221, 223
  trouble shooting, 229
Power operated front seats, 186
Power steering service, 266
Power window service, 326
Primary ignition circuit, 40
Propeller shaft
  service, 233, 361
  trouble shooting, 236
Pulse air valve system, 141

R

Radiator
  cap check, 131
  cap, pressure type, 127, 357
  filling, 132
  flow check, 132
Rear axle assembly,
  overhaul, 243
  removal, 241
  lubrication, 304
  service, 237
  trouble shooting, 245
Rear coil springs, removing, 251
Rear deck lid adjustment, 324
Rear main oil seal replacement, 108
Reconditioning valves, 85, 88
Relining brakes, 274
Rocker arms, 86
Rust prevention, 318

S

Seat belt, starter interlock
  system, 191
Self-adjusting brakes
  adjustment, 270
  servicing, 270
Shock absorber service, 247, 362
Single piston, disc brake, 280
Six-way seat, 186
Spark plug
  cleaning, 20
  gap, 20
  graphs, 16
  installation, 21
  original equipment table, 17, 18
  removal, 21

Spark plugs, 16, 351
Spark quick test, 15
Specifications,
  cooling system and crankcase, 347
  engine tightening, 346
  tune-up, 343, 344, 345
  Vega, Monza, Chevette, 363
  wheel alignment, 346
Speedometers, care, 183
Spring service, 247, 250
Stabilizer bar replacement, 262
Starter, 159
  adjustments, 159
  checks, 159
  interlock system, 191
  lubrication, 304
  service, 159
Starting circuit diagram, 162
Starting motor
  exploded view, 161
  removal, 162
  sectional view, 162
Starting motor and solenoid
  check, 161
Starting service, trouble
  shooting, 162, 163
Steering, 255, 259
  gear adjustment, 263
  gear lubrication, 304
  linkage, 261
  trouble shooting, 267
  wheel removal, 265
Stoplight switch, 182
Striker plate adjustment, 325
Supercharger, 340
Suspension, 247, 251
Synchromesh transmission
  trouble shooting, 228

T

Tail-stoplight and backup light, 181
Temperature indicator, 186
Theft deterrent system, 182
  wiring diagram, 183
Thermostatically controlled
  air cleaner, 58, 59, 67
Thermostats, 132
Three-speed Saginaw,
  disassembly, 208
Three-speed transmission,
  disassembly, 205

Timing
  belt replacement, 353
  case oil seal, 82
  case removal, 81
  chain replacement, 113
  gear replacement, 114
  ignition, 34, 350
Tire pressure, 305
Tire service, 301, 305
Tires, changing, 306
Tires, repairing, 306
Toe-in, 256
Toe-in adjustment, 259
Torque drive transmission, 225
Torque wrench, 104
Transistor ignition, 37
Transmission Controlled Spark
  system, 69
Transmission removal, 203, 215
Transmission service, 204
Trim assembly, removal, 325
Trouble shooting,
  alternator, 156
  brakes, 297
  carburetor, 64
  clutch, 201
  cooling system, 136
  emergency, 309
  engine repairs, 117
  fuel system, 64
  generator, 156
  ignition, 41
  lighting systems, 173
  Powerglide, 230
  propeller, shaft, 236
  rear axle, 245
  starting systems, 162
  steering, 267
  synchromesh transmission, 229
  10-SI Delcotron, 156
  transmissions, 229
  universal joints, 236
  wheel alignment, 267
Tune-up, first step, 9
Tune-up tips, 7, 349
Turbocharger, 340

Turbo Hydra-Matic, quick
  service, 217, 218, 225
Turbo Hydra-Matic
  transmission, 216
Turn signal, quick check, 180

U

Universal joint, 233
  lubrication, 304

V

Vacuum gauge, 13
Valve
  adjusting, 119, 354
  guide reaming, 92
  guides, 93
  lifter adjustment, 119
  lifter parts, 122
  lifters, hydraulic, 115, 116
  refacing machine, 88
  spring checks, 91
  spring compressing, 92
  spring installed height table, 91
  spring replacement, 91
  stem seal replacement, 91
  tappet adjustment, 120
Valves, reconditioning, 85, 88
Vega, Monza, Chevette, 349
Voltage regulator, circuitry, 150

W

Water leaks, 318
Water pump service, 135
Weather strips, 320
Wheel
  alignment, 255, 267, 361
  balancing, 262
  bearing adjustment, 300
  cylinders, quick service, 290
Windshield washer
  pump mechanism, 178
Windshield wiper
  and linkage details, 177
  motor details, 176
  service, 176
Wiring diagram, Engine
  compartment, 171, 192
Wood grain transfer, 327

MERCY FALLS

ALSO BY WILLIAM KENT KRUEGER

Blood Hollow
The Devil's Bed
Purgatory Ridge
Boundary Waters
Iron Lake

MERCY FALLS

WILLIAM KENT KRUEGER

ATRIA BOOKS
New York London Toronto Sydney

ATRIA BOOKS

1230 Avenue of the Americas
New York, NY 10020

Copyright © 2005 by William Kent Krueger

All rights reserved, including the right to reproduce this book or portions thereof in any form whatsoever. For information address Atria Books, 1230 Avenue of the Americas, New York, NY 10020

Library of Congress Cataloging-in-Publication Data

Krueger, William Kent.
   Mercy Falls / by William Kent Krueger.—1st Atria Books hardcover ed.
     p. cm.
   ISBN-13: 978-0-7434-4588-7
   ISBN-10:   0-7434-4588-0
    1. O'Connor, Cork (Fictitious character)—Fiction. 2. Private investigators—Illinois—Chicago—Fiction. 3. Rich people—Crimes against—Fiction. 4. Businessmen—Crimes against—Fiction. 5. Chicago (Ill.)—Fiction.
I. Title.

PS3561.R766M47 2005
813'.54—dc22

2004052905

First Atria Books hardcover edition August 2005

10 9 8 7 6 5 4 3 2 1

ATRIA BOOKS is a trademark of Simon & Schuster, Inc.

Manufactured in the United States of America

For information regarding special discounts for bulk purchases, please contact Simon & Schuster Special Sales at 1-800-456-6798 or business@simonandschuster.com

In memory of
Marilynne Miracle Krueger
and
Jane Jordan Browne,
two great women who have passed.

ACKNOWLEDGMENTS

First, a hearty thanks to all my cohorts in Crème de la Crime who, for a dozen years, have offered me the best in comradeship and critique.

I am so very thankful for Danielle Egan-Miller's decision to return to the business of being an agent, which she does so well.

For their editorial guidance and strong voices on my behalf, I owe a deep debt of gratitude to my editors, Emily Bestler and Sarah Branham. Thanks also to Anne Harris and Holly Bemiss of Atria, who have worked so hard with me to get the word out.

There are people who live the reality the rest of us draw on for our fiction. We are fortunate that they tend to be generous with their expertise and experience. Thanks to: former Pine County sheriff Steve Haavisto; Sergeant Jane Laurence of the St. Paul Police Department; Ramsey County Assistant Attorney Tami McConkey; and Connie Carlson and all her gang (cops and otherwise) in Prior Lake, Minnesota.

Finally, a big hug to Jim Theros and my friends at the St. Clair Broiler, staff and regulars, who make the place feel so much like home.

HOW IT ENDS

SHE WOKE NAKED on the bed, in a room she didn't recognize, her mind as clear of memory as the sky outside her window was of clouds. A huge pillow that smelled faintly of lavender cradled her head. She was too warm and drew back the covers so that she lay exposed on the white sheet like a delicacy on a china plate.

She tried to sit up, far too quickly, and the room spun. A minute later, she tried again, this time rising gradually until she could see the whole of the great bedroom. The bed itself was a four-poster with a canopy. The armoire a few feet distant was the color of maple syrup and carved with ornate scrolling. On the walls, in elegant, gilt-edged frames, hung oil paintings of Mediterranean scenes, mostly with boats and angry, blue-black seas. The magnificent red of the Persian rug matched the thick drapes drawn back to let in the morning light. None of this was familiar to her. But there was one detail that struck a welcome chord: an explosion of daisies in a yellow vase on the vanity. Daisies, she remembered, had always been her favorite flowers.

A clean, white terry cloth robe had been neatly laid out at the foot of the bed, but she ignored it. She walked to the daisies and touched one of the blossoms. Something about the fragility of the petals touched her in return and made her sad in a way that felt like grieving.

For whom? she wondered, trying to nudge aside the veil that, at the moment, hung between her perception and all her

1

understanding. Then a thought occurred to her. The birds. Maybe that was it. She was grieving for all the dead birds.

Her eyes lifted to the vanity mirror. In the reflection there, she saw the bruises on her body. One on her left breast above her nipple, another on the inside of her right thigh, oval-shaped, both of them, looking very much like the blue ghosts of tooth marks.

As she reached down and gingerly touched the tender skin, she heard firecrackers go off outside her window, two of them. Only two? she thought. What kind of celebration was that?

She put on the robe, went to the door, and opened it. Stepping out, she found herself in a long hallway with closed doors on either side, her only companions several tall standing plants that were spaced between the rooms like mute guardians. At each end of the hall, leaded windows with beveled glass let in enough daylight to give the emptiness a sense of benign well-being that she somehow knew was false. She crept down the hallway, listening for the slightest sound, feeling the deep nap of the carpet crush under the soles of her bare feet. At last she reached a staircase that wound to the lower level. She followed the lazy spiral unsteadily, her hand holding to the railing for balance, leaving moist fingerprints on the polished wood that vanished a moment after her passing.

She stood at the bottom of the stairway, uncertain which way to turn. To her right, a large room with a baby grand piano at its center, a brick fireplace, a sofa and loveseat of chocolate brown leather. To her left, a dining room with a huge crystal chandelier and a table large enough for a banquet. Sunlight from a long window cleaved the table, and in the bright gleam sat another vase full of daisies. Drawn by the smell of freshly brewed coffee, she moved through the dining room to the opened door of the kitchen beyond.

A carafe of orange juice sat on the counter near the sink, and next to it a glass, poured and waiting. The smell of the coffee came from a French-press coffeemaker that sat on a large butcher-block island. An empty cup and saucer had been placed on the block, as if she were expected. A book lay there, too, opened to a page that began, *I couldn't sleep all night; a foghorn was groaning incessantly in the Sound, and I tossed half-sick between grotesque reality and savage, frightening dreams.*

The sliding glass door that overlooked the veranda was drawn back, letting in the morning air, and she walked across the cool black and white kitchen tiles to the doorway. From there, she could see the back of the estate with its pool set into the lawn like a piece of cut turquoise. Beyond was the blue-gray sweep of a great body of water that collided at the horizon with a cornflower sky. Beside the pool stood a man in a yellow windbreaker with the hood pulled up. Although she couldn't see his face, there was something familiar in his stance. She stepped outside, not bothering to slide the door closed behind her.

It was a chilly morning. The cold marble of the veranda made her feet ache, but she paid no attention, because something else had caught her eye. A crimson billow staining the blue water. She descended the steps and followed a limestone walk to the apron of the pool.

The body lay on the bottom, except for the arms, which floated free, lifted slightly as if in supplication. The swimming trunks were white, the skin tanned. She couldn't see the wounds, only the blood that leaked from somewhere underneath, gradually tinting the turquoise water a deep rose.

The standing man turned his head slowly, as if it were difficult, painful even, for him to look away from death. The sun was at his back, his face shadowed, a gun in his hand.

She recognized him, and the thought of what he'd just done pulled her heart out of her chest.

"Oh, Cork, no," she whispered.

When he heard his name, his hard, dark eyes grew soft. Corcoran O'Connor stared at his wife, at her clean robe, her bare feet, her hair still mussed from a night she barely remembered.

"Jo," he said, "I came to bring you home."

1

*T*HEY HIT THE skunk just outside of town, and after that, they drove with the windows down. It didn't help much.

"I know what you're thinking," Deputy Marsha Dross said.

"How could you know what I'm thinking?" Cork replied.

"Because it's what I'd be thinking if I were you."

"And what's that?"

"That if I'd let you drive, this wouldn't have happened."

"You're not me," Cork said. "And that's not what I'm thinking."

"What are you thinking?"

"Just wondering if there's enough money in the budget for a new Land Cruiser." He put his head out the window and let the air clear his nose.

The road they were traveling had been traveled before by generations of Ojibwe and Voyageurs. It connected the Blueberry River with Iron Lake and had been an important passage in the days of the fur trade. The French had called it Portage du Myrtille, Blueberry Portage. To the Ojibwe, whom the white men often called Chippewa but who preferred the name Anishinaabe, which meant Original People, it was known as Maanadamon—Bad Trail—because it was a long portage with stretches of marsh and deep mud. And skunks. To the engineers who, in the mid twentieth century, had widened and graded it and laid down asphalt, it was called simply County Road 23. They'd killed the beauty of the

5

names, but they hadn't been able to destroy the stunning grandeur of the land through which it ran, the great North-woods of Minnesota.

The asphalt ended at the beginning of the Iron Lake Reservation. On the rez, the wide shoulders disappeared and the road became a narrow gravel track following a clear stream that threaded its way through vast stands of pine and rugged hills topped with birch trees and spruce.

As Dross slowed down, the skunk smell grew worse.

"Maybe I should take it through a creek or something," she suggested.

"With skunk, I think you just have to let it wear off. Maybe we'll put this unit out to pasture for a while." He scanned the road in front of them, looking for the turn he knew was coming up.

Autumn had started out cold that year. The sugar maples and sumac had turned early, a deep crimson. At sunrise, the eastern sky was often the color of an open wound and sometimes on crisp mornings the frost that lay over everything reflected the sky, and the whole land appeared to bleed. Warm weather returned in the first week of October, and for the past few days it had felt almost like June again.

"I love Indian summer." Marsha Dross smiled, as if hoping for a pleasant change of subject.

She was a tall woman, nearly six feet, and slender. Her hair was coarse and brown and she kept it short. She had a broad face, large nose. In her uniform and without makeup—something she never wore on the job—she was sometimes mistaken for a man. Off duty, she knew what to do with mascara and eyeliner and lip gloss. She preferred tight dresses with high hemlines, gold jewelry, and line dancing.

"Don't you love Indian summer, Cork?"

"Know where the term *Indian summer* comes from?" he asked.

"No."

"A white man's phrase. They didn't trust Indians, so when the warm days returned in late fall and it felt like summer but everyone knew it was a lie, they gave it a name they deemed appropriate."

"I didn't know."

"Yes."

"Yes, what?"

"I do love Indian summer." He pointed to the right. "Turn here."

"I know."

Dross pulled onto a side road even smaller and rougher than the one they'd just followed, and they slipped into the blue shadow of a high ridge where a cool darkness had settled among the pine trees. The red-orange rays of the setting sun fell across the birches that crowned the hilltops, and the white trunks seemed consumed by a raging fire.

"I wish you had let me take the call alone," Dross said.

"As soon as you hit that skunk, so did I." He smiled briefly. "You know my policy."

"I responded to a lot of calls on the rez when Wally was sheriff, and Soderberg."

"I'm sheriff now. Domestic disturbances can turn ugly, even between people as harmless as Eli and Lucy."

"Then send another deputy with me. You don't always have to go on the rez calls."

"When you're sheriff, you can do things your way."

Life, Cork knew, was odder than a paisley duck. Three months before he'd been a private citizen, proud proprietor of Sam's Place, a small burger joint on a lovely spot along the shore of Iron Lake. Flipping burgers was a vocation many people probably considered only slightly less humble than, say, rounding up shopping carts in a Wal-Mart parking lot, but Cork had grown fond of his independence. When a scandal forced the duly elected sheriff, a man named Arne Soderberg, from office, the Board of County Commissioners had offered Cork the job. He had the experience; he had the trust of the people of Tamarack County; and the commissioners happened to catch him in a weak moment.

Dross slowed the Land Cruiser. "The truth is, you love going out like this."

The truth was, he did.

"There," Cork said.

It was a small, shabby cabin set against the base of the ridge, with a horseshoe of poplar trees around the back and sides. There was an old shed to the right, just large enough for a pickup truck, but Cork knew it was so full of junk there was no way a pickup could fit. A metal washtub sat in the yard, full of potting soil and the browning stalks of mums that had frozen days before. A big propane tank lay like a fat, white hyphen between the cabin and the shed. Behind the shed stood an old outhouse.

Dross parked off the road in the dirt of what passed for a drive. "Looks deserted," she said.

The curtains were open and behind each window was deep black.

"Eli's pickup's gone," she noted. "Maybe they patched things up and went off to celebrate."

The call had come from Lucy Tibodeau who lived with her husband Eli in the little cabin. These two had a long history of domestic disputes that, more often than not, arose from the fact that Eli liked to drink and Lucy liked to bully. When Eli drank, he tended to forget that he weighed 140 pounds compared to Lucy's 200-plus. In their altercations, it was generally Eli who took it on the chin. They always made up and never actually brought a formal complaint against one another. Patsy, the dispatcher, had taken the call and reported that Lucy was threatening to beat the crap out of Eli if someone didn't get out there to stop her. Which was a little odd. Generally, it was Eli who called asking for protection.

Cork looked at the cabin a moment, and listened to the stillness in the hollow.

"Where are the dogs?" he said.

"Dogs?" Dross replied. Then she understood. "Yeah."

Everybody on the rez had dogs. Eli and Lucy had two. They were an early-warning system of sorts, barking up a storm when visitors came. At the moment, however, everything around the Tibodeau cabin was deathly still.

"Maybe they took the dogs with them."

"Maybe," Cork said. "I'm going to see if Patsy's heard anything more."

Dross put on her cap and opened her door. She stepped out, slid her baton into her belt.

Cork reached for the radio mike. "Unit Three to Dispatch. Over."

"This is Dispatch. Go ahead, Cork."

"Patsy, we're at the Tibodeau place. Looks like nobody's home. Have you had any additional word from Lucy?"

"That's a negative, Cork. Nothing since her initial call."

"And you're sure it came from her?"

"She ID'd herself as Lucy Tibodeau. Things have been quiet out there lately, so I figured we were due for a call."

Marsha Dross circled around the front of the vehicle and took a few steps toward the cabin. In the shadow cast by the ridge, everything had taken on a somber look. She stopped, glanced at the ground near her feet, bent down, and put a finger in the dirt.

"There's blood here," she called out to Cork. "A lot of it."

She stood up, turned to the cabin again, her hand moving toward her holster. Then she stumbled, as if she'd been shoved from behind, and collapsed facedown. In the same instant, Cork heard the report from a rifle.

"Shots fired!" he screamed into the microphone. "Officer down!"

The windshield popped and a small hole surrounded by a spiderweb of cracks appeared like magic in front of Cork. The bullet chunked into the padding on the door an inch from his arm. Cork scrambled from the Land Cruiser and crouched low against the vehicle.

Dross wasn't moving. He could see a dark red patch that looked like a maple leaf spread over the khaki blouse of her uniform.

The reports had come from the other side of the road, from the hill to the east. Where Cork hunkered, the Land Cruiser acted as a shield and protected him, but Dross was still vulnerable. He sprinted to her, hooked his hands under her arms, and dug his heels into the dirt, preparing to drag her to safety. As he rocked his weight back, something stung his left ear. A fraction of a second later another report came from the hill. Cork kept moving, his hands never losing their grip as he hauled his fallen deputy to the cover of the Land Cruiser.

A shot slammed through the hood, clanged off the engine block, and thudded into the dirt next to the left front tire.

Cork drew his revolver and tried to think. The shots had hit an instant before he'd heard the sound of them being fired, so the shooter was at some distance. But was there only one? Or were others moving in, positioning themselves for the kill?

He could hear the traffic on the radio, Patsy communicating with the other units, the units responding. He tried to remember how many cruisers were out, where they were patrolling, and how long it would take them to reach that cabin in the middle of nowhere, but he couldn't quite put it all together.

Dross lay on her back staring up with dazed eyes. The front of her blouse was soaked nearly black. Cork undid the buttons and looked at the exit wound in her abdomen. A lot of blood had leaked out, but the wound wasn't as large as he'd feared. It was a single neat hole, which probably meant that the bullet had maintained its shape, hadn't mushroomed as it passed through her body. A round with a full metal jacket, Cork guessed. Jacketed rounds were generally used in order to penetrate body armor, which Dross wasn't wearing.

Cork had choices to make and he had to make them quickly. If he tended to Dross's wounds, he ignored the threat of an advance from the shooter—or shooters—and risked both their lives. But if he spent time securing their position, the delay could mean his deputy's life.

He weighed the possibility of more than one assailant. The shots had come one at a time, from a distance. When he considered how Dross had fallen, the trajectory of the bullet that had pierced the windshield, and where the final round had hit the engine, he calculated they'd all come from approximately the same direction: from somewhere high on the hill across the road. The shooter was above them and a little forward of their position, with a good view of the driver's side but blind to where Cork crouched. If there'd been more than one assailant involved, a crossfire would have made the most sense, but so far that hadn't happened.

So many elements to consider. So little time. So much at stake.

He chose.

He holstered his revolver and leaned toward the deputy. "Marsha, can you hear me?"

Her eyes drifted to his face, but she didn't answer.

"Hang on, kiddo, I'll be right back."

In the back of the Land Cruiser was a medical kit that contained, among other things, rolls of gauze, sterile pads, and adhesive tape. Cork crept toward the rear of the vehicle. If he was right about the shooter's location, he should be able to grab the medical kit without exposing himself significantly to gunfire. *If he was right*. It was a big gamble. Dross gave a low moan. The blood had spread across the whole of her uniform, seeped below the belt line of her trousers. Still she looked at him and shook her head, trying to warn him against anything rash. Cork drew a breath and moved.

He reached around the back end of the Land Cruiser, grasped the handle, and swung the rear door open. He stood exposed for only a moment as he snatched the medical kit and the blanket, then he spun away and fell to the ground just as another round punched a hole in the vehicle and drilled through the spare tire, which deflated with a prolonged hiss. He rolled into the cover of the Land Cruiser.

While he put a compress over Dross's wounds, the radio crackled again.

"Dispatch to Unit Three. Over."

Cork glanced up from the bloody work of his hands. At the moment, there was no way to reach the mike. He tore another strip of tape with his teeth.

"Unit Three, do you copy?"

He finished tending to both wounds, then turned Marsha gently and tucked the blanket underneath her along the length of her body. He crawled to the other side, pulled the blanket under her, and wrapped her in it tightly like a cocoon.

"Unit Three, backup is on the way. ETA is twenty minutes. Are you still taking fire?"

Despite the blanket, Dross was shivering. Cork knew that shock could be as deadly as the bullet itself. In addition to keeping her warm, he had to elevate her feet. He opened the front passenger door and wormed his arm along the floor until his hand touched a fat thermos full of coffee he'd brought along. He hauled the thermos out and put it under the deputy's ankles. It elevated her feet only a few inches, but he hoped that would be enough.

Then he turned his attention to the son of a bitch on the hill.

He drew again his .38, a Smith & Wesson Police Special that had been his father's. It was chrome-plated with a six-inch barrel and a walnut grip. The familiar heft of it, and even the history of the weapon itself, gave him a measure of confidence. He crawled under the Land Cruiser, grateful for the high clearance of the undercarriage, inching his way to the front tire on the driver's side. From the shadow there, he peered up at the wooded hill across the road. The crown still caught the last direct rays of the sun and the birch trees dripped with a color like melting brass. After a moment, he saw a flash of reflected sunlight that could have come off the high polish of a rifle stock plate or perhaps the glass of a scope. If it was indeed from the shooter, Cork's target was 250, maybe 300 yards away, uphill. He thought about the twelve-gauge Remington cradled on the rack inside the Land Cruiser. Should he make an attempt, risk getting himself killed in the process? No, at that distance, the shotgun would be useless, and if he were hit trying for it, there'd be nothing to prevent the goddamn bastard from coming down the hill and finishing the job he'd begun. Better to stay put and wait for backup.

But his backup, too, would come under fire. Cork knew he had to advise them of the situation. And that meant exposing himself one more time to the sniper.

He took aim at the place where he'd seen the flash of sunlight, which was far beyond the effective range of his .38, but he squeezed off a couple of rounds anyway to encourage the sniper to reconsider, should he be thinking about coming down.

He shoved himself backward over the cold earth and came up on all fours beside the front passenger door. He gripped the handle and tried to take a breath, but he was so tense that he could only manage a quick, shallow gasp. He willed himself to move and flung the door open. Lunging toward the radio unit attached to the dash, he wrapped his fingers around the mike dangling on the accordion cord and fell back just as a sniper round slammed through the passenger seat back.

"Unit Three to Unit One. Over."

"Unit One. Go ahead, Sheriff."

"We're still taking fire, Duane. A single shooter, I think, up on a hill due east of our position, directly in front of the cabin. Which way you coming from?"

"South," Deputy Duane Pender said.

"Approach with extreme caution."

"Ten-four, Cork."

"Unit Two to Unit Three. Over."

"I read you, Cy."

"I'm coming in from the north. I'll be a couple of minutes behind Pender."

"Ten-four. Listen, I want you guys coming with your sirens blasting. Maybe we can scare this guy."

"We might lose him, Sheriff," Pender said.

"Right now our job is to get an ambulance in here for Marsha."

"Dispatch to Unit Three."

"Go ahead, Patsy."

"Ambulance estimates another twelve to fifteen minutes, Sheriff. They want to know Marsha's situation."

"Single bullet, entry and exit wounds. I've got compresses on both. I've put a blanket around her and elevated her feet. She's still losing blood."

"Ten-four. Also, State Patrol's responding. They've got two cruisers dispatched to assist."

"I copy that. Out."

Cork crawled toward Dross. Her face was pale, bloodless.

"A few more minutes, Marsha. Help's on the way."

She seemed focused on the sky above them both. She whispered something.

"What?" Cork leaned close.

"Star light, star bright . . ."

Cork lifted his eyes. The sun had finally set and the eastern sky was turning inky. He saw the evening star, a glowing ember caught against the rising wall of night.

From a distance came the thin, welcome howl of a siren.

Cork looked down at his deputy and remembered what she'd said: that he loved this work. At the moment, she couldn't have been more wrong. Her eyes had closed. He felt at her neck and found the pulse so faint he could barely detect it.

Then her eyes opened slowly. Her lips moved. Cork bent to her again.

"Next time," she whispered, "you drive."

2

"H<small>E MUST'VE SPLIT</small> when he heard the sirens."

Cy Borkmann looked across the road at the hill, which was a dark giant at the threshold of night. Cork, Deputy Duane Pender, and a state trooper named Fitzhugh had just come down from reconnoitering the top. They hadn't encountered the shooter, but they had found a couple of shell casings in a jumble of rocks overlooking the road and the Tibodeau cabin, in the area where Cork had seen the flash of reflected light off the sniper's rifle.

"Got word from the ambulance," Borkmann went on. They were standing beside his cruiser, a Crown Victoria parked a few yards back of the shot-up vehicle Cork had come in. At sixty, Borkmann was the oldest member of the Sheriff's Department. He was also the most overweight. He'd offered to climb the hill with the others, but Cork had left him behind to monitor the radio transmissions. "Marsha was rushed into surgery as soon as they wheeled her into the hospital."

"How's she doing?" Cork asked.

"She was still alive, that's all they said."

"Keep on top of it, Cy. Let me know when you hear anything."

Pender walked over from where he'd been conversing with the state troopers. He was young and brash, and Cork suspected not even experience would moderate his more irksome tendencies. "Christ, what's that smell? Skunk?"

15

Cork noticed it again, too, and realized that during the sniper's attack, he'd forgotten the odor entirely. "It's from the Land Cruiser," he said. "Marsha hit it on the way out."

Pender opened his mouth, probably to make a crack about women drivers, but wisely thought better of it.

Borkmann said to Cork, "I looked around while you were up on the hill. The two dogs you were wondering about? Dead, both of 'em. Rifle shot, looks like. They were carted around back and dumped out of sight. I'm thinking it's their blood Marsha was looking at."

"You check the cabin?"

"Quick look."

"Any sign of Eli or Lucy?"

"No."

"Let's hope that blood is from the dogs."

"Patsy located Larson. He was having dinner with Alice at the Broiler. He's on his way."

Borkmann was speaking of Captain Ed Larson, who headed the major-crimes investigations for the Tamarack County Sheriff's Department.

"I want to keep the scene clean until he gets here."

"You going to call BCA?" Borkmann asked.

"Soon as I'm back at the office."

It had been an assault on officers. Bringing in the state's Bureau of Criminal Apprehension was standard procedure, not only because of the organization's expertise and superior resources, but also to ensure that no local prejudice might warp the investigation.

Pender eyed the empty cabin. "Eli can get mean when he's drunk. Maybe that was him up there on the hill."

Cork had already considered that possibility. The call that had brought him and Marsha Dross out there had been made by Lucy to keep her from beating Eli ragged. Maybe Eli had retaliated in a big way. Anything was possible when love and hate became a heated jumble. But if Eli had been up there, if he had lashed out at his wife in a deadly way, where was Lucy?

Night was falling fast, flooding into the hollow from a sky salted with stars. Two more cruisers from the Sheriff's Department pulled up and several deputies got out wearing Kevlar vests and carrying assault rifles. The emergency response team. It had been fifty minutes since Cork's call for help had first gone out.

"Got here as quick as we could, Sheriff," Deputy John Singer said. "Took a few minutes to assemble the whole team." He was apologizing for what probably seemed to him like an inexcusable delay.

"That's okay, John. I think we're secure now, but why don't you post a couple people on the crown of that hill." Cork pointed toward the rocks where the sniper had taken his position. "I'd hate to have somebody start shooting at us again from up there."

"Done." Singer turned to his team and gave the order.

Fitzhugh, the state patrolman, left his vehicle and crossed the road to where the others stood.

"You need us any more?"

"No," Cork said. "Appreciate the assistance."

"Any time, Sheriff. Hope you get the bastard."

"Thanks."

Cork watched Fitzhugh walk away.

"Get on the radio, Duane," Cork said to Deputy Pender. "Have Patsy round up Clay and tell him to bring out a generator and floodlights. He can get them from the fire department."

Pender nodded and moved away.

"What did you see in the cabin?" Cork said to Borkmann.

"No bodies."

"You have to break in?"

"It was open."

"Figures. On the rez, nobody locks their doors. Any sign of violence?"

"Nope. Not the neatest housekeepers, but I'd say the mess in there looks pretty organic."

"Organic?"

"You know, rising naturally out of the elements of the environment."

"Organic." Cork shook his head.

"See for yourself," Borkmann said.

"I will. I want you to keep everyone away from the scene

for now. When Ed Larson gets here, and the generator and lights, we'll go over the ground carefully. Where'd you say the dogs were, Cy?"

"Behind the woodpile in back."

"Okay." Cork turned toward the cabin. He knew he risked contaminating the scene, but he needed to know if there were dead or injured people somewhere.

He lifted a pair of latex gloves from the box Borkmann had in his cruiser. He also borrowed the deputy's Maglite. Carefully, he skirted the area where blood had turned the dirt to a muddy consistency. He hoped it was only the mutts who'd bled. He made his way around the side of the cabin to the back. Behind a cord of split hardwood stacked between the trunks of a couple of young poplars, he found the dogs. They lay one on top of the other, thrown there, it seemed, with no more thought than tossing out garbage. They'd been shot through the head, both of them, straight on and at close range. Cork wondered if they'd come at their assailant and been killed in their attack, or if they'd sat there bewildered by their fate because whoever shot them was someone they'd trusted. He considered Eli again. Had the man finally gone over the edge, gone into a drunken rage as a result of Lucy's bullying, done away with his wife, and then killed his dogs? If so, why hide them like this? And where was Lucy?

It didn't feel right. A man like Eli might get drunk and riled up enough to kill his wife, but he'd never shoot his dogs. A sad statement, but Cork knew it to be true.

He returned to the front of the cabin and pushed the door open. Inside was dark. He located the switch on the wall and turned on the lights.

Eli's first wife had been a small, quiet woman named Deborah, a true-blood Iron Lake Ojibwe. She'd been good to her husband, had kept a clean house, and when ovarian cancer took her, Eli had grieved long and hard. His second wife was nothing like Deborah. As Cork stood in the doorway, he could see what Borkmann had meant about organic mess. The room was cluttered with magazines and newspapers, dirty glasses and plates, clothing left lying where it had been shed. The place had a sour, soiled-laundry smell to it.

He wove through the clutter to the kitchen, where he found a sink full of unwashed dishes. On the kitchen table lay a half loaf of dark rye and a butcher knife with a residue of butter on the blade. Next to the bread was a small pile of scratched tickets for the state lottery.

Cork checked the bedroom. It looked as though a struggle had taken place, the bed unmade, clothes tossed everywhere, but he suspected that was probably the norm. A few empty Pabst Blue Ribbon cans lay on the floor on the right side of the bed. Eli's side, he guessed.

The bathroom was in desperate need of a good scrubbing, but nothing struck Cork as particularly noteworthy.

He stood in the main room.

A sniper on the hill across the road. Two dead dogs behind the woodpile. No indication of violence inside the cabin, but no sign of Lucy or Eli, either. What the hell was going on?

"What happened to your ear?"

Cork turned and found Ed Larson standing in the doorway.

Larson wore gold wire-rims, little ovals that made him look bookish. His silver hair was bristle short, his face clean shaven, still a little pink, in fact, from the recent draw of a razor over his long jaw. He was dressed in a blue suit, white shirt, burgundy tie. His shoes were Florsheims, polished oxblood. During the brief tenure of the previous sheriff, Arne Soderberg, who'd managed to stay in office only six months, Larson had quit the department and taken a job teaching criminal justice studies at the community college. When the county Board of Commissioners tapped Cork to fill out Soderberg's term, he'd asked Larson to return, which the man had done in a heartbeat.

Cork touched the gauze he'd taped over his left earlobe to stanch the flow of blood where a sizable chunk of flesh was missing.

"Sniper round."

"Lucky," Larson said.

"Luckier than Marsha." Cork noted the man's clothing. "Awfully well dressed."

"Anniversary dinner. Thirty-fifth."

"Alice mad you had to leave?"

"She knows how it goes."

"You could've taken a few minutes to change clothes."

"The suit will clean." Larson looked at the room. "Struggle?"

"I get the feeling this is a natural state."

Larson walked cautiously into the cabin, watching where he stepped. "I talked to Cy outside, got a thumbnail of what's going on. I radioed Patsy to double-check the location of the call. Thought maybe it didn't actually come from here."

"Did it?"

"From right there." He pointed toward a phone on a low table next to the sofa, half hidden by a soiled, gray sweatshirt. "You didn't touch it?"

"Didn't even see it," Cork said.

"Door unlocked?"

"Yes."

Larson didn't seem surprised. "You check out the other rooms?"

"Yeah."

"Anything?"

"Not that leaped out at me."

Larson looked over his shoulder toward one of the windows. "It's getting pretty dark out there. What do you want to do about the hill?"

Two shell casings. Six, maybe seven shots fired. More casings to locate. Maybe other evidence as well.

Larson went on. "Cy says you've got floodlights coming. I hope you're not thinking of dragging them up that slope tonight."

Cork didn't answer. He didn't want to decide anything until he had an idea of what had become of Eli and Lucy.

"It's going to be a long night" was all he would say.

Larson turned back toward the front door. "I'll get my things and get started."

They both heard the screaming, and they went outside quickly.

An old puke-colored pickup was parked behind Borkmann's Crown Victoria, and Lucy Tibodeau had climbed out. She was trying to swing at Cy Borkmann while Pender did his best to restrain her. Cork hurried over.

"What's going on?"

"She wanted to go inside," Borkmann said.

"It's my damn house," Lucy hollered. She kicked at Cy but Pender pulled her back just in time. "What the hell's going on?" she demanded.

Eli's first wife had been like a fawn, small, soft, quiet. For his second bride, Eli had chosen a different animal altogether, huge and fierce. Lucy Tibodeau came from Fargo and, when Eli met her, had been dealing blackjack at the casino in Mille Lacs. She was short but big boned, with a lot of meat on those bones. Her hair was copper-colored, wiry like a Brillo pad. Her skin was splashed with huge brown freckles. Her eyes were green fire.

"Take your hands off me," she warned Pender, "or I'll bite your thumb off."

"Take it easy, Lucy," Cork said.

"Don't tell me to take it easy. You're crawling all over my place like a bunch of maggots and this son of a bitch has got his hands everywhere except up my dress. And he looks like he wouldn't mind going there next."

"Let her go, Pender."

The deputy did and stepped back quickly.

"What's going on?" Lucy asked, only slightly more civil.

"Where's Eli?" Cork said.

"I left him at Bunyan's. Last I saw of the little shit, he was kissing the lip of a whiskey glass."

"When was that?"

"Half an hour ago. What? Did he do something?"

"You've got the truck, Lucy. How's he getting home?"

"He can walk for all I care."

"Pender, drive over to Bunyan's. Round up Eli if he's there."

"Sure thing, Sheriff."

"What's going on?" Lucy said again, only this time with genuine concern in her voice.

"I was hoping you could tell me." It was hard to see the woman's face clearly. Cork opened the front door of Borkmann's cruiser and motioned Lucy to where the dome light would illuminate them both. "I'd love to know what happened after you called the Sheriff's Department."

"Called you?"

"At six-twenty, a call came from this location from a woman claiming to be you."

"At six-twenty me and Eli were playing pinochle at Bunyan's, like we do every Wednesday night. Hell, everybody knows that. We go for the walleye fish fry, then play a couple hours of pinochle."

A dark blue pickup rolled up and maneuvered alongside the other vehicles that crowded the narrow road. In the back sat a generator and some floodlights.

"You didn't call?" Cork said.

"Hell no." Something dawned on her, and she tried to pierce the dark with her eyes. "Where's our dogs?"

Cork didn't relish what he had to do, and when he spoke his voice sounded tired. "Somebody shot them, Lucy. I'm sorry."

All her spit and fire vanished in an instant, and devastation poured in to replace it.

Cork looked to Cy. "Would you see to Ms. Tibodeau. We'll need a full statement, but go easy." He turned and walked away.

Larson followed him. "Think she's lying?"

"Too simple to check. And why would she?"

Larson paused and looked up at the hill that was now a towering black shape hard against a soft night sky. "What's going on, Cork?"

"I'd say it was a trap."

"You guys got pulled out here to be shot at?"

"No," Cork said. "To be shot."

3

Cork left Ed Larson in charge with Borkmann backing him up. He intended to drive himself to the Aurora community hospital so that he could check on Marsha and have his ear tended to, but Larson stopped him.

"You shouldn't drive."

"It's just my damn earlobe," Cork said.

"It's a bullet wound and your body knows it and any minute may decide to overrule your stubborn brain. If that happens, I'd just as soon you weren't behind the wheel. Collins," he called to a deputy who was taking digital photos of the bullet-riddled Land Cruiser, "take the sheriff to the hospital. Radio ahead and let them know he's coming." He turned back to Cork. "You want us to call Jo?"

"No, I'll do that from the hospital. And I'll take care of contacting the BCA, too."

At the hospital, Cork told the deputy not to wait, that he'd have Jo give him a lift from there. Collins headed back to the rez.

In the emergency room, Cork ignored the admitting clerk and walked directly to the main hallway. As he approached the reception desk to ask about Marsha, he ran into his dispatcher Patsy Gilman, who was asking the same question.

Cork had hired Patsy during his first stint as sheriff. She was not quite forty, bright and funny, with deep laugh lines on either side of her mouth, and small intense eyes that noticed everything. She was good in Dispatch because she kept her head and her humor. As two of the only three women in the depart-

23

ment, she and Marsha Dross had formed a tight friendship, so much so that Patsy was to be the bridesmaid at Marsha's wedding, which was scheduled for the day after Halloween. Marsha was engaged to a big Finn named Charlie Annala.

"As soon as I knew they were bringing Marsha in, I called Charlie." She walked with Cork toward the surgery waiting area. "Then I called Bos and asked her to relieve me early. I didn't want Charlie to have to wait alone. You mind?"

She was still wearing her uniform, and there were dark stains under the arms. It had been a tough evening all around.

"Makes good sense," he said.

Cork knew he shouldn't feel this way, but he hated hospitals. They were places that did people good, that cured the sick and healed the injured, but it was also a place completely outside his control. He'd watched both his parents die in hospital rooms, and there hadn't been a damn thing he could do about it. Rationally, he knew that hospitals weren't about death, but whenever he entered the glass doors and caught the unnatural, antiseptic smell in the corridors, his heart told him differently.

They found Charlie Annala in the waiting room. He was sandy-haired, heavy, with a face made babylike from soft fat. He wore a forest green work shirt, dirty jeans, and scuffed boots. Cork figured he'd come straight from his job at the DNR's Pine Lake Fish Hatchery. He stood with his big, fat hands stuffed in his jean pockets, his head down, staring at the beige carpeting. There was a television on a shelf in a corner, tuned to one of the new reality shows. Cork figured Annala wouldn't have minded dealing with somebody else's reality at that moment. When he heard them coming, Annala looked up, not a happy man.

Charlie Annala was the protective type. Marsha didn't need that, but apparently she didn't mind, either. Maybe she appreciated that Charlie saw her in a different way than her male colleagues: saw the woman who liked, off duty, to show a little leg, line dance, and wear jewelry and cologne. Cork knew that her job was a sore point with Charlie, who was worried about her safety, a worry that, until this evening, Cork hadn't particularly shared.

Patsy rushed forward and threw her arms around the big man. "Oh, Charlie, I'm so sorry."

"Yeah," he said. He looked over her shoulder at Cork.

"Any word?" Cork said.

"Nothing since she went in. I haven't called her dad yet. I won't until I know how it's gone. What happened?" Charlie's eyes were full of unspoken accusations.

Patsy stood back, and let the two men talk.

"We're still trying to piece it together."

"What do you mean, 'piece it together'? You were there."

"At the moment, all I know is somebody shot her."

"Who?" He'd leaned closer with each exchange, putting his face very near to Cork's. There were deep pits across his cheeks from adolescent acne.

"I don't know," Cork said.

"Why not?"

"He was too far away, hidden in some rocks."

"Why her?"

Cork figured what he really meant was *Why not you?*

"When I understand that, Charlie, I'll let you know. I honestly will."

Patsy put her arm around Annala just as a nurse entered the waiting area. "There you are," the nurse said to Cork. "We've been expecting you in the ER." When he turned to her, she said with surprise, "Oh, my."

The shot that grazed his ear had opened a spigot of blood that had poured all over his shirt, and he looked like hell, as if he'd sustained an injury far worse.

"Keep me posted," he said to Patsy.

"You know I will."

Cork followed the nurse. He was beginning to feel his strength ebbing, and thought about what Larson had said. Maybe his wounded body was finally overtaking his stubborn brain. He hoped not. There was still so much to do.

He called Jo from a phone in the ER and asked her to pick him up, then he let them sew his earlobe closed.

She was waiting for him when he came out. She looked with alarm and sympathy at the gauze and tape on his ear. "What happened?"

"I'll tell you on the way."

Two blocks from the hospital, Jo pulled her Camry to the side of the street, parked in front of a fire hydrant, and listened. He told it calmly, almost blandly, but her face registered the horror of the scene.

"Oh God, Cork. How's Marsha?"

"She's still in surgery. We won't know for a while."

She gently lifted a hand toward the side of his face. "How's your poor ear?"

"Smaller."

"Does it hurt?"

"They gave it a shot. Can't feel much now."

She stared through the windshield. It was night and quiet and they sat in the warm glow of a street lamp. She put a hand to her forehead as if pressing some thought into her brain. "Why, Cork?"

"I don't know."

She leaned to him suddenly and held him tightly, and the good smell of spaghetti came to him from her hair and clothing. It was a quick dinner and a favorite of their children.

"Oh, sweetheart," she said. "I'll get you home and you can relax."

"No. I need to go to the department. I want to listen to the tape of Lucy's call."

It was a little before nine on a Tuesday night. Aurora, Minnesota, was winding down. Many of the shops had already closed. A good crowd was still visible through the windows of Johnny's Pinewood Broiler, and the air on Center Street was full of the tantalizing aroma of fried food. In front of the display window of Lost Lake Outfitters, against the buttery glow of a neon sign, stood old Alf Pedersen, who'd started the outfitting company fifty years earlier. Alf knew the most beautiful and fragile parts of the Boundary Waters, the great wilderness area north of Aurora, and although he'd guided hundreds of tourists in, he kept those places secret. In the next block, the door of Wolf Den Books and Gifts opened and a plank of light fell across the sidewalk as Naomi Pierce stepped out to close up. He couldn't hear it, but Cork knew that the opening of the door had caused a small bell above the threshold to jingle. He thought about the show that had been on television at the hospital. He didn't know whose reality that was, but his own reality lay in the details of this place, his hometown, details an outsider might not even notice. A tinkling bell, a familiar silhouette, the comfortable and alluring smell of deep-fry.

There was another reality for him as well. It was grounded in a maple leaf of blood on Marsha's uniform, the sound of glass shattered by a bullet capable of exploding his head like a melon, and the long, terrifying moments when he'd scrambled desperately to make sense of the absolutely senseless.

"You okay?" Jo asked.

"Yeah, I guess," he answered.

She accompanied him into the Tamarack County Sheriff's Department. Bos Swain, who'd relieved Patsy as dispatcher, buzzed them through the security door.

Bos was short for Boston, which was the name by which Henrietta Swain was known. As a young woman, she'd dreamed of going to college, specifically to Boston College, for reasons which she'd never divulged. Instead, she'd married her high school sweetheart, who went off to Vietnam and came back messed up psychologically. Bos had worked to support them and the two girls who were born to them, and although she never went to college herself, she sent both girls east, one to Barnard and the other to Boston College. When the girls were gone, she divorced her first husband and remarried, a good man named Tim Johnson who had a solid job stringing wire for the phone company. Although she didn't need to work to support herself anymore, she kept on as a dispatcher, drawing a county paycheck every two weeks, which she deposited in trust funds for her grandchildren's education. She was a fleshy woman, unusually good-humored, but the events of that evening had put her in a somber mood.

"I thought you were going to the hospital," she said to Cork in a scolding tone.

"I just came from there."

"How's Marsha?"

"Still in surgery when I left. Thanks for coming early so Patsy could be there."

"She seemed to be holding up real good, but I know it's tough for her. How's Charlie taking it?"

"Hard."

"Well, sure." She eyed his uniform and shook her head. "Jo, you ought to take him home so he can change those clothes. He's not exactly a walking advertisement for law enforcement."

Cork said, "I want to listen to the recording of the call that came from the Tibodeau cabin."

"Lucy's call?"

"That's what I want to know. Lucy claims it wasn't her."

Bos went to the Dispatch area, where the radio, at the moment, was silent. The public contact phone was linked to two different recording systems. The first recorded date, time, and the number of the phone from which the call had been made. The other system was a Sony automatic telephone tape recorder. It wasn't top-of-the-line—it had actually been donated to the department by the Chippewa Grand Casino when they'd upgraded to a digital recorder voice bank that fed directly into a computer—but it was a workhorse of a unit. Bos rewound the tape to the call that had purportedly come from Lucy. She played it, and they all listened. Then she played it again.

Patsy: *Tamarack County Sheriff's Department.*

The caller: *I'm telling you, if you don't get somebody out here, I'm going to kill the son of a bitch.*

Patsy: *Who is this?*

The caller: *Lucy Tibodeau.*

Patsy: *Where are you, Lucy?*

The caller: *At my goddamn cabin. And I'm telling you, you better get someone out here pronto, or I swear I'll kill him.*

Patsy: *Kill who?*

The caller: *That son of a bitch husband of mine.*

Patsy: *Eli?*

The caller: *You think I got another husband stashed in the woodpile, sweetie? Well, I wish to god I did, 'cuz the one I got ain't worth a bucket of warm spit.*

Patsy: *Where is Eli?*

The caller: *Outside, pounding on the door, hollering to let him in.*

Patsy: *You just stay put, Lucy. Take a few deep breaths. We'll have someone out there right away.*

The caller: *I'm warning you, the sheriff better get here real fast, he wants to avoid bloodshed.*

Patsy: *He's on his way, Lucy. You just relax, and don't you let that husband of yours rankle you, understand?*

The caller: *I ain't making any promises.*

The caller hung up.

Jo was the first to respond. "If someone's trying to sound like Lucy, they did a pretty fair job."

Bos nodded. "If I hadn't been leery, I'd have been fooled. I can see why Patsy didn't give it a second thought. Whoever it is, she's got Lucy's speech down pat. But it's someone younger, I'd say."

Cork had Bos play the tape once more. "Hear that?" he said, midway through.

"What?"

"Rewind it a bit." He waited. "Listen." He held up a finger, then dropped it suddenly. "Now. Did you hear it? A door closing in the background."

"Somebody came in?" Bos said.

"Or went out." Jo looked at Cork. "Either way, she wasn't alone."

"Pull that tape, Bos. We'll give it to BCA to analyze."

He went into his office and made the call to the Bureau of Criminal Apprehension office in Bemidji, explained the situation to the voice mail, then pulled out the clean uniform he kept in the closet. When he stepped back into the department common area, Jo looked at the uniform.

"You're not coming home," she said.

"No. I'll shower downstairs, change, and then I'm going back out to the rez."

"I wish you'd come home. You've got people who can handle the investigation."

"I need to be there. Don't wait up."

She kissed him and he could feel her restraint, her irritation.

"Be careful," she said, and left.

As he showered, he was conscious of his wound. The local

anesthetic was wearing off, and a dull ache crept in behind it. He put on the clean uniform and went back upstairs.

"I'm taking my Bronco," he told Bos. "Let Ed know I'm on my way."

"You really ought to get a radio in that vehicle."

He started for the door, but Bos called him back.

"Sheriff?"

He turned around.

"Somebody lured you out there."

"It looks that way."

"They wanted you dead. Or maybe Marsha."

"That's generally the reason they use bullets."

"My point is this," she said. "They didn't succeed. Does that mean they'll try again?"

FLOODLIGHTS LIT THE hollow with an unnatural glare, and the poplar trees around the Tibodeau cabin looked like a crowd of gawkers gone white with shock. Cork pulled up behind Cy Borkmann's cruiser and got out.

Ed Larson stood in the doorway of the cabin. He wasn't wearing the latex gloves anymore and looked as if he'd gathered evidence and was weighing the meaning. Or at least, that's what Cork hoped his look meant.

"Where's Lucy?" Cork asked.

"She and Eli went into Alouette to stay with his uncle. We took statements from both of them. They were pretty broken up over the dogs."

Cork glanced inside the cabin. "So, what did you find?"

Larson adjusted his wire-rims, not a good sign. Then he said, "Well," which nailed the coffin shut.

"Nothing?" Cork said.

"Not down here. Whoever it was, they actually wiped out the tracks leading back to the woodpile where they threw the dogs. Looks like they used a pine branch or something. I took prints off the phone, but I'm betting they're just latents from Eli and Lucy. Nothing on the shell casings you found earlier. We pulled the slugs out of the Land Cruiser but they're too mashed up to be of any use for ballistics. We're still looking for the round that went through Marsha. Doing a quadrant search of the ground surface right now, then I'll have the guys start digging. Come morning, we'll go over every inch of the hilltop where the shooter was. We bagged the dogs. If you think it'll be of any value, we can have them autopsied."

Duane Pender, who was working on the search of the ground, hollered.

"What is it?" Larson said.

Pender picked up something and held it up in the light. "It's a bell. A little jingly Christmas bell."

Larson walked carefully to the deputy and took the bell from him. It was a silver ball with a little metal bead inside that jingled when the ball moved. "It's new. Not dirty, so it hasn't been on the ground long. What do you make of it, Cork?"

Cork walked over. "Could be from a Christmas ornament."

"In October?"

"Or maybe from a jingle dress."

"A what?"

"For ceremonial dances. It may be nothing, but make a note of where you found it, Duane, and put it in a bag."

Larson followed him back to the cabin door. "Any word on Marsha?"

"She was still in surgery when I left the hospital."

"You don't look too good yourself."

Cork slumped against the door frame. The lights for the search were bright in his eyes, and he turned his face from them. "I keep trying to figure all this."

"I've been thinking," Larson said quietly. "Someone went to a lot of trouble to get you out here. Think about it, Cork. The call comes from the rez. Since you've taken over as sheriff, the old policy of you responding to most of the calls from out here is back in place. Marsha's driving the Land Cruiser. She's your height, more or less. She's wearing a cap. The sun's down, the whole hollow here is in shade. The shooter assumes it's you who gets out and he fires."

"Or she fires," Cork said.

"She?"

"I listened to the tape of the call when I was back at the department. It was a woman doing a pretty good job of sounding like Lucy."

Larson considered it while he scratched the silver bristle of his hair. "Whoever, they knew what they were doing. Two dead dogs, tracks erased, a well-chosen vantage point from which to fire."

"Why didn't he . . . she . . . set up a crossfire?" Cork said.

"That probably means the number of people involved is limited. Maybe just the shooter. Or the shooter and the woman he used to get you out here."

"A lot of speculation," Cork said.

"Without a lot of hard evidence to go on, you've got to begin your thinking somewhere. I'm guessing it's someone who knows the rez. They knew that Lucy and Eli would be gone, anyway. They were pretty sure it would be you who'd respond. Cork, this wasn't some sort of random violence. It was well planned and you were the target."

Borkmann strolled over. In the glare, his bulk cast a huge shadow before him. "We still got two men on that hill."

The moon wasn't up yet, but it was on the rise. "Might as well bring them down," Cork said. "I don't think we'll have to worry any more tonight. Maybe we should all call it a night. What do you think, Ed? Come back in the morning? BCA'll be here then. In the meantime, we can post a couple of men to keep the scene secure, and we'll send everyone else home. That bullet you're hoping to dig out of the ground'll still be there tomorrow."

"Cork?" Borkmann called from his cruiser. "Just got word from Patsy via Bos. Marsha's out of surgery and doing well."

Cork felt something begin to break inside him, a wall behind which an ocean of emotion was at risk of flooding through.

Ed put a hand on his shoulder. "I'll take care of getting things packed up here. You go on home and get some rest. We'll have a go at it again tomorrow."

He went back to the department and filled out an incident report, then stopped by the hospital one last time. Patsy had gone, but he found Charlie Annala asleep on the sofa in the waiting area of the recovery room. Someone had put a thin blanket over him. Shortly after midnight, Cork headed home.

By the time he turned onto Gooseberry Lane, the moon had risen high in the sky, a waxing gibbous moon, a silver teardrop on the cheek of night. His home was an old two-story frame affair with a wonderful front porch and a big elm in the yard. The whole town knew it as the O'Connor place. With the exception of college and a few years when he was a cop in Chicago, he'd lived in that house his whole life. In a way, it contained his life. He stood on the lawn a few moments, in the shadow the elm cast in the moonlight, trying to draw to himself the feel of all that was familiar. A light in his bedroom upstairs told him Jo had waited up for him. A soft glow drizzled through the window of his son's room, Stevie's night-light. His daughters' rooms were on the backside of the house, but it was late and a school night and he figured they would be asleep by now. He listened to the creak of the chains on their metal hooks as the porch swing rocked slowly in the breeze. He put his hand against the rough bark of the big tree that was as old as he and took in the dry smell of autumn.

Jo had left a light on in the living room so that he wouldn't walk into a dark house. He turned it off and headed upstairs, where he checked the children's rooms. Stevie was snoring softly. Jenny lay asleep with the headphones of her Discman still over her ears. Annie's pillow was over her head, and her right leg was off the bed. Cork took a moment and carefully settled her back in.

In his own room, he found Jo sitting up but asleep, a manila file folder open on her lap; her reading glasses had slipped to the end of her nose. She was a lawyer and she often brought her work to bed, one way or another. Cork decided not to wake her. He wasn't quite ready for sleep yet, anyway. Too much going on inside.

He went back downstairs and stood in the dark living room, feeling oddly alien in the quiet of the house, as if he'd been gone a long time and had lost touch with the details that created the mosaic of a normal day. He felt adrift, stranded in a place he didn't quite know or understand.

In the kitchen, he latched onto the cookie jar, an icon of familiarity. It was Ernie from *Sesame Street,* and it had been in the O'Connor house for more than a decade. Cork dipped into

Ernie's head and brought out a chocolate chip cookie, which he put on the kitchen table while he took a glass tumbler from the cupboard next to the sink. From the refrigerator, he grabbed a plastic gallon jug of milk and filled the tumbler halfway.

As he turned back to the refrigerator, the shatter of glass exploded the quiet of the kitchen. He hit the floor, let go of the jug, reached automatically for his .38. He scrambled across the linoleum and pressed his back to the cabinet doors below the sink, clutching his gun. *One of the windows?* he wondered. But a quick glance told him no bullet had come through any of the panes.

Then he saw the broken tumbler on the floor, the puddle of milk around the shards, and he realized he'd knocked the glass off the table. A simple accident due to his own carelessness, a small incident in a day full of enormous event. Still, it felt as if something had finally snapped inside him, the cord that had kept him from taking a long fall.

Finally alone, he drew his legs up, laid his arms across his knees, cradled his head, and with a violent quaking gave himself up to the dark emotions—terror, rage, regret—that had stalked him all night.

5

BOSTON WAS STILL on duty when Cork rolled in at first light.

She glanced at her watch. "You didn't sleep much," she said. "And you don't mind me saying so, you still look like hell."

"What's the word from Morgan and Schilling?" he asked, referring to the two deputies who'd been posted overnight at the Tibodeau cabin.

"Checked in every hour; nothing to report."

Cork poured himself some coffee from the pot in the common area before going to his office. He spent a few minutes typing a memo on his computer, printed thirty copies, and handed them to the dispatcher. Bos lifted the top copy, read it, and looked up.

"Everybody wears armor on duty now?"

"No exceptions," Cork said. "I want this memo posted on the board and I want every deputy to check off with initials so I know they've read it." He handed her another sheet on which he'd printed some instructions. "Give this to Cy when he comes in. I want him to brief everyone about last night. Duty assignments remain the same except for Larson's evidence team, who'll be out at the cabin. I'm taking a cruiser and heading to the rez."

She eyed him with maternal concern but said nothing.

He drove a Pathfinder that had been confiscated in a raid on a meth lab near Yellow Lake in August. It had since been fitted with a radio and was now an official part of the vehicle pool. He'd taken only a couple of sips of the coffee he'd poured himself earlier, so he stopped at the all night Food 'N Fuel and bought three coffees and several granola bars.

As he headed north out of town, a red sun inched above the ragged tree line on the far side of Iron Lake. In an autumn in which the whole earth had seemed the color of a raw wound, the water itself appeared to be a well of blood. Cork couldn't look at it without thinking of all the blood that had soaked the blouse of Marsha Dross's uniform. As much as possible he kept his eyes on the road and considered the question of who might want him dead.

He'd been sheriff of Tamarack County before, for a period of seven years. Things had happened near the end of that tenure, terrible things that had torn him apart and nearly shattered his family as well. His badge had been taken from him. He'd spent the next three years running Sam's Place and putting himself back together. Over time he'd begun to feel whole again and to believe that his life still had promise. In those first seven years as sheriff, he'd been responsible for a lot of people going to jail. On many occasions, he'd been threatened with reprisal, idle threats for the most part. Or so he'd thought.

Still, that was old business. Retribution was usually born of rage, and rage generally lost its heat over time. So an old grudge, while possible, didn't feel like a solid thread.

It was a chilly morning. In protected coves, the surface of Iron Lake was covered with a languorous mist. Russet leaves hung on the branches of the oaks. The tamaracks, brilliant yellow, seemed like plumes of fire exploding from the dark ground that edged the marshes. Normally, Cork would have reveled in the beauty of the woods, but as he sipped his coffee he was deep in thought, not only baffled over who'd want him dead, but wondering if Ed Larson would find anything useful at the Tibodeau cabin.

The deputies, Howard Morgan and Nate Schilling, knew he was coming, and they both stepped from the cruiser as he drew up and parked behind them. They looked tired, as though they'd had enough of sitting all night trying to fight sleep, as though they'd probably had enough of each other, too. He hauled out the other coffees he'd bought and the granola bars and offered them to his men.

"The java's probably a little cool by now, but it's pure caffeine. And take your pick of the bars."

"Thanks," Morgan said. He was the older of the two deputies, a seven-year veteran of the force and of Duluth PD before that. He was an easygoing sort, and Cork liked him.

The hill cast a shadow across the road. The sun would be a long time in reaching the hollow, hours before it drove out the cold that lay along the bottom. When the men breathed and when they spoke, clouds of vapor escaped their lips.

"Bos said everything was quiet last night."

"That's right, Sheriff." Schilling took a bite of a peanut butter—chocolate chip granola bar and followed it with a slug of coffee. Although he'd completed his schooling and training almost two years before, he was still considered a rookie. Usually, he had a little rose in his cheeks, but he looked pretty sallow at the moment.

"Nobody curious drop by?"

"Nobody we could see anyway," Schilling said. "After the floodlights got packed up, it was pretty dark. Could have been someone watching from the trees, I suppose."

"You suppose?" Morgan laughed so hard coffee dribbled out his nostrils.

"What's that all about?" Cork said.

"Nothing, Sheriff. Not a thing," Schilling said.

"Like hell. Cork, he was so scared somebody was taking a bead on us that he spent the whole night on the floor of the cruiser." Morgan wiped his nose with the sleeve of his uniform.

"Morgan, you asshole. It wasn't like that, Sheriff."

"You both wore your armor the entire watch?"

"Absolutely," Schilling said.

Cork figured it was a good thing Morgan was sporting his Kevlar vest, because if Schilling's eyes had been bullets they'd have blown holes all the way through him.

He stared at the dark side of the hill, where snakes of mist coiled and uncoiled among the pine trees along the base. "I'm going up, see what things look like on top."

"You're not waiting for Captain Larson?" Schilling said. When he saw Cork's face, he added, "I just meant that he's on his way. We got word from Bos just before you came."

"Hey, Einstein, the sheriff's got a radio," Morgan said.

"Oh, right."

"Just let him know where I am," Cork said.

He walked fifty yards down the road to the place where, the day before, he and Pender and the state trooper named Fitzhugh had begun maneuvering up the hill, moving under the cover of trees and exposed outcroppings, working their way carefully toward the rocks where the sniper had been. He wasn't wearing his uniform now. He'd put on old jeans, a forest green wool shirt with a quilted lining, and his Timberland boots. His badge was pinned on his gun belt next to his .38. And he wore a Kevlar vest.

The night had not been cold enough for frost, but the hillside was covered with dew, and his boots slipped on the wet rocks and wild grass. The top of the hill was maybe two hundred feet above the road. He was breathing hard by the time he reached the crown, puffing out clouds like an old steam engine. He hoped this was due mostly to the lack of sleep, but he was concerned that his age might also be an issue. He wasn't far from turning the corner on half a century, and although he was an avid jogger, he knew that age eventually caught up with everyone, even the swiftest runner.

Cork walked along the spine of the hill a hundred yards south to the jumble of rocks where they'd found the shell casings. The thin topsoil there had completely eroded away, exposing gray gneiss beneath that had been fractured by aeons of freeze and thaw. There were sharp edges to the rocks, and the shooter had covered his position with a bedding of pine needles. It was among the needles that Cork had found the shell casings the night before.

The road down the hollow took a right turn and followed a deep furrow just to the south where a thread of water called Tick Creek ran. North, the narrow access to the Tibodeau cabin was clear all the way to where it branched off the main road. Wooded hills stretched away in every direction. Pressing down above it all was the great blue palm of the sky. The shooter had chosen well, a vantage from which he could clearly see not just the cabin but also the approach of anyone traveling the road from the north or south.

He looked down at the pine-needle bed in the rocks and was puzzled.

The shooter had been careful in so many respects. Knowing Lucy and Eli's schedule. Calling from the cabin, then wiping away all traces of his or her presence. Choosing a position that was excellent not only because of its vantage but also because it lay on solid rock where no footprints would be left. So why did he ignore the shell casings? They were crumbs on an otherwise empty plate, impossible to miss. Had the shooter simply overlooked them? Or been suddenly rushed, worried by the sound of the sirens as Pender and Borkmann approached, and fled without taking the time for the last details?

Cork considered the dead dogs. He thought it likely they were killed first, then the shooter or the accomplice made the call and climbed the hill, probably the same way he'd come. Did the accomplice come, too? How did they leave? Cork walked toward the back side of the hill where the night before it had been too dark to go. The slope was gentler there, with more soil and long tufts of wild oats beneath the aspen trees. About fifty yards from the shooter's rocks, Cork found a spot where the incline increased suddenly and where some of the ground cover had been disturbed by a sliding shoe or boot. A few feet farther down was a scar in the soil where a whole bunch of oat stalks had been pulled completely out, as if someone had grabbed them in an attempt to prevent a fall. Below that, the bushes had been broken by the weight of a large object, perhaps a tumbling body. The shooter, or someone with the shooter, had taken a nasty spill.

Cork picked his way down the back side of the hill and reached the bed of Tick Creek. Fall had been dry, and this late in the season there was only a small trickle of water crawling along the bottom. A couple of hundred yards to the south, the creek crossed the road. That was the direction from which Pender had come the day before with his lights flashing and his siren screaming. Cork didn't think the shooter would have fled that way. North was different. Before it intersected County

23 a half mile distant, Tick Creek curved sharply away from the turnoff to the Tibodeau cabin, so that a cop coming from that direction would see nothing of the creek. Cork turned north. The banks were high and formidably steep from the cut of floodwaters that came with the snowmelt each spring, and they were crowned with a thick growth of brush and popple. Someone on foot could have climbed out, but not a vehicle. In a few minutes, Cork reached the bridge at County Road 23. The structure was made of creosote-soaked wood with a web of rusted iron railing along either side and decorated with painted graffiti. In the soft dirt of the narrow shoulder at the east end of the bridge, Cork found recent tire tracks.

Larson watched Cork approach on foot. "I thought you were up there." He pointed toward the hilltop.

Cork said, "I walked down the other side and around the hill."

"You needed the exercise?" came a voice behind him.

Cork smiled and turned as BCA agent Simon Rutledge stepped from the cabin.

Rutledge spoke like Jimmy Stewart, with a little catch in his throat and a naively honest tone that you had to love. He was in his midforties, an unimposing man with thinning red hair and a hopelessly boyish smile, but his appearance and demeanor belied a tough spirit. Cork had watched Rutledge question suspects. He never browbeat, never bullied. He offered them his sympathy, bestowed on them his neighborly smile, opened his arms to them, and, after he got their trust, almost always got their confession. Simon Rutledge was so good that whenever he interviewed a suspect, other agents referred to it as "Simonizing."

"How's it hanging, Cork?" Rutledge said. The two men shook hands.

"I've had better days."

"Bet you have. Where you been?"

Cork nodded toward the hilltop. "Our shooter left the back way. I found tire tracks at the bridge over Tick Creek on County Twenty-three. They'll photograph well, and I'll bet if we're careful we can get a good cast made."

41

"Mack," Rutledge called to one of his BCA evidence team who was digging in the ground in front of the Tibodeau cabin. He gave the agent directions to the bridge over Tick Creek. "Check out the tire tracks . . ." He glanced at Cork.

"East side, south shoulder."

"You heard him. Get good photos, and I'll be there in a bit to help with casting."

"On my way." Mack put his shovel down and headed for his state car.

"You take a look at the cabin?" Cork asked Rutledge.

"Yeah. But I know Ed did a good job on it, so I wasn't expecting much. I was just thinking of going up top to have a look where our shooter camped out. You see anything while you were up there?"

"I didn't look hard. Mostly I was thinking."

"Wondering who wants you dead?" Rutledge flashed a slightly diminished version of his smile but it still produced dimples. "I had a talk with Ed, and he's got a point about you being the target. You need to be thinking seriously about who'd want you in their gun sight."

"Any time you bust someone, deep down they want to bust you back," Cork said.

"Not everybody's got the balls for that. The question for you is who does?"

Two of Cork's deputies were helping the BCA people dig in front of the cabin. They put a shovelful into a metal sieve, sifted, tossed out rocks and other detritus, then repeated the process. They were looking for the round that hit Marsha Dross. Cork hoped they'd find it and that it would prove good for a ballistics analysis.

Rutledge walked to his car, an unremarkable blue Cavalier, and brought back an evidence bag that held the two shell casings Cork had found the night before. "Remington .357, packed with a hundred fifty grains, I'd say. Probably fired from something like a Savage One-ten. That would be my firearm of choice, anyway."

"Why? That's a game rifle," Cork said.

"With a good scope, one of those babies could make Barney Fife into an effective assassin. And up here, a Savage One-ten is as common as a snowmobile. Wouldn't raise any eyebrows like a more sophisticated sniper weapon might."

"You're saying it could be anyone," Cork said.

"Those tracks you found at the bridge might help narrow things a bit." Rutledge looked at Cork wistfully. "So?"

"So what?"

"Who wants you dead?"

6

CORK DROVE THE Pathfinder back to Aurora and parked in the lot of the community hospital. He checked at the reception desk, then walked to Intensive Care, where Marsha Dross had been moved. It was breakfast time for the patients, and the smell of institutional food that filled the hallways reminded Cork that he hadn't eaten that morning. He should have been hungry, but he wasn't.

He found Frank Dross sitting in a chair outside Marsha's room. Marsha's father, a widower, was a retired cop from Rochester, Minnesota. Like his daughter, he was tall and not what you would call good looking. He had a long nose, gray eyes, and gray hair neatly parted on the right side. He wore a black knit shirt and tan Haggar slacks with an expandable waist that was, in fact, expanded over a small paunch. Cork had met him several times and liked the man.

Dross stood. "Sheriff." He shook Cork's hand.

"How're you doing, Frank?"

"Better, now that I know Marsha's out of danger. They tell me you saved her life."

Saved her life? Maybe he'd kept her from dying in the dirt in front of the Tibodeau cabin, but he'd also been responsible, in a way, for the bullet that put her there.

"Do you know why yet?" Frank asked.

"We're working on that. How is she this morning?"

"Officially, she's listed in guarded condition. They got her hooked up to all kinds of monitors, but she'll be fine."

"Fine?" Charlie Annala came from Marsha's room. He didn't appear to be any happier with Cork this morning than he'd been last night. "Because of that bullet, she may never be able to have kids. *We* may never have kids. You call that fine?" He wore the same clothing as the night before. He hadn't shaved, and from his smell it was clear he hadn't showered, either. The skin seemed to hang on his face like heavy dough, and his bloodshot eyes looked fractured. "And the hell of it is, nobody can tell me why."

"Sometimes, Charlie, just being a cop is reason enough for people to hate you." Frank put a hand on his shoulder. "In the sixties, seventies, they called us pigs. It's not a job that gets a lot of respect. I told Marsha it wouldn't be easy, but it was what she wanted to do. It was always what she wanted to do." Frank gave Charlie a gentle pat. "It can be tough, being in love with a cop."

"Is she allowed visitors?" Cork asked.

"One at a time," Frank said.

"Mind if I go in?"

Charlie opened his mouth, about to object, but Frank said, "Sure. Keep it short, though, okay?"

The curtain was partially drawn. Cork walked to the end of the bed. An IV needle plugged into Marsha's right forearm fed a clear liquid into her body. She was hooked to a heart monitor and a machine that tracked her respiration as well. She lay with her head deeply imbedded in a pillow, the skin of her cheeks a bloodless white. Even so, she managed a smile when she saw Cork.

"Hi," she said.

"How are you feeling?"

She beckoned him nearer. He walked along the side and took the hand she offered.

"Drugged," she said. "Not feeling much." She squeezed his hand. "Thanks."

"Any time."

She shifted a little, tried to rise, but gave up. "The investigation?"

Cork looked out the window, which faced east. The hospital was on a small rise at the edge of town, and Iron Lake was visible beyond a line of birch trees that were like white scratches against the blue water.

"We're getting somewhere," he said. "We've got shell casings, and I'm sure we'll get a bullet for ballistics. We've got tire tracks, too."

"A suspect?"

"We're working on that."

"Eli and Lucy?"

"They weren't anywhere near the cabin last night."

She nodded faintly. "I've been thinking. You and me in our uniforms, in bad light, we probably don't look all that different. I think somebody knew you'd answer that call."

"I've been thinking that, too," Cork said. "We'll get him, Marsha."

"*Him?* A woman called in the complaint."

She was a good, smart cop. Even in her drugged state, she'd been putting the pieces together.

"Him, her, them. We're going to do our jobs and we're going to get them."

"You better." She smiled weakly and gave his fingers another squeeze.

"Rest," he said.

She nodded, closed her eyes, and let go of his hand.

It was clear to everyone—even Marsha, full of drugs—that Cork was the one the sniper had meant to take out. As he drove away from the hospital with the sunlight sliding off his windshield, he thought about the question Simon Rutledge had posed: *Who wants you dead?*

They'd talked about it for a bit at the Tibodeau cabin, gone over a few possibilities. Only one seemed plausible. The raid on the meth lab outside Yellow Lake had gone down in July, just two weeks after Cork took over as sheriff. He'd had very little to do with the investigation, but the bust resulted in a tragic afternoon for a family of criminals. Two men, brothers, Lydell and Axel Cramer, were inside an old Airstream trailer parked next to their rural home when Cork's people arrived and pounded on the door. The chemicals used to make methamphetamine were volatile. It was dangerous business.

The two brothers had panicked. There was an explosion, and flames engulfed the trailer. One man stumbled out, his clothing on fire. Cy Borkmann wrestled him down and rolled him in the grass until the flames were extinguished. The man was Lydell Cramer. His little brother Axel never made it out. Lydell was airlifted to St. Joseph's Hospital in St. Paul, where he awaited trial while recovering from third-degree burns over most of his body. He didn't talk much, but when he did it was all about getting even with "the pig-fucking cops" who'd killed his brother.

They'd kicked around the idea of Lydell Cramer and decided it was worth looking into.

Patsy, who was on duty in Dispatch, radioed Cork and told him Jo had requested he call her at her office. Instead of calling, he drove straight over.

The Aurora Professional Building was a newer, single-story brick construction on the west side of town. Cork pulled into the lot and went inside. He passed the offices of David Spender, DDS, and Francis Kennilworth, CPA. He came to Jo's office and went inside. The anteroom was empty, and the door to Jo's inner office was closed. A sign sat propped on the desk: BACK IN 5 MINUTES. HAVE A SEAT. Which probably meant that Jo's secretary had gone for coffee, and Jo was with a client. Cork was just about to sit down and wait when the inner office door swung open and a man stepped out. Cork had met him only once before, and he hadn't liked him.

Edward Jacoby was the kind of guy who smiled broadly and often but without a trace of goodwill. It was hard to know what was really behind that flash of teeth, but as it was, Jacoby's smile reminded Cork of a wound that showed white bone. Jacoby was in his early thirties, good-looking in a dark way. He had thick black hair, heavy-lidded eyes, the shadow of a beard across his jaw. He was small, but with a large upper body and thick neck, a man who worked out seriously.

When they shook hands, Jacoby's grip, like his smile, was not about being cordial. A class ring dwarfed the knuckle on his right pinkie. The pinkie of his left hand sported a chunk of gold set with a diamond. Cork had always thought a pinkie an odd finger on which to wear a ring, especially for a man.

"Good to see you again, Sheriff," Jacoby said.

"I hope I'm not interrupting anything."

Jacoby magnanimously waved off Cork's concern. "Not at all. I was just leaving. Heard you had some trouble last night. Everything okay?"

"Under control."

"I'm sure it is." Jacoby eyed him with a shade of concern. "Say, you look like you could use a good night's sleep. Want some advice? Melatonin before you go to bed. It's one of those hormones older people's bodies don't regulate very well."

"I'll keep it in mind."

Jacoby reached back and squeezed Jo's hand. "Always a pleasure, Counselor. Give me a call—you have my cell phone number, right?—after you've spoken with the RBC. I'm staying at the Four Seasons. You should have my number there, too. If you don't get me, just leave a message. Ciao," he said, and left.

Inside Jo's office with the door closed, Cork said, "I've met rabid badgers I liked better."

"You don't have to like him." Jo picked up a document and scanned it.

Cork sat down at her desk and began to rub the back of his neck, which had developed a slight crick. "Do you?"

"I've dealt with him for six months now. I'm almost used to him."

Starlight Enterprises, the company that employed Jacoby, provided management for casinos all over the lower Midwest and was eager to expand into Minnesota. Jacoby had been working hard for the past half year to make the Iron Lake Ojibwe one of the company's clients. Because Jo had often represented the interests of the rez and had worked on the casino from its inception, Oliver Bledsoe, who headed the tribal legal affairs office, had retained her to handle the negotiations. The Reservation Business Committee, which oversaw all financial dealings the rez conducted as an entity, had initially rejected the idea. The casino was just about to lose its fourth manager in as many years, however, and several members of the RBC had become vocal advocates for using Starlight to supply consistent, qualified management. They'd finally authorized Jo to come up with a contract that the RBC could put to a vote.

As light as a butterfly, she touched Cork's wounded ear. "How are you doing?"

"Holding up."

"You didn't sleep much."

"A lot on my mind."

"You left this morning before the girls were up. They were disappointed they didn't see you."

"There were things I needed to do."

She pressed her palm gently to his chest. "I understand, Cork, but they're scared. Their father could have been killed last night."

"I wasn't."

"And thank God for that. But they need some reassurance and it needs to come from you."

When he'd agreed to step in again as sheriff, Cork had promised himself and Jo that, as much as possible, his job wouldn't affect his family, especially the children. Deep down he knew it was a futile pledge. He was the son of a sheriff himself, and he understood what the job demanded. He'd said yes for the most selfish of reasons. He missed the badge. He missed the camaraderie that came with it, the challenge, the feeling that he was doing something that mattered. It was also satisfying to have the Board of Commissioners come to him, hat in hand, after the people of Tamarack County elected Arne Soderberg, a man as near to being a cop as a duck was to being an eagle. They'd screwed themselves royally, and they needed Cork. That felt good. Damn good. So he'd said yes knowing full well the sacrifices it would require of his family.

He took her hand and kissed it. "I'll be home for dinner, promise. I'll talk to them then. Was that all you wanted?"

"And this." She kissed him softly. "Take care of yourself out there, cowboy."

In the early afternoon, he drove out to Alouette on the Iron Lake Reservation to meet with the tribal council. Simon Rutledge followed in his state car.

Alouette was the largest of the communities on the reservation. Even so, there wasn't a lot to it. From one end of town to the other was just over half a mile. A few years before, the housing had been mostly trailers and HUD homes in desperate need of repair, but lately things had improved considerably thanks to the Chippewa Grand Casino that was owned and operated by the Iron Lake Band of Ojibwe. Typically, the tribal council met in the new community center, which had been built with casino money. In addition to the large room where the tribal council gathered and where meetings open to the reservation at large were held, the center housed the offices of a number of tribal organizations, a health clinic, a day care center, and a gymnasium. Cork had spoken earlier in the day with George LeDuc, chairman of the tribal council, and had arranged to meet with that body to discuss the incident at the Tibodeau cabin.

In 1953, Congress passed Public Law 280, which allowed responsibility for law enforcement on Minnesota Indian reservations to be transferred from federal jurisdiction to the state, if that's what the enrolled members wanted. The Iron Lake Ojibwe had chosen to be policed by the state's local authority, which was the Tamarack County Sheriff's Department. As sheriff and as a man part Ojibwe, Cork had always tried to be a judicious presence on the rez. For the most part, he'd succeeded. But this time he was bringing Simon Rutledge of the BCA with him, and he wasn't hopeful about how well that would go over.

Seven of the eight members of the council had managed to be there and were waiting in the meeting room. Seated at the conference table with George LeDuc were Judy Bruneau, Albert Boshey, Roy Stillday, Edgar Gillespie, Heidi Baudette, and Thomas Whitefeather.

"*Anin,*" Cork said as he entered, offering the traditional Ojibwe greeting.

He shook hands with LeDuc and the others and introduced Simon Rutledge all around. When everyone was seated again, he explained what had occurred at the Tibodeau cabin the night before. He also explained why Rutledge would be in charge of the investigation. He was pretty sure they'd all heard about the shooting—heard some version of what had gone down, anyway—but it was impossible to tell from their faces, which showed little expression. They simply nodded now and then as he spoke. He'd been to lots of meetings on the rez, tribal council and otherwise. When there were only Ojibwe— or Shinnobs, as they often referred to themselves—present, discussions were almost always heated, with long digressions and references to obscure relatives and old incidents that had little if any bearing on the issue at hand. With Rutledge there, an outsider and a white law officer to boot, the council's silence didn't surprise Cork in the least.

When he was finished, there was a long silence, then George LeDuc spoke. In the dark, LeDuc might have been mistaken for a bear, an old bear, because he was seventy and huge. Although his long hair was streaked with silver, he still had a powerful look and feel about him. Only two years before, he'd fathered a child with his third wife, Francie. He and Cork had been friends for a lot of years.

"First of all," LeDuc said in a gentle growl, "we're all real sorry about Marsha Dross. We sure hope she'll be fine." He paused a long time, looking implacably at Cork. "As for that chunk of ear you're missing, well . . ." He glanced at the woman on the far side of the conference table. "Heidi, there, told me a little while ago she thinks a few scars on a man is sexy, so maybe it'll prove a blessing in the end." He almost smiled. "We'll do everything we can to help Agent Rutledge with his investigation."

"George, it would help most if you could encourage anyone on the rez who might know something to step forward. Talk to Agent Rutledge, or give me a call at my office, if they'd rather."

"We'll get the word out," LeDuc promised.

Thomas Whitefeather, an old man who was not an elected member of the council but was a part of it because he was a hereditary chief, spoke up. "Should we be afraid for the safety of the people on the rez?"

Rutledge fielded that one. "Until we know for sure the reason for the attack on Sheriff O'Connor and his deputy, I'd advise that any suspicious activity you observe warrants concern. However, at the moment we're operating on the belief that this was an isolated incident. I'll be spending time here today, and later in the general vicinity of the shooting. I'll be available to speak with anyone who might be able to shed some light on what's happened."

Rutledge stayed after, but Cork left and walked to the Pathfinder with George LeDuc.

"You must've really pissed somebody off," LeDuc said.

"Looks like."

"Folks on the rez, we've been glad to see you back in that uniform. Most of us. We hear anything, Cork, you'll know. But don't count on anyone talking to your BCA friend."

"I already told him that, George."

LeDuc shook his head and his long white hair shivered. "Out here, you can always tell a white man, but you can't tell him much."

7

A LITTLE BEFORE three that afternoon, Larson strode into Cork's office. The sun was bright and cast a long blade of light with a sharp edge that cut across Larson's thighs as he sat down.

"What have you got?" Cork asked.

"A good cast of the tire tracks," Larson said. "Excellent casting, actually. Rutledge's people are going to do a pattern match and then we can start checking sales around here. We dug the bullet from the ground, and that's on its way to the BCA lab. We didn't find any more shell casings, or anything else on the hilltop."

"You saw the tracks down the back side of the hill?"

"There were definite signs someone had gone that way, but we didn't find a good boot print. You took Rutledge out to the rez?"

"Yeah. He's there now, interviewing, hoping he'll find somebody who noticed something unusual. Problem is, there's nobody for a couple of miles in any direction from the Tibodeaus' place," Cork said. "And even if they'd seen something, they're not going to tell Simon."

"He's good. Let's wait to see what he comes up with." Larson's mouth went into a tight line, as if he were trying to keep something from slipping through his lips. "Cork," he finally said, "you need to see Faith Gray."

Faith Gray, MSW, PhD, was the consulting psychologist retained by the county for a variety of purposes. She did psychological testing for certain positions and was also responsible for counseling any sheriff's personnel involved in an officer-related shooting until she was ready to certify that they were fit for duty.

"I didn't shoot anybody," Cork said.

Cork had been toying with the silver pen he'd used to work on the duty roster. The pen slipped from his hands. He bent to retrieve it and, when he came up, realized that Larson's dark eyes had followed every move.

"You were shot," Larson said. "I can get you the policy statement, but you ought to know what it says. You wrote it."

"All right." Cork put up his hand as if to stop an argument. "I'll do it."

"It would be a mistake to put it off."

"I said I'd do it."

Larson nodded, rose from his chair, and left.

Cork sat for a while, eyeing the telephone. Finally he lifted the receiver to call Faith Gray and noted, a little distantly, that his hand was shaking.

As he'd promised, he was home for dinner. Jenny had put in a meat loaf, Annie had done potatoes and a tossed salad, and Stevie had set the table. His children weren't always this organized or cooperative, but whenever the foundation of the family seemed threatened, they pulled together admirably. They greeted him with prolonged hugs, as if he'd been away on a long trip.

He stowed his gun belt on the top shelf of his bedroom closet and put his revolver in the lockbox there. He took off his uniform, donned jeans and a yellow chamois shirt, and came down to dinner looking like a man who might be doing anything for a living. Except that he had stitches closing the lobe of his left ear where a bullet had narrowly missed piercing his skull. They talked about what happened. The children asked about Marsha, whom they all liked, and they were glad she would recover. As soon as he could, Cork moved them on to other topics.

"Get any great college offers today?" he said to Jenny as he wedged off a piece of the meat loaf with his fork.

She'd taken her SATs early and had done extremely well, scoring in the ninety-fifth percentile. For several months, she'd been considering the schools to which she would make application, and had narrowed her choices to Northwestern, Stanford, and Columbia, none of which the O'Connors could afford outright. They'd filed a statement of financial need, and knew that much of the final decision of a college would rest on what kind of aid Jenny was offered. She was a straight-A student with a lot of extracurricular activities and honors. Through a state-sponsored program, she'd already taken a number of college-level courses at Aurora Community College and aced every one. On top of it all, she was part Ojibwe. According to her high school counselor, all of these things made her an attractive candidate.

It was Northwestern that Jenny talked about most.

"No, but Mom and I talked some more about going to Evanston to check out Northwestern's campus."

"Sounds like a wise idea." Then he said, "'Some more'?"

Jo said, "We've been talking about a short trip to Evanston for a while."

Cork paused with his fork halfway to his mouth. "Really?"

"We told you, Dad. Don't you remember?"

"Sure." Although at the moment, he didn't. "When?"

"That's one of the things we need to discuss," Jo said.

Stevie, who was seven, put down his glass of milk. He had a white mustache on his upper lip. "I told Roger Turppa that I had a sister in the twelfth grade and he said I was a liar 'cuz school doesn't go that high."

"It might not for Roger Turppa, if he's anything like his dad," Cork said.

"Evanston's not that far from South Bend," Annie said.

Everyone knew Annie wanted to go to Notre Dame. There'd never been any doubt. Although only a sophomore, she was already determined to secure an athletic scholarship in softball, and when Annie set her mind on something it usually came to pass.

"We'll talk about Northwestern—and Notre Dame—later," Jo said. "When your father's not so tired."

After dinner, Jo washed the dishes, Cork dried. He was just hanging up the dish towel when the front doorbell rang.

"Dad," Annie called from the living room. "It's for you."

Simon Rutledge stood at the door, his hands folded patiently in front of him, smiling as he watched Cork come from the kitchen.

"Smells good," Rutledge said.

"The kids fixed meat loaf."

"The kids?" Rutledge laughed. "Mine can't even follow a recipe for ice water. Let's talk outside, okay?"

Cork stepped onto the porch and closed the door. It was a blue twilight with a few clouds in the west lit with a faint rose glow. The air was cooling rapidly, and by morning, Cork figured, there'd be frost. Gooseberry Lane was empty, but the houses along the street were lit by warm lights from within. During summer, when the evenings seemed to stretch into forever, he loved to sit with Jo in the porch swing and watch Stevie play with the other kids on the block, their laughter a perfect ending to the day. He didn't have that feeling now.

"I didn't get a lot on the rez," Rutledge said.

"I figured."

"People seem pretty well split in how they think of you."

"They always have been." Cork put his hands on the porch railing and leaned against it lightly. "You know anything about my family, Simon?"

"Nope. Only know you."

"My grandfather was a teacher, opened a school on the reservation in a time when most Ojibwe kids got sent away to government schools. The BIA's approach was to do its best to rub out the Indian in Indians. My grandfather had friends on the rez and also in politics and he was able to keep a lot of children from being taken from their families. Know why he did that?"

"He appreciated the culture?"

"He was in love. With my Grandma Dilsey, who convinced him to do the right thing. He was a decent man, but it was my grandmother who guided his heart. People on the rez respected my grandfather but they loved Grandma Dilsey.

"My mother chose to marry a white man, too. And a law enforcement officer, to boot. My father was a man of strong beliefs. He tried to be fair, and I think he did a pretty good job of it, but not everybody saw it that way. A lot of white folks called him a squaw man behind his back, like they did my grandfather. The Anishinaabeg called him *odeimin*. Know what that means?"

Rutledge shook his head.

"Strawberry."

"Because of his sweet disposition?"

"His ruddy Irish complexion. Now here I am, a little Indian and a lot of Irish. When folks, white or Shinnob, don't like what I'm doing, often as not they blame it on my blood." Cork glanced at Rutledge who was looking at the sky. "You find anyone who seemed pissed enough to shoot me dead?"

"You know the Ojibwe. For all the emotion they showed, I might as well have been talking to sticks. Nothing they told me was very useful." He yawned. It had been a long day for him, too. "We've got an agent in St. Paul who's going to St. Joseph's Hospital tomorrow to interview Lydell Cramer. We'll see what he has to say for himself."

Cork heard the dismissive tone of his voice. "But?"

"I've got to tell you, the Indian connection seems pretty strong. Whoever the shooter was, he knew the territory, knew the Tibodeaus' schedule, and knew it would most likely be you who responded to the call."

"Could mean it's just someone who's a good strategist."

"You make it sound like a war."

"I don't think it's over. Do you?" Cork said.

Rutledge put his hands in his pockets, hunched his shoulders. "He went to a lot of trouble and didn't get what he wanted. No, I don't think it's over."

Cork looked up and down the empty street. "Then it *is* a war. What do we do in the meantime?"

"Follow up on the tire castings and see what ballistics can tell us about the weapon." He saw Cork scrutinizing the neighborhood. "Worried?"

"He drew me out where there wouldn't be witnesses. I don't think he'll try anything here."

"Even so, it might be best to confine yourself to your office for a while. No rural calls."

"I'm not going to hide, Simon."

"That's not what I meant."

"I won't be stupid."

"All right." Rutledge started down the porch steps. "I'll be in touch."

Cork watched the agent get into his car and drive away. Night was pressing hard against the last stubborn light of day. He stood a few minutes longer on the front porch, peering deeply into the places where night and shadow already met. He turned his back to the street, felt a prickle run the length of his spine, the brief anticipation of a bullet, then he stepped inside.

8

HE WAS FOLLOWING his father through a stretch of pine woods he didn't recognize, following him at a distance. Liam O'Connor loped ahead, a giant of a man, putting more and more distance between himself and his son with each stride. He broke through shafts of sunlight, flashing brilliant for a moment, all gold. In the next instant he dropped into shadow. Cork tried to call out to him, to bring him back, but his jaw felt rusted shut, and all he could push through his lips was a desperate, incoherent moan. He struggled to run faster, to catch up so that he could throw his arms around his father and hold him forever. From somewhere in the pine boughs above came the harsh taunts of crows. He realized that everything around him had been perfectly still until the birds shattered the silence, and he became afraid. The cawing turned into the rattle of gunfire, and he saw that it was not his father he was chasing but Marsha Dross. As he watched, blood bloomed on the blouse of her uniform and she fell. Cork fought to free his legs, which had sunk deep into a bed of pine needles that held him like quicksand. The gunfire again became the cawing of the birds, and the cawing became the ringing of the phone in his bedroom as he pulled himself awake.

"Sheriff?"

"Yeah."

"Sheriff, it's Bos."

Cork registered that it was Boston Swain, the night dispatcher.

"You awake?"

"I'm here. What time is it?"

"Three A.M. You're sure you're awake."

Cork wiped away tears but was quite sure he was awake. "What is it, Bos?"

"Sheriff." She paused a moment, perhaps waiting for Cork to affirm that his eyes were open. "It looks like we've got a homicide."

He'd gone to bed to a clear sky and a moon heading toward full, and he'd thought by morning there would be frost. Clouds had moved in during the night, however, and kept the temperature up. As Cork headed away from home, a light precipitation began to fall, more mist than rain, coating everything with a wet sheen. The wipers of his old Bronco groaned intermittently across the windshield, the headlights shimmered off glazed asphalt, and the tires hissed as they rolled. The road to the overlook at Mercy Falls wound through dripping forests that, in the dark morning hours, seemed primordial and menacing.

There were two parking lots for the overlook at Mercy Falls. The first lot was for the picnic shelter and the restroom blockhouse. The second lot, a hundred yards up the hill and hidden by a thick stand of aspen, was nearer to the falls but had no facilities. The lower lot was empty; in the upper parking lot Cork found three vehicles. Two were department cruisers. The other was a silver Lexus SUV with an Avis sticker on the bumper. Nearby, heard but unseen, Mercy Creek gushed through a narrows in slate-gray bedrock before tumbling one hundred feet into a small pool. The falls overlook was a favorite place for sightseers during the day. Officially, it closed at sunset, but at night it was a popular spot for couples to do what couples in parked cars had always done in dark, beautiful places. The deputies on night patrol would swing by occasionally, often enough to keep the local kids guessing.

The two cruisers had been positioned so that their headlights blasted over the SUV from either side. Cork parked in back of the Lexus and left the Bronco's headlights on. Morgan and Schilling stood in the mist, their jackets zipped against the damp chill.

"Watch your step," Morgan said as Cork approached.

Cork looked down and skirted a small puddle of vomit, yellow-white on the wet pavement.

Schilling looked pale and shaken. "On the ground, in front." He nodded toward the Lexus.

The man lay on his back. A Cubs ball cap was pulled down over the top half of his face, obscuring his eyes. His mouth was open in an unending yawn. Long splashes of blood, almost black now from clotting, clung to his cheeks like leeches. His shirt, a button-down light-blue oxford, was a stained, shredded mess, getting damp from the mist. His pants and black briefs had been yanked down around his ankles. His knees were spread wide, and his crotch and inner thighs looked as if someone had taken a big brush, dipped it in a bucket of blood, and painted his skin.

Schilling said behind him, "They didn't just kill him, Cork. They castrated him, too."

"You found him?"

"Yeah." Schilling blew into his hands and shifted on his feet as if he were freezing.

"You touch anything?"

"I checked him for a pulse, that's it."

Cork looked back at the puddle of vomit. "His?"

"Mine," Schilling said. "Sorry."

"How're you feeling now?"

"I've been better."

"Okay. Nothing gets touched until Ed gets here. In the meantime, Howard," he said to Morgan, "I want you to get on the radio and run the plate, make sure it's a rental. Then let's contact Avis and find out who rented it."

Morgan nodded and headed to his cruiser.

"What about me?" Schilling said.

Cork considered the body and the ground around it becoming wet as the mist grew heavy, turning to a light rain. He didn't want to disturb the scene, but he also didn't want the rain to wash away evidence.

"Pull your cruiser around in front, Nate, and park with your grille facing the grille of the SUV. Stay back from the body a good ten feet. Leave your headlights on."

While Schilling maneuvered his vehicle, Cork grabbed a ground cloth and length of nylon rope from his Bronco. With his pocketknife, he cut four cords from the rope, each a couple feet long. When Schilling got out of his cruiser, Cork handed him one end of the ground cloth.

"Tie the corners to your grille. I'll tie the other end to the SUV."

When they were done, the ground cloth provided a shelter that kept the rain from falling directly on the crime scene.

"Now what?" Schilling asked.

"Wait for me in my Bronco. I'll be there in a minute."

Cork went to Morgan's cruiser and spoke to his deputy through the open window. "How's it going?"

"Bos is making the call now. Captain Larson's on his way. Should be here pretty quick."

"Stay with it. I'm going to talk to Schilling."

"How's he doing?"

"Still a little pale."

Cork returned to his Bronco, where Schilling sat hunched on the passenger side up front. Cork killed his headlights, and the two men sat for a moment in silence.

"Ever seen someone dead before?" Cork asked.

"Only in a casket. Never like that."

"Tough, huh?"

"You've got that right."

"You want to smoke, go ahead."

"Thanks." Schilling pulled a pack of Marlboros and a silver lighter from the inside pocket of his jacket. He tapped out a cigarette, wedged it into the corner of his mouth, flipped the lid on the lighter, put the flame to the tip of the Marlboro. He shot a cloud of smoke with a grateful sigh.

Cork opened his window a crack.

"Didn't touch the body, right?"

"Like I said, only to check the pulse."

"When did you throw up?"

"Right after that. It hit me real sudden."

"Sure. So you threw up and radioed the call in immediately?"

"Yes, sir."

"What time was that?"

"I don't know exactly. A little before three, I'd guess."

Cork had given up smoking a couple of years earlier, but he still found the smell of the cigarette enticing. "Tell me about your night up to that point."

"Nothing to tell. Real quiet up till then."

"Routine check of the park? That's why you were here?"

"I ran Arlo Knuth out earlier. I just wanted to be sure he didn't come back."

Arlo Knuth was an itinerant who spent his nights sleeping in parks or on back roads or wherever he could get away with parking the old pickup that was his home.

"What time?"

"Maybe midnight. Maybe a little before."

"You always do that after you've run Arlo off? Come back later to check?"

"Sometimes, not always."

"What made tonight different?"

"I don't know. Just a feeling."

"Why the hard-on for Arlo? He's harmless."

"Park closes at sunset. He's not supposed to be here at night. No one is."

"Most deputies cut Arlo some slack."

"I figure it's the law. Park's closed, everybody should stay out. Hell, I run kids off all the time who are making out here. Why should Arlo be any different?"

"When you came back, did you check behind the restroom blockhouse down in the lower parking lot?"

"No, sir."

"Sometimes Arlo uses the blockhouse for cover. That way he can wash up first thing in the morning."

"I know. And I would have checked it out, but when I got here I found a dead man. Pretty well ended my patrol."

"Think Arlo could've been involved in this?"

The deputy looked down at his cigarette, which hadn't touched his lips since his first drag. "No, sir, I don't expect so. Like you say, he's harmless."

Headlights flashed through the trees as several vehicles pulled off the main road and came up the winding access.

"All right, tell you what," Cork said. "Finish that cigarette, then take a hike down the path to the lower lot, check the blockhouse, see if Arlo's still around."

Ed Larson pulled up in his Blazer and parked. Cork left Schilling and headed to the Blazer just as Larson got out.

"Early start to your day, Ed."

"Same for you," Larson said. "What have we got?"

"Male Caucasian. Multiple stab wounds to the chest. And castrated. That's it so far."

"ID?"

"Not yet. I didn't want to disturb anything until after you'd had a chance to go over the scene. Looks like a rental vehicle. We're running the plates, so we may get something soon."

"All right. Who found him?"

"Schilling."

"Where is he?"

"In my Bronco. He's pretty shook. When you see the vic, you'll understand why. Oh, and watch your step as you approach the Lexus."

Larson looked at the SUV. "I called Simon Rutledge. I figured as long as he was in the neighborhood. He'll be here in a bit."

"Good," Cork said.

Morgan stood beside his cruiser, arms folded, water dripping from the bill of his uniform cap. Cork went over, and together they watched as Larson's team arrived and set about their work. Morgan had started his engine and left it idling so that the battery wouldn't wear down while his headlights lit the scene. The exhaust gathered in a ghostly white cloud that crawled around and under the vehicle. A minute later, Schilling left the Bronco and started down the path to the lower parking lot.

"Where's he going?" Morgan asked.

"I told him to check behind the blockhouse for Arlo Knuth."

"Think Arlo's still around?"

"Worth checking out. And gives Nate something to do."

"Good idea. I still remember the first body I saw on duty." Morgan's face was lit from the reflection of all the light in front

of him. His mouth was in a grim set. "Traffic accident. Guy
went through the windshield, ended up on the other side in
pieces. I lost my lunch that day."

Ed Larson was kneeling under the ground cloth Cork and
Schilling had tied above the body. "Cork," he called.

Cork wasn't in uniform. He'd thrown on a pair of wrinkled
jeans and a green sweatshirt with MACKINAC ISLAND across the
front, slapped a stocking cap on his head, and shrugged into
his bombardier's jacket that was so old and worn it looked like
the hide of a diseased deer. The jacket was soaked dark from
the mist and his face dripped as he walked to Larson.

"What is it?"

"You told me his balls were missing," Larson said.

"They are."

Larson held his flashlight out to Cork. "Look in there."

Cork knelt beside Larson and shined the light into the cav-
ern of the dead man's mouth, which Larson held open with
gloved fingers.

"Jesus."

"They're not missing," Larson said. "They were fed to him
as a last meal." He straightened up. "We'll move him in a little
while to see if we can locate a wallet for an ID."

Cork had had a good look at the face. He swung the beam of
his flashlight down to the dead man's right hand, where a big
gold ring adorned the pinkie—an odd finger, Cork had always
thought, for a man to put a ring on.

"No need," he said quietly. "I know who it is."

65

9

Jo WAS SLEEPING soundly, and Cork hated to wake her. For a little while, he sat in a chair in the corner, a maple rocker they'd bought when Jenny was a baby. Over the years, they'd taken turns rocking one child or another back to sleep during long nights of illness or restlessness or bad dreams, and Cork had often drifted off himself with a small body nestled against his chest. He hadn't always been the father he wanted to be, but somehow his children had clung to their love for him, and he felt blessed. Blessed, too, with Jo, although they'd had their problems. The point was, he thought, looking at his wife's face half lost in her pillow, to do your best as a man—father, husband, sheriff—and hope that your mistakes weren't fatal and they would be forgiven.

He moved to the bed, sat down beside Jo, and touched her shoulder gently.

She made an effort to roll over. "You're back?"

"Just for a bit."

Her eyes struggled to stay open. "Who was it?"

When he'd left, all he knew was that there appeared to have been a homicide at the overlook for Mercy Falls. He had told her to go back to sleep.

"You awake?" he asked now.

"Almost."

"I need you awake for this."

66

His tone brought her eyes fully open. "What is it?"

"I have to ask you a couple of questions."

She sat up, her back against the headboard, her blond hair a little wild. She pulled the covers up to keep warm. "Go ahead."

"How well do you know Edward Jacoby?"

"I've met with him half a dozen times over the past few months. Why?"

"How much do you know about him personally?"

"Almost nothing. What's going on, Cork?"

"The homicide at Mercy Falls. It was Jacoby."

"Oh my God."

The mist had developed into a steady rain that ran down the windowpanes. Outside, the street lamp on the curb pushed a yellow light through the window, and shadows from the streaked glass lay over the whole room like gray stains.

"Jo, do you have any contact information we can use to notify someone?"

"Downstairs in my office."

She threw back the covers. She wore a sleep shirt, her usual attire in bed. This one was black. She went barefoot ahead of Cork.

Downstairs, she turned on the light in the office she maintained at home, sat down at her desk, and reached for her Rolodex.

"Do you know who did it?" she asked.

"No."

"Any idea why?"

"No." Cork sat in the chair Jo's clients used. "Do you want to know how?"

Jo glanced up, her blue eyes guarded. "Do I?"

"Pretty brutal."

"Then no." She flipped a couple of cards on the Rolodex, then looked across the desk at him. "All right. How?"

"Multiple stab wounds. And he was castrated."

"Oh Jesus."

"Still had his wallet with him, stuffed with cash, so robbery doesn't seem a likely reason. Did he ever say anything to you, Jo, that might be helpful here?"

"Like what?"

"There's a lot of feeling on the rez that runs both ways about Starlight taking over management of the casino."

"Cork, you can't think somebody on the rez would do this. Over a business issue?"

"I don't know, Jo. That's why I'm asking questions."

She found the card she was looking for and took it off the Rolodex.

"All right," Cork said. "What about his personal life?"

"I don't know much."

"Married?"

"I believe so."

"Happily?"

"I have no idea."

"Does he gamble?"

"I don't know."

"Has he ever talked about people here, what he might do when he's not meeting with you?"

"Not really, but . . ."

"What?"

"I have my suspicions." She sat back. "He had a pretty high opinion of himself, and he appeared to have a libido the size of Jupiter."

"Yeah? Why do you say that?"

"He hit on me every time we met."

Now Cork sat back. "You never told me."

"It wasn't important. I dealt with it."

"You think he messed around?"

"I think he was the type."

"He ever mention any names?"

"Not to me. Here." She leaned across the desk and handed him the card. It contained Jacoby's office number, his cell phone number, the number for his home phone and a mailing address at Starlight Enterprises in Elmhurst, Illinois.

"Mind if I keep this?"

"No, go ahead." She studied him with concern. "You look so tired. Any chance you can lie down for a while?"

"I'm going to the office."

"At least let me fix you some breakfast."

He shook his head and stood up. "I'll hit the Broiler when it opens. You go on back to bed."

"There's no way I can sleep now." She came around the desk and took him in her arms. "Marsha, you, now this. What's going on, Cork? Didn't we leave Chicago to get away from this kind of thing?"

He took her in his arms and savored the feel, the only solid hold he had on anything at the moment. "Damned if I know, Jo, but I'm doing my best to find out."

He waited until 7:00 A.M. to make the call to Jacoby's home phone. After five rings, the line went to voice messaging, Jacoby's own oily voice saying he and Gabriella weren't home, leave a message.

Cork did, asking Ms. Jacoby to call him as soon as possible. It concerned her husband.

He stepped out of his office. The day shift had checked in, and the deputies were waiting for him in the briefing area. He gave them the lowdown on Mercy Falls, told them about a few changes to the duty roster, and reminded them to wear their vests.

At eight, he tried Jacoby's number again. This time someone answered, a woman with a slight Latino accent. Puerto Rican, maybe.

"Yes?"

"I'd like to speak with Ms. Jacoby, please."

"She is not here." Her *is* came out *ees*.

"Do you know how I might reach her?"

"Who is this?"

"Sheriff Corcoran O'Connor. I'm calling from Aurora, Minnesota."

"Mrs. Jacoby is gone. She will be back tomorrow."

"Does she have a cell phone number?"

"I can't give that out."

"Who am I speaking to?"

"I'm Carmelita."

"Carmelita, this is an emergency."

Carmelita breathed a couple of times before replying, "Mr. Edward?"

"Yes. Mr. Edward."

"Sometheen happen?"

"I need to speak to his wife."

She paused again, again considering. "Just a moment." Her end of the line went quiet. Then: "She is on a boat on the lake. I do not know if you can reach her. Her cell phone number is . . ." Cork wrote it down. Then she said, "His father. You should call him."

"His name?"

"Mr. Louis Jacoby. You want his telephone number?"

"Thank you."

He tried the cell phone that belonged to the dead man's wife, but it was "currently unavailable." He punched in the number Carmelita had given him for the father. It was the same area code as Edward Jacoby's home phone. The call was picked up on the first ring.

"Jacoby residence." A man's voice, modulated and proper.

"I'd like to speak with Louis Jacoby, please. This is Sheriff Corcoran O'Connor."

"Just one moment, please." The elegance of his voice seemed to lend a formality to the silence that followed. Half a minute later: "May I ask what this is in regard to, sir?"

"His son Edward."

A very proper silence again, then: "This is Lou Jacoby. What is it, Sheriff?"

"Mr. Jacoby, I'm calling from Aurora, Minnesota. It's about Edward."

"What's he done now?"

"It's not that, sir. I'm sorry, but I have some very bad news. Are you alone?"

"Just tell me, Sheriff."

"There's no way for this to be easy. The body of your son was discovered this morning in a park not far from here."

"His *body*?"

"Yes, sir. Mr. Jacoby, your son is dead."

Cork hated delivering this kind of news and hated doing it in this way.

"How?" Jacoby finally managed to ask.

"At the moment, we're treating it as a homicide."

"Somebody killed my son?" It was not a question but a hard reality settling in.

A silence that was only emptiness filled the line.

Then Jacoby rasped, "Eddie, Eddie. You stupid little shit."

10

A LITTLE BEFORE ten, Cork visited Marsha at the hospital. Charlie Annala had taken time off from his job at the fish hatchery and was a constant companion. Marsha's father, Frank, was there, too. Marsha looked better, with more color in her face, and she was sitting up. She'd heard about Mercy Falls and asked for details. Cork told her what they had. Then he had to tell her that as far as her own shooting was concerned, he knew nothing more than he did yesterday. But Rutledge was waiting for results from the BCA lab that he was sure would be helpful.

A few minutes after noon, he met with Simon Rutledge and Ed Larson in his office.

Larson explained that they'd completed their investigation of the crime scene at Mercy Falls after daybreak when they had more light to work with. They'd gone over the interior of the Lexus, taken hair samples from the upholstery that didn't appear to match that of the dead man, and had found in the ashtray two cigarette butts with lipstick on them. They'd fingerprinted everything; it was a rental, so there was a shitload of prints to process, and that would take a while. The door handles, however, had been wiped clean.

"Tom got right on the autopsy. He completed it about an hour ago. He's working on the official report right now, but basically this is what he found," Larson said, reading from his notepad. "There were fourteen stab wounds, all in the upper torso. Death was the direct result of a single stab wound to the heart. The mutilation came after Jacoby was deceased. The stab wounds were all delivered by a sharp, slender blade seven inches in length. The same instrument was probably used in the castration."

"Sounds like a fillet knife," Cork said.

"That's exactly what Tom thought."

In addition to being a physician and the county medical examiner, Tom Conklin was an avid angler.

"Was he robbed?" Cork asked.

"Nearly five hundred in his wallet, along with half a dozen credit cards."

"What was he doing out at Mercy Falls late at night?"

"Good question," Larson said.

"No indication of a struggle?"

"No lacerations on his arms or hands that would indicate he tried to defend himself."

"So Jacoby was taken completely by surprise?" Cork said.

"I'm guessing the final autopsy report will show a high blood alcohol level. There was a nearly empty bottle of tequila in the Lexus. Probably it'll show other drugs as well. We found a stash in the glove box. Cocaine, Ecstasy, marijuana, and Rohypnol."

The date-rape drug. Also known as Roofies, Ruffies, Roche, and by a dozen other names.

"It's entirely possible that Jacoby was too high to put up a struggle," Larson said.

Rutledge picked it up from there. "Jacoby had some receipts from the Four Seasons Lodge in his wallet. While Ed and his people finished at the scene, I dropped by and spoke with the lodge staff. Jacoby was staying there. He was a big tipper, flamboyant guy, and it wasn't unusual for him to be seen returning to his cabin at night in the company of a woman."

"Description?" Cork said.

"Not any particular woman anyone could describe. But we'll do more checking. Also we'll try to put together a complete history of his activities prior to his death."

"We'll be going over his room as soon as we leave here," Larson said. "See what turns up there."

"The drugs in the SUV," Cork said. "How'd he get those? Did he bring them with him? Risk a search of his luggage or person at airport security? Or did he buy them here?"

Rutledge nodded thoughtfully. "The castration might point toward a drug connection. Not uncommon to see something like that in drug deals gone bad. It could be the drugs were the reason he was at Mercy Falls."

"Anyone around here would know we patrol the park," Cork said.

Larson made a note on his pad. "Still worth checking out."

"Jacoby worked for Starlight. Casino management, right?" Rutledge said.

"That's right. He's made half a dozen trips over the last six months trying to convince the Iron Lake Ojibwe to become clients. The RBC is going to vote on it pretty soon."

"RBC?"

"Reservation Business Committee."

"But it's been Jo who's dealt with him mostly, right?" Larson said. "Have you talked with her, Cork?"

"Some. About all she could offer was that he was probably a skirt chaser." Cork rubbed his eyes, which were so tired they seemed full of sand. "Fourteen stab wounds, castration, and drugs. Cigarette butts with lipstick. Could it be we're dealing with a woman? Considering all the drugs, maybe a woman in an altered state?"

"What about an angry husband?" Larson threw in. "Maybe he followed them to Mercy Falls?"

Rutledge said, "I've requested the phone records for his room at the Four Seasons. Also his cell phone records since he arrived in Aurora. That might tell us who he's been seeing here for pleasure."

"The casino's something we should take a hard look at, though," Cork said. "Starlight's not a popular notion with everyone on the rez."

"Unpopular enough for someone to kill Jacoby over it?"

"Jo doesn't think so."

"What about you?"

What he thought was that, in the end, the rez was simply a community of people, and people—white, red, brown, black, yellow—were all subject to the same human weaknesses, more or less. He would like to have believed that the heritage of the Anishinaabeg, the culture and its values, made them strong enough to resist the temptations that accompanied the new wealth the casino brought, but he knew it was wishful thinking.

"I honestly don't know," he finally said. "Let's do a background check on Jacoby, make sure he didn't simply bring trouble with him when he came."

"Here's something that's kind of interesting we found in his wallet," Larson said.

He handed Cork a business card. The logo was the Hollywood sign of legend, the one perched atop the Hollywood Hills. Beneath was printed *Blue Smoke Productions* with Edward Jacoby listed as a producer and an address on Wilshire Boulevard in Los Angeles. No telephone number.

"Jacoby made movies?"

"Or wanted people to think he did."

"Women?"

"He certainly seemed to like them."

Cork handed it back. "Something more to check on." He addressed Rutledge. "How're we coming on the rez shooting?"

"My guy in St. Paul went out to St. Joseph's Hospital first thing this morning and talked with Lydell Cramer. Says Cramer was so full of shit, his eyeballs were brown. Cramer claimed that although he was happy to hear about your difficulties, he had nothing to do with them."

Cork nodded. "Cramer would have trouble just figuring how to put butter on bread. I don't think he could pull off a hit like this."

"Let me finish," Rutledge said. "My guy does a routine check of the visitors Cramer's had since incarceration. Only one: A sister. Address is in Carlton County. She visited Cramer the day before the sniper attack on the rez."

"Could be just a coincidence," Cork said.

"Could be. But I think it's worth checking out. Carlton County's only an hour south, so I'm going down today to have a talk with her."

"All right. Anything from the lab on the shell casings we found?"

"They haven't run them yet for markings, but they've identified them as oversized Remingtons. Hundred and fifty grain. Could have come from almost anywhere. The shooter could even have packed the loads himself. We'll check out the local hunting and sporting-goods stores, but unless we get very lucky, I'm not hoping for much."

"What about the tires?" Cork said.

"Better luck there. They're Goodyear Wrangler MT/Rs. High-end off-road tires, almost new. If they came from around here, we have a good chance at finding out who bought them. I've got one of my team on that, but I'd like to give him some help. Can you spare anyone?"

"I'll swing Deputy Pender your way. He can be abrasive but he's also thorough," Cork said.

"Two odd occurrences in two days." Larson raised his eyebrows. "Any way they might be related?"

Rutledge shook his head. "I don't see anything that would connect them. One shows a lot of planning, the other has the look of impulse. Of course, at this point, I suppose anything is possible." He eyed Cork. "I imagine you've been racking your brain pretty hard. Anything rattle loose?"

"Not yet," he said.

"All right, then."

Rutledge stood up and Larson followed him out the door.

Cork sat for a while, trying to muster some energy. Beyond the window of his office, the gray rain continued to fall. Across the street was a small park. All summer, the Lion's Club had raised money for new playground equipment and had spent several days volunteering their own time to install it, heavy plastic in bright colors. The playground was deserted. Beyond the park rose the white steeple of Zion Lutheran Church, almost lost in the rain.

Cork went out in the common area to pour himself some coffee. Two men stood on the other side of the security window that separated the waiting area from the contact desk. Deputy Pender was listening to them and nodding. When he became aware that Cork was behind him, he said, "Just a moment, folks," and turned to Cork. "Sheriff, there are some people here to see you. They say their name is Jacoby."

11

HE SEATED THE two men in his office. The elder man had white hair, a healthy shock of it that looked freshly barbered. He was tanned, in good condition, and dressed in a dark blue suit and red tie, as if he'd come to chair a board meeting. His eyes were like olive pits, hard and dark. If there was sadness in him, they didn't show it.

"Louis Jacoby," he'd said in the common area when he shook Cork's hand. "Edward's father. We spoke on the phone."

He'd introduced the second man as his son Ben. Ben remained quiet as his father talked.

"You arrived sooner than I'd expected," Cork said when he sat at his desk.

"I have a private jet, Sheriff O'Connor. Tell me what happened to Eddie."

Cork explained the events of the preceding night and where the investigation stood. "I have some questions I'd like to ask."

"Later," the old man said with a wave of his hand. "I want to see my son."

"That's not a good idea, Mr. Jacoby."

"I'm sure he's right, Dad," Ben Jacoby said. He appeared to be roughly Cork's age, maybe fifty. There was a lot of his father visible in his features, but his eyes were different, not so dark or so hard.

"I want to see my son." Jacoby didn't raise his voice in the least, but his tone was cold and sharp, cutting off any objection.

Still, Ben tried again. "Dad—"

"I've told you what I want. I want to see Eddie."

Ben sat back and gave Cork a look that asked for help.

"I can't prevent you from seeing your son, but the autopsy's only just been completed. If you could wait—"

"Now," the old man said.

"I don't understand—"

"I'm not asking you to understand, Sheriff. I'm telling you to show me my boy."

Cork gave up. "All right."

He took the Pathfinder. They followed in a rented black DeVille driven by a man they called Tony.

In a few minutes, Cork pulled up in front of Nelson's Mortuary on Pine Street. It was a grand old structure with a lovely wraparound front porch. It had once been a two-story home and was still one of the nicest buildings in town. When the Jacobys met Cork in the drive, Lou Jacoby stood in the rain, looking the place over dourly.

"I thought we were going to the morgue," he said.

"The morgue's at the community hospital, and it isn't set up for autopsies."

For a long time, the mortician Sigurd Nelson had been the coroner in Tamarack County. That position didn't exist anymore. Most of Cork's officers had become deputy medical examiners qualified to certify death. The autopsies were now contracted to be done by Dr. Tom Conklin, a pathologist who'd retired to a home on Iron Lake. For years prior, he'd been with the Ramsey County ME's office in St. Paul. He still used Sigurd's facility.

Cork rang the bell and the mortician answered. He was a small man with a big belly and a bald head, in his early sixties. He greeted Cork, then glanced at the other people on the porch.

"These are the Jacobys, Sigurd. Family of the man Tom autopsied today. They'd like to see the body."

"That's not a good idea," Nelson said. "Tom's finished the autopsy, but he hasn't repaired the body yet."

"Is Tom downstairs?"

"No. He went out for a bite to eat. He was going to finish up when he came back."

"We'll come back," Cork said.

"We're here," Jacoby said. "We'll see him now."

"Lou Jacoby," Cork said by way of introduction. "Edward Jacoby's father."

Sigurd Nelson addressed the man firmly but civilly. "With all due respect, you don't want to see your son's body right now."

"If you try telling me again what I want, I'll shove one of your coffins up your ass. Take me to my boy."

It wasn't so much that Nelson was cowed by Jacoby. Cork figured he probably decided a man with that attitude and those manners deserved to get exactly what he asked for. The mortician allowed them inside. Ben Jacoby signaled for Tony to accompany them, and the tall driver followed.

Nelson led them down a hallway. He lived upstairs with his wife, Grace, but the first floor was all business and included a large room used for memorial services, several viewing rooms, and a display room for coffins. At the end of the hall, he opened a door and they followed down a flight of stairs to the basement, which was divided into a number of rooms, all with closed doors. Nelson went to the last room, swung the door wide, turned on the light.

"Wait here just a minute," he said and disappeared inside. Shortly, Cork heard the flap of a sheet snapped open and the rustle of linen being arranged, then Nelson reappeared at the door. "All right."

Cork had seen the room many times before. It always reminded him of a laboratory. The walls were sterile white, the floor shiny red tile. There were cabinets with glass fronts through which shelves of plastic jars and jugs and glass bottles were visible. In the middle of the room stood a white porcelain prep table. It was old. Cork knew most prep tables were stainless steel now. Near the table was a flush tank and a pump for the embalming fluids. Beneath the table, the red tile sloped to a large floor drain.

The body lay on the table fully covered by the sheet the mortician had just positioned. Dark stains spread slowly across the white fabric.

"It won't be pleasant," Nelson said.

Jacoby paid him no heed. He walked forward stiffly, reached out, and drew the sheet back from Eddie's head. His son's face was bloodless, chalk white, but relaxed as if he were only sleeping. Which might have been a perfectly acceptable sight had Edward Jacoby still had a whole head. In his autopsy, Tom Conklin had slit the skin along the back of Jacoby's head from ear to ear, pulled the scalp forward over the face, opened up the skull as neatly as a tin can, and removed the brain.

"Oh God," Ben Jacoby said, and looked away.

Cork had been present at a lot of autopsies, and the sight didn't bother him. He figured it would be plenty to turn Lou Jacoby away, but the man surprised him. He drew the sheet back completely, exposing the raw, open, empty body cavity.

"Dad." Ben reached to steady his father.

"Leave me be." Jacoby stepped back, faltering. A tremor passed through him like a quake along a fault line. His hands shook and his jaw quivered. He squinted as if a bright light had struck his eyes, but he uttered not a word as he walked from the room.

The driver had not come in but had hung back, waiting in the corridor.

"Stay with him, Tony," Ben said. He turned to Cork and Sigurd Nelson. "I'm sorry. He's a man who gets his way."

"We need to talk," Cork said.

"How about not here," Nelson suggested, and ushered them out.

In the hallway, Lou Jacoby stood staring down the basement corridor with its false light and its dead end. Tony leaned against a wall nearby. He appeared to be in excellent condition, with long black hair and an olive cast to his skin. He watched the elder Jacoby carefully, ready to help should he be needed.

"Take him to the hotel," Ben said to him. "I'll be along."

Tony said gently and with a soft Spanish accent, "Let's go, Lou."

"I'm sure the sheriff has questions."

"I'll take care of them, Dad."

Jacoby nodded. Despite all his earlier posturing, all his effort at control, he seemed suddenly weak and uncertain. He didn't move toward the stairway until Tony urged him forward with a hand on his arm.

"We'll be right up, Sigurd," Cork said.

The mortician turned off the light in the prep room, closed the door, and left them alone.

"I have some questions about your brother, Mr. Jacoby."

"Of course. And call me Ben."

Jacoby was a handsome man, a little taller than Cork and, like his father, tanned and in good physical condition. He had his father's thick hair. It was still mostly brown, but there was a hint of gray at the temples. His face was smooth, the bones prominent. When he spoke, it was with quiet authority, a man accustomed to being listened to, who didn't need to flaunt his power. Sometimes the rich were like that, Cork had learned long ago. A profound sense of the responsibility that went along with wealth and position.

"Edward was here on business, is that correct?" Cork said.

"As far as I know, that's the only reason he came to Aurora."

"For Starlight Enterprises?"

"I assume so, yes."

"What does he do for Starlight?"

"I'm not entirely certain, but a lot of it has to do with bringing in new business."

"What do you do?"

"I run an investment firm with my father."

"You and your father but not Eddie?"

"Eddie had other ideas about what he wanted to do with his life."

"Did he talk about his visits to Aurora?"

"Eddie talked a lot. It was hard to know what to listen to, so I usually didn't. In terms of his business here, there's an attorney you ought to talk to. Eddie dealt with her a lot, I believe. Someone named Jo O'Connor." He stopped and gave Cork a quizzical look. "O'Connor?"

"My wife."

"Convenient."

Cork shrugged. "Small town."

"I assume you've spoken with her."

"I have."

"Would you mind if I did also?"

"Why?"

"My father is a little numb at the moment, but he'll be expecting answers soon. I'd like to be able to offer a few. Is there a reason I shouldn't speak with her?"

"No," Cork replied. "In fact, if you'd like, I'll drive you there."

"I could take a taxi."

"Ben, this isn't Chicago. We don't have taxis. I'll be happy to take you."

Jo was busy with a client, and they waited a few minutes in the anteroom of her office. Her secretary, Fran Cooper, asked if they'd like something to drink. They both declined.

Jo's door opened and Amanda Horton stepped out. Amanda was a transplant from Des Moines who, Cork knew, was trying to buy lake property currently tied up in probate.

"Hello, Cork," she said.

"Afternoon, Amanda."

She gave Ben Jacoby an appreciative look as she left.

Cork watched her go. When his eyes swung back, he found his wife standing in the doorway of her office, her eyes huge, her mouth open in an oval of surprise.

"Ben?"

"My God," Jacoby replied with equal wonder. "Jo McKenzie."

12

JACOBY ACCEPTED THE coffee she offered him and sat in one of the chairs available for clients.

Cork took the other client chair. "So," he said. "Law school together."

"My second year." Jo put the coffee server back on the tray with the mugs she kept on hand, went behind the desk, and sat down.

"My last," Jacoby said. "But you still practice, Jo."

"You don't?"

"I never did. I do investments."

"In Chicago?"

"We're in the Sears Tower." He shook his head and smiled. "You look wonderful. You haven't changed at all."

"What are you doing here?" She furrowed her brow. "Jacoby. Eddie?"

"He was my brother. My half brother."

She folded her hands on her desk, then unfolded them. "I never made the connection. I'm sorry, Ben."

Jacoby looked at his coffee mug but didn't take a sip. "No reason you should be. You and I, we knew one another a very long time ago. And Jacoby's not that unusual a surname."

"I mean I'm sorry about Eddie."

"Ah, yes. You dealt with him, with the business he had here?"

"That's right."

"Then maybe you can help me."

"In what way?"

"Before Eddie left for Aurora, he told me this visit would be different, that I'd understand when he got back. I got a call from him yesterday, late in the afternoon. He said he was going to celebrate. He sounded as if he was already two sheets to the wind, so I didn't know how much more celebrating he planned on doing. I wonder if you have any idea what that might have been about? Business?"

Cork looked at her, too.

Jo chewed on her lower lip, something she only did when she was very nervous. "It's possible. He'd been working for months to get the Iron Lake Ojibwe as clients for his company. He presented me with the contract yesterday. The RBC won't vote on it for a while, but they're certainly favorably disposed at the moment. So maybe that was it."

Jacoby thought it over and nodded slightly. "Maybe. Nothing Eddie touched ever turned out right. I think he was in trouble with Starlight and needed this casino deal." He glanced at Cork. "Does that help you at all?"

"We'll be looking into the possibility that his murder is related to his stay in Aurora, certainly, but is it possible this was something tied to his life in Chicago?"

"You mean somebody came out here to kill him?" The skepticism in his voice was obvious.

"I'm just asking are you aware of any circumstances in his life that ought to be considered."

"Did you know Eddie at all?"

"I'd met him a couple of times."

"Did he strike you as a gentle soul?"

"I'd appreciate it if you'd just answer my question."

"Look, Eddie and trouble were old friends, but I'm not aware of anything at the moment that I would connect with this. I can easily believe, however, that while he was here he pissed off somebody enough to want him dead."

Cork was making notations in a small notepad he kept in his shirt pocket. While he wrote, Jacoby turned suddenly toward Jo.

"Kids?" he asked.

Jo hesitated. "Three."

"I have a son. His name's Phillip. He's in his senior year at Northwestern." He waited, as if expecting Jo to reply in kind.

There was an uncomfortable silence, and Cork finally said, "We have two girls and a boy. Jenny's a senior in high school. Annie's a sophomore. Our son Stephen is in second grade."

Jacoby spoke toward Jo. "Sounds like a nice family."

"We think it is," Cork replied. "Interesting that your son's at Northwestern. That's Jenny's first choice for college."

"She couldn't choose better as far as I'm concerned. It's my undergraduate alma mater." He set his coffee mug on Jo's desk. "Sheriff, do you need anything more from me right now? I'd like to go to the hotel and check on my father."

"Where are you staying?"

"The Quetico Inn."

"I'll take you there."

The two men stood up, and Jo after them. Jacoby reached across her desk and warmly took her hand. "It's good to see you again, Jo. I'm just sorry it couldn't have been under more pleasant circumstances."

"I'm sorry, too, Ben." She drew her hand back, and addressed Cork. "Will you be home for dinner?"

"I'll try."

"I'd like you there. For the kids."

"Like I said, I'll try." He kissed her briefly and followed Jacoby out the door.

In the Pathfinder, as Cork pulled out of the parking lot of the Aurora Professional Building, Jacoby said, "Do you believe in synchronicity, Sheriff?"

Cork made a left onto Alder Street and headed toward the lake. "If that's anything like coincidence, no."

"I prefer to think of it as the convergence of circumstances for a particular purpose." He looked out the window. They were passing the old firehouse that had been converted into a suite of chic offices. "Nice town," he said, and sounded as if he meant it. "Aurora. The goddess of dawn."

Cork said, "What kind of man was your brother?"

Jacoby looked at him. "You'll get a prejudiced answer."

"I'll work around the prejudice."

"He was the kind of man I'd rather have working for Starlight than for me."

"Why?"

"He had a style I strongly disagreed with. What's that wonderful smell?"

"It's Thursday, barbecued rib night at the Broiler."

Jacoby smiled vaguely. "What was last night?"

"Homemade meat loaf and gravy."

Jacoby gave his head a faint shake. "Must be comforting."

"To live in a small town and like it, you have to appreciate routine."

"Routine. There are days when I'd sell my soul for a little of that." The sentiment seemed sincere.

The main lodge at the Quetico Inn was a grand log construction that stood on the shore of Iron Lake a couple of miles south of town. Cork pulled up to the front entrance and put the Pathfinder in park. Jacoby reached for the door handle.

"I'd like to talk more with your family," Cork said.

"We'll be in town a couple of days." He gave the handle a pull, opened the door, and stepped out. He tossed Cork a bemused look. "Nancy Jo McKenzie. Who would've thought it? Good afternoon, Sheriff."

He meant to get home for dinner as Jo had asked, but when he returned to his office, he found the department besieged by the media, and he arranged for a press conference at the courthouse at five o'clock. He contacted Simon Rutledge, who agreed to be there, but Rutledge was delayed and the conference began twenty minutes late. Cork had prepared an official statement that included the first public announcement of the identity of the murdered man, and he dispensed the statement to all the reporters. News cameras had also been sent by network affiliates in Duluth and the Twin Cities. Simon Rutledge deferred to Cork on most questions, and Cork answered honestly what he could, indicating that evidence had been gathered and that they had leads which he declined to go into.

After the press conference, he met with Rutledge and Larson in his office. They didn't feel either of the investigations had made much headway.

"I'm expecting to have a fax of Jacoby's phone records by tomorrow. I'm hoping that'll give us some direction," Rutledge said.

Larson chimed in. "In the meantime, we've pulled prints from his room at the Four Seasons. The linen gets changed daily, and it appears he didn't sleep in his bed last night, but we've taken the bedspread and maybe we'll get something from that—hair samples, for example, that match those from the SUV."

"How about the cigarette butts?"

"Still being analyzed," Rutledge said, with a note of apology.

Cork knew that the resources of the state BCA crime lab were in great demand, and whatever was sent from Aurora would have to wait its turn.

"One thing, though," Larson said. "When I talked with the Four Seasons staff, they told me that in the past Jacoby stayed for only two or three days. This time, he'd been there more than a week."

"And this time," Cork said, "the RBC is getting ready to vote on a contract proposal for Starlight's services."

"A lot of heavy lobbying on Jacoby's part?" Rutledge said.

"We should find out. I'll head out to the rez first thing tomorrow and talk to LeDuc and some of the other members of the RBC," Cork said.

"Another thing to think about is Jacoby's libido," Larson said. "I talked to the staff at the Boundary Waters Room." He was speaking of the restaurant at the Four Seasons. "Jacoby ate late, usually after a couple of drinks at the bar, then he generally left the inn. He sometimes came back with company."

"He got lucky?"

"Or he was the kind who didn't want to be alone, even if it cost him."

"I talked with Newsome," Larson said. Then, for Rutledge's benefit he added, "The night bartender at the Four Seasons. Newsome said Jacoby had asked him once where a guy with cash could find himself a little company."

"What did Newsome tell him?" Cork asked.

"Claims he said he didn't know."

"How hard did you lean on him?"

Larson said, "There are a lot of people to talk to, Cork."

"I know there are, Ed." He took a moment, shifted his thinking to the incident on the rez. "Did your man or Pender come up with anything on those Goodyear tires?"

"Nothing. They'll widen their area of inquiry tomorrow."

"How about the ammo?"

"Nothing there, either. But we'll keep on that, too."

"Simon, anything from your talk with Lydell Cramer's sister?"

"I never got to her. She lives on a farm. The road's gated and locked. I wanted to get back here for the press conference, so I'll try again tomorrow, talk to the local cops, see what they can tell me."

They ended their meeting. As he was leaving, Larson said quietly to Cork, "How're you doing?"

"Tired. I imagine you are, too. But if you're worrying about my mental state, don't. And by the way, I have an appointment to see Faith Gray tomorrow."

"I wasn't worried, Cork," Larson said. "Just concerned."

13

Cork had called to say he wouldn't be home for dinner. Jo wasn't angry. She understood his situation. But she wasn't happy, either. The children helped with dishes, then turned to their homework.

Jo went into her office at the back of the house to do some work of her own. She was going over the file of Amanda Horton when the phone rang.

"I was hoping you would answer." The voice was low and certain, and she knew it instantly. "I need to see you."

"What for?"

"To talk."

"That's not a good idea."

"Please. Just to talk."

"We can talk on the phone."

"There are things you need to know. For your own good. Please."

She closed her eyes and knew even as she made her decision that it held all the potential for disaster. "All right. My office in the Aurora Professional Building. In fifteen minutes."

"Thank you."

She went to the living room, where the children sat among their scattered books and notebooks and pencils.

"I have to go to my office for a while. You guys okay?"

"Sure, Mom," Jenny said. "A client?"

"Yes." The lie felt like something piercing her heart.

The rain had ended in the afternoon, but a dreary wetness lingered. It was after seven, the sky a dismal gray that was sliding into early dark. The radio in her Camry was on, tuned to NPR, *All Things Considered,* but she wasn't listening. She turned onto Oak Street, pulled to the curb, and stopped half a block from her office. She sat with her hands tight on the steering wheel, staring through the windshield at an old tennis shoe abandoned in the street. It looked like a small animal cringing in the beam of her headlights.

She closed her eyes and whispered, "Christ, what am I doing?"

She heard the car approaching, the whish of the tires on wet pavement. A black Cadillac passed and half a block farther turned into the parking lot of the Aurora Professional Building. She took a deep breath and followed.

When she parked beside the Cadillac, he stepped out.

"This way," she said, and went to a side door where she used her key.

The hallway was quiet and dimly lit, but from somewhere she couldn't see came the sound of a buffer going over a floor.

"Cleaning staff," she said, more to herself than to him.

She led the way to her office, unlocked the door, stood aside to let him pass. Closing the door behind her, she walked to her inner office and flipped on the light. She turned around. He stood close to her, smelling of the wet autumn air.

"What do you want, Ben?"

He wore a light-brown turtleneck that perfectly matched his eyes and hair and pressed against his chest and shoulders in a way that made it seem as if the muscles beneath it were about to burst through.

He said, "A very long time ago I built a wall across my life. There was everything before you and everything after."

"Very poetic," she said. "And what? The wall crumbles now, our lives suddenly merge again? Ben, you left me, remember? How's your wife, by the way?"

"She's dead, Jo."

"Oh." She felt the knot of her anger loosen just a little. "I'm sorry."

"I've been a widower for a year. But even before that we

were . . ." He shrugged in his tight, expensive sweater. "The marriage was over years ago. It was never much of a marriage to begin with."

She slipped behind her desk, put the big piece of polished oak between her and Benjamin Jacoby. "I'm sorry your life didn't work out the way you'd hoped, but I put you behind me a long time ago. I went on with my own life. I've been very happy."

He came to the desk. "You never thought of me?"

She didn't answer.

"It's a big world, Jo. It's unthinkable to me that fate would bring us together again without a reason."

"Fate?" She laughed. "Ben, you never left anything to chance. How long have you known I was here?"

He looked deeply into her eyes. "I always knew it. I just never did anything about it. Then one night, we're having dinner at my father's house, the whole family. Eddie's talking about this casino deal he's working on in Minnesota, going on about the gorgeous lawyer he was dealing with. I ask him where this casino is. And bingo—Aurora. I don't know. With Eddie coming here, it made a difference somehow, connected us. Since then I've often thought about using him as an excuse to contact you, but I'm not egocentric or stupid enough to believe there could ever be anything between us again. I wouldn't be here now if it weren't for what happened to Eddie. I don't have any desire to complicate your life."

"You can't complicate it, Ben. You're not even a part of it."

"I'm not looking for that, Jo. My life hasn't been perfect, but it was the one I chose, and it's had its advantages." He moved his hand across the desk but stopped far short of touching her. "You haven't asked why I left you."

"It was pretty obvious. You were married within six months."

"The roads we take aren't always of our own choosing."

"What? She was pregnant?"

"There are other compelling reasons to marry."

"Love?"

"In my whole life, Jo, I've loved one woman. I didn't marry her."

91

"I don't want to go on with this conversation. But I do want to know why the charade? Why pretend that my being here was such a surprise?"

"I was afraid that I'd scare you. I know how crazy all this must seem."

Jo shook her head. "I haven't heard you say one thing so far that sounded real to me."

He looked genuinely hurt. "The wall, Jo, that was real. You did divide my life. For a while, you absolutely defined it. I'm not saying that I've thought of you every day for the last twenty years, but whenever I think about a time when I was happy, I think about the summer with you." He seemed to be at the edge of defeat. "Look, I'm in town for only a couple of days. Could I . . ." He faltered. "Could I ask a favor? A small one, I promise."

"What is it?"

"I'd like to meet your family."

"Why?"

"I'd love to see the life you've made for yourself."

"I don't think that's a good idea."

"Only you and I know the truth about us. It wouldn't be awkward, I promise. And maybe it would help with closure."

"After twenty years you need closure?"

"All right. Then just to satisfy my own damn curiosity. An hour of your time and your family's. Is it really so much to ask?"

"Yes, it is. I can't believe you don't understand that."

"There's so much you don't understand. So much you never will." He put up his empty hands. "I guess that's it."

"You said there were things I needed to know, for my own good."

"I was mistaken. They were things I needed to know, and now I do."

He turned and walked to the anteroom. At the door that opened onto the hallway, he turned back, his hand on the knob. He took a look around him, at the ordinary room where Fran Cooper worked and Jo's clients waited. "Do you like this?"

"I love it," she said.

His eyes held a look of wistful sadness. "I wish I could say that about what I do. I wish I could have said it, ever. Good night, Jo." He went out and closed the door behind him.

She waited until the sound of his footsteps in the corridor had faded to nothing, then went back into her office, sat down, and put her hands over her face as if she were trying to hide behind a small, fragile fence.

14

THE BAR AT the Four Seasons was a big room with a stone fireplace and wide windows that overlooked Iron Lake. On sunny days, the view of the marina and beyond was stellar, row after row of boats at rest on blue water, framed by the sawtooth outline of pines. But at night there was only darkness outside the window glass, and what people saw then was the reflection of the fire and themselves, and the room seemed much smaller.

Cork caught Augie Newsome in an idle moment, wiping down the bar. Newsome was a rubbery-looking man with a willowy body, long arms, and face like stretched putty. He wore Elvis Costello glasses and combed his hair in a gelled wave. He usually appeared to be on the brink of smiling, as if all the ironies of life were right in front of him and always amusing. Cork had known him a dozen years, ever since Newsome migrated up from the Twin Cities for reasons that only Cork and a very few others knew. During his first stint as sheriff, he'd given Newsome a break that had meant a difference in the kind of bars behind which the man spent his time.

"Sheriff," Newsome said brightly, wiping his way down the bar toward Cork. "What can I do you for?"

Except for a couple seated at one of the tables near the fireplace, the bar was deserted. It was Thursday, the night before the weekenders descended. The locals called them 612ers, because the vast majority of the tourists and the nonresident landholders came from the Twin Cities where for years those three numbers had formed the prominent telephone area code.

Cork said, "Ed Larson talked to you today."

"That he did. Asked about the dead guy out at Mercy Falls. Man, is that crazy or what? Right here in Aurora. Say, I understand Marsha Dross is doing fine. Glad to hear it. Her and Charlie Annala are pretty regular customers. Can I get you something?"

"I just need a few answers, Augie. You told Larson that Edward Jacoby asked you where he might find a prostitute around here. Is that correct?"

"He didn't use the word *prostitute*, but that's what he wanted."

"What did you tell him?"

"I told him the lake was all the entertainment most folks needed up here. If it was a boat he was looking to rent, or fishing gear, I could point him in the right direction."

"Augie," Cork said, leaning close so that his voice wouldn't carry to the couple near the fireplace. "I've got a dead man on my hands. I need you to cut out the bullshit and help me here. Whose name did you give him?"

Newsome looked pained that Cork didn't believe him. "Sheriff, I—"

"Augie, do I have to remind you about the incident in Yellow Lake?"

"All right. I gave him one name and that was a few months ago. Krisane Olsen."

"Where's she working these days?"

"She hangs out at the casino."

"One name, last year, that's it?"

"That's it."

"He never asked again?"

"He asked. I played dumb."

"Why?"

"Talk to Krisane, you'll understand."

"All right, Augie. Thanks."

"Guys like him, Sheriff, when they end up with their balls cut off, it's not hard to figure why."

Cork gave him a puzzled look.

"Talk to Krisane."

Augie Newsome walked down the bar to where a man in a Minnesota Twins T-shirt had just sat down on a stool.

The Chippewa Grand Casino was a blaze of lights among the pine trees a quarter mile south of the town limits just off State Highway 1. Before the Iron Lake Ojibwe purchased the land and built the casino a few years earlier, the area had been a county park. The lot was packed with cars when Cork arrived. Even in the worst winter weather or in the black hours of morning when the rest of the county slept, the casino lot was never less than half full. That so many people felt compelled to empty their pockets, blithely or in desperation, had always baffled Cork. He'd been among the most skeptical when the casino had first been proposed, and while he knew that its success was a blessing both to the Anishinaabeg and to the economy of Tamarack County, there was something about the enterprise that felt like wolves feeding on sheep.

He found Krisane Olsen sitting at the bar, smoking a cigarette, a glass of red wine on a napkin in front of her. She chatted with the bartender, Daniel Medina, a Shinnob from Leech Lake. Krisane wore a shiny lime-green dress with a hemline that barely covered her ass. There was gold, or more likely imitation gold, around her neck and wrists and dangling in big hoops from her earlobes. She was a small woman, nicely built, with cranberry-colored hair and a face done brightly to mask her fatigue. Days, she worked as a dog groomer. Nights, she worked even harder.

Cork had changed out of his uniform before leaving his office, put on a blue flannel shirt, brown cords, a yellow windbreaker. When he wanted information, the uniform often presented a barrier. People would talk to Cork, but they clammed up in the official presence of the sheriff.

"Evening, Krisane." He took the stool beside her.

"Oh Jesus." She sent a cloud of cigarette smoke heavenward.

"What's she drinking, Dan?" Cork asked.

"Merlot."

Cork pulled out his wallet. "Give her another on me and then give us some space, okay?"

"Sure thing, Cork."

"What do you want?" Krisane said.

"Information, that's all."

"Right."

"Know a guy named Eddie Jacoby?"

"Never heard of him."

"A little shorter than me, dark hair, nice physique. From Chicago. Wears a gold ring on both of his pinkies."

"Never laid eyes on him."

Medina brought the glass of merlot. Cork laid a ten on the bar, told him to keep the change.

When they were alone again, he said, "I've always been square with you, Kris. I know how it is when you're a single parent trying to make ends meet, and as long as you've done business quietly and safely and no one complained, I haven't bothered you. Isn't that right?"

"Whatever," Krisane said. She ashed her cigarette in a star-shaped tray.

"This is the deal. You play straight with me now or I'll arrange to have an undercover vice officer follow every move you make."

"You'd do that?"

"I just said I would."

"I've got a kid to worry about."

"Right now your biggest worry is me. Understand?" He turned on his stool and faced her directly. "Did you ever hook up with Edward Jacoby?"

She stubbed out her cigarette, dug out a pack of Salems from the small beaded purse she carried, and fished out another smoke.

"Well?"

She lit the cigarette and exhaled with a sigh. "Only once. Four months ago."

"Only once? He didn't look you up again?"

"He came looking all right. I didn't want to have anything to do with him."

"Why?"

"The guy was psycho. He liked to hurt people. Women, anyway."

"What did he do?"

"Come on, Sheriff."

"I need to know."

She rubbed her thigh nervously with her free hand. "He was into a rape thing. He wanted me to fight him—you know, struggle. But he got rough for real. I tried to stop him for real. He just beat me up and did what he wanted. When he was done, he threw the money on the floor. Is that what you wanted to hear?"

"Why didn't you come to the department and make a complaint?"

She gave him a withering look.

"Anything like that ever happens again, Kris, you come to me directly. Okay?"

She was twenty-seven years old. Cork figured that by the time she was forty, the dye would ruin her hair, the smoking would make her voice like the growl of a bad engine, and the hard life would burn her out, leave her with no more substance than the ash at the end of her cigarette.

"All right," she said.

"Where were you last night?"

"Here. Danny'll tell you." She nodded toward the bartender, who was laughing with a man farther down the bar.

"You were here all night?"

"I left at ten."

"Alone?"

She hesitated a moment. "No."

"But not with Jacoby."

"No way. You can ask Danny about that, too. He knows who Jacoby is."

"What time did you go home?"

"Around one."

"I may have to talk to the john you were with."

"Jesus, Cork."

"I didn't say it was for sure. But you'd better know who he was, or how to find out who he was."

"He had a room at the hotel here. I can give you the number."

"All right."

She seemed to think she'd given him everything she could and turned away.

"Krisane, is it possible he went to another working girl?"

She smoked her cigarette and didn't look at him, like they were lovers who'd just had a quarrel. "There aren't that many around here, and I made sure they all knew about him."

"Okay." He slid off his stool. "I meant it."

"What?"

"You ever have any trouble again like you had with Jacoby, I want to hear about it."

She studied the glowing end of her cigarette, finally gave a slight nod.

15

CORK CAME HOME late. Jo pretended to be asleep as he undressed for bed. He had to be exhausted, with so little rest since the shooting on the rez; but he lay for a long time, and although he was quiet, she knew his eyes were open and he was staring at the ceiling in the way he always did when he was worried. When he finally nodded off, she was certain his dreams would be troubled.

She couldn't sleep, either, but she didn't want to talk to him. Pretending sleep was easier than pretending other things. Like pretending she had never loved Benjamin Jacoby, loved him desperately.

Cork rolled over, his face, so familiar even in the dark, close to hers. She could feel the strong grip of his love around her, her own love covering him like a blanket.

So what was this unsettled feeling, this rumble of fear? Ben Jacoby was twenty years ago. She'd lived a whole life since then, a full life with Cork and her children at the center.

Oh God. Was it possible that even after all this time, after all her experience, there was still some ember alive in her heart, burning for Ben Jacoby? Could she still feel something for the man who'd abandoned her on a cold rainy autumn night twenty years before—abandoned her without explanation?

She'd met him at law school, the final semester of her second year. He was older, funny, brilliant, gorgeous. They'd become lovers.

She was living in a small apartment in a run-down building on South Harper in Hyde Park, an easy walk to the University of Chicago Law School. Ben worried that it was not a good neighborhood, but Jo, a military brat, assured him she knew how to take care of herself.

Although they often ate out, he had come to her place for dinner that evening. She was a horrible cook, but she knew how to make spaghetti and that's what she'd prepared. He brought a good Chianti. He looked tired when he stepped in, and when she kissed him, he seemed to hold back.

She took his wet overcoat. Cashmere. He always dressed well, as if he had money, or his family did, although he never talked about it. In fact, he never talked about his family at all. He claimed he was a man of the moment. He didn't discuss his past, never speculated on the future, his or theirs together. Jo had a brief glimpse into his life, however. Ben had a younger sister, Rae, a student at Bennington, an art major, a fine artist already from the things Jo was allowed to see. Rae worshipped her older brother. In the long summer of Jo's affair with Ben, Rae, home from college, had joined them on some of their outings. She'd once taken them through the Art Institute and proved to be a knowledgeable guide. Jo liked her immensely. Rae was under strict orders not to talk about family, and although she tried to hold to that, once in a while she let something slip. Often it was something harsh about "Daddy." In September, she returned to Bennington.

Jo wasn't reluctant to talk to Ben about her own life, her own past. About the rootlessness that went with being raised by a single parent, an army nurse. About her teenage rebellions, her drive to excel in everything she did so she could escape the alcoholic mother whom she referred to as The Captain. She'd confessed her fear that, like her mother, she drank too much, was too harsh in her judgments of people. Ben Jacoby had been a marvelous listener, something new to her in a man, and although his intellect was towering, she never felt it was a shadow he cast over her or anyone else. He was, in her experience, a rare, good man. And she loved him powerfully.

"Are you all right?" she asked that rainy October night.

"Just a little tired," he said.

On graduation from the U of C Law School, he'd taken a prestigious clerkship with a state supreme court justice, a demanding position, and he worked long hours.

"I have something for you." He handed her a cardboard tube.

"What is it?"

"Open it."

She popped out the metal cap and from inside pulled a rolled canvas. She moved to good light under a standing lamp.

It was a portrait of her. She sat on the green grass of Grant Park, in a white dress, looking at something to her right that must have pleased her because she was smiling. Behind her, Michigan Avenue was an impressionistic mist of suggested buildings and pedestrians. It was a beautiful painting, and she fell in love with it immediately.

"Oh, Ben, where did you get this?"

"I asked Rae to do it. I gave her a photograph."

"I love it. I absolutely love it."

She kissed him passionately, but again felt his reserve.

Often they made love before dinner. That night they simply ate, seated at her small kitchen table in the glow of candlelight, with the sound of rain against the windows.

"You're quiet," she finally said. "And you keep looking at me like I've just left on a train out of town. What's going on?"

He said, "Jo." One word, but oh, it was like a funeral bell.

She sat back in her chair as if he'd hit her. "It's over, isn't it?"

In the candlelight, she saw that his eyes were filled with tears. Men never cried when they said good-bye. They found some way to make it not their fault, to feel justified. They left behind a foul sense that somehow it was all wrong from the beginning, a mistake everyone was better off forgetting.

But not Ben Jacoby.

"You're the best thing that ever happened to me," he said.

"Then why?"

He shook his head and looked truly bewildered. "I wish I could say the thing that would make it all clear, but it's so complicated. It has nothing to do with you or with what I feel for you."

"Right," she said, not bothering to hide her bitterness.

He reached across the table and took her hands. "If I had a choice, I would stay with you forever."

"You always have a choice. It's clear you've made it."

"Not being with you will just about kill me." He gripped her hands so powerfully that he'd begun to hurt her a little.

"Just go," she said. "And here. Take this with you."

She gave him back the painting.

"That's yours," he said.

"I don't want it. I don't want anything to remind me of you. Take it. Take it, goddamn it."

He didn't argue, didn't try to wheedle from her one last time in the sack, didn't suggest a last glass of wine or a final kiss. But he didn't hurry, either. He left with an air of profound sadness, and when she was able to think about it later through the filter of time, without anger or hurt, she realized that he'd left with a sense of dignity, his and hers, somehow intact. And for that she loved him, too.

They hadn't made promises, but they'd been in love, and there had never been a clear reason for the ending. Time had helped put him behind her. Time and her marriage. She hadn't thought of Ben Jacoby in years.

That something inside her still responded to him—his presence, his voice, even the scent of him, the same after all these years—surprised her. There was something going on with her emotions over which she seemed to have no control. She knew she would never act on what she felt, but it still frightened her.

She studied her husband, sleeping restlessly beside her. There had been rough periods in their marriage, but they were in the past. And the truth was, she loved Cork, as much for all he'd committed to working through with her and forgiving as for all that had been effortless and good between them.

He stirred, moaned softly. She lifted herself, leaned to him, and gently kissed his lips. Although she knew his sleep was troubled, for a moment in his dreaming he smiled.

16

FIRST THING IN the morning, before the day watch came on, Cork met with Ed Larson and Simon Rutledge so they would have time to alter duty assignments for the deputies if necessary. Cork related his conversation with Krisane Olsen and suggested it would be a good idea to interview the other women in Tamarack County who were known to take money, even occasionally, for sex. He and Larson came up with the list, and Larson said he'd see to it. Rutledge expected the records for Eddie Jacoby's cell phone any moment. He hoped they might offer more leads. Cork wanted to talk with the Jacoby family, find out if Eddie might have said anything to them that would be enlightening about his activities in Aurora. Rutledge thought he would try again to interview Lydell Cramer's sister. The possibility of Cramer being involved in the rez shooting was thin, but until they got more lab results there weren't any other threads to follow. They agreed to stay in touch and to meet again around noon.

The overcast of the day before was gone, and the morning was bright and crisp as Cork drove to the Quetico Inn. For the last quarter mile, the road ran alongside the resort's Jack Nicklaus–designed golf course, where the grass sparkled with dew. All the holes appeared to be empty, but Cork spotted a lone figure jogging in the green apron between the thirteenth fairway and the road. He recognized Tony, Lou Jacoby's driver. He passed, slowed, pulled over, and stopped. As the man approached the Pathfinder, Cork got out to meet him.

"Good morning, Sheriff," he said brightly. His face was flushed and his long black hair was damp with sweat, but he seemed barely winded. He wore tight black Lycra pants and a light-blue windbreaker. "Paying a call on the Jacoby family?" He glanced toward the lodge in the distance, then down at his sports watch. "You'll find Lou eating breakfast. He has breakfast every day sharply at nine. Ben's probably with him. Or playing golf." Now Cork could hear very definitely the Spanish accent he thought he'd caught the day before.

"Golf?" Cork said, thinking the man's brother had just died.

Tony smiled. "It's a strange family, Sheriff."

"I didn't get your full name."

"Tony Salguero."

"You do something for the Jacobys besides chauffeur?"

"I almost never chauffeur. Mostly I'm a pilot."

"You flew the Jacobys out here?"

"Yes." He rubbed his thighs vigorously. "My muscles are getting a little stiff, Sheriff. Do you mind if I return to my run?"

"Maybe you could help clear up a couple of things first. You got here awfully fast yesterday. Lou must've called you right away."

"He did. I was sailing. I got the call on my boat."

"Sailing where?"

"I was returning from an outing to Mackinac Island."

"And you still made it back to Chicago to fly the Jacobys?"

"I had docked at a marina in Kenosha, Wisconsin, for the night. When Lou called, I arranged for a helicopter to O'Hare where we keep the jet."

"Couldn't he have used a different pilot?"

"He prefers me. And I told him I could get him here."

"When Eddie Jacoby came out, did you fly him?"

"Not usually. That was for his business, so his company took care of that."

"Commercial flights?"

He shrugged. "I guess so."

"What about this last time?"

"I flew him. He asked me as a favor. I don't know why this time was different. But I told him he was on his own coming home. I would be sailing."

That probably answered the question of how Edward Jacoby had come by the drugs in his SUV. He'd brought them with him.

"Look, Sheriff, if I don't start running again, I'll pull something. Okay?"

" 'Preciate your time."

"By the way," he said as he stretched down, grabbed his calves, and put his forehead against his shins, "when you get to the lodge, you're in for a surprise." He came up smiling enigmatically and took off at a run.

Cork parked in the lot and went into the main lodge. The Quetico Inn was on the national register of historic buildings. It had been constructed in 1928 by a consortium of celebrities that included, among others, Babe Ruth, and was intended to be a getaway for the rich and famous. The Depression pretty much quashed that idea, but the beauty and integrity of the lodge had been maintained, and during the crazy economic boom of the 1990s, the resort had been expanded into a conference center that included tennis courts, the golf course, an Olympic-size indoor pool, a marina, and a restaurant with the best wood roast in all the north country.

The restaurant, a large, sunny room with a million-dollar view of Iron Lake, had few diners. It was Friday morning; on Saturday, however, and again on Sunday, the place would be packed. The Jacobys sat at a table near one of the windows overlooking the lake. They weren't alone. A woman sat with them, listening intently to Lou Jacoby as he talked. When Cork approached, Jacoby looked up, and the talking ceased. A moment of cold silence, then Ben Jacoby spoke up.

"Sheriff, won't you join us?"

From the residue on the elder Jacoby's plate, Cork guessed he'd had the renowned eggs Benedict. Ben Jacoby had a bowl, nearly empty now, of fresh fruit and yogurt. The woman had eaten oatmeal. They all were drinking coffee.

Cork took the chair on the empty side of the table. The sun was at his back, and his upper body cast a shadow over the white table cloth.

"Dina, this is Sheriff Cork O'Connor," Ben Jacoby said to the woman. "Sheriff, Dina Willner."

The woman, who was seated to the right of Cork, extended her hand. "How do you do?"

Her eyes were green and smart in a face that was easy to look at. She had brown hair with highlights, cut sensibly short. She was slender and probably stood no more than five feet three or four, but Cork felt an undeniable power in her the moment he shook her hand.

"Fine, thanks," Cork said.

"Would you like something to eat?" Ben Jacoby said.

"I've had breakfast, thanks."

"How about coffee?"

The woman said, "You look like you could use some."

"You look only half-awake yourself," Cork replied.

"Red-eye from Chicago last night. I drove up from the Twin Cities this morning. Just got here. I'm a little shy on sleep."

"Dina is a consultant on security issues. I've asked her here to give you a hand with your investigation of Eddie's death."

"A hand?"

The waiter returned. He was young and blond, with a healthy blush to his cheeks. He wore a name tag that read *Jan* and below that *Finland*. For years, the Quetico Inn had hired staff from all over the world to help during high season. He asked, in English that sounded very British, if everything was to their liking and whether Cork would care to order something.

"Coffee," Cork said.

"Try the blintzes," Ben Jacoby said. "They're marvelous."

"Just coffee," Cork said.

When Jan from Finland had gone, Dina said, "Sheriff, I headed the Organized Crime Section for the FBI's Chicago office for seven years. Before that, I was with the Money Laundering Unit out of DC. And before that, I spent several years as an investigator for the Cook County prosecutor's office."

"Impressive," Cork said. "But we don't need another hand."

"My experience with rural law enforcement is that resources are always scarce. It's my understanding that at the moment you're conducting two major investigations."

"The BCA is helping."

"Let me ask you something. When you send evidence to the BCA, how long before they process it?"

"Depends."

"A week? Three? I have access to private laboratories that guarantee results within twenty-four to forty-eight hours."

"We can't afford—"

"I can," Lou Jacoby broke in.

"With all due respect, sir—"

"I'm going to cut through the crap." The old man pointed his fork at Cork. "I want to know who killed my son, and I want to be sure that no hayseed with a badge fucks things up."

"Dad," Ben Jacoby said.

"Am I clear, Sheriff?"

Cork felt heat rising, his face flushing, his stomach drawing taut. His anger must have been apparent because the younger Jacoby said quickly, "We're all a little tired and upset, Sheriff. I hope you can understand."

It took a moment, but Cork finally swallowed the words that had been ready to leap from his throat. Ben was right. They'd lost a member of their family. That kind of loss was confusing, and people often responded in ways that were, in the end, understandable and forgivable.

"I'm not here to interfere with your investigation, Sheriff," Dina said. "I'm here to offer resources that might not otherwise be available. Honestly, wouldn't you appreciate getting answers faster than they've been coming?"

"I'll consider it," Cork finally said.

The patriarch looked as if he were about to speak again, perhaps to shove something more down Cork's throat, but his son said, "Dad, why don't we give Dina and Sheriff O'Connor a few minutes alone to talk."

Lou Jacoby cast a look toward Dina that was clear in its message: *don't fuck up.* He stood up.

"Ben," Cork said. "Would you stay for just a moment?"

Lou Jacoby glanced at his son, seemed to weigh the request, and nodded. He turned and walked from the room.

Cork folded his hands on the table. "I won't tolerate any interference. Your father might have influence in Chicago, but here he's just another guest at the Quetico Inn."

"I understand," Jacoby replied. "And please accept my apology. As I said, he's upset. That's part of the reason I asked Dina here. Dad was insistent that he was going to stay through the end of your investigation. Believe me, he would make life hell. Dina not only has the background to be of service, but she's also infinitely easier to work with. If you decline her help, you'll find yourself dealing directly with my father. Do you really want that?"

"Like I said, I'll consider it."

Dina Willner listened impassively but smiled pleasantly whenever Cork looked her way.

"I'm wondering if you could clarify something for me, Ben. Eddie's your half brother, correct?"

"Yes. After my mother died, my father married Eddie's mother, Gwen. She passed away two years ago."

"Were they married long?"

"Nineteen years."

"Nineteen years? Eddie was what, thirty-five?"

"If you're wondering about the math, Sheriff, Eddie was a bastard child. Lou and Gwen didn't get married until he was fourteen."

"How did you feel about him?"

"What do you mean?"

"He was a half brother, born to what, your father's mistress? Was there any resentment?"

"For better or worse, he was part of the family. My father loved him. I love my father. So I tried to be a brother to Eddie. I admit that wasn't always easy."

"Why?"

"We saw the world in different ways."

"What was his way?"

"He saw everything in terms of Eddie. A rather limited view."

"So, he was a difficult sibling. How was he as a husband?"

"You should probably ask his wife."

"She's not here. And I'm sure you have an opinion."

"I thought the police dealt in facts."

"Here's a fact. Eddie was a womanizer. More than that, he liked to hurt women."

Jacoby didn't appear at all surprised. "Is that why he's dead?"

"It's certainly one of the possibilities. You say your father loved him. Did they talk about things?"

"What things?"

"Eddie's work, his life, his hobbies, his treatment of women."

"I don't know. I'll be happy to ask him."

"How about if I ask him?"

"You've seen him, Sheriff. You'd get nothing helpful from him right now."

"Mind if I ask you where you were the night Edward was killed?"

"You think I resented Eddie enough to kill him?"

"I'm just asking where you were."

"I was working on a business deal until very late, with several associates. I can give you their names."

"Not necessary at the moment."

Jan from Finland finally arrived with the coffee Cork had ordered. Cork ignored it and turned his attention to Dina, who'd been listening patiently to the conversation. "We have evidence taken from the SUV in which Eddie Jacoby was murdered. A couple of cigarette butts with lipstick prints. If we came up with other samples that we'd like to compare against, DNA or the lip prints, how long would that take?"

"Depending on the kind of samples, if we shipped them overnight express, we could have results within forty-eight hours of their arrival."

"Results that would stand up in court?"

"Absolutely."

"Meet me at the Sheriff's Department at noon. I'll introduce you to the other investigators. Remember, you're with us only so long as you're useful and stay out of the way."

Dina Willner gave a serious nod. "Understood."

17

*H*IS MEETING WITH the psychologist was scheduled for 10:00 A.M. and he was already five minutes late.

He said, "Thanks, Margaret," into the phone and hung up.

Cork had worked with Special Agent Margaret Kay of the FBI's Minneapolis field office on an important case over a year ago, one that had put both Jo and Stevie in mortal jeopardy. He'd called to ask a favor of her: would she be willing to check on Dina to verify the woman's claim about her background with the Bureau, and to supply any other background information to which she might have access? Kay had agreed to help.

Cork left his office and headed to the converted Old Firehouse where Dr. Faith Gray had her practice. The psychologist smiled pleasantly when Cork hurried in, and she offered him herbal tea. They sat in green stuffed chairs in a room with a big dieffenbachia in a corner and a lush Swedish ivy in a brown jute macramé hanger at the window. Filled bookshelves lined the walls, a garden of knowledge. Faith Gray's long hair flowed white like fast water down the middle of her back. Her eyes were bright blue and kind. She wore a long denim skirt, a white turtleneck, and an oval of turquoise on a long silver chain around her neck.

"How's that ear?" she asked.

"Itchy. I'll be glad when the stitches come out."

They chatted awhile, then she lifted her cup to her lips. "How have you been sleeping?"

"I sleep."

"Not well, I'd wager, from the look of you. Trouble going to sleep? Staying asleep?"

"Both," Cork said.

"Do you dream?"

"Yes."

"Any disturbing dreams?"

He related the recurring dream in which his father transformed into a wounded Marsha Dross and he couldn't save either of them.

She listened, nodded, then said, "Tell me about the shooting."

Cork said, "You know about that. I had Pender drop off the incident report, as you asked."

"Tell me about it anyway."

Cork went through it from the time the call came in from the Tibodeau cabin to the moment the EMTs rushed Marsha Dross away in the ambulance.

"Look at your hands," she said when he'd finished.

"What?"

The light changed as clouds passed across the sun and the room took on a gloomy cast.

"Look at your hands, Cork."

Her eyes drifted gently to his fingers, which were dug into the padded arms of the easy chair so hard, his fingernails had turned red and his knuckles white. He loosened his grip.

Her eyes moved next to the pendulum clock on the wall behind Cork. "Our time's up," she said. "I'd like to see you again."

"Faith, I'm pressed for time these days."

"Let me rephrase that. If you want to continue performing your duties, you need to come until I tell you not to. It's in the regulation, Cork, the one you and I wrote together."

Cork, Larson, and Rutledge met before Dina Willner arrived. He told them what FBI Special Agent Margaret Kay had reported to him, confirming Willner's background and excellent record. They discussed her involvement. Neither Rutledge nor Larson liked the idea of an outsider being a part of the team, but the speed with which she might be able to get evidence analyzed was very appealing. They'd dealt with law enforcement agencies at all levels, and working with a consultant, they decided, wouldn't be significantly different. They wanted to meet her in person before they agreed.

Promptly at noon, Willner entered Cork's office. After shaking hands all around, she said, "You have the look of probation officers. Honestly, I'm here to help in any way I can, to offer anything you need that might facilitate your investigation. I'm also here as an intermediary. Sheriff O'Connor's already dealt with Lou Jacoby, so he knows that Lou prefers a cattle prod to diplomacy. He'd make your lives miserable, believe me."

She looked refreshed, as if she'd managed a nap or taken a shower. She wore jeans, a yellow cable knit sweater, and hiking boots. Cork noted again that although she was modest in size, there was a surety in her manner that made her seem substantial, someone you could trust watching your back. That she was attractive didn't hurt in the least.

"Questions, gentlemen?"

"My only concern is maintaining the integrity of the investigation," Larson said. "I'd like you to agree not to pass along any information to Mr. Jacoby or anyone else without explicit permission from us."

"Agreed," Dina said.

"Anything else?" Cork waited a moment. "If not, then could you step outside for a minute, Dina?"

"Of course." She left the room and closed the door behind her.

"Well?"

"Her credentials seem all right," Rutledge said. "And the chance of getting faster lab results is attractive."

"As long as she doesn't interfere, I don't see a problem," Larson said.

"Simon?"

"Goes for me, too."

When Dina returned, she took a chair to the left of Larson and Rutledge.

The day had warmed. A few minutes earlier Cork had

opened a window, and the smell of fall drifted into the room. In the park across the street, children too young for school filled the playground, and their small high squeals provided an odd background music to the grim discussion taking place.

Larson reported that he'd talked to most of the women on the list of known prostitutes. They all knew about Eddie Jacoby's penchant for cruelty and claimed they'd refused to have anything to do with him. They were all able to account for their whereabouts the night he was killed.

"I haven't followed up on the alibis yet," Larson said. "But if we get anything that points us in that direction, I'll hop right on it."

Dina gestured at the accordion folder Larson held. "Is that Eddie's case file?"

"Yes."

"May I see it?"

Larson looked to Cork, who nodded, then handed it over.

Rutledge had finally received the fax of the records for Jacoby's cell phone. He'd made copies, which he supplied to everyone present. In the week Eddie had been in Aurora, he'd called a lot of folks on the rez, and had received calls from them. All the names listed with the phone numbers were members of the Reservation Business Committee. Some calls had also come from a pay phone located at the North Star Bar. Rutledge asked about it, and Cork told him it was an Indian bar in the middle of nowhere. Several calls had been made to the Chicago area, mostly to Starlight Enterprises, and one to Ben Jacoby's cell phone the afternoon Eddie died.

Cork said, "Jacoby told me about his brother's call. I'd like to know what they talked about, exactly what was said. Ed, you mind taking that one? I want to follow up on some of these calls to the rez."

"Sure. You want to come?" Larson asked Dina.

"I'd rather work the rez."

Cork said, "You go anywhere, it's with Ed."

She didn't argue.

Cork turned to Rutledge. "Any word from the BCA lab?"

Simon looked a little chagrined. "I called. They're backlogged. We probably won't get anything for another week at least."

"Do you have any of the cigarette butts left that you found in the SUV?"

"One."

Dina said, "I'd be happy to send it to our lab in Chicago. We could have a DNA analysis by this time day after tomorrow, guaranteed."

"I'll consider it."

She looked as if there was something more on her mind.

"Yes?" Cork said.

"I'm just wondering." She'd taken the autopsy report from the file and she tapped it with a polished nail the color of pearl. "I've been looking at this. Death was the result of a stab wound directly to the heart."

"Yes," Larson said.

"And it appeared that Eddie put up no struggle, right?"

"That's right. High blood alcohol content in his blood and traces of Ecstasy. He was probably pretty high."

"Hmmmm," she said.

"What is it?" Larson asked.

"Eddie Jacoby was in terrific physical condition. All the Jacobys are. Even drunk, even high on Ecstasy, even surprised, he'd fight, believe me. Unless . . ."

She put a finger to her lips and the men waited.

"The very first knife wound was the fatal one."

Larson thought it over. "That would require a lot of luck on the assailant's part."

"Wouldn't it," she said.

"Or someone who knew where to stick the knife, knew what would kill a man instantly." He rolled that over in his mind. "Maybe somebody put more thought into this than it might appear at first glance."

The men looked at one another, then at Dina.

"Of course, it could be a jealous husband, as you've speculated," she said. "But he'd have to be one cold, calculating son of a bitch with more restraint than most jealous husbands, in my experience, are capable of."

Larson nodded slowly. "So scratch jealous husband."

She waited a moment, then offered, "According to the autopsy, the wounds on the body came from a long, slender blade approximately seven inches in length," she said.

"Like a fillet knife," Larson suggested.

"Or a stiletto," she said. "So. An isolated rendezvous, prints wiped clean, a postmortem castration. I think we can scratch hysterical woman, even a lucky hysterical woman."

"For the moment, let's assume that Jacoby brought his own drugs and his murder had nothing to do with that," Cork said. "He'd been working to secure a contract with the RBC. It's a controversial issue on the rez." He paused as he realized something, and he looked at Dina. "You already decided this was about Starlight. That's why you wanted to go with me to the rez."

"Given everything we know at the moment, it seemed the best prospect," she replied.

Larson said, "What about those cigarette butts and his need for female companionship? Are we going to ignore that?"

"Maybe he was lured to Mercy Falls," Dina said.

Larson nodded. "It would be good to know if he was seen with anybody that night. I'll check his hotel again and the bars in town. Maybe somebody remembers something."

"Sounds good," Cork said. He moved on to the other investigation. "Anything more on the shooting, Simon?"

Rutledge shook his head. "We blanked on the tires. But I've been thinking. It's possible we're dealing with somebody who has a military background. A lot of strategy in the planning and setup. A good position to shoot from. The hardware to do the job. An escape route chosen to keep the shooter away from traffic at the cabin."

Cork said, "What about the shell casings he left behind? Not great planning there."

"I don't know. That is puzzling. It's as if the shooter was distracted from his mission."

"The shooter may not have been alone," Cork said. "The woman who imitated Lucy Tibodeau on the phone may have been with him. Maybe she panicked, and that was the distraction."

"I think we'd do well to look for someone with a good

knowledge of the Iron Lake Reservation who has a military background and a grudge against you, Cork," Rutledge said. "Do you know anyone who fits that description?"

"I could name a few Shinnobs who were Vietnam vets and weren't happy when I arrested them, but I can't imagine any of them wanting to kill me for it."

"What about a hunter rather than a soldier?" Dina said. "From what I understand reading the incident report, the sniper was two hundred and fifty, maybe three hundred yards from his target. That's not a difficult distance for a good hunter, especially one with a reasonable rifle and scope. I would imagine hunters in this area are quite used to having to adjust for upslope and downslope shots. And they probably have a good understanding of where to position themselves for maximum effect. Plus," she went on, "I think there's a fundamental problem with the military scenario."

"What's that?"

"Again, just from what I understand reading the report, the sheriff saw a flash of light off the rifle, maybe from the scope, maybe a plate on the rifle stock. A trained sniper would never let that happen. The scope would be hooded and any metal on the stock that might reflect light would be covered. It also seems to me that a trained sniper would have chosen a position on the west side of the hollow, in the shadow of the hill behind the cabin where sunlight in his eyes or on his weapon wouldn't have been an issue."

"A hunter," Rutledge said, and gave a slight nod. "The problem there is that this is a county full of hunters."

She tilted her head. "That is a problem."

There was a knock at the door. "Come in," Cork said.

It was the dispatcher Patsy Gilman. "I've got the flowers, Cork. I'm heading to the hospital."

"I'll be right with you."

"I'll wait," she said, and closed the door as she left.

The department had taken up a collection to buy flowers for Marsha Dross. Patsy wanted to deliver them before she had to report for her shift at three o'clock that afternoon. Cork had asked to go along.

He took his copy of Jacoby's cell phone records. "After the

hospital, I'll head out to the rez and have a talk with the members of the RBC."

"I'd still like to petition mildly that I come with you," Dina said.

Cork shook his head. "People on the rez will be reluctant to talk to me as it is. With you along, they wouldn't say a word."

"If you're going rural, Cork," Ed Larson said, "wear your vest."

Cork wasn't sure he would. He didn't want to sit down and talk with people if it appeared that he was dressed for battle. And this trip to the rez would be different from the one he'd made with Marsha Dross. This time, no one knew he was coming.

18

THE TOWN OF Alouette was the political and social center of the Iron Lake Reservation. That didn't mean there was much to it. A grid of a dozen streets, several still not fully paved. A new community center that housed the tribal offices and a health center. A Mobil gas station and garage owned by Les Standing. The Nanaboozhoo Café. And George LeDuc's store.

LeDuc's was a small general store in a clapboard building with scratched wood floors. The shelves held a little of everything, from bread to Band-Aids to bait and tackle. It was also the post office for the rez.

When Cork stepped in, LeDuc was behind the counter.

"*Boozhoo,*" LeDuc called out in greeting.

"*Boozhoo,*" Cork called back. "Good to see you, George." He walked to the counter where LeDuc was preparing the day's mail for pickup.

"Good to see you, too. Still alive." LeDuc grinned. The lines of his face deepened, but there was a vigor in his dark eyes much younger than his seventy years. "How's your deputy?"

"She'll be fine."

"Everyone on the rez is talking about that shooting."

"Anything come up I ought to know about?"

"Nope. Got us all scratching our heads. Eli Tibodeau, he's still real broke up over those dogs of his. Seems to me it had to be somebody just plain mean to do that to a couple of dogs.

And to shoot Marsha Dross. She's a good person. Like I said before, I hear anything, I'll let you know."

"I'm here about Eddie Jacoby, George."

LeDuc bound the mail in a bundle. It was all letters today—a lot of bills being paid, from the look of it. "That guy, he was bad news. Whenever I shook hands with him, I counted my fingers after to make sure I still had 'em all."

"From what I'm hearing, the rest of the RBC didn't feel the same way."

"You don't have to like a man to like what he's selling."

"You think a contract with Starlight Enterprises is a good idea?"

"Not necessarily with Starlight. But we sure been having trouble with the managers we've hired. Russell Blackwater, he stole us blind. Daniel Wadena couldn't stomach the politics. That guy come up from Mystic Lake, he was just plain incompetent. And now Kirby Hanes has just about everybody at the casino threatening to quit. We could use some good management."

"The RBC's been dragging its feet for months. Suddenly you're all hot for Starlight. Why the change of heart?"

"Lots of ways to change a person's thinking. A sound argument, for one."

"Jacoby put one forward?"

"It was sound. Like I said, we been desperate for good management for a while. But the man himself . . ." LeDuc shook his head. He reached under the counter and brought out a small canvas bag labeled U.S. MAIL. He put the bundled envelopes inside.

"Lots of ways to change someone's thinking, you said. Was money one?" Cork asked.

"When you're dealing with a weak person, sure. And there are people on the RBC who might bend pretty easy that way."

"Did he try to bribe you?"

"I don't bend easy, and everybody out here knows it."

"Hear of any arm-twisting?"

"I heard he tried with Edgar Gillespie."

"How?"

"I don't know. Edgar wouldn't say. But with his past, hell,

you wouldn't have to dig too deep to find a little buried garbage."

"Jacoby's been working on this deal for six months. Why all the sudden pressure? Did he lose patience?"

"He was an impatient man to begin with. Doing things on Indian time really burned him. I was surprised he waited so long to get tough. Edgar probably wasn't the only one he leaned on."

"Where would he get the information he'd need for that kind of leverage? I'm thinking a white man, especially a white man like Jacoby, asking questions on the rez, that would get around."

LeDuc's face was unreadable, but the fact that he didn't reply was an indication that it was an area he wasn't willing to explore with Cork.

"Well someone talked to him." Cork opened a jar of jerky that sat near the register, pulled out a piece, laid money on the counter, and began to chew. "Going with Starlight or not going with Starlight. You think someone would kill over that?"

LeDuc took the money, put it in the till. "I had me an uncle who was murdered during the Depression, stabbed to death by a man who wanted his shoes. That tell you anything?"

Cork had left the records for Jacoby's cell phone calls in his vehicle. What LeDuc had just said made him want to look at them.

"*Migwech,* George," he said as he turned to leave. *Thanks.* "Give my best to Francie."

"Tell Jo hello."

In the Pathfinder, Cork put his half-eaten jerky strip on the seat and checked the phone records. Several calls had been made to Eddie Jacoby from the North Star Bar. It was the kind of place where men who would kill for a pair of shoes did their drinking.

The bar stood at a crossroads just south of the rez, surrounded by thick woods and nothing else for miles. The regulars were mostly Shinnobs, although members of other tribal affiliations felt at home there. The common denominator was heritage and hard luck. Occasionally white folks stumbled in, hunters or snowmobilers who didn't know the lay of the land, but they didn't stay long. It was an old wood structure, the paint faded, walls spattered with mud churned up by tires spinning in the unpaved lot. The windows were small and crowded with signs advertising the booze inside. Not much light squeezed through, and the North Star was notoriously dark. When Cork opened the door, the smell of liquor greeted him. It wasn't the kind of place that served food, except for pickled pig's feet in a big glass jar and fried pork rinds and chips that hung on a rack. If it wasn't beer or straight whiskey or at most a boilermaker you wanted, you were better off going somewhere else. Coming in from the sunny afternoon outside, Cork had to wait a minute for his eyes to adjust to the dark. It was deadly quiet, which surprised him because there were several pickups in the lot. When he could see again, he realized the silence wasn't because the place was empty. All eyes were on him and all mouths were shut.

On the way to the North Star, he'd pulled over and taken a few minutes to change into his uniform, including his Kevlar vest. His .38 was holstered on his belt. He walked to the bar where Will Fineday, who owned the place, leaned a couple of beefy arms on a surface badly in need of refinishing.

Fineday had a face straight out of a nightmare. Twenty years earlier, an accident with a hockey stick had nearly cleaved it in half. Although doctors in Canada where the incident occurred repaired the bone and stitched the skin back together, the wound left a jagged scar like a huge fault line across his left cheek, nose, and right eye before it ended halfway up his forehead. He didn't see at all out of the damaged eye. That was the part of the accident that ended a promising NHL career as a forward with the Maple Leafs. Fineday came back to the rez, used the money from the settlement to buy the bar, and for two decades his freakish face had added a certain timbre to the place. He'd managed to secure the stick that had done the deed, and it hung above the bottles at his back. He'd been known to snatch it down and use the threat of it to end a disturbance or roust an unruly customer.

"I don't suppose you want a beer," Fineday said. His voice was soft for such a hard-looking man.

"Got somebody to watch the bar, Will?"

"Why? Arresting me?"

"We're going in back to talk for a while."

The crack across Fineday's face lightened as the skin around it grew an irritated red. After a moment, he straightened up and called, "Lizzie!"

A door in the corner behind him opened and his daughter stepped out.

Lizzie Fineday was twenty, pretty in a surly way, with long black hair and anger in her eyes. Growing up, she'd been a Walt Disney dream of Pocahontas, a pure beauty. She had a lovely voice, sang at school, at powwows. She'd always wanted to be an actress, but Lizzie had a problem, and the problem was drugs. Cork had begun picking her up when she was barely thirteen. At sixteen, she'd run away, headed for Hollywood. She got as far as Denver, where she was arrested in a raid on a crack house. Her father went to fetch her and he put her in rehab. In the four years since, her record had been better, but Cork knew from the things he heard on the rez that she wasn't clean, just careful. She was still pretty, but in a damaged, brooding way. At the moment, a large bruise marred her face, a purple shadow along the high bone of her right cheek. Her upper lip was puffy, too. She moved behind her father, and she didn't look directly at Cork.

Fineday started toward the open door, but Cork held back.

"What happened to your face, Lizzie?"

Her hand went automatically toward the bruise but stopped before she touched it. "Nothing."

"Just woke up and there it was?"

"I fell," she said, looking at the floor.

"You fall again, how about letting me know."

She didn't answer, just turned to the sink where beer glasses waited to be washed.

In the office, with the door closed, Will Fineday sat down at an old desk that was covered with the sports section of several newspapers. He didn't bother to clear them away.

"What do you want?" Fineday said. "Someone complain I water down the whiskey?"

Cork hadn't been invited to sit, and although there was an empty chair, he remained standing.

"The name Eddie Jacoby mean anything to you?"

"The guy who got himself killed at Mercy Falls, right?"

"You ever see him out here?"

"Can't recall."

"A pain-in-the-ass white man, Will. You'd recall."

"Then I guess I never saw him."

"Somebody called him from here several times, from your pay phone."

"The pay phone's outside. I don't see who calls."

"How'd Lizzie's face get bruised?"

"Like she said, she fell."

"Bullshit. You hit her?"

"I never hit Lizzie. And I'd kill anyone who did."

Cork knew this was true. Will Fineday's wife had died young, and the man had raised his daughter alone. He'd made mistakes, but hitting Lizzie hadn't been one of them. Although Fineday had a harsh face, his heart, at least where his daughter was concerned, was something else. Cork had accused him only in the hope of jarring something loose.

"Stone hit her?"

Cork was referring to a man with whom Lizzie was known to keep company. They slept together—everyone knew it—but no one thought of it as love. Stone wasn't that kind of man.

"Like I said, if he hit her, he'd be dead."

Cork thought about Lizzie's weakness for getting high and about the drugs that had been found in Jacoby's SUV. "Did Eddie Jacoby hit her?"

"I didn't kill that man, if that's where you're headed. I didn't even know him."

"Mind if I talk to Lizzie?"

"Yeah. In fact," Fineday said, pushing himself up, "you've done all the talking you're gonna do here. I don't want you bothering Lizzie or my customers. You got a warrant or something, fine. Otherwise, I want you out."

"Bother your customers?" Cork laughed. "Hell, Will, nothing short of a bazooka's going to bother them."

Fineday went ahead of him out the office door and put himself between Cork and Lizzie. Cork thanked him for his time,
gave Lizzie a nod, and started out.

Just as he reached the exit, someone gave a high squeal behind him and said, "The other white meat."

Cork kept right on walking, glad for the feel of the Kevlar
against his back.

19

C ORK HAD CALLED early in the afternoon to tell Jo he'd be late and not to hold dinner for him. She didn't feel up to making anything when she got home. When she suggested to the children that they all eat at Johnny's Pinewood Broiler, she got no argument.

Jo was fond of the Broiler, of how it was the center of much that went on in the community. A big bulletin board hung near the entrance, crowded with notices of local events. Everyone knew everyone else and warm hellos were thrown across the dining room. The aroma always made her mouth water the moment she stepped in, the smell of grease on the griddle, of deep-fry.

They took a booth near a front window overlooking Center Street. After they ordered, Jo and Jenny talked about college applications while Annie helped Stevie with the maze and puzzles on the children's place mat. Several people stopped by to tell Jo how awful it was, what had happened on the rez, and to ask did Cork have a clue who was responsible.

They were near the end of the meal. The waitress was clearing their dishes when Ben Jacoby appeared at the table looking tremendously pleased to see them.

"Hello, Jo. What a nice surprise."

She wasn't sure it was.

"I drove by with your husband yesterday. Smelled delicious. I wanted to stop in before I left. Is this your family?"

She introduced the children. "This is Mr. Jacoby."

"How do you do?" he said, addressing them all at once with a charming smile. He studied Stevie's place mat. "Looks like you solved everything. Good for you."

"Annie helped."

"That was nice of her." He turned to Jenny. "I understand you're interested in Northwestern. That's my alma mater."

"Really?" Jenny's eyes danced.

"My son's a senior there this year."

"Sweet," Jenny said.

"Sweet?"

"She means way cool," Jo interpreted.

"I'd be happy to talk to you, tell you anything you want to know. The only problem is that I'm leaving first thing in the morning."

"Oh." Jenny's disappointment showed. Then she brightened. "We're having pie at home. Maybe you could join us?"

"I'm sure Mr. Jacoby has other pressing matters," Jo said.

"Actually, no. I'd love some pie. That is, if it's all right with you."

She wasn't pleased, but there didn't seem an easy way out.

"All right," she said, reaching for her purse.

"I'll just follow in my car," Ben suggested. "How's that?"

He sat at the kitchen table with Jenny. Jo made coffee while Annie dished up the apple pie, which, she explained, she'd made herself from a recipe her aunt Rose had given her. Ben declared it delicious, the best he'd ever tasted. Annie blushed deeply under the compliment.

Stevie went out to play, and Ben told Jenny all about Northwestern. She asked about the writing program.

"I'm not familiar with it," he said. "You want to be a writer?"

"Doesn't everybody?" She laughed.

"Who are your favorite authors?"

"Anaïs Nin, Virginia Woolf, Louise Erdrich. And I absolutely love *To Kill a Mockingbird*."

"Doesn't everybody?" It was his turn to laugh. "Do you know Tillie Olsen?"

"Should I?"

"Read *Tell Me a Riddle*. I think you'll find it to your liking. Have you ever visited Northwestern, toured the campus?"

"No, but Mom and I have been talking about it."

"I'd be glad to show you around sometime. If you and your mom decide to come down."

"Really? That would be terrific."

Ben looked at Annie. "And you, I've heard, are an athlete. Softball, right?"

"That's my favorite, but I like all sports."

"Notre Dame fan?"

"Go Irish."

"It's not that far from Evanston to South Bend. You could probably talk your mom into visiting both campuses the same trip." He gave her a conspiratorial wink.

The back door opened and Cork stepped into the kitchen. His surprise at finding Ben Jacoby at the table with his family was obvious.

"Good evening," he said.

Jo rose to greet him, kissed his cheek. "We ran into Ben at the Broiler. When Jenny found out he graduated from Northwestern, she had to give him the third degree."

"Informative?" he asked Jenny.

"I've learned tons, Dad."

Jo said, "Have you eaten?"

"Grabbed a sandwich."

"How about some pie, then?"

Cork shook his head. "Looks like everybody's finished. Maybe later."

"Dad," Jenny said. "I'm going canoeing with Alexandra Cunningham tomorrow on Higman Lake. You said I could borrow the Bronco, remember?"

Cork said, "I'll leave the keys on the counter for you."

"Thanks."

"It's a beautiful evening out. Why don't we have our coffee on the front porch?" Jo suggested.

"I'd like that," Ben said.

"Can you stay, Cork? Or do you have to get back?"

"I'll stay."

The children cleared the table while the adults stepped out onto the porch.

"A porch swing." Ben smiled. "I've never actually seen one except in movies. May I?"

"Be our guest," Jo said.

He sat down and began swinging gently. Cork leaned against the porch railing. Jo joined him there.

"I hate to bring up an unpleasant topic, Cork, but did you make any headway on Eddie's murder today?" Ben said.

"Maybe. I need to follow up a couple of things before I know for sure."

"Promising leads?"

"Leads often look promising but end up nowhere."

"You must have a lot of patience."

"What he has," Jo said, "is obsession. Once he starts on an investigation, he can't stop until he's solved it."

"Bulldog Drummond, eh?" Ben laughed.

It was Friday evening, the sun had just set, and Gooseberry Lane was cradled in quiet and a soft amber light. In the O'Loughlin house across the street, someone played easy blues on a guitar. Stevie stood in the yard tossing a baseball into the air. It fell back into his glove with a little slap of leather.

"This is nice," Ben said. "All so very nice." He sipped his coffee. "I understand you were a cop in Chicago for a while, Cork. You ever miss the big city?"

"Never. This is my hometown."

"Mine is Chicago. I love it, but this is pretty damn fine, I have to admit. What about you, Jo? Miss Chicago?"

"No, but I would love to get down there soon. My sister lives in Evanston."

"Rose?"

"Yes. With her husband Mal."

"Convenient. Especially if Jenny decides to attend Northwestern." Ben scanned the street, the yards in late shadow, and gave a satisfied sigh. "All the arrangements have been made to fly Eddie's body home. We'll be leaving first thing in the morning. Jo, it's been a pleasure seeing you again. Cork, you're a lucky man."

The front door opened and Annie said, "Dad, there's a phone call for you. She said it's important."

"I'll be right there." He glanced at Ben. "Excuse me."

"Of course."

When Cork left, they fell into silence, but Ben didn't take his eyes off Jo. She wanted to say something but wasn't sure what, and was relieved when Cork returned.

"I need to go," he said.

"Business?" Ben asked.

"It was Dina."

"Dina?" Jo hadn't heard the name before.

"A consultant the Jacobys have brought in to help with the investigation."

Ben drank the last of his coffee. "What did she want?"

"She was a little circumspect, but she seems to think it's important."

"Should I come?"

"You're leaving tomorrow, Ben. I'll be consulting with Dina when you're not here, so I might as well start now. Anything important, she can fill you in."

"Of course."

Cork started toward the steps. "I might hit the office afterward, Jo. Don't wait up. Ben, I wish I could say it's been a pleasure, but this hasn't been pleasant business." He shook Jacoby's hand. "We're going to solve your brother's murder."

"I'm sure you will."

On the way to his Bronco, Cork said something to Stevie, who giggled. A minute later he'd backed out of the drive and was gone.

Jo glanced at her watch, then at the sky, where the light was fading rapidly. "I should bring Stevie in. It's time to begin winding down for bed."

As if he knew what was coming, Stevie suddenly bolted across the street and disappeared behind the O'Loughlins' garage. Jo guessed that he'd spotted Rochester, the O'Loughlins' cat, for whom he had a great affection.

"Winding down?" Ben asked.

"He gets into his pajamas, we have a cookie and milk together, then I read to him—or sometimes these days he reads to me. The kind of bedtime stuff you probably did with your son."

He stared into his empty cup. "Unfortunately, no. We'd probably have a better relationship if I had." He looked up, smiled a little sadly. "Thank you, Jo."

"For what?"

"I know my being here isn't your choice, but I appreciate that you let me come. It's good to see how happy you are."

"You're not?" she said.

"The last time I remember being truly happy was when I was with you. But that's the past. Or maybe just the nature of the past. Everything seems better in retrospect."

"You were the one who left," she reminded him.

"That I was." He stood up suddenly and put his cup on the porch railing. "I'd best be off. We leave early tomorrow. Good night, Jo."

"Good-bye, Ben."

He took her hand briefly, then left the porch. He glanced back once and waved. A minute later, he was in his car, heading down Gooseberry Lane in the same direction Cork had gone.

Jo stood for a little while, alone, aware of a feeling like loss, but a small one, in her heart. Then she turned on the porch lamp and called, "Stevie, time to come in."

Almost immediately her son appeared, loping through the growing dark toward the light of home.

20

CORK HAD NOT been happy to find Jacoby in his house, at his table, eating with his family. The man was an acquaintance from Jo's law school days, and what was the harm in offering him a little hospitality, particularly considering the circumstances that had brought him to Aurora? Still, it gnawed at him. Maybe it was just the surprise, because Jacoby's presence had been so unexpected. Maybe it was territorial, because his wife and children seemed to enjoy the man. Or maybe it was because he still didn't know what to make of Ben Jacoby. With rich people, Cork was always on the lookout for the power play. In his experience, people with money held the belief, however veiled, that there was nothing that was beyond the influence of their wealth. In Lou Jacoby, it was as obvious as if he'd worn a suit made of hundred-dollar bills. The old man was used to getting his way. It was possible the same skewed thinking existed on some level in Ben, but he was better at hiding it.

Cork met Dina at the bar in the Quetico Inn, where the Jacobys were staying. He could have invited Ben Jacoby along, but he didn't see any reason. Dina could report to her employers if they really wanted to know what was going on.

She sat next to a window with a view. A small candle burned in the center of the table. Dina was looking at the lake, which, as night crept in from the east, had turned a dark, velvety blue. A drink in one hand, she didn't turn when Cork's image loomed behind her own in the glass.

"Is it always this pretty?" she said.

"To me it is."

Cork took the seat across from her at the table, but she still didn't look at him. She had a nice profile; a small nose with a little squaring of the tip; soft, full lips; good bone structure. Her eyes, he'd noticed, seemed to change color with the light. They were now a dark, intense green.

"Pretty even in winter?" Those full lips formed a smile and she finally looked at him. She wore the sweater she'd had on in Cork's office earlier that day, but she'd done something to her face, defined the features with makeup that made her seem a different kind of woman from what he'd imagined at first, a little less business. He put that information in the Wait and See file in his mind.

"It has a different beauty in winter," he said.

"I guess I'll have to take your word for that. Buy you a drink?"

"Sure."

She signaled the cocktail waitress. Cork ordered whatever Dina was having. It turned out to be Glenfiddich on the rocks.

While he waited for his Scotch, he said, "So what have you got?"

"Who is Harmon LaRusse?"

"LaRusse? Why do you want to know about him?"

"Because a Chevy pickup registered to one Harmon LaRusse followed you all over the reservation this afternoon. Loved the sticker on the rear bumper. 'If this is tourist season, why can't I shoot 'em?'"

"How do you know he followed me?"

"He was parked down the block from the Sheriff's Department and he pulled out after you when you left this morning. I happened to observe him do this, and I tailed him."

"'Happened'?"

When she smiled, her green eyes danced. "I intended to follow you, too, but he beat me to it."

"I thought you were going to work with Ed Larson."

"A misconception on your part. Who is LaRusse?"

"A Shinnob, used to live on the rez. Big guy, goes by the nickname Moose. I busted him five, six years ago for a string of burglaries. He did a nickel at Stillwater. Must be out by now."

"A Shinnob?"

"Short for Anishinaabe. LaRusse is full-blood Ojibwe."

The Glenfiddich came. The waitress asked if Dina wanted another. "Later, maybe," Dina replied.

"He followed me everywhere?"

"The hospital, the store in Alouette, the bar."

"Son of a bitch."

"I can't imagine it has anything to do with Eddie Jacoby's murder, but it might have something to do with the shooting on the rez, and so it's really not my concern. But that bar you went to is."

"The bar?"

"I just came from there."

"You went to the North Star alone?"

"I wanted to ask a few questions."

"That wasn't smart."

"I got answers."

"You got answers at the North Star?" He didn't try to hide his skepticism.

"Here, let me show you a trick." She reached down, grasped the bottom of her sweater, and in one quick, fluid movement, pulled it off over her head. Underneath she wore a low-cut top of some thin scarlet material that hugged her body like a surgical glove. Under that was a push-up bra that offered up her breasts with enough cleavage to swallow the *Titanic*.

Cork dragged his eyes from her chest. "They teach you that at Quantico?"

"I learned that one in the field." She made no move to put her sweater back on.

"Going in alone was a dangerous thing to do."

"I wasn't alone." She reached down and lifted the right cuff of her jeans, exposing an ankle holster fitted with a small Beretta Tomcat. She let the cuff drop.

"Eddie Jacoby sometimes met a man named Stone at the North Star. You know him?" she asked.

Cork said, "I know him."

"What would Eddie want with him?"

"Stone's the kind of guy who'd traffic in anything. Drugs, guns, information. I'm guessing it's that last one he was selling to Jacoby."

"What kind of information would Eddie buy?"

"The kind that might be used to influence a vote of the RBC on whether to sign a contract with Starlight."

"How would Eddie know of him?"

"I don't know. Slime finds slime. It's entirely possible Stone was the one who made the approach."

She sipped the last of her Scotch and the ice clinked against the glass. The sound seemed to intrigue her and she stared for a few moments at the cubes, whose hard edges had been rounded by the Glenfiddich. Cork caught himself glancing again at her breasts.

"Did you see the girl behind the bar?" she asked.

"Lizzie Fineday."

"Somebody hit her."

"Will, that's her father, says it wasn't him. Probably wasn't."

"She have a boyfriend?"

"Stone has a claim on her. I wouldn't call it love. He's a hard man, but I don't think he'd hit Lizzie. Fineday would kill him. But get this. In the bar today, when I tossed Jacoby's name out there as a possibility, Fineday tossed me out."

"That so? It might be interesting to talk to her."

"I've been thinking the same thing," Cork said. He took a long, burning swallow of the Scotch. "Want to be there when I do?"

21

*T*HAT NIGHT CORK woke, looked at the clock on the stand beside the bed—1:47 A.M.—and realized he was alone. He got
up, stepped into the hallway. Downstairs a dim flow of light
came from the direction of Jo's office.

He found her sitting at her desk, staring across the room at
a window where the blind had not been lowered. There was
nothing to see but the empty glass, the vague reflection of the
room on the pane.

"You okay?" he asked.

"Couldn't sleep," she said.

"Something bothering you?"

She tilted her head back and laughed, not a mirthful sound.
"Now, why would you think that? Someone shoots Marsha
but they probably meant to shoot you. My client Edward Jacoby is brutally murdered. And you've stopped sleeping.
What's to worry about?"

He walked to her desk, sat in the client's chair. "Anything
else?"

"That covers it pretty well, I'd say."

"Tell me about Ben Jacoby."

She'd been asleep when he came home, or had seemed to be.
He'd been thinking about Jacoby a lot and wanted to talk to
her about him, but he hadn't wanted to disturb her rest.

"There's nothing to tell."

"Jo, I'm sleep deprived, not blind."

"Ben was a long time ago."

"Not from the way he looks at you."

She sat back. Her eyes went toward the window again, as if seeking some focus that was not her husband's face. "I knew him before I met you."

"So I gathered. Knew him well, I'd say. Better than just law school acquaintances."

She took a breath. "We had a relationship for several months."

"What happened?"

"He left. Married someone else."

He leaned forward. His body was tired and it was hard to sit up straight. "Why didn't you tell me about him?"

"He was in the past."

"You told me about others."

"I don't know, Cork."

"So tell me now."

She shook her head. "You're angry."

"No, I'm tired."

"Either way, it's not a good time to talk about this."

"I'd rather we did."

"He was twenty years ago. He'll be gone tomorrow."

"Were you happy to see him again?"

"I was surprised."

"You must have loved him a lot to be so afraid to talk about him," Cork went on.

He thought she was going to put him off again. Instead, her blue eyes settled on his face and she said, "I loved him very much. And he hurt me very badly."

Cork mulled that over. "Did you marry me on the rebound?"

"Has it ever felt like that?"

"No."

"When you became my life, I put Ben Jacoby away, far away."

"And now he's back."

"Not because I wanted him." She stood up, intending to take Cork into her reassuring arms, but her attention was drawn to something behind him, something that put fear in her eyes. "Someone's at the window."

He turned in his chair. The pane at his back still showed only the reflection of the office. Beyond that, only night.

"He's gone," Jo said.

"Wait here."

Cork ran from the room, down the hallway, and into the kitchen. He flipped the dead bolt, flung open the door and the screen, then plunged into the dark outside. He charged along the side of the house toward the backyard and stopped at the corner. Except for the oblong of light that fell from Jo's window onto the grass, there appeared to be nothing to see. He stood listening intently, peering at the hidden recesses of the yard. Nothing moved or made a sound.

He heard a sudden rustle behind him in the lilac bushes that edged the driveway, and he pivoted and crouched, thinking what an easy target he was in his boxers and barefoot. He tensed as if he could feel the night scope on him, and he imagined the chambered round, the finger squeezing. The bushes shivered again; he forced himself to be still, to wait. It was dark and his eyes were useless. He cocked his head, trying to catch the slightest sound, the slide of a rifle bolt or the shallow intake of the steadying breath before firing.

A small rocket launched itself from the lilacs. It stayed low to the ground, and Cork stumbled back, startled. The shape made a sudden right-angle turn and scrambled down the driveway. Cork leaped to where he could see the drive all the way down to the street. As the shape passed into the light of the street lamp, it was clearly defined: the O'Loughlins' cat, Rochester. Cork's legs went weak, and he leaned against the Bronco, which he'd left parked in the driveway.

Jo stepped out the kitchen door. "Are you all right?"

"Yeah. You didn't happen to get a good look at who it was in the window?"

"No. He was there and then he wasn't."

"He? You're sure it was a he?"

She thought a moment. "No."

He took her arm. "Let's get back inside."

He threw the dead bolt on the kitchen door and checked the lock on the front door. He made sure the blinds over all the windows were down and the curtains drawn. Upstairs, he took his .38 from the lockbox in his bedroom closet.

"Are you going to sleep with that?" Jo asked.

"Yes, but downstairs, on the sofa."

She eyed the gun with concern. "Do you think that's necessary?"

"I don't know what's necessary, and I don't want to take chances."

"All right," she said. "Want company?"

"I'll be fine."

He put on sweatpants and slippers, took his pillow and a blanket, and stretched out on the sofa in the living room. He put the revolver under his pillow, then lay for a long time listening and thinking.

He'd believed he was safe in town, but maybe he was wrong. And if he was wrong, it meant that his home wasn't safe. Not for him, not for his family. He would have to do something about that. Whatever it was, he'd figure it out in the morning.

His father stood at the top of a hill, facing the setting sun, his back toward Cork. Cork tried to call out, but his jaw was paralyzed and nothing escaped his mouth but a low, helpless groan. His father began to walk away, disappearing down the other side of the hill, as if the ground were swallowing him. Cork fought desperately to follow, clawing at a slope that lay in deep shadow. He came at last to a place where pine needles had been laid as bedding in a jumble of black rocks that were embedded with gold nuggets glittering in the sun. Then he realized they weren't nuggets but brass shell casings. He started to run down the other side of the hill, but shots were already being fired and he saw his father tumble. And then it was not his father on the ground but Marsha Dross with her eyes wide open in terror, her lips rapidly moving, whispering words that were like the soft slipping of feet over a rug. In the next instant he was awake, hearing someone come down the stairs in his house.

Jenny shuffled across the carpet to where Cork lay on the sofa.

"Daddy?"

"Morning, sweetheart."

She seemed surprised to find him there. "What happened?"

"Trouble sleeping."

"Again?"

He ignored her remark, saw that she was dressed in jeans, a green sweatshirt, a billed cap, and her hiking boots, and he remembered. "All set for your canoe outing?"

"Yeah. Thanks for letting me borrow the Bronco."

"Got the keys?"

"Right here." She held out her hand to show him.

"Have a good time."

"We will."

"When should we expect you home?"

"After dinner. We're going to eat at the Sawmill when we come off the lake."

"Got money?"

"Plenty."

She kissed his cheek, went into the kitchen, and a moment later he heard the door open and close.

Morning sunlight fired the curtain. He looked at the grandfather clock in the hallway. Seven-ten. He thought about getting up, but was so tired that he could barely move. Every muscle of his body ached. His head felt thick and fuzzy. But the dream he'd been having when Jenny woke him was still vivid.

Although he hadn't had a cigarette in a couple of years, he wanted one now.

He heard the kitchen door open and Jenny came back in.

"Dad?"

"What is it, Jen?"

"I can't get the car started. It won't even turn over. I think the battery's dead."

"More likely a loose cable. Let's take a look." He slowly rolled off the sofa.

Outside, the morning was bright and crisp. The day had a peaceful feel. Cork loved this kind of morning, the light in the sky gold and promising, the smell in the air sharp with evergreen.

The night hadn't been cold enough for frost, but there was a thick layer of dew on the Bronco's windshield. "Give me the keys," Cork said.

He got into the vehicle and turned the ignition. Nothing happened. He popped the hood latch and got out.

"Hop in," he told his daughter. "When I tell you to, try to start it."

Jenny slipped behind the wheel. Cork walked around to the front of the Bronco and lifted the hood. What he saw froze him.

"Jenny," he said.

"Try it now?" she called.

"No," he ordered harshly. "Don't turn the key. Just get out of the car."

"What?"

"Just get out, sweetheart," he said, trying to keep his voice even.

Jenny did as she was told, then joined her father and saw what he saw.

"Oh, Jesus. What do we do, Dad?" She whispered, as if afraid that speaking too loudly might be dangerous.

"We're going inside," he told her. "I'm going to call the Department and then we're going to wake everyone up and get them out of here."

22

*T*HE BOMB SQUAD from the Duluth Police Department advised that everyone within fifteen hundred feet of the O'Connor house be evacuated. Standard procedure. The Tamarack County Sheriff's Department barricaded the streets, and two yellow pumpers from the Aurora Volunteer Fire Department stood ready. The bomb squad indicated they would be there in ninety minutes. In the meantime, all there was to do was keep the crowd back and wait.

The deputies reported that most folks who evacuated had been cooperative. Cork himself encountered only one instance of outright hostility, this from Gunther Doktor, an old widower who'd lived on Gooseberry Lane forever. Doktor had turned his good ear toward Cork, an ear that sprouted hair like corn tassel, and said, "You O'Connors. Always been trouble." Still, he'd abandoned his house as requested, muttering as he shuffled to the end of the block.

Most other neighbors made it a point to tell Cork they were outraged by this personal attack, and if there was anything they could do to help, then just, by God, let them know. The Women's Guild from St. Agnes Catholic Church somehow got word of the situation and had very quickly set up tables outside the secured perimeter to offer coffee and juice, doughnuts, and banana bread to those for whom breakfast was now a long way off.

Jo and Stevie stood with the O'Loughlins in the street

under the shade of an oak with russet leaves. Jenny and Annie mingled with the crowd and Cork wasn't always able to see them. He would have preferred to keep his whole family in sight, but he had his hands full.

He stood beside a cruiser parked beyond the barricades at the west end of the block, and he talked with Cy Borkmann, Ed Larson, and Simon Rutledge.

Borkmann said, "Duluth bomb squad radioed their twenty. They just passed the casino. Maybe five minutes now."

Rutledge had been in such a hurry that he hadn't combed his hair, and he'd put his sweater on inside out. "Jo told me the guy wore a ski mask, that she couldn't see anything that might ID him."

"That's right."

"And you saw no one when you went outside to check?"

"Like I told you, Simon, only the cat. Rochester's smart, but I don't think he planted that dynamite."

Rutledge was the only one who smiled. "We'll want your Bronco for a while, so we can go over it carefully for evidence."

"If it's still in one piece when this is over, you're welcome to it."

The bomb detail arrived in a Duluth Police van with a trailer in tow. On the trailer was a large, heavy-looking metal canister. An unmarked car followed. Two men stepped from the van and another came from the car. The man who'd driven the van said, "Sheriff O'Connor?"

"Here."

"Sergeant Dave Gorman." Tall, tanned, early thirties, buzz cut, good shape.

They shook hands. He introduced his colleagues, Sergeant Rich Klish and Sergeant Greg Searson.

"Where is it?" Gorman asked.

"Down the street. Two-sixteen Gooseberry Lane. The Bronco in the drive with the hood up."

Gorman nodded. "So what did you see?"

"A white PVC pipe, three inches in diameter, maybe fifteen inches in length, capped at both ends."

"A timing device? Clock, watch?"

"I didn't see one."

"Where was the explosive placed?"

"On the engine block, near the battery."

"Wires?"

"Yes."

"Did you see where they connected?"

"To the battery."

"The battery?" Gorman glanced at the men who'd come with him. "You're sure?"

"With alligator clips."

"Was there a clothespin glued to the pipe?"

"Yes."

"Did you notice any fishing line?"

"Fishing line? I don't recall."

Gorman puzzled over that. Cork felt that he was letting the bomb technician down. He should have checked more thoroughly, but he'd been worried about getting his family and his neighbors out of harm's way.

"Okay. You're sure about the clothespin?"

"Yes."

Gorman went to the van, came back with a pair of binoculars. He looked for a minute toward Cork's house.

"The Bronco, huh?"

"Yeah."

He looked some more. "You like it?"

"I beg your pardon?"

"I'm thinking of getting one. I just wondered if it's been a good vehicle for you."

"Good enough that I'd hate to see it end up in little pieces."

"Well, we'll see what we can do about keeping that from happening." He turned to his companions. "Let's take the van in, Greg. Rich," he said to the man who'd driven the unmarked car, "you stay with the sheriff, keep him apprised."

Gorman and Searson got back into the van. Cork's people moved the barricade aside and let them pass. They drove to the end of the block and stopped a good five hundred feet short of Cork's house.

"They're parked in the cold zone, a safe distance from the explosive," Sergeant Klish said. He was much shorter than

Gorman, and older. He had a square face that seemed oddly unconcerned about the danger his colleagues might be facing.

"You go out on a lot of these calls?" Ed Larson asked.

"Sometimes two or three a day. Not usually this far north, though. A Bronco, you said, Sheriff?"

"That's right."

Klish nodded. "Probably too high for the camera on the robot. I'm guessing Dave'll suit up and go in for a look-see."

They watched as Gorman laboriously donned a heavily padded green suit with a high collar and large helmet. Slowly, he began to walk toward the Bronco down the street.

"Looks like he's taking it pretty careful," Cy Borkmann said.

"He's wearing eighty pounds of Kevlar plates," Klish replied. "He doesn't have any choice but to go slow."

Gorman reached Cork's drive and approached the Bronco. He stood for a while peering under the hood.

"He seemed interested in fishing line," Cork said. "What was that about?"

"You said wires were connected directly to the battery?"

"Yes."

"Every explosive needs a power source. In this case, that's the battery. With power already supplied, the only thing that's needed to detonate is to complete the electrical circuit. That's where the clothespin comes in. On this type of device, the electrical contacts are often thumbtacks pushed into the legs of the clothespin. What keeps them from connecting and completing the circuit is a thin piece of plastic or maybe cardboard that's been slipped between. The question is, how does the plastic or cardboard get removed so the tacks can make contact, complete the circuit, and detonate the explosive? The answer: fishing line. Secure one end of the line to the cardboard, the other to the hood. When the car doesn't start, the victim lifts the hood to see what the problem is, the fishing line gets pulled up, the cardboard gets yanked out, the thumbtacks connect, the circuit is completed, and . . . boom." He gave Cork a wistful look. "You're a very lucky man, Sheriff. All I can think is that the fishing line broke."

Cork nearly staggered under the thought of what almost

happened, thinking less about himself than the fact that Jenny had been with him.

"What's in the pipe?" Larson asked.

"Could be anything," Klish said. "Black powder, dynamite, even C-4, I suppose. They'll check that out next." He shook his head. "You know, the hell of all this is that it's a very destructive device, but simple to make. Instructions for it and bombs a lot more sophisticated are all over the Internet. Go figure."

Gorman backed away from the Bronco and, when he was a safe distance, turned and walked to the van. He returned to the Bronco with what Klish described as a portable X-ray machine. Fifteen minutes later, with Gorman at the van, Searson began assembling a tall stand with what looked like a rifle barrel on the end.

"They're going to shoot," Klish said.

"My Bronco?"

"Relax, Sheriff. They'll probably shoot just the battery, or one of the cables, to remove the power source. Then they'll probably shoot the device to break it open so they can take a look inside. What Greg's constructing is called a PAN disrupter. It's basically a remote gun. It has a laser beam for aiming, a barrel that'll fire anything from shot to a slug to plain water."

Half an hour and two PAN shots later, they sent the robot in to lift the explosive from the Bronco. Searson guided the small wheeled device back to the van where Gorman waited, still suited.

"Dave's going to remove the detonator, then he'll drop the explosive into the trailer for transport and disposal. You wouldn't happen to have a gravel pit around here, would you?" Klish inquired.

"Just west of town," Cork replied.

When Gorman was finished and the explosive was safely in the transport canister, he removed his suit and walked to where Cork and the others waited. He was drenched with sweat and looked beat. He carried a liter bottle of water, from which he frequently drank.

"What was inside?" Klish asked.

"Trenchrite. Four packs."

"That's a very common explosive," Klish explained. "That gravel pit of yours probably uses it. What about the fishing line, Dave?"

"It was there. Broken."

"I explained to the sheriff his good fortune."

"You were lucky on two counts," Gorman said to Cork. "The line broke, yes. But also whoever made the bomb inserted a dead blasting cap. It had already been used. Even if the line hadn't broken, there's no way that bomb would have gone off. That was one really stupid perp."

Within twenty minutes, the bomb team cleared out, heading with Cy Borkmann to the gravel pit, where they intended to dispose of the explosive. The barricades were removed, the pumpers went back to the firehouse, and the crowd dispersed. Cork told Larson and Rutledge that he'd meet them in his office in half an hour.

He walked his family home and checked his Bronco. The cable to the positive battery terminal had been severed and there were white PVC fragments everywhere, but the damage seemed minimal. Inside the house, everything felt different, as if they'd been gone a very long time.

"Everybody out of the kitchen," Jo said. "I'm going to make us something to eat."

The children mutely drifted toward the living room.

When they were alone, Jo said, "Why, Cork?"

"I don't know. But one thing is certain. I don't want you or the kids around until we've nailed this guy."

"I agree. I've been thinking. Jenny wants to see Northwestern and Annie's dying to have a look at Notre Dame. Why don't I call Rose, see if we can stay with her and Mal in Evanston?"

"That's a good idea."

"I don't suppose you'd come, too."

"You know I can't."

She accepted it with an unhappy nod.

"I'm sorry, Jo. Sorry about all this."

"Not your fault, sweetheart." She tried to smile.

23

CORK WAS SURPRISED to find Dina Willner with Larson and Rutledge in his office. He'd seen her among the crowd on Gooseberry Lane, but they hadn't spoken. She wore black jeans, a white turtleneck sweater, sneakers. She held a disposable cup from the Gas Pump Grill, an old gas station on Oak Street that had been redone as a gourmet coffee shop. Larson and Rutledge had cups, too. Several cream cheese *kolaches* lay on a paper plate on Cork's desk, next to another cup from the Gas Pump Grill. The aromas of the coffee and the pastries were wonderful, the first good thing that whole morning.

"Do you mind if I sit in?" she asked.

Cork glanced at Larson and Rutledge. "Any objections?"

"Fine by me," Rutledge said. Ed Larson nodded his agreement.

"I brought you some coffee," Dina said. "French roast, black, but there's cream and sugar if you'd like."

"Thanks." Cork sat down, took the coffee, put in half-and-half from a tiny container and a couple of packets of sugar lying next to the *kolaches*.

"What do you think?" he said.

"A dead blasting cap. My first guess would be somebody who doesn't know what they're doing," Larson said.

Rutledge pursed his lips skeptically. "They got everything else right. Maybe it was a bomb never meant to go off."

Cork put his coffee down. "Why try so hard to kill me at

the Tibodeau cabin, only to give me some kind of bullshit scare now?"

They were quiet a moment. Then Larson said, "A stupid prank?"

Rutledge scratched the back of his neck and didn't look happy with that possibility. "If it was, it's one that could land the prankster in jail for a good long time. He'd have to be way off the impulsive scale. Way too risky. There's substance here."

Dina sat forward, just a little, but the men's eyes turned to her. She spoke quietly. "Remember, you have two major investigations under way. Is it possible this incident has nothing to do with what happened on the reservation?"

"Are you saying it's related to the Jacoby murder?" Larson inched his wire-rimmed glasses higher on the bridge of his nose.

"I don't know. I'm just suggesting it's a possibility."

"Somebody warning me off the investigation?" Cork sat back, considering.

"You said yesterday that there are people on the reservation who might have been blackmailed by Jacoby. Maybe one of them is afraid of what you might discover. They don't want to kill you—maybe they're not that kind, or maybe because of your blood connection, I don't know—but they're trying to dissuade you from looking too closely."

"If it was meant as a warning, why no note?" Rutledge said.

"To whoever planted it, maybe what it related to was obvious. They're not seeing any of this from Cork's perspective, which is much broader." She lifted her cup but paused before sipping. "On the other hand, I suppose it could just be somebody who really wanted you dead but doesn't have the brains God gave a caterpillar."

"Who has access to that kind of explosive?" Rutledge said.

"Up here, lots of folks," Larson replied. "Mining, logging, and we've got a hell of a lot of construction going on, new roads. It wouldn't be difficult to steal."

Rutledge looked at Cork. "Maybe you should think about getting your family out of Aurora for a while."

"I've already taken care of that. Jo and the kids are going to Chicago to stay with her sister and husband."

"Good. So what now? Any ideas?" Rutledge took a bite of his *kolache* and chewed quietly.

Cork said, "I'll hit the reservation, talk to some people out there. If Dina's right—if it's somebody trying to scare me off the Jacoby investigation—maybe I can get a handle on that."

Larson nodded. "We'll do a complete canvass of your neighbors, find out if anybody saw anything helpful. While that's going on, I'm going to do a couple interviews related to the Jacoby murder."

"Who?"

"The night clerk at the Four Seasons. He's been gone camping the last couple of days, but I understand he's back. I'm hoping he might be able to shed some light on Jacoby's comings and goings the night he was killed. And we're still looking for Arlo."

"Arlo?" Dina said.

"Arlo Knuth," Cork explained. "A local character, lives out of his truck and sometimes sleeps in the county parks. He was at Mercy Falls earlier on the night Jacoby was killed. One of my deputies ran him off, but we should talk to him. Good luck tracking him down, Ed."

"I'll find him."

There was a knock at the door. Deputy Duane Pender stepped in. "Here's the information you asked for, Cork." Pender handed over a sheet of paper. "And we've got a gaggle of reporters gathering out there."

"Thanks, Duane. Keep them at bay awhile, and then I'll talk to them."

Pender left and Cork glanced at the sheet he'd delivered.

"I asked Duane to run a DMV check on Harmon LaRusse."

"Moose LaRusse?" Larson said. "Why?"

"He followed me yesterday when I was on the rez."

"Moose? I didn't know he was back in these parts."

"Neither did I. According to the Department of Motor Vehicles, he isn't. He's got a Minneapolis address."

"Tell me about this Moose," Rutledge said.

"A Shinnob from the rez. Big guy, big troublemaker," Cork said. "Five, six years ago, we busted him for a series of burglaries in the county. Judge gave him five years in Stillwater."

"Why would he be following you?"

"I have no idea, but I'm going to make a few inquiries today, see if I can find out. But the first thing, Simon, you and I should talk to the media. We'll need to cover both investigations. Then what I'm going to do is see if I can get to the bottom of those bruises on Lizzie Fineday's face, find out if Eddie Jacoby had anything to do with it."

Dina put her coffee down. "You said I could be there when you talked to her."

"I haven't forgotten."

Rutledge stood up. "I'm going to try to have that talk with Lydell Cramer's sister this afternoon, see if anything shakes loose there."

"Everyone stay in touch," Cork said.

24

THEY HEADED TOWARD the North Star Bar, driving between stands of aspen with leaves yellow as the sun. They turned onto Waagikomaan Road, a shortcut across the rez paved with oil and crushed stone. Cork drove into marshland where cattails bent under the weight of idle red-winged blackbirds.

"Waagikomaan?" Dina said.

"Not wag like a dog's tail. It's a soft *a*. Like in father."

She tried again, more successfully.

"It means crooked knife," Cork said. "See how the road cuts back and forth, trying to keep to dry, solid ground."

They moved out of the marsh and into a series of low, rocky hills covered with red sumac, balsam, and more aspen.

"Interesting country," Dina said.

"You don't know the half of it."

He could have told her. How the Canadian Shield, the stone mass that underlay everything there and broke through the thin topsoil in jagged outcroppings, was the oldest exposed rock on earth. How the glaciers two miles thick had crept across this land over the centuries, scraping everything down to that obdurate rock and leaving, as they receded, lakes as numerous and glittering as the stars in the night sky. How the land was still lifting itself up, released from the weight of that continent of ice, rebounding, a living thing unimaginably patient and enduring.

"It's pretty," Dina said. "If you like trees."

"You don't?"

"A city girl. I spent a lot of summers at Camp Wah-kee-shah, though. That's Wah with a soft *a*."

The windows were open, and the wind ruffled her hair, loose strands drumming her cheeks like tanned, restless fingers. Cork thought again what a remarkably pretty woman she was.

"Me and a bunch of kids like me, Jewish mostly, sent to camp to be out of our parents' hair."

"You didn't come away with an appreciation of nature?" he asked.

"Not at all. But I can braid a pretty mean lanyard. You were a Chicago cop for a while. What brought you back here?"

"This is my home."

"A lot of people leave home at the first opportunity and never look back."

"You, for one?"

He waited but she never replied. The wind smelled of pine sap and of the yellow dust the Pathfinder kicked up. The road cut through an open area blanketed with purple fireweed, the first thing to grow after a burn. Ahead of them, the sky filled in the gaps between the trees like blue water. Except for the road, the land felt untouched.

"There are problems in a small town, sure," Cork said. "You can't have a thought without everybody knowing it. If your family doesn't go back a few generations, you can spend your whole life here and still feel like an outsider. The nearest foreign film is five hours away. And yeah, the kids leave as soon as they can, go to college, into the service, whatever. But a lot of them come back eventually. Why? It's a good place to raise a family, a good place for kids to grow up."

"And that's important?"

"Are you married?"

"I was. At the moment, no."

"Any kids?"

"Just little old me."

"It might be tough for you to understand."

Dina was quiet for a bit, then said, "I understand."

They came out on County 33, half a mile south of the North Star Bar. Cork turned onto the asphalt road.

"I'm going to stay with the car," Dina said. "I'd just as soon keep our relationship out of the limelight. Out here anyway."

"Don't want to kill the potential of the push-up bra?"

"Or any of my other tricks," she said.

"Other tricks?"

"Don't ask." It sounded like a wisecrack, but she didn't smile. "If Lizzie's there, let me know. Maybe I'll come in anyway."

Cork pulled into the dirt lot and parked away from the half dozen vehicles already there, dusty in the morning sunlight. Inside, it felt like a dark cave. Johnny Cash was on the jukebox. Cork didn't see Lizzie Fineday or her father. Leonard Trueur was tending bar. He was a heavy man, slow, with fat hands and fingers, a shuffle for a walk. It was still early in the day and the bar wasn't crowded. A couple of Shinnobs Cork didn't recognize sat at a table under an old neon sign that said *Hamm's*. They weren't talking. Maybe they fell silent when Cork came in, but they also had the look of men who didn't say much anyway. Three others played pool in the corner, ball caps shading their faces. They glanced at Cork. He knew them. They went on with their game.

"*Boozhoo*, Leonard," Cork said, stepping up to the bar.

Leonard wiped the bar, a needless thing because at the moment no one sat there. In fact, the rag looked more in need of a good cleaning than the bar top.

"I'm looking for Will."

Leonard watched his fat hand moving the dirty rag and shrugged.

"Is he around?"

"Nope."

"Where is he?"

"Dunno."

"Lizzie here?"

"Dunno."

"Think I'll go up and knock," Cork said.

Leonard didn't offer an objection, and Cork headed toward a door to the left of the bar that opened onto a steep stairway leading to the second story. At the top of the stairs was a small landing and another door, this one closed. Behind it were the rooms where Will Fineday lived with his daughter. Cork knocked, put his ear to the wood, knocked once more, very hard. Finally he turned away and went back down.

The music had stopped. The men under the Hamm's sign hadn't moved. At the pool table, two men held their cues while the third hunched and lined up a shot.

"You guys seen Will or Lizzie?" Cork asked.

"Ain't seen shit, cousin," said Dennis Finn, the one bent over the green felt.

"How about Moose LaRusse?"

"The Moose? Thought you had him doing a stretch in Stillwater."

"He was here yesterday."

"News to me, cousin."

Cork looked to the other men, but no one met his gaze.

"*Migwech,*" Cork said to Leonard, who was still working the rag over the bar. *Thanks.* He walked back out into the sun.

He stood with his back to the bar, thinking. A couple of crows hopped around the Dumpster at the side of the building, looking for a way to an easy meal. A moment later, the door behind him opened, and Ernie Champoux, one of the men at the pool table, stepped out. He lit a cigarette, blew the smoke into the windless air. Champoux was a hard man, but his dealings with Cork had always been reasonable.

"Stone," Champoux said. Then he said, "Moose, him I ain't seen."

That was all. He went back inside.

Cork walked to his vehicle and got in.

"Lizzie not there?" Dina said.

"No."

"You find out where?"

"Maybe." Cork started the car and pulled away from the bar. "We're going to see Stone."

They drove awhile before Dina asked, "Why are you doing this?"

"Doing what?"

"An investigation on the reservation."

"I do most of the law enforcement work on the rez myself."

"Why?"

"My grandmother was true-blood Iron Lake Ojibwe. Things tend to go a little smoother because of that."

"What I mean is, I thought reservations were under federal jurisdiction."

He explained about Public Law 280.

"Lucky they have a sheriff who's part Ojibwe."

"Not everybody thinks it's such a good idea."

He turned north onto County Road 17.

"This Stone," Dina said. "What's he like?"

"Smart like a wolf. Balls of a grizzly bear."

"I don't know about bear balls. Is that good?"

"He's stripped himself of most everything you think of as common goodness. A lot of men like him are just plain stupid, and they're also afraid, which limits their impact. Stone's sharp, and if there's something he's afraid of, I don't know what it is. On the rez, there's the legitimate authority, the tribal council. If you want something that's less than legitimate, Stone is who you go to."

"I like a man who's a challenge."

"This guy's a land mine."

"As in 'Watch your step'?"

"Exactly."

"What about the noble red man?"

"Stone's real father was a decent guy. A Shinnob poet, actually. Got himself killed in a car accident on his way back from the Twin Cities when Stone was just learning to walk. His mother remarried, a white man named Chester Dorset, owned a string of Dairy Queens, had money. He was also a drunk, a brutal drunk, and I mean to tell you, Stone had it tough as a kid. One night, Dorset's loaded, lays into Stone's mother. Stone splits his stepfather's head with an ax."

"Sounds justified to me."

"Problem was, he waited to do it until his stepfather had gone to sleep. He was sixteen and certified to stand trial as an adult. Convicted of manslaughter one. Got eighty-six months and served every day of it in the prison at St. Cloud. That's where he got his name: Stone. His real name is Byron St. Onge, but his papers got screwed up. Somehow they dropped the *g* from his name and missed the period after Saint. He

went in as Byron Stone instead of St. Onge. Stone stuck."
Cork swerved to avoid hitting a red squirrel that scampered
across the road. "While he was in prison, his mother died,
destitute, because Chester Dorset's kids from his first marriage
got all his money. Stone's had a clean record since he got out
of prison, but I'm certain he's been involved in an enormous
amount of illegal activity. Smuggling for sure. Drugs, arms,
cigarettes."

"Cigarettes?"

"Back in the nineties. The Canadian tax on cigarettes was
high and Canucks were paying through the nose for a smoke.
They could buy smuggled cigarettes for a song. A lot of evidence suggested the tobacco companies were complicit in the
smuggling. I worked with ATF for months trying to get something on Stone. Nothing. Same with DEA and Customs. Stone
was way too smart to get himself caught. Knows the woods
along the border better than any man I can think of. And he
intimidates the hell out of anyone who might be inclined to
testify against him."

They'd been driving half an hour and were approaching the
northern edge of the Iron Lake Reservation where it butted
against the Boundary Waters Canoe Area Wilderness. Cork
turned off onto a road that was barely wide enough for the
Pathfinder. A few hundred yards farther, the road skirted a
long narrow lake that ended at the base of a ridge covered
with jack pine. A ragged thread of wood smoke climbed the
face of the ridge.

"Stone built his cabin himself, where he could see anyone
approaching from a good distance away," Cork said. "The land
on either side is mostly marsh, so it's almost impossible to
come at it on foot. And directly beyond that ridge is the
Boundary Waters. He's got himself a decent stronghold."

"Boundary Waters?"

"The Boundary Waters Canoe Area Wilderness. Over a million acres of forest along the Canadian border. On the other
side is the Quetico, another wilderness just as large. Easy place
for a man to lose himself, on purpose or not."

Cork pulled into the clearing where Stone's cabin stood, and
he saw Will Fineday's old Dodge pickup parked behind Stone's

new Land Rover. Both vehicles were covered with a thick coat of red dust.

The two men faced each other in the open in front of the cabin. Fineday gripped a tire iron in his huge hands. Stone, shirtless, held an ax. Fineday didn't look when Cork pulled up, but Stone's dark eyes flicked away for an instant.

Stone was smaller, but where Fineday had gone to fat, Stone was smooth rock under taut flesh. He wore his hair long, tied back with a folded red bandanna that ran across his forehead. He was handsome, and there was a certainty in his face, particularly his eyes, that most men found intimidating and women, Cork had heard, found exciting.

Near Stone was a flat-topped stump that he used as a chopping block, and around the stump lay sections of split birch waiting to be gathered and stacked. Stone's chest glistened, and the bandanna was stained dark with sweat. It looked as if Fineday had interrupted preparation for a winter supply of wood.

Cork walked to the men slowly.

"Will, Stone, what's going on?"

"None of your business, O'Connor," Fineday said.

"Looks to me like you're both ready to let a little blood, and that *is* my business. This have anything to do with Lizzie?"

Fineday didn't answer, but he said to Stone, "Let her go, or I swear I'll kill you."

"You think I'm keeping her here against her will, Will?" Stone laughed at that, the ax held easy in his hands, the split wood on the ground around him like killed things. "Why don't I just call her out here, then, and let's see." He yelled her name over his shoulder.

They all waited. The sun was high and unusually hot. The drone of blackflies, an oddity for so late in the season, filled the quiet. The insects lit on Stone's bare, salty skin and crawled over his hairless chest and shoulders. He seemed not to notice, although blackflies were vicious biting insects, one of the worst scourges of the north country.

"Lizzie," he called again, more harshly this time. "Get your ass out here, girl."

The door opened slowly and Lizzie Fineday stepped out.

She wore a bright blue knit sweater and wrinkled khakis. Her hair snaked across her face, wild. She hung back in the shadow of the cabin, smoking a cigarette. She stared at her father, then at Cork, as if she didn't quite understand their presence.

"Lizzie, you come on over here. I'm taking you home," Fineday hollered.

He took a step toward his daughter, but Stone moved to block his way.

"Ask her, Will," Stone said. "Stay right where you are and ask her if she wants to leave."

Fineday gave him a killing look. "Lizzie, you come home with me. You come home now. You hear?"

"You want to go home with him, Lizzie?" Stone asked.

The young woman smoked her cigarette, finally shook her head.

"See?" Stone said to Fineday. "If that's what you needed, you have it. You, too, O'Connor. She's not a minor. She makes up her own mind. She wants to stay, she stays." He finally shifted his gaze from Fineday and spoke to Cork directly. "Unless you have a warrant of some kind, it's my right to ask you to leave."

"Lizzie," Cork called to her, "I'd like you to step out into the sunlight so we can see you clearly. Do you understand?"

She didn't react immediately, but eventually she took a step forward into the light.

"Are you feeling all right?" Cork said.

She carefully drew the hair away from her eyes and nodded slowly.

"You see?" Stone said.

"If you come with us, I promise nobody's going to hurt you."

"Nobody's going to hurt her here," Stone said, then called out, "Lizzie, you want to go with these folks, you go."

She blinked in the bright sunlight but she did not move.

Fineday gripped the tire iron and cocked his arms like a batter in the box. "Stone, you fucking son of a bitch."

"Will Fineday," Cork said, "you've been asked to vacate this man's property. You'll do that or I'll arrest you for trespassing."

159

"He's got my daughter, goddamn it."

"Your daughter is here of her own volition. You heard her as clear as I did. Let it go, Will. Leave her be."

"Lizzie," he tried one last time, but his daughter turned away and went back into the cabin.

"Come on, Will," Cork said. "You need to leave. We all do."

Fineday stormed to his truck and sped down the narrow lane.

"I'm looking for a way to come back, Stone," Cork said.

"You find it, I'll be here." Stone lifted his ax and went back to chopping wood.

In the Pathfinder, Dina said, "Prison tattoos?"

She was speaking of the designs on Stone's upper arms and chest.

"Yeah," Cork said. "Inked them himself. The feather on each arm recalls the eagle feathers on a warrior's shield. The bear over his heart is because he's Makwa, a member of the bear clan."

"I'm sure I saw a thunderbird, too."

"You did. Bineshii. Thunderbird was one of the six original beings that came out of the sea to live with the Anishinaabeg. Unfortunately, every Shinnob that Bineshii looked at died, so Thunderbird was sent back to the sea."

"A Shinnob-killer. Interesting choice for a tattoo."

"Isn't it?"

Fineday was waiting for them where the road met the county highway. He stood with his legs spread, the long scar that cleaved his sandstone-colored face white as jagged lightning.

"He hurts her, and he's not the only one I'll come after," he said as Cork got out of the Pathfinder.

"At the moment, Will, the law's on his side."

"The white man's law. When did it work for me?"

"What's she running from? What's she afraid of? Help me with that and I can take her away from Stone."

"She's running from nothing."

"She just likes Stone's company, is that it?"

"I'll get her myself."

"He'll be watching for you. And think about this. You try

something, it's not only Stone you'll have to deal with, it'll be me as well. Wouldn't you rather have me on your side?"

"Fuck you, *chimook*."

Fineday spun away, climbed into his truck, and slammed the door.

"I'll be around to talk to you again, Will, you can bank on it. In the meantime, stay away from Stone."

Fineday sped off, kicking up a tail of dust and gravel.

"Did he call you a schmuck?"

"*Chi-mook*," Cork said, enunciating each syllable. "Ojibwe slang for white man. Not complimentary."

"But you're part Ojibwe. Doesn't that count?"

"When people are pissed at me, I'm not Ojibwe enough for the Ojibwes, and not white enough for the whites," Cork said.

25

Jo HAD SPENT the day calling clients, judges, rearranging court dates, appointments. Everyone understood, she told Cork. She'd washed clothes, packed, helped the girls and Stevie get ready to travel. Cork promised to call the high school and Stevie's teacher and explain the children's absence.

Dinner was a subdued affair: ham and cheese sandwiches, Campbell's tomato soup, chips. They talked quietly about Chicago, seeing Rose and Mal, visiting Northwestern and maybe Notre Dame. No one said a word about the dynamite in the Bronco. Afterward, they played a game of Clue. Stevie won, although Cork and probably everyone else knew a couple of turns earlier that it was Mrs. White in the study with the candlestick.

Cork read to Stevie, something he enjoyed doing. The book was *Hatchet,* about a boy lost in the wilderness who uses his own wiles and strength of character to make his way back to safety. Stevie's dark brown Ojibwe eyes locked on the ceiling as he imagined the scenes painted by the words, saw the story playing out in his mind. Eventually, his eyelids began to flicker, and when they'd closed for good, Cork kissed him good night on his forehead and turned out the light.

As he came downstairs, there was a knock at the front door. Cy Borkmann.

"Just wanted to let you know that we'll have someone posted out on the street all night," Cy told him.

"I never authorized that," Cork said.

"Nothing needs authorization. We're all off-duty. Just wanted to make sure everything here is secure until your family's off safe and sound."

Jo came to Cork's side and said, "Thank you, Cy. And please thank the others for us."

He smiled a little shyly. "Sure. Look, you all sleep well, okay?" He tipped his ball cap and lumbered down the front steps toward the curb where his truck was parked.

With Stevie in bed, the girls probed Cork for information on the dynamite and the rez shooting. He wished he could offer them something substantial—anything—but he admitted he had nothing.

It was after ten when he got the call from Simon Rutledge.

"I'm at the sheriff's office in Carlton. I've been down here all day. I think I might have something. My cohort in St. Paul called me, and guess who just happened to visit Lydell Cramer at the hospital yesterday. His sister. It seemed a big coincidence that each of her last visits preceded a threat to your safety, so I decided to reconnoiter her farmhouse. There's a good-sized barn, but there aren't any animals around. I watched a couple of guys go in and out of that barn all day long, one of them always sporting what appeared to be an assault rifle. I did some checking with the police in Moose Lake and found out Lydell's sister lives with a guy name of Harmon LaRusse."

"Son of a bitch."

"Exactly. Turns out the Carlton County Sheriff's Department has a big file on him. On Cramer's sister, too, and the other guy out there whose name is Carl Berger, an ex-con with a pretty long history of drugs and violence. Sheriff's investigators have had them under surveillance for a while, after a neighbor complained he'd been threatened. An IR thermal scan of the barn showed a lot of heat. Which might have been understandable if there'd been livestock inside."

"An indoor marijuana operation."

"Bingo. A big one. That's why I'm at the Carlton County sheriff's office right now. For the last couple of months, they've been putting together everything they need for a good bust. They've been holding off, thinking they might be able to intercept a sale. When I explained my concern about a possible connection with your incident on the rez, they agreed to go ahead ASAP. They're hoping for a no-knock first thing in the morning, if you'd care to be here."

"Got a go time yet?"

"Not until they're sure they've secured the warrant. Want me to call?"

"Yeah. Thanks, Simon. Good work."

"That's why I get the big bucks."

Cork hung up and turned to find Jo watching him. "What's up?"

He told her.

"You think this woman and Moose LaRusse might be responsible for the shooting and the bomb?"

"It's certainly a possibility we can't ignore."

"Oh God, I hope it's them and that you get them."

"I still want you away from here until we're sure. Besides, the girls are looking forward to visiting college campuses."

She put her arms around him, pressed her cheek to his chest. "I hate leaving, thinking you might still be in danger."

"I'll be fine. I *am* fine."

He locked the doors, checked the windows, turned out the downstairs lights, and briefly moved aside a curtain. Out front, Cy Borkmann sat in his truck drinking coffee from his big silver thermos. Upstairs, Cork looked in on his daughters, who were in their rooms, in bed but not yet asleep. He talked with each of them awhile, kissed them good night, then went to his own room, where quietly and rather gently he and Jo made love. For a long time after that, he lay with his wife in his arms. They'd never finished their talk about her past with Ben Jacoby, but at the moment it didn't matter. Cork knew that despite every threatening thing, past and present, he was the luckiest man on earth.

26

In the early morning shortly before sunrise, Jo drove toward a blood-red streak of sky, carrying away in her Camry everything that was most important to Cork.

After they'd gone, he approached Howard Morgan's Explorer, parked at the curb where Borkmann's truck had been the night before.

Morgan stepped out and stretched. "So they're off," he said.

"Thanks, Howard."

"No problem. Good to see them go. Safer, I mean."

"I know what you mean. Be glad to fix you some breakfast."

"Thanks, but I've been thinking for the last couple hours about a stack of blueberry pancakes at the Broiler. Then I got a bed that's calling my name."

Cork went back inside, pulled down a bowl from the cupboard, shook in some raisin bran. He was just about to pour in some milk when Rutledge called.

They waited in an oak grove a quarter mile north of the farmhouse. Four cruisers, an unmarked Suburban, twelve deputies, two DEA agents, Undersheriff Jeff McGruder, and Sheriff Roy Killen. Cork and Rutledge were there, too. The sheriff's people wore midnight blue Kevlar vests and camouflage outfits. A couple of the deputies smoked. They all watched the sheriff as he held the field glasses level on the

165

farmhouse. They should have gone in before this—they all knew it—but Killen had decided to wait. The problem was the mist.

The farmhouse was an old white structure with paint flaking off in leprous patches, a sagging front porch, and a satellite dish on the roof. Across the yard stood the barn, in far better shape than the house and painted a new dark red. Cork had been told that there were empty animal pens, but he couldn't see them because of the mist.

The buildings stood a quarter mile off the road, in a field long fallow, full of thistle and timothy gone yellow in the dry of late autumn. The mist did not quite touch the ground and reached only a couple of dozen feet into the air, so that everything about the scene seemed to exist in colored layers. Far away were the yellow grass, the gray mist, the blue sky. Nearer, the russet oak leaves, the midnight blue vests, the camouflage outfits. Enclosing it all was the waiting.

Killen didn't like the idea of going in with the mist still thick. He couldn't see the farmhouse yard at all. Someone looking out a second-floor window could spot the cruisers coming and take up a hidden position in the yard. He didn't want to risk his people. Better, he'd decided, to let the mist burn off. So they waited.

Traffic picked up on the rural highway that ran past the oak grove, many of the cars heading to a small white church built among Norway pines just visible in the distance. Around the church, the mist had already vanished, but it still hung thick over the fields and the farmhouse and the red barn.

After a while, Killen spoke to McGruder and the two DEA agents, then approached Cork and Rutledge.

Killen was near sixty, with freckles across his forehead and age spots on the back of his hands, retirement not many years away. "I don't know what it is with this fog but we wait much longer and the whole damn world's going to know we're here," he said. "We're going in. You two stay back. This is our business."

He went to his deputies, who'd stopped talking and had thrown down their cigarettes when they heard what Killen had said to Cork and Rutledge.

"All right, let's do it. Just like we talked about, boys. Quick and simple. Everybody do their job."

They moved to the cruisers, and as the doors shut, popping like muted gunfire, Cork heard the bell in the little church steeple to the north begin to ring, clear notes that carried far in the morning air.

An unmarked Suburban went first. It stopped at the chained gate that blocked the access to the farmhouse. A deputy leaped out, split the chain with a bolt cutter, swung the gate wide. A couple of seconds later the cruisers sped through, hauling ass down the dirt lane, disappearing into the gray mist.

The dogs had already given the bust away. They began to bark as soon as the cruisers turned off the highway. Cork and Rutledge, staying far back on the lane as they'd been instructed, heard the dogs going crazy as the mist ate the cars. A few moments later, gunfire erupted. From the rapid crack of the first weapon, Cork knew it was a heavy automatic of some kind. Shotgun blasts boomed from a second-floor window, something Cork and Rutledge could see above the top of the mist, and immediately the boards around the window frame exploded in chips and splinters as the deputies returned fire.

Rutledge drew his sidearm. "I can't just stand here and do nothing."

"If you're thinking of going into that mist, Simon, I've got to tell you it's a bad idea. Way too confusing. Your Glock'll be no good at a distance, anyway."

"I have to do something," Rutledge said. He swung out of the vehicle and ran.

Cork jumped out, too, calling after him, "Simon!" but the BCA agent had already vanished into the mist. "Shit," he said. He popped the tailgate open and pulled his Remington from its cradle. He grabbed several slugs, jacked five into the chamber, stuffed a few more into the pocket of his windbreaker. He stood by the Pathfinder, resisting the temptation to move forward, although every impulse pushed him in that direction. He waited, as Killen had told him to do, while the gunfire became sporadic and the sound of the automatic weapon ceased.

The mist had begun to lift, ragged white fingers reaching

toward the sky, then evaporating. The long grass of the fields became clearer by the moment. Cork glimpsed a slender figure sprinting from the farmhouse, a figure with long, dark hair, wearing a yellow sweatshirt, carrying a rifle, and making hard for the south end of the field.

He got on the radio, tried to raise Killen or McGruder, got no answer. He left the Pathfinder and gave chase.

The mist was spotty, heavy in some places, almost gone in others. The long grass was still wet with dew and slapped at the cuffs of his khakis. He cut at an angle he calculated would bring him to the fleeing figure somewhere near the fence at the end of the field. Behind him, the gunfire had ceased completely.

Barbed wire edged the field. When Cork reached the fence, he saw that the figure had stopped. The rifle lay against the wire as the figure bent and spread the strands to slip through. Thirty yards back, Cork went prone in the tall grass, put the stock of his shotgun to his shoulder, and sighted. The mist still lingered between Cork and the fence, but the yellow sweatshirt made an easy target.

"Police," Cork shouted. "Raise your hands."

The figure let go of the strands, surprised. A hand shot toward the rifle.

Cork hollered, "Don't touch the weapon."

The figure ignored him, swung back, and pulled off a round that went high and wide.

"O'Connor," Rutledge shouted from somewhere behind Cork.

The figure at the fence corrected its aim, pointed the barrel above the place where Cork lay, and sighted toward Rutledge's voice.

Cork fired. The figure took half a step back into the fence, then crumpled to the ground, leaving an arm snagged on the wire, raised as if in surrender.

Lydell Cramer's sister and Harmon LaRusse were killed in the exchange of gunfire at the farmhouse. The dogs, too. The man in the mist whom Cork had shot, Carl Berger, was taken to the hospital in Moose Lake, where he was listed in serious condition and in no shape to be questioned. Rutledge had no

doubt that these people were involved in the rez shooting because, in addition to the marijuana operation in the barn and
nearly a kilo of cocaine and a sizable stash of crystal meth in
one of the farmhouse bedrooms, the sheriff's people found a
cache of weapons that included a Savage 110GXP3 fitted with
a Leupold scope. Rutledge sent the firearm to the BCA for a
ballistics comparison.

It was going on two o'clock when Cork rolled into his parking space at the Tamarack County Sheriff's Department in Aurora. A little more than eight hours had passed since he'd said
good-bye to Jo and the children, but it felt like days. He was
bone tired, and the relief that came with finding the rifle that
had probably been used in the shooting at the Tibodeau cabin
was tempered by the memory of two bodies lying together in
the front hallway of the farmhouse in a pool of their mixed
blood. They'd made the choices that had brought them to that
end, but always in the stillness after violent killing there was a
hollowness inside Cork that held no sense of victory or justice
or right, only the empty absolute of death.

Ed Larson joined him in his office, along with Dina Willner.
The windows were open to a quiet Sunday afternoon. A slight
breeze out of the southwest kept the skies fair and the temperature pleasant. Beyond the little park that Cork could see
through his window, the bell tower of Zion Lutheran was
etched like a white tattoo against the body of the town.

"When will we know for sure?" Larson asked.

"Simon said he'd pull strings to get the ballistics done
ASAP, so maybe tomorrow or the next day." Cork sat forward,
rubbed his lower back. He opened the top right drawer of his
desk, pulled out a bottle of ibuprofen, and tapped out four
tablets.

"Let me get you some water for that," Dina said. She went
out and came back with a paper cup filled from the cooler in
the common area.

"Thanks." Corked popped the tablets in his mouth and
swallowed them down with the cold water.

"Headache?" Larson asked.

"Back," Cork said. "Wrenched it when I dropped to a firing
position out there in the field."

Larson glanced at Dina. "We might have something that'll make you feel better. Something on the Jacoby killing."

"Yeah? What?"

"Tell him your part first, Dina."

Willner wore a tight black sweater and formfitting black jeans that Cork figured she had to grease herself down to slide into. She looked good and fresh, as if she'd had plenty of sleep, something Cork envied.

"I went to the North Star Bar last night," she began.

"Another session with the push-up bra?" Cork broke in.

She ignored him. "I talked with a dumpy guy behind the bar, name was Leonard. He told me that on the night Jacoby was murdered, Lizzie Fineday was out but came back in around midnight beat up bad. Her father took her upstairs, then came down a short time later and went out, moving like a man on a mission. He wasn't back for closing, so Leonard had to do it by himself, which he says is unusual. Fineday always insists on closing."

"You got all this with a push-up bra? I may have to start wearing one."

Larson piped in. "I finally caught up with the night clerk at the Four Seasons. He told me that around eight or nine on the evening Jacoby was killed, Lizzie Fineday came into the hotel looking for him. He wasn't there, so she left a note."

"He didn't happen to see what the note said?"

"No such luck. But Jacoby comes in around eleven, gets the note, heads right back out."

"Think it's enough to bring her in?"

"It's thin," Larson said. "Especially since we'll have to go through Stone to get to her. But that's not all."

He nodded to Willner, who brought from her purse a little Baggie containing several cigarette butts.

"I did some Dumpster diving late last night," she said. "When I was in the bar the other night, I'd noticed that Lizzie chain-smokes. In the Dumpster, I found a bag of trash that had some mail with her name on it, and these cigarette butts. Doesn't absolutely mean they're Lizzie's, but her father doesn't smoke, and even if he did I doubt he'd be wearing lipstick, so it's a good bet they're hers. We're sending one of these and one of the hair samples taken from Jacoby's SUV for a DNA match."

"That'll take time."

Dina shook her head. "We're not sending it to your BCA lab. We're using a private lab in Chicago. Flying it out this afternoon. We can have the comparison in forty-eight hours."

Cork looked at Larson. "You okay with this, Ed?"

"It might not stand up in court, but if it is a match, it'll give us plenty for a probable cause pickup and hold. It'll get us past Stone."

"Lou Jacoby'll foot the bill?"

"Of course. And he's supplying the transport. Tony's already in the air on his way here. ETA in about an hour."

"Jacoby's private jet? We'll have to get down to Duluth for that."

Dina shook her head. "He's going to land at the local landing strip."

"The jet?"

"A small plane."

"All right," Cork said. Then to Larson: "You ever connect with Arlo Knuth?"

"Not yet. Every briefing I ask the watch to keep their eyes peeled for him, check all the usual places. Nothing so far."

"You know Arlo. He can make himself scarce when he wants to."

"But why would he want to? That's what I'm wondering."

"You don't really think he had anything to do with Jacoby's murder, do you?"

"No, but I'm thinking he might have seen something that scared him into hiding. I'd like to know what."

"Stay on it."

"You know I will."

With the cigarette butt and the hair sample in an evidence envelope that had been sealed and signed by Ed Larson, Cork drove Dina toward the county airfield, which was located in the little community of Flax on Lake Margery, three miles south of Aurora.

Flax consisted of a few private cabins, a combination restaurant and gift store called the Cozy Caribou Café, and a small gas station with a garage and mechanic, all situated within hailing distance of the lake and the airstrip. Cork parked near the café, and they got out and wandered toward the airfield. It was a simple affair, a single landing strip, a small control tower, several corrugated buildings that housed the local planes. The sky was blue and almost cloudless—a perfect sky for flying, Cork thought.

"So, you think Lizzie Fineday was with Eddie at Mercy Falls?" Dina said.

"Sure looks that way."

"Do you think she killed him?"

"If she was doped up and freaked out, I suppose I could see it."

"Know what I think? It was her old man. He went ballistic when he saw what Eddie had done, went to Mercy Falls, and killed him."

"Couple of things about that bother me. Why did Eddie hang around Mercy Falls after she left? And why didn't he put up a fight?" He gave a single shake of his head. "I'm laying odds it was someone who surprised him, someone he didn't expect, or at least didn't expect to have a knife."

"So you're back to Lizzie."

"Not necessarily. I think there was someone else out there, someone with a colder heart than Lizzie has. I just don't know who or why yet."

Dina checked her watch just as the drone of an engine came out of the sky to the southeast. "Right on time."

A plane appeared above the treetops, circled, and made its approach from the north. It touched down, and as it rolled off the runway onto an apron near Cork and Dina, the prop ceased to spin and the engine fell silent. Tony Salguero stepped out. "Sheriff O'Connor. Dina. I hope I haven't kept you waiting. You have the freight?" he asked.

"Here." Cork handed over the sealed envelope. He looked at the plane while Salguero signed the receipt. "The Jacobys' own a fleet?"

"The jet is Lou's," Salguero said. "This baby is all mine. I built her myself."

"How's Lou doing?" Dina asked.

Salguero inspected the envelope. "We buried his favorite child this morning, but you know Lou. A mule could kick him and he wouldn't grunt. He simply takes it out on everyone around him." Tony looked toward the Cozy Caribou Café. "I need something to eat before I head back. How is the food here?"

"Reasonably priced and mostly deep-fried," Cork said.

"Perfect." Salguero began long strides in that direction.

They sat on the deck in the cool air of early October, the only ones outside. The waitress was reluctant to seat them there, but Salguero insisted.

"I have been cooped up for hours," he explained with a stunning smile and Spanish accent.

Cork never drank on duty, but he decided that, having handed off the evidence envelope, he was done for the day. He ordered a beer. So did Dina.

"A hamburger, bloody," Salguero told the waitress.

"We don't serve them rare anymore. Health reasons."

Tony closed the menu and held it out. "I will sign an agreement. If I get poisoned, it's my own fault." The waitress didn't take the menu or put anything down on her pad. Salguero finally tossed his hands up. "All right, cook it any way you please, just make sure the beer is cold."

"Beer?" Cork said. He looked toward the plane Salguero had to fly back to Chicago. "Should you be drinking?"

"I have flown hundreds of thousands of miles, Sheriff, without a single incident. But tell you what. If I crash I will make certain it is into an empty field." He smiled pleasantly.

"Have you flown long?"

"My father had his own planes. He flew himself everywhere, to the pampas, the rain forest, wherever he had investments. From the time I was a young boy, I dreamed of flying."

"The pampas?"

"I am from Argentina. Buenos Aires."

Cork said, "How long have you worked for the Jacobys?"

"Five years. But I've known them most of my life. My father and Lou Jacoby are old friends."

"So you know them well?"

Salguero grinned, showing beautiful white teeth. "What do you want to know?"

"Everybody keeps referring to Eddie as Lou's favorite child. Near as I can figure, he was mostly a son of a bitch."

"No, Sheriff. He was a bastard. Born out of wedlock. That is no secret. But I also think he was born out of love. Eddie's mother was the true treasure of Lou's life, and I think that when he looked at their son, what he really saw was Eddie's mother. Would you not agree?" he said to Dina.

She shrugged. "That's one explanation. I'm more inclined toward the sick-puppy theory myself."

"What's that?" Cork said.

"Lou's other children have done just fine in their lives, become responsible adults. If Lou died tomorrow, they'd probably grieve but they'd be fine. Eddie was like a sick puppy, always needing Lou. But I think in his way Lou needed Eddie just as bad. Maybe, in fact, that's why Eddie never really grew up, never learned how to be a responsible man. Lou never gave him the chance to be one."

The waitress delivered the beers.

"I think I will have that burger to go," Tony said. "And do you have a men's room?"

"Inside."

Salguero followed her in.

Dina sipped her beer. "This is good."

"Leinenkugel's. Local favorite." He took a swallow from his bottle and looked where Salguero had gone. "So. Argentina. A story there?"

"Tony's family had money," Dina replied. "When the Argentine economy collapsed, they lost it all. Pretty simple."

Salguero returned just as the burger was delivered in a paper sack, along with a tab for the food and the beers. He threw money on the table.

"Your beer is on Lou," he said. Then to the waitress: "Sorry if I gave you a hard time, miss. I have a long trip still ahead of me."

She smiled into his handsome face. "You were no problem at all."

He picked up the evidence envelope and the burger sack and started toward his plane.

"Need to gas up?" Cork asked.

"There is an airport in Wisconsin midway that I use for that purpose." He opened the plane door, tossed the envelope and the sack inside, then looked back at Cork. "I don't know what it is that I'm taking back, but I hope it helps to find the person who killed Eddie."

"I'm sure it will."

Cork stepped away as the engine kicked over and the prop began to spin. Salguero swung the plane around and took off into the wind. He circled back, tilting his wings in salute as he flew over.

Cork said, "Lost a fortune and now he flies for the Jacobys. He seems to take it well."

"Doesn't he," Dina said, watching as the plane disappeared into the southeast.

27

*H*E DROPPED DINA at her car in the Sheriff's Department lot, then went home.

He couldn't remember the last time the house had been so empty. The air felt close, smelled stale, and he realized that he'd left without opening the curtains or lifting the windows. He spent a few minutes going through the rooms doing just that. On the desk in Jo's office, he found notes she'd scribbled to herself as she'd scrambled to rearrange her schedule. He sat in her chair and felt the slight indentation that over time she'd left in the cushion, and he thought how small her hips were and how good they felt pressed against him in bed. On the floor in Stevie's room lay a sheet of paper, crayons, and a pair of scissors. Stevie had drawn a crude face on the paper and colored it green. For Halloween, he wanted to be the Hulk and he'd been trying to make a mask, but his work had been interrupted. In the living room, lying open on an end table next to the sofa, was a book Jenny had been reading, *The Beet Queen*, her place marked with a tarot card that held the image of a skeleton. In the kitchen, as he passed Annie's softball glove hanging on a hook by the back door, he leaned to it and breathed in the smell of oiled leather. His family had been gone less than a day, but they'd left behind silence and a deep, painful loneliness that Cork was glad he would not have to endure for long. Every man's life ought to be about something, he believed, and he was comfortable with the knowledge that his was about family.

But so was Lou Jacoby's, apparently, a man Cork didn't admire in the least and with whom he felt he had little in common.

He didn't know what to do with that, so he let it go. He was exhausted, hungry, and couldn't get out of his mind the image of Carl Berger's right arm hung up on barbed wire. He went upstairs to shower, hoping it might refresh him a little. He thought that afterward he would go to the Broiler for dinner.

Half an hour later, as he was coming downstairs, the doorbell rang. When he opened the door, he found Dina Willner standing on his front porch, a grocery bag in one hand and a twelve-pack of Leinenkugel's in the other.

"I figured after the kind of day you've had, you might need a little company," she said. "So I brought dinner. Hope you like New York strip."

Cork's surprise probably showed on his face. "I don't know, Dina."

"Look, you just relax." She squeezed past him into the house. "I'll do the cooking. Just show me to the kitchen."

She twisted the caps off two beers, handed a bottle to Cork, and drank the other as she worked. She started charcoal going in the backyard grill and wrapped garlic bread in foil so she could heat it over the coals while she grilled the steaks. Then she began to prepare a salad of assorted greens, red onion, and avocado. She talked the whole while, pleasantly.

"People around here think a lot of your family." She took a long draw on her beer and tore up lettuce. "They tell me your father was the youngest sheriff ever elected in Tamarack County. That true?" She glanced at him, her brows lifted questioningly above her attractive green eyes.

"True," he said.

"I also heard that the hands on the clock tower of your county courthouse have been stopped for thirty-five years, frozen at the moment of his death. Is that true, too?"

"More or less." He told her the story. The escapees from Stillwater, the shoot-out in front of the bank during which his father stepped between a bullet and an innocent bystander. How the clock was hit about the same time by an errant round and the hands had never moved since. How the town viewed it as a kind of memorial to his father's selfless act.

"Board of Commissioners periodically discusses getting the clock fixed, but they never do anything. They say it's out of respect. I think they just don't want to spend the money."

"I think it's a wonderful tribute." Over her shoulder, she threw him a lovely smile.

The steaks sizzled when she laid them on the hot grill, and the good smell made Cork's mouth water. He realized how hungry he was, and how happy that Dina had come.

It was dark outside by the time they sat down at the kitchen table to eat. The steak was excellent: rare, tender, juicy. She'd dressed the salad with her own balsamic-vinegar-and-oil preparation that tasted of garlic, lemon, and pepper. It was accompanied by the garlic bread and more beer.

"How are you feeling now?" she asked.

"Better. Thanks."

She eyed him as she lifted her beer bottle to her lips. "Mind if I ask you a question? About this morning?"

He paused in cutting his steak. "All right."

"A shooting, that's a hard thing, I know. Still, I find it interesting that you didn't kill Carl Berger."

"It was a lousy shot."

"Is that so? With a rifle at thirty yards? People around here seem to think you're an excellent shot. Been hunting all your life." She put her hands on the table and almost imperceptibly leaned toward him, narrowing the distance between them. "I've been wondering if you really meant to kill him."

"Of course I meant to kill him. You never shoot unless you mean to kill. He was drawing a bead on Rutledge."

"You've killed two men. People here talk about that. Respectfully. Men, I gather, who were better off dead. I'm guessing it wasn't easy, but you did it. So I'm wondering what was different about this shooting."

"I'd rather not talk about it."

"I managed to get a copy of your statement, and I've gone over it. Stay with me for just a minute. The mist. A figure not clear to you. Panicked, afraid, finally cornered. A slender figure with long, dark hair. I think you might have been wondering if it was Lydell Cramer's sister, a woman you were about to shoot. Could that have made a difference?"

"It shouldn't have mattered."

"But it did." She reached across the table and laid her hand against his cheek. "It did, didn't it?"

"Like I said, I'd rather not think about it."

"I understand." She pulled her hand back slowly. "How about another beer?"

After dinner, they sat in the quiet of the living room. It was late—later than Cork had imagined he'd be up. He was tired, what with the beer and the weight of all that had occurred that day. He wanted to be alone, and at the same time he didn't.

"How's your back?" Dina asked. "You said you wrenched it this morning during the raid."

"Stiff. Hurts. A lot of it's probably stress."

"I can help that." She put her beer on the end table and moved toward the easy chair where Cork sat. "Lie down on the floor. Come on. I won't hurt you, I promise. That's right. On your stomach." She took her shoes off. "Now, close your eyes."

The next thing Cork knew, she'd stepped onto his back. She was surprisingly light or knew exactly how to distribute her weight, because she was anything but oppressive. With her toes and the balls of her feet, she started to knead his muscles, beginning with the small of his back.

"Oh my God. Where did you learn that?"

"Picked it up along the way."

"You know, this could be very effective in getting suspects to cooperate."

"There's something I'd like to tell you."

"Go ahead. I'll try to listen, but this is distracting."

"I was wrong about you."

"How?"

"I've worked with a lot of rural law officers. More often than not they're pigheaded, defensive, and incompetent."

"I hope I'm only pigheaded."

"I don't work well with just anyone, but I feel like we're working well together."

"That's interesting. I'm not sure I feel the same way."

He could sense her reaction in the momentary pause of her feet.

"What do you mean?" she asked.

"I can't help thinking that there are things about Eddie Jacoby you know but aren't telling."

"I can't. Client confidentiality."

"His? Or his family's?"

She didn't reply.

"Would you tell me if I wore a push-up bra?"

She laughed. "There is one thing I'll tell you about Eddie that might give you an additional glimpse of the man. When he was twenty-five, he received the distribution from a trust fund his grandfather had set up for him. Several million. Eddie always wanted to be a hotshot movie producer, so he invested in a production company in California, proudly told everyone he was in the movie business. You know what kind of movies he was making? The kind that show pretty young girls doing pretty ugly things. And he was proud of that. His partners ended up taking him, stole most of the fortune, though legally. His father refused to bail him out of that one. But he still has business cards with his Hollywood logo, and I know he doles them out and when he hits on women he uses some line about making them a star."

"Do they ever buy it?"

"I'm thinking Lizzie Fineday might have. I can't imagine any other reason she'd be with Eddie."

"Anything else you'd care to share?"

"I'm helping you all I can, trust me."

She stepped off him. He couldn't move, didn't want to.

"Better?"

Slowly he rolled over and looked up at her. She seemed taller from that perspective, even prettier, if that were possible. He did want to trust her, and felt himself inclined. But he also knew his thinking was being filtered through exhaustion and alcohol. And he couldn't forget the fact that, in the end, Dina worked for the Jacobys.

"I think it's good night now," he said.

"Don't get up. I'll see myself out."

While she put on her shoes, he gradually pulled himself off the floor and followed her to the door.

"We're closing in on the end, Cork," she said in the doorway. "Coming toward the home stretch. Once we bring Lizzie in, I think it will be over, one way or another."

She hesitated a long moment before heading into the night, as if there was something more she wanted to do or to say. Whatever it was, she thought better of it, and the last moment of their evening together was left empty. She went down the porch steps and walked through the light of the street lamp to her car.

He flipped the dead bolt, checked the other doors and windows, began turning out the lights, thinking all the while that if he loved Jo so much, why did he feel a small disappointment in the emptiness of that last moment with Dina.

He headed toward the stairs, but before he took the first step, the telephone rang. It was almost eleven o'clock. It was either the office or Jo, he figured.

"O'Connor," he said into the phone.

"You think it's over?" the voice at the other end said. "Think again. You're dead, O'Connor. You're so dead."

28

IT WAS THE quiet that woke her. That and Stevie's elbow burrowing into her hip. The elbow didn't surprise her: her son was a restless sleeper. But the quiet was an odd thing. Not quiet exactly because there were the usual city noises. Traffic early and heavy on Green Bay Road two blocks east, the rattle of suspension, the screech of brakes, the warning beeper on a truck backing up, probably collecting garbage. Like Stevie's elbow, these were expected things. What was unexpected was the silence of the birds. Spring, summer, and fall in Aurora, the birds began their songs and arguments long before dawn. Jo had grown so used to their chirp and chatter that she didn't even notice anymore. Except when it was missing. In Evanston, Illinois, that morning there seemed to be no birds at all.

It was the West Nile virus. Rose had told her the night before how the mosquito-borne disease had devastated the avian population all along the north shore of Lake Michigan, leaving birds on the ground under trees like fallen, rotting fruit. It was an awful image to spring to mind first thing in the morning, and the silence in the wake of all that death was disturbing.

She hadn't slept well, and not just because of Stevie's restless jerking. She missed Cork. She was relieved when he'd called the evening before and told her about the raid on the farmhouse in Carlton County, relieved that it ended the danger to him. She wanted so much to be with him then, to hold him. But he was safe, and that was the important thing.

Her nose lifted at the smell of coffee brewing, and she pulled back the covers and slipped from the bed, careful not to wake her small son. She threw on her robe and left the guest room of her sister's home. Rose lived with her husband, Mal, in the upper level of a duplex in a nice neighborhood at the north end of Evanston. The building was long and narrow, what Rose called a railroad car design. In front was the living room, connected by a long hallway to the kitchen in back. Off the hallway on either side were the bedrooms and the bath. Jo found Rose in the kitchen rolling dough on a cutting board while coffee trickled into a pot on the counter.

"Cinnamon rolls," Jo said. "The kids will love you. They've missed your cooking."

"And I miss their appetites. Mal appreciates my cooking, but eating's never been that important to him. All those years of self-denial, I suppose. Coffee's just about ready. Want some?"

"I'll get it," Jo said.

"Sit down, relax. This is my kitchen," she said proudly. She wiped her hands on her apron and went to the cupboard.

Jo watched her sister with amazement and pleasure. There was so much different about Rose now. She'd been plain and heavy all her life, but in the past few months she'd dropped weight, and a lovely color flushed her cheeks. There was a lively snap to all her movements, a joyous energy. This, Jo suspected, was due to love.

"Mal likes his job?"

"It's perfect. Basically the same thing he did before he came to Aurora, but he doesn't have to be celibate now." She laughed sweetly.

For seventeen years, Rose had lived with the O'Connors, most of that time in a cozy attic room, taking care of the household while Jo and Cork both worked the law from different angles. Near the end, Mal Thorne had come to Aurora. Father Mal Thorne, then. For nearly two years, he'd served the parish of St. Agnes. During that time, he began to question significantly his commitment to the Church, and in the fertile ground of that doubt, his love for Rose had grown until he could not deny it. She'd felt the same. Yet, it had taken the ac-tions of a madman to put her into Mal's willing arms and to convince him it was time to divest himself of his collar and cassock. They'd been married in a civil ceremony and had moved to Chicago, where Mal, as a priest, had once headed a homeless shelter run by the Chicago Archdiocese. He did the same now for a publicly funded shelter.

As Rose turned to bring the coffee pot to the table, Mal walked into the kitchen in his drawstring pajamas. He was medium height. His hair was light brown, thin, and cut close enough to see the tan of his scalp. In his youth, he'd been a champion boxer, middleweight—he still had scar tissue over his left eye and a nose that was crooked from having been broken several times—and carried himself in a way that suggested both power and grace. He smiled often and broadly and did so now.

"Good morning, ladies." He swept Rose into his arms and kissed her lavishly.

Rose held the hot coffeepot at a safe distance. When Mal stepped back, she said, "I was going to offer you coffee to wake up, but I see you don't need it."

"A beautiful day," he said, and opened his arms toward the window and the sunlight beyond. "Family here and Cork out of danger, blessings both. Where are the kids?"

"Sleeping," Jo said. "Even Stevie. It's been hard on them lately. They could use the rest."

"I'm sure." Mal sat down at the table, opposite Jo. "What's the plan for today?"

Jo hid a yawn behind her hand. The coffee was good, but rest would have been better. "I'm thinking that Jenny and I will take a look at Northwestern, since that's one of the reason's we're here."

"Good. Then tomorrow or maybe the next day we might drive to South Bend so Annie can have a look at my alma mater."

"She'd love that, Mal. She talked nothing but Notre Dame the whole way down."

"Is she still hoping for a softball scholarship?"

"She's determined."

Rose, who was forming dough strips into tight spirals for

the cinnamon rolls, said, "She's like you. When she sets her mind to something, she makes it happen."

The phone in the hallway rang. Mal got up.

"Sit down, I'll answer it," Rose said.

Mal kept moving. "You'll get the phone all sticky." In the hallway, he answered with a cheery "Good morning." Then: "Yes, she is. Just a moment." He put the receiver to his chest. "For you, Jo."

"Is it Cork?"

"No, but it's a man." He handed her the phone and went back to the kitchen.

It was Ben Jacoby. His voice sounded showered and shaved and sparkling. Jo still had sleep in her eyes.

"Ben? How did you know I was here?"

"Dina Willner."

Dina. The woman working with Cork to solve the murder of Ben's brother. It made sense.

"I'm sorry about the bomb scare, but I understand they got the bastards."

"Yes."

"That's wonderful. Look, I'm sorry to be calling so early. I have some good news. I talked with a friend of mine in the admissions office at Northwestern. If you and Jenny are available today, he can arrange a private tour of the campus."

"Today?" she said.

"Unless you have other plans. I'm sure he'd be willing to schedule anytime. I just wasn't certain how long you'd be staying."

"Today would be fine. Thank you, Ben."

"Also, I was wondering if you might be free for a drink tonight."

"I don't think so."

"A glass of wine and half an hour of your time."

"It's not a good idea, Ben."

"I understand, but . . ." He fell silent, and Jo didn't know if he was gathering himself for another attempt or had given up. "Look, there are things I need to say to you."

She moved into the front room, distant from the kitchen.

"Like what?"

"Give me half an hour."

"You'll have to do better than that."

"I want to tell you why I left."

"That's not important to me now."

"It might be, if you knew. One drink. One glass of wine. One last time. Please."

She considered a long time before replying. "All right."

"I'll pick you up. Seven?"

"Seven is fine, but I'll meet you there."

"Deal."

He gave her the name of a restaurant on Green Bay Road, and he gave her his cell phone number, just in case.

"Ben?" Rose said when Jo came back to the table.

"Jacoby. I told you about him last night. The brother of the man who was killed."

"That's right. Your old law school buddy."

Although they'd shared many confidences, Jo had never told her sister about Ben Jacoby, and as far as Rose and Mal knew, they'd simply been acquainted in law school. At some point, Jo intended to tell Rose the whole story, but not at the moment.

"He's pulled some strings to get Jenny a tour of Northwestern today."

"That's great," Rose said.

"He also asked me out for a drink."

"We'll be glad to watch the children," Mal offered.

"Thanks."

She reached for her coffee. Although she'd put Ben Jacoby behind her long ago, his sudden departure from her life had been a nagging mystery for twenty years. She cradled her cup in both palms and carefully sipped the strong French roast amid the deep quiet of the dead birds.

29

THEY ALL SAT in Cork's office and for a long time said nothing, just drank the good coffee Dina Willner had brought, and sifted through their own, silent thoughts.

"We won't know for a while if the rifle we found at the farmhouse is the same one that fired the rounds at the Tibodeau cabin," Simon Rutledge finally said. "So we need to assume this isn't just some goofball who wants to scare you and is using the situation."

"Anybody ever tell you, Simon, that you've got a real knack for stating the bleeding obvious," Ed Larson said.

Cork knew the tension in the room was the result of tired people once again having to step into the front lines feeling as if they'd gained no ground.

"The phone records will tell us where the call came from," he said.

"It came from nowhere that'll be of any help to us, I can tell you that right now," Larson said.

He took off his gold wire-rims and massaged the bridge of his long nose. Rutledge tapped the desktop with his fingertips as if sending out Morse code. Dina Willner stirred a white plastic spoon in her coffee. Cork, who'd hardly slept, sat with a notepad in his lap and read over and over again what he'd written about the voice on the phone the night before.

Low. Muffled, but precise. Male. Dispassionate.

Several manila folders lay open on the desk, all containing

documents related to the investigation of the attempts on Cork's life. They'd been gone over a dozen times and no one saw anything new there.

He got up and walked to the window, watched a man in the park let his small dog off a leash to run free. Ralph Grunke and his terrier, Sparks. Cork watched Sparks begin to sniff every tree.

"I've been thinking about this guy who called. He wasn't angry. He didn't seem emotional at all. I keep replaying what he said, how he said it. It was very calculated."

"Calculated for what effect? Just to scare?" Rutledge said.

"No, I think he meant it. But it was as if the personal element was missing."

"Like a hit?" Dina asked.

Cork thought a moment. "I don't know what a hit's like, but maybe."

"It's interesting," Dina said. "If it is a hit, why let you know it's coming? In my experience, that's pretty unprofessional."

Cork turned to her. "What exactly is your experience?"

She took the spoon from her coffee and tapped it clean against the side of her cup. She set it on Cork's desk. "I dealt with a number of contract killings when I was with the Organized Crime Section. It's seen as an expeditious way to cover tracks, silence a witness."

"Cover what tracks here? And if Cork was a witness, a witness to what?" Rutledge said.

"Got me." Cork headed back to his chair.

"Maybe it *is* a hit," Larson said. "But not by a professional. Whoever it is sure bungled the first attempt."

"And the bomb," Rutledge said.

"And now this announcement of further intent," Dina added. "I think Ed's onto something."

Cork sat down. A dull throb had begun in his head. Too little sleep. "Could it still be related to Lydell Cramer?"

"The connection with Moose LaRusse and the rez would sure point in that direction." Larson hooked the wire-rims over his ears. "He certainly could have supplied the information needed for the location of the hit."

"Was there someone we missed who was connected to the farmhouse?" Dina asked.

Rutledge shook his head. "Lydell's sister, LaRusse, and Berger. Those were the only ones the Carlton County sheriff's people observed out there."

"Does Cramer have any other relatives?"

"I've already put someone on checking that out," Rutledge said. "We'll follow up on the phone records as soon as we have them. You never know what might turn up."

"What about the Jacoby investigation?" Cork asked. "Anything new, Ed?"

"I've got the record of the calls Jacoby made and received on his cell phone. I'll be looking those over."

"I'd like a copy, too."

"Sure. And we're waiting to see if there's a DNA match with Lizzie Fineday and the evidence we got from Jacoby's SUV." He glanced at Dina. "Any idea when we might hear?"

"I don't expect anything until tomorrow."

"If it's a match, we go after Lizzie and I'll bet something will break." Larson sounded truly hopeful.

"All right. Let's see what shakes," Cork said.

As the others filed out, Dina stayed behind and closed the door. She crossed the room and sat on the edge of his desk. She smelled of herbal soap, a clean, fresh scent. "You get any sleep at all last night?"

"Barely."

"It might be a good idea to stay somewhere else until this is over. Anywhere other than home."

"I've thought about that."

"You could stay at my hotel, take the room next to mine. Among other things, I'm an excellent bodyguard." She waited, gauging his response, which was simply to stare at her. "The other alternative is I could stay at your place."

To that he shook his head. "Small town. Big talk."

"I'd sleep on the sofa." She drilled him with her wonderful green eyes. "Unless you wanted otherwise."

"I think I'll put a cot in here."

She gave a diffident shrug, slid off his desk, and headed toward the door. "Just keep it in mind."

He watched her leave, but not without a little stab of regret.

30

JENNY WORE A plaid wool skirt and a rust-colored turtleneck. Her blond hair was carefully brushed. She appeared, Jo thought, very collegiate, probably a look she would abandon once she was actually attending college. It was just fine for her meeting at Northwestern with Marty Goldman.

His office was on the second floor of a three-story brick building with white colonnades, a block off the main campus. He looked like he'd been an athlete in his youth, but over the years a lot of his muscle had gone to fat and spilled over his belt. He wore a light blue Oxford with a yellow tie, and he rose from his desk to greet them, the skin of his face pink and shiny.

"I understand we're your first choice," he said after they'd finished with the pleasantries. "We're always glad to hear that. Have you taken your SATs or the ACTs yet?"

"SATs."

"Do you recall your scores?"

Jenny told him.

"Very impressive," he said, with a lift of his brow. "What kind of extracurricular activities have you been involved in?"

"I'm the editor of the school paper, *The Beacon*. I've been on the yearbook staff for the past two years. I'm a member of National Honor Society, president of the Debate Club. I can go on," she said.

"That's just fine," he laughed. "What is it about Northwestern that attracts you?"

"The Medill School," Jenny said.

"Journalism," Goldman said with an approving nod.

"I want to be a writer."

"Well, we certainly have some fine authors among our alumni. And we have several writing programs in conjunction with Medill that might interest you."

The talk was interrupted by a knock at the open door. A wiry young man a little over six feet tall with neatly groomed dark hair and a brooding look in his eyes stood just inside the threshold. He wore pressed jeans, a navy sweater over a white shirt, penny loafers. He stood stiffly, as if waiting for an invitation.

"Phillip. Come on in," Goldman said, rising.

Phillip came forward with a stiff, military stride.

"Jenny, Jo, this is Phillip. I've asked him to give you a tour of the campus this morning. He's a senior. I'm sure he'll be able to answer any questions you might have. I've scheduled you for about ninety minutes. That should be plenty of time to see almost everything of interest and for a Coke or cup of coffee in the bargain." He looked at his watch. "I'll see you back here at twelve-thirty and we can talk a bit more. Phillip?"

"This way." The young man led them out.

Jo hung back as they headed toward campus, letting Jenny and Phillip walk side by side in front. She was proud of her daughter, of Jenny's confidence and goals, proud of the woman her daughter was and proud of who she was becoming. She relaxed and listened as the two young people talked. Jenny had a million questions. Phillip answered them all. He was polite, informative, but there was something in his voice that hinted at irritation, as if this were a small ordeal.

The Northwestern campus was beautiful, deep in colorful fall. The collegiate structures, the flow of students along the sidewalks, the energy of freedom that was a part of college— Jo remembered the feel of it from her own undergraduate years long ago. For her, college had been an escape. It wouldn't have mattered where she'd gone. Anywhere, just to get away. She'd ended up with a full scholarship to the University of Illinois in Champaign, a campus that rose out of cornfields. She'd come well prepared to stand on her own, having spent her life standing up to her mother. There'd been nothing about college that intimidated her. The academics had been routine. Sex, drugs, and books she juggled easily and graduated magna cum laude.

After that had come law school at the University of Chicago, her first great challenge. She'd put aside the drugs and she'd also put aside men. Then came Ben Jacoby. When he stepped into her life, she was ready for something permanent, and until he said good-bye, she'd thought he was offering it.

Watching Jenny ahead of her, she hoped her daughter would have a different experience. Someone who would care about her the way Cork cared about Jo. Not that a man was necessary, because she remembered only too well how alone she'd often felt even when she was with a man. Ben Jacoby had changed that. For the first time in her life, she wanted to be with someone forever. She'd never let a man hurt her before, but Jacoby had hurt her deeply.

Maybe everyone needed their heart broken once. Maybe it had been that kind of hurt that helped her appreciate Cork from the beginning. From their very first meeting in Chicago.

It was spring. She still lived on South Harper Avenue in Hyde Park in the apartment where several months before she'd shared her nights with Ben. She came home from working late in the D'Angelo Law Library to find that her place had been broken into and she'd been robbed of her stereo and television. She called the police. A uniformed patrolman responded. Officer Corcoran O'Connor.

He filled out an incident report, then he spent a while looking over her apartment inside and out. Finally he sat down with her.

"I've got to be honest with you. There's very little chance of recovering your stolen property. No serial numbers, almost impossible to trace. But I'd like to make some recommendations for the future. First of all, I'd get a better lock on your front door."

"He didn't come in the front door. He came through the window."

"I understand. But almost anybody could break in through

the front door if they were so inclined, so I'd get a good dead bolt. Now, about the windows. I think you should put bars on them."

"I don't relish the idea of living in a jail," she said.

"Ever been in jail?"

"No."

"It won't feel like a jail, I promise. I understand you object to having to barricade yourself, but that's the reality of your situation. In a way, you're lucky. This time, they only stole from you. Next time, they might be after something different."

"As in rape."

"Yes, ma'am."

"I don't know that I can afford bars on the windows," she said.

"You don't need them on all your windows. I've checked around back. You're on the second floor, so you're fine there. But in front, with the porch and that elm, you're vulnerable. Really, your landlord ought to be the one who puts them on. If you get flack from him, I know where you can get them at a reasonable price." He cleared his throat. "And I'd be glad to install them."

"You?"

"Yes, ma'am."

"Please stop calling me ma'am. And why would you do that?"

"I know you volunteer your time helping people who can't afford a lawyer. I've seen you in the storefront office on Calumet."

"Yes."

"You do it, I'd guess, because you believe it's the right thing to do. Considering your situation here, I just think it's the right thing to do."

She studied him. He looked a little older than she, maybe twenty-six or twenty-seven. His hair was red-brown, shorter than she preferred on a man, but that was probably a dictate of the job. He wasn't handsome, not like Ben Jacoby or many of the others she'd been with, but there was a sincerity in his face, in his words, in the sound of his voice, that was attractive.

"That's it?" she asked with a sharp edge of skepticism. "You'd do that without expecting something in return?"

He capped his pen and scratched his nose with it. "You cook?"

Halfway through the ninety minutes that Marty Goldman had allotted for the tour, Phillip took them out to a long, grassy point on which nothing had been built. Lake Michigan lay to the east, a stretch of blue that looked as enormous as an ocean. Several miles south, clear in the crisp air of late morning, rose the Chicago skyline, as beautiful as any city Jo had ever seen.

Jenny stared at it for a long time. "Now I know what Dorothy felt like when she saw Oz."

"This is where I come when I need to get away," Phillip said.

"You like it here?" Jenny asked.

"It's my favorite spot."

"No, I mean do you like Northwestern?"

There was a breeze off the lake with a slight chill to it. Jenny hugged herself, and Phillip, without making anything of it, moved to block the wind.

"I wanted to go to school in Boulder," he said. "I love to ski."

"Why didn't you?"

"This was my father's preference."

"That's the only reason? I'd never go somewhere just because my father wanted me to."

"Lucky you," he said coldly, and turned back toward campus. "We should be going."

They stopped at the student union. Jo ordered a latte. Phillip did the same. Jenny didn't usually drink coffee, but she ordered a latte as well. They sat at a table for a few minutes.

"What's your major?" Jenny asked.

"Pre-law."

"You want to be a lawyer?"

"My father wants me to be a lawyer."

"What do you want to be?"

"It doesn't matter."

"Because you're going to be a lawyer like your father wants."

"He pays the bills."

"I don't know," Jenny said. "To me, that sounds like a recipe for an unhappy life."

"You're a lawyer," Phillip said to Jo. "Do you like it?"

She didn't remember telling him that she was an attorney, but maybe it had come up in his conversation with Jenny and she'd just missed it.

"Yes, I do," she replied.

"I've never known a happy lawyer," he said. "We should be getting back."

At the door to the admissions office, he stopped. "This is as far as I go. I have a class to get to."

"Thank you, Phillip," Jenny said. "We really appreciate your time." She shook his hand.

"Look," he said, "I apologize if I seemed rude. I'm a little stressed these days."

"You were great," Jenny said.

"Yeah, well, good luck. If Northwestern is really what you want, I hope you get it. Nice to meet you," he said to Jo.

Inside, Marty Goldman's secretary asked them to wait a few minutes. Mr. Goldman was still with someone.

"How did you like the campus?" she asked. She was a small black woman who spoke with a slight Jamaican accent.

"It's beautiful," Jenny said.

"Isn't it? And your guide?"

"He was fine."

"Good. He's not one of our usual group. He was a special request, as I understand it. His father, I believe. You must be friends of the family."

"And what family would that be?" Jo asked.

"Why, the Jacobys, of course."

31

CORK PASSED MUCH of the morning going over the record of the calls made to and from Eddie Jacoby's cell phone in the days before his death, and also the record of his hotel phone. Jacoby spent a lot of time with a receiver pressed to his ear. It fit the image Cork had of the man, the kind who drove his SUV with one hand and constantly worked his cell phone with the other.

In the afternoon, he attacked the paperwork that had piled up. The budget was a huge concern. The investigations, which required an uncomfortable amount of overtime, were eating up officer hours and resources. He knew he was going to have to go to the Board of Commissioners, explain the deficit that was developing, and ask for additional money. Christ, he'd always hated that part of the job.

Shortly after the three o'clock shift change, Ed Larson came into his office. Like everyone these days, he looked tired. Behind his wire-rims, his eyes rode puffy bags of skin and seemed to be sinking gradually deeper into his face. He still dressed neatly and held himself erect.

"Got a minute?" he asked.

Cork looked at his watch. "Not much more than that. I have a session with Faith Gray this afternoon. I've already missed one appointment. She's threatened that if I miss another, she'll require a temporary suspension. The regs, you know."

"I was just wondering if you've had a chance to look over Jacoby's phone records."

"Yeah." Cork picked up the document. "Several interesting items."

"I thought so, too. Particularly that call from the pay phone at the North Star Bar on the night he was murdered."

"You're thinking Lizzie?"

"That's what I'm thinking."

Cork arched his spine and worked his fists into the tight muscles in his lower back. He wouldn't have minded another session with Dina and her magic feet. "We need to be careful," he said, grimacing. "We know Jacoby visited the North Star, but we don't have anything that connects him solidly to the girl."

"She was certainly looking for him."

"We don't know that she found him."

"The bruises."

"Fineday says she fell."

"And he went charging out of the bar after she came home from that 'fall.' I'm betting he wasn't headed to a movie. It had to do with Jacoby. We both know that."

"We can speculate, but we don't really know." Cork settled back with a sigh. "They're afraid of something, it's clear. I'd love to know what she was running from when she ran to Stone."

"From her father?"

"Maybe. But why? He's a hard man, sure, but he'd never lay a finger on her."

From beyond Cork's door came the squawk of the radio in Dispatch and Patsy's voice responding.

"Another thing about these phone records," Cork said. "Not a single call to his wife or from her."

"So?"

"If you were gone from Alice for a week, wouldn't you call?"

"Sure."

"So why didn't Jacoby? And why didn't she call him? I'm just wondering if we ought to look at that marriage. It's an old adage but a good one that murder begins at home."

"I'll see what I can find out." Larson adjusted his glasses and tapped the phone records in his hand. "He may not have talked to his wife, but Jacoby sure talked to a lot of other people. His office in Elmhurst. New York. Las Vegas. And where exactly is Kenosha, Wisconsin?"

"South of Milwaukee, on Lake Michigan. May be a casino there."

"Makes sense," Larson said. "He also made a lot of calls to members of the Reservation Business Committee. Have you had a chance to talk to them?"

"Nobody at length. But I will. I know Lizzie looks good for this right now, but we need to keep checking all the possibilities. Have you been able to get anything on Eddie Jacoby's background?"

Larson took a notepad from his pocket. "I spoke with his boss at Starlight, a guy named Clayton. He said Jacoby'd been with them less than a year. I had the sense he wasn't going to be with them much longer."

"Why's that?"

"He wasn't representing Starlight well. Securing a contract with the Iron Lake Ojibwe was important for his career with the company."

"If he was dealing with Stone, he had to be desperate."

"Clayton said he hired him as a favor to Jacoby's brother. I asked about his employment record. He worked a string of jobs before Starlight, none very long."

"Dina told me he was into moviemaking for a while. Porn."

"Doesn't surprise me. Was he still into it when he was murdered?"

Cork shook his head. "Lost all his money, apparently."

"I spoke at length with his family before they left. Jacoby was married, two kids. Lived in Lake Forest not far from his father. He wasn't an easy son or sibling, I gather."

"Anything specific?"

"According to them, only minor scrapes with the law, nothing serious."

"You ask them about substance abuse?"

"Considering what we found in the glove box of his SUV, it was one of the first questions I asked. They claimed it was a surprise to them."

"A surprise? I doubt he was just experimenting."

"So did I. I checked for any criminal record. Nothing in Illinois. I called the Lake Forest police. They gave me nothing. But I can't help thinking that for a guy with an appetite for drugs and beating up prostitutes, he seems to have a suspiciously clean record."

"Maybe the Jacoby money has something to do with that. And maybe we need to check on him through a less official channel. I have a friend, a guy named Boomer Grabowski. We worked out of the same division when we were cops in Chicago. Boomer's a private investigator now, a good one. I think I ought to give him a call, see what he can dig up on Eddie Jacoby. Hell, on all the Jacobys. It'll cost us, but the budget's already shot."

"If you think it'll help. And you're the one who has to beg the Board of Commissioners for more money."

There was a knock at the open door. It was Patsy.

"Call for Ed."

"Put it through in here," Larson said.

A moment later, Cork's phone rang.

"Captain Larson," Ed said. He listened. "I see." He glanced at Cork, and something flared in his usual cool blue eyes. He took a pen from the desktop and jotted a couple of notes on the back of the top sheet of Jacoby's phone record. "You're certain?" He nodded at the answer. "I appreciate it. Thank you very much." He hung up.

"What is it?" Cork said.

"BCA's been helping us run the prints we took from the inside of Jacoby's SUV. Got an interesting match on one of them."

"No kidding. Who?"

"Lizzie Fineday."

They rendezvoused at the opening to the narrow dirt road off County 17 that led to Stone's cabin. Cork and Larson had come in the same vehicle, the Pathfinder. Morgan and Pender had been patrolling the eastern roads of Tamarack County and had been dispatched to accompany. Dina Willner was there, too.

"Stone's going to see us coming a long way off. That's all

right. We have a suspect, and so a lawful reason to be here. He shouldn't give us any resistance," Cork said. "If he does, we take him down right away, cuff him, book him for interfering with the execution of a lawful order. Morgan, Pender, that'll be your responsibility. Ed and I will conduct the search and apprehension of Lizzie Fineday. And, Dina, you're here by invitation, and I'd like you to stay well back." He lifted the back door of the Pathfinder and brought out a dark blue Kevlar vest with SHERIFF'S DEPT. printed in white letters across the back. He tossed it to her. "Wear this."

She caught it and put it on.

"Everybody else armored up? Then let's roll," he said.

It was late afternoon, the air still, the woods quiet. They drove through a thick stand of aspen that smelled of leaves fallen, dried, crumbling to dust. Breaking from the trees, they followed the shoreline of the narrow lake. Sun glinted off the water in piercing arrows of light. At the far end, wood smoke rose from Stone's cabin, straight and white as a feather. Behind it, like a prison wall, stood the gray ridge. Cork led the procession, his window down. There was no way to move quickly enough to surprise Stone. Cork couldn't help thinking of the raid on the farmhouse in Carlton County, how badly things had ended. You never knew. That was the hell of it: even with routine procedures, things could go wrong. You tried to be careful, to consider all the options, choose the best approach, but so much was out of your hands, beyond your control. In the end, you made your choice and went in hoping. Praying never hurt, either.

"Movement in front of the cabin," Larson said. He lifted a pair of Leitz binoculars to his eyes. "Stone."

"What's he doing?"

"Waving, it looks like."

"At who?"

"Nobody I can see. Toward the ridge. Now he's stopped. He's looking this way. Son of a gun. He's waving at us."

"Us?"

"Looks that way. Wait."

They kept moving, getting closer. Larson finally lowered the field glasses and laughed quietly.

"What?" Cork said.

"He's not waving. He's casting. He's got a fly rod in his hand."

They rounded the north end of the lake and climbed a rise to the cabin. Stone stood in front of his place, fifteen yards from the chopping block. He held the rod in his right hand and, with a deft snap of his wrist, flicked the line out again and again toward the chopping block. At his feet lay a zippered canvas bag long enough and wide enough to accommodate several rods fitted with reels. He paid no attention to the approaching vehicles.

Cork pulled up behind Stone's Land Rover, which was parked in the shade of a paper birch. He got out and Larson did, too. The deputies halted farther back and exited their cruisers. Dina stayed in her Accord as Cork had asked.

"Afternoon, Byron," Cork said.

"Sheriff." Stone watched the thread of fishing line sail out. The end touched almost dead center on top of the chopping block. He wore olive jeans, a long-sleeved wool shirt also green but of a lighter shade, with the sleeves rolled up to reveal his powerful muscles. His black hair was tied back with a folded bandanna of gold and green. "Looks like D-day. What's with all the troops?"

"We're here for Lizzie."

"Too late. She's already gone."

"Where?"

"Search me. I went into Allouette after lunch. When I came back, she was gone."

"Did someone come to get her?"

"I don't know."

"Why did she leave?"

"Same reason she came, I suppose. It suited her."

Stone whipped his arm back and the line arced through the air, catching the sunlight along its whole length so that for an instant it appeared to glow as if electric.

"Byron, I have an order authorizing me to pick up and detain Elizabeth Fineday for questioning in connection with the murder of Edward Jacoby. That order authorizes me to search your property for Lizzie."

"Be my guest. Mind if I keep working on my technique?"

"Morgan, Pender," Cork said. "Keep him company while Captain Larson and I have a look inside."

"Sure thing, Sheriff," Morgan replied.

Cork saw that Dina had left her car and was making her way to the back of the deputies' cruisers, keeping them between herself and any threat Stone might pose. He wondered what she was up to.

He held the screen door open for Larson, who went into the cabin first. Cork had been inside twice before, once with ATF and a couple years later with DEA. The place looked as spotless now as it had on the other two occasions. Once the casino allotments began to be distributed to the enrolled members of the band, some Iron Lake Ojibwe had gone a little crazy, packing their homes to the rafters with all manner of junk, feeding appetites generated by the sudden wealth. Stone continued to live simply. The Land Rover outside was his only obvious extravagance.

He'd built the cabin himself, a simple square divided into four rooms: a main living area, a kitchen, a bathroom, and a small bedroom. The wide window in the living area looked toward the lake. Cork suspected the beautiful view wasn't the only reason for its location. Through that window, Stone could see anything approaching along the road. The walls were bare logs, no paneling to hide insulation. Stone had cut the trees, planed and notched the logs so that they fit perfectly. The winter wind could not penetrate. He'd drilled his own well, put in his own septic system, had done all the wiring and plumbing himself. The electricity came from his own generator. He probably had ignored codes, but no inspector ever bothered to check. When dealing with Stone, most people didn't sweat the small things.

They went through the cabin, found no sign of Lizzie, not even any evidence that she'd been there. They stepped back outside.

Stone hadn't moved. With the canvas bag of rods on the ground at his feet, he still cast his line at the chopping block. Morgan and Pender watched him closely, and no one uttered a word. Dina was lurking behind Stone's Land Rover.

"She cleaned up after herself pretty well," Cork said.

"Didn't she?" Stone replied.

"Morgan, you got a cell phone?"

"In my cruiser."

"Call the North Star Bar, find out if Lizzie Fineday is there."

Morgan started to turn.

"Cell phones don't work here," Stone said. He nodded toward the gray ridge at his back. "It's the iron in the rock. Interferes with the signal."

"Try it anyway," Cork said to Morgan. "If he's right, relay the request to dispatch and have Patsy make the call."

Morgan hopped to it.

"I'd like you to come with us into town, Byron, answer a few questions about Lizzie."

"Got a warrant? No? Then you know I don't have to go. I'm content here."

"All right. While she was here, did Lizzie say anything to you about Edward Jacoby?"

"Most of the time she slept. She needed the rest."

"You didn't answer my question."

"No. The answer is no."

"Her face was bruised. Did she tell you how that happened?"

"I believe she fell."

"She told you that?"

"That's what she said."

From behind Stone's Land Rover, Dina called, "What time did you get back from Allouette today?"

Stone turned his attention away from the fishing line to the woman. His eyebrows arched as if he were surprised, only just now aware of her presence. Histrionics, Cork knew, because Stone didn't miss a thing.

"I heard you were pretty," he said. "And that you like to flash your breasts around."

"When *did* you get back from Allouette?" Cork said.

"Couple of hours ago."

"Engine's still warm," Dina said to Cork.

Stone went back to his casting. "I left again and came back again."

"Where?" Cork said.

"Brandywine. Had business at the mill there. You can check. But what difference does it make? Am I a suspect?"

"Sheriff," Morgan hollered from his cruiser. "Patsy says Lizzie's not at the North Star. Will Fineday claims he hasn't seen her since he was out here the other day."

"If I wanted to protect my daughter, I'd claim the same thing," Stone said. "On the other hand, Lizzie's lived on the rez her whole life. She's got friends, other relatives. Seems to me you've got a lot of checking to do, Sheriff. I'd get started if I were you."

Cork looked back at the empty cabin. He thought about warning Stone that if he was hiding Lizzie he'd be in trouble, but he knew Stone didn't care. "Pack it up," he said to the others. "Let's get out of here."

Under Stone's intransigent eye, they turned their vehicles and headed back the way they'd come. This time Dina Willner led the way. At the junction with the county road, she pulled over and got out. The two cruisers rolled past and braked to a halt ahead of her. Cork drew alongside and leaned out his window.

"What is it?"

"The cast of the tire tracks out at the Tibodeau cabin. What kind of tires did you say those were?"

"Goodyear Wranglers. MT/Rs, I think. Why?"

"Stone's got Goodyear Wranglers on his Land Rover. MT/Rs, and they're new."

Cork looked over at Larson.

Larson said, "You think?"

Dina said, "At the Tibodeau cabin, you had two people, probably a man and a woman, involved in the shooting. They knew the reservation well enough to know the Tibodeaus would be gone. At least one of them understood how to plan an ambush. And they escaped in a vehicle sporting Goodyear MT/Rs. You told me Lizzie wants to be an actress. Could she do a pretty good imitation of Lucy Tibodeau, do you think?"

"I imagine," Cork said.

"And is Stone a decent shot?"

"Stone's an excellent shot. Been hunting all his life."

"I don't know why they'd do it, but they certainly seem to me like prime suspects in that shooting," Dina concluded.

"Why didn't you say something back at the cabin?" Larson asked.

"Did you see the canvas bag at his feet?"

"For his rods?"

"He never moved a foot from that bag. I'm betting it wasn't fishing rods he had in there."

"A rifle?" Cork said.

"It seemed like a possibility to me. And if he is the shooter, it's likely that he's using armor-piercing ammunition. It didn't seem prudent to challenge him at that point. People could have been hurt."

"Let's go back now," Larson said.

Dina shook her head. "I wouldn't if I were you. He saw me looking at the tires. He pretended not to, but he did."

"Would he know about the tracks he left?" Larson said.

"Our people have been all over the county asking about those tires." Cork thought it over. "Let's see if we can get a warrant and go in after dark."

32

BEN JACOBY POINTED toward a bright pinpoint of light in the sky just above the horizon.

"First star on the left," he said, "and straight on till morning."

They were seated in a booth at Lord Jim's, a restaurant at the exclusive North Lake Marina near Evanston, looking east over the inky evening blue of Lake Michigan.

"Neverland," Jo said.

"That's where I'd love to be headed." Jacoby sat back. "Rough day." He wore a gray suit, white shirt, blue tie. He'd come from the office, he said, although he looked freshly shaved. "But it's better now. And thanks."

"For what?"

"Agreeing to have a drink with me. How did it go at Northwestern? Did you like your guide?"

"He was quite a surprise."

"A pleasant one, I hope. He did it as a favor for his old man. A good son."

Jo noted that he spoke of Phillip with more enthusiasm than Phillip had shown when speaking of him.

"Did Jenny like the campus?" he asked.

"She was thrilled."

"Great. Look, if she needs anything, a recommendation, help with her acceptance—"

"She doesn't."

"I'm just saying that a word from me wouldn't hurt. And I'd be happy to."

"Jenny will get in or not on her own merit."

"Just like her mother."

He'd ordered Scotch for himself and for Jo a chardonnay. He drank and looked melancholy.

"Halston," Jo said, noting the scent of his cologne. "You still wear it."

"You bought me Halston on my twenty-seventh birthday. It's all I wear. Like Proust says, smells transport us in time." He sipped from his drink. "You ever miss Chicago?"

"Some things."

"Like what?"

"The blues bars."

"Blues bars? We never went to the blues bars."

"Cork and I," she said.

"Oh. Sure."

"Ben, my life in Aurora is good and I don't regret leaving anything behind."

He looked hard at her face, searched her eyes. Finally he said, "I'm happy for you, then."

A passenger jet flew overhead, banked south, circled back toward O'Hare, high enough that it caught the rays of the sun, which was already below the horizon, and for a few moments it glowed like a giant ember.

"I never told you why I left you," he said.

"No, you never did."

He shifted uncomfortably, watched the plane slide out of sight. "When I met you I was already promised to someone else."

"You were engaged?"

"Not exactly. It was an arranged marriage. There are still such things. I knew from the time I was very young that I would marry Miriam. My father had arranged it, an agreement with his business partner, Miriam's father. It was conceived as a union of great fortunes, and it was. Her family, my family, everyone wanted it."

"So, was I a complication or simply a diversion?" The acid in her tone surprised her, and she saw Jacoby flinch.

"You were love," he said. "I wanted to tell you, to explain everything, but there never seemed a right time. I always thought that in the end I might make a different decision. When I walked out that night, I knew I was turning my back on happiness. I told you I didn't have a choice, but I did. I chose family." He breathed deeply, his broad shoulders rising. "Sometimes when my father stood up for Eddie, protecting him after the schmuck had done another stupid or cruel thing, I'd shake my head and wonder. I have a son now, and I understand. People fall out of love, but family is different.

"You told me about your mother, the Captain, about how awful you had it growing up, all the moving and the drinking and the fighting. That was your experience. Mine was different. My father isn't perfect, but I grew up knowing he loved me, knowing my family loved me. The idea of turning my back on them . . ." He shrugged. "I just couldn't do it. So I gave you up. I gave up love."

"You could have told me all this then instead of just walking out."

"Would it have made a difference? Would it have hurt you any less? Would it have made me any less a bastard in your eyes? I'd seen you argue on behalf of your storefront clients. I didn't want you to dissuade me from what I believed to be the right thing. And you found happiness. You met Cork. Me, my whole life I've loved one woman, and I didn't marry her."

"People fall out of love, you said. But love also fades, Ben, especially if it isn't nurtured."

"That's not been my experience." He finished his drink and signaled for another. "I have a confession. When I found out that Eddie was dealing with you in Aurora, I imagined for a little while that I might be able to step back into your life, still somehow create everything we might have had together. Then I saw your family and Cork and how happy you are, and I knew it was stupid and impossible." He looked out the window, stared into the distance above the cold lake water. "In the end everything fades but family, doesn't it?"

His cell phone bleated and he answered it, listened, and smiled. "I'm at a bar, actually. You'll never guess who with. Nancy Jo McKenzie." He laughed. "No, really. Would you like to talk to her?" He glanced at Jo with a welcome humor in his eyes. "I'll ask but my guess would be no." He said to Jo, "It's my sister Rae. You remember her?"

"Of course."

"She's at my father's house. We're sitting shivah tonight for Eddie. Rae wants you to drop by so that she can say hello in person."

"I don't think so, Ben."

"We're just fifteen minutes away. Stay fifteen minutes and leave. It would be less than an hour out of your life."

"I'm not dressed—"

"You look fine. It would thrill Rae no end. Please."

Jo thought it over. "All right. Fifteen minutes."

Along Lake Drive in Lake Forest, the homes became palatial. Jacoby pulled through a gate and into a circular drive that was lined with cars. Jo, who'd followed in her Toyota, parked behind his Mercedes, got out, and joined him.

"Very rococo," she said, looking at the house.

"My grandfather had it built to remind him of Italy, where he studied as a young man. The happiest time of his life, he used to say. He came to America to seek his fortune, something that didn't make him very happy, I can vouch for that."

"Looks like he succeeded in making the fortune."

"He was a harsh man in a lot of ways, but he knew how to handle money." He took her arm and gave her a brave smile. "You ready for this?"

As they neared the front door, a Jeep Cherokee pulled into the drive and parked behind Jo's Toyota. A six-footer got out, attractive, with long dark hair, thirtyish.

"Just arriving, Ben?" There was a Spanish roll to his r's.

"Good evening, Tony."

Tony looked long and appreciatively at Jo.

"Tony, this is Jo O'Connor. Jo, Tony Salguero."

He wrapped Jo's hand very warmly in his own. "You're here because of Eddie? Did you know him well?"

"Not well."

"A pity, his death." Tony turned his attention to Ben. "By the way, that package I flew back from Aurora. Any word?"

"Aurora?" Jo said. "Minnesota?"

"That's right."

Ben said, "Tony flew some samples back yesterday for DNA testing."

"My husband is Sheriff O'Connor," Jo told her.

"Your husband?" He looked to Ben, then back to Jo, and smiled wickedly. "A long way from home, are you not?"

"What about the DNA?" Jo said.

"They were hairs taken from Eddie's SUV," Ben explained. "And a cigarette that had been smoked by a woman in Aurora. There's a lab here that's doing a match. Your husband thinks the woman might have been with Eddie the night he was murdered."

"What woman?"

"Her name is Fineday."

"Lizzie?"

"You know her?"

"I know who she is. Is she a suspect?"

"Dina reports that she's the focus of the investigation at the moment."

She was thinking like a defense attorney, thinking that Lizzie's presence in the SUV meant nothing in itself. There had to be more to tie her to Jacoby's murder.

Jacoby said to Tony, "Why don't we go inside. Gabriella is there, I'm sure."

A cadaverous white-haired man in a black suit opened the door for them all.

"Good evening, Evers," Jacoby said.

"Mr. Jacoby," Evers replied with a trace of a bow. "Mr. Salguero."

"Everyone here?" Ben asked.

"They come and go, sir. May I take your wrap?" he asked Jo.

"We won't be long," Jo said.

"Safer to surrender it," Ben advised her.

Tony left them as Jo removed her coat and handed it to Evers.

Beyond the expansive foyer, the house opened left and right onto huge rooms filled with people. Some of the guests wore black, but many—the family members, like Ben—had only a torn black ribbon pinned to a lapel or bodice. They didn't appear necessarily to be dressed for mourning, but all were dressed elegantly.

Ben led her into a room dominated by a Steinway baby grand. There were two mirrors in the room, both completely covered by fabric to block any reflection, a custom of sitting shivah, Jo figured. Seeing them arrive, a woman separated herself from a small group on the far side of the Steinway.

"Ben," she said, languorously drawing out the word. She took both his hands and kissed him on the cheek. Her hair, dark red and expensively cut, brushed against her shoulders. Her face, tight skin over wonderfully sculptured bones, was so skillfully made up, Jo guessed it had been done professionally. She carried herself with finishing-school panache. Although her dress was the appropriate color for the occasion, it was cut low enough to show off substantial cleavage with freckles like splashes of rusty water. She looked forty, although Jo had the feeling that she was much older. "I'm so sorry."

"Thank you, Rachel."

Rachel seemed to notice Jo as an afterthought. "I don't believe I've had the pleasure."

"This is Jo O'Connor. An old friend. Jo, Rachel Herschel."

"How do you do?" Rachel's eyes cut into Jo, but she forced a smile, then looked back at Jacoby in a knowing way. "Lovely," she said, with an edge of ice.

"Have you seen my father?"

"It seems to me he was heading toward the veranda. For a cigar, no doubt." She still hadn't let go of Jacoby's hands. "I'd love to have a moment to talk with you. It's been . . . a while."

"Call me," he said, extracting his hands and looking past her toward a set of French doors on the far side of the room.

"Of course." She gave Jo another lengthy appraisal, pursed her pomegranate-red lips, and turned abruptly back to the piano.

They made their way through groups that were like floating islands on the soft white sea of carpet. Everywhere it was the same. Jacoby was greeted heartily, sometimes greedily, and Jo was addressed through a veil of civility that barely hid the looks of appraisal and approval, as if she were something that had been bought at auction for a good price.

Jacoby finally reached the French doors and opened them for Jo to pass through ahead of him. Outside on the veranda, the air was cool. Jo could see the back of the estate stretching to the lake, the long expanse of lawn turned nearly charcoal in the fading light. The water of an unlit swimming pool flashed now and again with a reflection from the windows of the big house. In a corner of the veranda sat a man in a great chair of white wicker, the glow of a cigar reddening his pinched, narrow face, lighting a dull fire in his eyes as he stared at Jo and Ben Jacoby.

"Escaping, Dad?" Ben said.

"What needs taking care of is being seen to. Has there been any more word from Minnesota?"

"Nothing from Dina."

"What about that yokel sheriff?"

"There's someone here you should meet," Jacoby said.

"I don't want to meet anyone right now."

"This is Jo O'Connor. She's the wife of Sheriff Corcoran O'Connor in Aurora."

The cigar reddened considerably. "When your husband has the murderer of my son in jail, Ms. O'Connor, I'll gladly take back the *yokel*."

"I'm sure my husband is doing everything possible to make that happen."

"Why are you here?"

"I asked her, Dad. Her daughter's applying to Northwestern. They came to see the campus."

Lou Jacoby took the cigar from his mouth and studied the long ash beyond the ember. "You know each other?"

"I told you," Jacoby said. "We went to law school together."

"That's right." He seemed to be putting it together now. "You were Eddie's attorney in that town."

"Not exactly," Jo said. "I represent the Iron Lake Ojibwe. Your son was trying to negotiate a management contract with their casino."

"That have anything to do with his murder?"

"I can't imagine that it did, but that's really a question my husband should answer."

"Does he confide in you?"

"Sometimes. In this, he's told me nothing that you probably don't already know."

He slipped the cigar back into his mouth, took a long draw, and sent out enough smoke to temporarily obscure his face. "Then I don't really want to talk to you right now, Ms. O'Connor. You either, Ben boy. I'd rather just be alone."

"All right," Jacoby said dutifully. He opened the French doors and waited for Jo.

"Grief can be blinding," Jo said, standing her ground. "But at some point, you're going to have to take a good long look at the man Eddie was."

"You think I don't know? Hell, I know all about my son."

"And loved him anyway," Ben said bitterly.

"I told you, I want to be alone."

Without another word, Jacoby strode back into the house. In the corner of the veranda, the cigar flared and little points of fire lit the old man's eyes as he glared at Jo.

"He's got himself a little blond shiksa this time," he said. "A shiksa with spine."

Jo turned and followed Jacoby.

She caught up with him in another room where he'd stopped under a chandelier to speak with a black-haired beauty who had two young boys at her side. As Jo neared them, the woman looked her way.

"Jo," Jacoby said, "this is Gabriella. Eddie's widow."

"How do you do?" Gabriella spoke softly and, like Tony Salguero, with a Spanish accent. She offered a tanned hand with nails red as rose petals. A diamond tennis bracelet sparkled on her wrist.

"I'm sorry about your husband," Jo said.

"Ben told me you worked with Eddie in Minnesota."

"Not significantly."

"Mommy," one of the boys said. He was perhaps five years old, with his mother's black hair and fine face, his father's insolent eyes. "I'm *tired*. I wanna *go*."

"Find your cousin Mark, play with him."

"Mark's a dork," the other boy said. Similar features, older by maybe a year, bored out of his skull.

Gabriella smiled, leaned down, and kissed her son's black hair. *"Pobrecito,"* she said. "Find your uncle George, then. He will entertain you."

The two boys wandered off, defeated.

Gabriella turned back to Jo. "I'm sorry. Eddie kept business to himself, so I don't know anything what he was doing in Minnesota. I hope his death . . ." She hesitated. "I hope his death does not inconvenience you."

Inconvenience? Jo thought.

"Excuse me, please." Gabriella went in the direction her sons had gone.

"She's from Argentina," Ben explained. "Her family have been clients for years, but the economy there is shot to hell. My father and her father made the arrangements for the marriage. Eddie sure got the better end of that deal. Poor Gabriella, she had no idea what she was getting herself into."

"Jo!"

She turned as a woman swept toward her across the room. There was a bit of gray in her hair, a few lines at the edges of her mouth and eyes. Unlike so many of the other women Jo had seen that evening, she didn't seem especially concerned about fighting time and age. She was smallish, a little round, and had a wry smile on her face. Although two decades had passed, Jo had no trouble recognizing Ben's sister, Rae.

"This is wonderful." Rae threw her arms around Jo. "I can't believe I'm seeing you again after all these years. How are you?"

"Good. And you?"

"Marvelous. Couldn't be better." She looked Jo over and shook her head as if in disbelief. "Twenty years and you're still gorgeous. Come on, let's go somewhere and sit down. I want to hear all about you."

"What about me?" Ben said.

"Go have a drink, Benny. I'll fetch you when I'm done with her."

Before they could move, from outside came the crunch of metal and the shatter of glass. People crowded the front windows, and someone called, "Ben, you better get out there."

Jacoby moved quickly. Jo and Rae followed.

Outside, they found Phillip Jacoby standing beside a Jaguar that had plowed into one of the brick pillars that flanked the entrance to the drive. He was staggering a little but seemed unhurt. A woman, also unharmed, stood near him, her arms crossed as if she were cold.

Phillip pointed at the pillar. "That damn thing's been out to get me for years."

"You've been drinking," his father said.

"I'm still drinking." He reached into the Jag and hauled out a bottle of Cuervo Gold. He put his arm around the waist of the woman, several years his senior, with brassy gold hair and dressed in a tight midnight-blue dress that was too skimpy for the cool evening, though it did advertise very nicely her wares.

"This your place?" she said to Ben with a slur.

Jacoby extended his hand. "Give me your keys, Phillip."

"Like hell."

"Give me your car keys. You're in no condition to drive."

"My fucking car," Phillip said.

"My fucking insurance," Jacoby shot back.

"Come on, Phil baby," the woman in the blue dress said. "This is a drag."

"Don't worry, baby, we're getting out of here."

He turned toward the Jag. Ben caught his arm, spun him, and used his son's drunken disequilibrium to throw him to the ground, where he pinned him quickly with his knee against his chest. The young man struggled briefly, then gave in.

"I'll take those keys." Jacoby reached into the pocket of his son's pants and extracted a plastic Baggie and a key ring. He studied the Baggie.

"Ecstasy? A parting gift from Uncle Eddie?"

Phillip glared up at him, his eyes bloodshot, his nostrils wet with mucus. "Fuck you."

Ben stood up, taking his weight off his son. "Get up. I'm driving you back to campus. We'll drop your friend wherever she wants."

Phillip picked himself up. He kicked at the bottle of tequila, which had fallen from his hand when his father tackled him. "I'll walk." He spun away and staggered from the drive into the street.

His woman companion watched him go, then said in a quiet voice, "I don't want to walk."

"I'll call you a cab," Ben told her.

She seemed to realize how alone and out of place she was. She folded her arms across her thin body.

"Why don't you come inside and wait," Rae said. She turned to Jo. "I'd love to talk, but this probably isn't the best time. Maybe lunch tomorrow?"

"I'm at the zoo with the kids."

"What if I met you there?"

"All right."

"What time?"

"Eleven. At the sea lion pool."

"I'll be there."

Rae turned her attention to the woman, who'd made no move yet to go inside. "Come with me," she said gently. "It'll be all right."

Most of those who'd come out had, by now, returned to the house. The others followed Rae inside.

Jo walked to Ben, who was inspecting the damage to the Jaguar.

"I'll give him a few minutes to cool down and sober up, then I'll go after him." He shook his head. "I'm sorry. I didn't imagine this was the way the evening would end. I guess I've never been very good at endings, huh?"

"Good night, Ben."

She kissed his cheek softly and left him standing beside the ruined car, looking toward the dark that had swallowed his son.

33

THEY MOVED ON Stone's cabin after nightfall, before the moon rose. Cork, Larson, Rutledge, Willner, and a dozen deputies. They went silently, on foot, in armor, and carrying assault rifles, semiautomatic AR-15s. In the trees that crowded the dirt road, the black was almost impenetrable, but as they filed along the lake with the open sky above them, the ambient light of the stars lit their way. Ahead, the ridge behind Stone's cabin cut a jagged silhouette against the star-dusted sky. Several of the men, including Cork and Larson, had night vision goggles. They crept single file up the rise that led to the cabin, which was completely dark. Cork put on his goggles.

"His Land Rover's there," he whispered to Larson, who was donning his own goggles.

Cork scanned the yard, empty except for the chopping block. He signaled and four deputies, with Morgan in charge, slipped along the edge of the trees outlining the yard and took up positions behind the cabin. Four others, led by Larson, spread themselves out in front undercover or in prone positions with a good line of sight. Rutledge and Willner stayed well back. Cork and the remaining deputies cautiously approached the front door.

Unlike many Ojibwe on the rez and the rural people of Tamarack County in general, Stone kept no dog to bark a warning. This may have been because he was gone for long periods of time, disappearing into the Boundary Waters, and a dog would be neglected. Cork thought it might also have been that Stone was a man for whom companionship, even that of a dog, was not only unnecessary, it was unwanted. Whatever the reason, Cork was grateful for the absence of any animal that might sound an alarm.

The curtains across the front window were drawn shut. There was no porch. He walked the hard ground silently and put his ear to the front door, listened for a full minute, then stepped back. Schilling and Pender readied the battering ram. On his signal, the two deputies splintered the pine boards.

"Police," Cork shouted and rushed in. He glanced left, right. The room, luminescent green through the goggles, was vacant. The bathroom door was open, showing only empty space. "The bedroom," he said to the others, and motioned his deputies to flank the closed door.

He stood off to the side. "Stone, this is Sheriff O'Connor. I have a warrant for your arrest. Come out now with your hands in the air."

They waited. Cork's heart hammered in his chest. He wanted this to be over quickly and cleanly, without shooting, without blood.

"Lizzie, are you in there?" he called.

Still no response. Cork tried the knob. Although it turned, the door didn't open. Latched from the inside. Pender and Schilling had come into the cabin. He motioned them into position to use the ram. On his signal, they swung it forward and sent the door tumbling off its hinges. Immediately, they fell back, out of the line of fire through the doorway. Cork waited again, ready for gunshots, but heard only the heavy breathing of his own men. He waved the deputies to follow and swung into Stone's bedroom.

The room was empty, the bed made, everything left in neat order like a hotel room awaiting the next guest.

Cork unclipped the walkie-talkie from his belt. "All clear. Repeat, all clear. The chicken has flown the coop."

They drove the vehicles up from the county road and parked with the lights shining on the cabin. Cork and those in charge stood outside the glare. The moon wasn't visible yet, but there was a strong glow coming from behind the eastern hills. It washed out the stars on the horizon.

"Morgan's certain no one came or left between our visit this afternoon and the raid," Larson said. "The Land Rover's still here. Wherever Stone's gone, he's on foot."

"Into the Boundary Waters," Cork said. "I can almost guarantee it. He knows those woods."

"He can't hide there forever," Rutledge said.

Cork shook his head. "Stone's one of the few people who probably could."

"Maybe he's trying to make it across the border into Canada." Larson waved vaguely to the north. "Or slip out of the woods somewhere far away."

"And what? Start over?" Cork didn't hide his skepticism.

"What do you think, then?"

"I'm not sure. None of this has made a lot of sense so far."

Dina Willner spoke up. "What about Lizzie Fineday?"

Earlier, they'd checked with relatives and friends. No one admitted having any knowledge of her whereabouts. Cork believed Stone had lied that afternoon when he said she was gone.

"I think we can assume he has her," Cork said.

"Why would he take her?" Rutledge asked.

"I can think of at least three reasons. The best face to put on it would be that he's trying to protect her. Or that he's got a hostage if he's cornered."

"You said three reasons," Willner pointed out.

"He might be thinking she's the only witness against him in the shooting at the Tibodeau cabin and he'd rather not have her found. Period." Cork turned to Larson. "Any word from Borkmann?"

As soon as they were certain the area was secure, Cork had directed his chief deputy to drive to the North Star Bar, apprise Will Fineday of what was going on, and escort him to Stone's place.

"He's on his way with Fineday. ETA fifteen minutes," Larson said.

The cough of a gas engine turning over hit the quiet of the night, and a moment later, the engine settled into a steady thrum.

"Good," Cork said. "Schilling's got the generator going. Let's get some lights on inside."

Larson started in that direction with Cork right behind him, but Morgan called to him from a cruiser, "Cork, it's Bos on the radio for you," and the sheriff turned back.

"This is Cork. Go ahead."

"Sorry to take you away, Cork, but Jo just called. She's been trying to get hold of you. She sounded worried."

An hour before hard dark, he'd tried to call her. He didn't know what he might be walking into at Stone's cabin, and he wanted to hear Jo's voice, hear that the children were having a good time, that everyone was safe. Rose told him that Jo had gone out for the evening. A drink with Ben Jacoby. He'd chatted with his sister-in-law, then talked with each of his children. Jenny told him about her tour of Northwestern. Mr. Jacoby had arranged it, she said, had pulled strings. Cork told her that was a nice thing for him to have done. He told them all that he loved them, and at the end he thanked Rose for taking them in. "Should I have Jo call back?" she'd asked. "No," Cork had replied. "Not necessary. Just tell her I love her."

Afterward, he'd thought darkly, *Jacoby.*

"Any message, Bos?" Cork said over the radio.

"She just asked that you call her back as soon as you can."

"Did you tell her anything about what's going on up here?"

"Not a word. Didn't want her to worry. I told her you were on a late call. Routine."

"Thanks, Bos. Out."

Cork headed to the cabin where Dina Willner stood looking through the door as Larson moved about carefully inside, trying not to disturb the scene any more than Cork and his men already had.

"No sign she was ever here," Larson said, adjusting his wire-rims. "Was she hiding, you think, when we came this afternoon?"

It was a question with a hidden implication: that maybe Stone had already taken care of her for good, hidden the body somewhere, and cleaned away all trace of her presence.

"I don't know," Cork said.

He heard the cruiser coming up the road and headed down

to meet it. Before Borkmann or Pender could exit the vehicle, Will Fineday was out and charging at Cork like an angry moose.

"You found her?" he said.

"Not yet, Will."

"I'll kill him," Fineday said. "I should have killed him the other day."

"When she ran, Will, why did she come here to Stone?"

"She was scared, not thinking. Stone, he's a son of a bitch, but everybody's afraid of him. She thought he could protect her."

"From what?"

"You guys. She didn't want to talk to cops."

"We know she was in the SUV with Jacoby the night he was killed. Was it Jacoby who bruised her face?"

"The son of a bitch. When I found out, I wanted to kill him."

"Did you?"

It was clear Fineday understood the direction this was going. Cork could see the struggle in the man's head and his heart. The truth might land him a view cut by iron bars, but it might also save his daughter.

"You went to Mercy Falls that night, didn't you, Will?" Cork said it quietly, and not as an accusation.

The threads—fear, distrust, prejudice—that had held him from speaking finally snapped and he nodded. "He was already dead when I got there, lying on the ground, blood everywhere. Somebody had cut his balls off, too. Shame. I wanted to do that myself."

"Did Lizzie kill Edward Jacoby?"

"No, but I'd've understood if she did. The asshole beat her and raped her."

"She told you she didn't kill Jacoby?"

"Until I came back from Mercy Falls, she didn't even know he was dead."

"You believed her?"

"Yeah, I believed her."

"Did you do anything at Mercy Falls?"

"Like what?"

"Interfere with the scene."

Fineday studied the sky. "Maybe I wiped the door handles clean."

"'Maybe'?"

"I didn't want Lizzie's fingerprints there, okay? I picked up some beer bottles that might have had her prints on them."

"Nothing else?"

"Nothing, I swear."

"If you'd told me all this before, it might've saved a lot of trouble, Will."

Fineday's hard brown eyes leveled on him. "If you were full-blood or at least not a cop, maybe you'd understand." He looked toward the cabin. "Where are they?"

"We think Stone went north, into the woods."

"He knows the Boundary Waters better than anyone." Fineday's eyes traveled over the ridge that lay between the cabin and everything beyond. "He took her with him, didn't he?"

"Maybe."

"When I find him, I'll tear out his goddamned heart."

"Cork," Larson called from the cabin. "Something here you've got to see."

Cork walked to where Larson and Dina Willner awaited him at the door. "What is it?"

"Follow me."

Larson led the way to the bedroom and stepped over the door that lay on the floor, torn off its hinges. He leaned over the bed and pointed toward an indentation in the pillow.

Cork took a step and saw what Larson meant. A large-caliber rifle bullet had been carefully placed in the center of the pillow.

"Jacketed round," Cork said. "Just like the ones fired at the Tibodeau cabin."

"It didn't get there by accident," Dina said.

Larson glanced at Cork. "What do you think it means?"

Cork crossed to the back window, pulled aside the curtain, shielded the glass so that he could see beyond the reflection of the room light. He stared out at the black silhouette of the ridge.

"It means we've got a long night ahead."

34

Mal and the children had gone to bed, but Rose was waiting up when Jo got home. There was a low fire under the kettle on the stove and two mugs on the kitchen table, each with a bag of Sleepytime tea hung over the lip.

Rose turned up the flame under the kettle. "Have a good evening?"

"A weird evening."

"You can tell me all about it in a minute. First you need to call Cork."

"He called?"

"Yes. Not long after you left."

"What did you tell him?"

Rose looked a little puzzled by Jo's concern. "That you went out for a drink with Ben Jacoby. What is it, Jo?"

"Let me call Cork, then we'll talk."

She tried him at home and got voice mail. She called the sheriff's office and Bos told her Cork was on a call. Routine.

"Routine?" Jo said. "It's almost ten o'clock, Bos."

"I can radio and let him know you called. Want a call back?"

"Yes. Please. As soon as he can."

"Sure thing. Miss him, do you?"

"Like crazy."

"I'll let him know."

When Jo returned to the kitchen, the kettle was just starting to whistle. Rose poured hot water into the mugs and sat down at the table with her sister. All their lives, long before Jo met Cork, before Rose fell in love with Mal, it had been like this, the two sisters and tea. In the places their mother, an army nurse whom they called the Captain, had dragged them, the desolate bases, the bleak military housing. None of that mattered because they'd had the comfort of their love for each other, embodied in late night cups of tea and talk.

"All right," Rose said. "What don't I know about Ben Jacoby?"

Jo told her the whole story.

"And I thought I knew everything about you." Rose sipped her tea. "But your relationship with him was a long time ago."

"I thought so, too. Then I saw him in Aurora, Rose, and for just a little while all the old feelings, I don't know, tried to come back."

"And?"

"I let myself feel them. And I realized absolutely there was room only for Cork in my life."

"So what's the problem?"

"For Ben it's been different, all these years."

"He's carried a torch?"

"That's what he says. I need to talk to Cork as soon as possible. God only knows what he must be thinking."

Stevie wandered into the kitchen looking half asleep. "I had a bad dream."

"Well, come on, big guy, let's get you back into bed." Jo took his hand. "Thanks for the company, Rose. You know I miss you in Aurora."

"I miss you, too. If Cork calls . . . ?"

"Wake me."

She led Stevie back to bed, got ready herself, and slipped under the covers. She tried to stay awake, waiting for Cork's call. Finally, sleep overtook her.

The call she was waiting for never came.

35

AT FIRST LIGHT, the tracking dogs began sniffing the area around Stone's cabin. Stone's scent was everywhere, but the scent of Lizzie Fineday led straight through the trees, over the ridge that backed the cabin, to Bruno Lake. It was the first in a series of lakes that led deep into the Boundary Waters Canoe Area Wilderness.

The dogs halted briefly at a large dock on the southeastern shore of the lake, deep in the shadow of the ridge. Cork and the others stood at the end of the dock, breathing hard from the fast hike over the ridge, puffing out clouds of vapor into the cold, damp air above Bruno Lake while the dogs went on, working the ground along the shoreline.

"What do you make of it?" Rutledge asked.

"Big dock," Cork said. "There's no access to Bruno except on foot or by canoe. Not the kind of traffic that would require a dock. I think this is for floatplanes."

"For trafficking?" Larson said.

"That would sure be my guess." Cork briefed Rutledge on the investigations his department had conducted earlier with the ATF and the DEA. "We never saw any sign of smuggling, probably because this ridge provides perfect cover. You can't see the lake except from the air, and I'll bet the ridge blocks the sound of a plane engine."

The sun had risen enough to fire the far shoreline, and the mist on the water there looked like steam coming from a cauldron. In a stand of gnarled cedars fifty yards down the shore, one of the dogs began barking furiously.

Rutledge looked toward the cedars. "What's all that ruckus about?"

As if in answer, Deputy Schilling called from the trees, "Cork, something here you ought to see."

"What?"

"Looks like a grave."

A faint trail had already been broken through the brush along the shore. Cork followed and near the end climbed over a fallen and rotting pine. He stepped into the cedars whose smell was sharp in the morning air. Orville Gratz, who'd brought the dogs, had pulled his hound back. The animal sat on its haunches, tongue hanging out, looking where Schilling looked, at a mound of rocks that had been piled in the middle of the cedars. The mound was two feet wide and five feet long, and looked as if it hadn't been there very long.

"Lancelot followed the girl's scent here," Gratz said. He didn't sound thrilled with the discovery.

Cork said to Schilling, "Get Cy over here with the Polaroid."

For a minute, no one spoke. The other dogs were still moving along the shoreline, their barks punctuating the silence in the cedars. Then Rutledge said quietly, "The son of a bitch."

Schilling brought Borkmann and the Polaroid.

"We need shots of that rock pile, Cy," Cork said.

Borkmann was still sweating from the exertion of the climb over the ridge, but he positioned himself and shot from several angles.

"All right, let's see what's under there," Cork said.

He approached the stones, bent, and began removing them carefully, piling them behind him. Rutledge joined him. Within a few minutes, they'd cleared the rocks away and had exposed a small area of newly dug earth. It was only a few feet long, however, much too small to accommodate a body fully laid out. Cork and Rutledge dug in the dirt with their hands, slowly clearing a shallow basin. A flash of blue appeared. Cork remembered that the last time he'd seen Lizzie Fineday in front of Stone's cabin, blinking in the sun, she'd been wearing a sweater that same shade of blue. As they removed the soil, the sweater was revealed, but that was all. It quickly became clear that the indentation had been scooped only deep enough to hold Lizzie's sweater. Below that, the ground was undisturbed. Rutledge stood up, the cardigan sweater hanging from his hand, rumpled and dirty.

"I don't get it," he said.

"There's something in the pocket," Cork said.

"Anybody got a glove?"

"Here." Schilling handed him one, leather.

Rutledge put it on and removed a folded slip of paper from the sweater pocket. He opened it. Cork looked over his shoulder and saw what was written.

48 hours.

"Mean anything?" Rutledge asked.

Cork wiped his palms on his khakis and looked at his nails, which were packed with black dirt. He pulled his walkie-talkie from his belt and called to Howard Morgan, who was at Stone's cabin, and told him to send Will Fineday down to the lake. He turned to Gratz. "Did you bring Pook?"

"You betcha. Nestor's got him." He waved toward the sound of the other dogs.

"Bring her to the dock. You know what we need to do."

"Yah," Gratz said. "Come on, Lancelot."

Rutledge watched the man and dog trot away. "What now?"

"Pook's an air scent dog," Cork said. He turned and started out of the cedars. "Gratz'll take him onto the lake. If Stone dumped Lizzie's body in the water, Pook might be able to locate her."

"And if he didn't dump her there?"

"We keep looking."

The mist vanished. Where sunlight struck the lake the clear water turned gold. Under the dock, the lake bottom was a jumble of dark stones; nearer the surface a school of minnows darted, moving together like a shadow creature.

For two hours, Orville Gratz had crisscrossed the lake in a canoe with Pook, but the dog hadn't caught Lizzie's scent. The other two dogs had sniffed the entire shoreline of Bruno Lake without success. Cork stood on the dock looking north where the Cutthroat River fed toward Sugar Bowl Lake and the other lakes beyond. He chewed on a ham sandwich, one of a couple dozen he'd ordered brought out to feed the searchers, along with coffee and water. Everything had to be carted over the ridge.

"I don't get it," Rutledge said. He sat on the dock, running his hand through the crystal clear water. "This place is so remote, how could Stone manage a serious smuggling operation? The planes fly everything in fine, but it has to be moved out of here on foot or by canoe."

"For a hundred years, the Voyageurs moved millions of dollars of goods through here that way. Helped build a few fortunes," Cork said.

"Why did Stone do it?" Dina Willner asked. She stood near him, sipping coffee from a Styrofoam cup. "From what I understand, he has plenty of money coming from the distribution of the casino profits."

"It's not about the money," Will Fineday said.

"No?" Rutledge said. "What, then?"

"Fuck you," Fineday said.

Rutledge looked surprised by the response.

"No," Fineday said. "That's what it's about. Everything he does is just a way of saying fuck you. To me, to you, to his people. He doesn't need anybody, doesn't want anybody. To him, we're all weak, like sick animals to be preyed on." Fineday strode to the end of the dock and stood between Cork and Dina. "On the rez, some people call him *majimanidoo*. A bad spirit. A devil." He followed Cork's gaze north toward the mouth of the Cutthroat. "They're right."

Larson came down the trail from the ridge.

"What's the word from the plane?" Cork asked.

He'd arranged for a Forest Service DeHavilland to fly over the area and look for anyone in a canoe on the lakes or along the Cutthroat. The nearest official access to the wilderness was ten miles west. It was late in the season and few permits were being issued, so anyone in a canoe would be suspect.

"Nothing. They didn't see a blessed soul."

"Got the map, Ed?"

"Right here."

Larson unfolded a topographical map of the region for four

hundred square miles. "The dogs are getting nowhere. The search plane's a bust. What do you think?"

"He moved fast," Cork said.

"Does he still have the girl?"

"If he'd left her at the bottom of the lake, Pook would probably have picked that up. I think Stone's still got her," Cork said.

Rutledge ran his hand through the water, making ripples that were edged with gold. He eyed Fineday. "Did she go willingly?"

Fineday didn't look at him. His own eyes were glued to the north. "You don't say no to Stone." He rubbed the long scar on his face as if the old wound still hurt him. "Why would he take her? He doesn't care about her. She'd only get in his way."

"He has reason," Cork said. "Somehow it goes back to that cartridge on the pillow and the sweater in the ground."

Rutledge glanced up. "Why wouldn't he just make a beeline to Canada? He could be there by tomorrow."

"When he gets to Canada, where is he?" Cork said. "No better off, and he knows it."

"We could wait him out. Put a watch on every wilderness access. Make sure every police and sheriff's department's on the lookout. I know what you said about him being able to stay in there forever, but that was before he took the girl."

"Maybe that's why he took Lizzie," Cork said. "With the girl, he can't stay in there long, and he knows we know it."

"I don't get it," Dina said.

"She's a liability. He can't afford to keep her. It's like that hourglass in *The Wizard of Oz*. As soon as the sand runs out, Dorothy dies. I think that's what the note in her pocket was about. Forty-eight hours. He'll keep her for forty-eight hours. He knows we won't wait him out. He knows we have to try to find Lizzie before her time's up."

"He wants us to go after him?" Rutledge said.

"I think that's why he left the cartridge. He wanted it clear that he was the one who'd fired the shots at the Tibodeau cabin. Maybe he figured we were already on the road to figuring that out for ourselves. But he makes the declaration, he maintains control. I don't think he's trying to escape. I think he wants us to follow him into his territory. It's like Will says. 'Fuck you.'"

"Seems a stretch to me," Rutledge said.

"It's the kind of man Stone is. He'd get off pitting his power against ours."

"What are you going to do?"

Cork tossed the crust of his sandwich into the lake, and a moment later the bread disappeared in a flash of shiny green scales and a splash of silver water. "I'm going to give him what he wants. I'm going in after him."

Rutledge scratched the top of his head. His face looked puzzled and he spent a minute fishing through his hair. He studied something he'd pinched between his fingers. "Damn. I thought tick season was over." He flicked the critter into the lake and shook himself. "Feels like they're crawling all over me now. Look, I don't like the idea of anyone going in, Cork."

"I don't like it either, Simon, but I don't see any way around it." Cork pulled the walkie-talkie from its holster on his belt. "Morgan. Over."

"Morgan here."

"Howard, I want you to get some gear together for a trip into the woods. Enough for three men for two days."

"One canoe?"

Fineday said, "I'm going with you."

Cork started to shake his head, but he could see the determination on the man's face. He understood how he'd feel if it was his daughter out there.

"Make it two canoes and four men. I want everything ready to go by"—he looked at his watch—"oh four hundred."

"Ten-four. I'm on it."

"You're really going in?" Dina said.

"Yeah. But I think Simon has a good idea. We should put a watch on all the nearest accesses and float Stone's photo everywhere. Contact the provincial police in Ontario, too. Let them know Stone may be headed their way."

Rutledge still looked skeptical. "You think you can find him?"

"No." Cork turned away from the lake and started for the ridge. "But I know a man who can."

36

J<small>O'S FIRST OFFICIAL</small> date with Cork had begun at the Lincoln Park Zoo. It had ended at Rocky's on the lakeshore, where Cork picked up a sack of fried shrimp and french fries, which they ate while sipping beer and watching Lake Michigan slide into the deep blue ink of evening. In between, she found a man who was funny, gentle, smart, who came from a small town in Minnesota and had somehow managed, despite the awful things he'd seen as a cop on the South Side, to retain a belief in simple human dignity.

"You're a good cop?" she'd asked in jest.

"Depends on the situation. I try to be a good man first. Sometimes that might make me look like a bad cop, but I don't think of myself that way. You don't have to be a hard-ass to be in control of a tough situation. Connection, that's what I try for. Maybe it's because I'm part Ojibwe. Connection is very important."

"Ojibwe?" It sounded exotic, exciting.

"Or Anishinaabe. Some people call us Chippewa, but that's really the white man's bastardization of Ojibwe. Most Shinnobs I know aren't fond of the name."

"Connection," she said. "Are we connecting?"

"I think we are."

"Then why haven't you kissed me?"

He smiled, as if amused by her boldness. "When I was twelve and my father sat me down to talk about the birds and

231

the bees, one of the things he said to me was, 'Cork, always let the woman make the first move.'"

"Was it a good piece of advice?"

"Do you want me to kiss you?"

"Very much."

"Then it was excellent advice."

Through all the years, the hardships, even when they both stood at the painful edge of abandoning their marriage, she'd never forgotten that kiss or the promise it held for her.

As arranged, Rae Bly was waiting for Jo at the sea lion pool near the zoo entrance. She was so engrossed in watching the animals cavort that she didn't notice Jo, who finally touched her on the shoulder.

"Here you are," Rae exclaimed with a broad smile. "And these are your children?"

Jo introduced them and Rose, then sent them along saying she would meet them at the primate house in an hour.

Ben's sister wore sunglasses and a white cap with a bill that shaded her face. She carried a purse and also a long canister that hung by a strap over her shoulder "A lovely family, Jo."

"Thanks."

Rae waved toward a bench in the shade of a tree. "Shall we sit down?" When they were seated, she put down the canister, reached into her purse, and pulled out a silver cigarette case. She held it open toward Jo.

"I don't smoke."

"You used to. Pretty heavily, as I recall."

"I quit when I became pregnant with Jenny."

"I don't have children, so I'm still looking for that compelling reason. Unfortunately, smoking and painting are tied together in my thinking. Paint a little, smoke a little, paint a little. The truth is, I'm afraid to give it up. Maybe the art wouldn't come without it."

Jo settled back so that she was out of the sun. "You're famous, Ben tells me."

"Famous? I sell well, but 'famous' is something else entirely. I enjoy what I do, and that's what's important for me." She sent out a cloud of smoke, and waved it away from Jo. "I was so pleased to see you last night. You and Ben. It reminded me of that wonderful summer."

"That was a long time ago. A lot has changed."

"Some things. Ben still loves you. He always has."

"Twenty years ago he left me, Rae. Without a word of explanation."

"I know." She looked up at the blue sky, squinting through her dark glasses. "When I left for school at the end of that summer, I prayed Ben would marry you. I'd talked to him about it. I know he hadn't told you about Miriam, and he made me promise not to say anything. He was so torn between love and duty. For a little while I thought he would choose love. But Lou's a formidable obstacle for us all, and in the end, fate seemed to be on his side. In September, our mother was diagnosed with pancreatic cancer. She went quickly."

"He never said a word to me."

"How could he? Her dying wish was for him to marry Miriam, and he couldn't say no. If it's any consolation, he was miserable his whole marriage."

"What was she like?"

"Miriam? A horrible JAP. I'm Jewish, so I can say that. She was spoiled, self-centered, vain. What was important to her was the big house, the country club, the glittery life. She didn't love Ben any more than he loved her, but the life she had seemed to give her everything she wanted. Ben walked through that marriage with his eyes and his mouth closed. And his heart. God, it was painful to see."

"How did he endure it?"

"By doing what the Jacoby men have always done. Poured himself into the business, made money to support his family, found his pleasure in other women." She looked deeply into Jo's eyes. "When I saw how Ben looked at you last night, I thought about how everything might have been different."

In the silence that followed, she took a long drag off her cigarette.

"I brought you something," she said, brightening.

She lifted the canister, unscrewed a cap at one end, and pulled out a rolled canvas, which she gave to Jo.

"Open it," she said.

Jo spread the canvas and recognized the painting immediately. It was her, Jo, in the white dress, in Grant Park, twenty years ago.

"Ben asked me to do it for him before I left for school that fall. He wanted to give it to you as a gift. Then he ended things and gave it back to me and told me to get rid of it. He couldn't bear to look at it. I've kept it all these years. I'd love for you to have it."

"It's beautiful, Rae, but I can't."

"Please. It was always meant for you. It would give me great pleasure knowing that you finally have it." She put a hand on Jo's arm. "And honestly, if you decide you can't keep it, you have my blessing to sell it. Believe me, you could get enough for that canvas to send Jenny to Northwestern for a year. Take it, Jo, please. For me."

She didn't feel comfortable accepting, but she also felt that to decline, particularly in the face of Rae's strong insistence, was not right, either.

"All right. Thank you." She rolled it again and slipped it back into the canister. "So you've become the artist you always wanted to be."

"No thanks to my father." Rae laughed. "He disinherited me."

"Because you became an artist?"

"That and because I didn't marry the man he'd chosen for me." She dropped her cigarette and crushed it on the pavement. "My parents' marriage was arranged and was a dismal affair. Ben married the woman my parents chose for him, and I saw how miserable he was. I decided, come hell or high water, I was going to marry for love. And I did. George Bly, a wonderful man. It was George who urged me to follow my heart and to paint. He's an artist, too. Stained glass. My father cut me off financially and cut me out of his will. Big deal. George and I do fine financially. The important thing is that we love what we do and we love each other. Believe me, that's not typical for the Jacobys."

"What about Eddie and his wife? How was that marriage?"

Rae shook her head sadly. "That may have been the greatest travesty of all. You knew Eddie well?"

"Well enough to wonder about the woman who would agree to marry him. Ben told me she's Argentine."

"Yes. From one of the best families. She's beautiful, well educated, cultured, and broke. When the Argentine economy collapsed, her family lost everything. Once again, Jews became the target of old hatred and prejudice. Many of those who were able to emigrated—to Israel, Spain, the States.

"My father and Gabriella's father had been financial associates for years. The situation in Argentina developed about the same time Eddie hit marriageable age. No woman who knew him would marry him. My father understood that. He'd seen Gabriella and knew the plight of her family, and he arranged to marry the poor girl to Eddie. It got her out of Argentina, and Lou promised to help the rest of the family emigrate. Her parents chose to go to Israel. Her brother came here."

"I was impressed with her last night."

"She is impressive. She proved to be a dutiful wife, good mother, doting daughter-in-law. Lou absolutely adores her."

Jo detected a note of bitterness in that last statement. "Is that a problem?"

Rae pulled another cigarette from her silver case and lit up. "In his business dealings, my father's a powerful and perceptive man. In his personal life, he's clueless. He has no idea about real love. He mistakes subservience for affection. My mother didn't put up with his tyranny, and he ignored her. Ben tried to break free of his control, and Lou has never completely forgiven him. I defied him, and he all but banished me. See, my father's great weakness is this. He'll deny it with a vengeance but he needs desperately to feel loved, and feeling loved means two things to him. That you need him and that you obey him. Eddie's mother, Gwen, understood this perfectly. She played to it flawlessly. Dad loved her and gave her whatever she wanted. Eddie grew up doing the same thing, the little toady, and became the apple of Lou's eye. Gabriella's no slouch. She understood immediately which way the wind blows." She shot out a puff of smoke. "If I sound bitter it's only because, despite everything, I still love my father. And I pity his blindness and I miss his affection. So maybe, in the end, I'm just as screwed up as all the other Jacobys." She looked away as a tear crawled down her cheek from behind one of her dark lenses. "I'm sorry, I didn't mean for that to happen."

"That's okay," Jo said.

"You"—Rae laughed gently—"you would have made a great sister-in-law. Tell me about your life now. Everything."

They talked for an hour, then Jo looked at her watch and said it was time to meet Rose and the children. She stood up, slung the canister strap over her shoulder, and gave Rae a parting hug. As she walked away, heading toward the primate house, Jo couldn't help thinking that there were a lot of cages in the world, and not all of them had bars.

37

No one knew the true age of Henry Meloux. He was already old when Cork was a boy. Meloux was one of the Midewiwin, a Mide, a member of the Grand Medicine Society. He lived on a rocky, isolated finger of land called Crow Point that jutted into Iron Lake at the northern edge of the reservation.

Cork parked the Pathfinder on the gravel at the side of the county road, locked up, and followed a trail that began at a double-trunk birch and led deep into the woods. For a while, the way lay through national forest land, but at some unmarked boundary it crossed onto the reservation. Cork walked for half an hour through woods where the only sounds were the chatter of squirrels, the squawk of crows, and the occasional crack of a fallen branch under his boots. When he broke from the pine trees, he could see Meloux's cabin on the point, an old one-room log structure with a cedar plank roof shingled over with birch bark.

"Henry," he called, not wanting to surprise the old man, though surprising Meloux would be a rare thing. The Mide had a remarkable knack for anticipating visitors. If that failed, the barking of Walleye, Meloux's yellow dog, was usually warning enough. Meloux did not respond, and Walleye was nowhere to be seen. Cork approached the door, which stood open, and looked inside.

The interior of the cabin was always clean, though full of a hodgepodge of items that recalled other eras. On the walls hung snowshoes made of steam-curved birch with deer hide bindings, a deer-prong pipe, a bow strung with sinew from a snapping turtle. There was a Skelly gas station calendar forty years out of date, but the old man kept it because he admitted appreciating the young woman in the cheesecake photo whose breasts were big and round as pink balloons ready to burst. Resting on two tenpenny nails hammered into the wall was an old long-barreled Remington with a walnut stock. There was a sink but no running water, a hickory table and two chairs, a potbellied stove, and a small bunk. These were practically all the material goods Meloux possessed, but he was the most contented man Cork had ever known.

The open door didn't bother Cork. In good weather, Meloux often left the door ajar for fresh air to circulate inside. It also allowed Shinnobs to bring and leave for the old Mide offerings of respect and gratitude. Cork could tell from the sacks on the table that the recent offerings had been *manomin,* wild rice. In the Ojibwe language, August was Manomingizis, the Month of Rice. In the final days of August and into early fall, the Anishinaabeg poled through the fields in the lakes, knocking the ripe kernels loose and filling their boats. After the rice was prepared, some would be eaten, some sold, and some given as a gift, as it had been to Meloux.

A distant bark brought Cork around. He gazed toward the trail he had followed, and in a moment he spotted Walleye bounding from the pine trees, his yellow coat full of burrs. Meloux was not far behind. He walked slowly but erect, his hair like white smoke drifting about his shoulders. He wore bib overalls, a faded blue denim shirt, deer hide moccasins that he'd made himself. In his hand was an ironwood staff ornamented with an eagle feather, and over his shoulder hung a beaded leather bag. He smiled when he saw Cork but didn't change his pace. Walleye, however, ran ahead. When Cork knelt to greet him, the old dog eagerly nuzzled his palm.

"*Anin,* Corcoran O'Connor," the old man said in formal greeting.

"*Anin,* Henry." Cork eyed the bag hanging from Meloux's shoulder. "Let me guess: mushroom hunting."

"I have gathered a feast. I will make a fine soup with rice and mushrooms. Will you join me?" Meloux said.

"I have to decline."

The sun was directly overhead, beating down out of a cloudless sky. Meloux shaded his eyes with a wrinkled hand and studied Cork's face.

"You always come like a hungry dog, wanting something, but it's never food."

"Sorry, Henry."

The old man lifted his hand in pardon. "It's all right. Like a dog, you're always grateful for even a scrap."

"It's more than a scrap I need this time."

Meloux nodded. "Let me put away my harvest, then we will smoke and talk."

They sat at a stone circle that enclosed the ashes of many fires. Down the slope a few feet away lay the water of Iron Lake, crystal clear along the shore, blue and solid as a china plate in the distance. The old man had listened to Cork's story and now he smoked a cigarette hand-rolled from tobacco Cork had brought as a gift. Although he'd given up smoking more than two years before, Cork held a cigarette, too. The ritual he shared with Meloux had nothing to do with addiction.

"Stone," Meloux said. "Like a Windigo, that one."

In Anishinaabe myth, the Windigo was a cannibal giant with a heart of ice. The only way to kill a Windigo was to become one. Once you had succeeded in destroying the terrible creature, you had to drink hot wax so that you would melt back down to the size of other men. If that didn't happen, you were doomed to remain a Windigo forever. Thinking of how Stone had killed his monster of a stepfather, Cork believed he understood what Meloux was saying. Myths were simple things, but they cut to the heart of brutal truths.

"What do you want of me?" the old Mide asked.

"You've lived in *Noopiming* all your life." *Noopiming,* the Ojibwe name for the north country. "You know the woods better than anyone alive. Since I was a boy, I've heard stories of your prowess as a hunter. Henry, I need someone who knows the Boundary Waters and who can track the Windigo."

The old man smoked awhile. Indian time. Never hurried.

"That was when I was a young man. It has been too many years to count since I was on a hunt, and this kind of animal I have never hunted. Stone, he will be dangerous."

"Will you do it?"

Meloux finished his cigarette. He threw the butt into the ash inside the stone circle. "I'm old. Death and me, we've been eyeing one another for a while now. There's not much left that scares me. One last hunt, that would not be a bad thing, especially to hunt the Windigo." He used his staff to help himself stand. "When do we leave?"

38

WHEN THEY RETURNED from the zoo, Jo told the kids it was time to concentrate on schoolwork. Stevie was in the first grade and had no homework, so Jo gave him the book she'd brought along for just this occasion, *Johnny Tremaine*. Luckily, all the reading his parents had done at bedtime was paying off. Stevie loved to read. He took the book and settled onto the sofa without an argument.

Rose was down the hallway, in the kitchen.

"Did Cork call?" Jo asked as soon as she walked in.

"No. Worried?" Rose was washing her hands at the sink.

"He hasn't returned any of my calls."

"Try him again."

Jo looked at the clock. Two-thirty. He should be at the office, but she was hoping maybe he was home, resting. God knew he needed it. And if he was, should she disturb him? She decided to.

The phone rang five times, then voice mail kicked in.

"You've reached the O'Connors. We can't come to the phone right now, but if you'd leave a message, we'll get back to you as quick as we can."

It was Cork's voice. Not him, but the illusion of him. Still, she liked what she heard, his words warm with easy hospitality, a genuine goodness in his tone. Or maybe she only heard it because that's how she thought of him.

She'd left messages already and didn't leave another.

"Still no answer?" Rose said. "Maybe you should try his office."

"They won't tell me anything."

"They certainly won't tell you if you don't try."

Jo called the Tamarack County Sheriff's Department. Bos answered.

"No," she told Jo. "He's not in."

There was something in her voice, a hesitancy, Jo thought.

"What's wrong, Bos?"

"Nothing's wrong, Jo. Cork's been working hard on two investigations, you know. He's just out a lot."

"I've left him messages asking him to call me. He hasn't. That's not like him."

Bos didn't reply.

"Is Ed Larson in?"

"He's out in the field, too."

"Is anybody there but you?"

"We're a little shorthanded."

"Look, Bos, I've heard that Lizzie Fineday is a suspect in Edward Jacoby's murder. Is that true?"

"You know I can't talk about an ongoing investigation."

She went hot with anger. "Goddamn it, Bos. What can you tell me?"

"Not much, and you know it."

It was useless to strike out at Bos, who was just following Cork's instructions. Jo breathed deeply, let go.

"Will you have him call me?"

"Of course. Just as soon as he can. And, Jo"—Bos sounded like a soothing grandmother now—"if there's anything you need to know, I'll make sure you know it right away, okay?"

Rose went to the refrigerator and pulled out a pound of raw hamburger and a package of sausage. She was about to start making a meat loaf for dinner. "So what's going on?"

"I don't know. Bos is keeping something back, but I have no idea what." Jo's whole body felt stiff, and she rubbed the tense muscles on the back of her neck. "It's not like Cork not to call. Is he angry, do you think?"

"About what?"

"He knows that Ben and I have a past together. He knows that we were out last night."

"I think you should give him more credit."

"I know, but I feel like I'm stumbling around in the dark."

Stevie wandered in to ask about a word in his book. He saw Rose working at the kitchen counter. "Whatcha making?"

"Meat loaf, for dinner."

"Meat loaf! Sweet! You make the best meat loaf in the whole entire world." He ran back down the hallway to share the good news with his sisters.

Rose said, "Can you call someone else—not one of Cork's people?"

Jo leaned on the counter watching her sister shape the loaf. "I suppose I could call Ben."

"Why him?"

"He hired someone to consult on the investigation of Eddie's murder. He gets regular updates."

"Seems worth a try. You'll certainly be no worse off."

Jo tried Jacoby's cell phone, but got only his voice mail. She called his office and was told he was in meetings all afternoon. She left a message.

"What's in the canister?" Rose asked.

The children had asked, too, but Jo had put them off. Now she unscrewed the cap, took out the canvas, and showed it to Rose.

"It's beautiful," Rose said.

Jo told her the history and that Rae had insisted she accept the gift.

"What are you going to do with it?" Rose asked. "Given your history with Ben Jacoby, I can't imagine Cork would be thrilled to see that hanging in your home."

"I know. I've been thinking. What if I gave it to Ben?"

"That might be the best thing, if he wanted it."

"I'll ask him."

It was three hours before Ben called back, just as Jo had begun to set the table for dinner. The whole house smelled of savory meat loaf.

"I'm in traffic right now, Jo, and I'd rather talk in person anyway. What if I dropped by your sister's place?"

His tone sounded a little ominous, and if it was bad news he was going to deliver, she wanted to be somewhere the kids couldn't hear.

"Or," he went on, "if you'd rather, we could meet at my house. It's only about ten minutes from where you are now. I'll be there in half an hour."

Jo agreed and Ben gave her the address and directions. The house was on Sheridan Road, easy to find. She hung up.

"That didn't sound good," Rose said. She was at the stove, checking the potatoes. "What did he say?"

"It's what he didn't say, and how he didn't say it."

"Until you know the worst, anticipate the best."

Jo said, "It's already pretty bad because I have to leave in a few minutes, which means I'm going to miss the best meat loaf in the whole entire world."

39

"WHY MORGAN?" Schilling asked.

They were gathered at the dock on Bruno Lake. The gear had been loaded into the canoes, and Cork was looking over the map one last time with Ed Larson and Simon Rutledge. Meloux already sat in the bow of the lead canoe, and Will Fineday had settled into the bow of the second.

Deputy Howard Morgan looked up from where he knelt on the dock, retying the lace of his hiking boot. "Because I do the Boundary Waters a lot. Because I have a sharpshooter rating. Because I don't whine about assignments. And," he added, standing up, "because I'm a bachelor." He gave Schilling a light, friendly jab in the stomach.

"I just meant that I'd be willing to go."

"I know," Cork said, glancing from the map. He could have added one more reason it was Morgan who was going. That in a tight situation he'd prefer Morgan at his back.

"The chopper and the critical response team will be standing by," Larson said. "Give the word and they'll be there in no time."

"Sure you don't want a few more men along?" Rutledge asked.

Cork shook his head. "If I'm wrong about all this, we'd be taking deputies from where they're needed. If I'm right, we've got the CRT for backup."

"By the way," Rutledge said, "Dina asked me to give you this."

He handed Cork a gold medallion the size of a silver dollar.

"A Saint Christopher's medal?" It seemed an odd gift, because Cork knew Dina was Jewish. "Where is she?"

"She left right after you headed off to recruit Meloux."

Cork slipped the medallion in his pocket. "We'll check in hourly with our location," he told Larson.

"I wish I felt better about this." Rutledge eyed Meloux with a look Cork interpreted as skepticism of the old man's ability to be of any help.

"I wish I felt better about everything, Simon. And if you've got another idea for saving Lizzie Fineday, I'm still open to suggestions."

Rutledge only offered his hand. "Good luck."

Cork stepped into the stern of the lead canoe, and Morgan took the stern of the other. They pushed away from the dock and into the lake, paddling toward the Cutthroat River, which would take them north into the Boundary Waters Canoe Area Wilderness. Halfway across the lake, a great bird appeared in front of them, high up, the tips of its wings like fingers scraping against the hard blue ceiling of the sky. Meloux watched the bird closely.

"An eagle?" he asked.

"A turkey vulture," Cork replied.

"Too bad," the old man said, sounding disappointed.

"What's it mean, Henry?" Thinking that for some reason the turkey vulture was not a good sign.

Meloux squinted at the bird and said with a note of sadness, "That my eyes aren't what they used to be."

Cork knew that Meloux's physical senses weren't those of a young man, but it was a different sense he'd hoped for from the old Mide, something that came from a lifetime not just of hunting but of understanding the nature of human beings. He prayed that this sense was still sharp.

The Cutthroat took them to Sugar Bowl Lake a mile north of Bruno. It was a round lake ringed by high hills, hence its name. The sun was at their backs. Their shadows moved ahead of them across the water, and behind followed a deep, rippling wake. Cork watched the slopes carefully. On top of his pack, which was situated directly in front of him, was a pair of Leitz binoculars. Beside the pack rested a Remington Model 700 police rifle. Morgan had brought an M40A1 sniper rifle and scope, and Fineday, who'd hunted all his life, had brought his own Winchester. Before embarking, they'd held a conference regarding the wearing of the Kevlar vests each man had been issued. Meloux and Fineday, neither of whom had ever worn body armor, were clearly not thrilled with the prospect of the stiff armature. Morgan commented that the vests were generally uncomfortable and would be particularly so during the kind of prolonged physical activity that the canoeing and portaging would demand. He also pointed out that they had every reason to believe that Stone, if he fired at them, would use armor-piercing rounds. Cork told them he'd prefer it if they wore the armor, but he understood their objections and drew up shy of insisting. They were, however, to keep the armor handy at all times and not hesitate if he gave the order to suit up.

The afternoon was still, the only sound the burble of water that swirled with each dip of the paddle.

"Should we be concerned yet, Henry?" Cork said.

The old Mide scratched his head and thought an unusually long time. "Not here. Not yet."

The Cutthroat left Sugar Bowl via a series of rapids too shallow for the canoes. One followed the Cutthroat, the other veered west toward a little lake called Snail.

"Which way, Henry?" Cork said.

Meloux walked the trail along the Cutthroat, came back, and followed the other portage for a distance. He studied the rocky soil carefully, shaking his head with uncertainty. "Hard ground, no tracks," he said.

Morgan spoke quietly. "Up here, it's all hard ground and no tracks."

Meloux stood where the trails diverged, looking west, north. Finally he pointed along the Cutthroat. "I think Stone would go this way."

"You're sure?"

"He would go quickly and far enough so that you would not bring the dogs. So north."

"How far, Henry?"

Meloux shrugged. "We will see."

Morgan gave Cork a look of concern, but held his tongue. The men hefted their canoes and began to walk.

Sunset found them at Lamb Lake, hitting the end of a short thirty-rod portage as the light turned blazing orange and ignited a wildfire of color that swept over the aspen on the hills. Cork and the others stood in the shadow of tamaracks on the western shore of the lake, the water dark at their feet. Already they could sense the cold that would descend with the fall of night.

The afternoon had not gone well. At every juncture, every point where a decision about direction had to be made, Meloux seemed uncertain. He spent a long time studying each trail. He knelt, his old bones cracking, and peered at the ground. He rubbed his eyes with his gnarled knuckles and afterward seemed to have a bewildered look. Each time he finally pointed the way, Cork wanted to ask, "Are you sure?" But what would have been the use?

In Morgan's face, the concern was obvious. Had they put their faith in a man too old? He said nothing. Fineday, too, held his tongue, but Cork could imagine his worry. Were they losing his daughter?

Still, none of them had been able to say that Meloux was wrong, that Stone had gone a different way. But were they, Cork wondered, the blind following the blind?

Beyond Lamb Lake, their way would lie to the east, along a narrow flow called Carson Creek that fed out of the far shoreline. It would take them to Hornby, a huge lake with dozens of inlets. The most direct route across Lamb was through a channel between two small islands. Although it was difficult from a distance to judge their size, Cork recalled from the map that both islands were shaped roughly like bread loaves, the larger approximately one hundred yards long, the other half that size. It appeared that at one time they'd been connected, but the natural bridge had collapsed, its ruin apparent in the great stone slabs that broke the surface in the channel. On the larger island, a few jack pines had managed to put down roots, but they were ragged-looking trees, like beggars huddled against a cold night. The southern end of the island was dominated by a sharp rise thick with blood-red sumac.

"Do we go on?" Morgan asked.

"Hell yes, we go on," Fineday said. "We haven't found Lizzie yet."

"Henry?" Cork turned to Meloux.

"I would like to sit and smoke," the old man said.

Fineday spoke urgently, but not without respect. "We don't have time. She's still with him out there somewhere."

"Stone knows we're coming," Meloux said. "He will be patient now. We should be patient, too."

"I'll go on alone if I have to."

"If you have to. But consider how much more eight eyes can see than two. And there's one more thing." Meloux settled his bony rump on the trunk of a fallen tamarack. "I am tired."

"We'll break for a while," Cork said. "Then decide."

Not far off the trail, in a stand of quaking aspen, was an official Boundary Waters campsite. While Meloux smoked and ruminated, Cork checked the camp. When he came back, he sat beside Meloux on the fallen tamarack, rolled a cigarette, and smoked with the old man in silence. Morgan lay with his back propped against an overturned canoe, his eyes closed. Fineday paced the shoreline.

"How're you doing, Henry?" Cork asked.

"When I was a young man, I could read a trail across a face of rock. Now . . ." He took a deep, ragged breath.

Cork was concerned. It was obvious the day had taken a heavy toll on Meloux. He looked ready to buckle.

What had he been thinking, bringing an old man, a man of parchment skin and matchstick bones, on such a difficult journey, such a dangerous mission? Had he put the others at risk, and Lizzie Fineday as well? Should he have mounted an army of deputies and volunteers, swept into the woods hoping to catch Stone in a huge net? Would anything he tried have worked?

Meloux finally said, "We are near the end, I think."

"How do you know, Henry?"

"He knows he has gone beyond the dogs. The next lake is Asabikeshiinh."

Spider. The Anishinaabe name for the lake. Because of all the inlets like legs, Cork knew.

"It is a big lake, easy to lose someone who follows him," Meloux said. "But he does not want to lose us."

"What do you think he'll do?"

"He will set a trap. Or he will circle."

"Come up on us from behind?" Morgan's eyes were open now.

"It is a trick of bears, a good trick. So maybe that is what he will do." He spoke to Fineday. "Put your restless walking to use. Look carefully along the shoreline, in the soft dirt, for boot prints. Go that way." He pointed to his right. "You, Corcoran, go the other way."

"What about me?" Morgan asked.

"Go back down the trail and look for signs of his turning there."

Fifteen minutes later, they regrouped at the overturned canoes. None of them had found any indication that Stone had ever been that way. Another disappointment.

"It's getting dark," Fineday said. "We should keep moving. We can make Lake Hornby before nightfall."

"If he is behind us," Meloux said, "moving ahead will take us away from him. If he is ahead, he is waiting, and dark is not a good time to walk into his trap."

"We should stay here?" Cork said.

The old man said, "Yes."

There was no way to know for sure what Stone had up his sleeve. Ahead, behind, watching them from somewhere even now, perhaps. When Fineday didn't argue, Cork figured that he'd accepted Meloux's advice. It sounded good to Cork, too.

"Maybe I should park myself out of sight near the last landing, see if anybody's following," Morgan said.

"Not a bad idea, Howard."

"It's almost time for a radio check," Morgan reminded him.

"I'll do it," Cork said.

When he raised Larson on the radio, Ed's first question was "What's your twenty?"

"Lamb Lake."

"Any sign of Stone or the Fineday girl?"

"Nothing."

"Have you seen anything, anything at all, that would confirm you're on the right track?"

"That's a negative."

"Cork, you could be on a wild-goose chase. Or, worse, walking right into Stone's gun sight."

"I'm still open to suggestions." Cork waited for a reply, then said, "In the meantime, have the DeHavilland make one more pass over the area before it's too dark."

There was a grill at the campsite, but it was too risky to build a fire. Morgan returned having seen nothing, and they sat down to a meal of peanut butter sandwiches, dried apricots, and Hershey bars with almonds. Once the sun had set fully, the chill of the autumn night rolled in quickly. Although it had taken precious space in the Duluth pack, Morgan had brought a one-burner Coleman stove and a small propane tank. He boiled lake water and made instant coffee, which the men drank eagerly.

The sky was amethyst and still without stars. "You said he would circle or he would set a trap." Fineday spoke out of the growing dark under the aspens. His form was clear, but his face was almost lost. "What kind of trap?"

"Why does he have your daughter?" Meloux said.

"Because he's a son of a bitch."

"That," the old man agreed. "But if our sheriff is right, Stone has her for the same reason a hunter puts fish and honey in a bear trap. Have you ever built a bear trap in the old way?"

Fineday said no.

"You build it of brush. It does not need to be sturdy, so long as there is only one way for the bear to get in. Even a hungry bear will look for the easiest way. The hunter puts the fish and honey far back in the trap, and he sets a heavy log over the opening. When *makwa* walks in," Meloux said, using the Ojibwe word for bear, "the hunter springs the trap, the log falls, *makwa*'s back is broken. It is the fish and honey that are his undoing."

"Stone is counting on us wanting the girl," Morgan said.

Meloux sipped his coffee. "Would we be here if he did not have her?"

They heard the drone of the DeHavilland as it approached

and flew low overhead. It circled Lamb Lake, then headed north into the darkening sky.

A few minutes later, Larson radioed from base. The floatplane had nothing to report.

Cork stood up and said, "Going to see a man about a horse."

He started in the direction of the pit toilet. Although he took a flashlight, he didn't turn it on. He'd gone less than a dozen steps when he froze and listened. From the portage came the snap of twigs and the crack of dry leaves underfoot. Quickly he rifled through the possibilities. An innocent canoeist? But the floatplane had spotted no one on the lake behind them. An animal? A moose might make that kind of noise, so maybe. Stone? No, Stone would never give himself away so easily. Unless he was up to something.

Cork was too far from his weapon, but in the thin light he saw Morgan in a kneeling position with his rifle stock snugged against his shoulder. Fineday quickly brought his own rifle to the ready. Meloux was invisible, already part of the woods somehow. Cork dropped to the ground and kept his eyes on the portage, visible through the trees twenty yards away. The ground was littered with golden aspen leaves, and the scent of their desiccation should have been strong, but all he could smell was the coffee Morgan had made. He wondered how far that good smell had traveled. Had Stone picked it up?

From the lake came the cry of a loon and, nearer to Cork, the buzzing of a night insect the cold had not yet killed. He heard the approaching footfalls, the scrape of something huge pushing against the brush at the side of the trail, something that seemed to let out a small growl now and then as it came. Both Morgan and Fineday had their cheeks laid against the rifle stocks, sighting.

The black shape that appeared, rattling the underbrush, was like nothing Cork had ever seen. Nearly as tall and long as a moose, it lumbered along the portage toward Lamb Lake. Cork couldn't help thinking of the cannibal ogre, the Windigo.

The creature stumbled and let out a cry. Then it spoke.

"Shit."

Cork recognized the voice.

"Dina?"

He realized the truth of what he was seeing. No creature, but Dina Willner, portaging what looked to be an inflatable kayak, which was sometimes called a duckie.

She set the kayak on the ground, and as she did so, the heavy rubber siding scraped the underbrush, resulting in what sounded like a growl.

"I was surprised you stopped," she said, a little breathless. "There was still daylight."

Morgan and Fineday lowered their rifles. Cork made his way across the campsite.

"What the hell are you doing here?" he said.

"What I'm paid to do. Consulting."

On her back she carried a pack, and slung over her right shoulder was a scoped rifle.

"Jesus Christ, we almost shot you."

"With all that noise? You might not have known it was me, but I know you didn't think it was Stone."

"A visitor?" Meloux asked. He'd materialized from nowhere.

"Not for long, Henry. She's going back," Cork said.

Meloux shook his head. "Not tonight. Not with Stone in these woods."

Dina walked to him and gave her hand. "I'm Dina Willner."

"Henry Meloux." The old man appraised her, top to bottom, and nodded appreciatively. "You are small but you have the look of a hunter. Are you hungry?"

"Henry," Dina replied with a huge smile, "I'm absolutely famished."

"It was the last inflatable the sporting goods store had. Not the best, but I figured that for a couple of days, it would do." She'd eaten a sandwich and a handful of the apricots, and now she was sipping coffee Morgan had offered. "I stashed it on the other side of Bruno Lake before you all got started."

"You haven't answered my question," Cork said.

"You mean, why am I here?"

"That would be the one."

"Because I'm not one of your people and have to stay back. Because you wouldn't have let me come if I'd asked. Because this is the kind of thing I'm good at."

"How did you find us?" Fineday said.

"I'm an excellent tracker," she said. "Also, I bugged Sheriff O'Connor."

Cork thought a moment, then dug in his pants and pulled out the medallion she had passed to him through Simon Rutledge.

"Good old Saint Christopher," Dina said. "He never lets me down."

"The DeHavilland didn't spot you," Cork said.

"I have a radio tuned to your frequency. I made sure I was under cover whenever the plane was due to fly over."

"We need to let base know the situation." Cork turned to the radio.

He explained everything to Larson, said that Dina would stay until morning, then would be sent back. To which she shook her head with a definite no. Larson gave him the latest weather forecast—clear skies, cold temperatures—and then gave him the difficult news.

"Faith Gray says you have one more chance to keep your appointment with her before she orders your suspension."

"Christ, doesn't she understand the circumstances?"

"The circumstances don't matter, Cork. The language of the rule is clear. You ought to know. Your rule."

Cork signed off feeling tired, feeling as if there was too much on his shoulders at the moment.

With hard dark, the stars came out by the millions and the sky through the branches above the campsite looked as if it were full of a thin frost.

"At least the weather's holding," Morgan noted.

"A little snow would be good," Meloux said.

"Snow?" Dina sounded surprised.

"Just enough," Meloux said.

"We call it a hunter's snow," Cork explained.

"I get it. The tracks."

Fineday had been quiet. Meloux said, "Worry will not save her."

For the first time, Fineday spoke to Meloux harshly. "Sitting here won't either. We haven't seen a single sign of them. How do we know they came this way? They could be miles from here."

Meloux replied calmly, "If they are, what can we do? Better to believe that we have been guided well."

"By an old man with failing eyes?"

"By the spirits of these woods."

"That's what's been leading us? Spirits?"

"We have not failed yet," Meloux said. "There's no reason to distrust or despair."

Despite the old Mide's encouraging words, Cork wondered if he saw uncertainty in Meloux's dark eyes.

"So in the morning the plan is that we cut between those two islands, hit Carson Creek, and see what happens from there?" Morgan said. "Sounds a lot like the plan we followed today."

His tone was not accusatory, but his point was clear. All the evidence so far seemed to indicate that they'd spent their time in a fruitless hunt that had netted them nothing except tired muscles and the prospect of a long night on cold ground. Cork understood that as a working plan for the next day it lacked appeal.

"Until Henry says different, we stay on the trail," he said.

"You're the boss. Anybody want more coffee?" Morgan got up from where he sat on his sleeping bag and took the pan to the lake to fill it with water. It was dark and he carried a flashlight. A minute later he hollered, "Hey, look at this."

Cork and the others hurried to Morgan, who stood on the lakeshore near the overturned canoes. He pointed the beam of his flashlight at the water a few feet out. Something gold glinted in the light.

"It looks like a watch," Dina said.

Cork used his own flashlight to locate a stick, then he fished the watch from the lake bottom.

Fineday grabbed it from him. "It's Lizzie's. I gave it to her when she turned sixteen."

"Do you think she dropped it on purpose, to let us know?"

Meloux said, "She would drop nothing that Stone did not know about."

"Stone left it?" Morgan asked.

Meloux looked across the dark water of the lake. "Fish and honey," he said.

40

IT WAS SOFT twilight when Jo pulled off Sheridan Road onto a long drive that cut through a hundred yards of dark lawn. The tires growled over dun-colored bricks that had been used for paving. She pulled up to a house big as a convent, with a red tile roof and stucco walls. In every way, it rivaled the home of Lou Jacoby.

Ben met her at the door. "Come in. I just got home." He was still dressed in his three-piece pin-striped suit, looking handsome, distinguished.

She stepped inside.

"It's a little dark," Ben said. "I can turn on some lights if you prefer."

"No, I'm fine."

They were in a large entryway that opened left and right onto huge rooms.

"Where would you like to talk? In the parlor?"

"You have a parlor?"

"And a billiard room, a library, a study. With a candlestick and a lead pipe we could be a game of Clue. It's way too big, but it's what Miriam wanted. How about we sit in the kitchen? It's really the coziest room in the house."

He led the way through a large dining room with French doors that opened onto a wide veranda. Jo could see a long stretch of lawn, green and tidy as an ironed tablecloth, with a turquoise swimming pool as a centerpiece. A tall hedge marked the rear boundary, and beyond that lay Lake Michigan, dark silver in the evening light.

The kitchen, which Ben had called cozy, was larger than any room in Jo's house on Gooseberry Lane. The floor was black-and-white tile. There were long counters, a dozen cupboards, and a butcher-block island. A round table with chairs was set near a sliding door that, like the dining room French doors, opened onto the veranda.

"You must eat well," Jo said.

"Miriam hired fine cooks." Ben indicated the table. "Have a chair. Would you like a glass of wine?"

"Thank you."

"Red? You used to love a good red."

"I don't drink red anymore. It gives me a headache."

"Things change, don't they? How about a chardonnay?"

He took a bottle from the refrigerator and opened it. From a rack above one of the counters, he took two glasses that hung upside down by their stems.

Several books lay stacked on one of the chairs at the table. They appeared to be college textbooks.

"What are these?" Jo asked.

Jacoby carried the wineglasses to the table and sat down. "They're Phillip's. He's around the house somewhere. He got expelled from his fraternity, and he's staying here for a while until he can arrange for other housing."

Jo had no idea what transgression might result in expulsion from a fraternity, but her sense, given the *Animal House* image she held, was that it had to be significant.

"All right," Ben said. "Let's talk. What do you want to know?"

"You get reports from a woman who's helping with the investigation of Eddie's murder, is that right?"

"Dina Willner."

"So what's going on out there?"

He settled back and folded his hands, a movement that seemed designed to give him a moment to think. "How much do you know?"

"Not much. When I call the department, they're evasive. I'm sure they're just following Cork's instructions. My guess is that it's because he's involved in something that I'm not supposed to worry about." When she said it, she heard a flutter of anger in her voice, and realized how strongly she felt.

"If they don't want you to know, why hit on me?"

"Because you're not one of his people. You can do what you like."

He sipped his wine and thought it over. "They've identified the man they believe was responsible for the shooting on the reservation."

"I know that. Lydell Cramer. He was burned during the meth lab bust a few weeks ago."

"Seems they were wrong in suspecting him. They're pretty sure now that it was a man named Stone."

"Stone? You mean Byron St. Onge?"

"I believe that's his name."

"Why? Why in the world would Stone want to shoot Cork?"

"As I understand it, that's still unclear."

"They could have told me that. There must be more."

"There is. When this Stone realized they were onto him, he ran, disappeared into the woods with the woman they suspect in Eddie's murder."

"Lizzie Fineday?"

"That's right. Your husband's gone into the woods after them."

"Alone?"

"No, the girl's father went with him. Also an old man who's a guide of some kind, and one deputy."

"Oh, Jesus. No wonder they wouldn't tell me. Goddamn him." She looked away a moment. "You know, he loves this. He's in his glory."

"Dina indicated she was going to try to accompany them, officially or otherwise. If it's any consolation, if I had to go after a man like Stone, I'd want Dina there with me. She's very good at what she does."

"Tell me about what she does."

"We use her as a consultant on all kinds of security issues. Protective services, investigations. She's a crack shot, holds a black belt in some kind of martial art, has significant law enforcement experience. Really, Cork couldn't ask for better backup."

"So Stone ambushed Cork. And Lizzie may have killed Eddie."

"And once they're caught, it's all over." He held up his hands as if it were as simple as two plus two.

They heard coughing in the dining room, and a few moments later Phillip walked in. He wore a black terry cloth bathrobe and sandals and carried a big white towel. He seemed surprised to find Jo and Ben in the kitchen.

"Hello, Phillip," Jo said.

He glanced from her to his father, and a dark, knowing look came into this eyes. "Don't let me interrupt," he said. "Just passing through on my way to swim."

"Have you eaten?" Ben asked.

"Lasagna. Mrs. McGruder made a shitload. It's in the refrigerator if you're hungry. Nice seeing you again," he said to Jo as he slid a glass door open and went outside.

"Isn't it cold for swimming?" she asked Ben.

"I keep the pool filled and heated until the end of October. I swim every morning, and prefer to do it outside. The first of November I start swimming at my health club."

The light in the sky was thinning, and the kitchen had grown dark, but Jacoby made no move to turn on a lamp. He swirled the wine slowly in his glass.

"Rae told me she had a good long talk with you this morning."

"Did she tell you what she gave me?"

"No."

"A painting that you'd asked her to do twenty years ago."

"Grant Park? White dress?"

"That would be the one."

"I thought she got rid of that. God, I'd love to see it."

"I considered bringing it."

He looked genuinely disappointed. "There's something you ought to see, something I feel a little guilty about."

He led her from the kitchen through the house, down a long hallway past big empty rooms. The thick carpet seemed to suck all the sound from their feet as they walked.

"You and Phillip, you're here by yourselves?"

"When Phillip's gone, it's just me."

She followed him to a study that smelled faintly of cigars. He turned on a light switch and revealed a study with shelves of books, an enormous polished desk, an antique couch upholstered in leather, a fireplace. He went to the desk and, beckoning her to look, turned a framed photograph so that she could see the image. It was Jo, standing on the shore of Iron Lake, the water at her back shiny and blue as new steel. Jenny had taken the snapshot a year before for her high school photography class. She had framed it and given it to Jo as a Christmas present.

"That was in my office in Aurora," Jo said. "I couldn't imagine what had happened to it."

He lifted the frame and cradled it in his hands. "Eddie snatched it on one of his visits. I should have returned it, but I couldn't bring myself to do that."

"Did you ask him to take it?"

"No. He thought of it as a gift to me." His face turned pensive. "Jo, I have a confession. When I found out someone had tried to kill Cork, I thought for a while Eddie might have been behind it. For God knows what reason, Eddie wanted desperately for us to be as close as true brothers. I wondered if, in his thinking, killing Cork would open the way for me to have you. A kind of gift from him to me. I know it sounds crazy, but that's exactly the kind of guy Eddie was."

"What would you have done if that had been the case?"

"Honestly, I don't know."

He held out the photograph toward her reluctantly, and she saw the sense of loss in his eyes as she took it.

"I'd like you to have Rae's painting, Ben."

He looked stunned.

"If you'd like it."

"It was meant for you, Jo."

"Twenty years ago it was meant for me. My life is different now. Honestly, Ben, I wouldn't feel comfortable with it hanging in my home in Aurora. Do you understand?"

"I suppose."

"Would you like it?"

"Very much."

"Would you accept it?"

"I'm sure it's a valuable painting. What if I paid you for it?"

"I'd rather it remained a gift."

"Thank you, Jo," he said.

"What if I brought it by tomorrow? About the same time? Say, six?"

"I could pick it up at your sister's place on my way home from the office."

"I'm not sure what will be happening there tomorrow night. I'd rather the kids didn't ask a lot of questions. It would be best for me to come here."

"All right, then. Six."

There was a splash outside and Ben drifted to the window. Jo could see Phillip swimming laps with strong, even strokes, his body a long, lean silhouette against the glaring lights in the pool.

"He loves to swim," Ben said. "He says when he's swimming, all his problems go away for a while."

"Problems?"

"He has more than his share. His mother's dead, he hates his father."

"How do you know?"

"Because I was the kind of father my father was."

"And you hate Lou?"

"Why wouldn't I? He's arrogant, rude, demanding. He cheated on my mother, disinherited my sister, loved Eddie beyond all reason." He gave a small, derisive laugh and shook his head in futility. "You know, I can still remember when I was a kid how even one word of praise from him was the best thing imaginable."

He moved nearer the window and watched his son glide through the turquoise water to the end of the pool, climb out, and quickly grab the towel to dry himself. Then Phillip slipped his robe and sandals on and headed back toward the veranda.

"I should go," Jo said.

Ben nodded and led her back through the vastness of a house that seemed to hold nothing but a silence waiting to be shattered.

The children and Mal had gone to a movie. The teakettle had just started to whistle on the stove when Jo walked in.

Rose poured boiling water over the herbal tea bags in the cups on the kitchen table, then sat down with Jo, who told her what she'd learned from Jacoby.

Jo didn't touch her tea, but the aroma, the soothing scent of apple and spice, registered in her senses. She wished she could give in to the pull of that smell, which seemed to come from a place of calm, of placid domesticity that was out of her reach at the moment. All she felt was irritation and worry.

"No wonder they wouldn't tell me anything. He's done it again, Rose. It's that damned cowboy mentality of his. That's the part of him I hate."

"If you were to ask me, I'd say it's also part of what you love about him," Rose said. "He's certainly come to your rescue on occasion. And mine."

"I know, I know." She lifted her cup, sighed into her tea.

"You're worried, Jo, and that's understandable. Why don't you call Aurora again. Now that you know what's going on, maybe they'll be more forthcoming. It's worth a try, don't you think?"

She was right, of course. Jo used the phone in the kitchen.

Bos was on duty. Jo told her what she understood of the situation and pressed Bos for more details.

At the other end of the line, Bos hesitated, then seemed to come to a decision. She told Jo that the search party consisted of Cork, Morgan, Meloux, Fineday, and now Dina Willner. They hadn't had any contact with Stone or Lizzie. Last check in was at twenty-two hundred hours, ten o'clock, and everything was fine.

"Why did he do it, Bos? Why didn't he just wait for Stone to come out?"

"He was concerned about the Fineday girl. He believed that if he didn't locate her quickly, Stone might kill her."

"Did it have to be him?" She hated herself for the question, for the whining way it came out. Of course Cork felt it had to be him, and that was all that mattered. "Bos, you call me with anything, good or bad, you hear?"

"I hear, Jo."

She hung up, closed her eyes, breathed deeply. The whole kitchen was suffused with the smell of the tea.

"Sometimes," she said, "I wish . . ." She let it drop.

Rose stood up and put her freckled arms around her sister, offered a comforting embrace. "I know, but would you have him be less than he is?"

"Of course not."

They sat at the table again. Jo sipped her tea. "Morgan. He's a good officer, and Cork trusts him. And Meloux as a guide, that's a godsend. He's old, but he's tough."

"There you go. God has sent good people along with Cork."

They heard Mal returning with the children. "I don't want the kids to know, Rose. Tomorrow, when you go to South Bend, I'm going to stay here and wait for word on Cork."

"A good idea."

That night, after Stevie had gone to bed, Jo stood for a few minutes at the window, listening, thinking of the unnatural quiet that came with the mornings since the birds were dead. West Nile virus was a merciless killer.

A breeze rose up, and outside the leaves of the trees murmured softly, as if to remind her that there were those things, like the wind, that moved swiftly and could not be killed.

Jo thought of Cork and the others with him. "Dear Lord," she prayed, "let them be the wind."

41

THE MOON, BEFORE it rose, put a glow in the sky above the trees, as if a lost city lay blazing somewhere in the distant forest. Under the aspens on Lamb Lake, Cork and the others prepared for sleep.

"What about Stone?" Dina asked. "Will he sleep?"

"It has been a long day for him, too," Meloux said. "He will sleep."

"To be on the safe side," Cork said, "we'll stand watches, two hours each. Howard, Will, Dina, and me, in that order."

Meloux said, "I don't sleep so good anymore. I can watch, too."

"If you're up, you can help whoever's on watch stay awake."

Morgan took his rifle and walked to the shoreline as the moon began to push up out of the trees. Cork and the others settled into their bags. Cork didn't think Stone would try anything that night, but who really knew? It would have been comforting to have more deputies there, but Stone could probably elude an army if he wanted. It was best this way, to try to draw him out. Someone had to do it. Still, he couldn't help feeling the weight of the responsibility like an anchor on his chest. He was glad Jo didn't know what he was up to. Or the children.

He was surprised when Dina shook him awake.

"Your watch," she said.

He rolled out of his bag, his body stiff from the hard ground.

Moonlight lit the woods, casting a net of silver and shadow all around. The air was cold, and he unrolled his fleece-lined jean jacket, which he'd used as a pillow, and put it on.

"Anything?" he asked.

"Only a beautiful night," Dina replied. "I'm not ready to sleep yet. Mind a little company?"

Cork arched his back, working out a kink that felt as though a horse had kicked him. He sat down beside Dina on the fallen trunk where earlier Meloux had smoked. On the lake, the silhouettes of the two islands were clear, the water in the channel between them sparkling like a swatch of black velvet sewn with a million sequins. Occasionally a soft breeze came out of the west and the aspen leaves rustled with a sound like the running of fast water.

"I never have nights like this," Dina said. "All my nights echo off concrete."

"But you like being a city girl. Or so you said."

"I could get used to this."

"Why are you here, Dina?"

She stared at the lake, then at the sky, and finally turned her face to Cork. Her skin was milk white in the moonlight and flawless. "People around your town tell me that even when you weren't sheriff you helped take care of some pretty troubling situations. Not because the responsibility was yours officially, but because that's who you are. I understand that."

"Nature of the beast?"

"Something like that. Also, I thought that when you found Lizzie, having a woman around might help."

"If you like this kind of thing so much, why did you leave the FBI?"

"Men and money. Too many of the first, too little of the second. By men, I mean flaming assholes with enormous egos. Now I only do what I want to do."

"And you do this kind of thing a lot?"

"I hunt people, yeah. Usually I find them. That's something I'm good at. I also protect people. I'm good at that, too."

Cork realized that his breath had started coming out in faint clouds. Soon, he knew, the frost would start to form, the leaves becoming brittle.

"What aren't you telling me?" he said.

She looked surprised, perhaps a little too theatrically so. "What do you mean?"

"Your story makes sense up to a point."

"What point?"

"That you're here out of the goodness of your heart, some protective sentiment about Lizzie. You're smart, you're tough, and you're not about public service and goodwill toward people. So why are you here?"

She smiled coquettishly. "Maybe I'm worried about you."

"Right," Cork said.

"Stranger things, Horatio . . ." She leaned over and kissed him lightly on the cheek. "See you in a couple of hours." She stood up, but when she turned, she let out a small, startled cry. "Henry."

Cork swung around and saw that Meloux stood very near, his dark eyes fixed on the lake.

"What is it, Henry?"

"I have been thinking about the bear trap." Meloux walked forward and waved toward the two islands. "Only one way in."

Cork followed his gesture and saw how the moon lit the water in the channel, a glittering path between the two black formations. He thought about it. The most direct way to the portage on the other side of the lake. The stone slabs breaking the water, requiring a slow, careful passage. He understood that whatever moved between the islands would be an easy target.

"You think he's on one of the islands, waiting for us to pass?"

"If his heart is set on killing, it would be a good place."

"How can we be sure?" Dina asked.

"Somebody needs to check it out," Cork said.

Dina shook her head. "Even if you headed there now, you'd be a sitting duck in all that moonlight."

"If he's awake and watching." Cork studied the island. "But if he's awake and if he's watching, he'll be looking this way and not watching his back."

Meloux laughed quietly. "You are thinking like the bear now."

"You're going to circle around behind him?" Dina said.

"It seems to me like the best approach."

"Not alone."

"I'm not risking anybody else." Cork scanned the eastern sky, still heavy with night. "How long before first light, Henry?"

"An hour," the old man said. "Maybe less."

"Then we should get started." He woke Fineday and Morgan and explained to them what was up.

"I'll go," Fineday said.

"It's already decided, Will."

"I'm not going to just sit here and see what happens."

"That wasn't what I had in mind." Cork looked toward the sky. "It'll be light soon, and if Stone's waiting for us, he's sure to be watching. We need to make certain his attention stays focused here."

"How?" Morgan asked.

"I think someone should cook breakfast. The wind's blowing toward the island and the smell ought to get his attention. There should appear to be a lot of activity going on."

"I don't want to sound pessimistic," Dina said, "but what if he shoots you, slips off the island, and gets away?"

"We need to close the back door, make sure he stays there. That's where Will comes in. And you, Howard. As soon as you can see enough to make your way through the woods, I want each of you to circle the lake from a different direction, post yourselves about two-thirds of the way around on either side, someplace where you have a clear view, a clear shot if Stone tries to leave. Dina, you'll be seeing to the same thing from this side. That way, you'll each have a third of the lake covered. As soon as we confirm that Stone's on the island or as soon as any shooting starts, you'll be responsible for radioing base, Dina, to get the critical response team out here right away."

"What about you?" Dina said.

"I'll be leaving very soon to paddle to the back side of the island."

"I already told you, in the moonlight you'll be a sitting duck."

"The moon's low enough that it casts a shadow of the trees

267

onto the lake, see?" He pointed toward a black, ragged lip of deep shade that lay over the water all along the western shore. "If I stay in the dark there, keep to the shoreline, and circle carefully, Stone shouldn't be able to see me."

"You hope," she said.

"Whatever we do, there's risk. You and Meloux, you'll have to make it look good, like we're all still one happy family here at the campsite."

Meloux nodded thoughtfully. "It is a good plan, Corcoran O'Connor. Worthy of a good hunter."

"Thanks for the vote of confidence, Henry. Let's roll."

The first thing he did was to contact base, explain the situation, and make sure that Larson had the CRT standing by. There were only three walkie-talkies. Cork took one and gave the other two to Morgan and Fineday. He tuned the radio to the same frequency so that initially Dina could communicate with the others, then change frequency when she needed to communicate with base. He checked his rifle, stuffed extra cartridges into his jacket pockets, and with Morgan's help quietly set one of the canoes on the water.

"Half an hour to first light," he said to Dina. "As soon as Howard and Will take off, get a fire going, start something cooking, anything."

"How does peanut butter and jerky sound?"

"Awful. But see what you can do to make it smell good, okay?"

Meloux said, "I can think of a few tricks."

"Thanks, Henry."

"Good luck." For the second time that morning, Dina gave his cheek a kiss.

Morgan said, "I wish you good luck, too, but don't expect a kiss from me."

Fineday offered his hand. "Thank you, Cork. I owe you."

"All right, then."

He stepped into the canoe, shoved off, and dipped the paddle. A few strokes out, he glanced back. In the dark among the trees, his companions had become nearly invisible. He glanced toward the islands and hoped the same was true of him.

Lamb Lake was an oval with a circumference that Cork

roughly calculated to be about two miles. If he didn't care about noise, he could easily make the trip to the backside of the islands in twenty minutes, but paddling quietly took more time. He was painfully conscious of the gurgle of water that accompanied each paddle stroke. Once, because he couldn't see clearly in the shadow of the trees, the canoe bow scraped a rock with a disquieting rumble.

In a while the birds, those that had yet to migrate and those that never would, began to sing, to call, to argue, to declare territory. Cork hoped the noise would help mask his own sound and he bent harder to the paddle.

By the time he slid around the southern end of the lake, out of the protective shadow of the tree line into moonlight, a faint evanescence had crept into the eastern sky, the promise of morning. The Northwoods began to take shape like a photo tediously developing. Cork glanced toward the campsite. A yellow tongue of flame licked among the trees there, and he knew that Morgan and Fineday had begun their mission. They were spreading a net across Lamb Lake, and if they were lucky they would snag Stone in it. If they were very lucky, no one would be hurt. But Stone was well named, and Cork was a realist. He would be satisfied if Lizzie and all those who'd come with him to look for her made it out of the Boundary Waters safely. He tried not to think of himself beyond the point of his own mission, which was simply to find out if Stone was on one of the islands, waiting. The possibility that they might have anticipated correctly and actually surprise him fueled Cork's tired body and brain. He felt remarkably ready.

A rat-gray light seeped over the lake. When Cork reached the shoreline almost directly opposite the campsite, the whole woods had emerged in particulars. Individual trees stood out, irregularities of the shoreline became obvious, distant hills were distinct. And everything had color. The green pine boughs over red-brown trunks, yellow meadow grass, silver reeds in the shallows. A breeze barely strong enough to ripple the water touched Cork's face, and he smelled a campfire. Along with it came the aroma of frying fish. Meloux, he knew. God bless him.

He slipped his walkie-talkie from the holder on his belt. He had set the volume low so any noise that might slip out wouldn't announce his presence. He spoke into it quietly.

"O'Connor, here. I'm in position on the eastern shore and just about to head to the big island. As soon as I know anything, I'll report. Out."

Cork had cautioned the others not to respond, not to risk any sound that might jeopardize him unless it was absolutely necessary.

Three hundred yards of water lay between him and the islands. Once he started toward them, he was, as Dina so aptly described it, a sitting duck, an easy target for even a lousy hunter, and Stone was a dead shot. But there was nothing else to be done now, and he dug his paddle into the water and shot forward.

Far across the lake, the first direct sunlight touched the tops of the aspens that enclosed the campsite, and the leaves glowed as if they were molten. Fish fed in the water all around Cork's canoe, flashes of scale and fin that left rings spreading on the still surface.

Cork headed for the larger island, toward a small indentation surrounded by pines. The shoreline there appeared to be free of rocks, and he hoped he could land without bumping the canoe against anything that would cause a sound. The part of the island dominated by the jack pines was to his right, and the hill covered with sumac rose to his left. As he approached, he saw no sign of Stone or of a canoe that would have brought him there.

Ravens flapped about in the crowns of the pines, their caws grating harshly against the quiet that lay over the lake. As Cork neared them, the birds seemed to grow more agitated, hopping along the branches, shrilly protesting. He drew up to the island and back-paddled to slow his approach. The bow kissed land and he stowed his paddle. Lifting his rifle, he disembarked and eased the canoe farther onto solid ground to anchor it. He hunkered down and listened. In the treetops, the ravens had fallen suddenly and ominously silent, but they still followed him with their black eyes as he slipped along the edge of the tree line. He saw no indication of Stone or Lizzie, no evidence that any human had ever set foot there. The ground under the pines was thick with brush and he knew there was no way to move through silently. Instead, he hugged the shoreline, edging toward the rise where the blood-red sumac grew.

He'd half circled the island when the walkie-talkie on his belt crackled to life.

"I see her. I see Lizzie."

Although Cork had turned the volume low, in the silence on the island Fineday's voice exploded like a firecracker.

"She's on the shore. Christ, I think she's dancing."

Cork fumbled with the knob and turned the walkie-talkie off completely. He did a quick calculation. If Fineday had set himself up as planned and could see her, it meant that Lizzie must be on the far side of the sumac-covered hill. That she was on the island didn't necessarily mean that Stone was with her, but probably it did, so Cork no longer had a purpose in staying there. His mission had been accomplished. He could leave, make a judicious exit, but he couldn't bring himself to do that.

Lizzie dancing? What was that all about? What did Stone have up his sleeve?

He bent to the ground and began to crawl up the slope on all fours, snaking his way among the woody stalks of the sumac. The leaves hid him, but they also blinded him. As he neared the top of the hill, Lizzie's voice came to him, singing. Something about sunny days, clouds. Then he realized it was the *Sesame Street* song, the opening ditty his own children had grown up singing. Lizzie's voice was sweet, almost innocent, a little distracted. Cork took a risk and stood a moment, lifting his head and shoulders above the sumac branches.

There she was, dancing in a large patch of dry grass that grew between the sumac and the pines. It was less a dance than a simple swaying as she sang. Her eyes were closed and she seemed to be moving inside her own small, safe world.

Safe? Cork wondered. Where the hell was Stone?

The rifle barrel that kissed the back of his neck was cold. Stone, in his coming, had been absolutely silent.

"If you move, O'Connor, if you even twitch, your head is gone."

Cork felt a tug on the rifle in his hand.

"Let go nice and easy," Stone said. "That's right."

The rifle slid from Cork's grasp and he heard a soft rustle as Stone laid the barrel against a sumac bush.

Stone said, "You had me confused. I couldn't figure why you'd stop for breakfast or risk tipping me off with a fire. So I put Lizzie out there, thinking you'd come for her. I didn't realize you were already here until I heard that squawk box on your belt. By the way, I'll take that, too."

Cork handed it over his shoulder. "I've got people all around the lake, Stone. There's no way you're getting off this island."

"I'll take my chances."

Lizzie looked up from her patch of yellow grass and smiled. The sun was not high enough yet to strike her face, but there was a kind of light dancing there nevertheless. She lifted her hand dreamily and waved.

"What's she on?" Cork asked.

"What isn't she? That girl's a walking pharmacy."

"You brought her along just to use her?"

"That's what happens to the weak. They get used, preyed on, eaten. Basic law of nature."

"So what now?"

"Now you die."

"Why?"

"Are you afraid to die?" The question had a sneer to it.

"It might help if I knew why."

"Why? Stupidest question you can ask. Never gets answered. Nobody ever told me why that son-of-a-bitch stepfather of mine beat me like a dirty rug. When they locked me up for killing him, nobody ever told me why. When my mother died alone and dirt-poor, nobody ever gave me a reason why. So I stopped asking a long time ago, and the question became how. How to survive."

"What did I do to you?"

"You personally? Nothing."

"But this is personal."

"It is now."

Now, Cork thought. But not at first?

"You have me," he said. "You have what you want. Why not let Lizzie go?"

"So that your death will have meaning and purpose? I don't think so. I like the idea of you dying for no good reason at all."

"You want to know the only thing I regret, Stone? That I won't see them shoot you down."

"You mean like I'm going to shoot you? You think that's what I'm going to do? Hey, man, I tried that once. I'm glad it didn't work. Too removed from the kill."

The rifle no longer pressed its deadly agenda into Cork's neck. Behind him, he heard the ruffling of cloth. A moment later, Stone said, "Turn around."

A sharp, blinding edge of sun now cut into the blue above the trees, and Cork blinked against the glare. Stone had removed his shirt and stood bare chested, his prison tattoos dark green on his tawny flesh. They reminded Cork of parasitic worms that grow unseen inside a man but eventually reveal themselves through the skin. In the grip of Stone's right hand was a hunting knife, its seven-inch blade glinting with an icy light.

"When I was in Stillwater, I dreamed of the day I'd feel the twist of a blade in a cop's heart. I'm going to like this. I'm going to like the look on your face when you feel it, too."

He lunged. It was a feint, really, not a killing thrust. He was testing Cork's reaction. Perhaps he had expected Cork to retreat, jump back. If so, he was surprised. Cork met Stone's outstretched arm with a quick knife-hand blow that drove the weapon down and away and made Stone stumble. Cork followed with a kick to the man's knee. Stone bent but he didn't topple. It was enough for Cork. He turned and fled through the sumac, a desperate swimmer in a crimson sea. He heard Stone huffing at his back, crashing through the brush behind him. Cork raced across the grass where Lizzie danced and he headed for the lake. With a long arcing dive that took him beyond the rocks of the shoreline, he split the surface. The shallows dropped away quickly to a jumble of stone slabs that littered the lake bottom ten feet down. Cork swam deep, planted his feet on the gray stone, and turned to meet his adversary.

He'd done all this without thinking, but somewhere in his brain was the knowledge that water would equalize them, slow Stone's hand as it wielded the knife, handicap them both equally in their need for air.

Stone came with a splash, trailing a wake of bubbles and white water. He swam straight for Cork, using both arms to propel himself. Cork watched the knife hand, and when it was drawn back at the end of a stroke, he thrust himself from the bottom and caught Stone before he could bring the blade into striking position. Without hesitation, he went for the man's eyes, driving the fingers of his right hand into a socket. Even in the muffle of deep water, Stone's bellow was a roar. He curled, kicked out, landed a boot in Cork's ribs.

Once more, Cork used the opening to retreat. He clawed to the surface and stroked hard to shore. Hauling himself onto the island, he sprinted past Lizzie, who watched him fly by with her eyes wide, as if he were some mythic creature or spirit, a *manidoo* that had sprung from the lake. He hit the sumac and made for the hilltop and the rifles there. He didn't look back to see if Stone was at his heels, but put all his energy into the race for a weapon. When he grabbed his rifle, he spun around.

Stone had not bothered to pursue him. He'd stopped where Lizzie, in her clouded state, had watched the struggle. His big bare left arm pinned her to him with an iron grip, and in his right hand the blade of the knife pressed against her throat. Her eyes were no longer dreamy but full of terror as she comprehended that her death was no farther away than a twitch of Stone's hand.

"She'll go first, O'Connor. You know I'll do it. Drop the rifle."

Cork did.

"Come down here. We still have business, you and me."

Cork descended, brushing aside the blood-red sumac leaves. He stepped onto the grass.

Stone's left eye socket was a raging red and already swollen nearly shut. "You try to run again, I'll kill her."

Anger like acid pulsed through Cork, rage that Stone would use the girl this way. The hell with all the reasons Stone was the man he was. He would be a better man dead.

"Turn her loose and let's get to it, you son of a bitch," Cork said.

Stone flung Lizzie aside. She tumbled to the ground with a small cry. Stone set his mouth in a line that showed teeth—a grin or grimace, Cork couldn't say. Stone's hard body tensed and the muscles swelled under his taut skin. His good right eye, the pupil dark as an empty grave, regarded Cork intensely. Cork readied himself. Stone let out a scream, a kind of war cry, and charged, galloping across the grass, his knife lifted high, gleaming in the morning sun as if white-hot.

Then his chest opened, a portal that spouted blood, and he fell, collapsing far short of where Cork stood. At the same instant, the crack of a rifle shot broke over the island. Cork looked toward the lake. In the bow of a canoe, paused midway between the campsite and the big island, sat Henry Meloux. In the stern knelt Dina Willner, cradling a rifle and still squinting through the scope. In the heat of the battle, neither Cork nor Stone had seen them coming.

Blood wormed from the entry wound dead center between Stone's shoulder blades. Cork turned him over. The exit wound in his chest was the size of a man's fist, the edges ragged with fragments of white bone. His mouth hung open and his eyes looked stunned. It was illusion, for Stone felt nothing now, not surprise or bitterness or betrayal. He was dead. Simply dead.

Cork sat down, suddenly too weak to stand. He watched Meloux and Dina Willner paddle toward the island. Lizzie lay in the grass, crying softly. Cork thought he should go to her, offer comfort, but he couldn't move. The canoe touched shore. Meloux climbed out and after him came Dina. The old Mide went to the girl and spoke to her in a low, gentle voice.

Dina sat down beside Cork.

"Thanks," he said.

"I told you. It's what I'm good at."

The *whack-whack-whack* of chopper blades came from the distance. The critical response team.

Meloux left Lizzie, who'd ceased her weeping. He walked to the body, sat crossed-legged beside it, and in his ancient, cracked voice began to sing, guiding Stone along the Path of Souls.

Cork was soaked and shivering now.

"Cold?" Dina asked.

"Freezing."

"Here. Let me help."

She put her arms around him, offering her warmth, for which he was grateful. He was even more grateful for the gift she'd already given him. His life.

42

FIRST THING, CORK called Jo.

"Hey, gorgeous."

"Cork!" she said, her voice full of joyous relief.

"Bos told me you'd talked to her."

"Oh, Cork. Thank God. I was worried."

"I knew you would be. That's why I didn't tell you I was going."

"Did you get Lizzie?"

"She's fine."

"And Stone?"

"We brought him in. Not alive."

"Does that mean it's over?"

"Not entirely. I still think someone hired Stone to kill me, and I still don't know who."

She was quiet. "So they may try again?"

"It's certainly a possibility." He wanted to give her more, an absolute reassurance, but that wasn't something he could offer. "How are the kids?"

"Fine. Rose and Mal took them all to South Bend today to visit Notre Dame. I stayed. I didn't want to miss this call."

"You mean if it came."

"I knew it would. Cork, when can we come home?"

"Soon, I hope. We'll be interviewing Lizzie shortly. Maybe we'll know more after that. I have to go, sweetheart. Things still to do."

"I know. I love you, cowboy."

"I love you, too."

Lizzie Fineday had been fed a decent meal and coffee, and was coherent. Although she distrusted cops, she was grateful for what Cork and the others had done and was willing to talk. She waived her right to counsel but asked that her father stay with her during the questioning.

Stone, she said, had enlisted her help to play a joke on the local cops, something she didn't mind doing. He told her that afterward they'd do a little Ecstasy. The afternoon of the shooting, they'd parked his Land Rover at the bridge over Tick Creek. He got out and told her to wait five minutes, then follow him on foot to the Tibodeau cabin. She'd wondered about the rifle he took with him, but not much. On the Iron Range, everyone seemed to have a rifle. Just as she started for the cabin, she heard two shots. She didn't know what that was about.

"The dogs," Cork said. "He shot the Tibodeau dogs."

She started crying, and they waited to go on until she'd calmed down.

She made the call from the Tibodeaus', imitating Lucy's voice, not a difficult thing. Almost anyone could do a decent impersonation of Lucy. After that, Stone had her climb the hill with him and they waited. She'd asked about the Ecstasy. He told her to be patient, gave her some grass to smoke in the meantime. She lay down on the top of the hill. It was evening by then, and she remembered staring up and thinking how soft the sky looked, like a big bed with dark blue silk sheets. She was tired and was almost asleep, when she heard the car from the Sheriff's Department coming down the road. She got up and saw that Stone had the rifle to his shoulder and was sighting. He started shooting. She freaked and ran. She barely remembered stumbling down the backside of the hill, and then she was standing in the dry bed of Tick Creek, crying uncontrollably, with no idea where to go. Stone came charging down the hill, grabbed her arm, yanked her after him, and they ran for the Land Rover. After they drove away, he told her if she said anything to anybody, she'd go to jail for sure. She was confused and scared.

"Did he tell you why he shot at the sheriff and deputy?" Simon Rutledge asked.

He'd said a guy paid him.

"He didn't tell you the guy's name?"

He hadn't.

"Did he say anything at all about him?"

Nothing she could remember.

Rutledge asked a few more questions about Stone, then Ed Larson said, "Tell us about your relationship with Eddie Jacoby."

She met him in her father's bar when he went there to see Stone. Jacoby made passes at her, the usual kind, and she didn't pay much attention. He gave her a business card, one with a Hollywood logo, and told her he could get her into movies. She still didn't want to have anything to do with him. She got weird vibes from him, creepy.

"But the night he was murdered, you went looking for him at his hotel. Why?"

Because after the shooting at the Tibodeaus', she was scared. She'd decided it was best to get out of town, and she thought maybe Jacoby was being straight with her and could get her to Hollywood. She left him a note saying if he was interested in partying to meet her at Mercy Falls.

"Why Mercy Falls?"

It was isolated and easy to find. She didn't want anyone to know she was seeing Jacoby, didn't want it to get back to Stone. When he showed up, she got into his SUV. They snorted a little coke. He gave her a beer. They drank, talked. He touched her. She didn't like it, but she wanted to get out of Tamarack County and she thought he might be her ticket. She felt trapped in the SUV, so she got out and went to the overlook. She was feeling woozy, light-headed. Jacoby joined her, began going at her again with his hands. She got tired of it and tried to push him off. He seemed to like that and began getting rough. He hit her, then he hit her again. She tried to make him stop, begged him. He pushed her down, fumbled with her jeans, worked at pulling them down. She fought him, and then he really laid into her. She remembered the blows, but she didn't remember any pain. Everything seemed to go kind of distant.

She stopped talking, and Cork and the others waited. Will Fineday's eyes were hard as agates, and deep hollows ran beneath his cheekbones. The scar on his face had turned bone white.

"Did he assault you sexually?" Larson asked gently.

She cried again, huge sobs that wracked her body, but she managed to say yes.

They took a break from the questioning. Cork asked if she'd like something to drink, a Coke maybe. He got one from the machine in the waiting area. She drank a little, and when she seemed calmer, they continued.

She didn't remember him leaving, but she remembered being alone at the overlook, hearing the water of the falls, feeling the ground very cold under her. Then a strange thing happened. An angel spoke to her.

"An angel?"

That's what it had seemed like because of her voice. Gentle, kind.

"*Her* voice? It was a woman?"

Yes.

"What did she look like?"

She didn't know. The night was dark, the moon gone, and she wasn't thinking clearly.

"But a woman, you're sure?"

She thought so.

"What did she say?"

It sounded like "Poor vaceeto."

"'Poor vaceeto'? Vaceeto, is that a name?"

She didn't know.

Larson looked at the others. "Vaceeto?"

They shook their heads.

"What happened after the angel spoke to you?"

After a little while, she roused herself. Her pants were down and she pulled them up. She could see Jacoby's SUV still parked in the lot. She was afraid, so she ran like crazy to her own car, locked the doors, and got out of there fast. She drove straight home.

"Edward Jacoby was stabbed to death. Do you know anything about his murder?"

She said she didn't.

"Did you see him again before you left the parking lot?"

No.

"When we tried to locate you for questioning, you'd gone to Stone's place. Why did you run to him?"

She'd gone to Stone because she didn't want to talk to the police, and Stone promised he'd keep them away. He also promised to keep her high. That was something she very much wanted. To be high and to forget.

She broke down again. This time she couldn't stop crying.

Cork said, "Let's call it a day."

"An angel?" Rutledge said.

They sat in Cork's office. Larson, Rutledge, Willner, and Cork. It was almost noon. Cork had changed into his spare uniform, and he'd eaten a ham-and-cheese sandwich and had drunk some coffee. He was tired. The food and the coffee helped a little, but sleep was what he needed most. Days of uninterrupted sleep.

"'Poor vaceeto.' Mean anything to anybody?" Larson asked.

"A name? An endearment?" Rutledge said.

"Not a personal endearment, apparently. It didn't mean anything to Lizzie."

"It was a woman, yes?" Rutledge said.

Larson cleaned his glasses with a small soft cloth he kept in his wallet for that purpose. "Between the beating and the drugs, Lizzie was pretty far gone, so who knows. Think Jacoby slipped a little Rohypnol into her beer?"

"That would be my guess. It's what you found in the glove box of his SUV."

"A woman," Larson said. "A passerby?"

"Who just happened to be there at midnight, and who just sympathized and left her?" Rutledge shook his head. "I don't think so."

"How about a prostitute, then? Maybe beating and raping Lizzie Fineday wasn't enough and Jacoby brought in some extra entertainment."

"That's a possibility. And maybe it was the prostitute who killed Jacoby, defended herself with a knife."

"There's another possibility," Dina Willner said quietly.

The men waited for her to go on.

"Stone." She looked every bit as tired as Cork felt, but her brain still clicked along magnificently. "He's the thread that ties together Lizzie Fineday and Edward Jacoby. We know he had a personal relationship with Lizzie, and Cork believes he had a business relationship with Jacoby. He was certainly a man capable of a brutal killing."

"Why would he kill Jacoby?"

"He seemed like a man who didn't need a lot of reason. It could be that his relationship with Jacoby had soured. Or maybe he didn't like what Jacoby had done to Lizzie."

"She said the angel was a woman," Rutledge pointed out.

"She was drugged and beaten. I'm just saying it might be worth checking out."

Larson said, "I'll have my people go over Jacoby's SUV again, looking for any evidence that might link Stone to that vehicle."

"I think we should also have another talk with the working girls," Rutledge suggested.

Dina eyed Cork. "We still don't know who asked Stone to do the hit. A favor for a friend, Lizzie said. Moose La-Russe?"

"How's Carl Berger doing?"

"Alive, but not able to talk yet," Rutledge said.

For a lot of reasons, Cork was glad that the slug he'd fired into the man on the farm in Carlton County hadn't killed him. "When he can talk, let's squeeze him for answers."

Cork had listened to most of the discussion without comment. Partly because he wanted to take in carefully what was being said. Partly because he didn't have anything to add. And partly because he was so tired, his brain felt like a chunk of cement.

Larson said, "Cork, you need some sleep."

"I'm thinking about that. First, I'm going to take Meloux home. Then I'm going to take a bath. Then I'll take a nap."

"Don't forget, you've got a mandatory meeting with Faith Gray this afternoon at four. This one you can't miss."

"I'll be there."

"What about Lizzie Fineday?" Rutledge asked.

"Release her into her father's custody," Cork said.

"You don't think she'll run?"

"Look where it got her the first time. We should make it clear to Will that he's responsible for her until the county attorney decides if he wants to charge her with anything."

They filed out of his office, but Dina stayed behind.

"After that nap you say you're going to take, I'd love to buy you a drink. Maybe even a steak," she said.

"I'll do the buying. I owe you big-time."

"I won't quibble with that."

"I think we should put the drink and steak on hold for today. You look like you could use a good rest, too."

"Me? I'm just getting my second wind." She laughed lightly. "If you change your mind, just whistle." She winked, turned, and sauntered from the room.

Henry Meloux was waiting in the common area. His statement had been taken, he'd eaten, and now he was sitting in an office chair, his head lowered, his chin resting on his chest, sleeping. Cork touched his shoulder gently.

"Henry, I'm taking you home."

Meloux blinked, then was wide awake and smiling. "Good," he said. "I need to lay these old bones down for a while." He got up from the chair.

Cork said to Patsy, who was on Dispatch, "After I get Meloux back to his cabin, I'm going home. No calls unless it's urgent, okay?"

"Sure, Cork. Get some rest."

They'd managed to keep the media in the dark about the operation in the Boundary Waters. Larson and Rutledge were preparing an official statement that would be released that afternoon. There were still a lot of unanswered questions in Tamarack County, foremost among them who killed Eddie Jacoby, but for a little while Cork thought he could step back and take a rest. He was looking very much forward to closing his eyes for a few hours.

Meloux nodded most of the way. When Cork pulled to the side of the road where the double-trunk birch marked the path to Crow Point, the old man roused himself and prepared to take his leave.

"Let me walk with you a bit, Henry."

The woods were quiet that day, the air warm and full of the musty smell of fall. For a while, they walked without speaking, the only sound the dry rustle of fallen leaves under their feet. Meloux moved slowly and Cork couldn't decide if it was weariness or simply that for Meloux there was almost never any need to hurry.

"Stone," Meloux finally said. "He was of the People in blood only. He did not understand the Anishinaabe spirit." He shook his head. "He might have been a great warrior, but a warrior fights for honor and for others. Stone's heart was too small. There was room only for him."

They reached Wine Creek, which was little more than a reddish iron-rich thread of water so late in the dry season. Meloux paused before crossing.

"Stone is on the Path of Souls, but I think he still weighs on you, Corcoran O'Connor. Or is it something else?"

"I can't help thinking, Henry, that maybe if we'd all done something different, stepped in a long time ago, Stone might have ended up a different man."

"Probably. But better? He spent much time in *Noopiming,*" Meloux said. "This land can guide a man, young or old, to a peaceful place. Stone was like his name, blind, deaf, hard to the good he was offered here." The old man took a long look at Cork. "I think there is something else."

"It's not finished, Henry. Stone wasn't at the heart of what's been going on. There's still so much I don't know, don't understand."

"I think you will," the old man said. "You are like a snapping turtle that does not let go. It also helps that you have a thick shell." He reached out and with his knuckles gave Cork a playful rap on his head.

Cork smiled. "*Migwech,* Henry," he said in thanks.

"No," the old man responded. "Thank *you*. You have given me one last good hunt to remember."

Meloux turned away, crossed the creek, and headed toward his sanctuary on Crow Point; to Walleye, who would be patiently waiting and would greet him eagerly; to a meal of wild rice and wild mushrooms; and finally to bed. That last part sounded so good, Cork wished he were going with the old Mide.

But he knew he still had miles to go before he slept.

Fucking miles.

43

Marsha Dross lived on Lomax Street, in a little white house with flower boxes on the front porch and green shutters on the windows. There was a For Sale sign on the lawn. Marsha and Charlie were planning to buy a home when they married, to start their life together in a new place large enough for a family. As soon as he returned to Aurora, Cork stopped by Marsha's house. She'd been released while he was in the Boundary Waters, and he wanted to tell her firsthand where the situation stood.

Her father opened the door. He wore a plain white shirt with gray slacks and black suspenders. He had on black socks, no shoes. A pair of black-rimmed reading glasses were nestled on the bridge of his broad nose. A folded paper, the *Duluth News Tribune,* was in his left hand. With his big free right hand, he waved Cork inside.

"Thanks, Frank," Cork said. "They told me at the department that Marsha had been released from the hospital. Is she here?"

"In her bedroom. Heard you had a little excitement."

"A little. All right if I talk to her?"

"Just let me make sure she's awake and decent."

Frank went down the hallway.

To anyone who knew Marsha, her house was a pretty fair reflection of the woman. Neat, uncluttered. Needlework hung framed on the walls, an art form that had been a favorite of her mother. A few lush plants, just enough to make the rooms comfortable. Finished floors with hand-loomed rugs. It was a nice place, but given her upcoming marriage, Cork could understand why she'd sell.

"Go on back," Frank said when he returned. "She'd love to see you."

Marsha's room was full of sunlight that made her face bright. Her hair was brushed, and she appeared to have put on a bit of makeup. She wore a clean white T-shirt and had the covers tucked around her below that. She was sitting up, her back propped against a pillow. She smiled when Cork walked in.

"You're looking better," he said.

"I wish I could say the same for you."

"Last couple of days have been a little rough."

A small white wicker chair had been placed next to the bed for visitors, and Cork sat down.

"We got him," he said.

"I know. Patsy called. What she couldn't tell me was why he did it."

"He died without saying directly, but I'm almost certain it began as a hit."

"Who hired him?"

"We're working on that."

She registered no emotion. She was in bed, recovering from a wound that had nearly killed her, that had jeopardized her hope of ever giving birth to a child; yet, here she was, accepting with a simple nod that Cork still had no idea who had ordered the attack or why. He wondered if it was because she understood that knowing wouldn't change her situation, or because she believed that eventually what was hidden would be revealed, that Cork would find the answers. Maybe it was both, because Marsha was strong and she believed in her work and in her colleagues.

"Doctor says in six weeks I can be back on duty."

"What's Charlie think of that?"

"Charlie's decided that he'd rather have a wife who's in a different profession. We've called off the wedding."

"I'm sorry, Marsha."

"It would have been an issue eventually. Better to deal with it now. You look beat. You should go home, Sheriff."

"I'll keep you in the loop, I promise."

He stood up and Marsha put her hand over his on the bedspread. "Going into the Boundary Waters after Stone, that was a stand-up thing to do."

"Thanks."

Frank was waiting at the front door to let him out.

"She told me about Charlie," Cork said.

"She's strong," Frank replied. "In every way. She'll be fine. And Charlie? Truth is, I never thought he was the right guy for her anyway. Thanks for stopping by."

Cork shook Frank's hand, then headed out into the sunshine of that fine fall day. The screen door creaked on its hinges, and a moment later he heard the soft slap of wood on wood as it closed behind him.

He finally went home. Upstairs, he tugged off his clothes, stepped into the shower, and stood for a long time hoping the hot water would melt all the tension in his muscles. While the water ran, he considered the situation as it now stood, sifting through what he knew for an understanding of what he didn't.

The shooting at the Tibodeau cabin was a hit, arranged by some guy. According to Lizzie Fineday, Stone hadn't been any more specific than that. Some guy. Moose LaRusse? Who was doing it for Lydell Cramer or Cramer's sister? Then why hadn't Stone referred to LaRusse as a Shinnob, more common among the Ojibwe? And so far, was there any substantial evidence linking Moose LaRusse or Lydell Cramer directly to Stone? The connection was certainly possible but yet to be proven.

Who else had a connection with Stone?

Eddie Jacoby.

Okay, Cork thought as the water started to parch his skin, suppose it was Jacoby behind the hit. Why? Generally speaking, murder, when it was planned, was either for vengeance or gain. Had he done something to Jacoby to warrant his hatred? He barely knew the man. So what about gain? Was there something in Cork's death that would benefit Jacoby? Did Cork stand in the way of Jacoby's scheming to get a contract for Starlight? He couldn't think how. What could Jacoby possibly gain by killing him? Cork had nothing. Jacoby came from a family that had everything.

He stepped out of the shower and toweled off, then went to the sink, intending to lather up and shave his two-day bristle. He opened the medicine cabinet and a jar tumbled out, which he managed to catch before it hit the floor. It was the Noxema Jo used every night to cleanse her face, a simple object, but as he held it in the palm of his hand he felt a solid and profound connection with the woman he loved. He seemed to be at the bottom of a deep emptiness and wanted nothing more at that moment than to have Jo there beside him. He took a deep breath and put the Noxema back.

He reached for his razor but stopped.

He realized there was something he had that one of the Jacobys wanted, but it wasn't Eddie.

Ben Jacoby wanted Jo.

Hadn't he felt it the night Jacoby sat at his kitchen table? Hadn't he seen it in Jacoby's eyes whenever he looked at her?

Cork hesitated. Was this crazy thinking? Was this lonely, jealous, tired, crazy thinking?

He tried to slow himself, to consider it carefully, step by step. Stone had been hired to kill him. Eddie Jacoby had a relationship with Stone that included dealings of a potentially criminal nature, so arranging a hit was not out of the question. Ben Jacoby was responsible for getting his half brother hired by Starlight. Had he been planning this for some time, plotting to use Eddie's presence in Aurora to set up the hit? Was he capable of such a cold, calculated act? Hell, who exactly were these Jacobys?

"Grabowski Confidential Investigations."

Boomer Grabowski spoke words the way a rock crusher spit out gravel.

"Boomer, it's Cork O'Connor."

"Again?"

After Boomer and Cork worked together as cops in Chicago, Cork left the force to move to Aurora. A few years later,

Boomer had taken an early medical retirement because of an accident that left him with a leg that was next to useless, and he had opened his own private cop firm. A lot of time had lapsed without the two men talking, then a few months ago Cork had called Boomer for some help with a situation that was tied to Chicago. Now he was calling again.

"What kind of mess you in this time?" Boomer said.

"I need you to check on some Chicago people for me, Boomer."

"It's what I do."

"It's a family. Jacoby's the name. I'm most interested in Benjamin Jacoby and his half brother Edward Jacoby. Eddie was murdered here a few days ago. We still don't know who the perp is or the motive." Cork filled him in on the details, then gave him the addresses for all the Jacobys, including the father, Lou.

"Money," Grabowski said when he heard where they lived. "What do you want to know?"

"Anything and everything. Where'd the money come from, where does it go. Connections. These are people used to manipulating the world to their advantage, Boomer."

"They think they're bad dudes, huh? So I should be careful?" He gave a callous laugh. "You want dirt?"

"If that's what comes up."

"Always comes up with money. When do you need it?"

"An hour ago."

"Done."

Boomer hung up without a good-bye.

Cork looked at the clock on the stand beside the bed. 1:15 P.M. More than three hours before his appointment with Faith Gray. He decided to lie down for a while, close his eyes, nap if he could. He set the alarm for four and stretched out on the bed.

An instant later, the telephone woke him. Cork rolled over, groped around on the nightstand.

It was Boomer on the line.

"You hit the jackpot, buddy."

"What are you talking about?"

"Those Jacobys you're interested in."

"You have something already? I just called."

"Four hours ago."

Cork looked at the clock. It was ten after five. "What have you got?"

"I called Adam Gabriel. Remember him?"

"Sure. Nice guy, worked out of Central, last I heard."

"He's in the north burbs now, with Highland Park. Currently assigned to work with NORTAF."

"Never heard of it."

"Northern Illinois Major Crimes Task Force. Provides investigators for a number of northern communities. Gabriel says Eddie's pretty well known to the local constabulary, although if you talk to them, they'll swear his record is clean. He's never been formally charged with anything, and the feeling Gabriel has is that it took a lot of family money to keep him out of trouble. Fat envelopes under the table to a badge in the right position. You know how that goes. Appears to be a family tradition with these Jacobys."

"How so?"

"American branch began in the late teens. Guy name of Albert Jacoby comes over from somewhere in Europe, ends up in Chicago, associated with Jake Guzik."

"Greasy Thumb Guzik? Capone's financial wizard?"

"The same. He never gets his hands soiled with the dirty work because he's got a knack for handling finances. And not just for Capone. Made a lot of money for the mobsters, and made himself rich in the process. His only son, Lou, continues the family business but distances himself from the underworld, or so it appears. Does millions in legit transactions, but a lot of people in the know think he never completely severed those early, dirty ties. You know how it is. Even if a rat dresses in Armani, the stink of the sewer is still all over him. Cork, these Jacobys reek."

"What about his son Ben?"

"I don't get the sense of the old man's ruthlessness, but they're in business together and I can't believe he's not complicit. Does the apple ever fall far from the tree, buddy?"

"Any active investigations?"

"There have been from time to time but nothing at the moment, according to Gabriel."

"Good work, Boomer."

"All in knowing who to ask."

"There's someone else I want you to check on."

"Your dime."

"A security consultant out of Chicago. Her name's Dina Willner."

The sound at the other end may have been a cough or a quick, harsh laugh, or just a catch in Boomer's gravelly voice. Then he said, "What's Willner got to do with this?"

"The Jacobys brought her in to be sure Tamarack County's bumbling law enforcement didn't blow the investigation into Eddie's murder. You sound like you know her."

"Oh, yeah. I know Dina."

"So tell me."

"I'll tell you what's official, then I'll tell you what I think, what a lot of us security consultants think.

"She's good. And expensive. A thoroughbred background as far as law enforcement goes. Great record with the Bureau. Her client list probably reads like a who's who of Chicago's richest and most powerful families. Does very personal business for them."

"*Personal* meaning?"

"Now we get into speculation. You had a chance to observe her in action?"

"I have."

"Note anything unusual?"

"Like what?"

"That she could probably hold her own against a platoon of Navy SEALs."

"I've seen enough to be glad she's on our side."

"Is she?"

"Cut to the chase, Boomer."

"A lot of us in the business don't even carry a piece. Word is, Dina Willner travels with an arsenal. I'm saying that *consulting* is a delicate word for what Dina does."

"Which is?"

"Among other things, she's probably not above doing a hit."

"You know that for a fact?"

"I told you, speculation. She's good, she's discreet, and she

works for only the best-positioned people, so she's also protected. Ask a cop, and she's clean as a whistle. Ask me, I'd say
watch your back."

"She saved my life, Boomer."

"Bully for you. I don't know what happened, but if I were
you, I'd take a good look at the circumstance, make sure that it
is what it seems."

"You've been a big help, buddy."

"Bill's already in the mail. You need anything else, just
holler."

Cork swung his legs off the bed and stood up. He walked to
the window. It was late afternoon. He'd missed his appointment with Faith Gray. That meant a mandatory suspension
until Faith agreed to recommend he be permitted to resume his
duties as sheriff, and in the meantime Ed Larson would be in
charge of the department. Cork knew he'd fucked up, fucked
up pretty major, but he had other concerns on his mind. So
when, a few minutes later, he received a call from Larson in-
forming him that, in accordance with departmental regulations, he had been relieved of duty pending psychological
evaluation and a recommendation for reinstatement, he was
not alarmed.

"Faith said she'd be willing to work you in tomorrow, Cork.
Considering the circumstances, she's been very understanding,
but her hands are tied. It's the regs."

"I know, Ed. I'm okay with it."

"Well, hell, there's nothing to be done about it now. You
might as well go back to sleep," Larson advised. "Let me know
what you arrange with Faith."

"Anything new on the Jacoby murder?"

"Nothing so far."

When he hung up, Cork had no intention of going back to
sleep. He paced his room for a few minutes, going over questions in his mind. Then he reached for the phone.

"Dina? It's Cork O'Connor."

"I thought you were out for the count."

She sounded a little groggy herself, as if he'd awakened
her.

"I napped some. Got my second wind. Thought if you were

still interested, I'd love to buy you that drink and steak I promised."

"When?"

"Say, six-thirty? I'll meet you in the bar there at the Quetico Inn."

"It's a date." She sounded awake, and she sounded pleased.

44

THE DAY, WHICH began so well with Cork's call that he was safe, was destined to end in a nightmare.

When she hung up the phone, Jo felt an enormous weight lifted from her, felt as if she were floating. Cork was out of the Boundary Waters, tired but alive. She gave a prayer of thanks, then called Mal's cell phone. Rose answered, said that they were on the interstate halfway to South Bend. Jo told her the good news, declared that she felt like getting drunk, like celebrating, and proposed that she whip up a gourmet Italian dinner that night—spaghetti and meatballs, the one thing she knew for certain how to make. Rose sounded skeptical but agreed, and said to expect them between six and seven.

Most days in Aurora, she found an hour to slip away from her office and work out at the YMCA, but she hadn't exercised at all since she'd come to Evanston. She knew she needed an outlet for all the energy that filled her now, so she put on a sports bra, a T-shirt, and her Reeboks, and stretched in the living room for fifteen minutes. After that, she doffed her blue warm-up suit and drove along Green Bay Road to Kenilworth, then east to Sheridan Road. She parked on a side street in front of a house decorated with jack-o'-lanterns and ghosts and witches in anticipation of Halloween. She locked her car and began a relaxing jog on the sidewalk heading north. The homes on the eastern side of Sheridan, huge affairs with vast grounds, sat with their backs against Lake

Michigan. Those on the opposite side were still grand, but all the windows seemed like jealous eyes glaring at the greater splendor across the road. She passed Ben Jacoby's house and kept running.

A long time ago, Jo had dreamed of being a part of this kind of wealth. Her desire had had little to do with money, but was instead a desperation to rise above the drab, unhappy existence that had been her adolescence. She'd driven herself to be the best at everything, to get into a first-rate law school, and for a while to be on the partner track of one of the top law firms in Chicago. It had been her great fortune, she believed, to marry a man of a different ambition, whose life had been rooted in a small town buried deep in the remarkable beauty of the Minnesota Northwoods. She'd never regretted abandoning the chance for a splendid estate on Sheridan Road in favor of the cozy house on Gooseberry Lane.

As she ran through the glorious morning light, through the deep shadows of trees on fire with autumn color, with the lake silver-blue in the distance, she knew absolutely that her life with Cork couldn't have been more satisfying or full.

She spent the afternoon napping, catching up on the sleep she'd missed the night before worrying about Cork. At five-ten, she took the cylinder with Rae's painting rolled inside and headed out. She stopped at a grocery store and picked up a few items she needed to make the spaghetti dinner, then went to Ben Jacoby's home. She rang the bell, waited, and rang the bell again.

Phillip Jacoby opened the door. He smelled of alcohol.

"Ah, Ms. O'Connor. I was told to expect you."

"Your father's not here?"

"He's been delayed. He asked me to play host until he arrives." He stood back and welcomed her inside with a deep bow and a sweep of his hand. "Would you like to wait on the veranda? That's where I've been hanging out. It's a lovely afternoon, warm for this time of year, don't you think?"

He led her through the large dining room to the French doors that opened onto the veranda. The view was stunning, the long carpet of grass set with the blue swimming pool, the low hedge at the back of the property, the lake beyond. He offered her a chair at a white wicker table and she sat down. "May I get you something to drink? Myself, I'm having a martini. Several, actually."

"No, thank you."

"Oh, come on. How about a martini?"

"Nothing, thank you."

"A Coke at the very least. Dad would never forgive me if he thought I'd neglected you."

"A Coke, then. Diet, if you have it."

"Coming right up." He walked a bit unsteadily toward the sliding door that opened onto the kitchen.

She took in the view, checked her watch, wondered how long Ben would be. A notebook lay open on the table, and on top of it a book facedown. A bookmark had been slipped between the pages near the end. She turned it so that she could read the spine. *The Great Gatsby.*

"For my American lit class," Phillip said, returning from the kitchen. "A big bore, if you ask me." He held a tumbler in one hand and a martini glass in the other. "Here you go. Diet, just as you asked." He handed her the glass and sat down in a wicker chair. "Did you have a good time the other night?"

"Last night?"

"No, at my grandfather's house, the night the stone pillar attacked my Jag."

"I'm sorry. That must have been difficult for you."

"If by *difficult* you mean humiliating, then yes, it was."

She thought about pointing out that Ben had simply been worried about Phillip's safety but decided it wasn't her place to defend or explain the father to the son. She drank her Coke.

"You know, I have to give my old man credit. He knows how to choose his women."

"I'm an old friend of your father, nothing more."

"Is that why he has a picture of you on the desk in his study?" He held up his hand in surrender. "Sorry. None of my business."

She looked again at her watch.

"Somewhere you have to be?"

"I'm just wondering what's keeping Ben."

"Oh, it could be anything. He's a very important man, my father. You'd be surprised, all the excuses he's found over the years not to come home." He sipped his martini. "How's the Coke?"

"Fine, thank you."

"So. Your daughter—what's her name?"

"Jenny."

"That's right. Jenny. Is she, like, all in love with Northwestern?"

"At the moment, it's her first choice."

"But you'd let her go anywhere she wanted?"

"Within reason. A lot depends on financial aid."

"It must be a bitch being poor." He shrugged. "Me, I could afford to go anywhere. But here I am, stuck in my own backyard because it's where my old man went to school. You think I look like him?"

"Yes."

"Everybody tells me that, as if it's a compliment."

"You don't think it is?" She was suddenly feeling a little ill. Where was Ben?

"I don't want to be him," Phillip said with venom.

Jo put her hand to her head, feeling dizzy.

Phillip said, "You don't look so good."

"I don't feel well. I think I need to lie down."

"Sure. Let me help."

He took her arm and eased her up. She could barely stand. He walked her inside.

"Oh, my," she said, and her legs gave out.

Phillip caught her in his arms and lifted her.

The room seemed out of focus. She tried to gather herself, but everything was swimming. She was aware of stairs, of rising, then a soft bed beneath her and Phillip looming into view near her face.

"You think my father is an important man," he said, his voice distant. "Sure you do. All his women think that."

She wanted to tell him once and for all that she was not one of Ben Jacoby's women, but she couldn't make her mouth form the right words.

"By the way, my father called and canceled your rendezvous. He asked me to look after you, to give you anything you need."

She felt his hand on her breast and she wanted to scream, to fight him off, but she could not move.

"That's what I'm going to do," he said. "I'm going to give you exactly what a woman like you needs."

45

CORK ARRIVED AT the Quetico Inn well in advance of six-thirty and spent a while talking to Dick Granger, the desk clerk on duty. After that, he sat down at a table with a good view of the lake and the marina. The sun had just set and, reflecting the fiery afterglow in the sky, Iron Lake was a vast expanse of burning water.

Dina walked in a couple of minutes later, dressed in a black knit top and black slacks, flashes of gold at her ears, and a chain with a small diamond at her throat. Her clothing was simple but displayed nicely every slope and curve. Cork stood up and pulled the chair out for her.

"I can't remember the last time a man did that for me," she said. "So you changed your mind about dinner."

"The house felt too big and too empty." Cork took his own seat.

"I know that feeling well."

"I decided I needed company."

"And it was mine you wanted." She sounded flattered.

The cocktail waitress came.

"What'll you have?" Cork asked.

"Cutty," Dina said. "On the rocks."

"Two," Cork told the waitress.

Dina put her purse, a small black beaded thing, on the table, then folded her hands and gazed at Cork. "Out in the Boundary Waters, there were moments when the thought of good Scotch and a thick, rare steak was just about all that kept me going. I didn't imagine I'd be sharing it with you."

"A nice surprise, I hope."

"Very nice."

"It was quite a surprise for me," Cork said. "You showing up out there like that. And certainly lucky."

There was a candle on the table, a small votive in a glass jar. The reflection of the flame danced in Dina's eyes.

"Lucky for both of us. If Stone had killed you, I'd . . ." She gave a slight shrug. "I'm just glad he didn't." She gazed out the window at the lake. "I'm beginning to understand what it is you love about this country. It's beautiful and it's dangerous. That's an attractive combination."

"The land is just the land. It is what it is. The danger comes from people who go into it with the wrong attitude. Good people without a proper respect for what the Boundary Waters demands. And not-so-good people whose reasons for being there are at odds with the spirit of the place. I've seen both end in disaster."

The drinks came. Cork lifted his glass. "To friends," he said.

"Friends," she echoed, and sipped her Scotch. She glanced at him curiously, maybe a little shyly. "I've been wondering about your change of heart this evening. Was it only the empty house?"

For a moment he didn't answer. "In the Boundary Waters my way of looking at things changed."

"Changed how?"

He studied his hands. "Out there on Lamb Lake, I started to see life as a fuse getting shorter by the minute."

"And?"

He finally looked at her directly, looked into her dancing eyes. "I liked the feel of your arms around me."

She'd been drinking her Scotch. Her hand slowly descended as if it had taken hold of a heavy weight. "I liked how that felt, too."

Cork said, "We could take our drinks up to your room."

"My, that's quite a change."

"It was just an idea."

"Not a bad one, if you ask me."

301

Cork left plenty of money on the table for the Scotch and a good tip. They walked from the bar together, past the front desk, to the elevator, which opened the moment Cork pressed the button.

Inside, after the doors had closed, he said, "I don't know what you're wearing, but it's a wonderful fragrance."

"It's called Black Cashmere."

She reached out, touched his cheek, started to lean toward his lips just as the elevator stopped.

Halfway down the hall, she slipped her card into the key slot, opened the door, and stepped inside.

"Nice room," Cork said as he followed her in.

He crossed to the window. Outside, evening had descended fully, and the fire on the lake was gone. The water had become nickel colored in the dusk. When he turned back, Dina had put her glass on the stand beside the bed. She hadn't bothered to turn on a lamp, and in the dim light of the room she eyed him intently.

"I don't do this as a rule," she said.

She came toward him carefully, as if walking the dangerous edge of a high cliff. Her eyes never left his face.

When she was very near she said, "I told you that men don't interest me much. But when I find one that does, I'll let him do anything." Her smell, partly the Black Cashmere but also something else, better than perfume, profoundly human and female, enveloped him. "Anything."

He put his glass on the windowsill, reached out and took her. She pressed herself to him, breasts and stomach and hips and thighs, and her arms went around him like soft rope binding them together. She lifted her face hungrily toward his lips. He bent, felt her hot, Scotch-scented breath break against his face.

And the phone rang.

"Ignore it," she said in a hoarse whisper, and arched more tightly against him.

"It might be important."

"Nothing's more important right now than this."

Cork slowly drew away. "Answer it. I'll still be here."

She relaxed, let out an exasperated sigh, and released her

hold. At the nightstand, she grabbed the phone from its cradle. "What?" she said, with great aggravation. She listened. "Thank you. I'll take care of it later." She listened a bit more, rolled her eyes. "All right, all right. I'll be down in a minute." She hung up. "There's some sort of problem with my credit card. Apparently it can't wait."

"Go ahead," Cork said. "I'll make myself comfortable."

She returned to him, cupped his face with her hands, and kissed him. "This won't take long, I promise."

As soon as she was out the door, Cork hit the closet, found her suitcase, and opened it. Empty. He checked the shelf, the floor. He went to the bureau, yanked the drawers open one by one, riffled through her clothing. Kneeling, he looked under the bed, then stood up and headed to the bathroom.

When Dina came back a few minutes later, he was standing at the window again. The sky outside was almost dark and Iron Lake was the color of an ash pit.

"False alarm," she said. "You Minnesotans are very nice, but what you don't know about doing business would fill an encyclopedia." She sauntered toward him. "Where were we?"

She was still a few feet distant when Cork brought from behind his back the black ski mask. She stopped abruptly and considered first the mask, then Cork.

"I found it in the bottom of your cosmetics case," he said.

"In this country, you can never be sure about the weather," she replied in a leaden voice.

"It's the one you wore the night you planted the explosives in my Bronco."

"Were you looking for that, or just on a fishing expedition?"

"*Why?*" Cork spit the word. "Why bring my family into it?"

"Take your clothes off."

"What?"

"Take your clothes off. I want to see if you're wearing a wire."

He didn't move.

"Do you want to talk or not?"

He undressed. Sport coat, shoes, socks, shirt, pants. He laid everything on a chair. When he was down to his boxers, Dina said, "That'll do."

"Now tell me why," he said.

"I don't know why you think I can answer that question, but maybe I can help your thinking a little, provide a dispassionate perspective. For example, it might be productive to think about the explosive itself. If I recall, it was made with a blasting cap that was dead, yes?"

"You know it was."

"So it couldn't possibly have detonated. Now, it might be that the person who put it in your Bronco was simply stupid. On the other hand, it might be that it was never intended to hurt anyone."

"Then why was it put there?"

Dina picked up her glass from the nightstand and finished the Scotch with a clink of ice against the empty glass.

"All right," Cork said, addressing her silence, "let me do a little speculation. Let's say the device wasn't intended to kill anyone. What did it accomplish? It caused me to lose a lot of sleep. It certainly confused the situation. Were either of those the point? Or was it to separate me from my family, send them scurrying to Chicago? I'm thinking this because the night before the bomb was planted, Jacoby was at my house. He learned all about my family. Jenny and Northwestern, Rose and Mal in Evanston. He even knew Jenny was planning on using my Bronco the next morning. I'm thinking that a man like Jacoby believes he can manipulate anything and anyone to get what he wants. So he has someone—someone, let's say, like you—plant a bomb—or a nonbomb—to scare me into sending my family his way so that he can be with them, comfort them when word of my demise reaches them. Tell me I'm wrong."

"I enjoy seeing a fanciful mind at work. Go on."

"That's what the hit was about, I think. To get me out of the way because another man coveted what I have. It wasn't Lydell Cramer who wanted me dead. It was Ben Jacoby. And he used his brother Eddie to broker the deal. Now, your part in all this is still a little uncertain. What were you supposed to do? In the event that Stone couldn't complete the hit, were you instructed to kill him, make sure he didn't talk?"

"I was hired to make sure the investigation into Eddie's

death wasn't mishandled. Period. When I came here, I didn't know anything about Stone."

"Then why this?" He shook the ski mask at her.

"You've overlooked something obvious. It could be that the point of the bomb—or nonbomb, as you appropriately call it—was to ensure that your family was out of harm's way."

"Is that what Jacoby told you? Or did you even care, so long as he paid you enough? Out of harm's way, sure. And my wife right into his waiting arms."

"Not every outcome of an action can be predicted. It seems to me that whether Jo stepped into someone's waiting arms was entirely up to her, wasn't it? And as for killing Stone, when I pulled that trigger, I pulled it for only one reason."

In the little illumination that still fell through the window, he saw anger in her face, and perhaps hurt. He almost believed her.

"Tell me I'm wrong about Ben Jacoby," he said.

"It's an interesting speculation. Do you have any substantiating evidence?"

"He's a thorough man, but I'm sure he's slipped up somewhere. I'll find out where."

He went to the chair and began to dress.

Dina watched him. "What are you going to do?"

"Let Jo know who Ben Jacoby is. Then I'm going to figure how to nail him."

"Be careful, Cork."

He pulled on his shoes, tied them, and stood up. "You're worried about me?"

"Your family's safe. You need to think about yourself."

It took a moment for him to weigh her words and her tone. Then he understood. "He offered you the contract on me, didn't he?"

"If I wanted you dead, I'd have let Stone finish the job on Lamb Lake."

He still held the ski mask. He threw it to Dina.

"I should have it checked for explosive residue, and I should have your luggage and your car checked, too. If I were a betting man, I'd bet we'd come up with something. But you saved my life. Consider my debt paid."

As soon as he returned home, Cork called Evanston. Rose answered. Her "Hello?" sounded anxious, and when she knew who it was, her voice took a serious nosedive to a bleak octave.

"What is it?" Cork asked.

"I was hoping you were Jo."

"Why?"

"Well," Rose said hesitantly, "she seems to be missing."

46

ROSE EXPLAINED THAT they'd come back from their day in
South Bend to an empty house. Jo had left a note on the
kitchen table saying she was going out to buy some wine, had
an errand to run, and would be back before six. On the note,
she'd put the time she left, five-ten. She still hadn't returned.
There was also a message waiting on Rose's voice mail, from
Ben Jacoby, left at five-fifteen, apologizing to Jo for having to
cancel out. Something important had come up. He was sorry
and promised to be in touch.

Jacoby again, Cork thought.

"Cancel out on what?" he asked.

"I don't know, Cork."

"Was she going to meet Jacoby?" he asked.

"She didn't say a word to me about it."

"Did you try her cell phone?"

"Yes. She doesn't answer."

"How about Jacoby? Did you call him?"

"We don't have his number," Rose said. "It was blocked on
our caller ID, and when we tried directory assistance, they
told us it's unlisted."

"I have it," Cork told her. "I'll call."

"Oh, good. Let me know what you find out."

In his wallet, he had the card Jacoby had given him when
the man came to Aurora after Eddie's murder. Only his business number was printed on it, but on the back Jacoby had

written the number for his cell phone. Cork punched it in.

The phone rang at the other end. Jacoby didn't answer. The recorded voice said the customer was not answering calls at this time but a message could be left. Cork left one telling Jacoby to call, it was urgent, and he gave his cell phone number.

After a minute or two of hard, desperate thinking, he called the Quetico Inn and asked to be connected with Dina Willner. She didn't answer. He called the front desk.

Dick Granger told him Dina had just gone into the dining room. Should he page her?

"No. Just make sure she doesn't leave before I get there."

He called Rose and told her he'd had no luck with Jacoby, but he knew someone who might have a better idea how to get in touch with him. He'd let Rose know.

"How're the kids?" he asked before he hung up.

"Mal and I are downplaying this, but if we don't find her soon they'll know something's wrong."

"Do what you can, Rose. And thanks."

He found Dina seated near the fireplace, a glass of red wine in front of her, a thick New York strip bleeding onto her plate.

"This is a pretty good steak," she said, "and if you don't mind, I'd just as soon enjoy it alone."

"You told me my family's safe. You lied."

"Oh?"

"My wife's missing. She went to meet Jacoby and hasn't come back."

"Does she have a cell phone?"

"She's not answering it."

"What about Ben?"

"No answer there, either."

"Did you try his townhouse?"

"I don't have that number."

With an exaggerated effort, she reached into her purse and brought out a pen and a small notepad on which she wrote two phone numbers. "The first number is his townhouse, the second is his home in Winnetka."

"Thank you."

Cork stepped away from the table and tried the numbers. He didn't get an answer at either of them, but he left messages saying basically "Where the hell is Jo?" He turned back and found Dina watching him. Her steak was getting cold.

"What now?" she asked.

"I'm going down there."

"How?"

"Driving, I guess."

"Long drive alone."

"At this point, it'll be just as fast as trying to get a flight out of Duluth or the Twin Cities."

"How much sleep have you had?"

"Thanks for your help," he said grudgingly, and turned to leave.

"Wait." She wiped her mouth carefully with her napkin. "I'll go with you."

"I don't need—"

"You try driving to Chicago alone right now and you'll be a danger to yourself and everyone else on the road." She stood up. "You know what I'm saying is true. If you want to get to Chicago in one piece, let me help."

The weight on him felt enormous. Worry, sleeplessness, a long drive in the night with only his fear and uncertainty for company. He knew she was right, but didn't trust her motives.

"Look," she said. "Whether you believe it or not, I've always been on your side. And think about it. If I'm riding shotgun, am I going to shoot you while you're going seventy?"

He gave in because her logic was sound, and he knew he needed help to get to Chicago.

"Give me a few minutes to change and I'll meet you in the lobby," she said.

While she was gone, he called Rose and told her he was coming. She didn't try to argue him out of it. He instructed her to call the area hospitals in the meantime.

He phoned Ed Larson at home and filled him in.

"You really think there's reason to be concerned, Cork?"

On a normal day, maybe not, but Cork couldn't remember the last day his life felt normal.

"I'm going, Ed. That's all there is to it."

"We'll hold down the fort here. Keep me posted."

Dina came down dressed for business—black jeans, black

sweater, black sneakers, and a black windbreaker. A large black purse hung over one shoulder.

"Let's do it," she said, and hit the door ahead of him.

Cork glanced at his watch. It was almost nine o'clock. He figured if the roads stayed dry, if a cop didn't pull him over for speeding, if he didn't hit a deer, he'd be in Evanston in just under eight hours.

A lot of ifs.

They didn't talk much at first. Cork kept hoping his cell phone would chirp any minute and it would be Rose with word that Jo was fine and there was a good explanation for her disappearance. What that explanation would be, he couldn't imagine. Maybe her cell phone battery had died, although that was not like her. Why didn't Jacoby answer his phones?

"You have connections on the Evanston police force?" he asked Dina.

They were outside Duluth, heading over the bridge on the interstate into Superior, Wisconsin.

"I have connections on every police force."

"How about calling to check out accidents with injuries." He waited a beat, then added, "Or fatalities."

She talked to a guy she called Red, shot the breeze for a minute, then ran her request past him. She gave him Jo's name, the car make and license plate number, which Cork fed to her. It didn't take but a minute for Red to respond. Nothing involving Jo or even an unidentified victim. So far, it had been a quiet night in Evanston.

"How about Winnetka?" Cork said when she'd completed the call. "You know the cops there?"

"Couple."

"Think you can get them to send a patrol to Ben Jacoby's place?"

"What'll I tell them?"

"That some fuckhead rich bastard thinks he owns the universe and everyone in it."

"What'll I tell them?"

Cork let out a breath that momentarily fogged the windshield in front of him. "That there's an emergency, and Ms.

O'Connor needs to be contacted and we believe she's at the Jacobys', who aren't answering their phone. You can embellish as you see fit."

She did a nice job of embellishing and got a promise that a patrol car would swing by. It was, apparently, a quiet night in Winnetka, too.

"Today, after we came out of the Boundary Waters, did you give Jacoby an update?" Cork asked.

"That's part of what he pays me for."

"So at this point, he knows everything?"

"Everything we know."

"Is there anything you know that I don't?"

"Nothing that would help right now."

"Do you think Jacoby knows anything that would help right now?"

"Ben Jacoby always knows more than he tells."

She was quiet, staring out the window as the empty streets of Superior slid by. It was an old port town on the harbor, and its glory days were a memory. In the daylight, everything about the place seemed gray. At night, it looked even worse.

"When I told him about the Fineday girl's recollection of the night Eddie was murdered, something happened. I could hear it in his voice." Dina seemed to be addressing the door window, or her own faint reflection in it.

"What did you hear?"

"Like lock tumblers clicking into place. I think he put something together."

"What?"

"I don't know. But he told me I was done in Aurora."

"Except for killing me, if you wanted the contract?"

In her seat, she pivoted toward him angrily. "Just who the hell have you been talking to about me?"

"A reliable source."

"Let me guess. One of my colleagues in the security business."

"Someone I trust."

"Who repeated shit he knows nothing about."

Cork swerved to miss a black cat with glowing green eyes that had frozen in the headlights. "So that was nothing but a lucky shot on Lamb Lake?"

"I train for that kind of shot. That doesn't mean I enjoy it."

"And Jacoby didn't offer you a contract on me?"

"Go fuck yourself."

They took US 53 south out of Superior and in a while were skirting the Brule River State Forest. There wasn't much traffic and the road seemed to tunnel through the trees into endless black.

On the seat beside him, Cork's cell phone bleated. He picked it up. Rose was calling.

"We've tried all the hospitals anywhere near here, Cork, but nobody will tell us anything. They say legally they can't. But they're also saying that if Jo had been admitted and they were looking for nearest relatives, you'd have been notified. So I guess that's one way of saying she's not there."

"Okay, Rose. That's good. Evanston Police Department said they have no report of her being involved in an accident. And we've got someone checking out Ben Jacoby's house in Winnetka right now."

"What if she's not there?"

"Then we'll keep looking."

"The kids are scared, Cork."

"I don't blame them."

"Shouldn't we notify the police that she's missing?"

"They won't do anything, Rose. Not for at least twenty-four hours. Adults disappear all the time for their own private reasons." It was a line he'd delivered many times as a cop to a worried husband or wife. The truth was, most people showed up, came back after they'd had time to think things over. "Do what you can for the kids, okay, Rose? And thanks. If you hear anything—"

"I know."

Cork put the phone down beside him.

"Nothing?" Dina asked.

"Nothing." Cork swung around a slow-moving Voyager, the speedometer at eighty when he pulled back into the lane. The broken white lines came at him like tracer bullets from a machine gun. "You think I'm wrong about Jacoby wanting my wife?"

"I've never met your wife." She laid her head against the

seat back. "But I know that people kill for less compelling reasons than love."

"A man like Jacoby, does he even understand love?"

"We most desire what we can't have."

"Desire's not love."

"No," she said. "It isn't."

Her phone rang. She answered and listened. She said thank you and hung up.

"Winnetka PD. A couple of uniforms stopped by the Jacoby residence on Sheridan Avenue. Phillip Jacoby answered the door. That's Ben's son."

"I know," Cork said.

"He told them Jo wasn't there, that he hasn't seen her at all and he's been home all evening."

"Was Ben Jacoby there?"

"The cops talked to Phillip, that's all I know."

"Does he lie?"

"I don't know anyone who doesn't. Do you?"

In Eau Claire, they stopped for gas and Cork drove through a McDonald's because he hadn't eaten all day. Dina took the wheel and guided them to I-94, which would take them to Chicago. Cork ate, barely tasting the food. All he could think of was Jo. Where the hell was she, and was she safe?

And when that became almost unbearable, he thought about Jacoby and wondered what Dina had said that made him want her off the investigation.

47

THEY TOOK TURNS driving, nodding off briefly when they weren't behind the wheel. Once, Cork jerked awake with a terrified suck of air.

"Bad dream?" Dina said, shifting her attention momentarily from the road ahead. "You have a lot of those?"

"Tell me someone who doesn't." Cork rubbed his eyes and directed her to pull off at the next exit. He was ready to drive.

He wondered what was true about Dina Willner. How much of her had Jacoby bought? Was she really along to keep him from sleeping at the wheel or mostly to keep him in her sight for Jacoby? He was tired, knew that his judgment was off, and decided if he couldn't trust himself it was best to trust nothing.

They hit Evanston around five-thirty and fifteen minutes later pulled up in front of Mal and Rose's duplex. There was a faint glow in the eastern sky, but under the trees on the street where Cork parked, night still held solid. Most of the homes were dark. Upstairs in the duplex, a light shone behind the curtains.

Mal opened the door and hugged Cork in welcome. Rose was right behind him.

"Anything?" he asked. He'd checked in by phone only an hour earlier, but he still hoped that good news might have arrived.

"Nothing," Mal said.

"This is Dina Willner." Cork stepped aside. "She's been helping with the investigation in Aurora. She offered to come along and make sure I didn't fall asleep at the wheel."

"Won't you come in?" Rose said to her warmly. "I've got coffee."

"Thanks. I could use a cup."

Inside, Cork asked, "The kids?"

"Asleep," Mal said. "The girls have been up most of the night but they finally conked out a couple of hours ago."

"Let them sleep," Cork said.

They sat around the kitchen table, hunched over the coffee Rose poured. Jo's note lay in front of Cork. He could almost hear her voice in her carefully handwritten script.

"I feel so helpless," Rose confessed. "I don't know what to do."

"Let's start with what we know," Cork said. "She left to meet Ben Jacoby, but before he called to cancel. Did you save Jacoby's message?"

"Yes."

"Let me hear it."

Rose brought him the phone and punched in the number for voice mail. She tapped in a security code, then a code to replay the message, and handed the phone to Cork.

"Jo, it's Ben. I apologize, but something extremely important has come up that I have to take care of right away. I won't be able to meet you. I'm hoping you haven't left yet, but just in case you have, I'm going to call Phillip and let him know to expect you. You can certainly leave the painting, but I'd much rather you gave it to me personally. Again, I'm sorry to bail on you at the last minute. Honestly, this is business that can't wait. I'll be in touch."

Cork handed the phone back to Rose.

"Time on the message is five-fourteen. And the note Jo wrote said she left at five-ten."

"Yes," Rose said.

"So he just missed her." He looked at Dina. "You said you updated Jacoby about Stone. When did you talk to him?"

"As soon as we came out of the Boundary Waters. Later I gave him a full update on what we learned from Lizzie Fineday."

"About Eddie's murder?"

"That's right."

"What time?"

"I don't know. Around five, I'd guess."

"And when you talked to him, you had the feeling things seemed to fall into place for him, right?"

"That's the feeling I got, yes."

"A few minutes later, he calls Jo, cancels their meeting, and rushes off to take care of something that can't wait. Something that had to do with Eddie's murder?"

Dina nodded thoughtfully. "If I were you, that's the first question I'd ask when I see him."

"Second," Cork said. "The first thing I'm going to ask is 'Where the hell is Jo?'"

He stood up and took his mug to the coffee pot on the counter.

"Okay," he said, pouring himself a refill. "She was headed to Jacoby's place. He has two residences. A townhouse near downtown Chicago and a home on Sheridan Avenue in Winnetka. Her note says she'll be gone less than an hour. I'd say that eliminates the townhouse. During rush hour, it would take at least that long just to get there. So I'm betting it was the house on Sheridan."

"The uniforms who talked to Phillip said she hadn't been there."

"Maybe Phillip lied."

"Why?"

"I don't know, but it's the only solid lead we have, so that's where I'm starting." He grabbed his yellow windbreaker from where he'd draped it over the chair back.

"What are you going to do?" Dina asked.

"Pound on the door, or on the kid, until I get some answers."

When Cork pulled off Sheridan onto the private brick drive that led to Ben Jacoby's palatial home, the sky along the horizon above Lake Michigan burned with a warm orange glow that was dawn. The trees of the estate, a mix of yews and Catawba and maples, were eerily quiet, and Cork, as he stepped from the Pathfinder, realized that there were no birds in them and wondered where they'd all gone.

Curtains were drawn across the windows. The panes reflected an empty sky. At the end of the drive, which circled a small fountain edged with dewy grass, Cork spotted the garage doors, three of them, each with a row of glass panes roughly at eye level. He walked to the doors, Dina a step behind him, and peered in. It was an area large enough to accommodate four vehicles. Currently it was full. There was a Mercedes, a Jaguar with a smashed front headlight, a Lincoln Navigator, and a blue Toyota Camry with Minnesota plates.

"She's here."

"And that's Ben's Mercedes," Dina said.

He went back to the Pathfinder, opened the glove box, and took out his Smith & Wesson .38 Police Special and a box of cartridges. He filled the cylinder and snapped it shut.

Dina watched him. "You're not going in shooting."

"If this isn't a kidnapping, I don't know what is."

She put a hand on his arm. "Cork, what if she's here because she wants to be?"

"If that were true, she would have called. She wouldn't want Rose or the children to worry. Or me."

He approached the front door under the portico and tried the knob. Locked. He stepped back, looked left and right, turned toward the south corner of the house.

"I'm going around in back, see if I can find an open door," he said in a low voice.

"Why don't we just ring the doorbell?"

"You wait here," he said. "And don't ring the doorbell. Not yet."

He started across the lawn, the heavy dew soaking his shoes and the cuffs of his pants. He tried to move carefully, to keep his breathing steady while he battled fear and a mounting rage. Though his brain was fried from exhaustion and worry, he kept focused on the one thing he knew absolutely: Jo was somewhere inside this house, and she was not there because she wanted to be.

He turned the corner and lost sight of Dina. Trimmed bushes grew against the length of the house and Catawba branches reached above him. It seemed as though he'd entered a long, dim hallway that opened at the end onto the back lawn.

He'd gone less than halfway when shots rang out, two of them. Without thinking, Cork dove for the cover of the bushes and lay in the dirt, gripping his .38. He scanned what he could see of the estate, which wasn't much. In his mind, he replayed the sound of the shots. They'd come from ahead, from somewhere behind the house, out of his line of vision. He decided that they were probably not meant for him.

The quiet had returned immediately, pressing so heavily on Cork that he felt as if he were underwater. He forced himself to move and in a crouch went forward. At the back corner, he peered around the edge of the house. The yard was empty. He saw a pool, a small pool house, stairs that led up to a veranda. A black robe hung over the back of a lounge chair beside the pool.

He hugged the wall, edging his way toward the stairs. He finally pushed from the house and swung his revolver toward the veranda, which proved to be as empty as the yard. He looked at the pool, at the rose-colored stain spreading across the water. He crept nearer and bent over the edge. The body lay on the bottom, eyes closed, two dark plumes rising from somewhere underneath, near the middle of the back.

He didn't hear her but felt her presence. He turned his head and there she was, gripping a white robe closed over her breast, her hair a tangle, her feet bare, her blue eyes wide with astonishment.

"Oh, Cork, no," she whispered.

He was so happy to see her, he wanted to cry.

"Jo," he said, "I came to bring you home."

48

"HEY, CORK. Long time no see."

Adam Gabriel closed the door and offered Cork his hand. He stood six feet tall and was slender, with curly blond hair and a serious look in his face.

"What are you doing here, Adam? I thought you were with Highland Park."

They were in an interview room of the Winnetka Village Police.

"I'm also assigned to NORTAF. We float all over."

"That's right. I remember Boomer saying that."

"Good old Boomer." Gabriel allowed himself a brief smile, then sat down across the table from Cork.

"Good to see a familiar face," Cork said.

"They've been rough on you?"

"Just doing their jobs. You've got yours, too. They send you in to play good cop?"

Gabriel gestured toward the Styrofoam cup that held coffee, which was cold now. "Want something besides that?"

"I'm fine."

"You look like you could use sleep. I understand you drove all night."

"A lot of ground between me and Jo to cover. I'd love to be with her right now."

"She's in good hands, Cork. With someone from SANE. Sexual Assault Nurse Examiner program."

319

"I know what it is."

"Sure."

"How's Lucille?"

"Back in school. Almost fifty and she's finally finishing her degree. Never too late, huh?" He folded his hands on the table. "So this is what I understand. You came down here because Jo disappeared. You went to Jacoby's because of the message on Rose's phone. By the way, I didn't know she'd moved back down here. Happy to hear she's found a good man."

"We all are."

"So you and Willner head to Jacoby's. You see Jo's car in the garage, ring the bell—"

"We didn't ring the bell."

"Did you knock?"

"No. I tried the door."

"Which was locked?"

"Yes."

"So you started looking for another way in. You were on the south side of the house when you heard the shots and dove for cover in the shrubbery. Because you thought you were being shot at?"

"That's right."

He nodded in an understanding way. "Skittish. After that business on the reservation in Minnesota, it makes sense. How's the ear?"

"Doesn't bother me anymore. Stitches'll be coming out pretty soon."

"How long did you stay there in the shrubs?"

"Couple minutes."

"No more shots?"

"No."

"Then you continued to the backyard, which was empty."

"Except for Jacoby on the bottom of the pool."

"You saw no one leaving the scene?"

"No one."

"You told the other detectives that you thought Jacoby was dead. You think about pulling him out, checking for a pulse?"

"No."

Gabriel seemed a little troubled with that. "You know dead when you see it?"

"Jo came from the house at the same time. I was more concerned with her."

"And besides, you figured it was Jacoby who'd kidnapped her, right?"

"I didn't want him dead. I just wanted Jo back safely."

"But things got out of hand. I can understand how that might happen."

"Look, Adam, I know you have to do this. I didn't shoot Jacoby."

"But you did have a gun."

"Which I didn't fire. Winnetka Police can easily confirm that. They swabbed my hands for residue. They decide to have it analyzed, it'll show negative. But I'm sure they told you all this already."

"Cork, they're searching for gloves."

"Gloves?" He thought about it a few seconds and understood. "They found the gun that killed him. Let me guess. A throw-down?"

"That's right."

"Adam, you know me. You know I'm not a dirty cop."

"I told them that. But they don't know you, Cork. They're looking at a guy who believed his wife had been kidnapped, who believed Jacoby was responsible, and who charged in on his own, thinking he'd save her. On top of that, he's a guy who's currently suspended from his duties as sheriff pending psychological evaluation."

Cork sat back, weary to the bone.

"It would have helped if you'd told them about that last part."

"They ready to charge me?"

Gabriel shook his head. "Timing and motive are strong, but they don't have any physical connection between you and the throw-down. Plus, you've been extremely cooperative."

"Are they going to hold me?"

"No. But they want you to stick around for a while. You know the drill." Gabriel breathed a deep sigh. "There's something else, Cork. Phillip Jacoby came in a while ago with his lawyer, Lawrence Blumenthal. He's admitted that he had sex with Jo, but says it was consensual."

"Consensual?" Cork almost leaped from his chair.

"That's his statement. He says his father came home, found them together. Jo had had too much to drink and had passed out. Jacoby was extremely upset and sent Phillip to stay with an old friend who just happened to be Lawrence Blumenthal, one of Chicago's best defense attorneys. Blumenthal insists that Phillip was at his home when Ben Jacoby was murdered."

"Money makes everything so much easier, doesn't it?" Cork said bitterly.

"When Boomer called me yesterday, I wish I'd known what all this was about. I'd have been happy to help."

"That was yesterday, Adam." He reached across the table and shook Gabriel's hand. "And you *have* helped."

Dina Willner was waiting for him.

"You look like the walking dead," she said. "Why don't I give you a ride back to your Pathfinder. We need to talk."

While the police were questioning Dina, one of her operatives had delivered her car to the village police station. It was a red Ferrari, and she fit into it as if she'd been born in the driver's seat.

"I saw Phillip at the police station, but they wouldn't let me talk to him," she said.

Cork told her what he'd learned from Gabriel.

"Consensual? That's ludicrous." Her voice was pitched with anger.

"Adam says his attorney's one of the best in Chicago."

"Blumenthal's good, but Phillip's got a history of date rape. The Jacobys' hired me last year to make a Rohypnol situation go away."

"Do the police know that?"

"The police know all about the Jacobys, but money's an enormous protective moat."

She stopped at a light. The Ferrari purred under her like a contented lion.

"There are things I haven't told you, but now that Ben's dead, I think I should."

The light changed. She shifted and accelerated with a roar of the powerful engine.

"I can understand why you thought it was Ben who was responsible for Stone trying to kill you, but you're wrong. He didn't know anything about it. Eddie was mostly all about Eddie, except where Ben was concerned. He looked up to Ben, desperately wanted his approval, wanted to feel like they were true brothers. The trouble was, he was the kind of guy who fucked up everything he did.

"Eddie knew about Ben and Jo. When he turned up dead and Ben went to Aurora and heard about the ambush on the reservation, he didn't believe it was just a coincidence that Eddie was there when it happened. He was afraid Eddie might have done something stupid, like arrange the hit. I wasn't hired just to make sure the investigation was handled correctly. I was hired to find out if what Ben feared was true."

"And if it was?"

"My first priority was to make sure you and your family were safe. Then, if Eddie was responsible, identify the person he hired for the hit and intervene discreetly. Dissuade that person any way I could and keep the Jacoby name out of it."

"Tall order."

"I'm well paid."

"So I was wrong about Ben Jacoby wanting my wife?"

"I don't know about that. Ben always struck me as a man who never had a handle on happiness. If Jo made him happy once, maybe he would have given almost anything to get her back. He might even have been just fine if it had to be over your dead body, so long as he wasn't responsible, but he wasn't the kind of man who'd have had you killed for it."

"You seem to know Jacoby pretty well."

"In my business, people tell me their secrets."

"You're paid to keep those secrets. Why are you telling me this?"

"Call it a moral imperative. Anyone who'd care is dead. Ben, Eddie, Stone. And with everything that's happened to you and your family, I think you deserve to know the truth.

But if you ask me to testify in court, I'll refuse. You understand?"

"Sure."

"However, I can give you the name of the girl and her family in the date rape incident. I'd bet it wouldn't take anything at all to make them turn on the Jacobys."

They were on Sheridan, not far from Ben's place.

"So who killed him?" Cork said.

"Until you told me about Blumenthal, I'd thought it might have been Phillip. An argument, maybe."

"If Blumenthal's telling the truth, Phillip's off the hook. From what I've gathered, Jacoby was probably shot with a throw-down, so that would indicate a planned killing."

"Ben was a powerful man. I'm sure he had enemies. Maybe his murder didn't have anything to do with the rest of this business."

Cork shook his head. "Think about it. After you called him with your report on Lizzie's interview, he canceled his meeting with Jo and went somewhere. You said it yourself, that he put something together. What was it he figured out? That might be clear if we knew who he went to see."

"You think his death had something to do with Eddie's murder?"

"It's the only connection I can see at the moment. It's all too closely related to be just coincidence."

Dina pulled onto the brick drive that led to Jacoby's home. The crime scene team was still there, but the media vans were gone and the neighbors had all retreated back into their own big houses. She pulled up to the Pathfinder, still parked where he'd left it earlier that morning.

"Cork, I'm not on the Jacoby payroll anymore. Eddie, Ben, they're not my worry now. But you are." She reached into the glove box, pulled out a business card, and gave it to him. "If you need me for anything, call."

"Listen," he said. "That was a lousy thing I pulled in Aurora. I'm sorry."

"Done in a good cause," she replied, then smiled wistfully. "'Of all sad words of tongue or pen, the saddest are these, it might have been.'"

She leaned over, kissed his cheek, watched him get out, then growled away in her Ferrari, a car that cleaning up the messes made by people like the Jacobys had paid for.

By the time he arrived at the clinic, Jo's examination was over and she'd gone home with Rose.

At the duplex, he found the women gathered around the kitchen table—where else?—drinking tea. The long night of despair had left them with puffy, dark-circled eyes and faces still pinched with worry. Jo was safe, but Cork suspected that for Jenny and Annie the ordeal was not over. It was clear they knew what she'd been through, were probably even now imagining it, living it in their own minds, feeling the filth of it on their own bodies. What had happened to their mother had been the kind of thing that happened to other women, other families, in other places, but here it was at their table, the monster of all fears, and Cork understood that for a while it would shadow their world.

He kissed Jo and held her.

"They kept me a long time," he said. "I would have been there."

"It was fine. Rose was with me."

"Thank you." He spoke over Jo's shoulder to his sister-in-law. "Where's Stevie?"

Rose said, "Mal took him to the park. He doesn't really know what's happened."

"Good. Hi, guys." He kissed both his daughters as he circled the table toward an empty chair.

They smiled bleakly.

"Would you like some tea?" Rose offered.

"Sure, what the hell. Wouldn't happen to have a cookie to go with it?"

"Chocolate chip."

"Rose, you are an angel."

He looked at the two most dour faces at the table and he spoke especially to them. "You know, in the last week I've been shot at, threatened with a bomb, attacked with a knife. Your mother's gone through her own terrible hell. But here we are together around this table, and I can't remember a time when I've felt so lucky. Rose," he called, "cookies all around. And don't stint on the chocolate chips."

Smiles like small bright caterpillars crawled across his daughters' lips.

Later, in the privacy of the room Jo had shared with Stevie, Cork held her for a long time.

"I'm sorry," he whispered into her hair.

She spoke, her breath soft against his cheek. "The truth is, I don't remember anything. I only have vague impressions, like a bad dream. I suppose that's lucky."

"It may hit you later."

"Probably."

"I have to see Faith Gray when I get back to Aurora. Maybe you should, too."

"All right."

"I wish I could have kept it from happening."

She drew back just enough to look into his eyes. "How could you? It was such a predatory act, who could have predicted it?"

"It's not the first time Phillip's done something like this, Jo. I'm going to do everything I can to make certain he doesn't prey on anybody else."

"Do they have any idea about Ben? Who killed him?"

"Not yet. I get the feeling they'd like to pin it on me."

"They can't possibly suspect you."

"If I were them, I'd consider me a pretty good suspect. Jo, Dina told me some things I think you ought to know."

They sat on the bed in the room she had shared with Stevie, and he told her everything he knew.

"All this," she said, "because Eddie Jacoby thought he could make a gift of me."

"It's a possibility."

"All this death."

He touched her cheek, felt her heat, her life flowing into his fingers. "We're not dead, you and me."

"But Ben is. Why him?"

"I don't know."

"I want to leave here, Cork. I want to go home."

"The Winnetka police would like us to stay awhile. They'll have more questions when they're finished with the crime scene and start looking at the evidence."

"I've told them everything I know."

"So have I, several times. They'll ask again. Before we talk to them we should have a lawyer. And there's something else, Jo."

He told her about Phillip Jacoby's assertion that she had consented to the things he'd done.

"That little son of a bitch," she gasped.

"So for a while, we sit tight and see what develops and make sure that we're prepared to face the worst."

She felt the tears welling, her throat closing. "Shit doesn't just happen, does it, Cork. It happens and happens and happens."

"Here," he said. He kissed her hands, lifted them, and waved them gently over their heads.

"What was that?" she asked.

"A shit shield."

She was laughing quietly when the knock came at the door.

"Cork?" Rose called. "There's a call for you."

Jo followed him to the kitchen, where he took the phone and said, "Yes?" He listened, looked concerned. "I'll be right there." He hung up.

"What is it?" Jo asked.

"That was Lou Jacoby. He wants to see me."

49

Cork parked on the drive that circled in front of Lou Jacoby's Lake Forest estate home.

"I swear to God," he said, killing the engine, "the North Shore has more castles than the Rhine."

He'd tried to convince Jo not to come, but she'd insisted, telling him that now that they were together, she'd be damned if she'd let anything separate them.

Evers, Jacoby's houseman, answered the bell. He looked tired but still maintained the rigid formality his position required.

"The O'Connors," Cork said. "Mr. Jacoby is expecting us."

Evers led them down a long hallway to the rear of the house, where a small, lovely woman with black hair and a Latin look awaited them. She seemed familiar, but Cork couldn't recall where he'd seen her before.

"I'll take it from here," she said to Evers.

"Of course." The houseman vanished back into the vast silence of the place.

"It is a pleasure to see you again," she said to Jo. Then to Cork: "We have not met. I am Gabriella Jacoby, Eddie's widow."

She spoke a foreign accent he'd recently heard, and he realized where he'd seen her before. In the face of a pilot.

"Do you have a brother?"

"Yes."

"Tony Salguero?"

"Do you know Antonio?"

"I've met him."

"He is a good brother." She smiled briefly, then lapsed into a somber tone. "I told Lou this was not a good idea, but he insisted. I warn you, he is out of his head with grief. He will probably say things that will sound crazy. You may leave now, and I will explain it to him."

"If he wants to see me," Cork said, "let him see me."

She reached for the knob, hesitated as if she were going to speak again, perhaps argue the wisdom of proceeding, then she opened the door and stepped ahead of them inside.

The room was mostly dark and smelled of an old man and his cigars. The only illumination came through the slits of partially opened blinds over the long windows. In the far corner, bars of light like the rungs of a ladder fell across a stuffed chair and its occupant. Jo's eyes climbed each rung until they encountered the red eyes of Lou Jacoby staring back. He wore a dressing gown that hung open over his chest, showing a white undershirt. His legs were bare, his feet slippered. His hair was a wild spray of white. He seemed smaller than the last time she'd seen him, as if Ben's death had taken away something physical from his own form. He held a glass that contained ice and a hickory-colored liquid. A smoking cigar sat in a standing brass ashtray to his right.

"I knew you were trouble the moment I saw you with him." The voice came from the darkness beneath his red eyes, from the mouth Jo still couldn't quite make out.

"I'm sorry about your son," she said.

For a moment, he didn't reply. Then: "The sons should bury the father. That's how it's supposed to be."

Gabriella crossed to him and stood at his side, her hand protectively on his shoulder. In the slatted light, her shadow fell over the old man and swallowed him.

"You wanted to see me," Cork said.

"If I were a younger man, I'd stand up and beat you to death with my own hands."

"I didn't kill your son."

"Lou has been told about the police investigation," Gabriella said. "He knows about the gun they found. What they call a throw-down, I believe. They told him it is something policemen have been known to do to get away with murder."

"Not this cop. Have you talked to Dina Willner?"

"She has been mysteriously silent to our inquiries," Gabriella replied.

"It's not enough you kill my son," Jacoby spat out. "You slander my grandson, too, with your lies."

"I understand your grief," Cork said. "But don't let it blind you to the truth."

With difficulty, Jacoby rose from his chair. "I'm not a man of idle threats. An eye for an eye. You hear me?"

"Mercy," Jo said, speaking softly into the dark of the room. "It falls like the gentle rain from heaven, Mr. Jacoby."

"Not in this house, woman." He said to Gabriella, "Get them out."

Gabriella came forward and placed herself between the O'Connors and the old man. "It's time for you to go."

"We've done nothing to you," Jo said.

"You've done everything short of killing me. Get out."

Jo turned away, then Cork. Gabriella followed them out and led them toward the front door.

"I warned you," she said.

"Have you even tried to help him understand?" Cork said.

"You saw him. When he's ready to listen to reason, I will reason."

As they neared the door, they saw Evers blocking the way, arguing with someone standing just outside.

"What is it?" Gabriella said.

Evers stepped aside, and Jo saw Rae Bly framed in the doorway.

"I was trying to explain that I have my instructions."

"To keep me out?" Rae's voice was a sharp blade of indignation. "I don't believe it."

"That's all right. I will take care of it," Gabriella said.

Evers stepped back, turned, and walked away, stiff as a zombie.

Gabriella addressed her sister-in-law. "It is true. He does not want to see you."

"Does he even know I'm here?"

"I told him that you called. He won't see you. If you try to talk to him now, you will only be hurt by him. When he is ready, I will let you know."

"I'm his daughter, Gabby."

"As am I now. And we must think of him. Later he will see you. It will be all right, I promise, *pobrecito*. Now, good day to you all."

Cork and Jo stepped outside.

Rae stared at the door that had closed against her. She wilted and then she wept. "Ben, Ben. Oh, Benny."

Jo put her arms around her. After a minute, Rae pulled herself together.

"I'm sorry," she said.

"That's all right."

"I didn't get all the details, but enough to say I'm sorry for what happened to you, Jo. It's shameful, but that's the Jacobys. Did Lou see you?"

"Only long enough to threaten us," Jo said.

"Don't take him lightly."

"This is Cork, my husband."

"I figured."

"Rae is Ben's sister."

"I was sure he'd see me. We're all we have now, each other."

"Apparently, he thinks he has Gabriella, too," Cork said.

"Will you be all right?" Jo asked.

"No, but that's not your concern. You have your own problems. And the Jacobys," she said bitterly, "we take care of our own affairs."

They left her, a small figure standing alone in the shadow of her father's great house.

50

FROM ROSE AND Mal's duplex, he called the number on the card Dina Willner had given him.

"I just came from Lou Jacoby's," he told her.

"And you're still alive?"

"Not for long, from the way he's talking."

"Cork, Lou doesn't just talk."

"Gabriella Jacoby says you've been silent on what happened at Ben's place."

"Silent? I've been trying to reach Lou but Gabriella is screening everything. I can't get through to him."

Cork heard the frustration in her voice, a rare emotion in his experience. He realized how tired she must be, too.

"How's Jo?" she asked.

"Doing remarkably well, considering."

"Strong woman. How about you? Are you all right?"

"Jo's safe. I can handle everything else."

"I'll get to Lou somehow, explain things, Cork. That's a promise."

He was exhausted, but he spent the afternoon at a park on the lake with his family, pushing Stevie on the swings, talking with his daughters about Northwestern and Notre Dame, watching Jo—who seemed, in spite of what she'd been through, calm as the water on the lake that day. Twenty years before, he had proposed to her on Lake Michigan, on a dinner cruise, an evening that had changed his life and taken it in the best of directions.

He sent Jenny and Annie off to play with their brother while he sat on a blanket with Jo.

"I've been thinking about Gabriella," he said. "And her brother. And about an angel who spoke to Lizzie Fineday."

"An angel?"

"In Lizzie's confused recollection anyway. What was it that Gabriella called Rae this morning? *Pobrecito*? What does that mean?"

"If I recall my college Spanish, it means something like 'poor little one.'"

"Lizzie said her angel called her 'poor vaceeto.' Could it be that the angel spoke Spanish and what she really said was *pobrecito*?"

"You think Gabriella was Lizzie's angel?"

"When I called Edward Jacoby's home the morning after he was murdered, his housekeeper told me that Mrs. Jacoby wasn't there. She was on a boat. Tony Salguero told me he was sailing on Lake Michigan. Because I didn't know there was a connection between them, I didn't put it together at the time, but what do you want to bet they were on the same boat? How difficult would it be to anchor somewhere not far from an airfield, fly to Aurora, take care of some pretty gruesome business, and get back to the boat in time for Lou Jacoby's call the morning after Eddie was murdered?"

"I don't know. How would you prove something like that?"

"They had to leave a trail. Dock somewhere, file a flight plan, gas up, land and park a plane. If they tailed Eddie out to Mercy Falls, they had to have a vehicle of some kind. A rental, maybe? There's got to be documentation for some of this somewhere. It should just be a question of tracking it down."

He stood up and called to the children. He hated to end the picnic, but there was work to be done.

First he called Ed Larson, who had already spoken with the Winnetka police and knew about what had happened to Jo.

"Christ, Cork. I'm so sorry."

"Yeah."

"I'd love to get that Jacoby kid alone somewhere."

"Won't happen, Ed."

"How's Jo doing?"

"Holding her own."

"Look, I do have two pieces of good news."

"I could use some about now," Cork said.

"First, Simon Rutledge was finally able to talk to Carl Berger. Looks like we'll be amending the complaint against Lydell Cramer to include conspiracy to commit murder. Berger says that Cramer used his sister and LaRusse to arrange to have Stone do the hit at the Tibodeau cabin. The motive was revenge, pure and simple.

"Now for the second piece of good news. We finally found Arlo Knuth. He'd gone on a bender and wound up in the drunk tank in Hibbing. I talked to him. He says that after Schilling ran him off, he parked behind the blockhouse on the lower level at Mercy Falls. Around midnight, he saw two vehicles head to the upper lot near the overlook. Right behind them came a third vehicle that parked in the lower lot. Two people got out and hiked up the stairs toward the overlook. They came back down half an hour later and left. Arlo says he left right after that. The place was getting too busy."

"Was he able to give you a description?"

"No, but he did give us something very interesting. Whoever those two people were, they spoke Spanish."

"*Pobrecito*, Ed."

"What?"

Cork told him about Gabriella Jacoby and Antonio Salguero, and explained his thinking about Eddie's murder.

"The Salgueros lost everything in Argentina. Marrying Eddie Jacoby gave Gabriella a handle on another fortune. With her husband dead, she probably stands to get her hands on a significant chunk of change. Insurance, at the very least. Maybe she even moves up a notch in the old man's will."

"They'd been married for years. Why kill Eddie now?" Larson asked.

"Maybe she waited until she was solid with his father. She's given Lou grandchildren, weaseled her way next to his heart. I'd bet she and Tony have been thinking about it for a while.

Could be that Aurora's isolation seemed to offer the opportunity they'd been hoping for."

"And the hick cops they figured would do the investigating."

"Probably that, too. Look, it's a lot of speculation, I know."

"Makes sense, though."

"When Dina gave Ben her report on our questioning of Lizzie Fineday, Jacoby must have known what 'poor vaceeto' was really all about. He took Dina off the case in the hope of keeping her ignorant, and I'll bet he canceled his rendezvous with Jo because he went to see Gabriella or Salguero, to confront them."

"Didn't want the police involved?"

"Exactly. A family matter. The family name at stake. Something like that. There's a lot of digging to do, Ed."

"I'm on it, Cork," Larson said. "I'll keep you posted."

The next call was to Dina Willner's cell phone.

"Tell me what you know about Tony Salguero," he said when she answered.

"Handsome. Educated. Refined. Daring."

"Daring? What do you mean?"

"He flies. He sails. Like his father, he's a world-class big-game hunter. He was in the Argentine military for a long time, an officer."

"Special training?"

"I could find out. Why?"

"I want to know if he's the kind of man who'd know where to thrust a knife to kill somebody instantly."

Dina's end of the line went silent a long moment. "As in Eddie Jacoby."

"Exactly."

He told her what he knew and what he suspected.

"Gabriella and Tony together." She was quiet, probably rolling the idea around in her thinking. "Gabriella was a better woman in almost every way than Eddie could have hoped for. Murder might not have been on her mind at first, but I imagine anybody married to Eddie would, over time, begin to think about it seriously."

"There's something else," Cork said. "I think Ben suspected.

335

I think that's why he took you off the case. 'Poor vaceeto.' He put it togther right away."

"God, why didn't I?"

"It had been a hard day, remember?"

"Still . . ."

"Look, with your connections, any way you could find out quickly who Ben called after he talked to you yesterday afternoon?"

"You're thinking he called Gabriella or Tony?"

"And then went to see them."

"That's why he canceled on Jo. Cork, do you think they killed him?"

"Not necessarily themselves. They may have had it done. Ed Larson's working on the connection with Eddie Jacoby's murder. Once we have that, Winnetka PD might be persuaded to look at them for Ben's murder as well. Given the ties between the Jacobys and local law enforcement, it might be best not to tip our hand too early."

The silence again. Then: "It feels so cold, Cork."

He thought about Gabriella, the shadow she'd cast over Lou Jacoby that morning, her control. It may all have started as a way to rid herself of a man no woman in her right mind would want, but it was different now, huge and malevolent. It had probably taken the life of Ben Jacoby, and Cork could feel the menace at his own back, in Lou Jacoby's ignorant vow, "An eye for an eye."

"Watch yourself, Cork."

"You, too."

He put the phone down. He'd made the calls in the front room of the duplex, away from the rest of the family who were all gathered in the kitchen around the table talking and laughing. He could hear Mal and Rose, each of the children, and Jo. He thought about the Jacobys, the various reasons they had married—money, position, beauty, prestige, duty. For all its pain, all its uncertainty, all the terror of the power it wielded, love was still, in Cork's book, the best reason.

He started toward the kitchen, toward the laughter that was a song, toward the love that was everything.

51

HE HEARD THE phone ring, looked at the clock beside the bed, wondered who would be calling at two in the morning. In the hallway, the floorboards creaked, and Mal Thorne said, "Hello?"

He didn't say anything else. A minute later, a cupboard door squeaked open in the kitchen, followed shortly by the rattle of glass in the refrigerator.

Cork threw back the covers, pulled on his pants, and slipped from the room where Jo lay sleeping.

The kitchen light was on. Mal stood at the counter near the sink, a glass of milk in one hand, a cold chicken leg in the other. He held up the leg. "There's more in the fridge if you're hungry."

"No, thanks."

Mal wore a white T-shirt, red gym shorts, white socks. "Trouble sleeping?"

"Can't get my eyes to close. My brain won't stop working. Who was on the phone?"

"Nobody there. Second time tonight. Would it help you to talk?"

"Maybe."

Mal used the chicken leg to point toward the kitchen table. "Confessional's open."

Cork sat down. His feet were bare and cold on the linoleum.

"I've been thinking about everything that's happened recently," he said. "A lot of what's occurred I understand now, but I'm having trouble understanding my place in all this."

"How so?"

"Jo's a wonderful woman."

"You won't get an argument from me on that."

"She didn't want me to take the job as sheriff, Mal."

"Did she tell you that?"

"No, but I knew. She's always been afraid of the effect it's had on our family."

"Cork, if you're going to start blaming yourself for what's happened—"

"It's not that, Mal. It's a realization. I was doing fine running Sam's Place. It's a pretty location there on Iron Lake. I grilled good burgers. I set my own hours, closed up at night, went home, and what did I have to worry about except making sure there were enough potato chips for the next day? Now I lie awake worrying about everything. The department budget, county politics, the safety of my people." He glanced toward the hallway. "The safety of my family."

"Why did you take the job?"

"I told myself there were good reasons, but in the end it was pride, plain and simple."

"I suspect there was more to it than that, but I understand what you're saying. So what are you going to do?"

The fridge kicked on, and the hum grabbed Cork's attention. He looked at the refrigerator door, which was decorated with photos, mostly ones Jo had sent of the children and her and Cork.

"I'm going to quit. When I get back to Aurora, I'm going to tender my resignation."

Mal took a bite from the chicken leg and didn't seem inclined to argue.

The phone rang in the hallway.

"There it is again," Mal said. "The caller who isn't there." He got up to answer. "Hello?" He paused. "Yes, he is. Just a minute." He brought the cordless into the kitchen. "It's Dina Willner, for you."

"Dina, what's up?"

"Make sure the lights are out, then carefully look out the front window."

Cork said, "Kill the lights, Mal."

Mal did as Cork asked and followed him to the front room. Cork parted the curtains a crack.

"What am I looking for, Dina?"

"Black Malibu two houses down, far side of the street."

He located it parked in a place where the streetlights didn't quite reach. "I don't see anything. Wait." Inside the Malibu, a match flared, lighting a cigarette perhaps. "Okay, I make 'em."

"They've been watching for a while."

"Who are they?"

"Lou threatened you this morning. I'd say he's making good on that threat."

"A hit?" Cork eyed the Malibu fiercely. "Where are you?"

"In the alley back of the duplex. Get dressed and get out here. You have a firearm, bring it."

"Winnetka PD took it."

"Then just get out here."

Cork handed the phone to Mal.

"What is it?"

"See the black Malibu? Dina thinks there's someone in it who's been paid to kill me."

"Jesus, Mary, and Joseph. Let's call the police."

"Wait, Mal. There's not much they could do at this point but roust the guy. If it *is* a hit, that would only delay the inevitable."

"What are you going to do?"

"Dina's out back. I'll talk to her. Maybe we can come up with something. Don't wake anybody."

Cork went to the bedroom, dressed quietly, put on his windbreaker, and paused a moment before he walked out. Jo lay on her side, the top sheet half covering her face. She looked peaceful, and he wanted her to stay that way. He closed the door silently as he left.

In the kitchen, Mal said, "Take the back stairs. I'm going to keep an eye on the guy out front. You know Dina's cell phone number?"

Cork gave it to him.

"He moves, I'll let you know."

"Thanks, Mal."

Outside was a small landing with a flight of wooden stairs that led down to the backyard. Cork descended, crossed the yard, and went out a gate near the garage. Dina was parked in the alley, in a dark blue Honda Civic.

"What happened to the Ferrari?" Cork asked when he got in.

"This car doesn't shout when I'm on surveillance." Her eyes shifted to the mirror, then back to the alley in front of her. "Among the calls I made after we talked this afternoon were a few discreet inquiries about Lou and those threats he made. Couple hours ago I got a call back. Lou got things going fast. There's a contract on you. Half a million is what I was told."

"He wants me dead pretty bad."

"Half a million is nothing to Lou. It gets worse, because it's not just a hit, Cork. It's a bounty. It's open season on you. Whoever gets to you first."

"If I'm hit, Lou Jacoby's the guy the cops will look at."

"He's old. He's lost everything. Probably in his thinking, his life's over. He goes to jail or even to death row, big deal. I know Lou. He won't hesitate to do what he feels he has to. That includes collateral damage, Cork."

"My family?"

"Or whoever happens to be with you at the time. Half a million dollars is a lot of incentive not to be neat."

"What if we brought in the police, Adam Gabriel, say, and NORTAF?"

"What can they do until somebody actually tries something? You know how that goes. Even if they wanted to help, they can't watch your back twenty-four-seven. And we both know there are badges up here on the Jacoby payroll. You deal with them and everything gets funneled right back to Lou.

"I worked a case in New Jersey. We had a witness sequestered in a farmhouse outside Passaic. Somebody—a badge, we suspected—leaked the location. The place got hit with three rocket-propelled grenades. Killed the witness and two federal agents. You don't want that to happen to your family." She looked grim and sorry. "You need to find a safe place to disappear for a couple of days."

A flare of anger shot through Cork, seemed to explode in his brain. He slammed his fist into the dashboard. "I'm not running, Dina. I'll talk to Lou Jacoby, pound a little sense into that old man if necessary."

"You barge in, you really think he'd back down? Hell, he'd probably shoot you himself." She put a hand gently on his arm and spoke calmly. "Right now you need to back off. Let us gather enough evidence to convince Lou to listen to reason. With Ed Larson working his end and me here, we'll have what we need in a couple of days, I promise."

"A lot of homicides never get solved."

"A lot of homicides don't have me working the case."

He knew she was right, knew that an irrational act in response to another irrational act usually spelled tragedy.

"A couple of days, Cork, that's all."

In the dark inside the Civic, he stared into her eyes.

"Trust me," she said.

Her cell phone chirped. She looked at the display. "It's coming from the duplex." She answered. "Yeah?" A few seconds and she said, "Thanks," and broke the connection. "Shit."

"What?"

"The Malibu's on the move."

Behind them, a car screamed into the alley. Its headlights blasted over them. Dina jammed the Civic into gear and shot off with a squeal. The car was far more powerful than it looked, and Cork figured she had customized the engine, added muscle. She hit the street at the other end, took a hard right. Cork looked back as the black Malibu fishtailed into sight. Dina cut up side streets and blazed down alleyways. She worked gradually east, putting distance between them and the car in pursuit. Finally she skidded to a stop in a driveway behind a high hedge. She killed the engine and the headlights. They sat a moment and the Malibu shot past, roaring into the dark at the far end of the street.

"You need to disappear and you need to do it now," she said.

"Where?"

"Pick a direction and go. Do you have any money?"

"Not much."

"Here." She reached under the dash and something clicked. A small compartment popped open next to the glove box. She reached in and pulled out a stack of bills. "There's twelve hundred. I keep it for emergencies. Take it. And take this, too." She reached down, pulled up the cuff of her pants, removed her .32 Beretta from the ankle holster, and handed it to Cork.

"I can't even say good-bye to my family?"

"The choice is yours, but I think it's risky. Obviously the guys in the Malibu weren't alone. Somebody tipped them off that you were in the alley. No telling how many people are on you or where they are. I'll let Jo know what's going on."

He gave a nod and they were both quiet.

Dina sat back with a tired sigh. "Lou, Eddie, Phillip, Gabriella, Tony. My God, what you must think of us Jews."

"It's got nothing to do with religion or culture. It's just a screwed-up family. You find those everywhere. Irish Catholics, Ojibwe—hell, probably even among the Bushmen of the Kalahari."

At the end of the block, the black Malibu crept into view like a panther stalking its prey.

"I'll lead them on a merry chase," Dina said. "You make yourself scarce."

"Once again you come to my rescue."

"I'm a sucker for a pretty face. Get going."

He opened the door, slid out.

"You have my number. Let me know where you end up. Good luck, Cork."

Dina backed from the drive and turned on the headlights. As soon as the Malibu squealed in her direction, she shot off. Cork hunkered in the dark of the hedge while the Malibu sped past. He waited until the sound of the two engines had faded into the distance before he walked to the street.

Dawn seemed far away. At that moment, everything did.

EPILOGUE

A SOLITARY TWO-LANE *highway splits the marsh. To the right
and left, brittle reeds disappear into a dingy, low-hanging mist.
A fragile light falls over the scene, the day almost breaking. The
marsh is silent. The birds have fled south or been killed by the
virus, or perhaps it's something about the place itself that in-
hibits their song, for there is the feel of abandonment here, of
death, like an old battlefield or a cemetery.*

*Far to the west rises the dark square of a barn wall and the
slope of a roof. It seems like an ark floating on a dun-colored sea.
East there is nothing but the empty slate sky and the reluctant
dawn.*

*He walks in his windbreaker with his shoulders hunched, each
breath of cold air a reminder that autumn is making its last
stand. He knows what will follow is a killing season.*

*He hears the rattle long before the mist around him begins to
glow from the headlights, and then the truck passes, an old
pickup, the bed fitted with rickety slat-board sides. Thirty yards
beyond him the brake lights flash. The truck slows, stops. As he
approaches, he sees that the bed is filled with feed sacks stacked
half a dozen high in neat rows, and a contraption of wood and
metal with gears and a long handle whose purpose is unknown to
him. He opens the door. The smell of manure greets him.*

*"Hop in." The man at the wheel beckons. He's in overalls and
his boots are caked. "Where you going?"*

"North," he says as he climbs in and slams the door.

"Whereabouts?"

"Just north."

"Big place, that." The man grins in a friendly way and gears into the mist.

In a moment, the truck is lost, heading north, which is indeed a big place, but not big enough.